# Beginning OpenOffice 3
## From Novice to Professional

Andy Channelle

Apress®

**Beginning OpenOffice 3: From Novice to Professional**

**Copyright © 2009 by Andy Channelle**

ISBN-13 (pbk): 978-1-4302-1590-5

ISBN-13 (electronic): 978-1-4302-1591-2

Printed and bound in the United States of America 9 8 7 6 5 4 3 2 1

Trademarked names may appear in this book. Rather than use a trademark symbol with every occurrence of a trademarked name, we use the names only in an editorial fashion and to the benefit of the trademark owner, with no intention of infringement of the trademark.

Java™ and all Java-based marks are trademarks or registered trademarks of Sun Microsystems, Inc., in the US and other countries. Apress, Inc., is not affiliated with Sun Microsystems, Inc., and this book was written without endorsement from Sun Microsystems, Inc.

Lead Editors: Michelle Lowman, Frank Pohlmann
Technical Reviewer: Bruce Byfield
Editorial Board: Clay Andres, Steve Anglin, Mark Beckner, Ewan Buckingham, Tony Campbell,
    Gary Cornell, Jonathan Gennick, Michelle Lowman, Matthew Moodie, Jeffrey Pepper, Frank Pohlmann,
    Ben Renow-Clarke, Dominic Shakeshaft, Matt Wade, Tom Welsh
Project Manager: Richard Dal Porto
Copy Editors: Julie McNamee, Elliot Simon
Associate Production Director: Kari Brooks-Copony
Production Editor: Candace English
Compositor: Patrick Cunningham
Proofreader: April Eddy
Indexer: Brenda Miller
Artist: April Milne
Cover Designer: Kurt Krames
Manufacturing Director: Tom Debolski

Distributed to the book trade worldwide by Springer-Verlag New York, Inc., 233 Spring Street, 6th Floor, New York, NY 10013. Phone 1-800-SPRINGER, fax 201-348-4505, e-mail orders-ny@springer-sbm.com, or visit http://www.springeronline.com.

For information on translations, please contact Apress directly at 2855 Telegraph Avenue, Suite 600, Berkeley, CA 94705. Phone 510-549-5930, fax 510-549-5939, e-mail info@apress.com, or visit http://www.apress.com.

Apress and friends of ED books may be purchased in bulk for academic, corporate, or promotional use. eBook versions and licenses are also available for most titles. For more information, reference our Special Bulk Sales—eBook Licensing web page at http://www.apress.com/info/bulksales.

The information in this book is distributed on an "as is" basis, without warranty. Although every precaution has been taken in the preparation of this work, neither the author(s) nor Apress shall have any liability to any person or entity with respect to any loss or damage caused or alleged to be caused directly or indirectly by the information contained in this work.

*For Alison.*
*Finally it's done!*

# Contents at a Glance

## PART 1 ■■■ The Applications

## PART 2 ■■■ Working Across Applications

# Contents

# PART 1 ■■■ The Applications

# PART 2 ■ ■ ■ Working Across Applications

# About the Author

**ANDY CHANNELLE** is a writer, designer, and educator. He has written on the subject of Linux, open source, and other technical stuff since 2000 and teaches new media and journalism students at the University of the West of England. He writes regularly for publications, including *Linux Format* and *Mac Format* in the UK, and has had work published all over the world.

In the past, Andy has worked as a magazine editor, TV and film reviewer, technical author, information architect, new media consultant, web designer, and strawberry picker.

More recently, Andy has become involved with the production end of new media with a number of small-scale intranet projects at the University of the West of England and the deployment of a community-based web site for Spike Island (http://www.spikeisland.org.uk) built using Drupal and a variety of other open source software.

On those occasional moments when not working, Andy likes playing the drums and guitar, reading novels and books on the history of science or philosophy, and losing at games of Mario Kart. He's been in the middle of writing a ground-breaking novel since 1999.

# About the Technical Reviewer

**BRUCE BYFIELD** is a journalist who writes about free and open source software. He got his start by writing about OpenOffice.org and now writes regularly for *Datamation*, Linux.com, and *Linux Journal*.

# Acknowledgments

First of all, I must thank my wife Alison and the kids—Alice, Olivia, and Tom—for their patience as "the book" consumed my waking thoughts and most of my time. It's not the first project that has achieved this feat, but it does take the biscuit for being the largest. Of course, families don't exist as islands, so thanks also to the various Channelles, Doddridges, and Scarbroughs who have been enthused, excited, or just plain tolerant of my talking about work all the time.

In fact, tolerance has been shown in abundance by my colleagues at *Linux Format* (Andrew, Paul, Nick, Graham, and Mike), Spike Island (Lucy, Lori, Paul, and Karen), sts-solutions (Fiona and Amy), and the University of the West of England (Phil Hargreaves, Mark Barton, and Cluna Donnelly) who have graciously put up with late work or late me.

Thanks to everyone at Apress who had a hand in getting this book out (and took a punt on a first-time author), including Frank Pohlmann, Michelle Lowman, Richard Dal Porto, Elliot Simon, and Julie McNamee (sorry about being late!). Thanks also to Bruce Byfield for sensitive and rigorous technical reviewing and an ability to see where I'd left out something blindingly obvious.

The process of writing so much and staring at a computer screen all day, every day (and night) for months would probably not have been bearable were it not for Radio Paradise (http://www.radioparadise.com), The Daily Show, The Guardian, Slashdot, TechCrunch, the BBC, Facebook, and Google.

Finally, there would have been nothing to write about without the brilliant, brilliant work of the OpenOffice.org developers and community. Thanks!

# Introduction

Office suites are one of the most popular types of software, and most computer users will, at some point, find themselves staring at the user interface of a word processor, spreadsheet, or presentation package. Traditionally, office suites have been quite expensive packages, but thanks to the generosity of Sun Microsystems and a massive community of developers, writers, and testers, there is an alternative to shelling out hundreds of dollars or taking the risks (computer viruses, law suits) associated with downloading and running pirated editions of commercial software. OpenOffice.org (which is both product name and web address) is a piece of software that offers access to the most common features used in office environments, and some of the more uncommon ones too. In addition to being a great collection of applications, one of the revolutionary things about this "business class" software is that it costs less than your daily paper. In fact, anyone—individuals, businesses, charities, governments—can download and install OpenOffice.org for absolutely nothing. And this isn't trial software; it's not restricted in any way. Who said there's no such thing as a free lunch?

## A Tiny Bit of History

The suite started out as a proprietary product called StarOffice developed by StarDivision in Germany, but this changed when it was purchased by Sun Microsystems in 1999. Sun released the software under a permissive license in 2000 in the hope of gathering a community of developers around the application that would then build and improve upon it, allowing it to emulate the success of other open source projects such as the Mozilla browser suite, which spawned Firefox. The intention of the project is to compete with Microsoft Office, and it therefore borrows much of the structure of Microsoft's flagship suite and also supports its file formats. The latest version of OpenOffice.org can open files created using Microsoft Office 2007.

OpenOffice.org's native formats—collectively called the Open Document Format (ODF)—have been adopted as an international standard and are in use across a growing range of applications.

The latest version of OpenOffice.org has been released for Windows, Linux, Solaris, and, for the first time, as a native OS X application. Previously, it required users to run within an X terminal session. So with this version, it's now possible to deploy the suite across an organization regardless of the operating system choices. The software itself is divided into five main sections covering word processing, spreadsheets, presentations, database building, and illustration. These are complemented by a selection of smaller applications and a growing range of third-party plug-ins, which extend the available features considerably.

The StarOffice name lives on in Sun's "official" version of the OpenOffice.org suite.

# The Applications

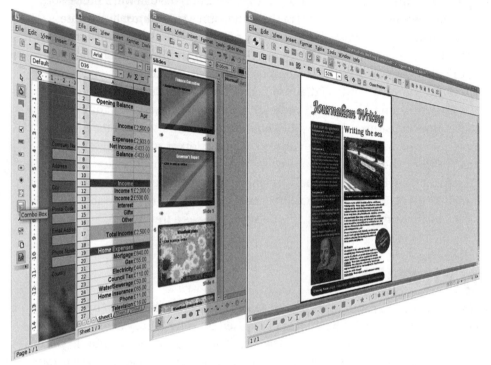

*Writer* is, for most users, the core of the application suite. It can be used for a wide range of text-based tasks from newsletter design and thesis writing to posters, flyers, and book production. Writer is also a very usable web-editing package that is ideal for creating templates for e-mail newsletters. Its equivalent in the Microsoft Office suite is Word, and Writer can open and save documents in both Microsoft's `.doc` format and `.docx` format from the latest version of Word. In addition to printed output, Writer also outputs standard PDFs, Rich Text (RTF) documents, HTML, and many other current and historical formats. The first three chapters of this book deal with documents in Writer.

*Calc* is the spreadsheet element of the software, which will be familiar to anyone who has used Microsoft Excel. Calc can open and save Microsoft Excel's `.xls` file format and includes support for the vast majority of the functions available in that package. In addition to being useful in large-scale accounting work, Calc includes options useful in managing household budgets, performing small business tasks, and producing table data for the Web. Chapter 4 works through the tools and options in Calc.

*Impress* is a presentation package that ships with all the tools you might find in Microsoft PowerPoint. As with the other parts of the suite, Impress opens and saves the ubiquitous Microsoft Office formats, in this case .ppt, and compares well with the competition. Impress features a large number of usable animations, effects, and transitions, and can use the many PowerPoint templates available on the Web, making the job of building engaging presentations a breeze. Impress can also output presentations in various formats suitable for distribution on the Internet or through more traditional channels, and it dynamically integrates data from other parts of the suite. Chapter 5 explores Impress.

*Draw* often seems like the black sheep of the OpenOffice.org family, but its extensive graphical prowess provides other parts of the suite—especially Writer and Impress—with some useful design tools. The package's collection of standard shapes, lines, and fills makes it ideal for building flow chart diagrams and editing clip art for adding to word-processing documents or presentations. Chapter 6 runs through a basic Draw project.

*Base* is the newest element of the system and allows users to build, edit, and query small and large databases. These databases can be anything from a small address book of club members—perfect for creating mail merges in Writer—to more extensive asset-management applications complete with forms, multiple views, and role-based queries. Despite its power and complexity, you can build and manage small-scale projects in Base without advanced technical knowledge. Chapter 7 features a simple Base project capable of being adapted to much broader applications.

Although these applications are strong individually, the common OpenOffice.org core and the ability to take elements from one document and insert, paste, and migrate them into another makes this a powerful package.


## About This Book

This book is divided into project-based tutorials that have been designed to expose as many of OpenOffice.org's individual tools and features as possible. Although the projects may seem quite specific, the processes and tools discussed are transferable to many other office tasks. The projects themselves are based on real-world scenarios and will guide you from the basic options available in the suite to more ambitious uses. Additional tips and guides are included outside of the main text to help take your experience of the software even further beyond the tutorials.

This is not a book for elite hackers, rather it's aimed at those approaching OpenOffice.org for the first time with the intention of getting the most out of the suite in the shortest time. You may have experienced other office suites, in which case, you'll find many tools in expected locations, but it's not a prerequisite. In fact, many of the skills, tools, and processes we'll work through will be useful way beyond OpenOffice.org, and after you've mastered this, you should be able to sit down at any basic application on Windows, Linux, or OS X and feel confident that, with just a little exploration, the application will behave as you want.

The first part of the book is perfect for those who've been given a horribly tight deadline to put together a report, chart, or presentation or to format a long essay because it covers the most commonly used parts of the OpenOffice.org package. It begins with basic word-processing document creation and then moves on to cover the tools available that will allow you to create smart, consistent documents, spreadsheets, presentations, databases, and illustrations with the least effort.

After we've covered the main applications themselves, Part 2 looks at various ways of dropping content from one application into another, looks at document and author management, runs through the methods of output, and takes a quick tour through some of the essential extensions for the suite.

The screenshots used in this book were taken on a Linux PC (running Ubuntu Hardy Heron 8.04), but the key combinations, menu structures, and options are applicable to both Windows and Mac OS X, although on the latter, the Ctrl key should be transposed to the Apple key directly to the left of the spacebar.

## Conventions Used in This Book

Graphical user interfaces can be difficult to represent in written form, but the method used in this book is as follows:

- Menu entries are shown with a ➤ between each element. You should follow from left to right; for example, File ➤ Save As launches the Save Document dialog box. Many menu entries contain an ellipsis, and for the purposes of visual clarity in the text, these have been removed from the written commands.

- Many options in the applications have associated key combinations. These are joined together with a + sign. For example, Ctrl+S saves a document, whereas Ctrl+Shift+S launches the Save Document dialog box.

- And finally, although OpenOffice.org is a perfectly serviceable name for an application, we'll often shorten it to OO.o, and individual applications within the suite will be referred to by their shortened names—Writer, Calc, and Impress.

Anything else will be explained in the text because, well, we need to crack on… there's so much to do!

# PART 1

■ ■ ■

# The Applications

Let's crack on then. Part 1 runs through the five core applications of the suite with a bit of a bias in the first three chapters toward Writer, the word processor. These three chapters each start with a very basic document and then use the tools and options available in Writer to create something much more sophisticated. In the course of these jobs, you'll explore many of the ways in which Writer can be used to make document creation and editing not only more versatile but also easier through the use of automation, saved styles, and document variables. Writer gets the lion's share of space in Part 1 because, as well as being the most used part of the suite, the dissection of the interface and customization options in this application are also relevant to the rest of the suite. Along with being a journey through Writer, these chapters also explore OpenOffice.org itself.

After we leave Writer behind, you should be ready to explore the rest of the suite without too much assistance on customization and optimization. This is the perfect time to introduce Calc, the suite's spreadsheet. Calc is capable of everything from home budgets to corporate accounts; we'll be heading for something in between—an adaptable accounts system for a small business.

Impress is the presentation package that is capable of some very smart results. We'll be going through the process of building a basic presentation, turning that into a template, and outputting documents in a variety of formats.

We'll then move on to Impress's twin, the illustration package Draw, before finishing up with a small, uncomplicated project built with Base, the newest member of the OO.o family. Databases are often regarded as hideously complicated things with no relevance to everyday life unless you're a big business or club. In fact, OO.o's Base application can be used to build something as small as an address book or a home inventory.

After completing the tutorials in this book, you will have the confidence to create a selection of different document types for a variety of uses and also have the skills necessary to apply those procedures and ideas on your own projects. You will also be able look beyond the basics and explore. Remember, the Undo button is always just two clicks away.

# CHAPTER 1

# Writer: Basic Documents

**W**e'll begin in the obvious place with a run through the core applications in the Open-Office.org (OO.o) suite beginning with Writer, and then moving on through Calc, Impress, Draw, and Base.

If you have two hours to prepare for a seminar presentation, feel free to leap into the Impress section straight away. However, it might be a good idea to read through the following annotations that explain the user interface conventions used in OO.o. Although the screenshot is from Writer, most of the interface elements are consistent across applications (see Figure 1-1).

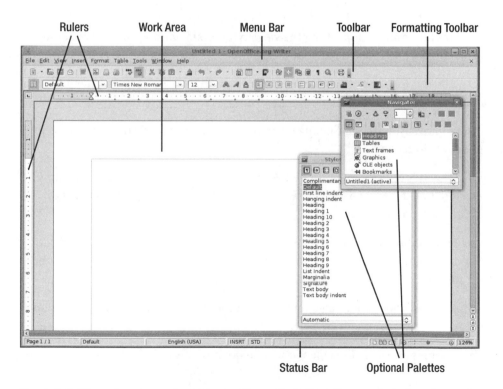

**Figure 1-1.** *The advantage of using an office suite is that the user interface is consistent across the different elements.*

# Menu Bar

The *menu bar* (see Figure 1-2) is standard across most desktop applications. Almost all of Writer's tools are accessible via these menus, and most of the options available have keyboard combinations assigned to them. For example, to quickly save a document, you could choose File ➤ Save or simply press Ctrl+S.

**Figure 1-2.** *The menu bar*

The menu system in OO.o is configurable via Tools ➤ Customize, so you can redesign the whole application to look like your favorite package. The menus are described here:

- *File*: Deals with file operations such as opening, saving, and closing documents, but also contains the document properties section and print options.

- *Edit*: Allows you to cut, copy, and paste as well as find and replace particular words or phrases.

- *View*: Provides options for setting the view in the main window and also opening and closing Writer's various toolbars.

- *Insert*: Allows you to add things to the page, including frames, images, headers, footers, and breaks in the text.

- *Format*: Allows you to make changes to everything from pages and paragraphs to individual characters.

- *Table*: Provides options for adding tables to a document. Tables can be used to present data like a spreadsheet and also to position elements when it comes to building web pages.

- *Tools*: Enables you to configure OpenOffice, configure the user interface of Writer (or another of the applications), perform a word count, and set up options for the spell checker.

- *Window*: Allows you to manage multiple documents or multiple views of the same document.

- *Help*: Provides access to the OpenOffice.org documentation.

# Toolbar

The *toolbar* contains a range of commonly used shortcuts for opening, saving, and adding various elements to your documents. The toolbar is divided into logical regions, which, from left to right, are file operations, output, spelling, clipboard features, formatting, inserting, and searching (see Figure 1-3). As with the menus, these are completely customizable from Tools ➤ Customize.

**Figure 1-3.** *The toolbar*

Although the default view of Writer displays two toolbars, many more toolbars are available that contain tools for performing specific tasks such as designing forms, adding rich media to web pages, or offering more control over elements such as line spacing and bullets or numbers. These can all be accessed using the View ➤ Toolbars menu entry. Once added to a page, they can be dragged from the edge of the page and either left as a floating toolbar (which means they will have a standard Close icon in the top right of the window) or docked to another edge of the window. Docking a toolbar to the top or bottom of the screen renders it as horizontal, whereas docking to the left or right edge positions the icons vertically.

# Formatting Toolbar

The *Formatting toolbar* is a specialized toolbar used to make changes at either the character or paragraph level. This element is actually context sensitive, so in most cases, a version similar to this will be displayed. However, if you were editing a picture, configuring a frame, or drawing a shape, the Formatting toolbar would display a toolset relevant for that task.

The Formatting toolbar in Figure 1-4 is the standard text model, which has options for changing the font, font size, style, justification, indents, and color options. The disclosure arrow to the far right of the toolbar offers quick access to customization tools for that particular toolbar.

**Figure 1-4.** *Context-sensitive Formatting toolbar*

# Rulers

*Rulers* provide a visual guide to your page (see Figure 1-5). By default, the rulers are set to increment in centimeters; however, you can change this to inches, millimeters, and even points and picas through the application preferences (see Figure 1-6).

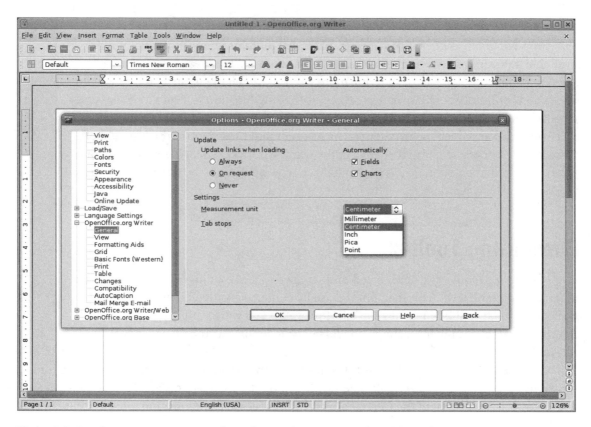

**Figure 1-5.** *Rulers*

**Figure 1-6.** *Set the measurements to the value you're most comfortable with.*

To access these preferences, choose Tools ➤ Options, click the OpenOffice.org Writer disclosure arrow on the left edge of the window, and choose General. Alternative measurements are available in the drop-down list. You should notice the Tab stop value (i.e., the distance the Tab key will move your cursor across the page) updates automatically to reflect the measurement change. Select the appropriate value, and click OK.

At the left edge of the horizontal ruler is a pair of marker icons that can be used to visually define the indentation used in the document. The lighter colored space shows the usable area of the page. The top icon can move independently of the bottom one, which sets the first line indent. The bottom icon defines the standard paragraph indent (it has a companion on the right side of the ruler), and it can be simply dragged and dropped to the right place. You can create a hanging indent by dragging the top icon to the left of the bottom icon (see Figure 1-7).

This method of creating paragraph indents is quick but imprecise. More refined control is available via the options available by choosing Format ➤ Paragraph.

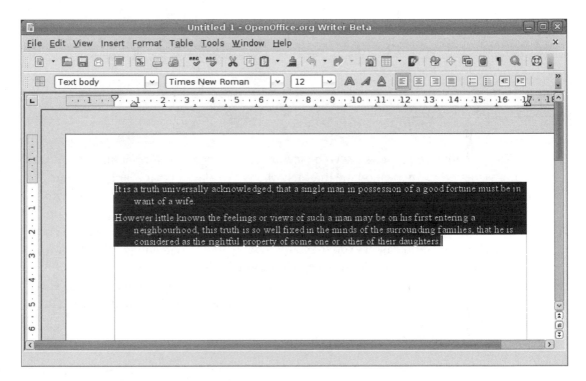

**Figure 1-7.** *Use the ruler widgets to make a hanging indent.*

# Work Area

The *work area* is where your document is displayed (see Figure 1-8). Writer features a number of display modes, which are accessed through the View menu. The standard view is a so-called WYSIWYG (what you see is what you get) view, which means the text and images onscreen attempt to represent the look and feel of the final document, including headers, footers, and page numbers. A more accurate rendition can be seen by choosing File ➤ Page Preview.

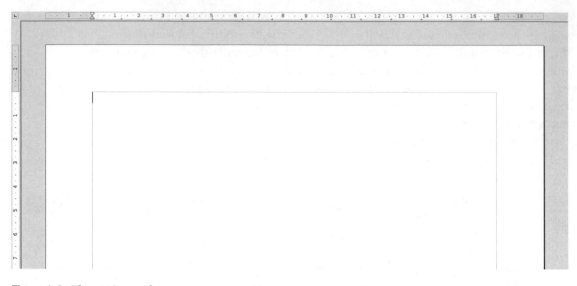

**Figure 1-8.** *The main work area*

The two other main views are Web View and Full Screen. The former displays documents as they would appear on the Internet, whereas the latter is excellent for writers who prefer not to have the distractions of toolbars, menus, and palettes onscreen with their words. The work area can be zoomed to various levels by choosing View ➤ Zoom. Options available here include Fit Width and Height (i.e., full page), Width, Optimal, or Variable. The last option allows you to set the zoom level as a percentage. This edition of Writer also allows you to see double-page spreads in the full-page view.

In some parts of the application suite, notably in Impress and Draw, the main Formatting toolbar is augmented by a set of drawing tools arranged across the bottom of the screen.

## Optional Palette

During normal use, most of Writer*'s* facilities are available through either menus or toolbars; however, some options launch a new palette with a further set of tools (see Figure 1-9). The advantage of these palettes is that they can be freely positioned on the screen and, when necessary, removed completely with the click of a mouse. Examples of optional palettes include text styles, the document Navigator, and the bibliographic database.

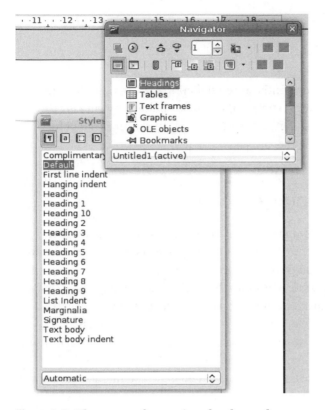

**Figure 1-9.** *There are a few optional palettes that you may leave open as you work.*

These palettes behave just like ordinary application windows, which can be minimized, maximized, and removed. However, they always stay on top of the main Writer window. The Navigator may become more useful as you investigate the powerful document creation options in OO.o because it provides ready access to the deep structure of a document. For example, when working on a long document with chapters, sections, and subsections, the Navigator can display these elements in a hierarchy, so that selecting the element takes you directly to that section for editing. Navigator also presents a list of (labeled) images, making it easy to select a picture even if it's obscured by other page elements.

# Status Bar

The *status bar* at the bottom of the window (see Figure 1-10) is mainly informational, although it does have a few user editable options. Most useful are the mode switch in the center of the bar that changes editing from inserting (i.e., preserving the existing text) and overwriting; the selection options; the page mode; and the zoom slider, which allows you to zoom in and out of the document without having to visit the menu. Note the two small notches on the slider; these correspond to the Whole Page view and the Page Width view.

| Page 1 / 1 | Default | English (USA) | INSRT | STD | | | | | 126% |

**Figure 1-10.** *The status bar*

In the very center of this bar is the currently selected dictionary. This should conform to the default language of your computer system, but it can be changed by clicking the language name and selecting a new language. If your language isn't listed, select More to access more language options.

# Creating Your First Document

The word processor is one of the core applications for almost every type of computer user. Whether you're writing a novel, report, dissertation, or just a shopping list, a decent word processor, such as Writer, is a good thing to have around.

At its most basic, you can launch Writer, click into the work area, and begin typing. Words will appear on the screen within a representation of your page, and these can be highlighted (click and drag across your selection with the mouse) and then adjusted in a variety of ways using the Formatting toolbar. The options on the Formatting toolbar (from left to write) allow you to apply a style to the text (we'll cover these later); change the font and size; make the text appear bold, italic, or underlined; change the alignment; create a list; change the indentation of the paragraph; or adjust the color or highlighting of the text.

Your first project is based on producing a letterhead for a small business or solo trader. You'll add a small graphical flourish, the essential address details, a space for a reference number, and a footer. After the design is satisfactory, you'll save the whole thing as a template for use the next time you need to write a letter.

## Create the Page

To begin, launch the application by either selecting the Start Center or Writer from the Start menu. The former launches a new window containing icons for each of the individual applications—choose Writer to get started—whereas the latter takes you straight to the application itself. Either way, a new document is displayed onscreen using a default page size and margins setup.

### READY FOR LAUNCH

The first time you launch OO.o, you are prompted for your name (this can be used to automatically add details to documents), and given the option of setting automatic application updates and registering the software with the OO.o project. Although I recommend using both of these options, neither is mandatory.

The first task is to set up the most fundamental elements of your document, the page size and margins. To do this, choose Format ➤ Page, and select the Page tab. A number of predefined page sizes (A4, Letter, etc.) are available via the Format drop-down list, and you can also define a new page size using the Height and Width options (see Figure 1-11). Page sizes that are higher than they are wide are Portrait (and will thus be defined as such), and pages that are wider than they are high are Landscape. You can switch these around using the two buttons below the page dimensions. For this document, choose A4.

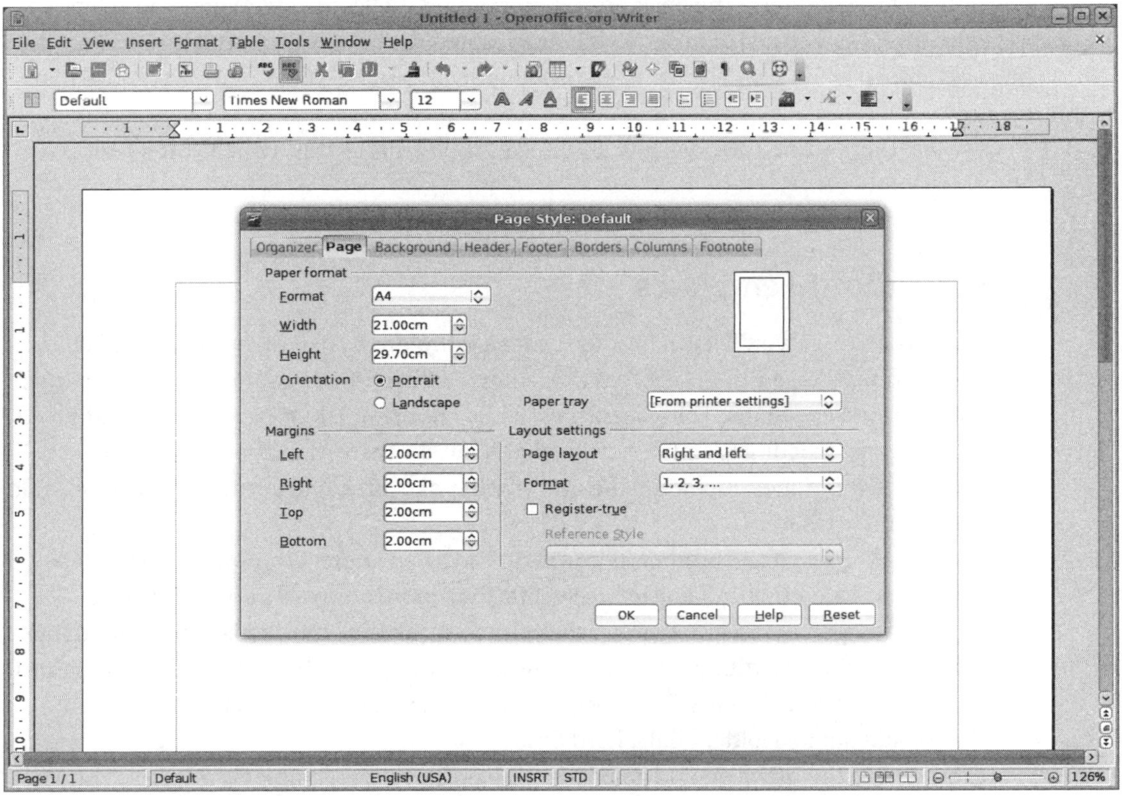

**Figure 1-11.** *The Page Style window is used to define the dimensions of the document.*

At the bottom left are the margin values for the page, which can be altered either by clicking on the increase/decrease arrows or by simply typing new numbers in the spaces. You can also use the Tab key to move from one value to another, which automatically highlights the next number ready for editing. For this document, use 2.54cm all round, as this equates to about an inch.

Next move onto the Layout settings, where you can set up how the pages will be displayed, that is, as either a series of left or right pages, right and left (as in a book or magazine), or mirrored. The two first options are good for single-sided short documents or individual pages; with Right and Left, you can set master objects such as page headers and footers independently for left and right pages. Finally, the Mirror option allows you to design on one side and have those changes mirrored on the opposite page. For example, a page number that appears on the left edge of the left page appears on the right edge of the right page. Because this is a simple letter, choose Only Right from the list.

The Format option defines how automatic page numbers will be displayed when added to a document. The choices are pretty straightforward.

The final option of interest in this dialog box is the Register-true check box. This is a typographical tool that attempts to line up the text on both sides of a page so the reader doesn't see the shadow of the back side when reading the front side. When you select Register-true, the text style chosen in the drop-down list will be anchored to a grid on the page regardless of its size. This can be problematic on simple documents, so ignore that for now.

Many other options are available in the Page Style dialog box, which you'll learn about in Chapter 3.

## A Word About Templates

Later in this chapter, you'll learn how to create a template based on the style of this particular letter. But it's worth noting that OO.o ships with a few templates, albeit templates designed for presentations. These are accessed by choosing File ➤ New ➤ Templates and Documents. Existing templates are available under the various headings, and custom-made templates, including the one you'll make later, will eventually be accessible in the MyTemplates folder.

Fortunately, the OO.o community comes to the rescue here. From within the New ➤ Templates and Documents dialog box, select the Get more templates online link (see Figure 1-12) to open a web browser on a web site that contains hundreds of downloadable templates covering everything from text documents and spreadsheets to presentations and labels. I've selected the Professional Templates Pack II, (available in English or German) and downloaded it to a folder on the hard disk.

Close down the browser, and go back to OO.o. Close the Templates selector, choose Tools ➤ Extension Manager from the menu bar, and select Add. This launches the system's file browser, and you can navigate and select the recently downloaded file that has the extension .oxt. Click the Open button, read and accept the license agreement, and then wait for just a few seconds as the extensions are installed.

Finally, close the Extension Manager, and choose File ➤ New ➤ Templates and Documents to see the collection of new available templates that are all housed under sensible headings.

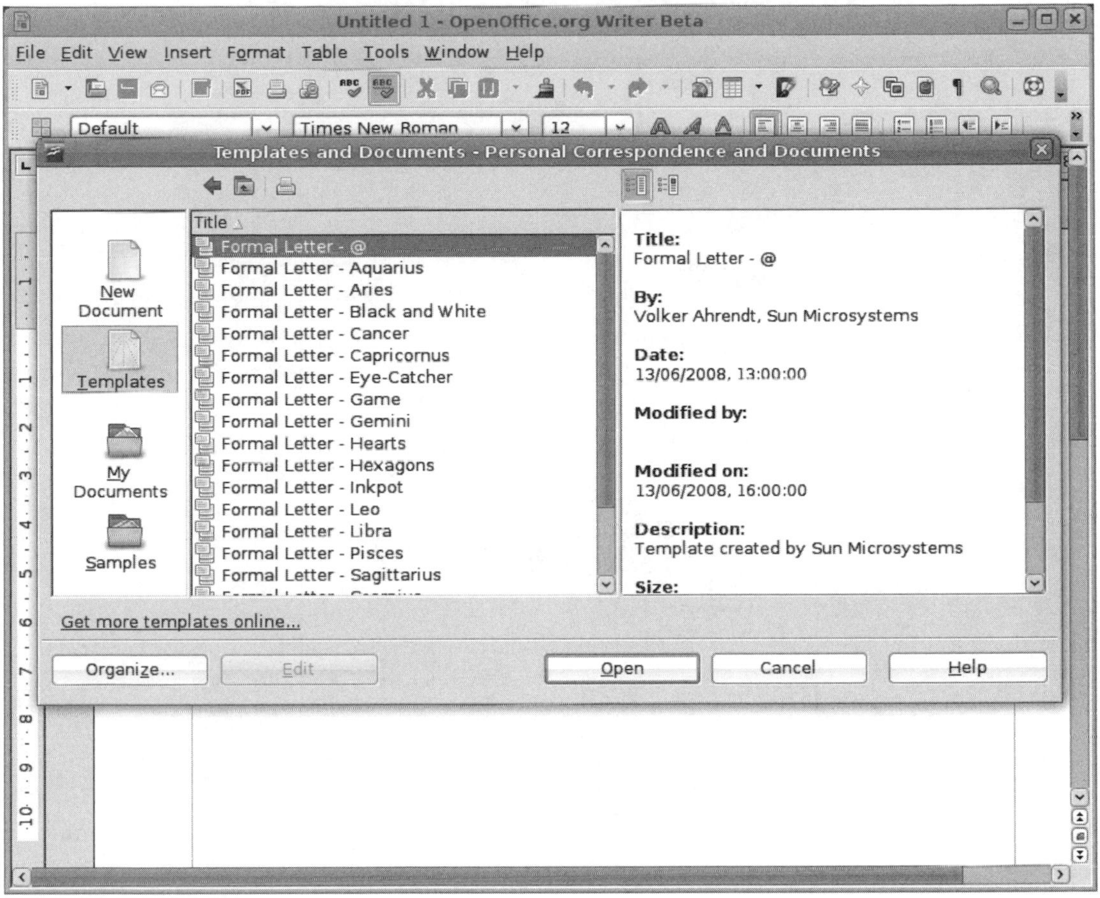

**Figure 1-12.** *The Web is a good source of new templates.*

## Add and Format the Main Text

Now that you have a suitable page set up for a letter, you can add some text (see Figure 1-13). Add the name, recipient address, your address, date, salutation, reference, text, signoff, and your name using the default font and hard returns (i.e. press the Enter key) after each line.

You can format sections of this letter by highlighting the text you want to effect and then choosing the appropriate options. To begin with, adjust the size and position of the first element to make it look more like a letterhead by highlighting that and choosing 24 from the Font Size drop-down list (third from the left on the Formatting toolbar). You can also draw more attention to this particular element by making it bold. With the text highlighted, click the B icon on the Formatting toolbar or press Ctrl+B. Finally, select the Centered icon from the Formatting toolbar (or press Ctrl+E) to center the new heading.

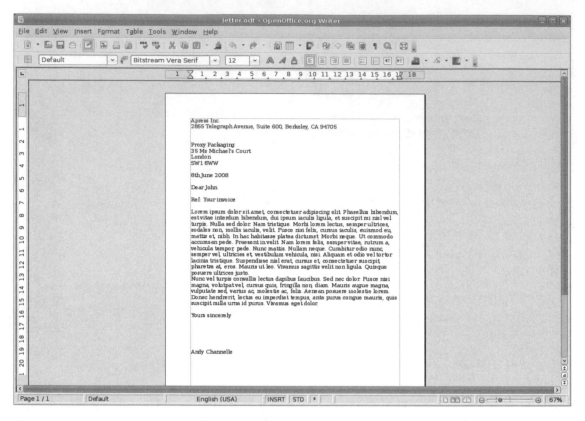

**Figure 1-13.** *If you launch the application and begin typing a letter, you'll end up with something like this.*

Next you need to reposition your address so it's flush with the right edge of the page by highlighting the whole address and then clicking the Align Right button or pressing Ctrl+R.

---

■**Note**  You can highlight text using just the keyboard. You can move around the document with the Up, Down, Left, and Right cursor keys, and if you hold down Shift, these movements will select the text. For example, Shift+Right Cursor Key selects the letter to the right of the cursor. However, pressing Ctrl+Shift+Right Cursor Key, you can select the whole word to the right of the cursor. Putting a cursor at the far left of a paragraph and pressing Shift+Down Cursor Key selects the whole line.

---

Although you can leave the address set right, it might look better set as a single line below the centered letterhead. Highlight the address, and choose Edit ➤ Cut (or press Ctrl+X) to cut the text to the application's clipboard. Now click below the letterhead text, and choose Edit ➤ Paste (or Ctrl+V) to paste the text back in. Obviously, it will be written across a lot of lines, so position the cursor on the left of each line, press Backspace, add a comma between each element, and then click the Centered icon to center the text.

Next, make the Reference section bold, and you're ready to move on to the main text.

## Introducing Paragraphs

Most of what you've done so far has worked with small amounts of text, but you can also effect large changes with just a few clicks. One of the methods often used to mark out paragraphs is to indent the first line of each paragraph. In Writer, this can be accomplished through the Paragraph dialog box, which is available by choosing Format ➤ Paragraph (see Figure 1-14).

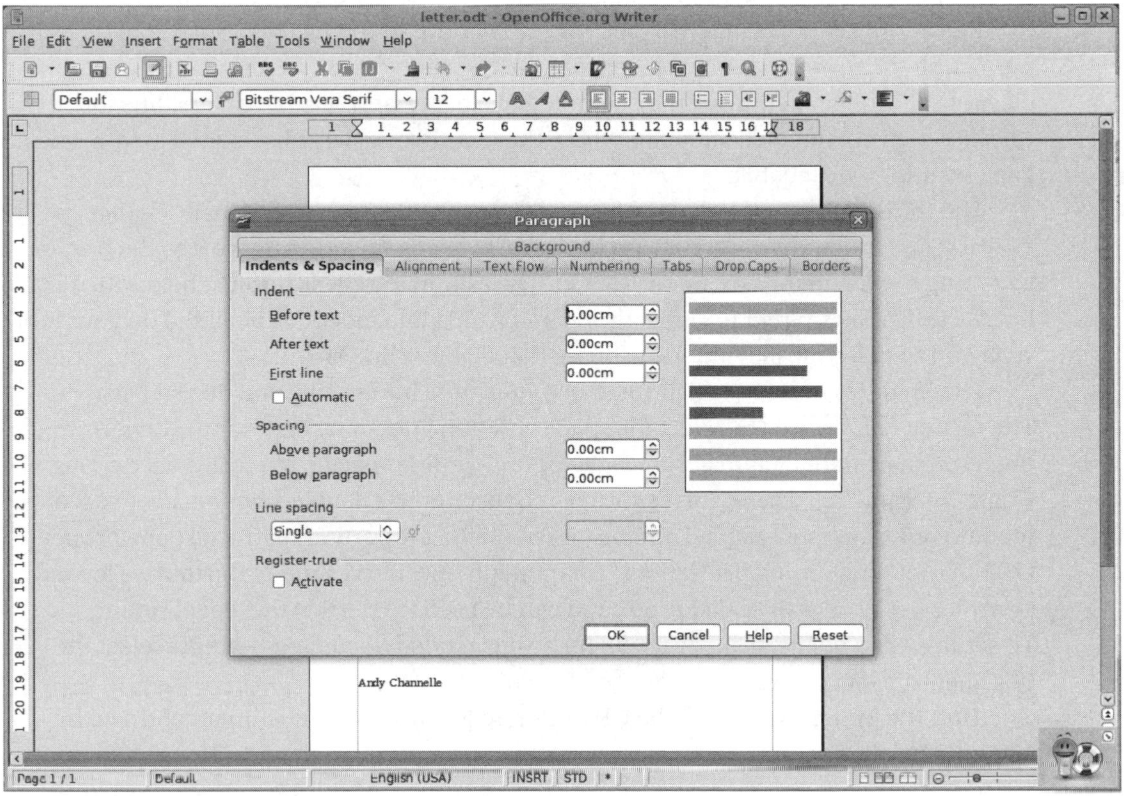

**Figure 1-14.** *We'll be revisiting the Paragraph dialog box later, but for now we're just interested in the Indents & Spacing section.*

There are two levels of formatting in Writer: character level and paragraph level. When working on the character level, for example, selecting a font or making some text bold, then every part of the text that is to be changed needs to be selected. When working on the paragraph level, as you are here, it's enough to just click anywhere inside the paragraph to be changed. If you're formatting multiple paragraphs, the selection (click and drag with the mouse) needs to touch each paragraph to be changed. You don't have to worry about selecting every single character.

Although the Paragraph dialog box contains a lot of options under various tabs, we're sticking with Indents & Spacing for the moment.

The top section deals with *indents*, which are the distances between the edge of our work area and the text itself. The Before text option defines the gap between the left edge and the text, whereas the After text option deals with the right. Earlier you saw how you can alter these values visually using the widgets on the ruler, but this method offers far more control.

The Spacing section allows you to define the gap that appears before or after each paragraph. Usually you'll only use one of these options, but there are exceptions such as when adding subheadings to a piece of text. For this letter, I've set a small gap Below paragraph to create a visual break between each section of text. In most cases, a more elegant solution to identifying the beginning of a paragraph is to have a first line indent (discussed next), but on documents where the text covers a large horizontal area, a small gap can improve readability.

The third option in this dialog box, and the one you're going to actually change, is the First line indent. We can increase the value by using the up arrow next to the box, or by typing a value in the box. Enter **1.50cm**. The Automatic check box just below the First line section allows Writer to define the "perfect" first line indent value based on your font style and size. It overrides any value defined in the First line box.

The final two options, which you'll use later, are Line spacing and Register-true. The former can be used to adjust the space between lines of text in various ways, from the blunt instrument approach of single- or double-line spacing (typically, a letter has single-line spacing, whereas an essay or a manuscript has double-line spacing to accommodate notes) to more refined options based on the proportions of the text or a proper DTP-like leading setting. The latter is a paragraph-specific version of the tool we looked at earlier in the Page Style dialog box and can be used to override the global setting. To set this—it's not particularly useful for a single-sided document—simply select the Register-true check box.

After the indent is set, click the OK button to go back to the document and see the effect of the change.

## Personalizing the Interface

As you advance through Writer, you'll be revisiting the Paragraph dialog box quite often. You can save some time by adding a new icon to the Formatting toolbar to launch the dialog box and also giving it a keyboard shortcut.

Usually there are levels of keyboard shortcuts in use on most computer systems. First, there are systemwide shortcuts that work across many applications. These include things like Ctrl+S for saving, Ctrl+C for copying, and Ctrl+P for pasting. The second-level shortcuts are suite-specific; Ctrl+B makes selected text bold in all of the OO.o applications (and in many other office suites), but launches, for example, a text options box in Adobe's InDesign. The third level is application specific, such as using Ctrl+1 to apply a particular text style to some selected text.

Although you can assign any combination of keys to almost any task in OO.o, it's best to steer clear of the most common combinations when defining or redefining shortcuts using the following method.

To do the former, choose Tools ➤ Customize, and select the Toolbars tab (see Figure 1-15). Under the OpenOffice.org Toolbars section, choose Formatting from the drop-down list, and scroll down the long list to find Paragraph. Click Paragraph, and a new icon will appear at the far right of the Formatting toolbar. You can change its position by clicking the up arrow next to the list; the higher it appears in the list, the farther left it will be on the toolbar.

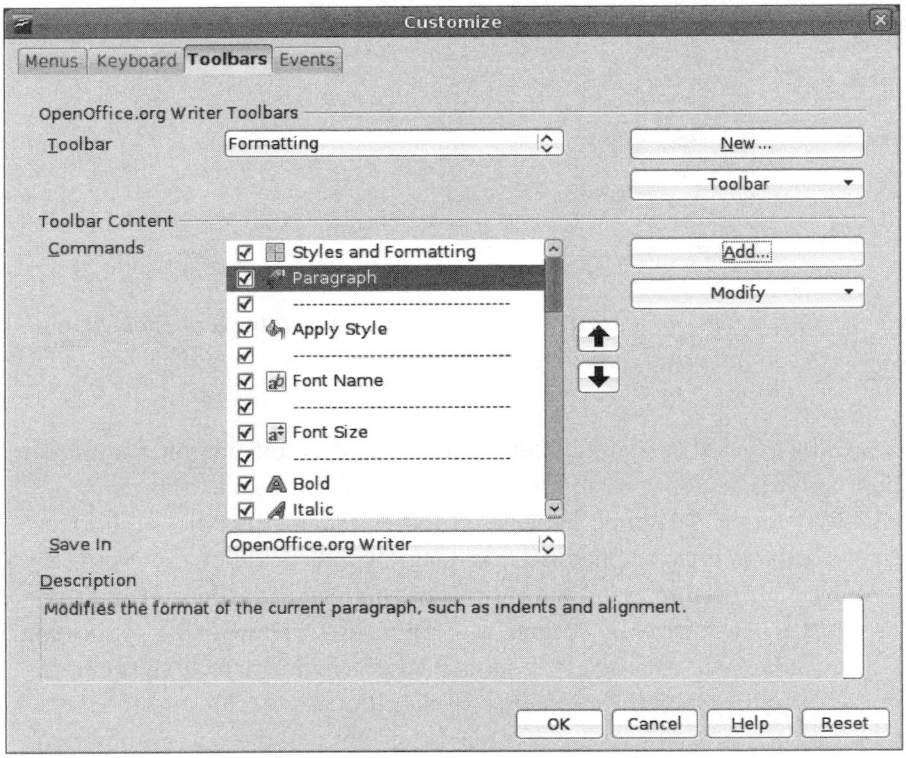

**Figure 1-15.** *The Paragraph button has been added to the Formatting toolbar next to the styles drop-down list, making it much quicker to access.*

The keyboard shortcut is again added by choosing Tools ➤ Customize, but this time, you choose the Keyboard tab. Although hundreds of options are available here, the process is actually quite simple, as you can see in Figure 1-16.

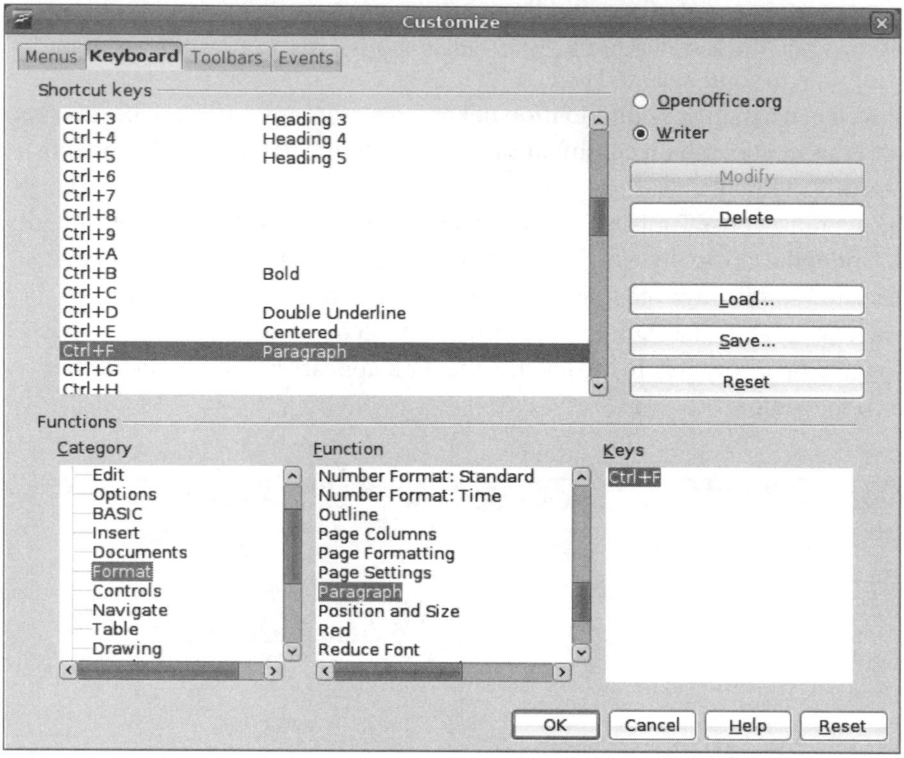

**Figure 1-16.** *Commands can be bound to any keyboard shortcut, making it possible to replicate the workflow of your favorite applications.*

Start by choosing a vacant key combination to contain the command from the Shortcut keys section. Ctrl+6 is free, so you can use that. It might seem sensible to choose something like Ctrl+P for the paragraph settings, but that is a standard keyboard shortcut for printing, so it's better to opt for something that doesn't conflict. With the shortcut defined, you can now add the command using the three windows at the bottom of the dialog box, which is just an alternative way of looking at the menu structure of the application.

In the Category pane, select Format to repopulate the Function pane in the center. Scroll through the list until you find Paragraph, and click it.

Click the Modify button on the top right of the dialog box, and the key combination will be bound to the command. Note that commands can be bound to any number of key combinations, but each shortcut can only have one command.

You can also edit a shortcut; for example, if you wanted to bind Ctrl+P to the Paragraph options, you find the shortcut in the list, reconfigure the Functions at the bottom of the dialog box, and click Modify. More importantly, if you're working with OO.o across a number of computers, you can save reconfigured shortcuts by using the Save button, moving the file to the second machine, and importing them with the Load button, which means there's no need to duplicate a lot of effort across machines. You can also restore the default combinations using the Reset button.

Any changes you make are written to the system only when you click the OK button, so if you mess things up, just select Cancel to revert to the pre-edited state.

Now the all-important paragraph options are just a button or shortcut away; but while you're editing the user interface, think about the other tools that might be useful on one of the toolbars or that might need to be moved. The entire interface can be edited through the Customize option. Moreover, if you only need regular access to a particular button for a short time, you can hide previously added buttons from a toolbar (and, obviously return them) by clicking the down arrow at the far right of any toolbar, selecting Visible buttons, and then deselecting the appropriate option. This is different from removing a button using Tools ➤ Customize because the button is not completely removed; you can add it again by going back to the Visible buttons and reselecting the tool.

## COMMON KEYBOARD SHORTCUTS

- Ctrl+B: Bold

- Ctrl+I: Italic

- Ctrl+U: Underline

- Ctrl+Shift+P: Superscript

- Ctrl+Shift+B: Subscript

- Ctrl+C: Copy selection

- Ctrl+X: Cut selection

- Ctrl+V: Paste selection

- Ctrl+A: Select all the text

- Ctrl+R: Align text right

- Ctrl+L: Align text left

- Ctrl+E: Center text

- Ctrl+P: Print

Refer to the appendix for more keyboard shortcuts.

## A Word About Toolbars

The primary use for a word processor is creating largely textual documents, so the developers of any piece of word-processing software have, as their primary goal, the desire to make creating and editing text easy. This means ensuring that the most commonly used tools are always available.

However, many users need more extensive tools as their documents become more sophisticated, and Writer can accommodate this growth with the addition of no fewer than 20 other toolbars.

Most of the toolbars are set up to cover very specialized work such as adding formulae, building web forms, and adding hyperlinks, but others, such as the Drawing Tools and Bullets and Numbering, can provide quicker access to particular tools than using menus and dialog boxes. All toolbars can be enabled or disabled by choosing View ➤ Toolbars. They will either appear as docked toolbars—that is, they will be appended onto an existing toolbar—or they will be floating free (see Figure 1-17). You can undock a toolbar by clicking on the dotted vertical line at the left of the toolbar (this is also true for the two default toolbars) and dragging out to the page. The toolbar then becomes a regular window that can be placed anywhere on the screen. Redocking involves dragging a free-floating toolbar back into the space at the top of the window.

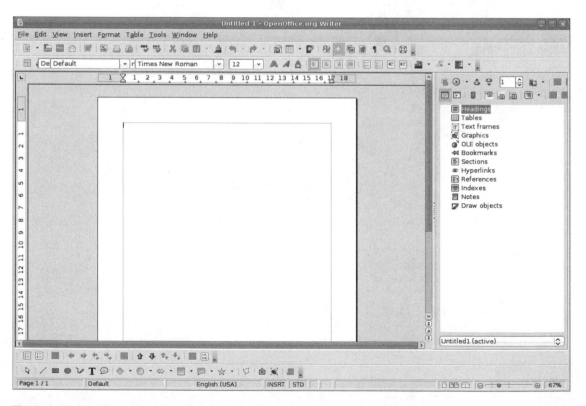

**Figure 1-17.** *Toolbars can be either free-floating or docked to any edge of the screen.*

If the top of the user interface is getting cluttered, you can drag any toolbar to any edge of the main window, and it will be docked to that edge. Many applications place a selection of drawing tools along the base of the window, and you can re-create the experience by enabling the Drawing toolbar (View ➤ Toolbars ➤ Drawing), which will default to the base of the window.

If none of the available toolbars suit your requirements, new ones can be built from scratch, which become accessible (either locked, movable, or floating) in the same way as the pre-made ones.

---

■**Caution**  It's important to remember when you're adding, removing, and editing the Writer user interface (or any other part of the suite) that the purpose of productivity software is to increase productivity. If your computer screen is totally obscured by buttons and widgets that you might use once every three weeks—or even just once a week—you might think about simplifying things a little.

---

## Saving

With your basic document created, you now need to save it to the hard disk. Choose File ➤ Save as, navigate to the desired location on your disk, and input a file name. After you click the Save button, the document will be written to the disk and can be opened by choosing File ➤ Open. As you work, save the most recent version of your document by pressing Ctrl+S or choosing File ➤ Save. For peace of mind, OO.o performs an autosave periodically and can also be set to make a backup of the document that can be recovered in the event of a crash. In fact, OO.o has some pretty smart crash recovery systems, which means you won't lose too much work should anything unforeseen happen.

You also can take a snapshot of the document, which allows you to return to a previous version (this is especially useful if you're going to make a radical, experimental change) by choosing File ➤ Versions. This launches a new dialog box with a large area (which will eventually hold the different versions of the document) and a series of buttons on the right. Click Save Version to create a new snapshot and close the window. Save the document in the normal fashion as you're working and then save a new version using the same method when necessary. You can roll back to a new version by selecting it from the list and clicking Open. You can also compare versions, delete old versions, or set the software to create a new version whenever the document is closed. All of these versions are saved with the document.

# Template Building

Templates are one of the most versatile tools available in OpenOffice.org. They allow users to create designs that can be reused again with new content, thus saving you time. The template system is common across all applications in the suite, so you can build templates for text documents, spreadsheets, presentations, and even databases.

## Add Placeholders

The purpose of using word-processing software, as opposed to a manual typewriter for example, is to reduce the need to perform repetitive tasks such as inputting the same address or date on every letter you write. Now that you've created a simple letterhead, you'll remove the unique content from it, replace that with a series of placeholders, and then save the whole thing as a template that can be reused over and over again (see Figure 1-18). This means that the next time you need to write a letter, you can open the template, add the unique content again, and save it as a new document without the fear that you're saving over some other important document.

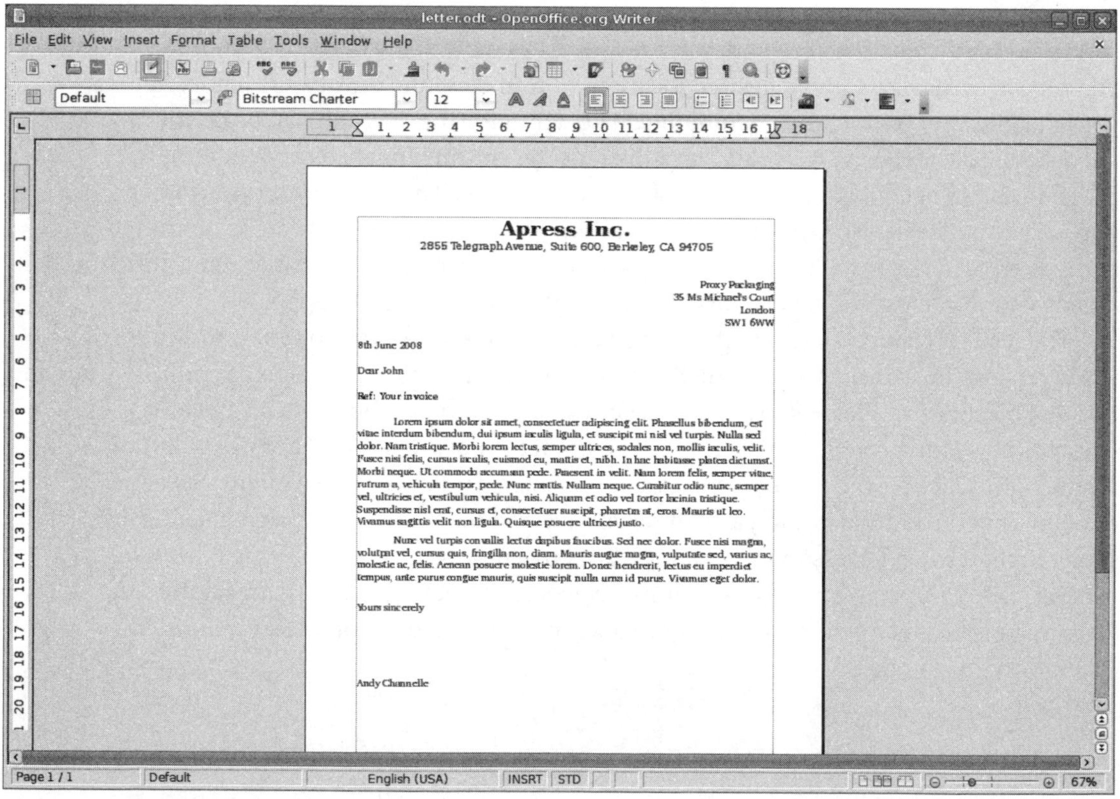

**Figure 1-18.** *From very plain text, we've added a little style. We'll save even more time by creating a template from this document for all of our letters.*

You'll start from the top of the document and work down, changing items as you come across them. The recipient address is likely to be variable data—that is, it will change on every letter—so you need to add placeholder text. This text includes a description of what the placeholder should contain, which disappears when the element is clicked, and is formatted so that any added text assumes that format.

Highlight the first line of the address in your letter and then choose Insert ➤ Fields ➤ Other to launch the Fields dialog box. Placeholder is a predefined variable field that is accessible under the Functions tab, so select Placeholder to reveal the three-column configuration box. The Type of field we're adding is a Placeholder and the Format is Text. On the right side of the dialog box, in the Placeholder text box, you can add the text that will appear as the placeholder in a fetching green, encased in <> angled brackets and, just in case you don't realize their special use, highlighted in gray. Anything typed into the Reference text box that appears below the Placeholder text box will be displayed as a tool tip when you or some other user hovers over the placeholder text; it's especially useful if you're designing for another user and you want to offer some instruction or advice on the placeholder's content (see Figure 1-19).

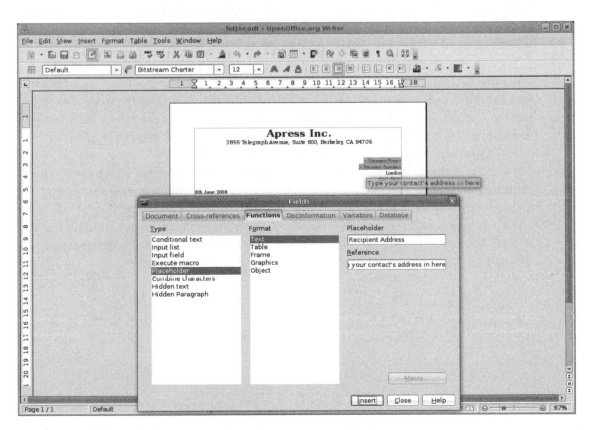

**Figure 1-19.** *Tool tips are especially useful if you're designing a document that is destined to be used by someone else.*

The Fields dialog box is entirely "live" so you can keep it open while working on the actual document beneath it. This means that with the window open, you can select each part of the address in turn, define the Placeholder and Reference elements, click Insert, and see that placeholder added over the top of the selection. Complete the recipient address by adding details such as town or city, postal/ZIP code, and phone number, and then close the Field dialog box.

The placeholders can be formatted in the same way as any other text—simply highlight and adjust—and so can be designed to fit in with the rest of the document. When you reuse the template at a later date, you'll be able to click a placeholder and begin typing, and whatever you add will assume the location and formatting of the placeholder text.

## Choose the Date

The date is next down the page, and there's a special field available for just this purpose. Because this field should dynamically update as you create new documents, instead of hard-coding the date into the page, you're going to add a date field by selecting Insert ➤ Fields ➤ Date. This adds a standard format date to the document and adds the gray background to indicate that this is a field. You need to make a few changes by double-clicking on the date to open the Edit Fields dialog box.

This box consists of three columns, but you can ignore the left column. The Select column has two options: Date (fixed) and Date. Selecting the former inserts today's date into the document, which stays the same regardless of when you edit the letter. This is not really appropriate for a template, so select Date to ensure the document includes the current date. From the multitude of date formats in the third column, choose MMMM DD YYYY, which will display Christmas Day as December 23 2008.

If none of these options suit, you can also create your own format by scrolling to the bottom of the options list and choosing Additional formats. This opens up a more extensive dialog box where you can make more radical changes to the date.

Here again you'll see the list of available formats, but at the bottom of the window is an area for creating a totally custom date field (see Figure 1-20). The various elements you can add are shown in Table 1-1.

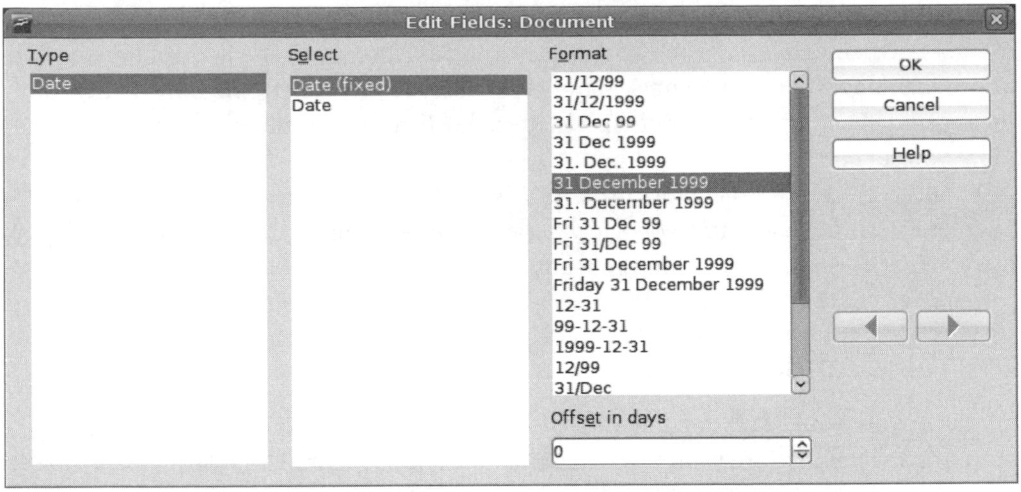

**Figure 1-20.** *Many date options are available, but if nothing fits the house style, then you can create custom dates.*

**Table 1-1.** *Date Elements Are Given Representative Codes*

| Code | Description | Example |
|------|-------------|---------|
| NN | Short day | Fri |
| NNNN | Full day | Friday |
| DD | Numerical day | 25 |
| MM | Short month | Dec |
| MMMM | Full month | December |
| YY | Short year | 08 |
| YYYY | Full year | 2008 |
| HH | Hour | |
| MM | Minute | |
| SS | Second | |

You can also delimit each element with any character. For example, to create 12/23/08, you would enter MM/DD/YY, but to add a more formal dateline, you might have NNNN MMMM DD YYYY, which would render as Thursday December 25 2008. The options for adding hour, minute, and second information are likely to be useful in a spreadsheet but can usually be ignored in letter writing.

Now you need to add placeholder elements for the salutation and reference because these too are likely to change on each new letter. You'll also select the body of the text and put a placeholder there. Remember that this placeholder will inherit the formatting from the present text, so when you write a new letter, it will automatically retain the first line indent you set earlier.

Finally, you'll add placeholder text for the signoff (with a short note in the tool tip about letter-writing etiquette), add a few punctuation elements to save typing them every time you use the template, and you're ready to save.

## Save the Template

Ordinarily, you would save documents as documents, as you did earlier in this chapter, but in this special case, we want to save as a template (see Figure 1-21). This means that the next time the document is opened, it will open as if it were the first time, and users will be prompted to supply a new file name when they attempt to save it. If you saved as a document, edited the text or replaced the placeholders, and clicked Save, it would automatically save over the original—you don't want this to happen as that would destroy your previous work!

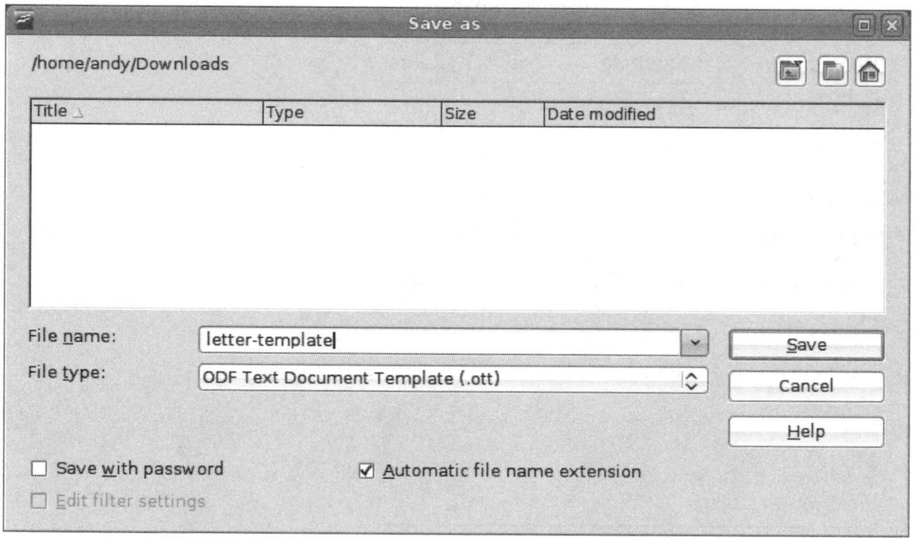

**Figure 1-21.** *Save the document using the correct template format so that you can create a new document from it at a future date.*

Templates can be saved to any location, but if you want them to pop up in the My Templates section of the New Document selector, they need to be saved from within OO.o or manually moved to the correct location.

To save within OO.o, choose File ➤ Template ➤ Save. Select the MyTemplates folder, and provide a name for the template. Click Save to add the template to the folder. To make changes to the template name or the location of a particular file post-creation, choose File ➤ Templates ➤ Organize. This will launch a two-paned organizer window where individual files can be moved around or deleted (see Figure 1-22).

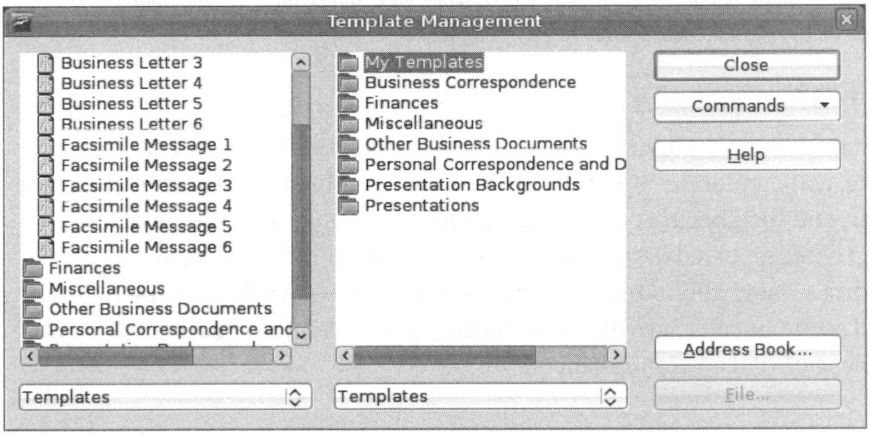

**Figure 1-22.** *Organize templates by moving them between folders.*

## TEMPLATE LOCATIONS

The location of the template files that make up the My Templates collection varies from system to system.

### Windows

Windows stores templates in C:\Documents and Settings\username\Application Data\OOo3\user\template.

### Linux

Linux users need to save in ~/.openoffice.org3/user/template, which is a hidden directory. The simplest way to get the template into the right location is to save it first to your desktop or documents folder, and then manually move it. After the template is saved, open up your File Manager, and select View ➤ Show Hidden Files. If you're already sitting in your home directory, a bunch of folders should have appeared, including the one you need. Navigate through this in the usual manner until you open the /template folder, and then drag the previously saved file into there. Remember to hide hidden files again if you're not a fan of filesystem clutter.

### OS X

The new Mac OS version of the application stores its templates in /Users/username/Library/Application Support/OpenOffice.org-aqua/3/user/template.

---

■**Note**  You can set your own location for templates, which makes it much easier to add and remove them. Go into Options (Tools ➤ Options), open the OpenOffice.org section by clicking the little plus (+) icon next to the label, and find the Paths section. Choose Templates, click the Edit button, and click Add. This launches a standard file selector where you can navigate to an existing directory or create a new one. This new location is added to the default location, which means you'll retain access to the suite's included templates while being able to manage custom templates much more easily. Make sure you select the radio button next to the new path to set this as the default save location for new templates.

---

To test that everything's working, open up Writer, and select File ➤ New ➤ Templates and Documents. Look under the MyTemplates tab, and your blank letter should be there. Select this letter, and then begin adding content. The placeholder text should be clickable, so you can enter repeated detail without having to either delete or format anything. The other important thing about this method is that when you save the document for the first time, it will automatically Save As, which means there is no risk of accidentally overwriting some piece of vital correspondence.

## Checking Through a Document

Writer contains a selection of tools designed to help you create great documents and present a professional image to the world. And despite being fairly simple documents to design, when drafting a letter, which these days tends only to be used for very important things, you don't want bad spelling and a flaky layout to let you down.

By default, Writer has the Auto Spell Check tool turned on. This feature draws a wavy red line under any misspelled words. Right-clicking such a word opens a context-sensitive menu (see Figure 1-23) offering a selection of words you may have intended to use and also a few other options with which you can add the word to a dictionary if it is correct or set the language correctly if, for example, you're attempting to use the word "colour" and the document is set to US.

If the red wavy lines are annoying, switch off the Auto Spell Check (which is in the fourth section of the main toolbar) and, after the document is finished, use the normal spell checker (Tools ➤ Spellcheck, or press F7). This launches a dialog box where each "incorrect" word is shown with options for selecting a different word or redefining the current selection as correct (see Figure 1-24). The Ignore Once button will move over a word by highlighting it again if it appears in the text. Ignore All will note the word as acceptable on a document-wide basis and will not highlight it again.

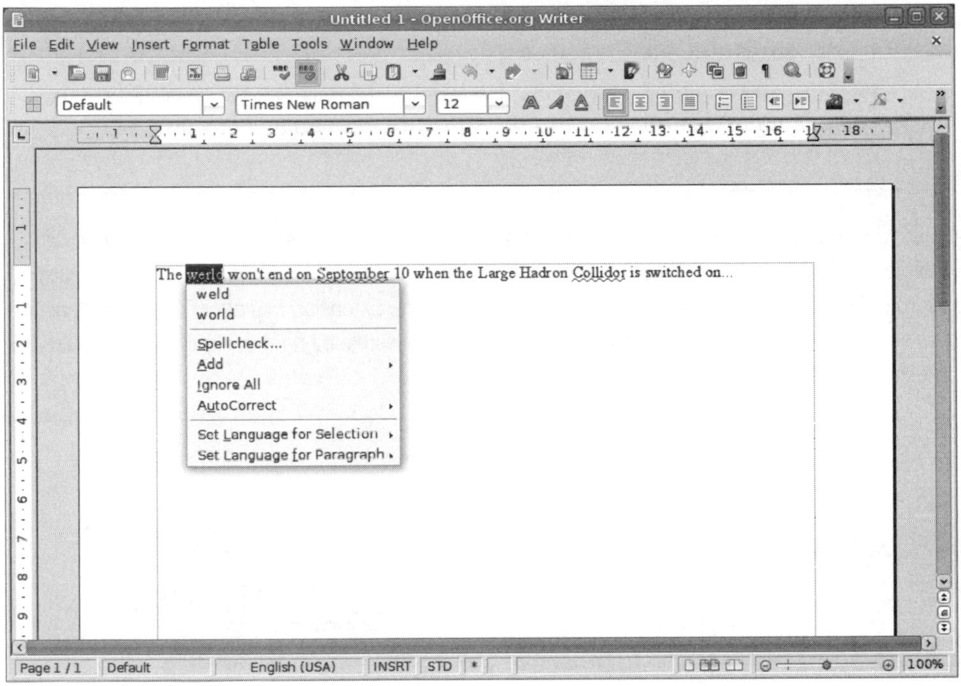

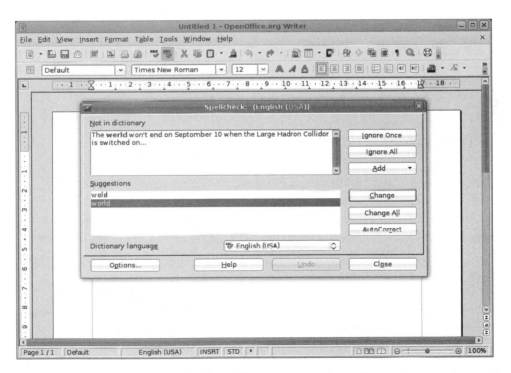

**Figure 1-23.** *The right-click menu offers a selection of words "close" to the incorrectly spelled one.*

**Figure 1-24.** *The Spellcheck dialog box allows you to go through every incorrectly typed word in the document.*

The Add button adds the highlighted word to the standard dictionary, and the Auto-Correct button adds the word, and the selected "correct" version to the AutoCorrect dictionary. This latter tool is really useful if you consistently spell a word wrong (we'll cover this more in Chapter 3), and you want the software to change it as you type.

---

**Tip** If your version of OpenOffice.org is not displaying the wavy spelling lines, it could mean that no dictionaries have been installed. Dictionaries in many languages can be downloaded from the OpenOffice.org web site as .oxt files. These can be added to the software using the Extension Manager (Tools ➤ Extension Manager) as shown in Figure 1-25. Once added, a dictionary is accessible by right-clicking and choosing Tools ➤ Spelling and Grammar.

---

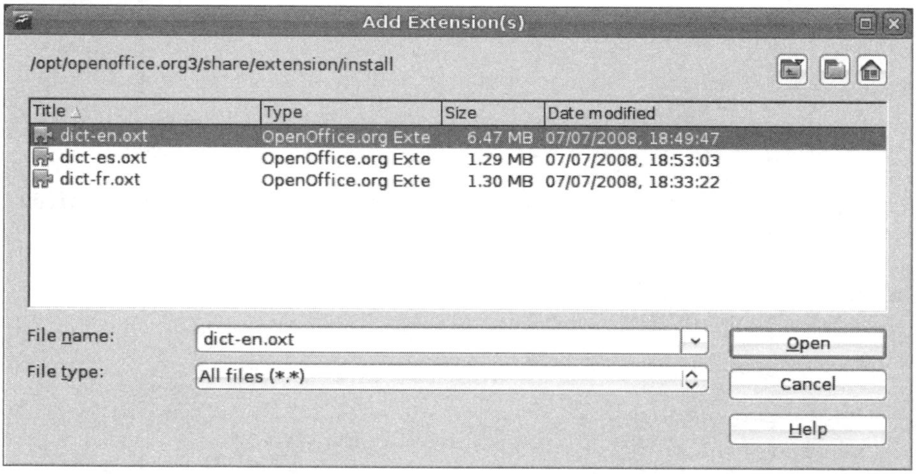

**Figure 1-25.** *OpenOffice.org can have a number of dictionaries installed at one time.*

Another presentational problem that often besets word processor documents is incorrect spacing between words. For example, in the day of the typewriter, users got into the habit of adding two spaces after a full stop (after a period). When using a type-writer with a fixed-width typeface, this might have made sense, but in the age of dynamic fonts, it's unnecessary. Finding an instance of two spaces within a document can be quite a challenge, but there are two ways you can eliminate them.

The first is to choose View ➤ Non Printing Characters to expose all of the hidden parts of the document—the spaces, paragraph returns, soft returns, and tabs—allowing you to comb through the text and remove anything that is out of place (see Figure 1-26). The text remains editable in the normal way, and when printing, will print as normal.

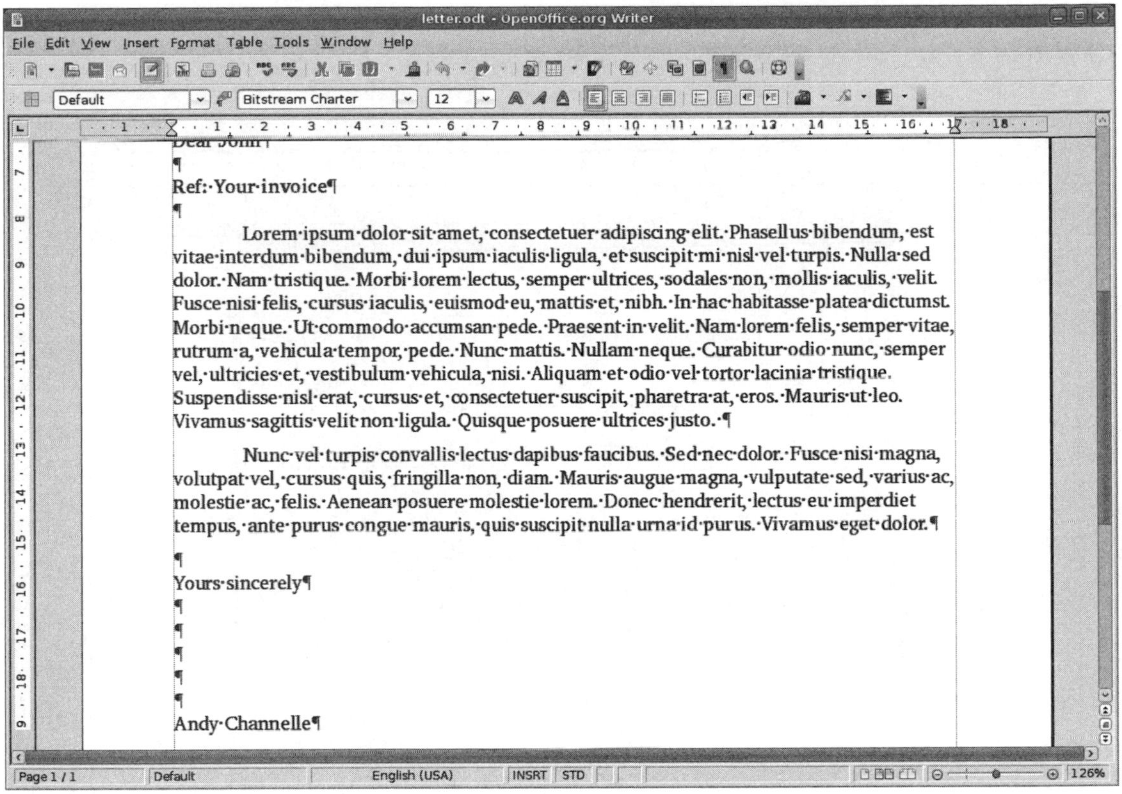

**Figure 1-26.** *The dots in this screenshot represent spaces. Each "hidden" character in a document has its own symbol that can be used for search and replace.*

The second way to remove annoyances such as double spaces, especially if there are a lot of them in a single document, is to use the Find & Replace option under the Edit menu. The top text area of this dialog box contains the text you need to find, and the bottom area contains its replacement (see Figure 1-27). After these have been added, use one of the buttons on the right to find and replace single entities or use Replace All to replace all instances of a certain term at once. The Match Case option is useful when you want to change, for example, "Hope" (the town) but not "hope" the concept. The Whole words only option is useful if you want to change "Man" to "man" but don't want it to affect "Manchester" or "Manager."

Of course, the Find & Replace option can be used to make more drastic changes as well. For example, you may write a novel with the lead character called Harry. If, 55,000 words in, you decide his name should be John, Find & Replace will save a lot of effort. And if you ensure that Whole words only is not selected, it will also change "Harry's" to "John's," just as using the Match case option will ensure that the sentence "The boss used to harry his staff . . ." doesn't become "The boss used to john his staff. . . ."

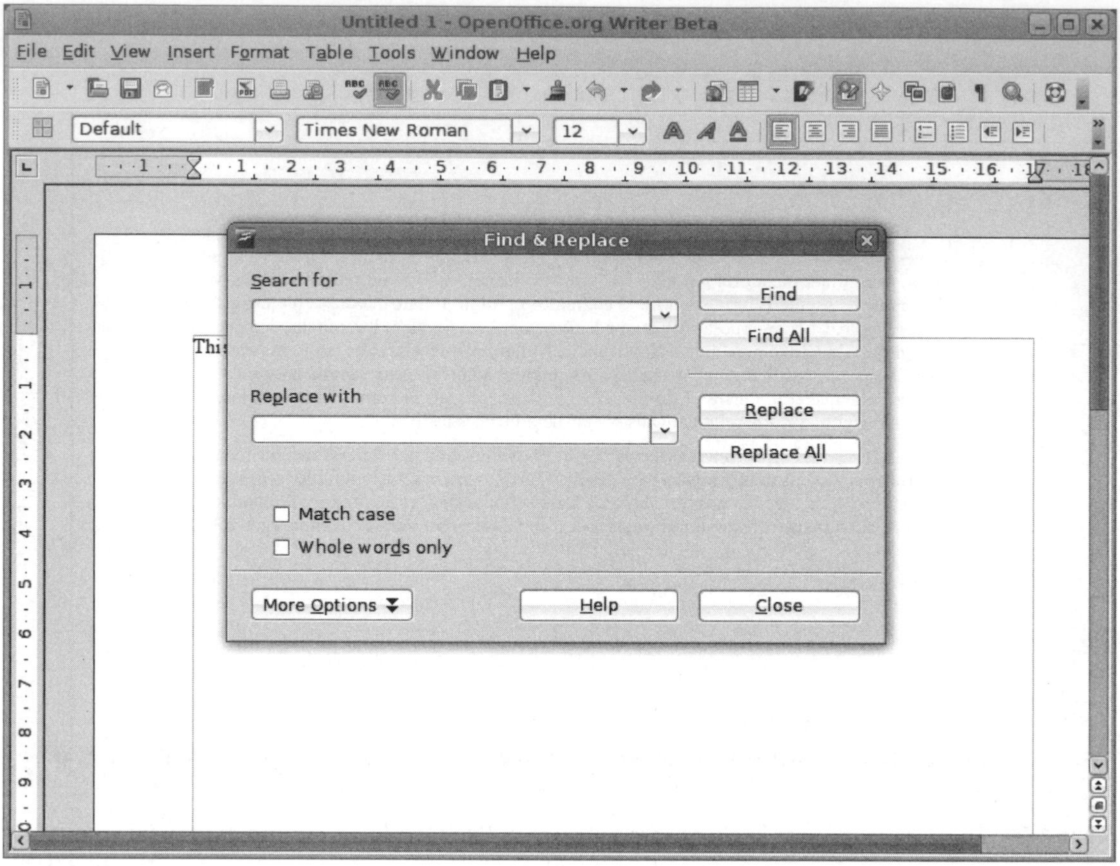

**Figure 1-27.** *Use the Find & Replace feature to make large-scale textual changes to a document.*

## Printing

The final stage of any production—well, any traditional production—is printing out a hard copy. First, however, you can get a better idea of how the final result will look by using the Preview button (the eighth button from left on the main toolbar) or by choosing File ➤ Page Preview. This displays a more accurate rendition of the page.

The Print button (next to the Preview button), the File ➤ Print menu, or the Ctrl+P shortcut key will launch the standard Print dialog box. You can select a printer, set the page size, define the number of copies, and set the pages to be printed in this dialog box (see Figure 1-28). Options relating to the selected printer are accessible from the Properties button, while the Options button has many things to change, including preventing graphics from being printed, setting left- or right-only page printing, or turning off backgrounds. These options can be useful for proofing documents without wasting ink and time. Click OK to initiate the printing process.

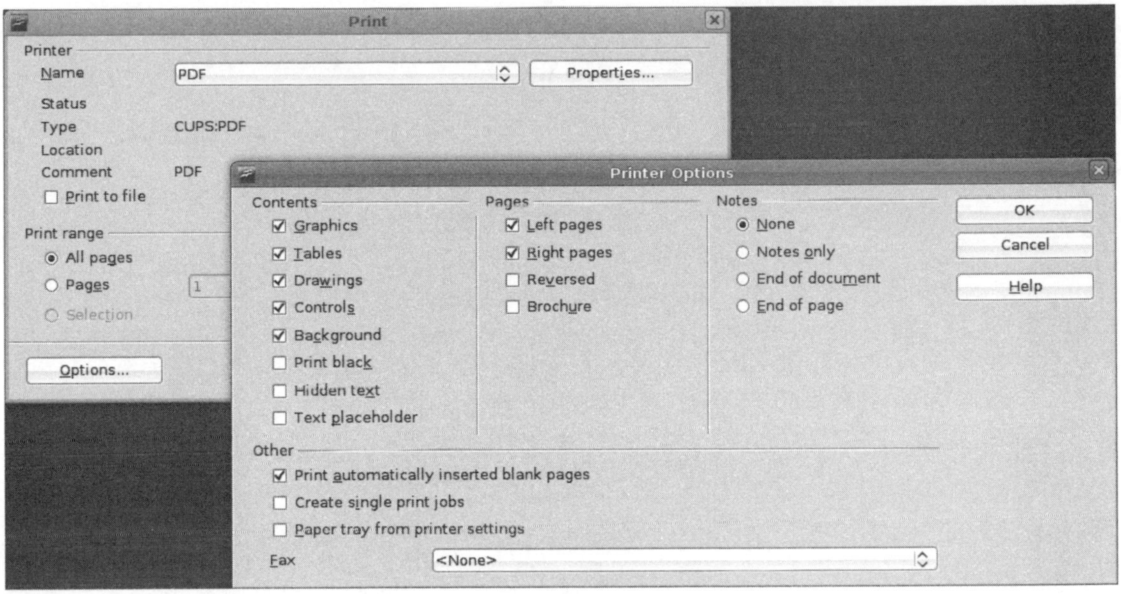

**Figure 1-28.** *Comprehensive printing options provide good control over how your final document appears.*

# Recap

In this chapter, you've used OO.o Writer to create a basic text-based letter. You've made some simple alterations to the format of characters and paragraphs and made a few changes to the application's interface to put important tools a few clicks away. You've taken this letter, removed all the unique content, and repurposed it as a template that will save time in later uses. Finally you've delved into the Placeholder text system—in readiness for more extensive edits later—and changed the way that OO.o deals with dates at the document level.

In the next chapter, you'll work with some of these elements again, but this time, you'll focus on a more design-intensive document and adding some graphical flourishes.

# CHAPTER 2

∎∎∎

# Design Using Writer

We've looked at the basics of Writer document creation, but the application is capable of so much more (see Figure 2-1). In fact, you have a set of design and layout tools at your disposal that, just a few years ago, would have beat a thousand dollar professional publishing package. In this chapter, we're concentrating more on bringing text and imagery together to create something much more stylish than a few blocks of text. And this is perfect preparation for the next chapter where we'll draw together the whole Writer toolset to create a newsletter with columns, graphics, colors, and photographs.

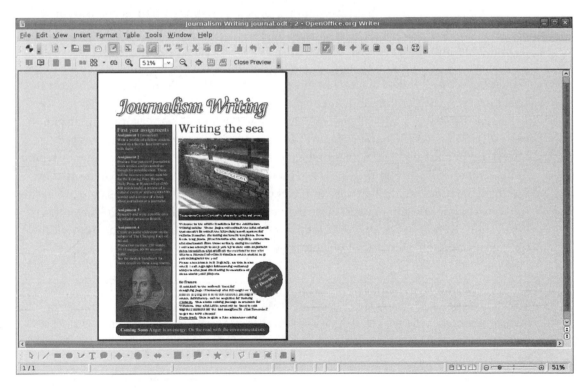

**Figure 2-1.** *Writer is capable of much more than simple letters. In some areas, it even rivals dedicated desktop publishing packages.*

Although the end result may be a newsletter, the processes and tools you'll use to create this page are perfect for any document that requires a little more visual style than a simple piece of text; from flyers and menus to bookmarks and class handouts. This change of emphasis from simple text to design involves introducing a few new concepts into the mix. Frames, which can contain any kind of content, are discussed later in this chapter, whereas paragraph styles, which allow you to automate many elements of the presentation process, are covered briefly next but will be examined in much more detail in Chapter 3. In addition, Draw has some page layout features that may be useful if a design seems too ambitious for Writer. See Chapter 6 for more on this.

# Multicolumn Text

In our previous document, we followed the conventions of a letter that had a single column down the center of the page. To add a little flexibility to the next project, you'll begin with a two-column page. After you've created a new document (File ➤ New ➤ Text Document), select Format ➤ Page to define the page size and margins, and then click the Columns tab.

Writer is very flexible about its columns, allowing anything up to 99 columns on a single page and allowing you to set widths either automatically or on a column-by-column basis. Five common layouts are offered at the top of the window; they can be used as is or as a starting point for more editing. Adding columns to a document can give it a more "newspapery" feel, but be aware that three columns on an A4/letter page is probably the maximum you should aim for. Larger pages can obviously take more columns.

Below these five icons are the configuration tools; there is a measurement box for each column (use the left and right arrows to see anything beyond the three visible boxes). Editing the width of a column involves either using the up/down arrows or typing a value in the box (see Figure 2-2). These values can obviously not add up to more than the available space, so the software won't let you design unfeasible widths, and increasing the width of one column beyond these boundaries will automatically shrink any others. If you want to create a number of columns with an equal width, choose the AutoWidth option (the manual width boxes will be grayed out).

---

■**Note**  If you've added content to a column-based layout, and the text features masses of hyphens on the right edge of each column, look at the font settings or column widths for a remedy. There are a lot of hyphenation settings to play with by choosing Format ➤ Paragraph, under the Text Flow tab. See Chapter 3 for more on advanced paragraph formatting.

---

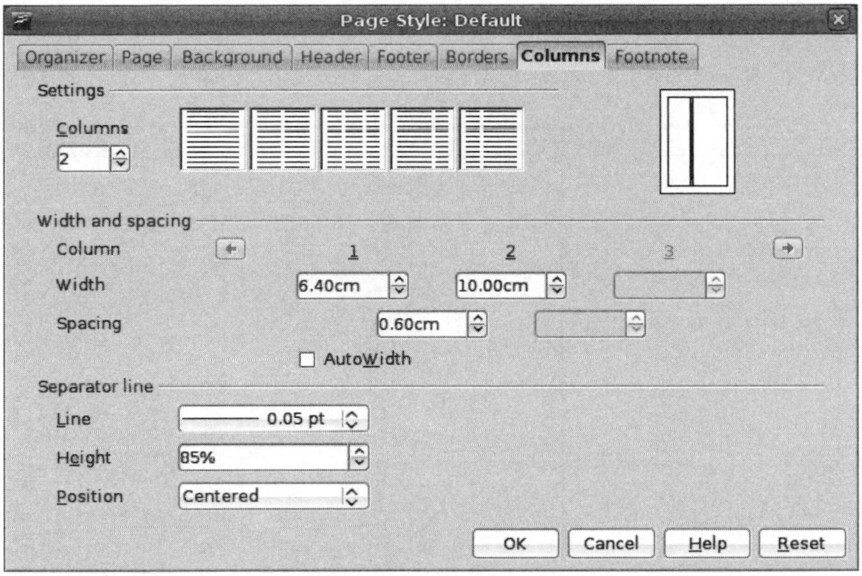

**Figure 2-2.** *Writer is capable of sophisticated multicolumn design, and to save having to design your own, the software has a set of premade layouts available at the click of a button.*

Beneath the Width values are the Spacing values that define the gap—or gutter in design-speak—between each column. Studies have shown that when readers are following a long horizontal line of text on a page, they frequently lose their place, so the use of columns and gutters can improve readability significantly. A gutter needs to be wide enough to make it clear to readers that they should not continue along the current line. For reference, a typical newspaper uses a gutter of between 0.4 and 0.5cm between each column, whereas books have a larger gutter. Set yours to 0.6cm because you'll be adding an extra separator between the two areas of content.

In the Separator line section of the dialog box, there are options for setting the width of the line and its height. Selecting anything but 100% for the latter will automatically enable an alignment option where you can choose to set the separator at the top or bottom of the page or center it vertically. Onc thing missing here is the ability to define a particular line type (dotted, dashed, etc.), so leave your line in place for the moment, but note that you'll be replacing it later on.

For this project, you're going for a two-column asymmetric layout, with thc lcft column taking up 6cm and with spacing of 0.6cm. Now add a 0.05cm line between columns, set it to 85% of the page height, and align it to the bottom of the page (see Figure 2-3).

This sort of design divides the page neatly into three regions; there is space at the top for a masthead or large title, the smaller left column is set to contain publication and address information, and the right column is for some actual content. This is the perfect layout for a community or church newsletter, school brochure, internal communications, or formal business flyer.

**Figure 2-3.** *This asymmetric layout gives you quite a few options when it comes to importing a selection of different stories.*

Normally, Writer expects text to flow in particular ways. For example, if you begin typing (or pasting text) in this page, the words go across the left column creating new lines as it reaches the right edge of the column until it hits the bottom of the page; the text then flows into the right-hand column and continues on down the page until it reaches the base of that page, and then a new page is added to the document following the design of the first page with the text in the left column, and on and on. However, you'll be working using the DTP (desktop publishing) methodology, which means actually creating the three regions mentioned earlier so that the various bits of content stay in their own frames.

## The Title Frame

You'll start by adding the textual element that will dominate the page in a new frame. This element is ordinarily the title of your publication or a section title. Frames are what make the DTP-like functions of Writer possible because each one can contain anything from text or images to drawings and spreadsheets. They're like having a lot of small individual pages on top of the main page. Choose Insert ➤ Frame to launch the Frame dialog box. The Frame dialog box is divided into three sections, but we're really only interested in the right-hand section at the moment (we'll come back to the other parts shortly). In the right-hand section, you'll notice that, by default, your new frame is set to Anchor To paragraph. Any frame that is anchored to a paragraph moves up and down with its host as you edit or add text above it. This will be useful later on, but we want the title frame anchored to the page. An object in Writer is typically anchored to a particular place in the text, for example, a paragraph or character. By anchoring to the page, the object will stay where we place it, and text can—if configured to do so—wrap around the object.

Select To page and click OK (see Figure 2-4). The underwhelming result is a little frame near the top of the page. However, you can resize this to more impressive dimensions by clicking it to reveal eight grab handles and dragging these to the right places on the page. It's also possible to move the entire box by clicking anywhere within the box and dragging.

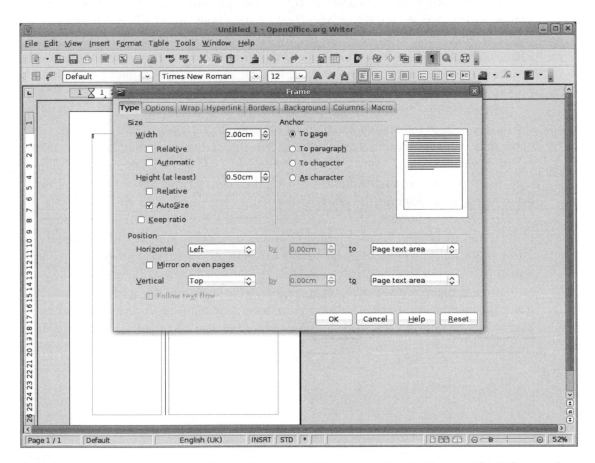

**Figure 2-4.** *Frames can be anchored to various parts of the content, but for the most flexibility, anchor this frame to the page.*

■**Note** The first time you edit text frames in Writer can be a little frustrating because the method of grab-bing them may seem random; it's not. It's just that all frames in Writer have two methods of editing to deal with the distinction between the object and its content. The most obvious example of editing an item is clicking the edge of a frame and resizing the object with the frame handles or repositioning it on the page; but item editing also includes things such as the border, the background, and the frame's relationship with the rest of the page. All of these options (which we'll discuss further in this chapter) can be accessed by double-clicking the frame.

You can edit the content of the frame by clicking inside it and getting straight to work on the text. Of course, if you've previously selected a frame for item editing and want to edit the content, you first have to click off of it, that is, click somewhere else on the page before clicking inside the box again.

This frame needs to go across the top of the page (from margin guide to margin guide), and the base should fall a few millimeters from the top of the vertical line between the columns. You probably noticed that Writer automatically adds a black border to text frames, which we don't want. Getting rid of the border is an "item" edit, so click one of the frame edges to go into item mode and then double-click the frame. This launches the Frame dialog box that you used earlier to add the frame. Before getting rid of the borders, this is a good opportunity to refine the position of the box—your eye may be good, but it's probably not perfect—using the bottom section of this dialog box.

Writer's standard method of defining position is to base it on the edge of the page. In this case, you need to make sure that the Horizontal and Vertical values on the Type tab of the Frame dialog box are set from Left and Top, respectively, and that the figures in the boxes match the margins set when creating the page. If you can't remember these num-bers, you can also position the frame relative to the Page text area (using the drop-down list on the right) and setting the value to 0.00cm.

Now select the Borders tab (see Figure 2-5). In this tab, you can define which edges of the frame are bordered, the style of any borders, their color, and the gap between the frame edges and your content. At the base of this window, there is also an option to add a shadow to the box, but ignore that for now.

For this project, we want a newspaper-like title, so switch off the borders completely, (selecting the first icon under Line arrangement), and click OK. Now click off the frame box in your document, click inside it, and type a title for the document.

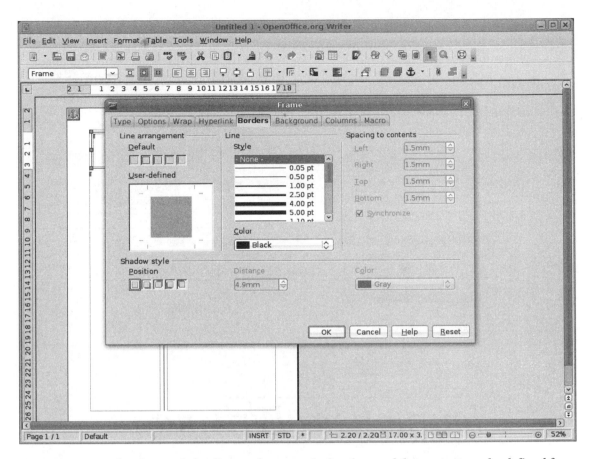

**Figure 2-5.** *Frame borders and the distance between the borders and the content can be defined for each edge.*

# Advanced Text Editing

Now that you have a title, you need to make it a bit larger so it stands out from the rest of the text that will be on the page. To do this, highlight the text, and increase the size using the font size drop-down list on the Formatting toolbar. The drop-down list offers preset sizes, but you can be more precise by entering any size using the number keys. You may also want to change the default Writer font to something a little more stylish by selecting the right look from the font drop-down list.

---

■**Tip** Typically fonts for printing are measured in "points," and the higher the number, the larger the text. In the past, most fonts were designed to follow a standard size, which meant that 72 points roughly equaled 1 inch in height. However, this is not so standard now, and 72 points in one font may be significantly smaller or larger than another.

---

Writer has more options available to improve the look of your text beyond this simple editing; to access the extended toolset, highlight the title, and choose Format ➤ Character. This launches the familiar Character dialog box where you can make a few more changes; the dialog box launches with the Font tab highlighted (see Figure 2-6). The Font tab contains the same range of tools available on the Formatting toolbar but also has a preview so you can see changes made in real time.

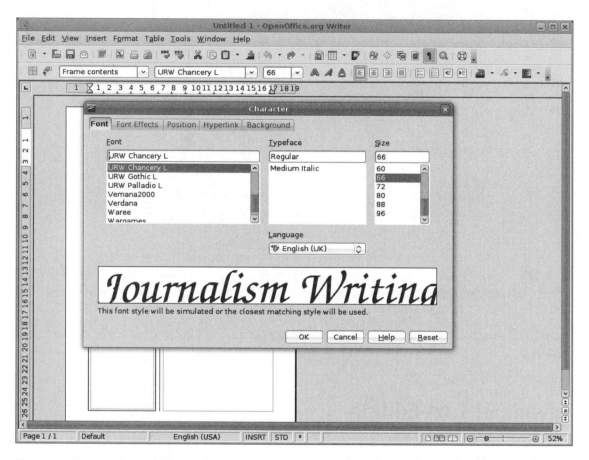

**Figure 2-6.** *You can select a font from the main interface and from the Character dialog box.*

In the Font Effects tab, you can make some fairly dramatic changes. It's easy to go overboard with these effects and create something messy, so take care, especially when using small font sizes. On the left are the Strikethrough and Underlining options, featuring a range of different types of line and color, and the Font color option. On the right, there are some case Effects—that is, they change the case of selected letters to uppercase, lowercase, title case (each word has an initial capital), or small caps—Relief effects (embossed and engraved), and then some miscellaneous effects such as Outline, Shadow, Blinking, and Hidden. The Outline and Shadow effect combination works well for titles, so select those check boxes as shown in Figure 2-7.

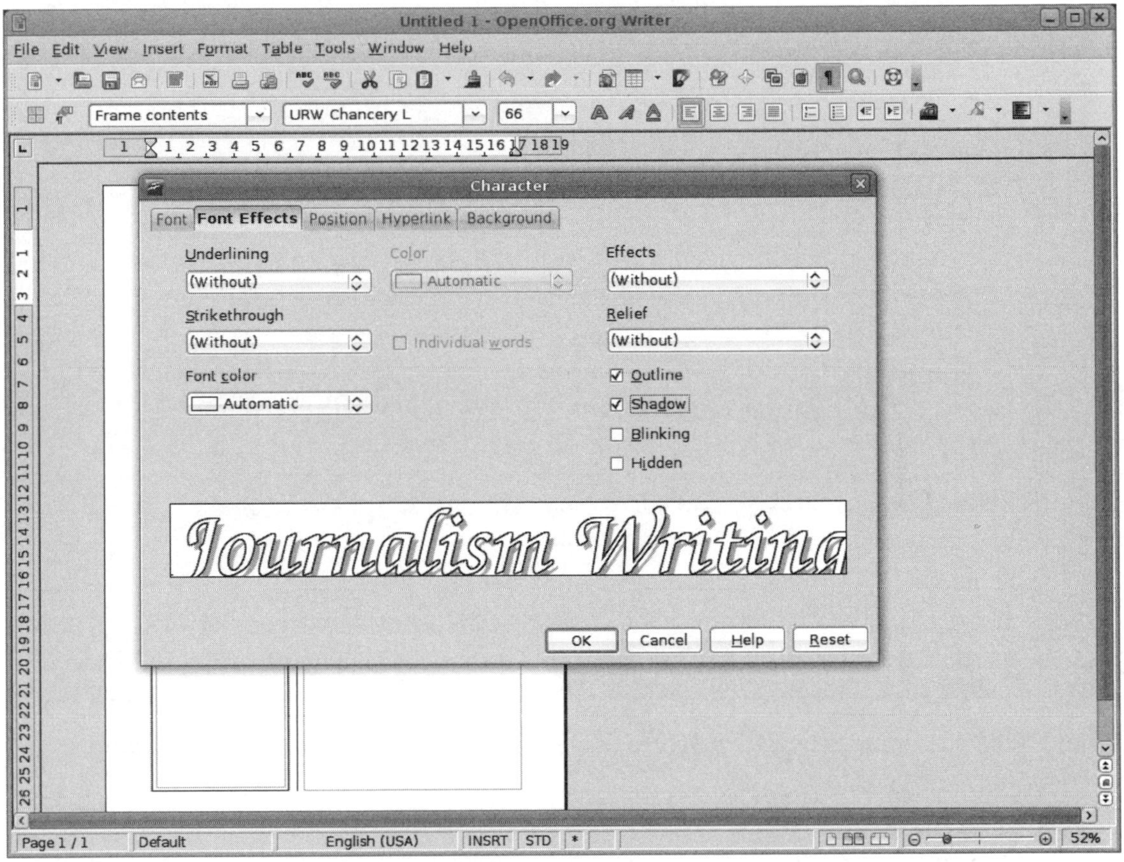

**Figure 2-7.** *The Outline and Shadow effects work well together on our newsletter title.*

The Position tab provides a great deal of control over how the text is positioned not just in terms of superscript and subscript but also in the spaces between individual letters, the width of each letter, and the rotation of the text (see Figure 2-8). There is an impressive amount of control here, as well as some sensible default options for those more interested in the words themselves. For example, in the Subscript and Superscript options, you can define how far to scale the letters and how far from the baseline to move them; by default these values are set to 58% and 33%, respectively, but you can create some interesting effects by playing around with these settings.

Rotation/scaling settings are available in the center of the dialog box.

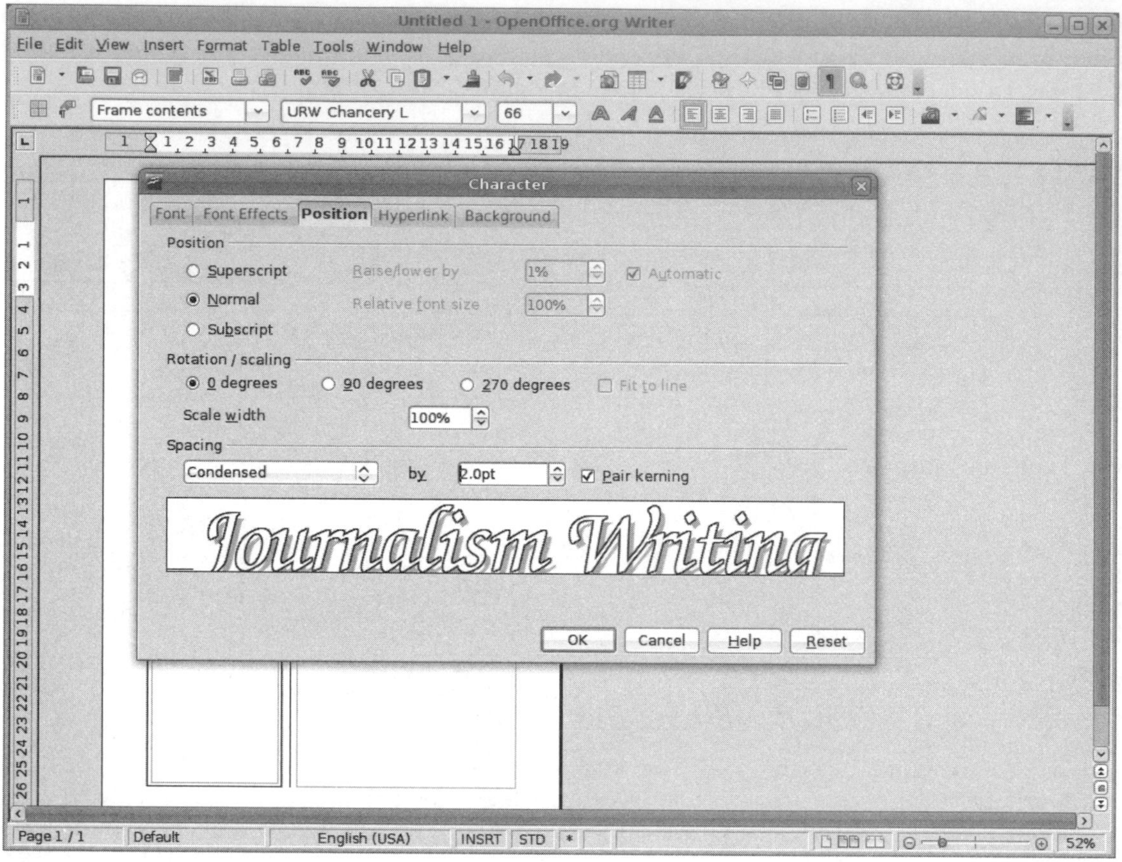

**Figure 2-8.** *When outline fonts are condensed, clashing letters are dealt with in a stylish manner. Overlaps are joined together.*

Ordinarily, rotation is restricted to 0, 90, or 270 degrees (horizontal, vertical bottom-to-top, and vertical top-to-bottom), and the Fit to line option—which is grayed out until a rotation value has been selected—squishes the line of text vertically into the same height it occupies horizontally.

The scaling options increase or decrease the width of the letters (the value of 100% is Writer's standard setting), whereas the Spacing section options expand or condense the gaps between the letters. Pair kerning, which is only available on some fonts, pays particular attention to letter pairs such as "Wo" and "fi," which can often cause problems. Kerning is the process of pulling pairs of letters together to reduce ugly gaps in a word. By using these options, you can fit your title effectively in the space at the top of the page. There are two approaches to this; you can either reduce the size of the font slightly and then increase the spacing until the text fills the space, or you can increase the size of the font until the text goes over two lines and then reduce the spacing to get it back to one line. The latter adds the most impact to the title, whereas the former is good for giving space to subheadings.

| TEXT FORMATTING TERMS |
|---|

- *Bold*: Makes the text thicker to add emphasis. Bold text takes more space on a line than regular text.

- *Italic*: Slants text forward slightly, at its most basic. In practice, though, a real italic font is not just slanted but may also be slightly more ornate.

- *Underline*: Adds a solid line under the text. It too can be used to add emphasis, but most modern design tends to steer clear of it as italic is a far more elegant solution.

- *Strikethrough*: Denotes something that should be removed by putting a solid line horizontally through the center of the text.

- *Superscript*: Reduces the size of the font and raises slightly from the baseline of the text. Used for adding suffixes to numbers in dates ($21^{st}$, $3^{rd}$), in mathematics ($10^2$), and to denote a footnote or bibliography entry.

- *Subscript*: Like superscript, reduces the size of the text but drops it below the baseline. Often used to define chemical structures ($h_2 0$).

■**Caution**   As with font effects, it's easy to overuse spacing and horizontal/vertical font scaling, which results in an unprofessional-looking document. Use your eye to compare what's on the screen with the kind of output you're used to looking at. Does your text look odd? Are the letters easy to distinguish?

# Edit Frames

Frames can be used to add as many text boxes (and other objects) as you like to the page. In addition to the title box you built earlier, you'll add two text boxes in the main content area, reflecting the column design of the page, and add a third just beneath the title for the publication's subtitle. You'll position these using the margin guides.

The left-hand frame will be colored in the final production, and the text will be inset slightly in the box so it doesn't clash with the edges. There are two ways you can accomplish this job: you can use the paragraph options (see Chapter 1) to add indents to the left and right edges of the text and then add a little space to the top paragraph, or you can add a four-sided border to the frame and then inset the contents all around the box. To do the latter, double-click the box, choose the Borders tab, and set the All Four Borders options in the Line arrangement section as shown in Figure 2-9.

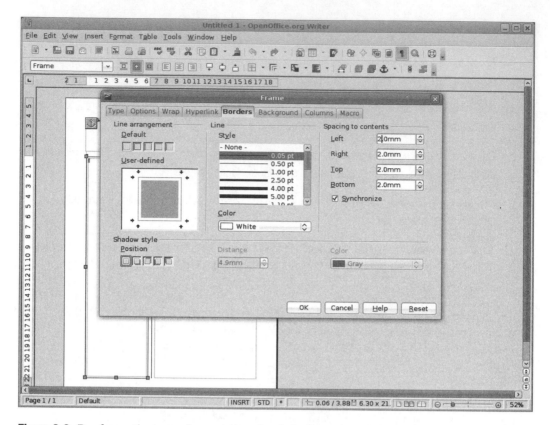

**Figure 2-9.** *Border options can be set using the default or user-defined method.*

With that selected, choose the line width (0.05pt) and Color (White), and then define the Spacing to contents on the right-hand side at 2.0mm all round. The purpose of choosing a white border is so that when you color the frame (later in this chapter), it won't look out of place. (You could also make the border the same color as the frame background.)

At the base of the Borders settings is an option to add a shadow to the box. Selecting one of the positions (bottom-left, top-right, etc.) enables the Distance and Color settings, providing a lot more control over the look of the shadow. You don't need this now, but you might come back to it later.

For now, populate the two main frames with some placeholder text to get an idea of what the final layout will look like.

# Placeholder Text

The type of placeholder you'll use is called "lorem ipsum" text, which is designed to simulate the look of written English (so you can make an intelligent guess at how many words each part will accommodate) while not actually making any sense. The text we've used was cut and pasted from a website called the Lorem Ipsum generator (http://www.lipsum.com/), but we can make the process of adding this text with the addition of a special OO.o extension.

Extensions are covered in detail later, but briefly, an *extension* is a small program or macro that integrates with Writer, or some other element of the suite, and adds a feature that might be slightly too "niche" for the OO.o developers to worry about. One such extension is the Lorem Ipsum generator, which uses the Lipsum website to generate dummy text for your layouts. The extension is available from http://extensions.services.openoffice.org/project/Lorem_ipsum_generator. Download the file, which has an .oxt file extension, and save it somewhere on your disk.

In any OO.o application, go to Tools ➤ Extension Manager, select My Extensions, and click the Add button (see Figure 2-10). Now use the normal file browser to find the downloaded .oxt file, and click Open. The extension appears under the My Extensions disclosure arrow; its status should automatically be set to Enabled, but if not, click the Enable button, and then click Close. Because of the way this extension integrates with OO.o (it adds a new menu entry), you'll have to shut down and relaunch the application to see the fruits of your labor.

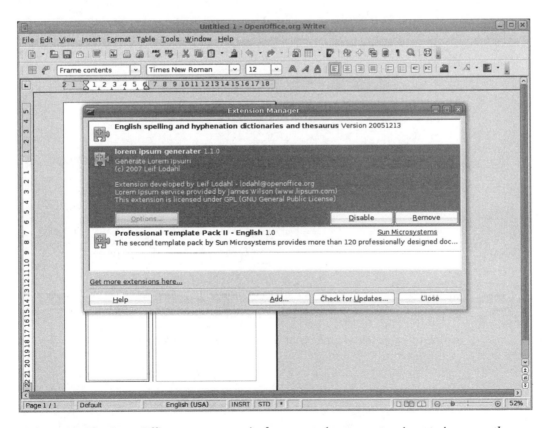

**Figure 2-10.** *The OpenOffice.org community has created many extensions to improve the toolset for specific user groups, including designers. See Chapter 11 for more on extensions.*

So, in a restarted Writer, select the appropriate frame, and choose View ➤ Toolbars ➤ Lorem Ipsum to add the LI toolbar to the Writer user interface. (or you can simply add the button to an existing toolbar as described in Chapter 1). For some reason, the icon is a crash test symbol; click it, define how much text you want in either words, paragraphs, bytes, or lists, and click Generate (see Figure 2-11). The placeholder is added to wherever the cursor was before the Generate button was clicked.

When the placeholder text is in these frames, you can define the font, size, and paragraph settings to make everything look good before you even have to worry about the actual content. When you add the real words, the formats will be inherited from the placeholder text.

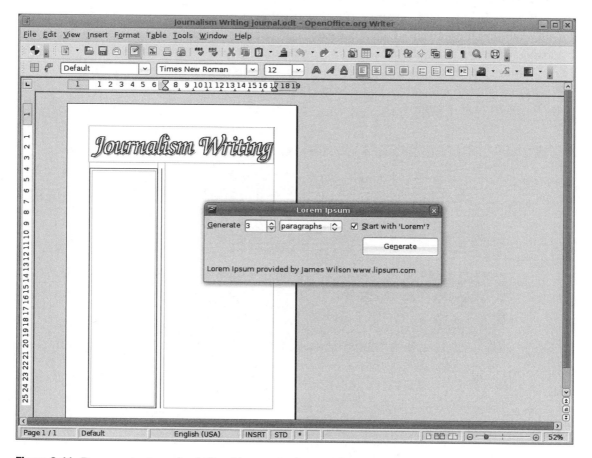

**Figure 2-11.** *Dummy text can be defined in particular word or paragraph lengths.*

## WORD COUNTS

Writer's word count is accessible from Tools ➤ Word Count. This will launch a two-part dialog box; the top section reveals the number of words and characters in a selection, and the bottom section does the same for the entire document. Of course, if you have nothing selected, the top half won't have any useful information.

On longer projects, such as scripts, books, or dissertations, the section word count is absolutely vital, but it's also useful to get an overview of the entire project.

More statistics, including the number of paragraphs, pages, images, and tables in a document, are available by choosing File ➤ Properties ➤ Statistics.

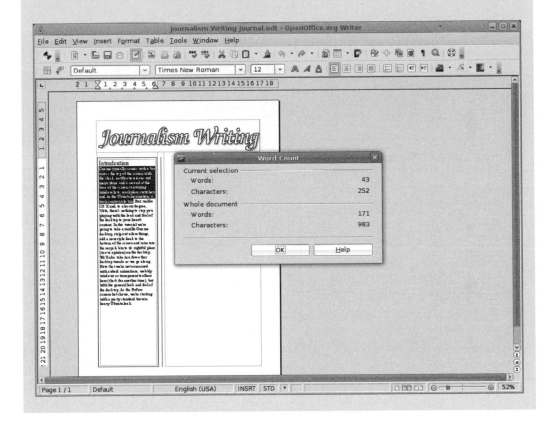

# Colors

Almost any document can be enlivened with a splash of color, and you can add some sparkle to almost any element on a Writer page.

## Text

Text is so important that it gets three separate types of color options: type, highlight, and background. Most obviously, the type color changes the color of the font on the page. Highlight a piece of text, and click the text color icon to open the selection dialog box. The Font color dialog box is a movable palette rather than a simple drop-down list, which makes it easy to leave open for experimentation (see Figure 2-12). Changes in text color only affect highlighted text, but if you choose a new color before selecting text, the cursor becomes a paint bucket, and you can paint across a text selection to change its color. You'll notice, also, that if you have a shadow, and the text is black, the shadow will be a faded gray; but when using any other color, the shadow will be black.

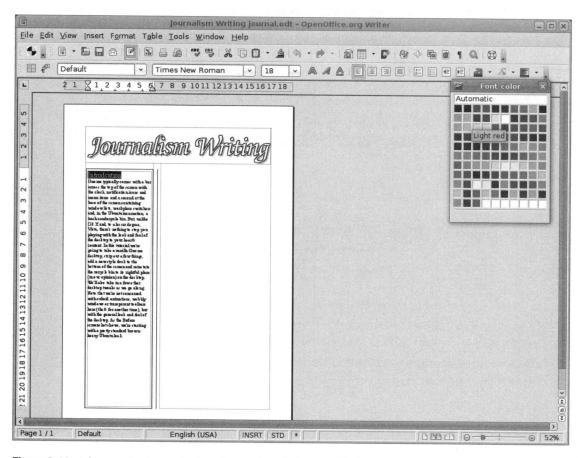

**Figure 2-12.** *A large selection of colors have already been added to the system. Hover the mouse over a color to see its name.*

The Font color dialog box contains just over 100 colors (hover over a color to see its name), but you can also add more hues in the Options settings (Tools ➤ Options). Under the OpenOffice.org settings (at the top of the list on the left), select Colors. Colors in OO.o, in common with most computer applications, are usually defined by mixing a combination of red (R), green (G), and blue (B) light. There are 256 degrees of brightness for each of these, giving you a potential palette of 16,777,216 colors ranging from white (255, 255, 255) to black (0, 0, 0) and all points in between. It's best to begin with a color that is close to what you need rather than starting from scratch, so pick a color from the available palette, re-edit the values to get it just right, add a new name in the Name field, and click the Add button (see Figure 2-13). Your new color will then be available whenever the Font color dialog is opened. If changes need to be made, revisit this dialog box, select the color to be edited, and click the Modify button. Changes made will then be reflected not just in the palette but also in any page element using that color.

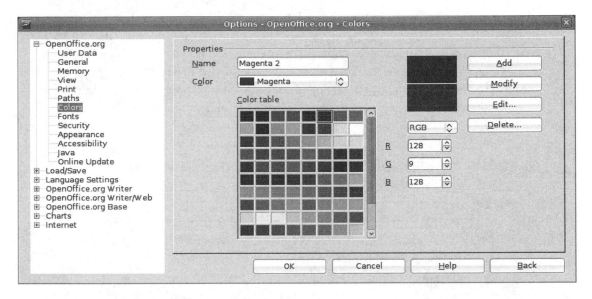

**Figure 2-13.** *The color-editing box*

**■Note**  In the color-editing box, just above the R, G, and B settings, you'll see a drop-down list; click this, and select CMYK to define your color using the cyan, magenta, yellow, black system, which tends to be used by professional printers. RGB (Red, Green, Blue) is how colors on a screen are defined. If your document is destined for output by a printing bureau, it may be best to define your colors using this system, especially if you're working with a particular selection of colors.

## Highlights

The highlight color is used to pull out a word or phrase from a piece of text, just as you might with a traditional highlighter pen. Select some text, and click the highlighter button and the text will be picked out in a bright yellow (the default color). You can choose other hues by using the drop-down arrow to launch the color selector. Obviously, particular color combinations (black text, black highlight, etc.) won't work well, so Writer changes the text to black or white depending on the strength of the chosen highlight; darker backgrounds will have white text, and lighter ones will have black text. These options are based on the "Automatic" text color—at the top of the color selection box—and will be overridden by any changes made to the text color.

## Background

Whereas highlights work on individual characters, words, or phrases, the Background color option highlights entire paragraphs. It uses the same methodology: make a selection (in this case, simply clicking anywhere in a chosen paragraph), and choose the color (see Figure 2-14). Again dark colors will force the text to white, and light colors will force it to black. As with any paragraph formatting, the background color is automatically assigned to following paragraphs as you type until the color is changed or No Fill is selected from the chooser.

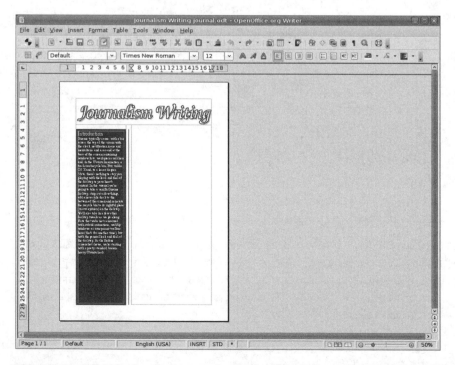

**Figure 2-14.** *Bold blocks of color can be used to highlight particular areas of the page.*

## Frames

You can also set various color options for the frames you've created (see Figure 2-15), and these are available by either double-clicking a frame or by choosing the appropriate option from the Formatting toolbar. As you saw earlier, you can color both the line of the border and the background of the frame itself. Your layout demands that both colors be the same for now. After a frame has been created, it can be saved as a frame style, which makes it easy to apply the same format to every frame in the document. Styles are covered in detail in Chapter 3.

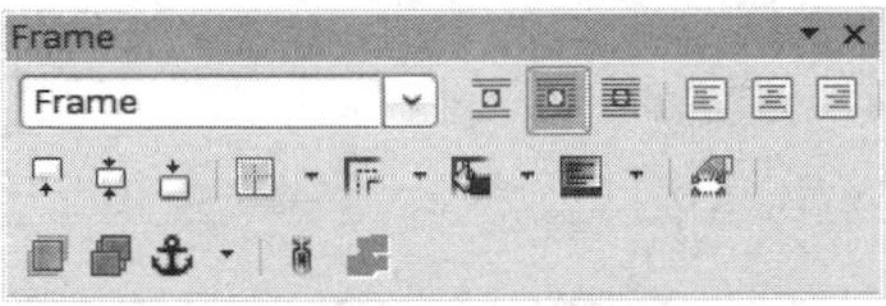

**Figure 2-15.** *Launch the Frame toolbar using View ➤ Toolbars ➤ Frames.*

Note that if you have the text in this frame set to Automatic, it will change to white text if the background color is dark and will remain black on a light background. Override this coloring by selecting the text inside the frame and defining a color as discussed previously.

# Inserting Graphics

So far you've been working with text and color, but now its time to introduce a little imagery. The process of actually adding a picture to the page is very similar to what you've previously done with frames, and it begins with choosing Insert ➤ Picture ➤ From File. Writer is capable of importing a wide range of bitmap and vector pictures, and it also has tools that allow you to create graphics (as discussed in this section and Chapter 6) directly on the page.

You'll start by adding an image to the left column, so click into the column, and choose Insert ➤ Picture ➤ From File. Now navigate to the location of your image (preferably a photographic image for this section), and select it. If you're looking for a particular image in a sea of DCFSxxx-xx.jpg, click the Preview button to get a glimpse of the pictures before importing (see Figure 2-16).

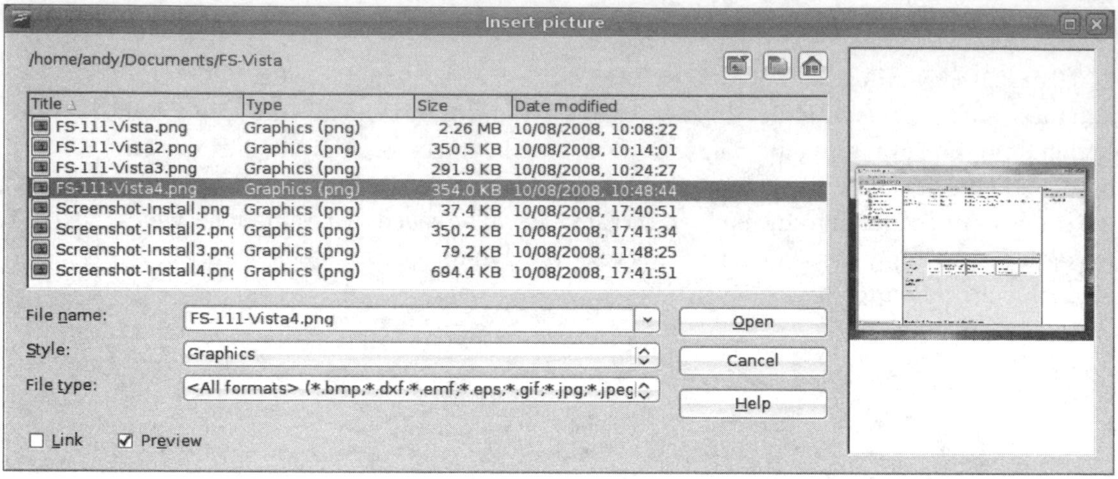

**Figure 2-16.** *Use the Preview button to get a look at a selected image before importing.*

By default, the software imports the image into the page, but you can also link the image to its original file by selecting the Link option. The advantage of this is that the picture will be reloaded onto the page every time the document is opened, which means if you edit an image in an external application, these changes will be automatically reflected in the version on the page. Click the OK button. The image will be added to the page. By default, Writer anchors the image to its paragraph, meaning if you begin adding text above the image, the image will move down the column. This is useful in many situations, but to get more freedom for your layout, you need to anchor it to the page.

Double-click the image. From the Type tab, set the anchor point To page, and click OK. This detaches the picture from the paragraph it was in, allowing you to drag and drop it anywhere on the page. Clicking the image also reveals a set of handles on each corner and edge that can be used to resize the picture.

When you drag to resize, hold down the Shift key to force the image to retain its proportions; of course, if you want to squash or stretch the picture, don't hold any key down. For more refined control over the size and position of the picture, double-click to access the Picture dialog box again (the Type tab should be selected), and edit the height, width, and location numerically. Again, if you want to retain the aspect ratio of the image (which is usually important), select the Keep ratio button before making any edits.

As with the frames created earlier, the position of the graphic, by default, is defined in relation to the top and left edges of the page, but you can change this using the drop-down lists in the Position section.

Sometimes, such as when adding screenshots to a book page, you may want to anchor an image to a paragraph and then have this image move with the text. To do this, change the Anchor setting from To page to To paragraph as shown in Figure 2-17, and then, in the Position section, click Follow text flow. You can still adjust the position of the image, but it's much easier to manage if you change the Horizontal positioning from the edge of the page to the left or right paragraph border; this is especially true when working across multiple columns.

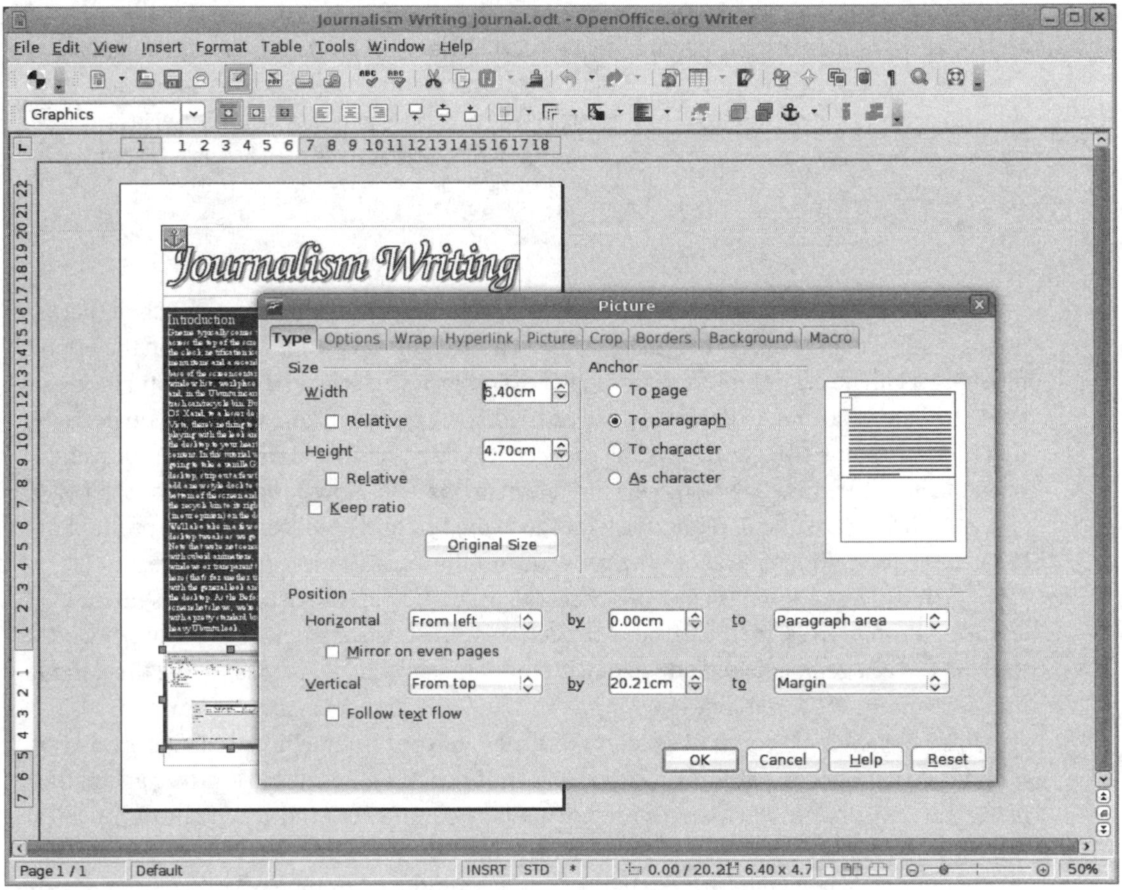

**Figure 2-17.** *Adding images to a page uses the same positioning features you've previously used to add frames.*

Before we dismiss the Picture dialog box, check out the Crop tab, which does exactly as you might imagine and a little bit more. There are three sections in this tab, a preview window, and a big button to set the image to its original size (i.e., 100%). We'll go from top to bottom.

## SUPPORTED IMAGE FORMATS

These formats can be divided into bitmap and vector formats. The former, such as those with a `.jpg`, `.png`, or `.tif` file extension, are used for photographic images, whereas the latter, such as `.wmf`, `.eps`, `.emf`, and so on, are described in terms of mathematical properties rather than as a collection of pixels.

Bitmap: JPG, BMP, GIF, PCD, PCT, PCX, PGM, PNG, PPM, PSD, RAS, TGA, TIFF, XBM, XPM

Vector: DXF, EMF, EPS, MET, PBM, SGF, SGV, SVM, WMF, SVG

The advantage of using a bitmap is that the detail available in the image is restricted only to the capabilities of your camera or scanner. The disadvantages are that bitmap images scaled up way beyond their original size will look awful and that file sizes of big high-quality pictures tend to be quite large. Vector illustrations, in contrast, can have small file sizes and can be scaled to any size with no loss of quality.

The Left, Right, Top, and Bottom values in the Crop section affect how much of the image is seen on the page. When using a linked image, this operation won't crop the original, meaning it can be easily recropped later. For example, if you select Keep scale and increase the Left value, a portion of the image will be hidden on the page; conversely, if you decrease that number, some white space will be exposed. It's also possible to use this mechanism to scale the image within the box by selecting Keep image size. Now as you increase the Left value, the image is expanded into the left edge of the box and, therefore, will be omitted from the page. This method uses a lot of scope to distort the image, so use it with care.

The middle section has a proper percentage scale; keep the aspect ratio safe by ensuring both figures are the same. The section at the base of the window can be used to scale the image to a particular size (with the same caveats as before) using the default measurements of the application.

If, by any chance, you make a complete mess of your image or its box, it's always possible to get back to where you started by either clicking Reset and starting again, or by using the Cancel button. Changes are not actually committed to the page until you click the OK button; they can also still be undone using Edit ➤ Undo.

In addition to playing with the location and cropping of an image, Writer also has some editing tricks. To get to these, select the image you want to edit, and choose View ➤ Toolbars ➤ Picture to launch a small but very compact toolbar (see Figure 2-18). Like any other toolbar this can be free-floating or can be docked to any edge of the main Writer window.

**Figure 2-18.** *This deceptively small toolbar holds a lot of power to edit images on the page.*

This tiny toolbar is dominated by a drop-down list of image styles that can be used to change the picture to a grayscale, black and white, or watermark, which increases the brightness and reduces contrast, making the image suitable for use as a background picture (see Figure 2-19).

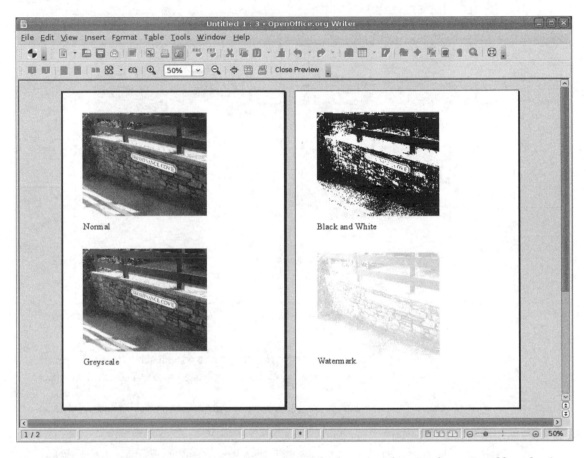

**Figure 2-19.** *These effects are entirely nondestructive, which means they can be reversed by selecting the Normal option at any time.*

To the left of the drop-down list are two buttons; the first opens up the Picture dialog box for positioning, cropping, and so on, whereas the second contains a collection of icons that can be used to apply various effects to the picture (see the sidebar for examples), including smooth, sharpen, posterize, and pixellate. These filters are not a real substitute for a full-fledged image-editing package, but for quick jobs (especially sharpening up an image that's been reduced in size), they're ideal. Each filter has a selection of options that is revealed when the filter is selected from the list.

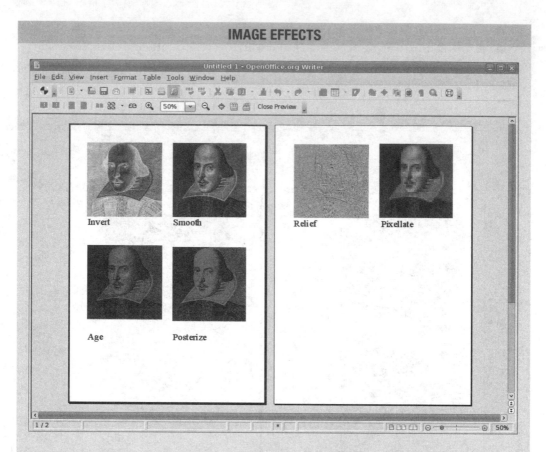

The following image effects can be used to make rapid changes to a document but should be used sparingly. Major image editing is a job for a more specialized application such as Photoshop or Gimp.

- *Invert*: Changes the color values of every pixel in the image to their complete opposite. For example, white becomes black, green becomes red, yellow is changed to blue, and so on.

- *Smooth*: Antialiases the image slightly (i.e., adding colors to areas of high contrast) to make them appear less distinct. Very useful for making curves look smoother.

- *Age*: Attempts to simulate the aging process on a photo. This filter fades color, adds scratches and dirt, and introduces some other color elements.

- *Posterize*: Reduces the number of colors in an image, sort of simulating the process of creating a screen print. Colors can be reduced down to four.

- *Relief*: Attempts to make the image look like an engraving by highlighting areas of high contrast. This effect is really hard to use well.

- *Pixellate*: Enlarges the pixels in the image, which has the effect of obscuring detail. Good when creating screenshots of financial software or removing faces or license plate details from a picture.

To the immediate right of the drop-down list is a Color icon that launches a Color edit window offering very fine control over color composition of the image, including its brightness, contrast, and the RGB values in the image. Using this toolbox, you can, for example, knock back the image by increasing the brightness to 20% and decreasing the contrast to -40%, and then turn the blue element up to 100% to create a light blue watermark-type image (see Figure 2-20), which fits in nicely with the rest of the design.

**Figure 2-20.** *Editing the brightness and contrast and then increasing the value of a single color allows you to make a useful watermark image, which can sit behind some text without adversely affecting readability.*

Next to the Color icon, you'll find the Transparency settings with a range of 0% (completely opaque) to 100% (completely transparent), followed by the Flip Horizontal and Flip Vertical buttons that mirror the image along either the horizontal or vertical plane.

# Building an Image Gallery

Many projects and publications rely on images such as logos, signatures, and photos that are used over and over again. Fortunately, Writer makes it simple to work with recurrent images without having to constantly import them from some obscure location through its gallery feature. The gallery allows you to corral a lot of images together in themes and then use drag and drop to add elements to the page.

The package comes with a selection of prebuilt themes, including backgrounds, icons, and even sounds, but they all display an obvious web-editing bias, so you'll create a new one to go with the example publication.

To begin, open the gallery by selecting its icon from the main toolbar or choose Tools ➤ Gallery. A new section opens at the top of the main Writer window that is populated with web-style tilable backgrounds. On the left is a list of available galleries, and the location of the gallery objects is set out across the top. One of the prebuilt themes is labeled My Theme (see Figure 2-21) and is totally devoid of content. Rename it by right-clicking My Theme, selecting Rename, and then providing the new name for the gallery: Newsletter. Click OK to go back to the gallery, and then you can begin adding to it.

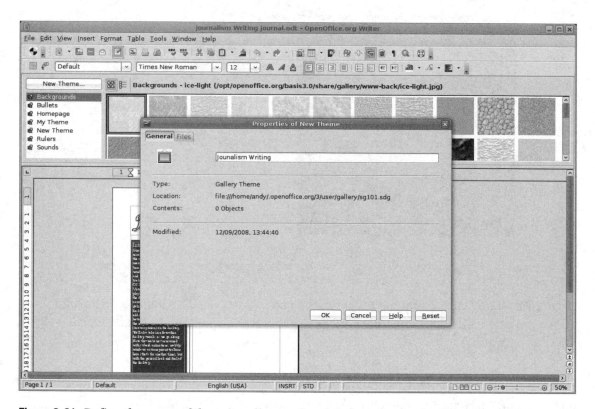

**Figure 2-21.** *Define the name of the new gallery and note its location on the filesystem.*

There are two ways to add to the gallery. First you can right-click the gallery name again and select Properties. The General tab is displayed (with another opportunity to change the name); click the Files tab, and then select Add (see Figure 2-22). This launches the standard file selector with which you can navigate to the location of an image, select it, and click OK to add the image to the gallery. If you've assembled all of the required images in one location, select Find Files instead, and then use the file browser to navigate to that folder. Select OK, and the main section of this window is populated with a list of files within that directory. Now you can select individual files (click the Preview button to see thumbnails of the images) and click Add, or just click Add All to put every image in the folder into your gallery.

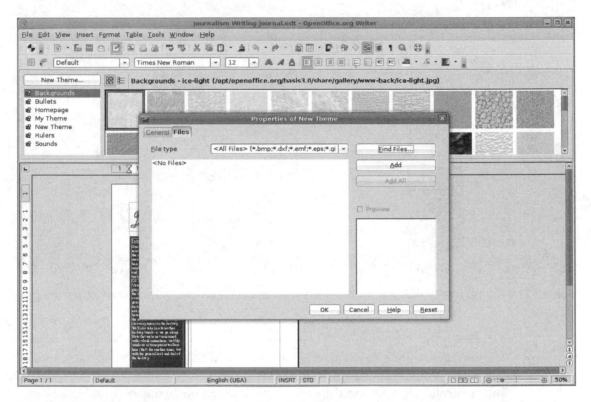

**Figure 2-22.** *Use the file manager to manually add an image or a selection of images to the gallery.*

The second method simply involves dragging images from any file browser and dropping them into the gallery window.

Note that neither of these methods copies the image to a new location; they simply create a link to the original image, which means if you remove or edit the original image, those changes will occur in the gallery.

To take an image from the gallery to the page, drag it onto the page and drop it (see Figure 2-23). It will then be configured exactly as any other imported image, that is, set as anchored to paragraph with no border and totally uncropped. All the editing options mentioned previously are also available. You can also set it as a link (meaning, once more, that any changes made to the file will appear on the updated page) by right-clicking an image and selecting Insert ➤ Link or by holding Ctrl+Shift as you drag the image onto the page.

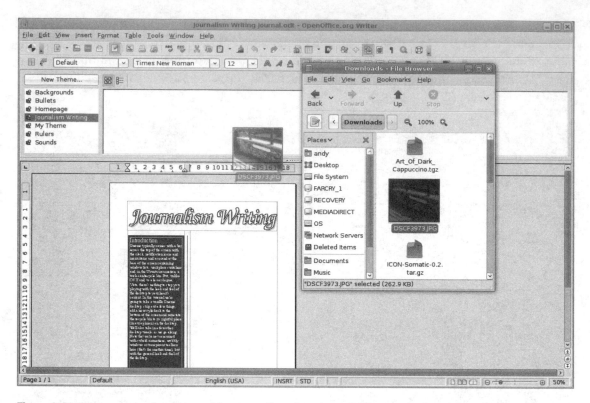

**Figure 2-23.** *Pictures can be dragged into a gallery from any folder on the hard disk or even from the Internet.*

The third item on the Insert menu allows you to add an image to the page or a paragraph as a background. (See Chapter 7 for more on this.)

The menu also provides some file options such as renaming the file, deleting it from the gallery (a move which won't delete the file from your system), and previewing a larger version.

If you want to see an even bigger preview of the image, choose the Preview option (see Figure 2-24) and then resize the gallery window by clicking and dragging the bar between the gallery and the main window down the screen; the preview image resizes dynamically. Close the gallery by reselecting its icon from the toolbar or by choosing Tools ➤ Gallery.

In addition to images, galleries can also hold media files for use in web pages and presentations.

---

■**Tip**  Get a better idea of what the final printed product will look like by clicking the Page Preview button next to the Print icon (see Figure 2-24). The current page will be displayed with all guides, frame borders, and paragraph marks removed.

---

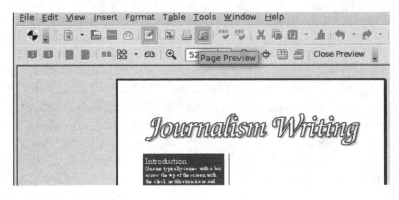

**Figure 2-24.** *The Page Preview button*

# Using the Illustration Tools

So far, you've added text, imagery, and other visual content to your document and divided up the page to present a hierarchy of content to the user. Now you're going to add a final touch using a few of Writer's illustration tools. The tools included in Writer are a subset of those available in the full Draw package (see Chapter 6) and, in the right hands, are capable of professional results. You're just going to add a few basic shapes as a way of introducing a trio of useful design tools: transparency, word wrap, and layer arrangement.

Start by adding the Drawing toolbar to the interface (View ➤ Toolbars ➤ Drawing) to expose the various shapes, lines, and primitives available. The majority of buttons (essentially all but the first on the left and the four on the right of the toolbar) can be used to add new shapes, text, or lines to the document. Buttons with the small arrow to the right of the icon have more content available, which you can see by clicking the arrow and then selecting the item (see Figure 2-25).

**Figure 2-25.** *Click and hold an icon in the Drawing toolbar to see more options.*

So, for example, to add a puzzle shape to your document, you click the Symbol Shapes icon's disclosure arrow and select the cloud shape. The cursor changes to a crosshair, and you can draw the cloud shape onto the page by clicking and dragging as shown in

Figure 2-26. As with images, holding Shift while dragging leaves the shape in its original proportions (this is more important for squares and circles than puzzle shapes). After you have the right shape, release the mouse button, and the shape is added to the page filled in the default color and outlined with a thin black line.

After the shape has been created, the Formatting toolbar changes to give you immediate access to the most useful tools, including the line- and fill-editing options. The quickest way to change the color is to simply select a new one from the drop-down list on the Formatting toolbar (this is a long list of all the system colors and any custom hues mentioned previously); however, more options are available in the Area dialog box, which is accessible by clicking the Pen icon next to the color drop-down list.

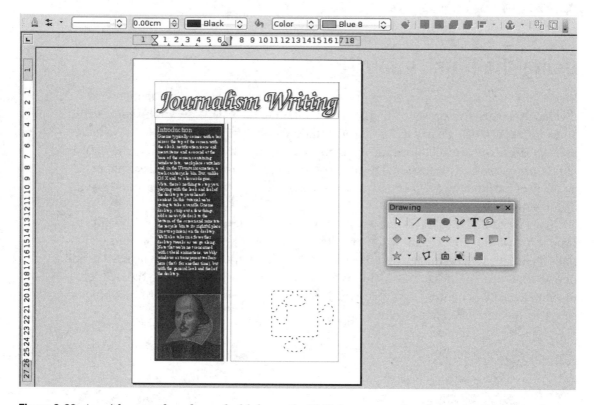

**Figure 2-26.** *As with any other shape, hold down the Shift key as you drag to retain the original proportions of the shape.*

The Area tab of the Area dialog box offers a few basic options and contains a drop-down list to select the type of Fill to apply to the shape (see Figure 2-27). Fill types are None, Color Gradient, Hatching, or Bitmap, and the second section of this tab changes depending on your choice. For example, selecting Color displays the list of colors mentioned earlier, whereas selecting Gradient offers a list of predesigned gradients and one extra control to set the number of increments used to get from one color to the other.

Select Gradient from the drop-down list, choose one of the available fills, and click OK. The fill is added to the shape.

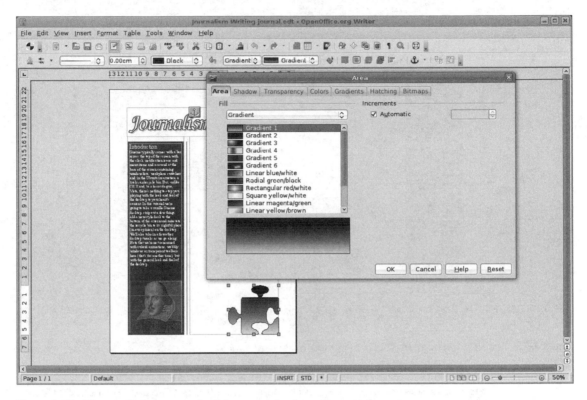

**Figure 2-27.** *The gradient system builds on a selection of premade patterns.*

More editing options are available in the other tabs, so select the shape again and then click the Pen icon to re-edit the area fill. In the Gradients tab, there are six gradient types—which flood an area with a fill that shifts from one color to another in up to 128 steps—including Linear and Radial, as well as options to change the start and end color, the prominence of one color over another, and the angle or center point of the gradient (see Figure 2-28). The workflow in here involves taking an existing gradient from the list, editing the parts that need changing, and then appending it to the available gradients by clicking the Add button. You'll be prompted to input a new name for the gradient, and then it will be added to the list and can be selected as normal. Click OK to change the fill on the shape.

---

■**Tip** If you make use of a lot of custom gradients, make sure you take them with you when upgrading your OO.o installation. In the Gradients editor, use the Disk icon to save your gradients list to your home directory. This can then be reloaded into a new version of OO.o using the Load icon.

---

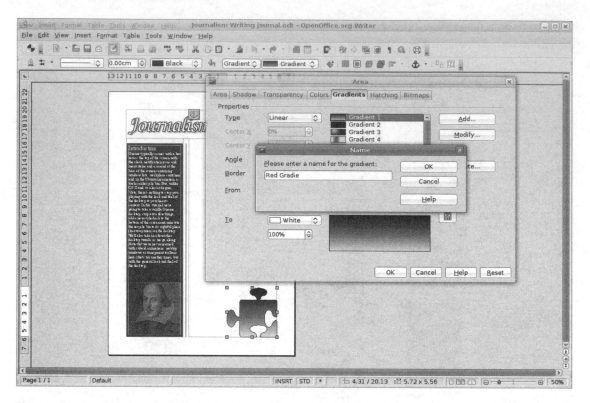

**Figure 2-28.** *The first black gradient has been adapted and saved.*

Another option is to make the shape transparent, allowing the content beneath to show through. To do this, go back into the Area dialog box, and select the Transparency tab. At its simplest, you can apply a uniform transparency to the entire shape (again, 0% is completely opaque, 100% is completely transparent), but there is also a gradient option featuring the same six gradient types available as fills and configurable start and end transparency values. In this example, create a rectangle, fill it black, and then set a linear gradient to run from 100% to 0% (top to bottom). Beneath this, add another black box ready for a caption, which creates a nice glossy look on the main image.

Now use the Circle shape tool to add a circle to the page, remembering to hold down Shift to create a perfect circle. Double-clicking the shape inserts a cursor into the shape ready for text. One thing to remember when putting text into a shape is that the text will not automatically wrap to the contours of the shape, so you'll need to use the Enter key to make new lines.

Previously, you went through the process of rotating text to 90- and 270-degree angles, but by using the text shape tool (the sixth icon from the left), you can add a text box to the document and then rotate it to any angle you like. Begin by selecting the text icon. The cursor becomes the crosshair again, and you can draw a rectangle onto the page just as you would a shape. This becomes the boundary for the text you're going to add, and, unlike inside a normal shape, the text automatically wraps when it gets to the right edge of the box.

Most of the text formatting options you need are available in this type of text object, including the usual indent and spacing options, so this could be used for very long passages of text, as long as they're restricted to a single page. When we click the Rotate icon (next to the Color drop-down list), the handles on the corners and edges of the selected box change to little red circles as shown in Figure 2-29. Grab any one of these, and move the mouse in the direction you want to rotate the text. You can also add a numerical rotation by right-clicking the box, selecting Position and Size, and entering a figure under the Rotation tab. Note that the text remains editable; double-click it to edit the actual content.

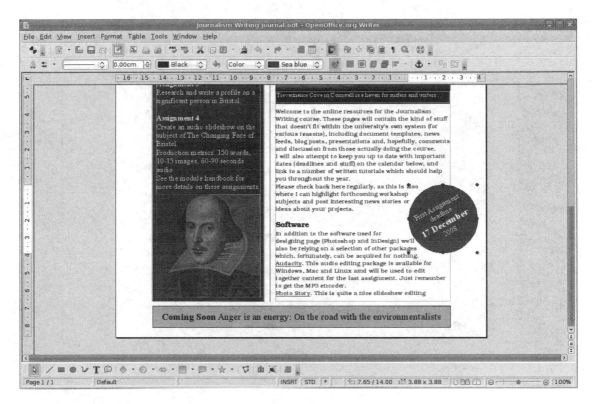

**Figure 2-29.** *The Rotate tool provides more extensive options for twisting and turning text shapes from the Drawing toolbar.*

To change the color of the text, highlight it, right-click, and select Character from the context-sensitive menu. Under the Font Effects tab, select a new color from the drop-down list, and click OK. The font is recolored. Previously, I mentioned the distinction between the item and its content, and this is also true of this kind of text object, although the method of selection is the opposite way around. Single-click to edit the item, and double-click to edit the content.

Examples of item-editing options include setting the gap between the border and text (right-click ➤ Text); filling the background with all the options mentioned previously (note, however, that the transparency affects the background of the box but not the text (as shown in Figure 2-30); adding a shadow (see Figure 2-31); and adding a border (right-click, choose Position and Size, select Slant & Corner Radius, and input a figure in the radius box to add some Web 2.0 stylings to your document as shown in Figure 2-32).

We've also added a circle using the Ellipse tool (remember to hold down the Shift key to keep the ellipse perfectly circular), colored it blue to match the left-hand column, and positioned it on the right side of the page with a few lines of text.

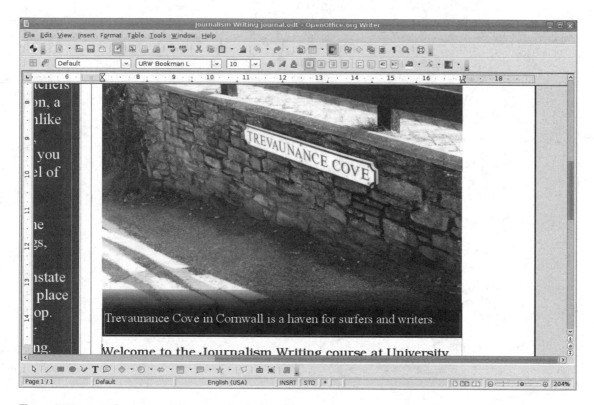

**Figure 2-30.** *Any element on the page, including shapes, frame backgrounds, and text, can be filled using the comprehensive fill tools.*

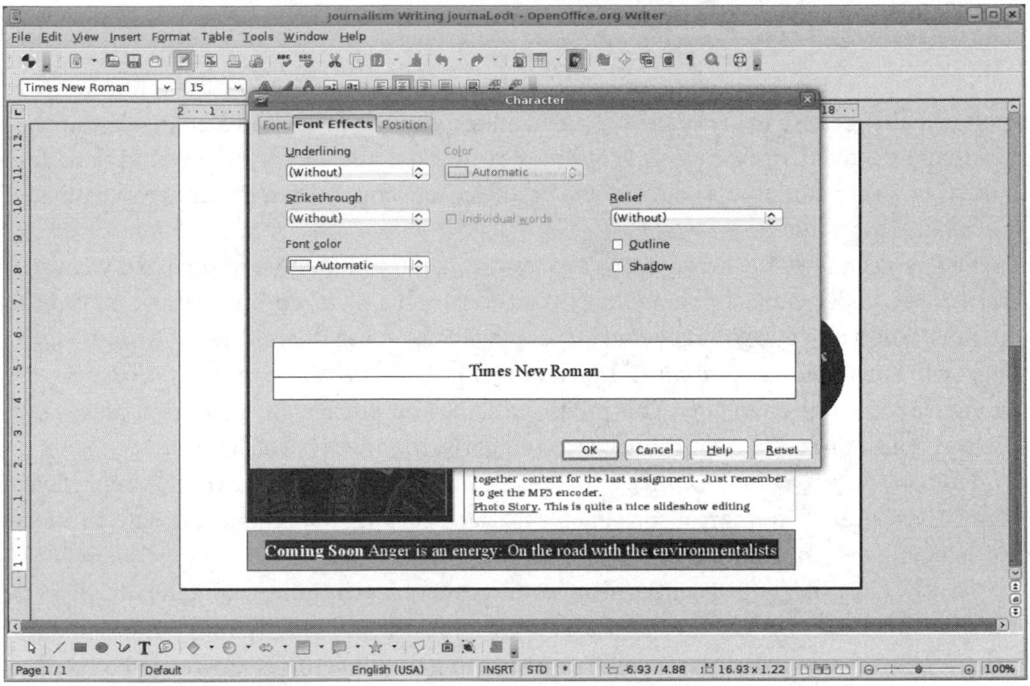

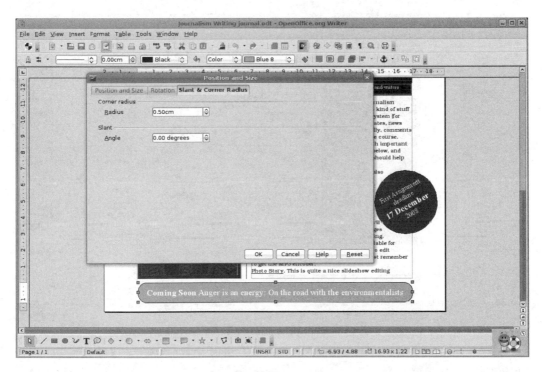

**Figure 2-31.** *Text inside Drawing objects can have its color edited using the context-sensitive (right-click) menu and selecting Character ➤ Font Effects.*

**Figure 2-32.** *Change the radius of an object's corners using the Position and Size settings.*

# Arranging the Page

You now have a lot of content on the page, so it's time to start thinking about how to re-arrange it all. Because many of the elements on the page have been placed inside frames, these can be moved, resized, and recolored very quickly; however, you may find that, due to the way Writer constructs pages, some parts may obscure others. There are two tools you can use to fix this.

First, you can use the Arrange options to restack page elements, so the parts we want to see are actually visible. Imagine that as you construct a page, adding frames, pictures, and illustration objects, you're laying these things one on top of another. The topmost object will inevitably obscure the parts underneath. This is where choosing Format ➤ Arrange menu comes into play. This menu contains four entries. Bring to front places the selected object on top of everything else; Bring forward moves it one level up the layers; Send to back puts it at the bottom of the stack; and Send backward moves it a single layer down. These four options are also available by right-clicking the object you want to affect, and selecting the Arrange menu.

To select an object that is underneath some other object or frame, hold the Alt key as you click above the object. Shift+Alt+click cycles in the other direction from bottom to top.

The second option that is vital when rearranging things is the Text wrap, which tells Writer how an object (a frame, a picture, a shape) should interact with everything below it in the layer stack. There are six basic options here as shown in Figure 2-33.

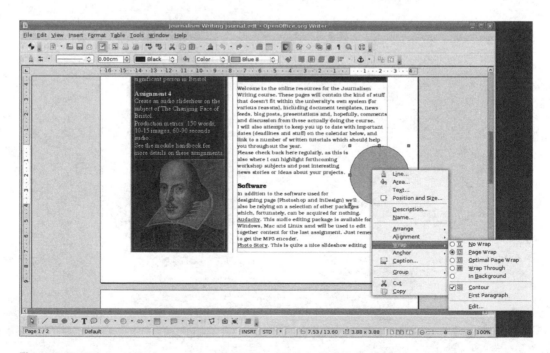

**Figure 2-33.** *To wrap the text around an object, right-click, select Wrap, and choose one of the options.*

No wrap puts text before the object and after it, leaving a gap where the object itself is. This is useful in logical breaks in the text and covers most or all of a column. In our example, though, it just looks awful (see Figure 2-34).

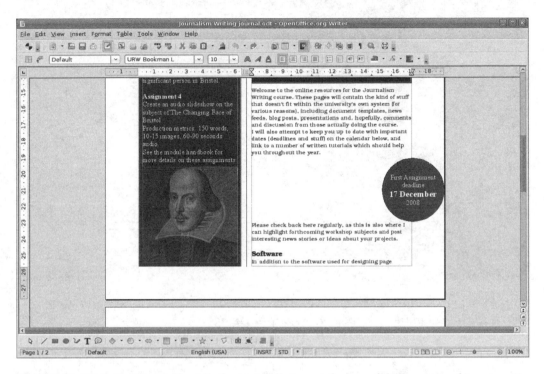

**Figure 2-34.** *With No Wrap selected, the text will stop at the top of the image and resume at the bottom. This is useful if an image fills a column completely.*

Page Wrap attempts to follow the contours of the object. For example, if a square shape is placed in the center of a piece of text, the text is knocked out by the object but still appears on both sides of it, meaning the reader has to leap from one part of a sentence to the next across the shape or image.

Optimal Page Wrap attempts to solve this problem by only wrapping along one edge of the object as shown in Figure 2-35.

The Through option places the object on top of the text and doesn't make it wrap at all. In effect, the object obscures the text as shown in Figure 2-36, so you better make the object transparent if you want to see the text!

In Background also doesn't knock out the text, but the object is placed behind the text as shown in Figure 2-37, like the watermark you created earlier.

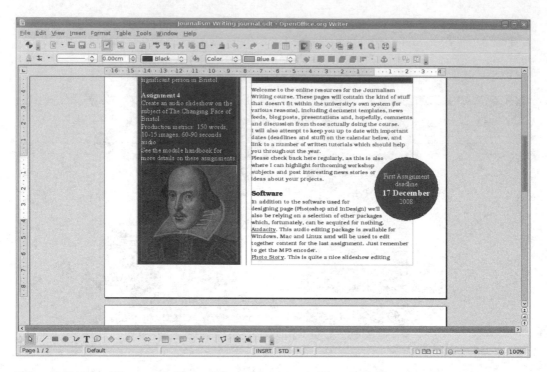

**Figure 2-35.** *Page Wrap and Optimal Page Wrap make the text follow the contour of an object. The latter only wraps around one side of an image.*

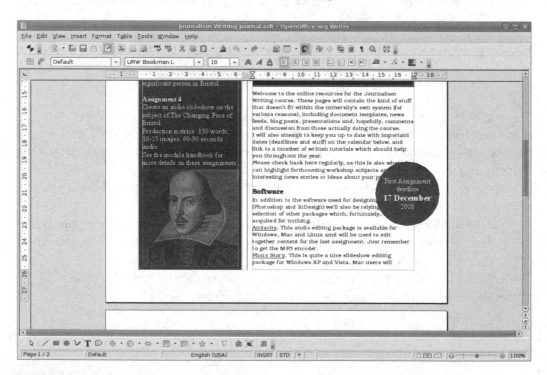

**Figure 2-36.** *When using the Through option, the object obscures the text.*

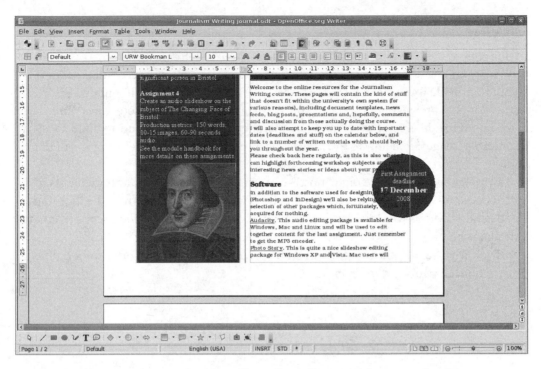

**Figure 2-37.** *The In Background option allows the text to run right across the object.*

The last option—Contour—is only available by right-clicking and choosing Wrap ➤ Edit. This gives you the opportunity to configure the text wrap a little more fully, for example, by specifying how far the text should be away from the object (see Figure 2-38). On square/rectangular objects, there are options for the Top, Bottom, Left, and Right, whereas on circular objects, a single value works all the way around.

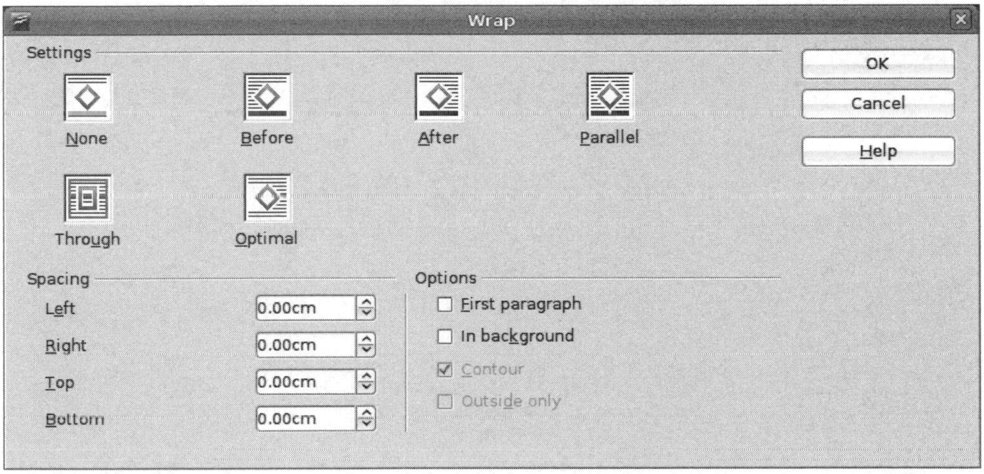

**Figure 2-38.** *More extensive wrapping options are available via the Wrap ➤ Edit menu.*

# Recap

In this chapter, you have designed the first page of a newsletter using a range of design tools in OO.o Writer. You've structured the page using an asymmetric, double-column layout to provide three distinct content areas. These areas were then populated with frames for text, images, and captions. You also learned about the various ways Writer can be used to add color, texture, and transparency to a document; how to build a gallery of reusable images; and how to rearrange objects on the page without losing site of the content.

The next chapter is once more mostly concerned with text—the raw ingredients of any document—but you'll use a range of techniques to automate many of the jobs that can be really tedious when working on long documents or on many documents that have a similar structure.

If you want to take the design further and prepare the newsletter project for online distribution, skip forward to Chapter 7.

■ ■ ■

# CHAPTER 3

# Writer Automation

**W**riter, as we've seen, can be used for a lot of different tasks, but it really comes into its own when working on long, complex documents such as dissertations, reports, and even books. These documents have "words" at their heart, and Writer is fundamentally a word processor designed for the purpose of writing and editing text. Letters can be written in any old text editor, for example, and high-end DTP software will do a better job of dealing with design-intensive documents such as magazines, newspapers, or posters. But Writer's main purpose is allowing a user to compose, edit, and organize words. The elements discussed in Chapters 1 and 2 such as frames, images, and paragraph formatting feed into this, and an understanding of these processes provides a good basis for moving onto the options available for automating the organization and production of a finished document.

The document you'll be working on in this chapter is a long piece of academic writing (see Figure 3-1), which will allow you to explore many of the automation and document management facilities in Writer. And although this is a specific form of writing, the techniques you'll be using to create it are equally useful in other tasks, including letter writing and newsletter design, where consistency is important. For example, in Chapters 1 and 2, you manually formatted paragraphs and page elements using various tools and options. With Writer's style system, you can take that formatting and turn it into a "style" that can then be applied across a document, to other documents of the same type, or, in the case of the newsletter, in future issues. Any word-processing task that is likely to be repeated can benefit from a little automation.

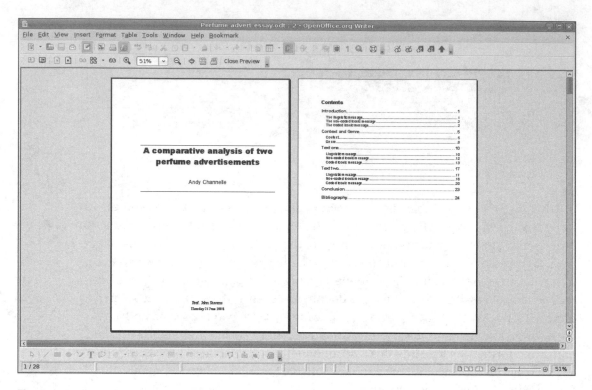

**Figure 3-1.** *Writer's raison d'être is the production of long and complex documents such as reports, essays, and dissertations.*

# The Basic Page

The letter you created in Chapter 1 took you a little way down the road to automation by starting with a template; in this chapter, you'll create and edit a cascade of styles, using the information OO.o keeps about the author, setting up styles to make it simple to build a dynamic table of contents (TOC), and adding references using Writer's built-in bibliographic database. You'll also start with a much more complicated basic page, so begin by choosing File ➤ New ➤ Text document and then go into the page formatting section (Format ➤ Page).

---

**Note**   The example is based on a single page style, but using the following techniques, you can create any number of page styles to add more variety to the document. When using multiple page types, use the Organizer tab to define how one page style might follow another. For example, if you're working with different left- and right-hand styles on your spreads, you'll need to set the Next style (in the Organizer tab) options to reflect this design.

---

Our first stop is the Page tab, where you'll define the page size (A4 again) and set the margins (see Figure 3-2). Increase the size of the left margin to allow a reviewer or marker to add comments or other marginalia, and under the Layout settings, change Page layout to Right and left because you'll only be printing on one side of the document, and it will be bound along the left edge. If you were printing on both sides, the logical choice for the page layout would be Mirrored.

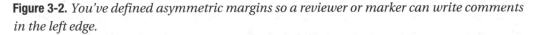

**Figure 3-2.** *You've defined asymmetric margins so a reviewer or marker can write comments in the left edge.*

Margins are an important part of a design and can have a real effect on readability. For example, very narrow margins make a page look busy and may force the reader to cover part of the text with their thumbs. Wider margins can look more "luxurious" and also make the lines of body text narrower, and therefore easier to read, which could help with navigation through the text.

The next stop in this dialog box is the Header tab (see Figure 3-3). The header is a piece of information that appears at the top of every page in the project; usually it is reserved for the document title or author name. Select the Header on button to enable the rest of the options. Increasing the Left and Right margin sizes actually decreases the horizontal space for the header as the 0.00cm option matches the borders already set. The Spacing option defines the gap between the header and the main text; a more spacious gap can look more formal but obviously results in less space for the document text. Finally, you can fix the height of the header, which is good for consistency, or allow it to expand or contract depending upon the content. Fix the Height at 0.60cm to mirror the spacing between the header and text.

As with the header, you'll also add a footer (under the Footer tab) that will run along the base of each page. Stick with the same dimensions.

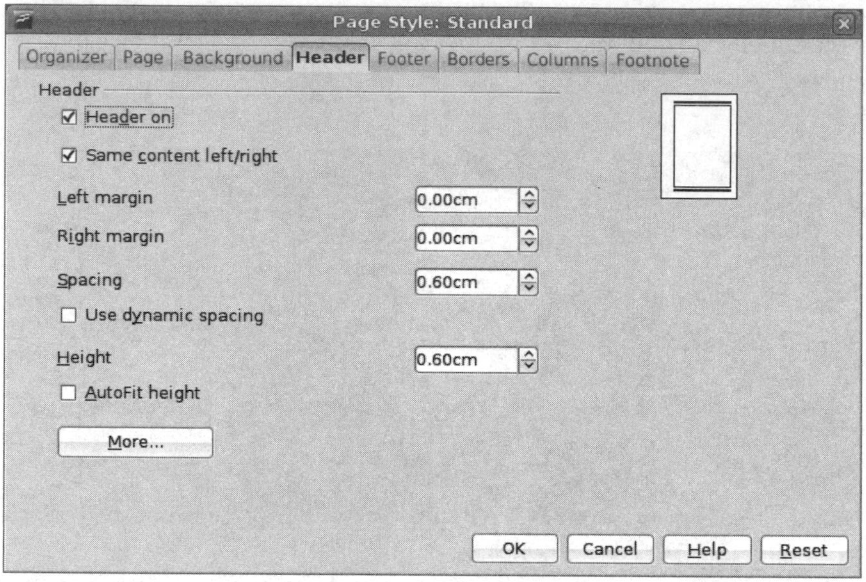

**Figure 3-3.** *The header is a persistent presence along the top of each page in the document.*

Finally, for this section, you'll define a space for footnotes. It's important to define this space, especially in academic writing because the default is the Not larger than page area option, which means a long footnote would take up an entire page. By setting a limit on the size, extra information is flowed to the next page in the footnote space.

In addition to setting the maximum size for a footnote, this tab also has the option to set the spacing between the text and the footnote, and an option to put a division line between the two parts (see Figure 3-4). As with the column lines (see Chapter 2), these are defined as a percentage of the width of the work area and can be aligned to the left, right, or center of the page.

After this is done, click the OK button to go to the page where you'll see faded margin lines marking out the content area and the header and footer space.

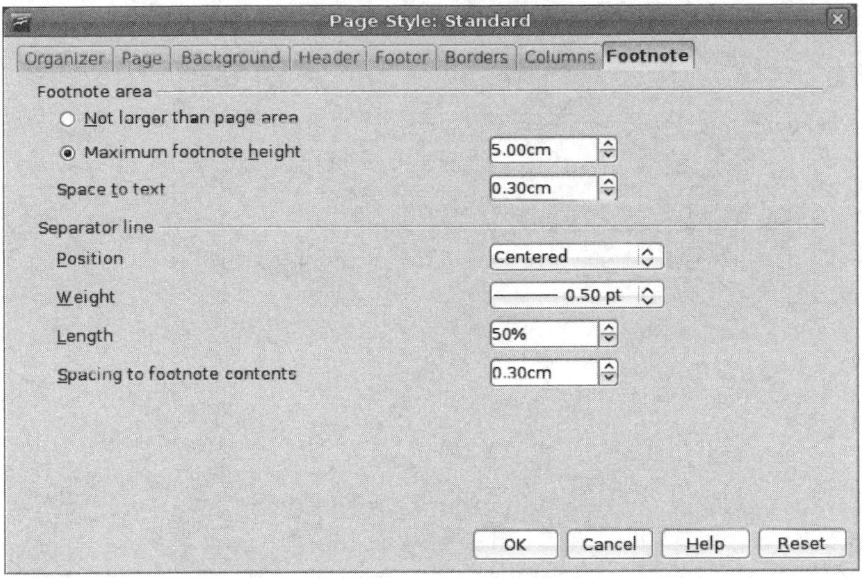

**Figure 3-4.** *Add a space for footnotes so that they don't become too prominent on the page.*

# Document Properties

In the interests of being well organized, you'll now add details to the document properties system. This information not only makes it easier to find this particular document (or documents of this type) but also allows you to make large-scale changes to the document at a later date. To access this section, choose File ➤ Properties. As with other configuration elements in OO.o, this is a tabbed dialog box.

The General tab provides information such as the document author, the date and time it was created and last modified, the size of the document in bytes, and the amount of time spent editing this particular document (a good idea if you are designing a book and being paid by the hour!). The Author name is taken from OO.o's User Data, which is accessible by choosing Tools ➤ Options, and clicking the User Data entry on the left.

On the Description tab, you can define many elements of the document, such as the title (often different from the document's file name), subject, and a series of keywords (see Figure 3-5). The latter can make finding and organizing multiple documents easier within your filesystem later on; for example, all documents featuring the keywords "key indicators" and "2008" could be found more easily with keywords than by having to make sense of the document contents alone.

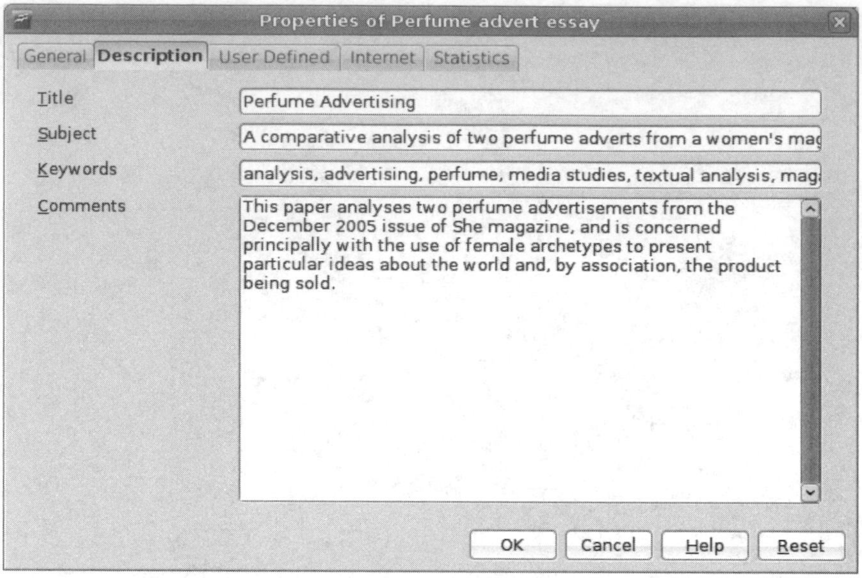

**Figure 3-5.** *Document properties can be used to manage files but are also useful for making significant changes to some elements of the document.*

The Comments field can, again, be used to add information useful for searching and classifying the document without having to read the entire thing. For example, in academic writing, it might contain the abstract, and in business, it could be an executive summary of main points or even just a list of things needed to finish the project.

The User Defined tab is especially useful because it allows you to create four new classes of data, which can be assigned a field name (see Figure 3-6). Fields can be entered into the document, and then every instance of that piece of information can be edited simply by altering one text element at a later date. Add two pieces of information in the fields labeled Info 1 and Info 2 by simply typing the information in the text areas in the dialog box. This method could be used to edit, for instance, the lead character in a novel or a location in a play; in this example, you're going to insert a publication name and an academic supervisor. Before leaving this section, you can make the user-defined information a little more meaningful by clicking the Info fields button and giving the two fields you've created better names so that they're easier to manage later.

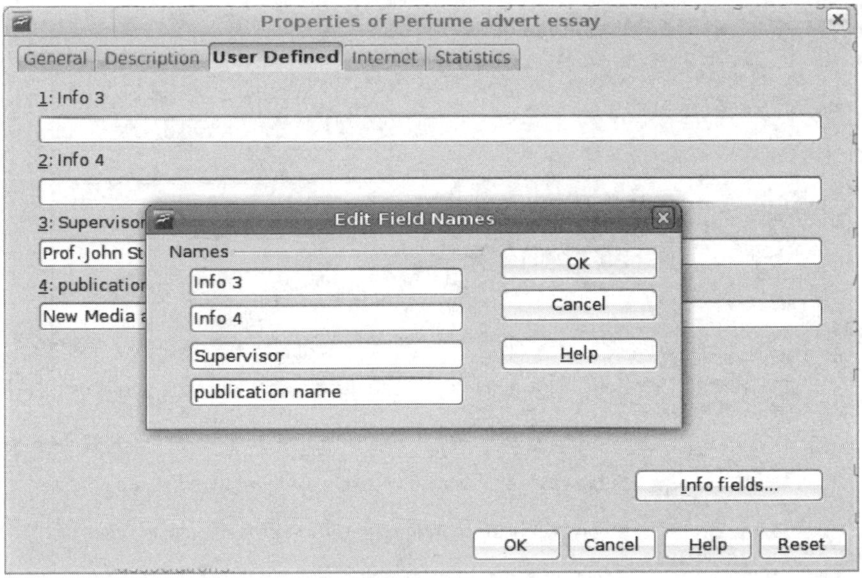

**Figure 3-6.** *Add a few user-defined properties. These can be inserted into the document later.*

After all the information has been added, click the OK button.

The last part of setting up your page is to add a few details to the header section of the document. You could simply click anywhere in the header and begin typing away, but you can also be a little more sophisticated than that. You'll begin by adding the document title (which you've just defined) by clicking in the header, choosing Insert ➤ Fields ➤ Title, and then aligning this to the right of the page by clicking the right align button in the Formatting toolbar. To format this using the Styles and Formatting palette, select Special Styles from the drop-down list at the bottom of the palette, and then edit the Header style.

The second element to go in the header is the author name, which you can add by choosing Insert ➤ Fields ➤ Author (see Figure 3-7). This data will be added immediately to the right of the document title. Click in between the title and author name, and press Tab twice, forcing the title all the way over to the left, while retaining the right alignment for the author name. Now format the header text with the desired font and font size, and you can move on to actually editing text.

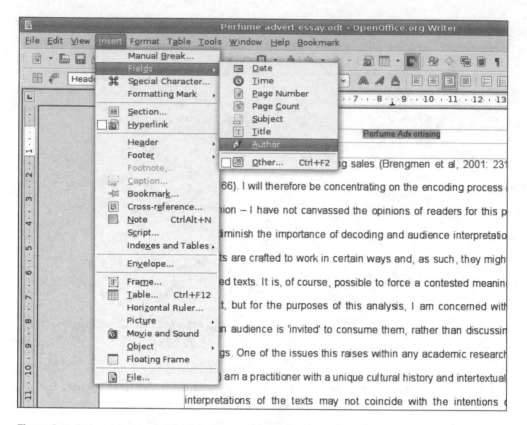

**Figure 3-7.** *Document variables are inserted into the text using the Insert ➤ Fields menu entry.*

# Adding Style

At this point in the example, the text is written, so you can run the spell checker (Tools ➤ Spellcheck, or F7), and you're ready to start formatting. During this stage in the editing process, it's important to start on an even footing, so select the entire document (Ctrl+A), and select Clear formatting in the style drop-down list on the Formatting toolbar.

To begin exploring text styles, you'll use the predefined styles in the palette, so major headings will be styled with Heading 1 and subheadings with Heading 2, and then you'll edit those style individually to conform to the eventual look of the document.

Every single style element is available using this method of document construction. So, for example, you can ensure that each major section of the document begins on a new page. Right-click Heading 1, select Modify, and click the Text Flow tab (see Figure 3-8). In the Break section—which we previously ignored—click the Insert button to enable the various options, and make sure the drop-down selectors are set to insert a page break in the Before position.

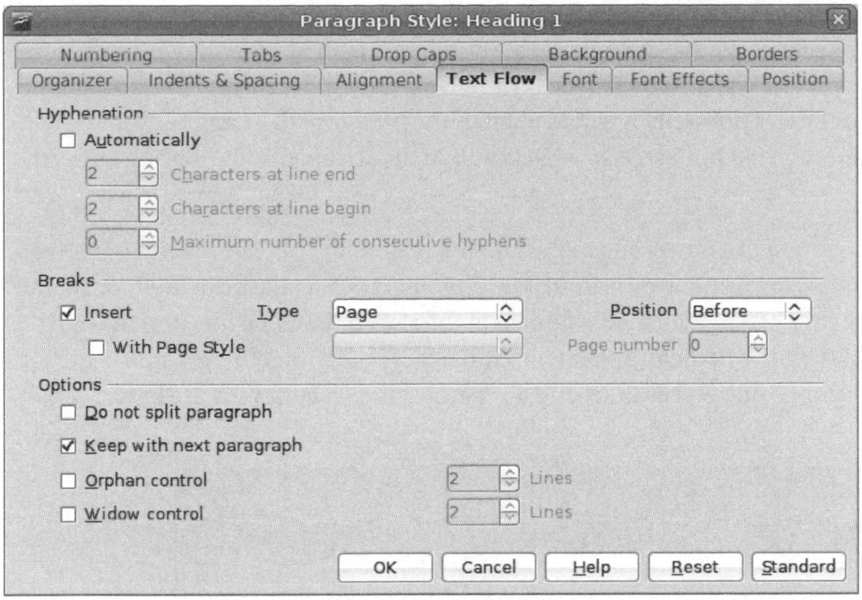

**Figure 3-8.** *Edit existing text styles by right-clicking the name in the Styles and Formatting palette (Format ➤ Styles and Formatting).*

Click OK, and, then as you scroll through the text, you'll notice that each section—we defined this with the Heading 1 style—now starts on a new page.

Next you'll create a base paragraph style for the majority of the document by formatting a single paragraph in the desired way. So highlight the first real paragraph of the document, and choose Format ➤ Paragraph. There's a lot to do in here, so we'll go through the important tabs in turn.

**Indents & Spacing**. We looked briefly at this tab in Chapter 1, but this is where you can set left, right, and first-line indents for the paragraph and also set how much space appears between the end of one paragraph and the start of the next. You can also set the line spacing, so select Double, which is standard for this kind of document. Set the first-line indent to 0.50cm.

**Alignment**. Text can be either aligned left, aligned right, or justified, which means the software introduces tiny space changes into the text to line up the left and right edges of the text to the margins. The jury is still out on whether justified text is easier to read or whether it makes for a better-looking document, so this choice comes down to personal preference. For this example project, use the justified option, which bring a few more elements into play. Most significantly, you can define how the last line of a paragraph falls, with options to set it left, centered, or right. Left is the most common option. Selecting Justified for the last line means that, regardless of length, it will be forced to align to both edges—via a process called forced justification—which can introduce large gaps. The other option is to select whether a single word should be justified. The Text-to-Text setting is used to define how Writer will deal with two pieces of text with different font sizes on different lines. Ordinarily it would align to the baseline (the imaginary line where the bottom of the text sits) but can also be set to align to the top, middle, or bottom of the two elements.

**Text Flow**. This section can have a big impact on the readability of your text. The Hyphenation options allow you to stop words from being hyphenated at all (the default) or set the minimum number of letters that should appear at the start or end of a line and the maximum number of hyphens that can appear in sequence (see Figure 3-9). As a rule, a higher number is good for the first few options and a lower number is better for the latter.

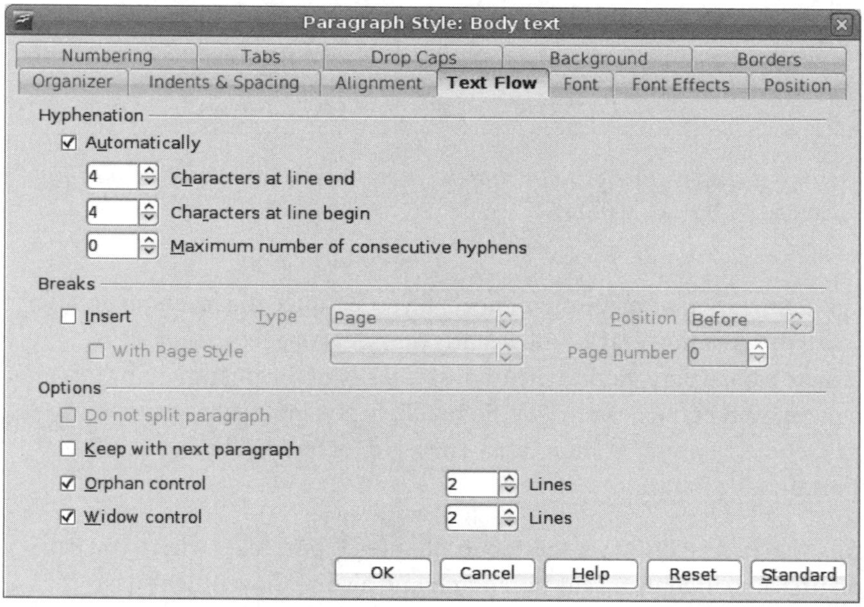

**Figure 3-9.** *Configure hyphens, widows, and orphans using the Text Flow tab. This can make quite a difference to the look of a document.*

You can safely ignore the Breaks section for now (although we'll return to it shortly) and move on to the Options section. Selecting Do not split paragraph means that any paragraph formatted with this style will not ever split over a page break; this is useful for some paragraph types—headline, for example—but not for a body text format.

Keep with next paragraph is also useful for headlines because it ensures that the head-line doesn't appear at the bottom of a page with no text beneath it. Finally the widow and orphan control can prevent a paragraph from starting on the last line of a page or column (a widow) or ending on the first line (an orphan) with options for setting the number of lines that should always start or end a page. For instance, if the Widow value is set to 2 lines, a paragraph that falls on the base of a page with a single line is shifted to the next page. A similar situation with an orphan causes a line to be taken from the preceding page and placed at the top of the next so there is a complete line before the last line of the paragraph. For clarity, widow and orphan control is always desirable (see Figures 3-10 and 3-11).

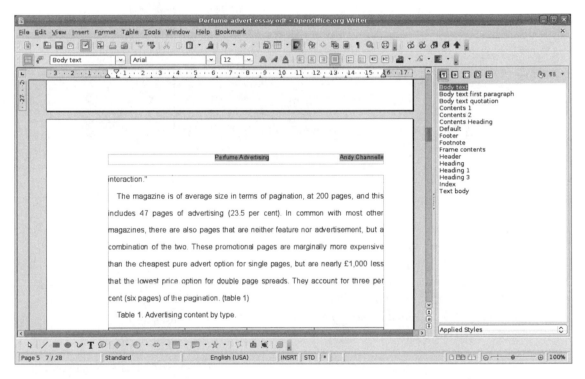

**Figure 3-10.** *Orphans, where a paragraph ends on the top line of a new page or column, can make a document look unprofessional.*

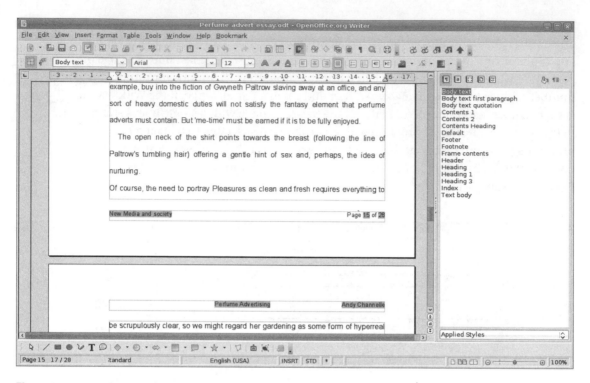

**Figure 3-11.** *A widow is when a new paragraph starts on the last line of a column or page. The Text Flow options can be used to control these.*

**Tabs**. Tabs are something of a holdover from the old world of manual typewriters, and with sensible use of first-line indents, they should be largely unnecessary, but it's worth knowing how to set them in case you need to line up a few columns of data and don't want to create a table or embed a spreadsheet. To match the first-line indent created earlier, add a tab position at 0.50cm by editing the Position element on the left. You'll return for more extensive tabs editing shortly.

So now you have a formatted paragraph that you can use as the basis for a first style. To do this, open the Styles and Formatting palette by either pressing the F11 key or choosing Format ➤ Styles and Formatting, and then highlight the first paragraph. Across the top of the Styles and Formatting palette, a range of icons appear that show (from left to right) paragraph, character, frame, page, and list styles. Select the first icon to display the list of premade styles (see Figure 3-12).

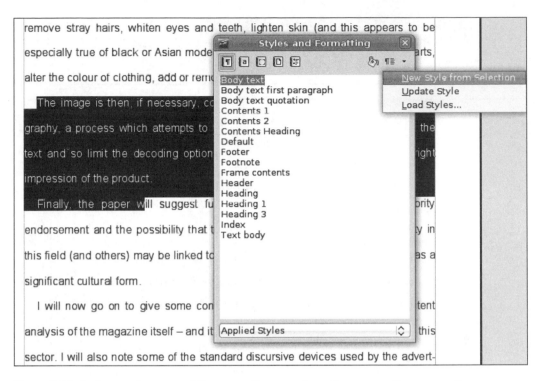

**Figure 3-12.** *Styles can be created from text formatted on the page or from scratch.*

Double-clicking one of these styles applies that style to the selected paragraph, so you don't want to do that. Instead, click the icon on the far right, select Create new style from selection, input a name (for this example, "Body text"), and click OK.

---

■**Tip**  New styles can be created from scratch by right-clicking anywhere in the Styles and Formatting palette and selecting New.

---

The new style is appended to the list and becomes selectable. Because this will be the most commonly used style, apply it to the entire document by pressing Ctrl+A to select all, and then double-clicking the new style.

Obviously, this is not the look we want (see Figure 3-13). For example, it's common practice when creating a long document with a first-line indent on paragraphs to have no indent on the first paragraph after a heading or subheading, so we need to add some variety.

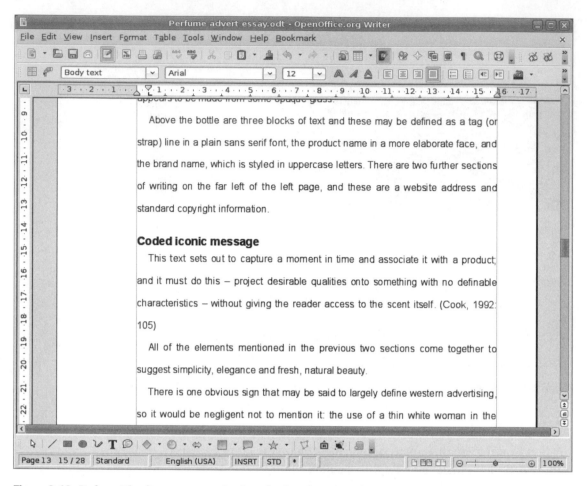

**Figure 3-13.** *Before: The first paragraph after the heading has the same formatting as each other paragraph.*

The logical thing to do is to adjust the formatting of a first paragraph and then create a new style from that, but there is an even more efficient way to achieve the same results. In the Styles and Formatting palette, right-click the Body text style, and select New. This clones the original style, gets it ready for a slight bit of editing, and launches the Paragraph style dialog box. In the Organizer tab, provide a new name for the style (for the sake of simplicity, it's best to name this style something related to the original so it appears next to it in the palette), and ensure that both Next Style and Linked with are configured with Body text. The former option means that if you write a paragraph using this style (called Body text first paragraph) and press the Enter key to start a new paragraph, the Body text paragraph is automatically selected. The latter option is very important because it allows you to cascade the style.

AutoUpdate, accessible from the Organizer tab, is also an important option to be aware of because it can lead to some confusion if you don't understand how it works. Ordinarily, changes to a style have to be made by selecting it in the palette and clicking the Modify option. However, with AutoUpdate on, any changes made to *any* paragraph configured with that style are automatically propagated across every other instance of the style.

Next, move onto the Indents and Spacing tab, and remove the first-line indent. This means that the style you're working on now is exactly the same as Body text, except it doesn't have the first-line indent. Go back to the Organizer tab to see a list of the unique elements of this style. Now click OK to add the new style to the list, highlight the first paragraph of the text, and select the style (see Figures 3-14, 3-15, and 3-16). The result should be a piece of text exactly the same as the second paragraph, but with no first-line indent.

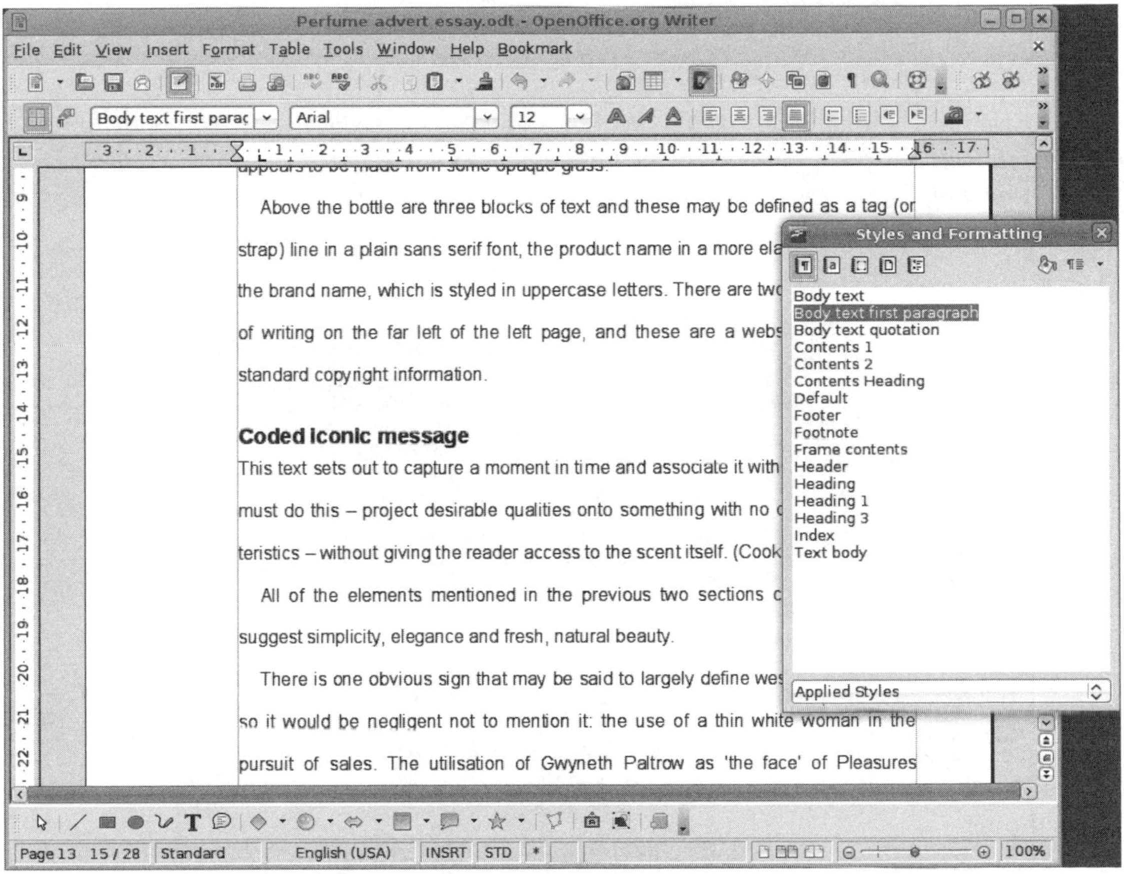

**Figure 3-14.** *After: Having made a few changes to the style (see Figures 3-15 and 3-16), you now have a first paragraph that looks slightly different.*

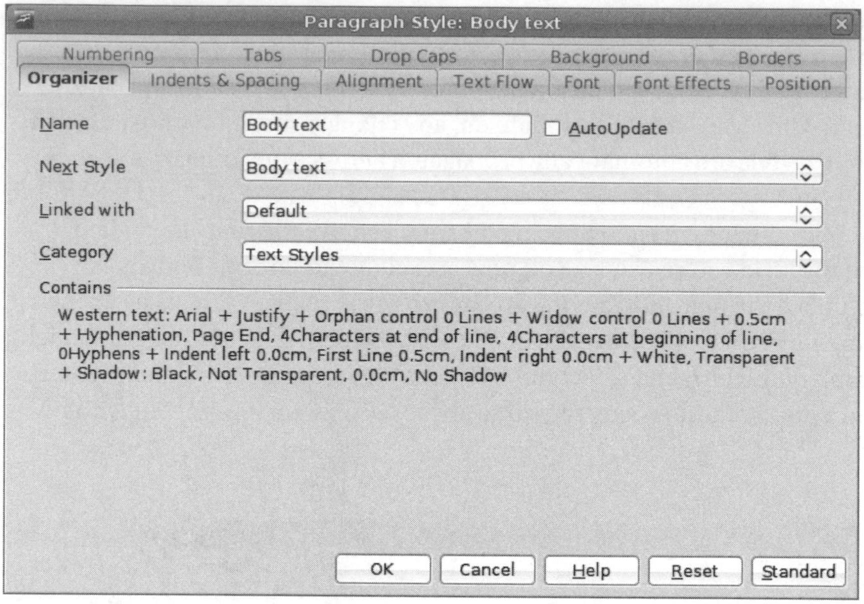

**Figure 3-15.** *The long-form definition of the style takes up the lower part of the Organizer tab. This covers every element of the text from the font size and alignment to the justification and line spacing.*

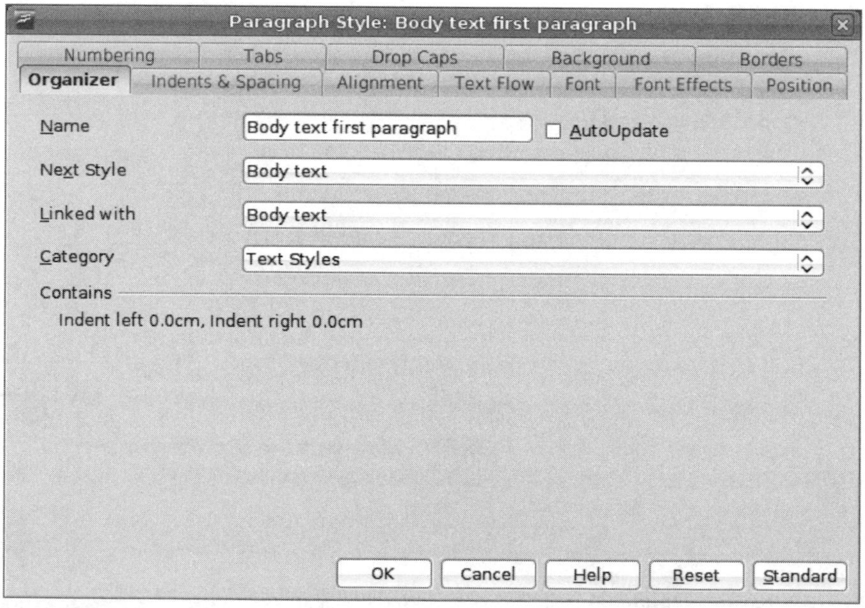

**Figure 3-16.** *In contrast to Figure 3-15, this definition is very short. Because it is linked with Body text, it only needs to control the elements that are different.*

Now create a third style based on the first one for quotations (single line spacing and left/right indent of 0.50, to match the first-line indent of the Body text style), and save that too. To apply the style, click into the paragraph that needs styling, and click on the appropriate style. When working on long documents, this select-then-click routine can get a bit tedious, but fortunately Writer has a Format Painter option. Simply choose the second from right icon at the top of the Styles and Formatting palette (the tool tip will say Fill format mode when the mouse is hovered over it), select the appropriate styles (see Figure 3-17), and then click each paragraph in the document that should be formatted in that way.

**Figure 3-17.** *The Styles and Formatting palette can be altered to reflect the type of editing being carried out.*

It's also possible to define a keyboard shortcut to apply a style. Choose Tools ➤ Customize, and select the Keyboard tab. Find an empty key combination in the top part of the dialog box, select it, and define the Category (Styles ➤ Paragraph Styles) and Function (Body text first paragraph) before clicking the Modify button and binding the style to the key combination. Now you can click into a paragraph, use the shortcut, and the format will be applied. It's probably wise to limit this method to a few very commonly used styles; otherwise, you may end up getting lost in all the combinations.

With the entire text formatted, there's a slight problem with the spacing of the quotation body text; where the single line spacing of the quotation text meets the double line spacing of the body text, there is quite a tight space. You can fix this by right-clicking the quotation style in the Styles and Formatting palette, selecting Modify from the menu, adding a little space (say, 0.50cm) in the Below paragraph section, and clicking OK. This is where styles really show their time-saving nature because every paragraph formatted with the Quotation body text style will now be altered to reflect the change, saving you the work of going through the document and changing every instance.

■**Note** The benefits of using the tools available to manage styles and formatting in Writer, and indeed the rest of the suite, can't be overstated. A document created on these principles will be easier to manage and edit and will look more consistent, and thus professional, allowing you more time to concentrate on the difficult job of writing engaging or informative text, rather than worrying if the subheadings are all the same size. Although style definition may seem to be one of the more boring aspects of document design, it not only makes your final output (all your final output if the styles get reused in templates) look better but can also save serious time in the future. For example, combine a document with ready-defined styles and the templates method discussed in Chapter 1, and you start the document creation process with all the tedious stuff already done!

# Cascading Styles

At the beginning of this section of styles, you created a style called Body text and then added two more styles that were based on this. Having finished the main text for the document, now let's change the Times New Roman base font, which looks a little formal, to something that gives the essay a touch of modernity. You could select the entire text and change the typeface to Arial (or something similar) but that will obviously change headings and subheadings too.

The smart way to do this is to right-click the Body text style, select Modify, adjust the typeface using the Font tab—change font, size, color (under Font Effects)—then click the OK button, and watch as the paragraphs formatted with this styled are instantly reformatted. The real magic, though, is that the styles based on this style will also be updated to reflect the change. So with just a few clicks, you've edited three individual styles without messing up any of the headings.

All headings, meanwhile, are based on the style labeled Heading, so changing the font in that will change the font in all your headings. Smart.

In addition to paragraph styles, you can also create character styles in the same way, and these differ by only affecting the selected text, whereas paragraph styles will affect the entire paragraph. For example, it is common practice to present publication names in italics, so you can find a piece of text, italicize it using the Italic button on the Formatting toolbar, and then select the Character Styles button (second left) in the Styles and Formatting palette. Now you can use the icon on the far right to create a New style from selection, give it a name, and click OK. Navigate to the next publication name, highlight it, and click the appropriate style in the palette. As with the Paragraph styles, this seems like quite a long-winded way to make a small change, but it will pay dividends later on. Promise!

**Note**  Deleting the premade styles included in OO.o is hopelessly complicated, so we're not going to bother doing it. It's much better to adapt available styles to your needs than start digging around in configuration files. User styles, however, can be deleted by right-clicking the style and selecting the Delete option.

If you've created a complete set of styles and don't want to be swamped with standard styles, use the drop-down menu at the bottom of the Styles and Formatting palette to select Custom Styles. To get back to the original list, choose Automatic.

# Table Making

Occasionally a document will feature some kind of data that would be most appropriately presented in a table—sales figures, projected growth, and so on—and Writer has a useful selection of table-editing tools that can do quite a lot before you have to migrate to the Calc spreadsheet. Tables are covered in more detail later—skip ahead if you have an insatiable desire or pressing need to organize tabulated data—but for now, let's look at the three most common ways of inserting a table into a document.

Method one is essentially the same as inserting a frame or image, except we choose Table ➤ Insert to launch the configuration dialog box (see Figure 3-18). In this dialog box, you can define the number of column (horizontal) and row (vertical) elements in the table and insert a header for the table that can contain labels for the columns. If the Header option is selected, a new button is enabled that will add an extra header section at the top of a page should the table span two pages. By default, the table takes up the entire width of the page, frame, or column into which it is inserted; the columns are equally spaced, and the rows expand to accommodate the information put into them. Selecting Don't split table makes sure the entire production appears on a single page. The Border check box puts solid division lines between each cell.

If you're feeling particularly pushed for time, a number of predesigned table styles are available via the AutoFormat button with good options to match most color schemes. The AutoFormat options are actually a good place to start if you want to go beyond simple white backgrounds and black lines. You can also create an AutoFormat based on a table design you've created. After a table has been formatted, choose Table ➤ AutoFormat and select the Add button. Provide a name for the creation, and it will be added to the list of available designs. This can be used to ensure that all tables in a single document or series are consistently formatted.

The second way to add a table is also the quickest. Select the drop-down arrow to the immediate right of the Table button on the standard toolbar, and drag the mouse to define the number of columns and rows needed (see Figure 3-19). Once clicked, a table with those dimensions will be inserted into the document at the cursor point and will range right across the available space.

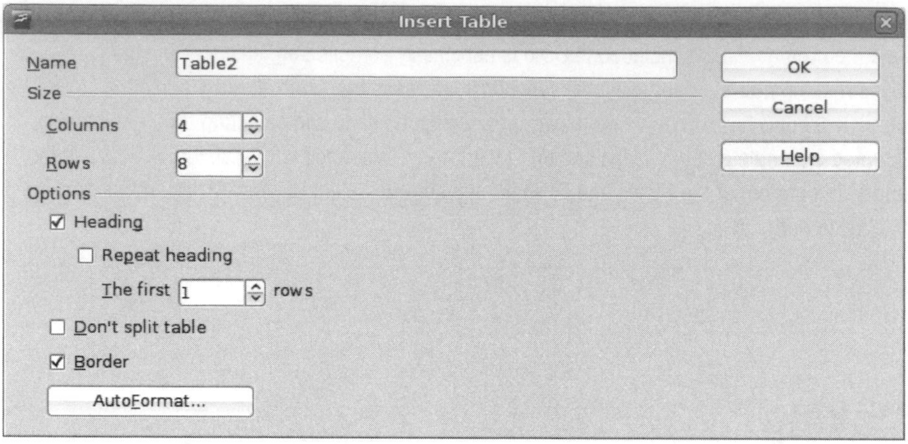

**Figure 3-18.** *Insert a table into a document with Table ➤ Insert, and then define the rows and columns to be included.*

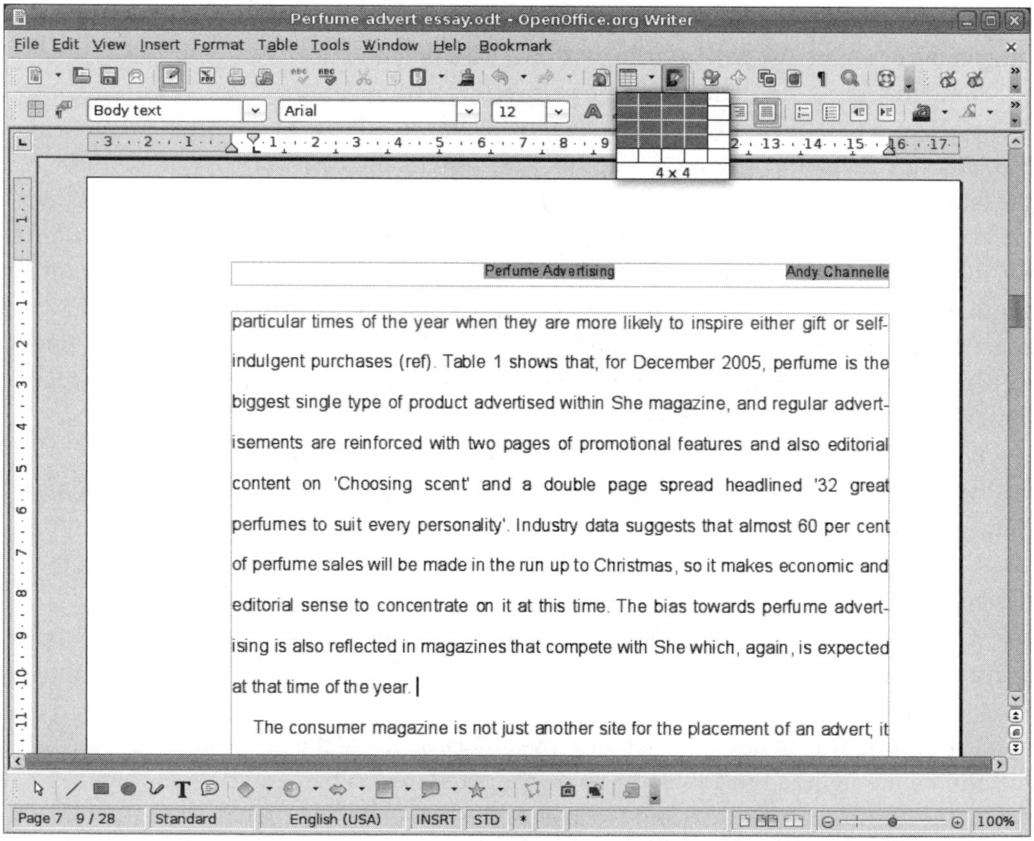

**Figure 3-19.** *Use the dedicated button on the Toolbar to quickly add a table to a document. Use the visual representation to define the number of rows and columns.*

## BASIC TABLE FORMATTING

Clicking anywhere in a table causes the Table editing toolbox (a floating toolbar that can be anchored to any part of the Writer window) to appear. We'll look at most of the options in here later, but for now, we just want to add a hint of color to the header of the table so it's obviously not part of the data.

One important point to remember is that edits made in this toolbox will affect the cell, row, or column that the cursor is in. So to change the color of the header, you need to click into the leftmost column and drag across the rest of the header row. This selects just that row (you can also hover the mouse close to the far left or right border so it becomes an arrow and just click), and then you can add a background color by opening the chooser (the fifth icon on the top row) and picking a color. Each of the highlighted cells assumes that color.

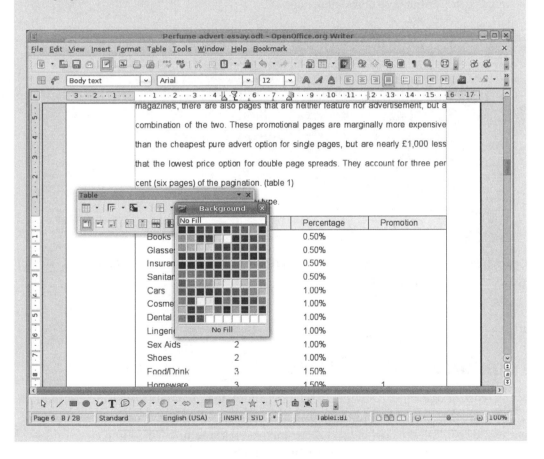

The third and final method—the one you'll use in this example—is especially good when the data is already present in a document. For example, you have a set of statistics that are arranged in the following manner:

Firefox [tab] Konqueror [tab] Opera [tab] Internet Explorer
Gecko [tab] WebKit [tab] Presto [tab] Trident3.0 [tab] 4.1 [tab] 9.5 [tab] 8.0

and so on. This is known as tab-delimited data because the tab key marks one element out from the next. Turning this kind of data into a table involves highlighting all of the parts with the mouse and choosing Table ➤ Convert ➤ Text to Table. This launches a dialog box with the same options as previously mentioned but with the addition of a section where you can set the delimiting character (see Figure 3-20). This has various options, such as Tabs, Paragraph (Enter key), Semicolons, and Other, where you can input any textual element as a delimiter, which means you can deal with just about any kind of data. In this case, selecting the Header element turns the first line of the data into column headers. AutoFormat is also available here.

**Figure 3-20.** *Tab-delimited text can be added to a document as a table with the Table ➤ Convert ➤ Text to Table option.*

# Footnotes and Endnotes

Many types of writing rely on notes to clarify a point, to offer supplementary information that might look out of place in the body text, or even just to give the reader a web address without disrupting the flow of text. There are two main methods of adding these notes—footnotes, which go at the base of the page the anchor is on, and endnotes, which are positioned at the end of the text—and Writer is happy with either. Of course, you can make your own frames at the bottom of pages for footnotes or type endnotes manually, but this goes against our "let the computer do the difficult stuff" mantra. By allowing Writer to organize the notes, you won't have to worry about ensuring frames stay with their corresponding note numbers, or that the numbers themselves become jumbled up during the editing phase.

To add a footnote or an endnote to a piece of text, click the point where the anchor needs to go (i.e., the text being "footnoted"), and select Insert ➤ Footnote. This launches a small dialog box that allows you to define how the note is anchored to the text and whether you're using a footnote or an endnote (see Figure 3-21). Choose Automatic to have a number assigned to the note and anchor, or choose Character to use some other device such as an asterisk. If you opt for Automatic, Writer will also deal with the numerical order of the notes. The Character option allows you to define an anchor character to the text, which is referenced in the footnote. For example, the first note might have an asterisk (*), the second might have a dagger (†), and the third a double-dagger (‡).

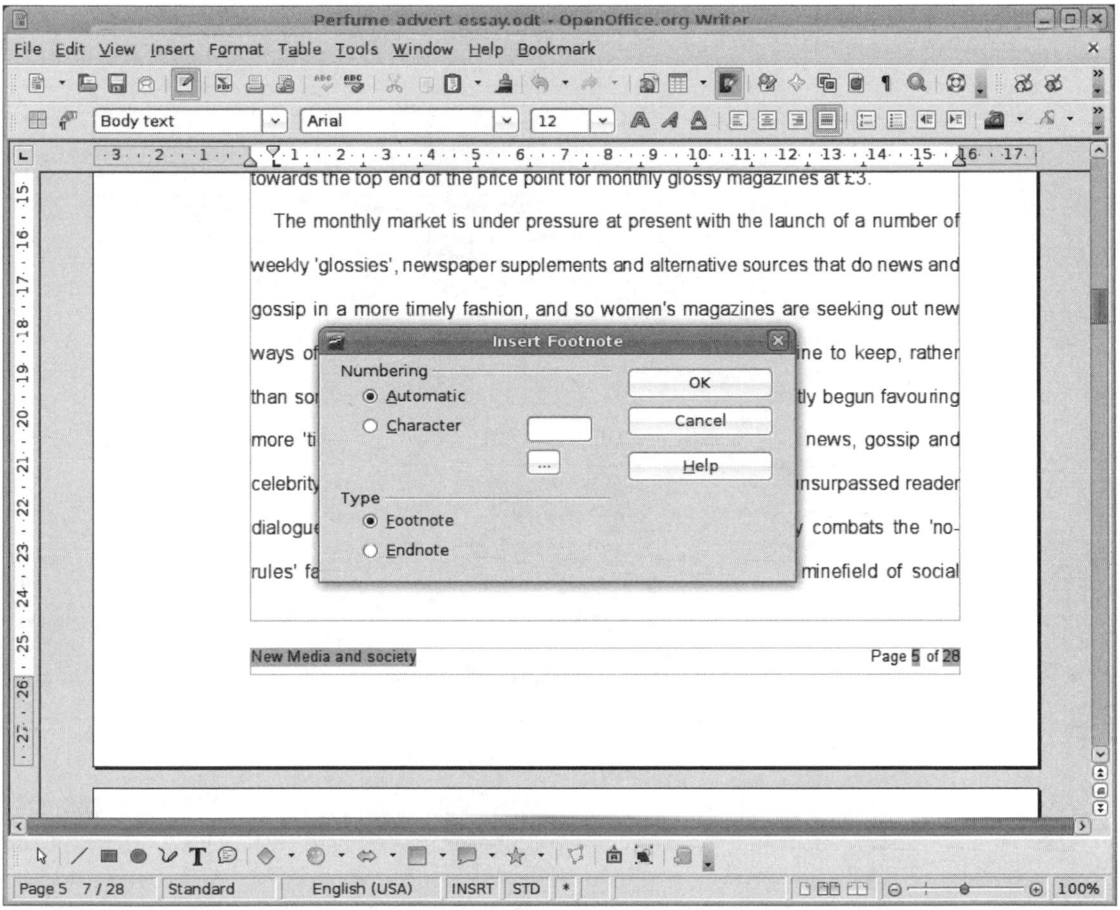

**Figure 3-21.** *Footnotes sit at the bottom of the page, which contains the anchor text, whereas endnotes are positioned at the end of the main text.*

Click OK to add the anchor to the text, create a box ready for the footnote/endnote in the appropriate place, and insert the cursor ready for writing. Note that there is a pre-defined style for Footnotes in Styles and Formatting, which is automatically applied to the text in the footnote. This means you can nip in and edit the format by opening the Styles and Formatting palette, right-clicking Footnote ➤ Modify, and then refining the style to fit the rest of the document.

■**Note**  If you use a lot of footnotes, it could be worthwhile to add the Insert Footnote Directly (or Insert Endnote Directly) button to the standard toolbar because this will provide one-click note entry. Select Tools ➤ Customize ➤ Toolbars. Select the standard toolbar, click Add, and look under the Insert category for the appropriate entry (see Figure 3-22). Click Add again, then click Close, and the icon will be added to the tool-bar. Now when you want to add a note, click the icon and begin typing.

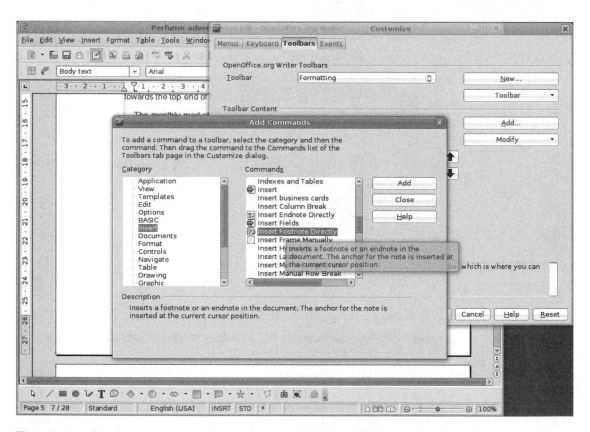

**Figure 3-22.** *Add a button to the toolbar and make inserting footnotes a one-click process.*

After the note has been added, however, mouse over the anchor to see a tool tip of the note (see Figure 3-23), or click the anchor to go straight to the content—especially useful for endnotes—and edit as normal, and then click the anchor in the note itself to go back to the original place. You can also edit the note type by clicking just ahead of the anchor in the text and choosing Edit ➤ Footnote. In this way, you can turn a footnote into an endnote and vice versa.

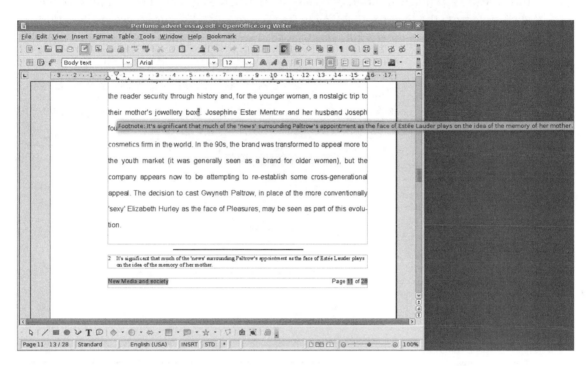

**Figure 3-23.** *Hover over an anchor to see the contents of a footnote.*

# Text Automation

Writer has a few options available for the automatic input of textual elements. We already looked briefly at some page variables earlier when defining the page settings—we'll go through a few more soon—but there are also AutoText and AutoCorrect. The former allows you to automate the insertion of text, images, and other content, whereas the latter monitors your efforts at typing and tries to make everything a bit easier.

Let's begin by adding the most commonly used page variable—the page number— while taking a broad overview of the available options. The page numbers are going to be in the page footer and aligned on the right, so click in the footer area of any page, click the right align button on the Formatting toolbar, and define the font. Remember, good-looking documents usually don't have more than two fonts, so stick with the same one used in the header area. Now choose Insert ➤ Fields ➤ Page number to add the page number to the footer. Note that any text inserted before or after the page number variable will appear in that position on each page, which makes it possible to add some text (Page 1) or visual flourishes (-1-). In some business reports, it might also be useful to let the audience know how many pages they have to read, so the page number section might read Page (Page number) of (Page count), where Page count is another variable accessible from the Insert ➤ Field menu (see Figure 3-24). Because these are variables based on the document structure itself, it will always be completely accurate.

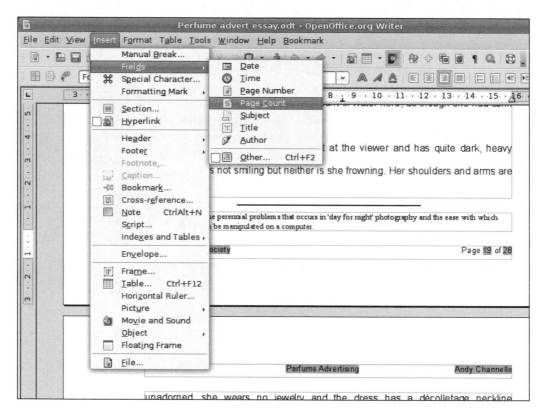

**Figure 3-24.** *Page numbers are one of the most commonly used variables in any word processor.*

You can also add the publication data you defined right at the beginning of the document by clicking to the left of the page number, choosing Insert ➤ Fields ➤ Other, and expanding the Custom menu using the disclosure (+) icon. Under here we find the User Generated fields created when editing the document properties. Select Publication name, and click Insert (see Figure 3-25). Again, two presses of the tab key shifts this variable to the left of the page.

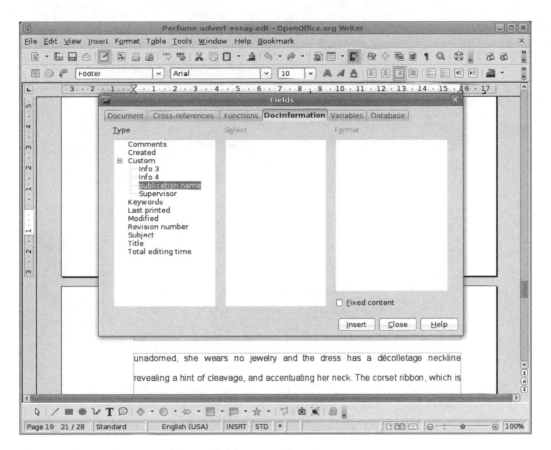

**Figure 3-25.** *Inserting one of the variables created earlier*

With these variables now set, you can quickly change the title of the document, the author, and the publication name by going back into File ➤ Properties and changing the data.

## AutoText

In Chapter 2, you built a small gallery of images that can be reused over and over again. One of the limitations of the gallery concept is that although it's good for adding graphics and sounds, it doesn't have the facility to insert snippets of text. Fortunately, this is exactly what AutoText does. More importantly, you can create a piece of text (complete with images and tables if necessary) and then turn that into a piece of AutoText with ease. Let's start with a simple piece of text.

Throughout this document, the phrase "Estée Lauder/Elizabeth Arden" must be typed. This is an annoying piece of text because it has a lot of initial capitals, the forward slash in the center, and that accent over the first lowercase "e." Start by highlighting the text string, and then choose Edit ➤ AutoText (or press Ctrl+F3) to open the configuration dialog box (see Figure 3-26).

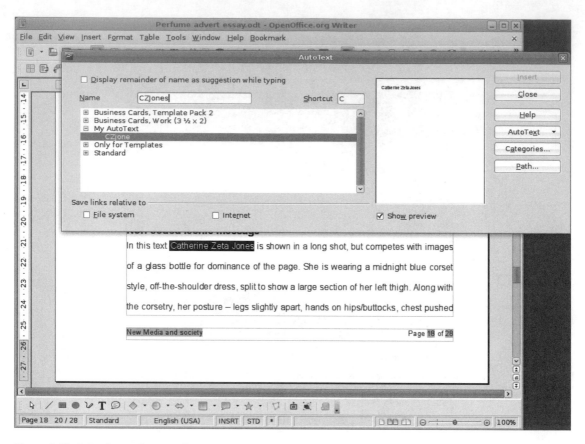

**Figure 3-26.** *Words or phrases that are used often in a document can be added automatically using the AutoText feature.*

Before you build the first entry, let's look at one of the standard AutoTexts. Click the disclosure icon (+) next to Standard, scroll down until the Sincerely entry is visible, and click the Preview check box to see what the actual AutoText content looks like. Select this to display the structure of the text. Near the top of the window, you'll see the name of the AutoText and the keystroke that invokes it—in this case, SI. As with the default styles mentioned earlier, you can't edit or delete these, but you can come back to edit user styles later.

Now, click the minus icon (-) next to Standard, and click the entry labeled My Auto-Text. The top elements become editable, allowing you to specify a name (which doesn't have to be the same as the text string) and shortcut to stand in for the text. Try to think of something memorable that is at least a little related to the words or phrase to be replaced—if you spend two minutes trying to remember if the shortcut for Sun Microsystems is SM or SMS, you may as well just type the text! When those elements are defined, choose AutoText ➤ New, which saves the entry to the system, and then click Close to get rid of the dialog box.

Adding a piece of AutoText simply involves typing the shortcut, for example, SI for Sincerely, and then pressing the F3 key. If you've tried this with Sincerely, you'll see that Writer doesn't just put the text in but also adds a hard return ready for the next piece of text. Anything that can be added to a Writer document— links, images, graphics, tables, and so on—can be enclosed in an AutoText entry. It can even manage variables.

## AutoCorrect

A second kind of automatic text entry is the AutoCorrect feature, which automatically corrects commonly mistyped or misspelled words and does a whole lot more. Access the dialog box by choosing Tools ➤ AutoCorrect, and feast your eyes on all those tabs (see Figure 3-27). We'll go through them one-by-one.

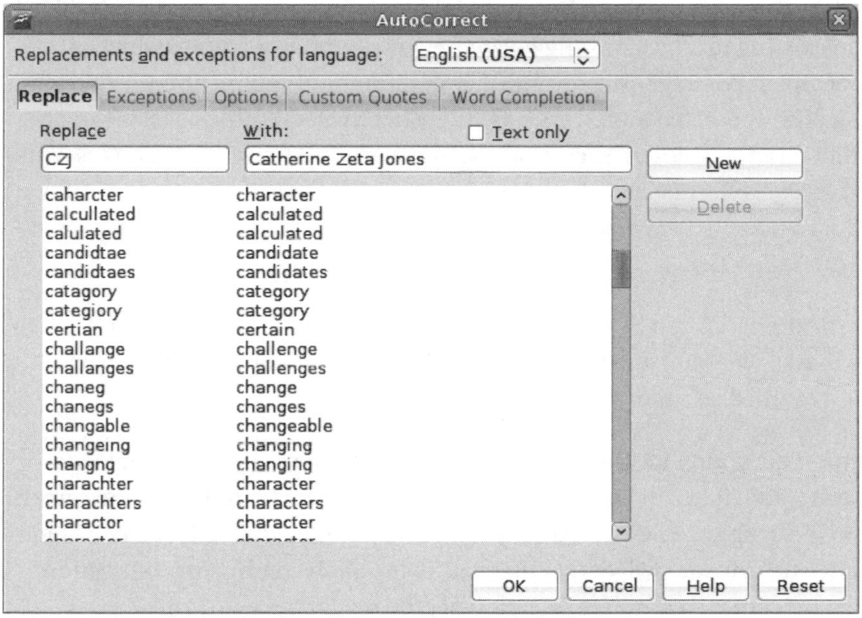

**Figure 3-27.** *AutoCorrect can replace commonly misspelled words with their correct versions or long phrases with a few initials.*

**Replace**. This is the most obvious task of AutoCorrect. If you type "becuase" or "drive-ing," it will replace them with "because" and "driving," respectively. It also makes light work of the copyright symbol—just type (C)—the registered trademark symbol—type (R)—and decent-looking arrows—type --> or <--. You can also add your own entries, so if you always spell "Pontefract" wrong, add the incorrect spelling (Pontifract) to the left-side text area, put the correct spelling in the right area, and click the New button. A new entry will be added, and next time you're writing about the town in the North West of England,

Writer will remember the correct spelling so you don't have to. You can also set these to automatically add an initial capital letter to city or country names (replace canada with Canada) or use it as an alternative to the AutoText system (replace MSFT with Microsoft).

**Exceptions**. Sometime we spell words nontraditionally on purpose, especially when using abbreviations and acronyms. You might want to write "approx" instead of "approximately," for example, or you might mention (musical) CDs or OO.o, and this is where we can prepare for those times. The latter is important because Writer typically treats words that have two capital letters at the beginning as a typing error, so common two-letter acronyms that might have a plural version—the aforementioned CDs—or technical terms such as MHz will get through the filter.

**Options**. This is where you can define just how diligent the AutoCorrect tool is at monitoring your mistakes. There are two ways to work with this, which are reflected in the two columns of check boxes. Marking an option in the [M] column means that the option will be applied to existing text by choosing Format ➤ AutoFormat ➤ Apply (which is great when importing or pasting text from another document); marking the [T] column means that text will be corrected as you type. Options here will do things like automatically make the first letter of any sentence a capital and replace a typed web address with an active, clickable link, but they can also be used for quick formatting because text enclosed in asterisks (like *this*) will be made bold, and text enclosed in underscores (_like this_) will be underlined.

**Custom Quotes**. Content created in a standard text editor may not use proper curly single or double quote marks. Enabling the options here will ensure your quotes are never straight, which is regarded as a more professional finish.

**Word Completion**. This option has the potential for serious time saving but can take some getting used to and, it has to be said, is more useful to those who stare at the screen while typing. It's a little like predictive text on a cell phone. When enabled, you can begin typing "conn," and the software will define that you're probably aiming for connection, which is in the list of words to complete. As you type, the rest of the word will appear on the line reversed out with a blue background; pressing Enter will complete the word. Moreover, by clicking the Append space check box, the software will also add a space at the end of an automatically entered word except—cleverly—if the next character typed is a punctuation mark. This is one of the options that often throws users and requires a bit of discipline to be used effectively.

If the Enter key feels wrong for completing the word (it does for many), use the Accept with drop-down list to select another key such as Tab, Space, or the right cursor key. You can, of course, turn off completion by deselecting the option at the top of the dialog box. The options at the bottom allow you to configure the minimum word length to be completed (autocompleting a three-letter word is a bit pointless) and also the number of words Writer will add to the list.

# Document Breaks

Although the text in the example document is now looking pretty good, there are a few important omissions, particularly the title page and contents page, and this presents a problem. If you were to click at the beginning of the text and add a couple of page breaks (Insert ➤ Manual Break ➤ Page) that would give you the space needed for these two important elements, but it would also add the header and footer to both pages (which you don't want) and make the main text begin on page 3 instead of page 1.

Styles—this time Page Styles—come to the rescue. Open the Styles and Formatting palette again, and click the Page Styles icon (fourth from the left). Use the new style icon on the far right, and select New style from selection to create a new page style based on the default you created at the start of this project. Give it a name (for this example project, use the innovative "Standard"), and click OK.

To create a new style, right-click anywhere in the list, and choose New to launch the normal page definition dialog box. Use the same values and margins as the main page, but make sure that headers and footers are not enabled. Call this one "Front." Finally, do the same thing again, and call the next page style "Contents."

You now have three page styles, and you're ready to add a new page to the beginning by choosing Insert ➤ Manual Break and selecting the Page break option (see Figure 3-28). Under the Style heading, choose Standard—the style the page after the break will adopt— enable the Change page number check box, and ensure the number below it is set to 1.

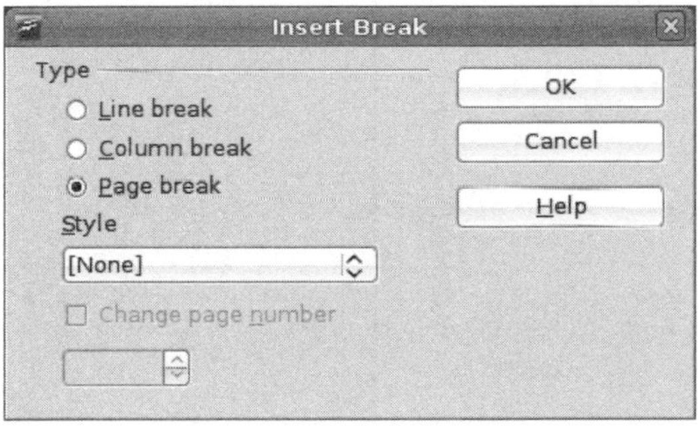

**Figure 3-28.** *Force a document to break in a particular place using the Insert ➤ Manual Break menu.*

When you click the OK button, a new page will be added to the document using the Standard style, but if you look at the footer of the first two pages, you now have two pages labeled "1." Not good. However, if you click somewhere inside the new first page and then double-click the Contents page style, the Header and Footer (along with the confusing page number) will disappear. You can now do another new page, but this time choose Contents as the Style, click OK, click inside the first page, and double-click the First Page style.

You now have two blank pages ready for new content, and page 1 actually begins on page 3. For the front page, create a new frame (Insert ➤ Frame), anchor it to the page, remove the border, and position the frame as a band across the center of the page. Into this frame, put the document's title (choose Insert ➤ Field ➤ Title) and, beneath that, the author name (choose Insert ➤ Field ➤ Author), and then format them appropriately.

You can add a new frame near the bottom and add the Supervisor variable and the date (choose Insert ➤ Field ➤ Date), and you've created a title page that can be updated using the document properties quite simply (see Figure 3-29).

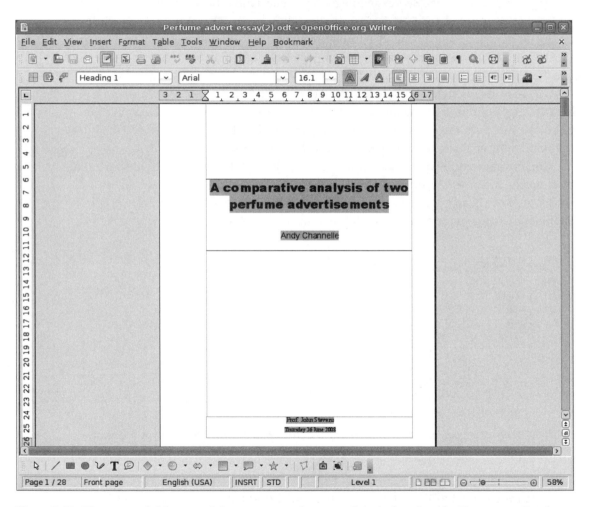

**Figure 3-29.** *The cover of this type of document can be created entirely using the Document Properties set earlier.*

# Table of Contents

Now some of the effort made earlier is really going to pay off, and you'll use Writer's styles and formatting system to build and maintain a dynamic table of contents to go near the front of the document. Again, let the computer do the heavy lifting, which makes sure that the contents page is always up to date because we don't have to worry about manually updating page numbers or chapter, section, and subsection titles.

To begin, click in the page set aside earlier for the contents, and then select Insert ➤ Indexes and Tables ➤ Indexes and Tables. On the left of this complicated-looking dialog box is a preview of what the completed contents page should look like (see Figure 3-30). It has a lot of elements that we won't be covering for the moment, so we're really concerned with the text entries at the top.

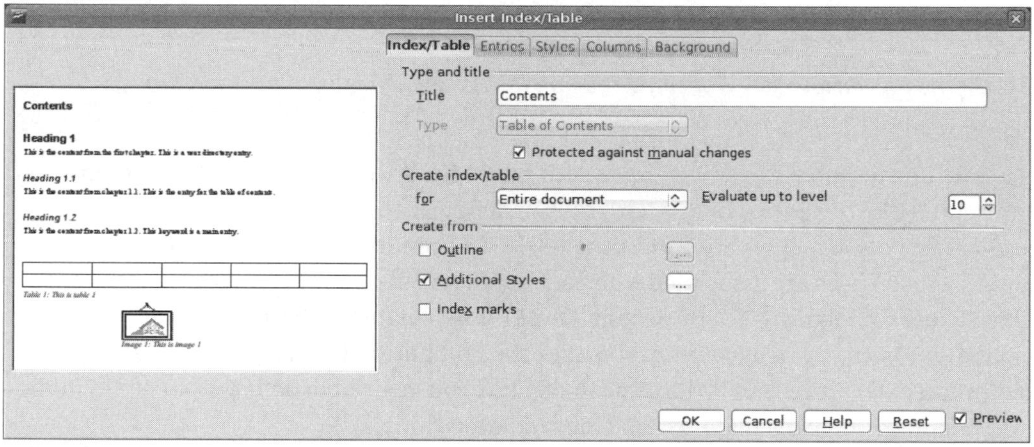

**Figure 3-30.** *Use Insert ➤ Indexes and Tables to access the table of contents options.*

Under Type and title, choose Table of Contents, and provide a title to go at the head of the list. Ensure Protect against manual changes is selected (make the computer work) and then deselect Outline in the Create from section. This latter choice is necessary because when creating the document a few user-defined styles were used in the headings, so you want to be able to define entries using that scheme. Click Additional Styles, and, for the moment, deselect Index marks. You can now define the structure by clicking the ellipsis button (...) to the right of Additional Styles.

You now have a list of available styles and a dialog box containing a horizontal ruler and two arrow boxes at the bottom (see Figure 3-31). This is where you define the structure with the numbers across the top representing the "levels" in the table of contents. You move styles to the right level using the arrows. For example, in the example document, the section headings were styled with Heading 1, so select that, and move it to position 1. The subheadings are styled with Heading 3, so shift that into position 2. Click OK.

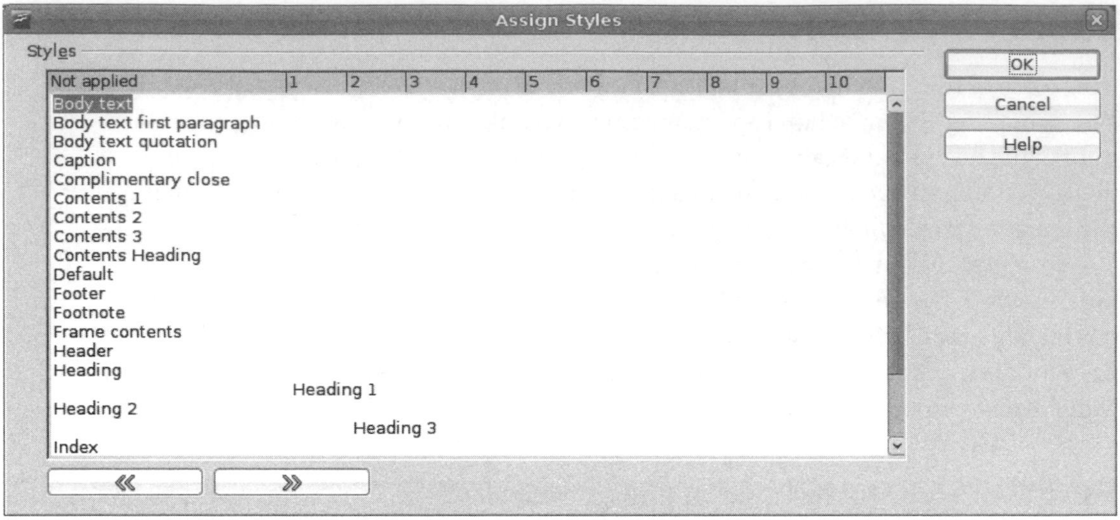

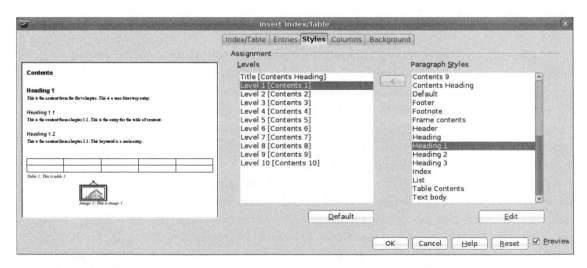

**Figure 3-31.** *Define the various levels of content using the Assign Styles configuration box.*

The Entries tab is already set up for our purposes, so ignore that for the moment, and move on to the Styles tab. In this tab, you can define all the stylistic elements of the TOC, and the work is just like editing any other style. The column on the left of the window shows which styles are associated with each level, and the one on the right shows available styles (see Figure 3-32). By default, Level 1 is associated with Contents 1, so select Contents 1 from the right column, and click the Edit button to access the normal styles definition dialog box. This is the same dialog box you've used to define other styles in the document, so you can edit fonts, spacing, and everything else.

**Figure 3-32.** *Each element of the TOC has its own editable style.*

The table of contents is dynamic, which means we don't have to edit the table itself because it will update to reflect changes made to the text (see Figure 3-33). To see this in action, scroll through the document, and edit one of the section headings. This automatically makes the table of contents out of date, so go back to the head of the document, right-click any part of the TOC text, and select Update Index/Table. The entries will now reflect the content of the document. The right-click menu also offers access to the main dialog box (Edit Index/Table) where the levels, styles, and everything else can be refined (see Figure 3-34).

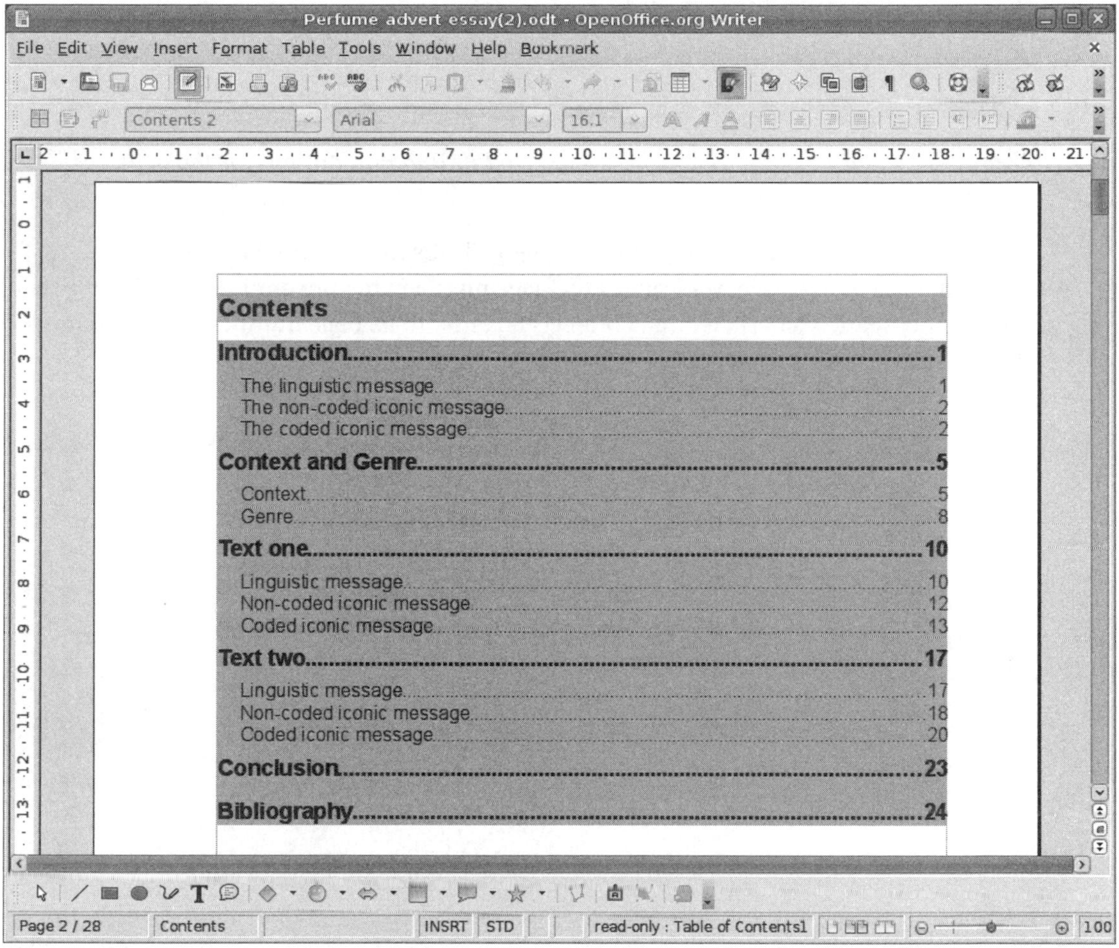

**Figure 3-33.** *Once created, the TOC is a dynamic object built on the contents of the rest of the document.*

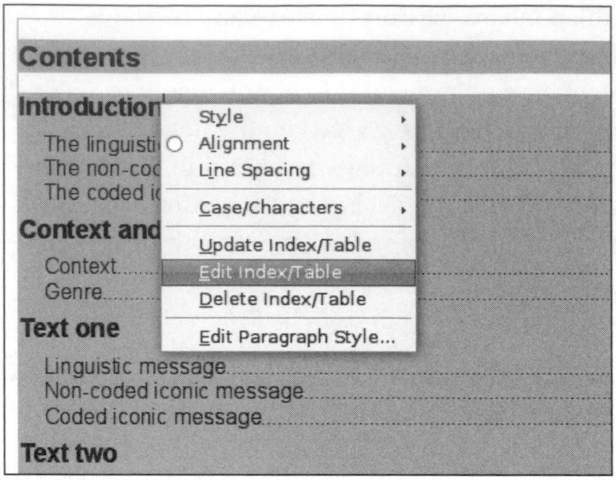

**Figure 3-34.** *Right-click the TOC to access the Update and Edit options for the page.*

Writer can deal with many different styles of TOCs through the Entries tab (see Figure 3-35). For example, you can set the page numbers to appear first, alter the appearance of the "leader" character that connects an entry to its page number, or even remove the leader.

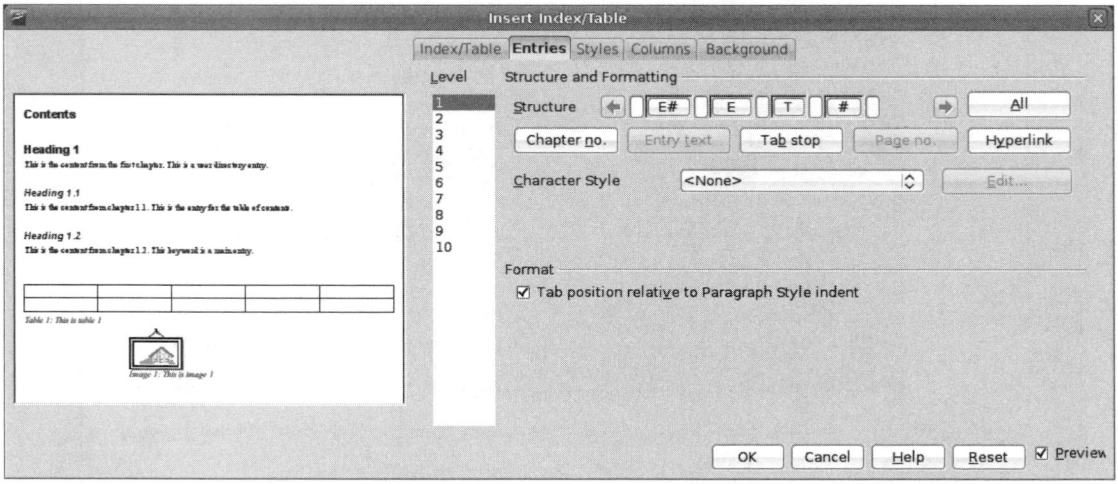

**Figure 3-35.** *The Entries tab allows you to make large-scale adjustments to the structure of the table of contents.*

The Entries tab looks really complicated, but it's not that bad really. The boxes in the center of the page define the way that each entry is displayed. To change the structure of the top-level part of the TOC, select 1 in the Level column, then select each structural element (the boxes) in turn, and press Delete. Now click the first empty box, and select the element name that you want to include first. For example, select Page No to have that as the first part of the line of text, click in the second box, and select Entry Text to insert the text that will accompany the page number. A space has been added before the Entry Text so it's not too close to the number (see Figure 3-36). The Hyperlink button will add a link to the page, making it possible to jump straight there by clicking the link.

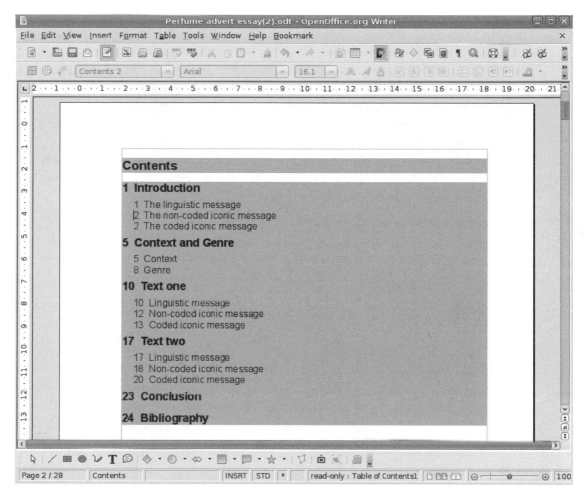

**Figure 3-36.** *The final result is a TOC with a markedly different visual style.*

# Recap

In this chapter, we've looked at some of the ways you can automate many of the difficult jobs that arise when creating complex documents—basically getting the computer to do the hard work so you don't have to. You've created styles and substyles enabling you to make global changes to the look and feel of a document with just a few commands, and then used these styles as a basis to build a table of contents that can be updated quickly and without lots of small edits. We've also looked at how to automate the management of staple essay and report elements such as footnotes and endnotes.

The great thing about doing all of this is that it's really a job that needs to be done from start to finish only once. As soon as the text is finished, saved, and printed, it would take just a few minutes of work to remove all of the content of the document and save the whole thing as a template ready for the next job. All the styles will be saved, as will the location of variables such as author name and title, meaning the process of setting up a second essay or report will be done in half the time.

In the next chapter, we'll rest our literary brain for a moment and adopt a more numerate outlook as we enter the world of the spreadsheet and OpenOffice.org Calc. However, if you have a tight deadline, skip ahead to Chapter 10 for more on Writer in an academic setting with an exploration of the bibliography system built into the software. And take a look at Chapter 11 to find out about some of the extensions that can make working with Writer a more  fruitful experience.

# CHAPTER 4

# Spreadsheets with Calc

Although word processing may be regarded as the core application in any office suite for general users, spreadsheets are starting to find their way into more homes, classrooms, and offices as users discover the benefits of organizing data in more useful ways. And that, in a nutshell, is what a spreadsheet does; it takes pieces of information entered by either humans or some process and then allows the user to display and interrogate it to make something meaningful.

In this chapter, you'll use OpenOffice.org's Calc program to create a couple of simple projects, including a very basic accounting spreadsheet and a more ambitious home budget system. These two jobs will allow you to explore the most commonly needed tools in the software to input and arrange information and to create charts that will display this data in a more visual way.

A spreadsheet is made up of cells (individual units of data) that are arranged into rows (left to right), columns (top to bottom), and worksheets. A single spreadsheet could contain main worksheets that are accessible via the tabs at the base of the main window. The software's power comes from the fact that you can run an operation such as finding the average value of a range of cells, and then feed this into other operations, and then on to other operations, and so on. And with this chain of relationships defined, you can change one of the earlier values (that fed into the first averaging operation) and see how that small change propagates through the rest of the spreadsheet. For example, in a household budget, you can see how a change in the monthly cost of gas will affect the chances of a two-week vacation in France next year (see Figure 4-1); whereas in a business account, it allows an accountant to monitor income or model cash flow for the forthcoming quarter.

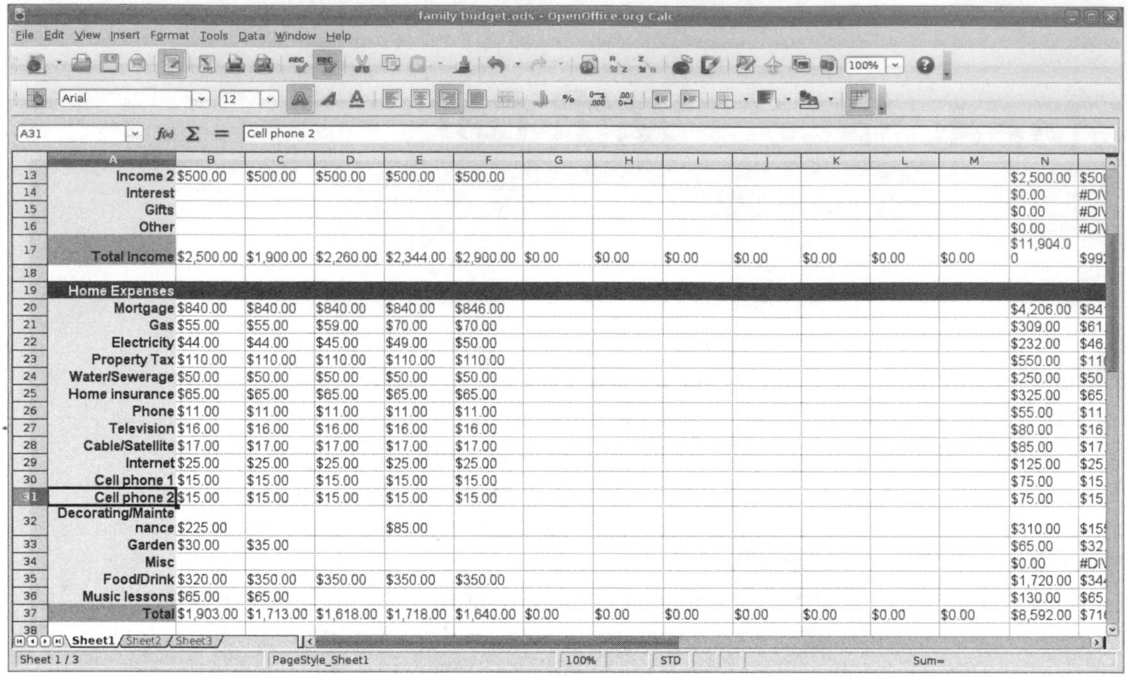


| | A | B | C | D | E | F | G | H | I | J | K | L | M | N | |
|---|---|---|---|---|---|---|---|---|---|---|---|---|---|---|---|
| 13 | Income 2 | $500.00 | $500.00 | $500.00 | $500.00 | $500.00 | | | | | | | | $2,500.00 | $50 |
| 14 | Interest | | | | | | | | | | | | | $0.00 | #DI |
| 15 | Gifts | | | | | | | | | | | | | $0.00 | #DI |
| 16 | Other | | | | | | | | | | | | | $0.00 | #DI |
| 17 | Total Income | $2,500.00 | $1,900.00 | $2,260.00 | $2,344.00 | $2,900.00 | $0.00 | $0.00 | $0.00 | $0.00 | $0.00 | $0.00 | $0.00 | $11,904.00 | $99 |
| 18 | | | | | | | | | | | | | | | |
| 19 | Home Expenses | | | | | | | | | | | | | | |
| 20 | Mortgage | $840.00 | $840.00 | $840.00 | $840.00 | $846.00 | | | | | | | | $4,206.00 | $84 |
| 21 | Gas | $55.00 | $55.00 | $59.00 | $70.00 | $70.00 | | | | | | | | $309.00 | $61 |
| 22 | Electricity | $44.00 | $44.00 | $45.00 | $49.00 | $50.00 | | | | | | | | $232.00 | $46 |
| 23 | Property Tax | $110.00 | $110.00 | $110.00 | $110.00 | $110.00 | | | | | | | | $550.00 | $11 |
| 24 | Water/Sewerage | $50.00 | $50.00 | $50.00 | $50.00 | $50.00 | | | | | | | | $250.00 | $50 |
| 25 | Home insurance | $65.00 | $65.00 | $65.00 | $65.00 | $65.00 | | | | | | | | $325.00 | $65 |
| 26 | Phone | $11.00 | $11.00 | $11.00 | $11.00 | $11.00 | | | | | | | | $55.00 | $11 |
| 27 | Television | $16.00 | $16.00 | $16.00 | $16.00 | $16.00 | | | | | | | | $80.00 | $16 |
| 28 | Cable/Satellite | $17.00 | $17.00 | $17.00 | $17.00 | $17.00 | | | | | | | | $85.00 | $17 |
| 29 | Internet | $25.00 | $25.00 | $25.00 | $25.00 | $25.00 | | | | | | | | $125.00 | $25 |
| 30 | Cell phone 1 | $15.00 | $15.00 | $15.00 | $15.00 | $15.00 | | | | | | | | $75.00 | $15 |
| 31 | Cell phone 2 | $15.00 | $15.00 | $15.00 | $15.00 | $15.00 | | | | | | | | $75.00 | $15 |
| 32 | Decorating/Maintenance | $225.00 | | | $85.00 | | | | | | | | | $310.00 | $15 |
| 33 | Garden | $30.00 | $35.00 | | | | | | | | | | | $65.00 | $32 |
| 34 | Misc | | | | | | | | | | | | | $0.00 | #DI |
| 35 | Food/Drink | $320.00 | $350.00 | $350.00 | $350.00 | $350.00 | | | | | | | | $1,720.00 | $34 |
| 36 | Music lessons | $65.00 | $65.00 | | | | | | | | | | | $130.00 | $65 |
| 37 | Total | $1,903.00 | $1,713.00 | $1,618.00 | $1,718.00 | $1,640.00 | $0.00 | $0.00 | $0.00 | $0.00 | $0.00 | $0.00 | $0.00 | $8,592.00 | $71 |

**Figure 4-1.** *Calc is the ideal choice if you need to organize a family's annual budget, and it costs less than a "home finance" package.*

# The Basics

When you select the spreadsheet option from the Start Center or manually launch Calc from the Start menu, you'll notice the familiar divisions in the interface. Across the top are the menus, and below that are two toolbars similar to those seen in Writer. Many of the options available in Calc use elements from the other parts of the suite. For example, defining the borders of cells uses the same options that you used to add borders to cells in tables and even in text frames in previous chapters, and the various text options that appear in Writer are available here as well. One of the major additions in Calc is a third toolbar called the Formula Bar. This is where formulas can be constructed and where individual cells are edited. Ordinarily, the Formula Bar has five parts: the name box, which identifies the currently selected cell; the Function Wizard, which is designed to make defining functions easier; Cancel and Accept buttons to enact, or not, a function; and the input line, which can be used to add or edit a function manually.

Dominating the rest of the window is the sheet itself. This is divided into rows, which are labeled with numbers, and columns, which have alphabetical headers. When navigating a spreadsheet, it's vital to remember that cells are always referred to with the column value first; that is, F21 signifies the column F and the row 21, whereas A1 is the first cell in the sheet. You can see the reference for any cell by selecting it and looking for the value on the Formula Bar. If the rows in a sheet go beyond row Z, then it will follow the sequence AA, AB, AC, AD, and so on. The rows, of course, simply increment normally. Under this scheme, a spreadsheet can contain thousands of cells.

The most recent version of OpenOffice.org Calc has increased the number of columns available in a spreadsheet from 256 to 1,024, making much larger sets of data, and thus more complex actions, possible. As mentioned earlier, a single spreadsheet could contain multiple worksheets, and although these may work as individual datasets, they are also linked, so you could, for instance, take the data from sheet 3, cell A3 and have that work in sheet 1, cell F4.

## Editing and Selecting

The most basic operations on the spreadsheet are inputting data and selecting cells. The simplest way to do the former is to click inside a cell and begin typing. As the words or numbers (spreadsheets don't have to contain just numbers) appear in the cell, they also show up in the input bar just above the main window. After text has been added, deselecting a cell can be accomplished in a few different ways. Clicking into another cell deselects, as does pressing the Enter key. Tapping Tab moves the cursor onto the next cell to the right; whereas the up, down, left, and right cursor keys move the cursor one cell in the appropriate direction.

In Figure 4-2, I've created a short list of names and e-mail addresses in columns with named headers. I've changed the color of the headers by using the Background color option on the toolbar. Note that the e-mail addresses have become clickable by default, meaning if you select one, it will launch your e-mail client ready to send that person a message.

Selecting cells follows the logic of making selections in most common file managers, including Windows Explorer.

Select a single cell by clicking it with the mouse or using the Tab and cursor keys. To add to or edit a cell's content, either double-click the cell, or select with a single click and begin typing.

Select multiple adjacent cells by either clicking and dragging the mouse over the required cells, or by clicking in the first of the selection and then Shift-clicking in the last. For example, you could select everything between A1 and G3 by clicking A1 and Shift-clicking G3.

Select multiple nonadjacent cells by clicking the first and then Ctrl-clicking each subsequent cell.

You can also select an entire row (or selection of rows) by clicking the row labels ranged along the left edge of the window; select a whole column by clicking a column heading at the top of the window; or select the entire table (useful for making universal changes to font size) by clicking in the small rectangle where the row and column labels meet.

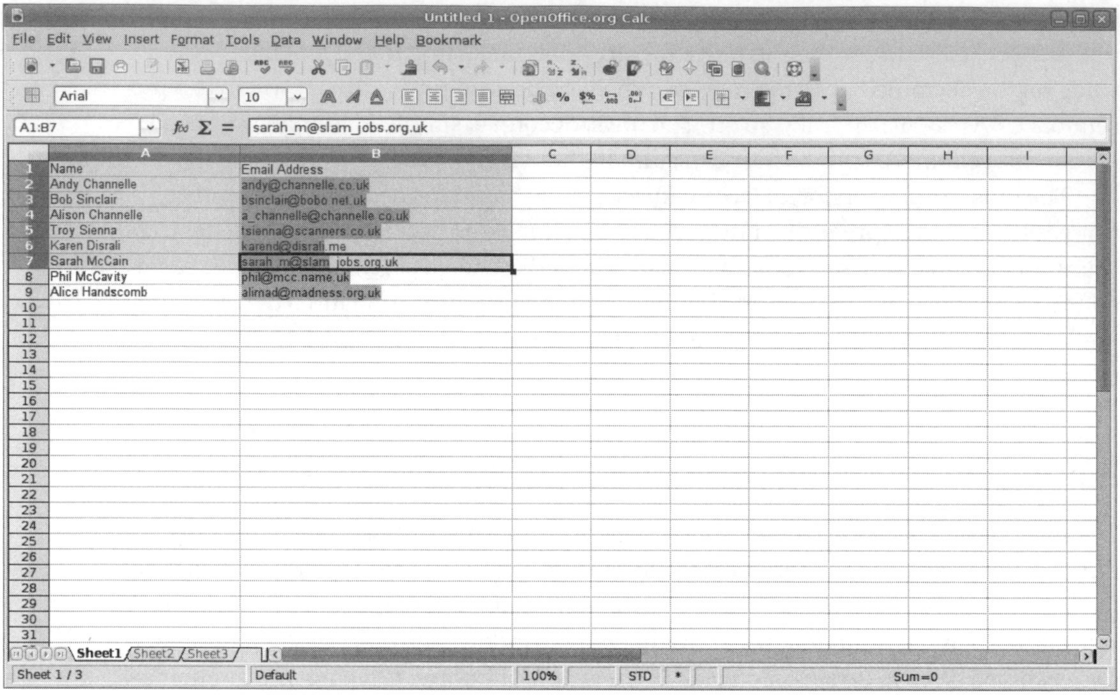

**Figure 4-2.** *Cells can be selected by clicking and dragging the mouse over the area to be formatted.*

## Sorting Data

In our example, data has been entered in quite a haphazard way, which can make it difficult to find a particular record. Fortunately, you can sort these names and e-mail addresses into a more orderly list.

Select all of the data in both columns, including the headings in A1 and A2. Now choose Data ➤ Sort to launch the Sort dialog box. This has three spaces for defining sort criteria (see Figure 4-3). Click the first drop-down list, which contains entries that reference the column headers. Calc assumes that the top column content is the header, which is why it's important to make sure those parts are selected before sorting. Select Name from this list, and click OK. The content of the spreadsheet is reordered alphabetically. Note that if you only select the Name column, only that column will be sorted, meaning your names and e-mail addresses will no longer correspond. If this happens, choose Edit ➤ Undo to get back to the original state.

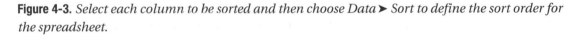

**Figure 4-3.** *Select each column to be sorted and then choose Data ➤ Sort to define the sort order for the spreadsheet.*

## SPREADSHEET OR DATABASE?

Both spreadsheets and databases are designed for organizing and visualizing data, but which should you use for your project? For those that require complicated financial or numerical sorting, the spreadsheet is the obvious choice, whereas those managing a lot of variable information (text, lists, images) will find a database more suitable. In the middle, there are projects such as address books, client lists, and home inventories that would work well in both. In these cases, scale and requirements should be your guide.

### Use a Spreadsheet When

- The nonnumerical dataset is going to have less than 50 entries (rows).

- The scope of the information collected has less than 10 elements (columns).

- There are no big image needs.

- The collected information doesn't need to integrate with other applications in the suite.

- You're uncomfortable with the perceived "difficulty" of a database.

### Use the Database When

- You're collecting large volumes of data, that is, thousands of cells.

- Multiple users will be entering information.

- The data will be used elsewhere in the suite, for example, in a mail merge.

One useful thing to remember is that it is entirely possible to extract the contents of a spreadsheet as a CSV file and build a database on that, and that the contents of a database can be loaded into a spreadsheet.

## Create a Spreadsheet

For many users, setting up a complex(ish) spreadsheet can be quite exciting because the functions often appear to be magic, but actually adding data can be quite tedious. It's important, however, to be diligent because you'll only get out of any piece of software what you put in, so for a spreadsheet to provide an accurate view of a person's or company's finances, the right information has to be entered to base that view on. Yes, it can be boring, but after the data are in there, you can sort things and make charts, which is exciting. Maybe exciting is the wrong word, but it can be interesting to visualize all those numbers.

You may also find some templates on the Internet that could save some work, but even if you find a template that does exactly the job you want, knowing how things happen inside the cells is very helpful.

Let's begin by creating and formatting a simple spreadsheet, which can then be used to examine the chart options in Calc. We'll then move on to the more ambitious project that uses functions and sums.

So begin by choosing File ➤ New ➤ Spreadsheet, and add some data similar to Figure 4-4.

To create the title cell, select everything between C1 and I1, and then choose Format ➤ Merge Cells. You can then center the title text and format it using the Formatting toolbar.

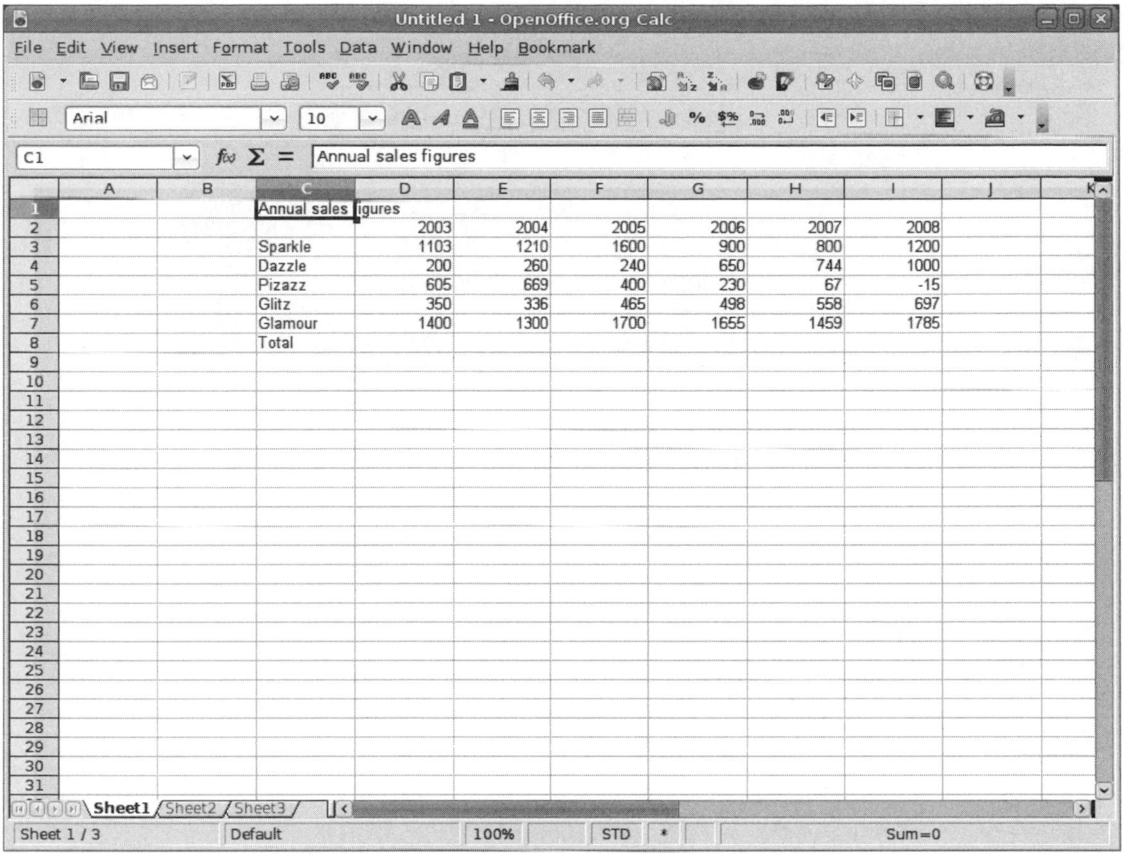

**Figure 4-4.** *This spreadsheet features a typical array of information such as labels and figures, though the formatting could do with some work.*

The new, more manageable spreadsheet contains sales figures for five stylish products over six years. Before you actually investigate the charts, let's make this display of raw data a bit more readable. By default, Calc squashes up cells to get as much onscreen as possible, but for this example, this is not an issue, so you can create a bit more space around the data. Select the entire spreadsheet by pressing Ctrl+A, choose Format ➤ Row ➤ Height, set the height to 1.00cm, and click OK (see Figure 4-5). Now choose Format ➤ Column ➤ Width, and set the value to 3.00cm before clicking OK.

---

■**Note**  Just as there are some predefined text formats in Writer, Calc has a number of premade spreadsheet formats. These are accessed via the Format ➤ Autoformat option. To apply the appropriate format, you select it from the list on the right and click OK. It's also possible to add new Autoformats based on a currently selected table by using Add and supplying a new name.

---

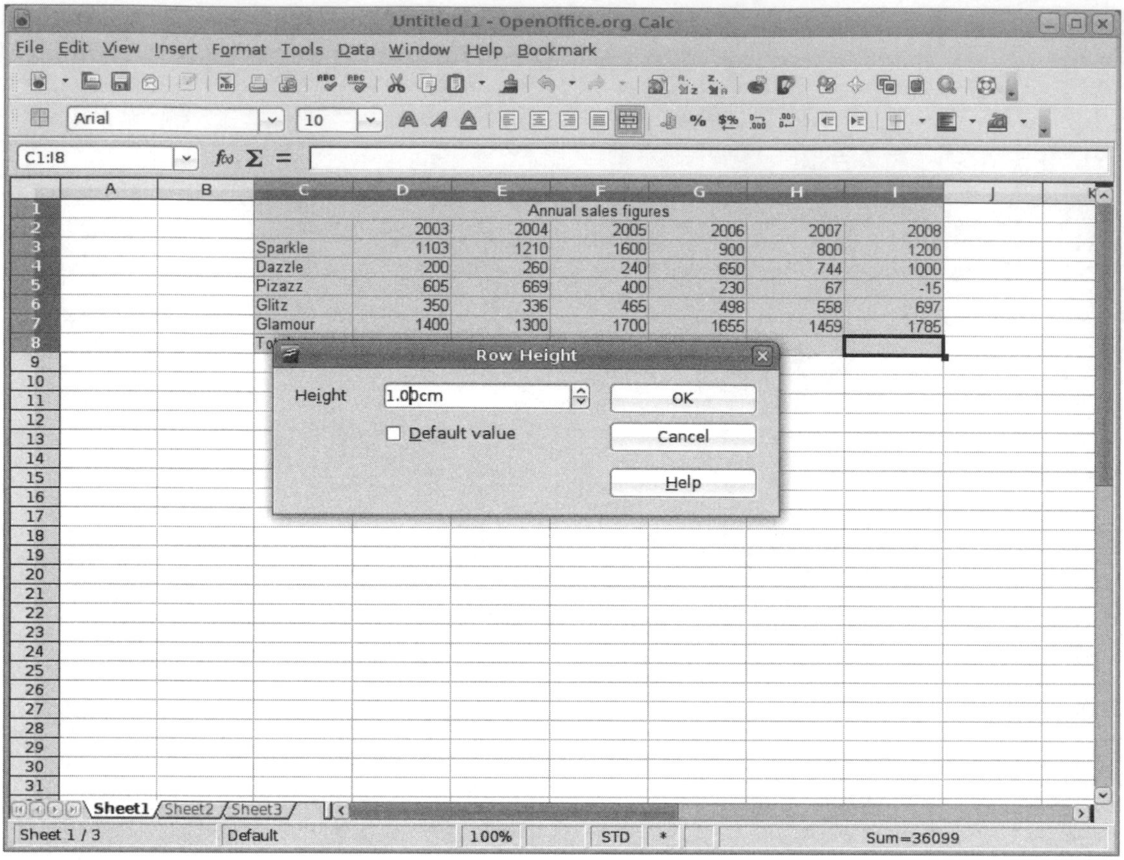

**Figure 4-5.** *Row height*

Select just the table now, and choose Format ➤ Cells. This launches the main cell configuration box where you can define a lot of the visual elements of the spreadsheet. We'll look at the content formatting in more detail later, but because this example deals with sales, click the Numbers tab, and change the Category to Currency. This formats figures in the cell in the style of the default currency format, which, in turn, is defined by the default language and location of your OO.o installation.

Move on to the Font tab, which offers a subset of the main font options, allowing you to select a font, size, and weight (bold, italic, etc.). More options, including font color, are available under the Font Effects tab.

In the Alignment tab, the top part allows you to define how content sits within a cell, with options for Horizontal and Vertical alignment (choose Default and Middle, respectively), whereas the middle section allows for some interesting rotations, and the bottom part defines what happens when text is too big for a cell (see Figure 4-6). Selecting Wrap text automatically enables the Hyphenation active option, and the Shrink to fit cell size option does drastic things to font sizes if too much material is entered into a cell.

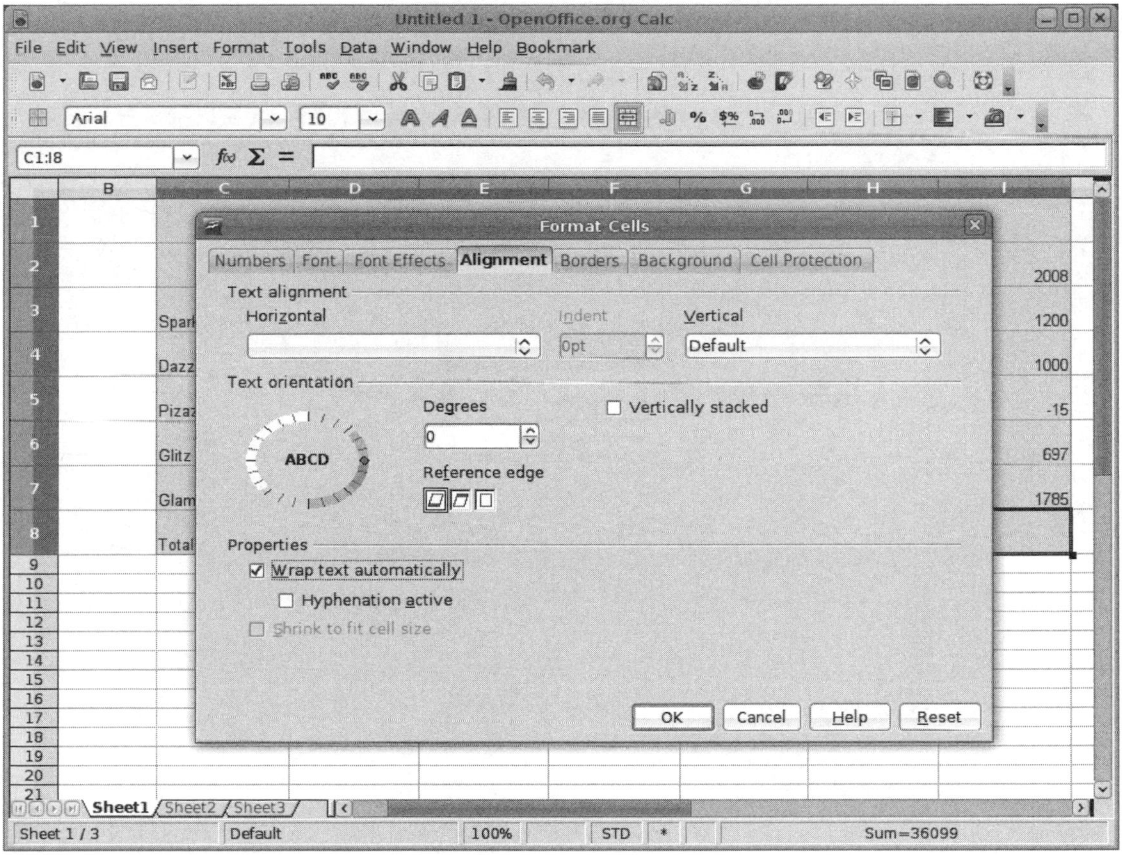

**Figure 4-6.** *The Wrap text automatically option stops bits of text from disappearing off in the edges of a cell.*

Select the Borders tab to set how the current selection is enclosed with lines (see Figure 4-7). One thing that can be confusing is that the lines selected here are applied to the current selection, so in this example, if you chose the second default line arrangement in the Borders tab, a solid line would be applied to the outer edge of the whole table, but if you had selected a single cell, that would be enclosed. This makes it possible to do many interesting things with lines, including ruling off along vertical or horizontal axes. The center column allows the selection of various line styles, widths, and colors, whereas the right-hand section can be used to inset the contents of the selected cells. By selecting the Synchronize check box, all four values are linked. Increase this value to 1.00mm to avoid any clashes with the cell edges. You can safely ignore the final two tabs in this dialog box because you'll color the backgrounds individually, and we'll look at Cell Protection later. So click OK to see the effects of your edit.

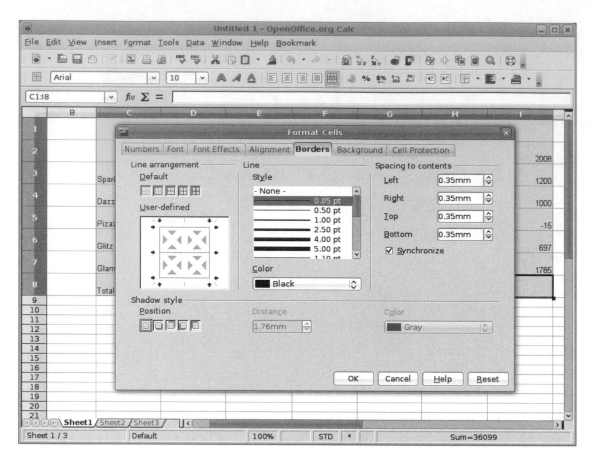

**Figure 4-7.** *Defining cell borders in Calc is similar to setting up table or frame borders in other parts of the suite.*

## Add Functions

At the base of each column, you'll add a function that takes the figures and performs the most basic calculation, that is, adds them together to give a total. Select the cell at the base of the first data column. In the data bar (above the main window), type **=SUM(X:Y)**, where *X* represents the first data cell in the column (in this case, C2) and *Y* represents the last data cell (in this case, C5). After you press Enter, the function is replaced with a figure that represents the sum of those cells (see Figure 4-8).

To make things easier, Calc also includes a Function Wizard, which is covered in the "Adding Some Logic" section later in this chapter.

Later you'll use more complex functions, but for the purposes of this simple spreadsheet, =SUM is adequate, and we can move on to creating a chart based on this information.

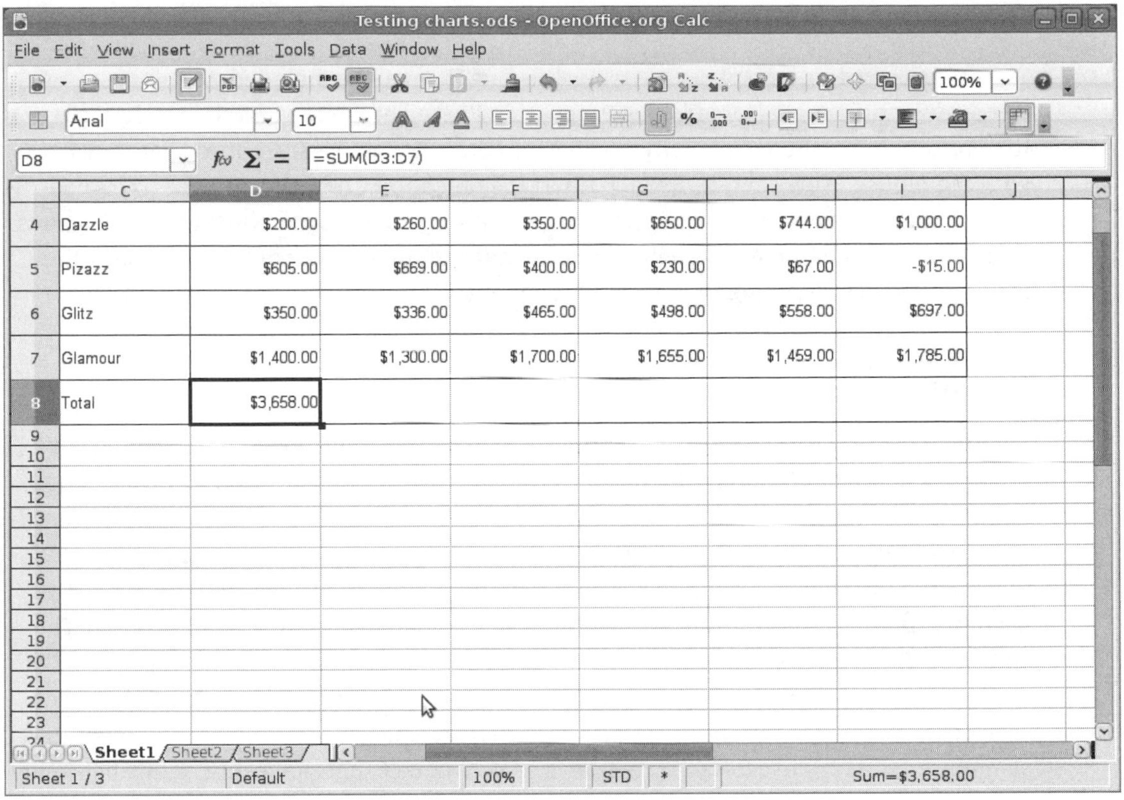

**Figure 4-8.** *Spreadsheets are so powerful because they can take information from a range of cells and add, subtract, average, or perform many other functions.*

## COLOR CHARTS

When you create a new chart in Calc, it draws upon a selection of 12 default colors. This color scheme has been designed to offer a good degree of separation—in terms of hue and brightness—for colors that are likely to end up next to each other on the chart. This is all good, but what if the result needs to conform to your firm's corporate colors? Fortunately, it's easy to change the colors.

Choose Tools ➤ Options to launch the main configuration dialog box, and then skip down the list of sections on the left until you get to Charts. Open the menu by clicking on the disclosure arrow, and select Default Colors. To change one of the Data Series colors, click it on the left side, and then select a new color from the palette on the right.

If nothing in the palette takes your fancy, click the OpenOffice.org disclosure arrow, choose Colors, and add some new colors manually. When you revisit Charts ➤ Default Colors, the new ones will be just a click away.

# Your First Chart

To create a chart, you first have to define the data that will be included. In this case, this is everything in the spreadsheet except the title cell at the top and the total cells at the bottom. Make the selection by clicking and dragging across the appropriate cells with the mouse. Now choose Insert ➤ Chart to launch the Chart Wizard. This is a good hand-holder, and you may be tempted to click through every option just to see the goods. This method of chart creation will work (and you can re-edit later on, as you'll see), but it's a good idea to examine the selectable elements.

## Chart Type

Your first decision is what kind of chart to use. Calc provides nine basic types, which are selectable in the right window, but each type has its own variations, often involving some 3D look. As discussed earlier, the charts will be built using the default colors, but you can change this at a later stage. The Chart Wizard is actually dynamic, so as you make changes, they should be reflected automatically in the chart on the spreadsheet, although you may need to shift the wizard window slightly because the default chart size is rather small. The choice of chart type will depend on both the data in the spreadsheet and the audience. For example, a simple bar chart or scatter graph is useful for showing a change over time such as the growth of a product or increased sales, whereas a pie chart is better for highlighting elements of data relative to each other, such as in a market share snapshot or the division of an income source. After you've picked a chart type and variation, click Next (see Figure 4-9).

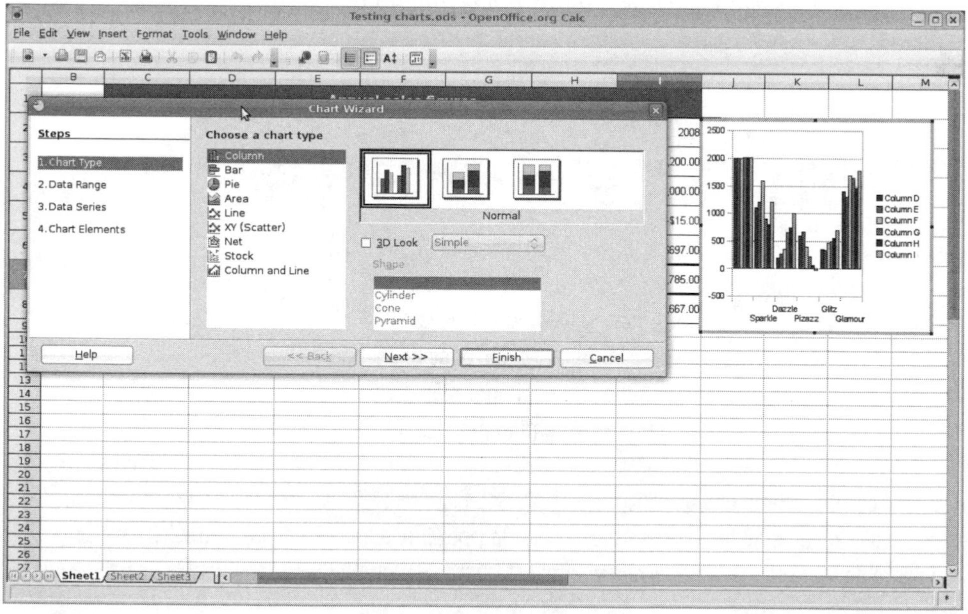

**Figure 4-9.** *Calc contains an array of different chart types, which is useful because what suits a sales chart won't necessarily suit an expenses chart.*

## Data Range

In the next section, you'll define precisely what data will feed into the chart. Changes made here can have a fundamental effect on the way the final chart is presented so it's worthwhile to explore the various options. I've already done the difficult part of defining the data using the mouse, which is represented in the Data range input box as a piece of code: $Sheet1.$C$2:$I$7. This code defines the sheet ($Sheet1) and cell range ($C$2:$I$7) to be charted, and you can edit this by hand.

Below this are two sets of options. The first defines the grouping of results by either row or column. Your choice here depends on how the chart is supposed to be perceived. In the example, you could group results by product, which makes growth or decline apparent across the range, by selecting the Data series in columns option (see Figure 4-10). The alternative (Data series in rows) would group elements by year showing relative performance over time.

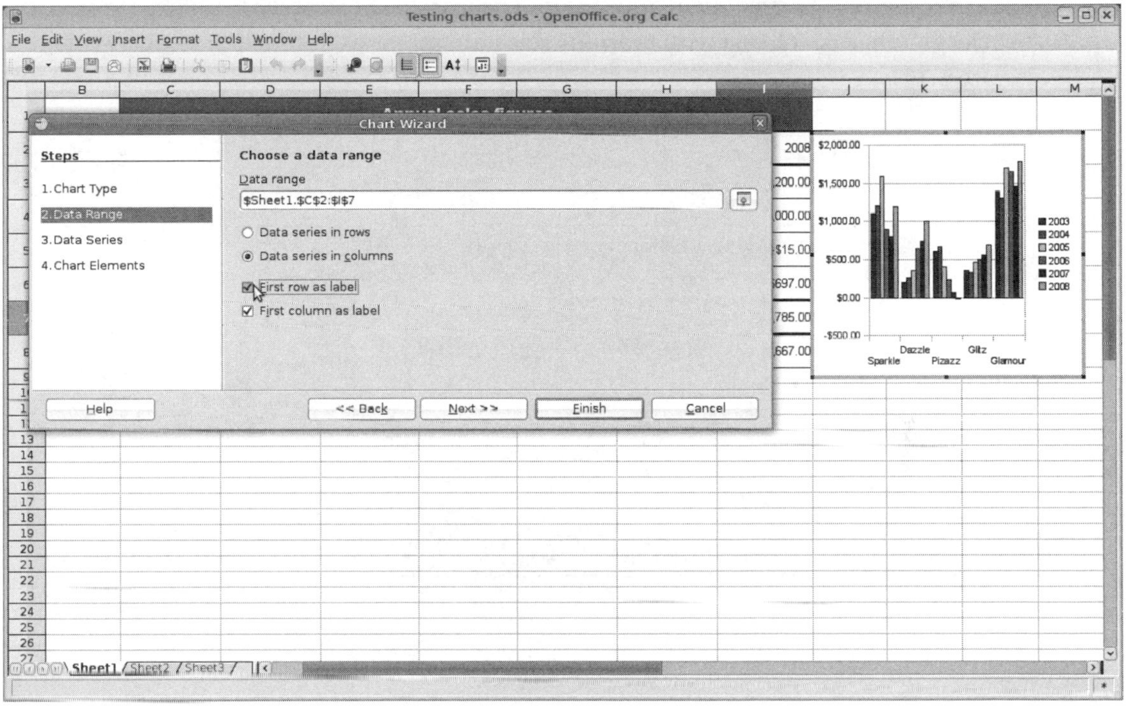

**Figure 4-10.** *In addition to redefining the data range, you can set up axis labels in this section of the Chart Wizard.*

Finally, you can choose to use either row or column headers as labels individually or together. Deselecting one of these will label elements Data series 1, Data series 2, and so on, allowing you to redefine them later. This will be useful when you build a chart on a more extensive or selective basis.

## Data Series

The Data Series screen allows for the refinement of the data in the chart. This is where, for example, you can change the names of the labels or adjust the display of data from a column, a row, or even an individual cell. On the left are the data series, and on the right the ranges that define them. The important thing to remember about this is that everything has to be defined in terms of its location on the spreadsheet. So, for example, if your columns were headed Apr, May, Jun, Jul, and so on, but you wanted the chart labeled April, May, June, July, you can't just add those details. Instead you would need to create cells elsewhere on the chart with the correct labels and then define those in the Range for Name setting; that is, $Sheet1.$H$7 might contain the text "April."

The other important thing, especially if you're less cell-minded and more visual, is the small icon to the right of the input bars. Click the icon next to the Range for Name section, and the dialog box shrinks to give you access to the spreadsheet, making it possible to click the cell needed to name the range. To return without selecting anything, click the (slightly changed) icon once more. The icon next to Categories allows you to select a range of cells using the various selection methods outlined previously (see Figure 4-11).

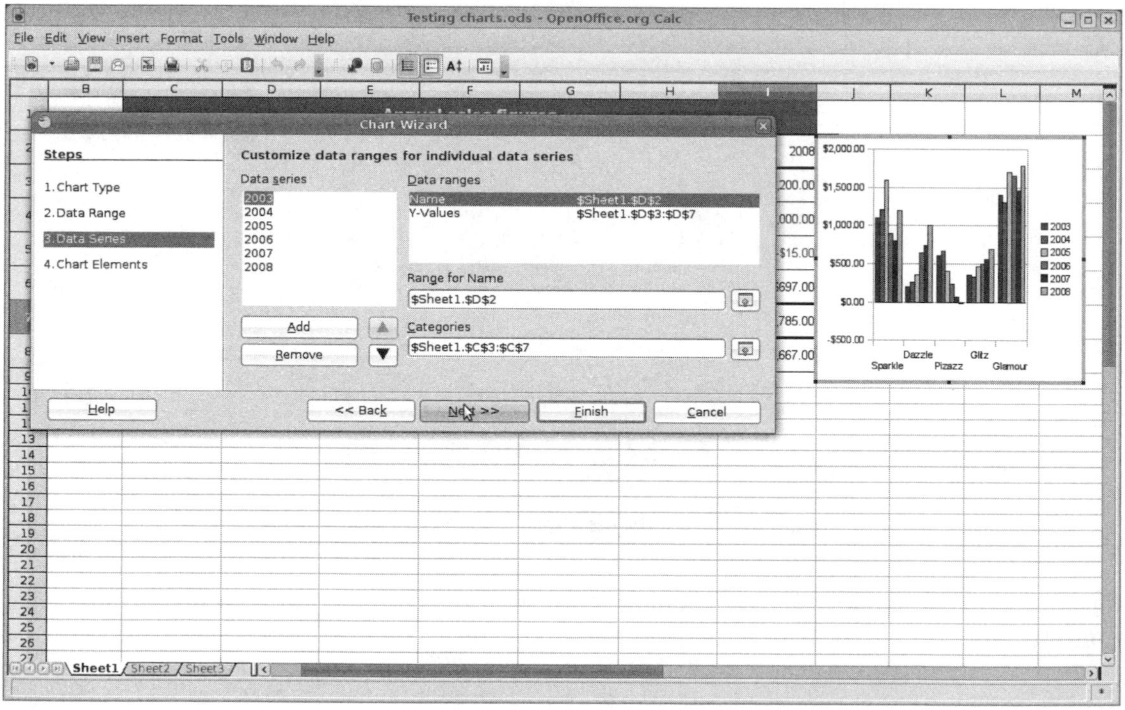

**Figure 4-11.** *Accept the default values in this window.*

## Chart Elements

The final section uses a different methodology in that it's not possible to use cell values for its various parts. For most charts, there will be four title spaces available: Title, Subtitle, X axis, and Y axis (see Figure 4-12). Remember Y defines the label for the columns, and X defines the rows. Leaving these spaces empty leaves more space for the chart but could reduce legibility slightly, so experiment to get the most satisfying result.

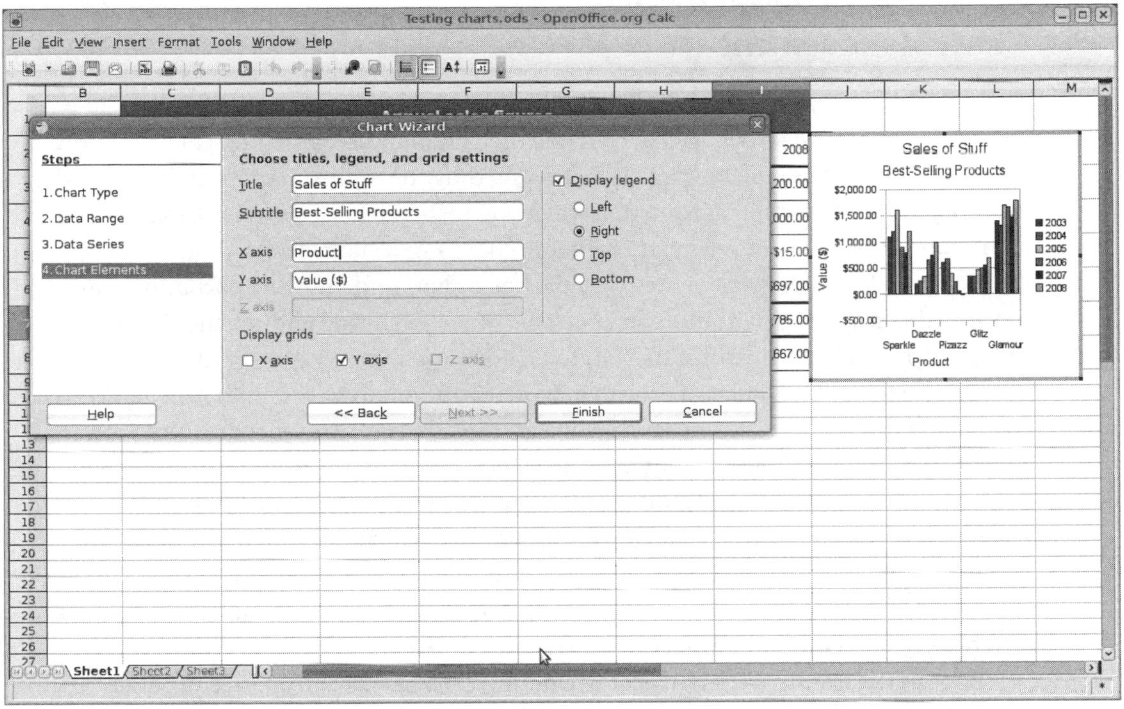

**Figure 4-12.** *Add titles, subtitles, and axis labels to improve legibility.*

On the right of the dialog box is the Display legend check box, which allows for the provision of more data and, in this example, takes its values from the column headers. It can be removed altogether or set to appear at any of the four edges of the chart.

Finally at the bottom of the window are options for displaying the axes themselves. Enable or disable using the check boxes. In column charts, where the bars are going vertically, removing the y-axis lines can reduce legibility quite substantially because the reader has to try to marry the top of the line to the values on the edge of the chart—of course, this is great for obscuring poor figures—and the same is true when removing the x-axis lines from a bar chart. No one likes to see both.

After you've defined and refined all of these elements (you can skip back through the wizard using the navigation area on the left of the window), click Finish to see your chart in all its glory.

Despite looking like a graphic, the chart is linked intimately with the data. To see this in action, select one of the data cells, and change its value. The length of the bar in the chart adjusts to reflect this change after a short pause. You can also define a chart based on an empty spreadsheet and then populate the spreadsheet later.

## Chart Management

The default chart size is, well, small, but it is resizable just like any other "object" in an OO.o project. To resize, click once to enable the grab handles, and then click and drag these to the required size. We can also click and drag the entire chart itself to some other location on the spreadsheet. Note that when you resize a chart, the relative sizes of bars are retained because this is a living, dynamic chart, not a static illustration.

You can do much more to pretty up the basic chart and, more importantly, make it more usable from a visualization perspective. To begin editing and see the Chart toolbar (which will appear at the top of the window), double-click anywhere on the chart.

The Chart toolbar makes it easy to make broad changes to the chart (see Figure 4-13). By clicking the first icon, for instance, you can change the chart type; the third icon removes grid lines; the fourth switches the legend on or off; the fifth sets the text elements to scale as the chart is resized; and the last icon resets every element within the chart to its default position—good for making things normal again after a lot of experimenting.

In edit mode, you can hover over one of the bars and see a tool tip description of what it refers to. Clicking on an object (e.g., a column) while in edit mode selects it and also highlights in the spreadsheet what the column refers to.

Back in the example chart, click once on the 2005 bar for the Sparkle product to select that product across all the years, and the entire 2005 column is highlighted in the spreadsheet. Click the 2005 Sparkle bar again to select just that bar, and only two cells (the year label and the data cell) are highlighted in the spreadsheet.

After a bar (or bar set) has been selected in this way, it is editable in the same way as many other objects in OO.o. The main editing options are available by right-clicking the element. The first entry in this menu is Object Properties, and selecting this opens up a new tabbed dialog box where you can make some changes. Begin by selecting the Area tab, which is where you can change the color of the bar using the standard color selector or, by using the drop-down list, apply a gradient from the presets, hatching, or a bitmap (see Figure 4-14). Again by selecting an individual bar within a set, you can change the color of each bar individually, perhaps to highlight one particular figure, within a set.

Be wary of going overboard with bells and whistles on a chart because the goal is to make the chart concise and readable rather than flashy.

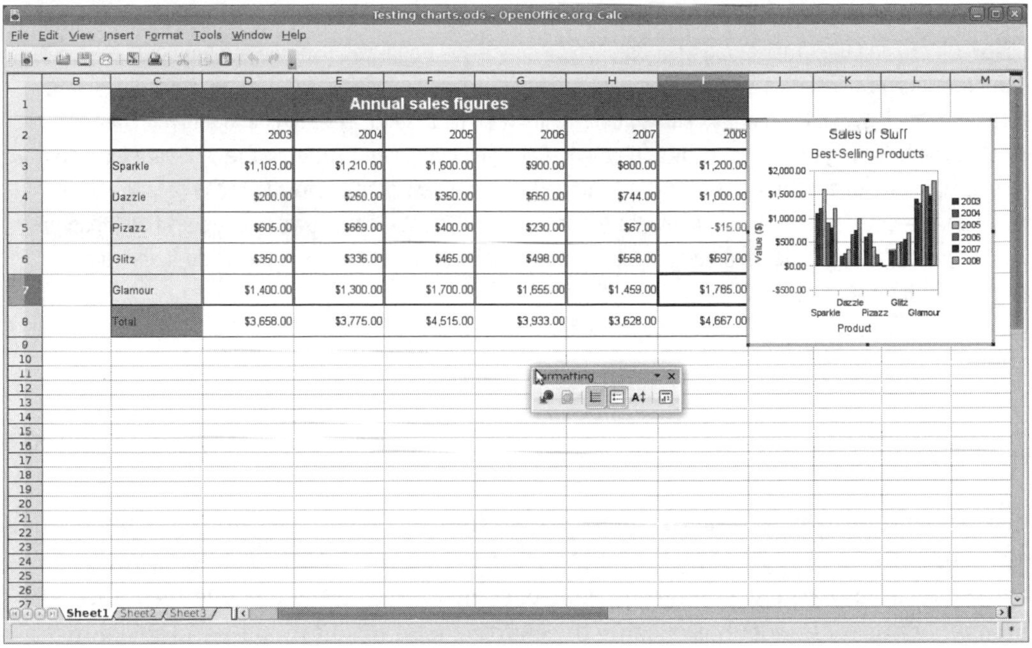

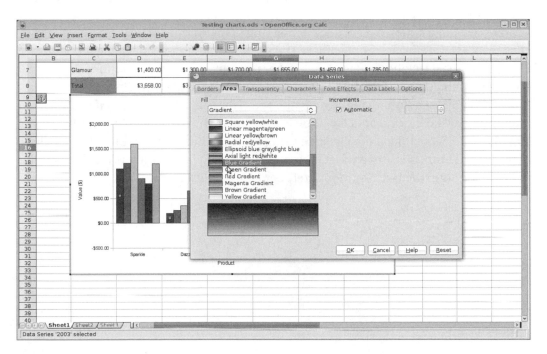

**Figure 4-13.** *The Chart toolbar is usually docked to the top edge of the screen, but it can be dragged off to float free.*

**Figure 4-14.** *The common gradient system can be used to increase the design palette in Calc's charts.*

---

■**Note** Perusing the Gradient menu in Calc, you'll notice one thing: you can't create new gradients. Don't fear, however; there's a very simple way around this small omission. OO.o works across a shared core of technology, and part of this shared core is the Area fill system. This means that if you want to create swanky new gradients to apply to charts in Calc, you can go into Writer or Draw, create a random object, click the Area fill button, select Gradient, and define a new gradient to add to the palette. When that's done—you don't need to save the Writer or Draw document—shut down and restart Calc, load up the document, and get back to editing the chart. Any gradients created in the trip outside Calc are now available in the list.

---

### Text

Just as you right-clicked a bar to edit its properties, you can do the same with any textual element of the chart, including the labels, legend, and various title elements. You can add consistency to the sales chart by right-clicking each of the text elements in turn— *remember* this is after double-clicking the chart to get into edit mode—and selecting Object Properties from the menu. Because you've selected a text object, the properties available are going to be slightly different. The Borders and Area tabs configure the borders and background for the individual text elements, which can be useful if you're designing for a dark background, but for this example project, the more interesting tabs are to the right of the box.

The available options will change depending upon the type of text selected. Right-click the x axis, for instance, and choose Object Properties to see the dialog box shown in Figure 4-15. Select the Characters tab, where options are available for font size, style, and weight, and then go into Font Effects to set the color of the text. The Label tab has a smart widget for adjusting the angle of the text. This can be quite useful if you're attempting to shoehorn a lot of labels on a chart full of thin bars. Set the angle by dragging the small icon around the circle, or using the input box next to it to add the angle in numerical form. These two widgets are linked, so changing one alters the value/angle in the other. After the text is appropriately configured, click the OK button.

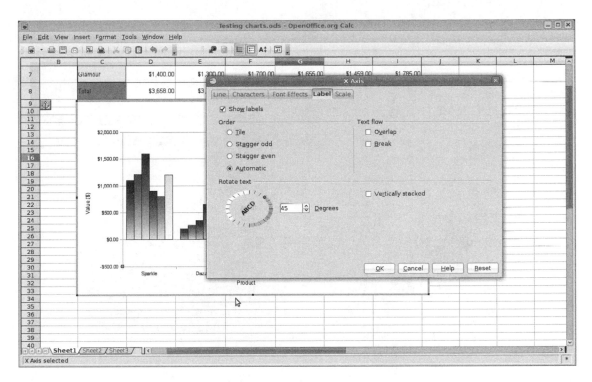

**Figure 4-15.** *Sometimes rotated text can improve the look of a chart, especially if you're attempting to shove a lot of information into a small space.*

## Scale and Error Bars

The example chart looks great, but there's still something that isn't quite right. The negative statistic on the chart is a rather minor -$15, but the negative number on the chart's y axis goes to a more alarming -$500, which could give the impression to the audience (and charts should always be built with an audience in mind) that you're anticipating bigger losses in the future. The -$500 is there because Calc has worked out the "best" scale for the columns based on the data and offered up a selection of divisions at intervals of 500. Fortunately, all of these elements are editable.

Right-click the y axis, choose Object Properties, and go into the Scale tab. All of the options under Axis scale will be set to Automatic, and the one you're most interested in sorting out is labeled Minimum. Deselect the Automatic check box next to Minimum, and then, in the value box, replace -500 with a less troubling amount such as -100 (see Figure 4-16). You can also set the Major and Minor intervals here, which affect the actual figures that will appear on the axis. When defining these parts, think carefully about the numbers you use, how they will divide up the chart, and the figures that will display. For example, doing odd things with the setting could mean your axis features confusing divisions ($1,545 or something) that don't improve the readability of the chart.

At the bottom of this window are options to display the scale marks either inside or outside the axis lines.

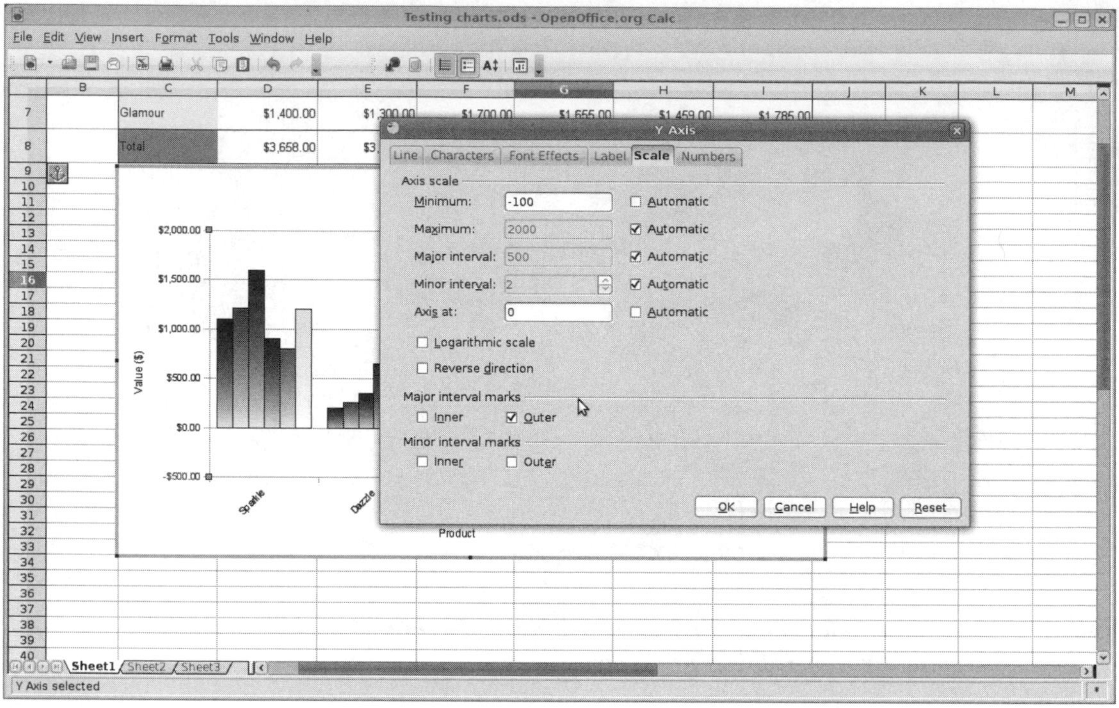

**Figure 4-16.** *The axis of a chart can have an impact on the impression your data makes. Large negative numbers look bad.*

There are many ways to edit elements on the charts, including the Formatting toolbar and the menus. When a chart is double-clicked, dramatic changes occur under the Insert and Format menus, especially when attempting to make broad changes to a chart. For example, one of the new features in Version 3.0 of Calc is the ability to add *error bars* to a chart. These simply suggest the margin of error in any element with an icon that looks like a capital I. There are two ways of adding error bars to a chart. First, right-click a bar set and select Insert Y Error Bars. A new dialog box launches offering a few options, including the error categories; whether to show positive, negative, or both bars; and some parameters. If you had done a survey, and the margin of error was ±5%, then you could add error bars to the chart by selecting Percentage as the Category and then use the Parameters setting to raise the Positive value to 5. Note that with the error indicator set to positive and negative, the plus and minus values are linked. Now click OK to see the error bar added to the selected chart element (see Figure 4-17).

Now, you could do the same thing for all the bar sets, but it would be much quicker to select the whole chart with a double-click and choose Insert ➤ Y Error Bars. Configure as you did previously, and click to see the bars applied to all the bar sets (see Figure 4-18).

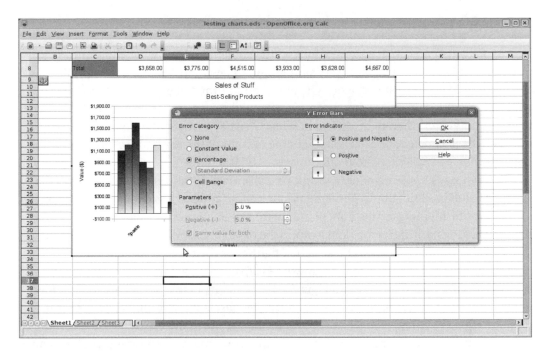

**Figure 4-17.** *Error bars, an important statistical tool, are new in Version 3.0 of Calc.*

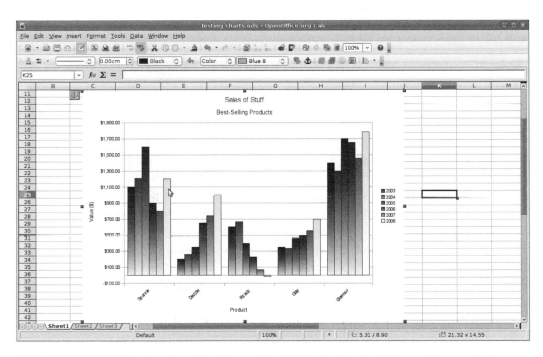

**Figure 4-18.** *With the exception of some gentle text formatting and the gradients, this is a standard bar chart style.*

## Another Dimension

One of the ways you can make charts look a little cooler—if that's what you want—is to give them a 3D makeover. This is very simple, adds a few more visualization options to the roster, and can also aid legibility. Of course, done wrong, it can look a mess, so use your judgment when adding that extra axis. To add the z axis to the current chart, select it with a double-click, then right-click, and select Chart Type. Keep the Column style chart, but click the 3D Look option. This changes the options at the top of the chart type window, offering—in this case—four different types of 3D charts.

You can also choose to render a simple or realistic chart, the difference being that the simple version has lines drawn on all intersecting edges and has less detailed shading on the extrusions (the bit that isn't the front of the chart). The Shape section allows you to define the shape of the bars themselves and features the default box, cylinder, cone, and pyramid.

Make some changes, click OK, and then right-click the chart again. The change to 3D added some more entries to the context-sensitive menu. Select 3D View to launch the 3D View dialog box as shown in Figure 4-19. The Perspective tab allows you to move the chart around in 3D space using X, Y, and, if you deselect Right-angled axis, Z rotation. Rotation is defined using degrees, and the bigger the figure entered here, the more extreme the view angle. The Z rotation is an important option to get right if you're using it because, through the use of perspective, it can make obvious distortions to the data.

The second tab, Appearance, offers another chance to choose between Simple and Realistic rendering or, by using the trio of check boxes, a combination of the two.

---

■**Note** During onscreen editing, the Object Borders option can lead to quite ugly results, but these are smoothed out during printing.

---

The last tab is also the most fun because it allows you to change the illumination of the 3D scene. Using the light bulb icons, you can define up to eight light sources (see Figure 4-19). Click a light bulb icon once to select it, and then click again to enable or disable the light. Below these icons are two color selectors; the top one defines the color of the currently selected light source, whereas the bottom one works on the ambient light of the whole scene and has the most effect on the way color is viewed. When a light source is enabled and selected, the large view port allows you to position the source with the mouse. This works just as light would in nature, so if the source is placed behind the chart, the face of the chart seen by the viewer will be in silhouette, whereas placing it in front of the object will light it up more fully.

Using a combination of the light source and the positional options you can create some quite stylish charts (see Figure 4-20). However, it's vital never to lose sight of the fact that the purpose of a chart is (usually) to make some aspect of the dataset clearer to an audience; a beautiful production that obscures that information may not be seen as a success.

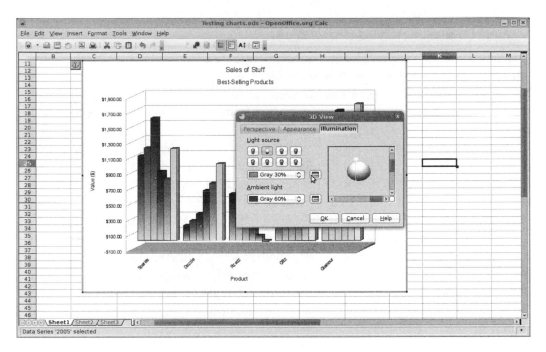

**Figure 4-19.** *3D charts can be lit from any direction and can also be rotated along the x, y, or z axis, which makes it easy to make a mess. Be careful.*

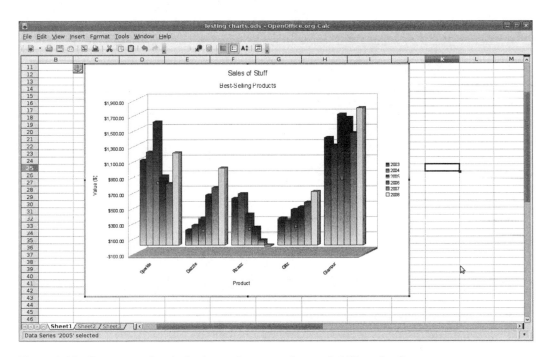

**Figure 4-20.** *If you use 3D wisely, it can improve the readability of a chart.*

# Creating a Family Budget

Now let's build a small family budget spreadsheet that can be used to plan for the year ahead. This will be divided into three sections. At the top, you'll have a broad overview of the family finances, and then below this, sections dealing with income and expenses. The top one, as you might expect, will take the values from the second and third section to create this overview.

To begin, choose File ➤ New ➤ Spreadsheet, and then, in the first row, select the cells A to O by clicking in the A1 cell and dragging the mouse to O1—the standard way to select a range of cells—and then releasing. The selected cells will change color to highlight their selected status. Now choose Format ➤ Merge Cells. This makes the selection one large cell, which is ideal for a title, so type the name of the project in the cell.

You can edit the text in a cell almost exactly as you did in Writer. For example, select the just-typed title, and, in the Formatting toolbar, select a different font, font size, or style. At the far right of the Formatting toolbar, the normal color selectors can be used to define the background and font color; the former changes the background color of the currently selected cell. This example uses a nice financially prudent green with bold white text for the title (Figure 4-21).

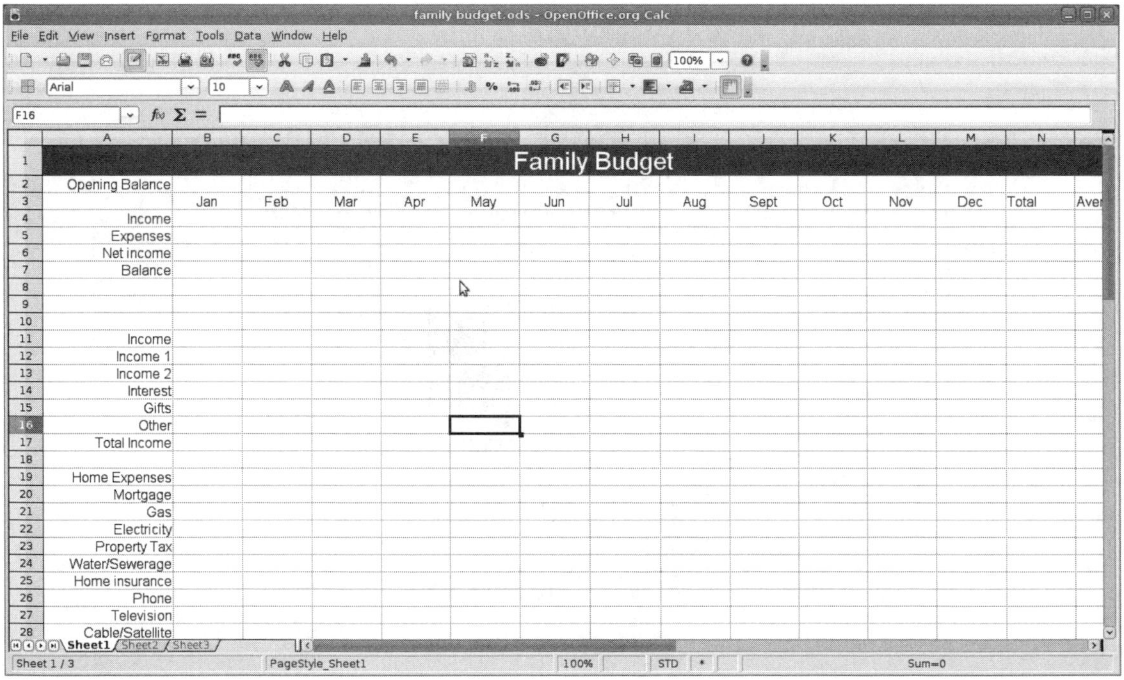

**Figure 4-21.** *It's always a good idea to think about the structure of a spreadsheet before adding information or formatting, and also try to build space for growth.*

The 15 columns you'll use for this example provide space for titles, 12 months, totals, and averages for each of the elements you're going to define.

In the first available cell (A2), enter a title for the Opening Balance, this will be the amount in the bank at the start of the year, and then input the words **Total** and **Average** into cells N3 and O3, respectively. These are simply labels, so you don't have to worry about any sort of formatting yet. You can also add the labels for the other parts of the overview section now, so starting at B3, enter the names of the months, and then, in column A, add labels for Income, Expenses, Net income, and Balance (see Figure 4-22).

You may notice that the columns don't expand to find the contents of cells, but you can increase the width of a column by clicking the dividing line between, for example, A and B in the header and dragging the mouse to get the appropriate size. As the mouse moves, a tool tip marks out the size using the default measurements.

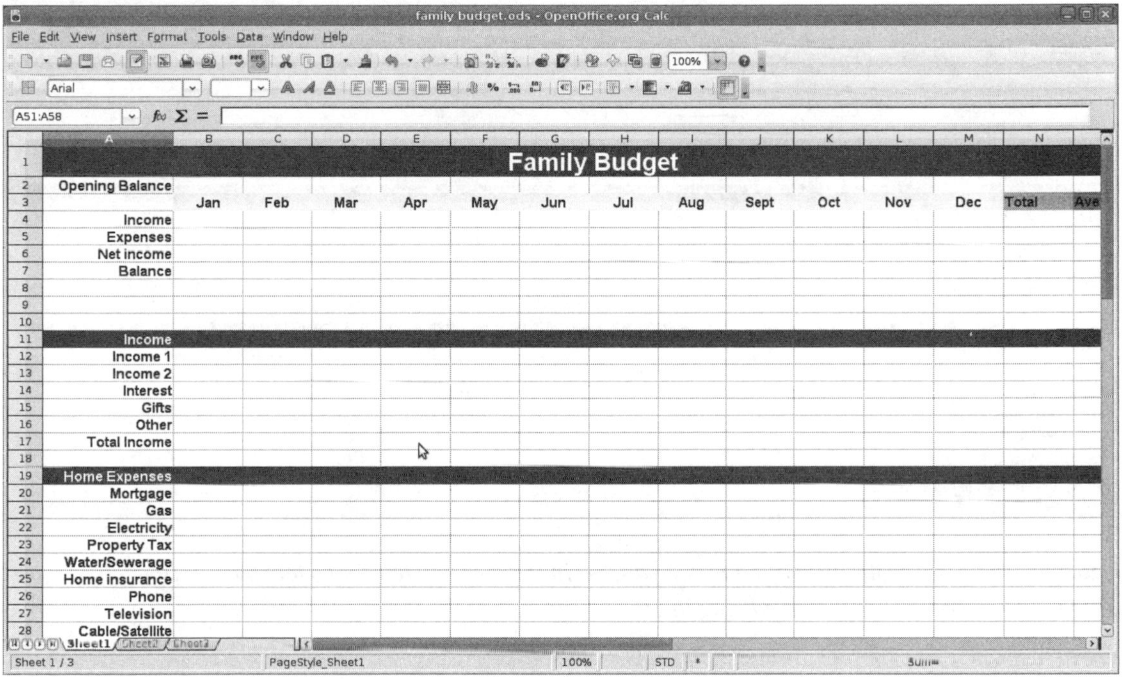

**Figure 4-22.** *By adding a little background formatting to the months, they become easier to navigate.*

As shown in Figure 4-23, you can increase the size of the text in the main label boxes in column A and for the months, make them bold, and add a subtle background color to the cells to improve readability. You can also expand column A to accommodate the text. With the overview section defined, you can now do the same job on the Income and Expenses sections farther down the sheet. The process is exactly the same—you just need to think how you're going to divide all the sections up—except that the column headers are already defined. Unless you're running a massive portfolio career, the Income section is likely to be rather short, but the Expenses section can be as vague or as detailed as you like. Obviously, the latter is going to provide the best information but will also take the most work. In this example, things are divided up slightly so you can see how much is spent individually on home, transport, and financial services, and a row labeled Total has been added at the bottom of each section. This last addition has two functions, first it allows you to see how much each part of your life costs but also, more importantly, makes it easier to set up the various mathematical functions in the spreadsheet. And that's what you need to do next.

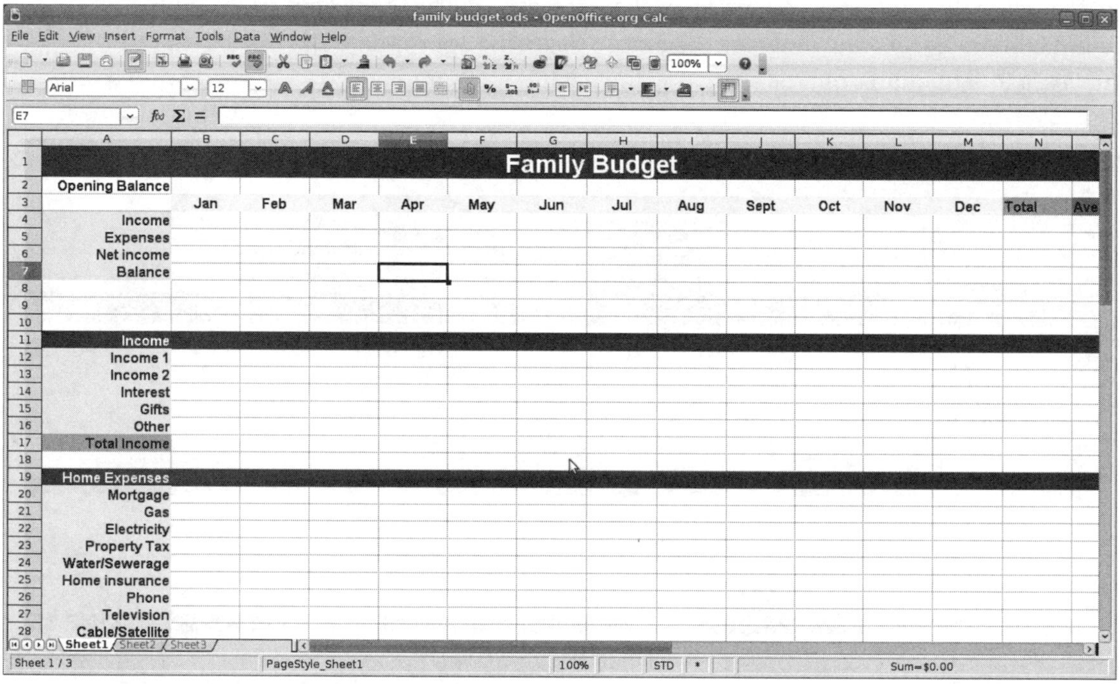

**Figure 4-23.** *A little growing room has been added in the rows by leaving a few blanks in each section. This may save a little formula editing later.*

## Adding Some Logic

So far, everything you've done has been about defining labels and constructing a visual look for the spreadsheet. However, the really important part is defining relationships between cells so that the sheet can begin to function. You'll begin with a simple bit of addition, and as it's such an easy job, you can do the whole thing manually. This process involves selecting a target cell (i.e., where the information is going to go), defining the function, and then setting the sources for the function to work with.

Begin by clicking into the cell to the left of the one labeled Total Income in the Income section. This is the target, and it will contain a function that will add together all the income sources for April.

`=SUM(B12:B16)`

This is a three-part function. The first part (`=`) denotes a function, and the second (`SUM`) defines it; in this case, it means add the following values together. The third part (`(B12:B16)`) tells Calc to use everything between cells B12 and B16 as the source. You could do the same with the more long-winded (`B12;B13;B14;B15;B16`), but using the colon (`:`) symbol allows you to define a range by selecting the start and end points, rather than individual cells. Of course, being able to define a noncontinuous range of cells is useful, but we'll come to that shortly. When simply adding together two numbers or cell references, it's not necessary to add the `SUM` element, just use `=B1+B2`.

---

### FUNCTIONS

Spreadsheets work using functions—that is text strings—that define relationships between individual cells or a collection of them. All functions have a common format: `=FUNCTION(formulas)`. The `FUNCTION` element, which is always written out in capitals, could cover everything from adding (`SUM`) and averaging (`AVERAGE`) numbers to defining days (`DAY`), duration (`DURATION`), and annual interest values (`NOMINAL`). We've used lots of simple functions such as `=B1+B2`, but they can become quite complex, for instance `=(F$5 - ($I$2*$C$2))*POWER($I$3,$A18-E18)`, and even hideously complicated. Inevitably, the more complex these things become, the more opportunities there are to introduce errors.

---

■**Tip** Working on a spreadsheet and can't find a calculator? Just select an empty cell, type `=number/operator/number`, and press Enter to do a quick calculation. Available operators include add (+), subtract (-), multiply (*), and divide (/). For example, `=23*34` will return 732, whereas `=23/34` will return 0.68. Meanwhile, `=23+34+56+87` will return 200.

---

Now define the Total box for each of the Expenses sections under the first month. You'll add `=SUM(B20:B36)` to B37, `=SUM(B41:B46)` to B47, and so on until each section's total has been defined (see Figure 4-24). In addition to typing these values, you can also add them with the mouse or by using the Function Wizard. To do the former, select the target cell, type the **=SUM** function and the brackets, use the mouse to select the first part of the range, and then Shift-click the final part. This method can also be used to select a noncontinuous range of cells, which is what you need to do in the overview section of the sheet.

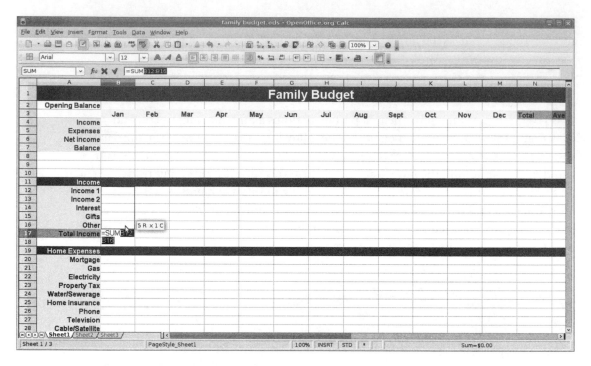

**Figure 4-24.** *As before, we begin with a few simple sums to add various cells together.*

To use the wizard, select its icon from the function bar. Select the SUM function from the Functions section by double-clicking (you may need to select Mathematical from the Category drop-down list first). Numbers or cell values can be entered either directly into the formula at the base of this window, in the number sections by typing, or by selecting one of the number sections and then clicking the appropriate cell on the spreadsheet itself. Use the icons to the right of the number sections to hide the wizard window while making a selection.

All of these methods of data entry are fine, and what is most comfortable for some users may not be best for all. Seasoned users are likely to enter common functions manually, but the wizard is still useful for long creations (see Figure 4-25).

You need to insert the total income value into the overview. Of course, you don't know that total income value, but you do know that it will be, for April, the value of cell B17, which, as you saw earlier, is the value of everything between B12 and B16. You could add =SUM(B12:B16) again to the income total, however, it's more efficient not to replicate the sum but rather to add =B17 to the Total Income section, telling Calc to display the value of B17 (see Figure 4-26).

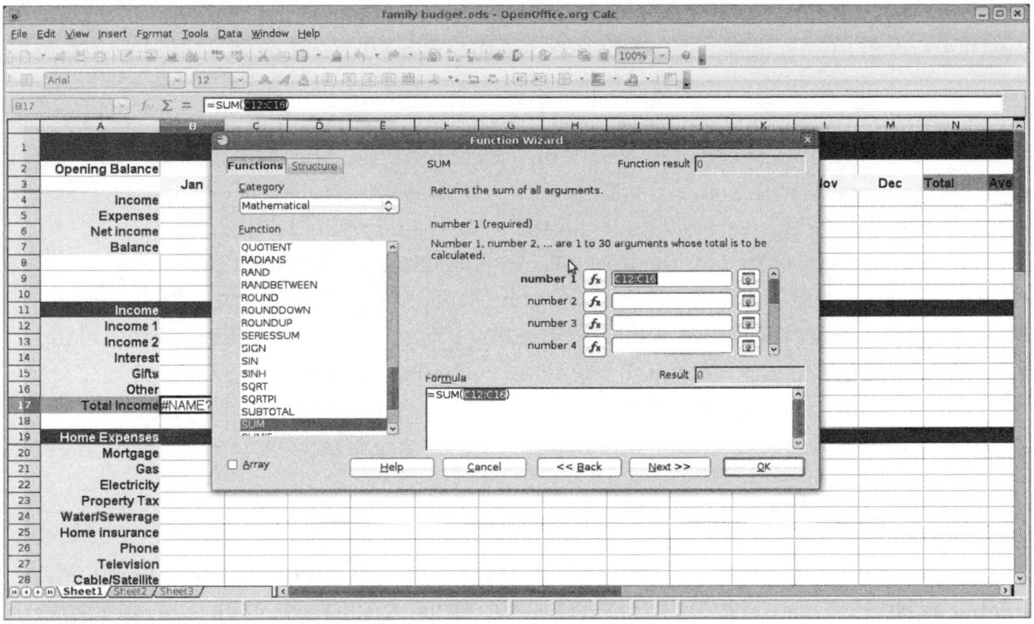

**Figure 4-25.** *The Function Wizard is useful on complex entries, but for simpler functions it's usually easier to just type it out.*

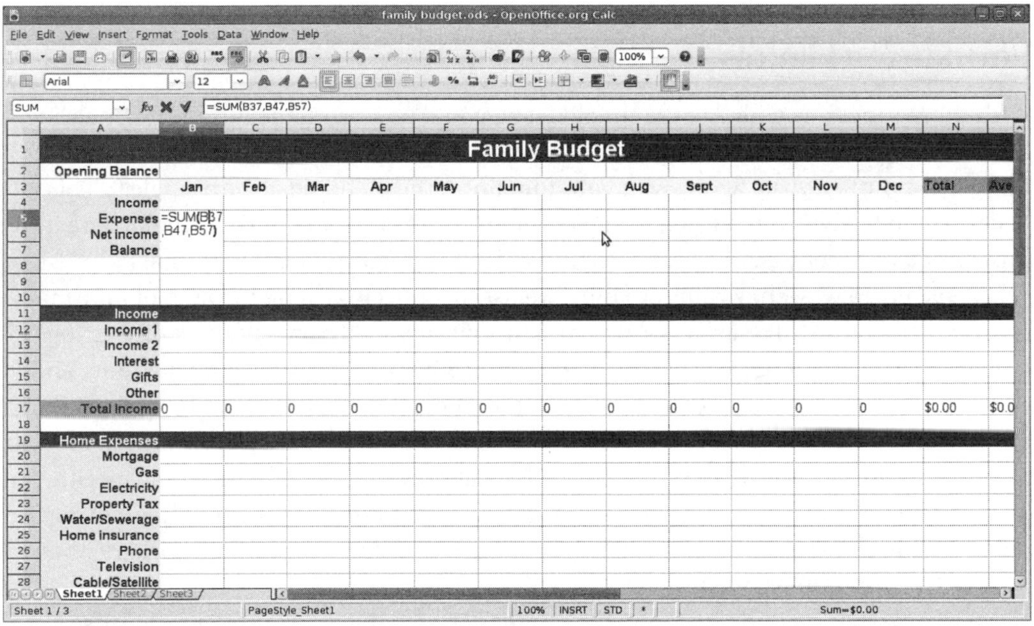

**Figure 4-26.** *Having tallied up the various Expense sections, you can now add all of those together to get a total of totals.*

The total expenses value is slightly more complex because it needs to add together the totals of all the expense subsections. Using the manual method, you could type out the function, setting it to take the values from a noncontinuous range by separating each cell value with a semicolon (;) character. With a full spreadsheet, however, it may be easier to do it visually. In this case, select the target cell, and type the function. Now select each cell that needs to feed into this function while holding the Ctrl key (Apple key on a Mac), as you click the cell value to be added to the function.

The total expenses box for the Apr column now contains the function =SUM(B37;B47;B57), meaning it will take the values from cells B37, B47, and B57, and add them together to get the total expenses. Note that if you add rows to these sections later, the function must be updated to reflect the new position of these totals.

Now do a function on these totals, by simply subtracting the expenses from the income in the cell labeled Net income.

=B4-B5

You've simplified the function here by using a standard minus sign (as you would in a calculator). This also works with other basic arithmetic functions, including adding (+), multiplying (*), and dividing (/).

The final part of the overview is the monthly balance, which has to take the net income value and add it to the opening balance. In the first month, this function is =B6+B2, —B6 being the net income for the month and B2 being the opening balance.

## Formatting Figures

With these functions added to the spreadsheet, you'll now see some numbers appearing in the Apr column (or whatever you labeled the first real data column). Unless something has gone seriously wrong with your functions, these should all be a single 0. This is because you haven't yet plugged in any numbers. But before you put any actual data into the spreadsheet, let's take a short diversion to look at different number formats.

Typically in western writing systems, we use symbols to denote the kind of information being displayed. For example, we use a format such as $xx,xxx.xx when discussing US dollars, but we might use xx/xx/xxxx when noting dates or xx:xx:xx to note the time, and these formats can have a profound effect on the calculations that Calc will perform on our data. This is because at its basic, currency is usually decimal, whereas time is built around the numbers on a clock (60/12), and date information varies depending on the month. So if we're talking about cash, the sum 97+23=120 (which potentially needs to be reformatted as $1.20); if we're talking about time, 8+8=4; and if we're considering February, then 25+7=03/04 (or 04/03 in the UK).

Fortunately, you don't have to worry about defining these base systems because Calc has a ready supply of commonly used number systems available, making it easy to ensure that you always have the right format.

The example you're working with is a very simple spreadsheet where all of the usable data is currency-based, so you can define every cell at the same time. Select the whole sheet by clicking the rectangle where the row and column labels meet and then choosing Format ➤ Cells. Ensure that the Numbers tab is highlighted, and then scroll through the Category list on the left to find Currency. Click this to see a set of standard format options in the central column. At the head of this column is a drop-down list providing access to most major world currencies. Select yours and then refine the formatting by choosing the most appropriate-looking entry from the format list.

Just below this is a pair of useful options. Selecting the first renders negative numbers (commonly known as debt) in red, whereas the second ensures a "thousands" separator is included in large numbers.

As you investigate these options, take a look at the changes happening in the format code along the bottom of the window. In here, everything to the left of the semicolon defines positive numbers, whereas everything to the right defines negative numbers, making it possible to totally redefine the way figures are displayed. Briefly in the example (see Figure 4-27), the first section ([$$-409]) defines the currency type as US dollars, and the second section (#,##0.00) defines how the figures are displayed, in this case 1,250.00. After the semicolon, the same information appears, with the addition of [RED] to render the text red and a leading minus sign.

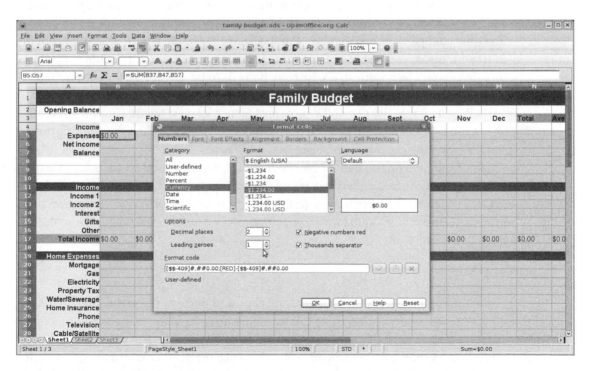

**Figure 4-27.** *In any kind of operation, it's important to define the correct number format.*

Calc has options for date, time, currency, percentage, basic numbers, scientific, fractions, and user-defined. We'll examine a few more of these later. For now, make sure you've selected Currency and that the format code represents the way you're used to seeing money represented. Click OK, and the previously plain numbers in that first column should now look something akin to $0.00.

## Some Copy and Paste Magic

The example spreadsheet now contains a lot of empty cells and one column (Jan in this example) with most of the functions added. However, it would be a bit tedious if you had to redo all that work for the rest of the months. Luckily, Calc is quite smart when it comes to cut-and-paste operations. Click in cell B6. The input bar should display its contents as =B4-B5. Select the entire B column below the month heading (in this example, it's B4:B57) and then choose Edit ➤ Copy (or press Ctrl+C) to copy the contents to the clipboard.

Now click into the C column below the month heading, and choose Edit ➤ Paste (or press Ctrl+V). The contents of the clipboard are pasted into the column, but if you select cell C6, you should see that the function actually says =C4-C5 because Calc realized keeping the B values didn't make any sense. You can do a similar paste job for the rest of the columns individually, but it's quicker to select the first cells of the remaining months (D4:M4) and then choose Edit ➤ Paste to do the whole lot at once. Note that if you select H6, the function will be rendered as =H4-H5, J6 will be =J4-J5, and so on.

The only change you need to make is in the balance section, where B7 should contain =B6+B3 (the month's net income + the opening balance), but C5 should not have =C6+C3 because there won't be a value in C3. Instead, it needs to be =B7+C6 (the balance from last month + the net income from this month). After this function is defined, select and copy it, and then paste it into the rest of the monthly balance spaces. Again, you can select all the rows from D7:M7 and have the function updated as needed. When the warning pops up about overwriting existing data, select Yes (see Figure 4-28).

A pair of columns on the right of the sheet offers a running total and averages for the year. The total cell can be defined just as you did earlier: the B row features the function =SUM(B4:M4), which is simply copied and pasted into the other sections down the spreadsheet.

To create the average value for row B, you simply use the AVERAGE function and the usual range option (B4:M4):

=AVERAGE(B4:M4)

Press Enter, then select the cell again, and copy and paste to the various sections of the sheet. You will notice as you paste this formula into rows of the spreadsheet that don't have data—which is most of them—that instead of the expected $0.00 value, you get a #DIV/0! error as shown in Figure 4-29. This is because the average command is attempting to divide by zero, which isn't possible, so an error is displayed. When data is added to the sheet, these errors disappear, but you can do some cosmetic work to make things look cleaner. There are two ways to do this, using either conditional formatting—which looks best—or with the number format, which is the correct way of doing things.

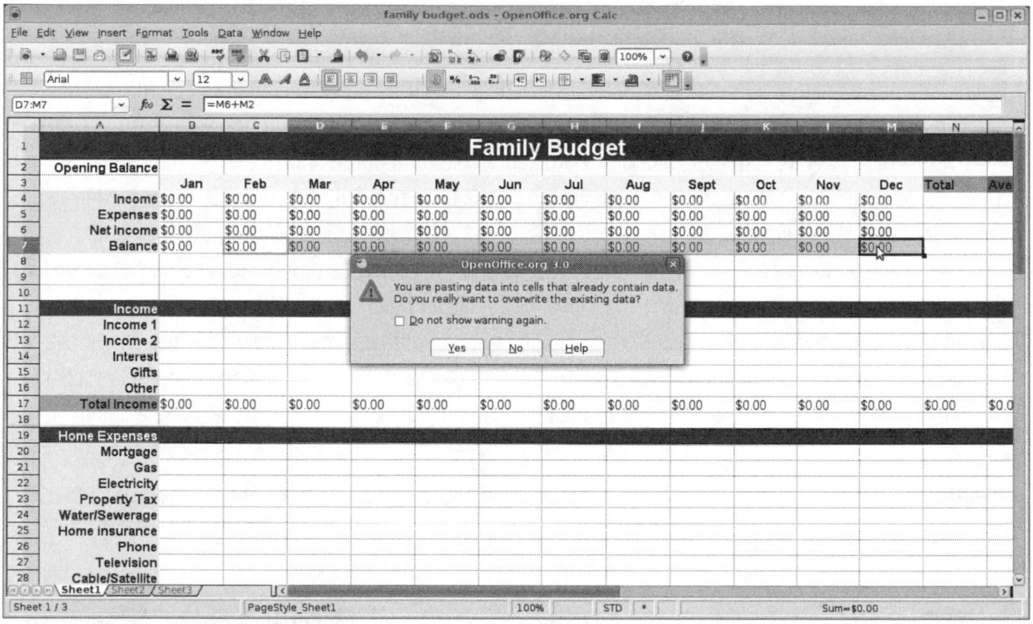

**Figure 4-28.** *Copying and pasting data across a range of cells automatically updates formulas to reflect their new location.*

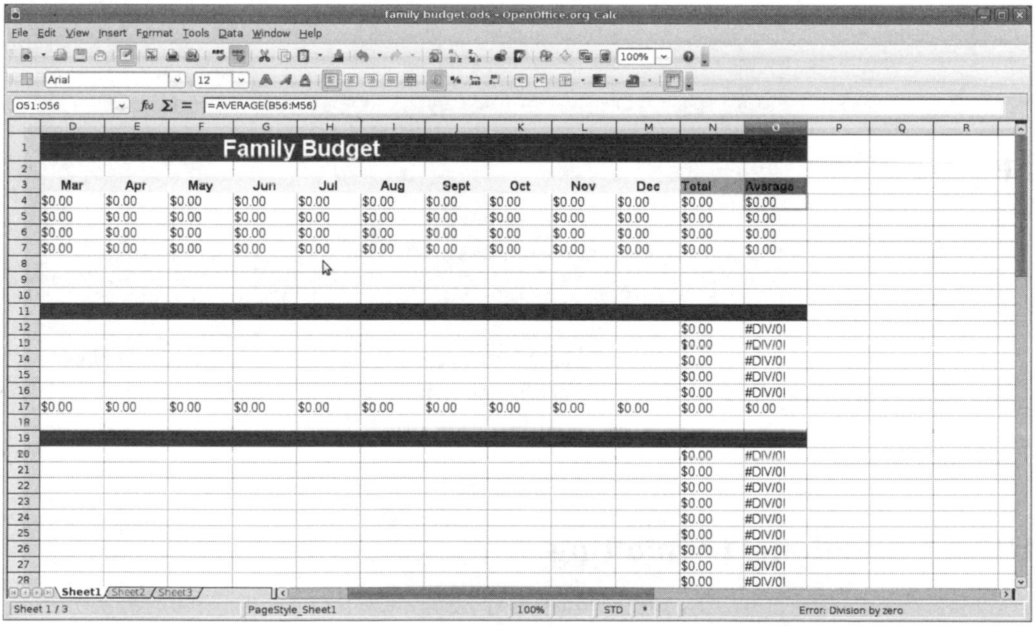

**Figure 4-29.** *These errors occur because the software is attempting to divide by zero, an impossible operation.*

## FREEZING HEADINGS

Spreadsheets often start out small and then become huge unwieldy things as data are added. This can cause a few navigation problems as you constantly scroll around the sheet to match up labels with data. Fortunately Calc has a brilliant solution to this problem in the form of the Freeze tool. At the click of a mouse, you can fix a column, row, or both onscreen, meaning that only cells beneath or to the left of the freeze location will scroll.

For example, to freeze the column headings—so you can match up months to data farther down the table—click the row number below the month headings and then choose Window ➤ Freeze. A thick line appears below the month headings, and scrolling now only affects cells below this line. To remove the freeze, choose Window ➤ Freeze once more. To do the same for the row headings on the left, click the column letter immediately to the right of the label column, and choose Window ➤ Freeze again.

Finally, to create both row- and column-based freeze points at the same time, click the cell that defines both the top and left of the freeze, and choose the Window ➤ Freeze command.

## Using Conditional Formatting

You can get rid of the clutter by hiding it using a very powerful feature called *conditional formatting*. The principle behind conditional formatting is very simple: if the value of a cell fits a particular pattern, then apply a particular style. The use of the word "style" here is deliberate because the conditional formatting system relies upon the same Styles and Formatting system you've used in Writer and will use again in Impress.

To begin, create the style to apply to the numerous "0" cells by choosing Format ➤ Styles and Formatting or by pressing F11 to open the Styles and Formatting palette. In Writer, there were a lot of styles already defined, but Calc has far fewer.

Create a new style by selecting the New Style from Selection button, which is in the center of the trio on the right. This launches the Cell Style formatting dialog box, which has an array of tabs across the top. First visit Numbers, and ensure that Currency is selected from the left, and the display conforms to the desired formatting.

Next go into the Organizer tab, and provide a name for the style—in this case, Zero— and then select the Font Effects tab. Select the Font color drop-down list, select White, and then click OK (see Figure 4-30).

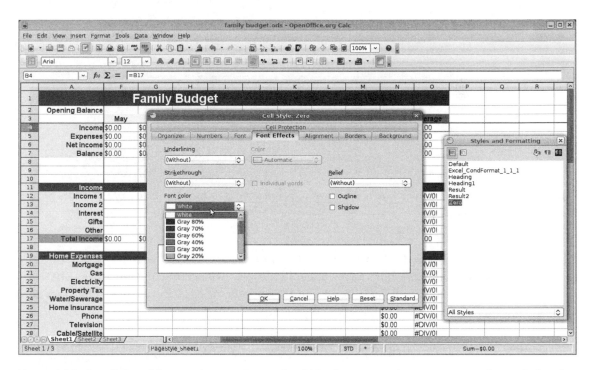

**Figure 4-30.** *Conditional formatting can be used to hide those annoying #DIV/0! entries and also the masses of $0.00 cells.*

This is a universal setting, so select the entire sheet, and then choose Format ➤ Conditional Formatting. In this simple dialog box, you'll define the single condition to look out for—it can handle three—and the style it should use. Ensure the Condition 1 box is selected, and then move onto the definition itself. The Condition 1 check box has three drop-down selectors and an input bar as shown in Figure 4-31.

In the first drop-down list, make sure the Cell value is option is selected because you're working on the results rather than the functions.

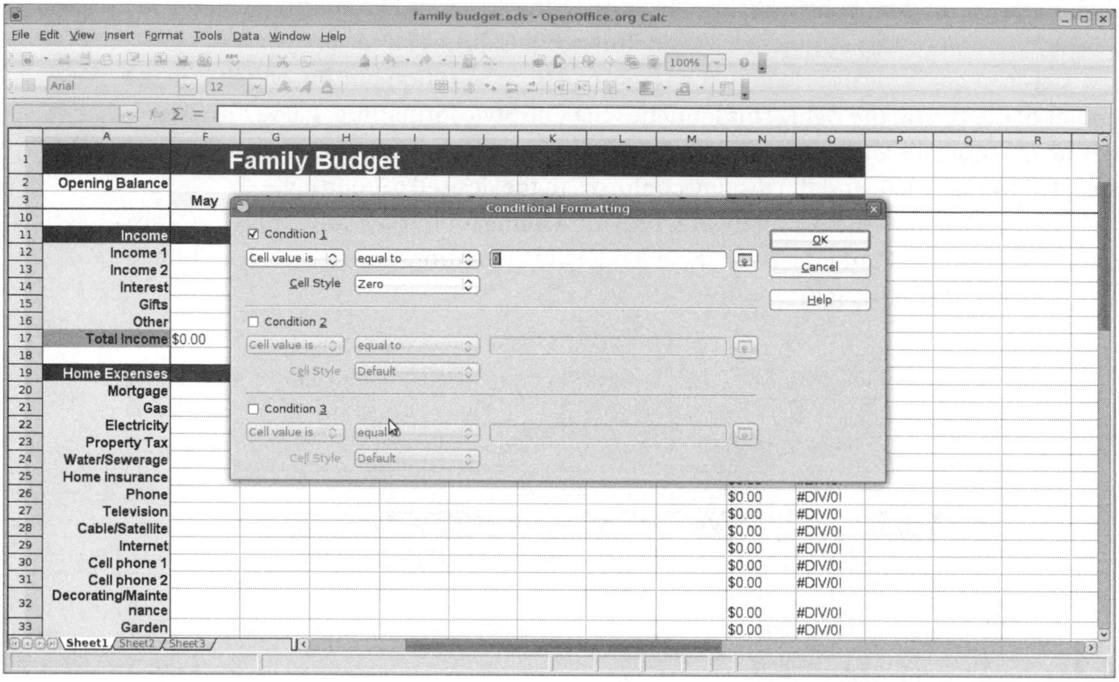

**Figure 4-31.** *The best way to approach conditional formatting is to think in terms of sentences that will "work" on the data.*

In the second drop-down list, select equal to, and then type **0** into the input bar. That's the condition defined, so use the third drop-down list to select the previously made style labeled Zero. Click the OK button, and marvel as all the numbers disappear!

### MORE USES FOR CONDITIONAL FORMATTING

Conditional formatting is extremely useful in a number of situations. For example, teachers could collate class grades in a spreadsheet and set conditions so that if a grade falls below 50%, the cell turns red (if cell value is less than 50 format using Style A), turns pale pink if the grade is between 50% and 60% (if cell value is between 50 and 60, apply Style B), and turns blue if the marks are above 60 (if cell value is more than 60, apply Style C).

Or it could be used to mark off past and upcoming deadlines: if cell value is less than TODAY(), apply Style A, but if cell value is less than TODAY()+3, apply Style B. In this case, anything dated before today—that is, it's gone past—will be highlighted in one way, anything dated within the next three days will be highlighted differently, and anything more than three days out will be left alone.

You'll now use conditional formatting to create zebra stripes on the main window, that is, alternating lines of color to make navigation a little easier. To do this, open the Styles and Formatting palette (Format ➤ Styles and Formatting), and create a new style. Call this **Odd Rows**. Click OK, then right-click Odd Rows, and select Modify. Select the Background tab, and choose a suitable color, something quite close to white so it won't overpower the spreadsheet. Click OK, and then do the same routine, this time calling the new style **Even Rows** but leaving the color white.

Now select the range of cells that are going to be altered—remember, you can select the entire sheet by pressing Ctrl+A—and then choose Format ➤ Conditional Formatting.

Add two conditions based on the Formula is option rather than the Cell value is option:

In Condition 1, select Formula is, input **MOD(ROW();2)=1**, and apply cell style Odd Rows.

In Condition 2, select Formula is, input **MOD (ROW();2)=0**, and apply cell style Even Rows.

These are quite interesting formulas because they use the modulo (MOD) function, which finds the remainder following the division of one number by another (see Figure 4-32). Expressed in normal language, the formulas say "If the row number divided by 2 leaves a remainder (1) then apply the Odd Rows style" and "If the row number divided by 2 leaves no remainder (0) then apply Even Rows." So the even row numbers, which are divisible by 2, will be formatted differently from the odd numbered rows, which, when divided by 2, leave the number 1.

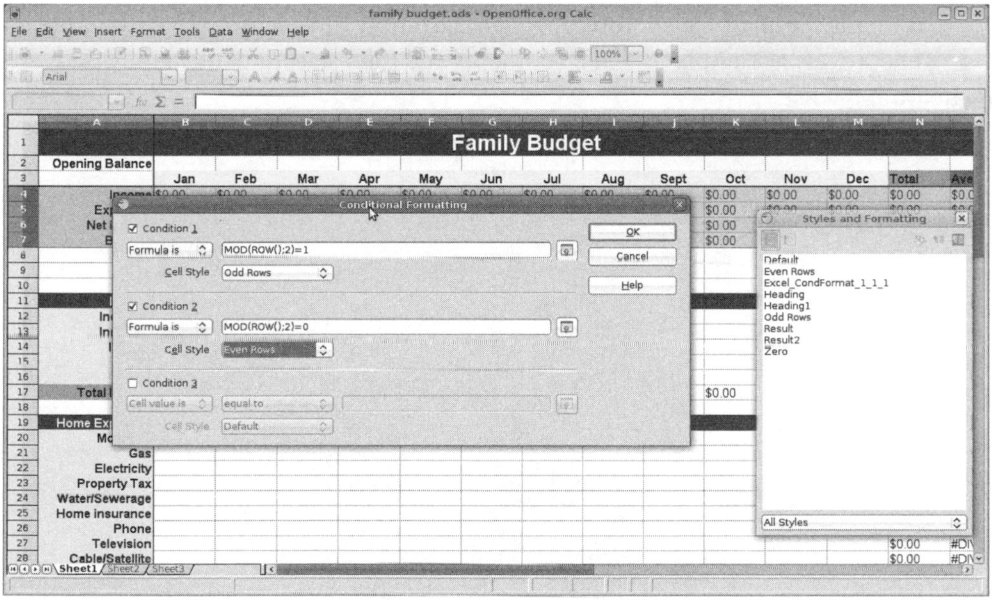

**Figure 4-32.** *The modulo function can be used to format the look of odd or even rows to create a zebra effect on the spreadsheet.*

To take this a little further, the condition "Formula is ISODD(ROW()+COLUMN())" with an appropriate cell style would create a checkerboard pattern.

## More Number Formatting

Although conditional formatting is flexible in a lot of situations, a more elegant solution to this particular problem is to make a small addition to the number formatting we looked at earlier. For example, select the whole table again, remove the conditional formatting (Format ➤ Conditional Formatting, uncheck Condition 1), and then choose Format ➤ Cells to get to the formatting dialog box. Choose the Number tab.

You're going to make a small addition to the format code at the bottom of the window. At the end, include either of the following: ;# or ;"". The note below the code will change to "User-defined," and a new entry will be added to the User-defined category allowing this to be reused later. If you want to change the note, just click the note icon to the right of the format code bar, and press Enter.

After you click OK, the $0.00 values disappear once more, but the divide-by-zero errors are still displayed. You can get rid of those by redoing the conditional formatting "when Cell value is equal to #DIV/0! use style Zero," which was created earlier. Easy.

## Saving for the Future

As with Writer projects, this is the kind of document that can be reused over and over, so you can save it as a template before adding any information (see Figure 4-33). Choose File ➤ Templates ➤ Save, and then double-click the MyTemplates entry, provide a name, and click OK. With the template saved, you can begin the family budget afresh next year by choosing File ➤ New ➤ Templates and Documents and then selecting the Family Budget template from the list.

After the template is saved, you can begin to add data to the spreadsheet itself.

| | Jan | Feb | Mar | Apr | May | Jun | Jul | Aug | Sept | Oct | Nov | Dec | Total | Ave |
|---|---|---|---|---|---|---|---|---|---|---|---|---|---|---|
| **Family Budget** | | | | | | | | | | | | | | |
| Opening Balance | | | | | | | | | | | | | | |
| Income | $0.00 | $0.00 | $0.00 | $0.00 | $0.00 | $0.00 | $0.00 | $0.00 | $0.00 | $0.00 | $0.00 | $0.00 | $0.00 | $0.0 |
| Expenses | $0.00 | $0.00 | $0.00 | $0.00 | $0.00 | $0.00 | $0.00 | $0.00 | $0.00 | $0.00 | $0.00 | $0.00 | $0.00 | $0.0 |
| Net income | $0.00 | $0.00 | $0.00 | $0.00 | $0.00 | $0.00 | $0.00 | $0.00 | $0.00 | $0.00 | $0.00 | $0.00 | $0.00 | $0.0 |
| Balance | $0.00 | $0.00 | $0.00 | $0.00 | $0.00 | $0.00 | $0.00 | $0.00 | $0.00 | $0.00 | $0.00 | $0.00 | $0.00 | $0.0 |
| **Income** | | | | | | | | | | | | | | |
| Income 1 | | | | | | | | | | | | | $0.00 | #DIV |
| Income 2 | | | | | | | | | | | | | $0.00 | #DIV |
| Interest | | | | | | | | | | | | | $0.00 | #DIV |
| Gifts | | | | | | | | | | | | | $0.00 | #DIV |
| Other | | | | | | | | | | | | | $0.00 | #DIV |
| Total income | $0.00 | $0.00 | $0.00 | $0.00 | $0.00 | $0.00 | $0.00 | $0.00 | $0.00 | $0.00 | $0.00 | $0.00 | $0.00 | $0.0 |
| **Home Expenses** | | | | | | | | | | | | | | |
| Mortgage | | | | | | | | | | | | | $0.00 | #DIV |
| Gas | | | | | | | | | | | | | $0.00 | #DIV |
| Electricity | | | | | | | | | | | | | $0.00 | #DIV |
| Property Tax | | | | | | | | | | | | | $0.00 | #DIV |
| Water/Sewerage | | | | | | | | | | | | | $0.00 | #DIV |
| Home insurance | | | | | | | | | | | | | $0.00 | #DIV |
| Phone | | | | | | | | | | | | | $0.00 | #DIV |
| Television | | | | | | | | | | | | | $0.00 | #DIV |
| Cable/Satellite | | | | | | | | | | | | | $0.00 | #DIV |

**Figure 4-33.** *When the budget basics are finished, save it as a template (File ➤ Templates ➤ Save) so it can be used over and over.*

## Charts in Complex Tables

With information added to the spreadsheet, it's time to find a new way of looking at the expenditure data that has accumulated. You're now going to build a series of charts, one for each month of the year, to visualize spending habits. In the Home Expenses section of the spreadsheet, select the label and Apr columns to begin with—on the example sheet this is A20:B36—ignoring the total at the bottom.

Choose Insert ➤ Chart, and choose Pie chart as the chart type. In the next section, ensure that First column as label is selected, and then select the Chart Elements section to add a title/subtitle to the chart. Finally click Finish to create a pie chart showing April's Home Expenses as shown in Figure 4-34.

Now select the chart, and copy with either Edit ➤ Copy or Ctrl+C, and then paste with Ctrl+V to create a replica of the April chart. Double-click this to select it, and then right-click ➤ Data Ranges, and select the Data Range tab. Under the section labeled Data ranges, select Y-Values as shown in Figure 4-35. With this selected, you can now edit the Range for Y-Values input box, replacing the letter B (denoting the B column) with C, so the chart takes the values from the C column, which is May. Leave the categories value as it was to retain the pie chart labels. The only thing wrong now is the subtitle, which says April instead of May. Select the chart with a double-click, and choose Insert ➤ Title to edit the title or subtitle.

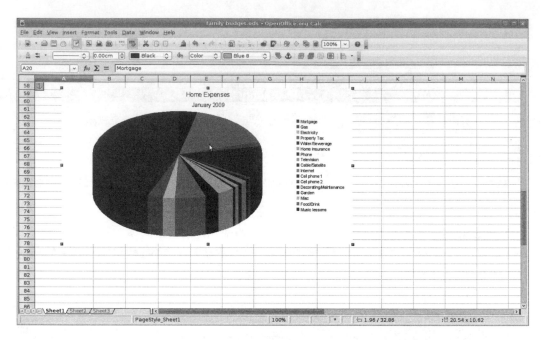

**Figure 4-34.** *Pie charts are great for seeing how household expenses are divided up.*

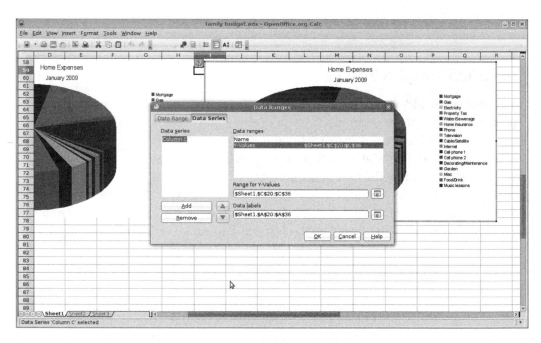

**Figure 4-35.** *Change a few settings to re-create the pie chart for each month of the year.*

Do this for each month, and you'll have a series of pie charts showing the proportion of income spent on household expenses.

## Cell Validation

In the Calc projects you've done so far, all of the cell content has been either set as static text—headers or labels—or as numerical information. Occasionally, however, the contents of a cell should be limited to a selection of responses. For example, if you were creating a job-tracking spreadsheet for a freelance designer, you might want a Client column to contain one of a small selection of options.

In this example, the Client column will go into B, so click the header to select the entire column. Now choose Data ➤ Validity, and, under the Criteria tab, click the Allow drop-down list and select List as shown in Figure 4-36. In the Entries box, type in each client name followed by pressing the Enter key. You can change a few other options— allow blank entries and show the selection list—and then click OK. Now, when a cell in the Client column is selected, a drop-down arrow appears, allowing the user to select an entry from a list (see Figure 4-37). This could be used to define any type of limited content, including months, team names, venues, and so on.

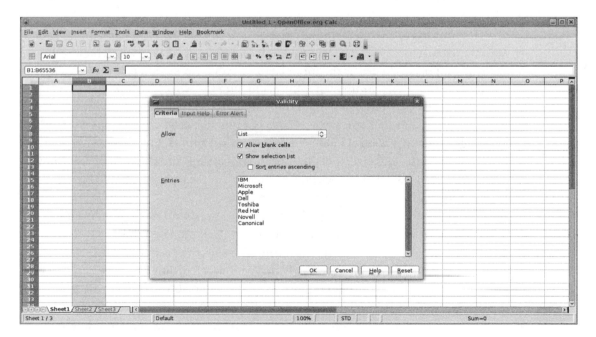

**Figure 4-36.** *Cell validation is useful when you want to ensure consistent data are entered into the spreadsheet.*

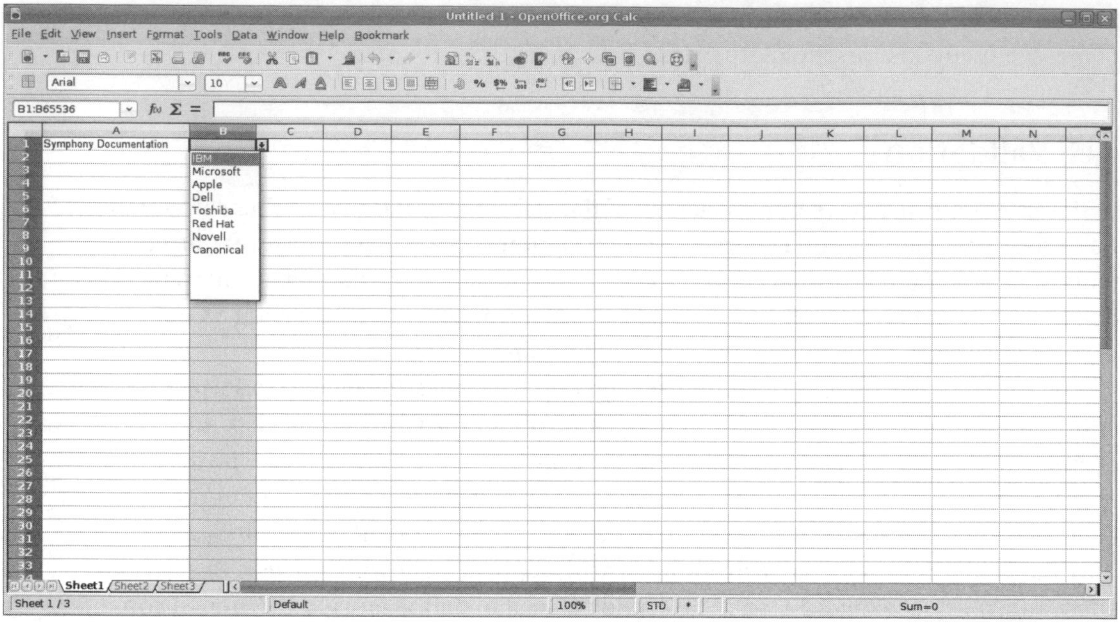

**Figure 4-37.** *When users encounter a validated cell, they can enter data via a drop-down list of potential entries.*

Another useful tool under the Data ➤ Validity window, especially when building a spreadsheet for others to use, is the Input Help window. For example, if you want to remind the freelance designer to invoice the client after the work is completed, you might create a column labeled Completed that is formatted to receive date information. To remind the user to send an invoice when filling out this cell, select the Complete column using the header, choose Data ➤ Validity, and select the Input Help tab. Type a title in the top section and the message/tool tip in the lower section, and then enable the Show input help when cell is selected check box. As the user works on the sheet, selecting a Complete cell to add a date will display the reminder.

The Validity system can also be used to force users to enter information in a particular format, for example, as a date, time, decimal, or cell range. In these cases, it's very useful to create an error message to inform users that they've made a mistake. This option, again, is defined for a particular cell range and is accessible by choosing Data ➤ Validity and selecting the Error Alert tab in the Validity dialog box (see Figure 4-38). Ensure that the Show error message when invalid values are entered check box is checked, and type out a title and error message in the spaces provided. There are four different approaches you can take to errors, which are available in the drop-down list. The Stop option displays the message when invalid data is entered and offers an OK button to dismiss the warning. When this button is clicked, the cell is cleared, which means it's impossible for the user to enter the wrong data type. The Warning and Information options display the error text but offer both OK and Cancel buttons. The cell is cleared if the user selects Cancel. Finally, the Macro button runs a macro (see Chapter 11).

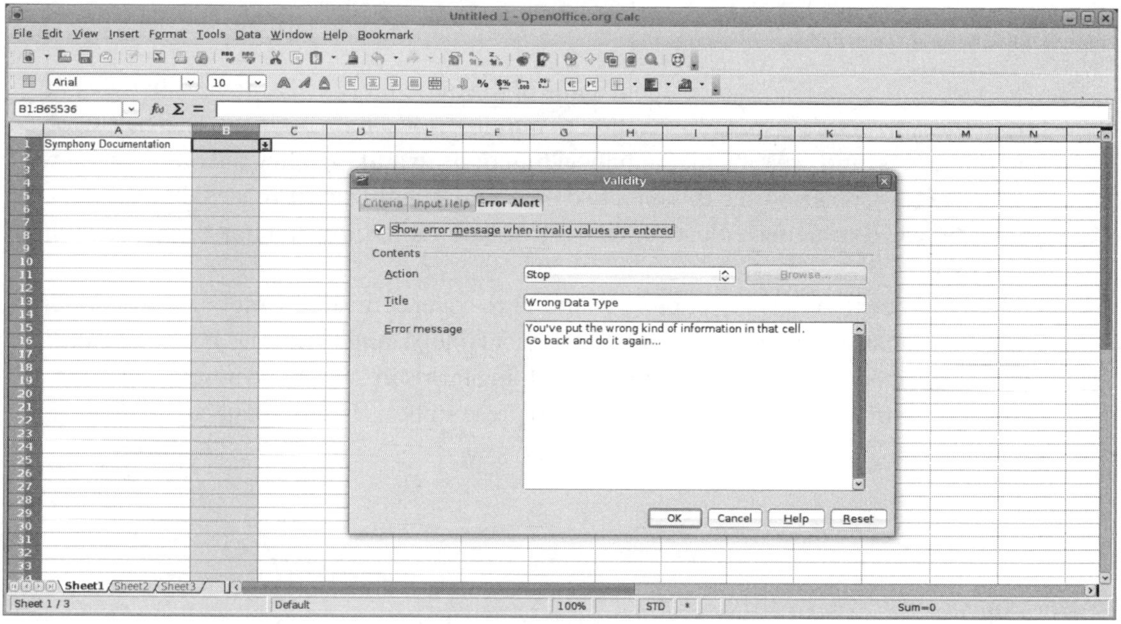

**Figure 4-38.** *Custom error messages are especially useful if you're designing a spreadsheet for others to complete.*

# Saving and Exporting

Calc is able to save spreadsheets in a variety of formats, including its native OpenDocument (.ods) and the Microsoft Excel format up to and including the latest OOXML (.xlsx) files from Office 2007 and 2008 for Mac. A spreadsheet can also be exported as HTML, which is excellent for building static archives of data or exporting for inclusion on a web page, or as a PDF, which is useful when sending fixed data via e-mail. PDF also has some excellent security options (see Chapter 9). All of these options are available under the File menu.

---

■**Caution** Although Calc supports the majority of functions used by Microsoft Excel, there are some that are not supported, and vice versa. In our simple examples, we haven't encountered any of these, but it's worth noting that the more complex a spreadsheet becomes, the more likely incompatibilities are to appear.

If you're migrating a significant volume of information to Calc from another application, as a precaution, keep the original applications around until everything is tested and found to be satisfactory.

---

The best method for exporting charts is cut and paste. Taking a chart to Draw, for example, makes it possible to edit the look of the chart and then export this in a wide range of formats while retaining the link with Calc (see Chapter 10).

# Recap

In this chapter, you've learned about some of the basic tools and functions in Calc and used these to create a small application to monitor household budgets. This has involved defining cells, and creating mathematical functions to add together cell ranges and create averages. You also used this data to create a number of charts to visualize the data in different ways, and then edited the charts to create something that improves readability and style.

We'll return to Calc in Chapters 10 and 11 to cover some of the more esoteric functions available, add macros to automate particular jobs, and look at ways of exporting data to different applications, including building forms in Writer and adding dynamic charts to Impress to ensure data included in presentations is kept totally up to date.

# CHAPTER 5

# Impress: Stylish Presentations

**K**nowing how to put together a concise and engaging presentation is becoming an essential skill in business and academic situations. Having a smart slideshow does three essential things in these situations: firstly, it allows the presenter to give the audience a range of information that would be tedious to run through verbatim; secondly, it forces the presenter to boil down his or her information to a few well-chosen bullet points; and finally, it provides a large area for the audience to focus on while the presenter shuffles his or her notes.

In this chapter you'll start by creating a short presentation using text, links, and images based on the Impress Blank template. You'll be introduced to some, but not too many, animations, such as point-by-point builds and slide transitions, and then you'll add some visual interest by creating a theme to underpin this, and future, presentations. In the final part, you'll look at the tools Impress offers to assist the presenter in delivering a slideshow or outputting it for later distribution (Figure 5-1).

**Figure 5-1.** *Presentations are all about effective communication, and while Impress won't make you a great presenter, it can help focus your mind on the message and give your audience an additional view of your thoughts.*

# Creating a Basic Slideshow

From the OpenOffice.org Start Center's Create a new section, select New Presentation. You'll run through the wizard, beginning with an Empty presentation. Select this option and click Next to go into the Slide selection part (Figure 5-2). There's not much going on in here, so ensure that the Slide design section is set to <original> and that the output medium is set to Screen. If you install any additional templates from the Web, they too will be accessible from the Slide design section. The main part of the window is given over to a preview of, well, a blank slide, so click Next to move onto the default transition. Use the Effect drop-down list to choose Fade smoothly, and make sure the duration is set to Medium. With these settings, the transition from one slide to the next will take under a second and won't be too jarring or flashy.

In the lower section, leave the option at Default, because this means the slideshow will be advanced when the presenter either clicks a mouse button, presses the spacebar, or manually advances with an onscreen icon.

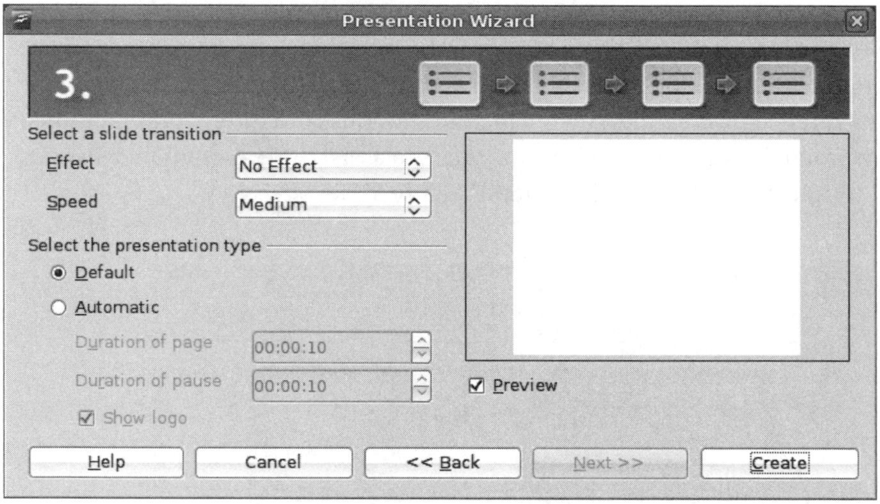

**Figure 5-2.** *The presentation takes you through the initial presentation design. To create a blank presentation, just choose Create on the first screen.*

It's also possible to create automated slideshows by selecting Automatic, with the first timing setting how long each slide will be displayed and the second one setting the length of gap between one presentation and the next. The automatic presentation tools could be used to build an advertising slideshow (or series of slideshows) to be displayed on a screen in a building's foyer.

Finally click Create to launch the application and get editing.

**■Tip** Another way to begin a presentation is by creating an outline in Writer and making that the foundation for a new presentation. To do this, create an outline in Writer using the Heading styles to define the main points of the presentation. Click File ➤ Send ➤ Outline to Presentation to open up Impress with the outline already added to the outline section (see the later section "Presentation Structure" for more on the outliner).

## The Interface

As with Writer and Calc, the screen is divided up into regions, with toolbars running across the top (you can, of course, edit and reorganize these as much as you like), but the work area is itself split into three areas (Figure 5-3).

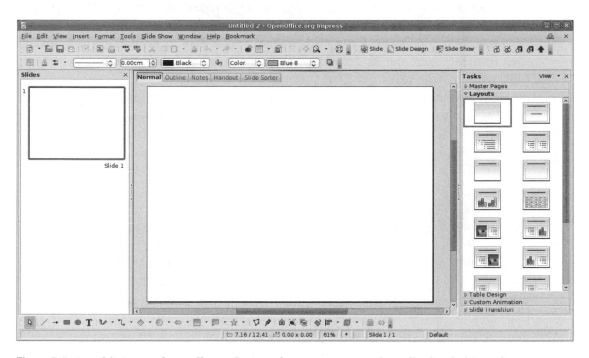

**Figure 5-3.** *In addition to the toolbars, the interface on Impress is broadly divided into three columns, though when designing slides you may want to turn off the two outside panes.*

## Slide Pane

On the left is the slide organizer window—called the Slide Pane. In here you see thumbnail images of all the slides in the presentation in a vertical list. In addition to providing quick access to any slide in the production, this is where you can reorder slides on the fly. The playing order is top to bottom, and it can be edited by dragging a slide and dropping it to a new position within the list. As you drag the slide, a thick black line will appear in between existing slides to show where the drop is going to land. The numbers in this column are always consecutive, so if Slide 1 is moved to a location between Slides 4 and 5, it will become Slide 4 (4 will become 3, 3 becomes 2, etc.). Thus you always know where a slide is going to appear in the list. If you prefer names to numbers, it's possible to change the name of a slide by right-clicking on a slide and selecting Rename Slide from the menu. Of course, if you change the position of the slide once its name has been changed, the name will move with it, though numbered slides will be reordered appropriately. In the right-click menu, you'll also notice options to delete the slide, hide it, enter the design or layout dialog box (see the later section "Presentation Structure"), or adjust the transition.

A small diamond-shaped icon below a slide denotes that a transition has been set to work on that slide, and, as the position of the icon suggests, the transition affects the "out" portion of the slide to which it is attached.

As you add more slides to the production, this window will acquire a scrollbar, but if you need more space to edit an individual slide, this pane can be removed by clicking View ➤ Slide Pane. Do the same thing to bring it back. You can also resize the pane by clicking and dragging the border between it and the work area.

## Work Area

The work area dominates the interface of Impress, and this is where you can design individual slides. In addition to the actual slide, this part of the interface has five tabs at the top providing immediate access to the main parts of the software that are used to create rounded presentations. Most of the time you will be working in the Normal tab, but there will be some jobs to do in the Outline tab, which is great for building a basic presentation structure without having to worry about the aesthetics; the Notes section, which can make delivering the presentation smoother; the Handout section, where you can devise some audience-centric notes; and the slide sorter for making last-minute edits to a presentation. As you move through these tabs, you'll notice that the interface changes quite a lot depending on the tab and, in many cases, the tool being used.

When working on an individual slide, it's usually a good idea to remove as much from the work area as possible. Switch off the surrounding panes via the View menu.

In addition to the tabs, it's possible to access these various elements from the View menu. We'll look more at these shortly.

## Task Pane

This is where most of the configuration goes on. The Task Pane (Figure 5-4) is divided into collapsible palettes (expose one by clicking the small disclosure arrow next to the title) covering areas such as slide layout, transition, table design, and build in and out—that is how elements appear and disappear on the page. It's possible to remove some or all of these collapsible menus by clicking the View menu at the top right and then selecting or deselecting the item you'd like to change. For example, if the presentation is unlikely to contain tables, click View ➤ Table Design to remove that element and leave more space for the part that might be needed. You could also remove the whole thing by clicking View ➤ Task Pane, by clicking the cross icon on the top right, or by detaching the pane from the main window (View ➤ Undock Task Pane).

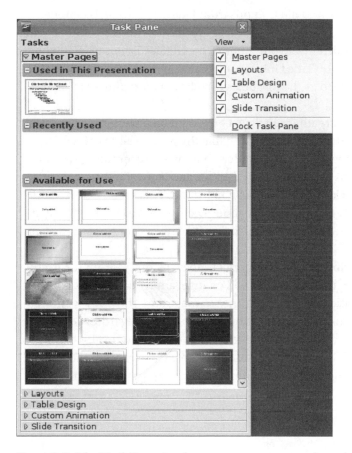

**Figure 5-4.** *The Task Pane is where you can access such options as transitions, tables, and animations. This pane can be undocked from the interface and floated free.*

At the bottom of the window is a configurable toolbar featuring the drawing tools you saw in Chapter 2 and, below this, the status bar. The status bar in Impress is largely informational, but the exception is the view percentage space, which can be right-clicked to zoom in and out of the currently viewed slide. The available options include the ever-useful Entire page and Page width.

## Adding Content to a Slide

The basic element of any slideshow is the single slide, so you'll start by creating one of those. When the application first launches, the work area is dominated by a blank slide. In the Task Pane, ensure that Layouts is selected so you can see the various basic slides available for use. All of these slides have preset regions for titles, text, and images but can also accommodate charts from Calc and illustrations from Draw. These can be applied to a slide with a single click on the appropriate slide and are very useful. You could begin with a clean slate and use the Blank Slide layout. But this could raise issues when it comes to creating a theme later, so select the Title Only layout, which, in the icon view, has a single line of text across the top. Do as the text box says (click to edit) and add the title for your presentation.

You can also add a subtitle by creating a new text box. With only your eye as judge it is really easy to create slides that are lopsided, so enable the grid—a series of regularly spaced dots on the page—to give yourself a better idea about where everything should go. This is the same grid system that is available in both Writer and Draw. First click View ➤ Grid ➤ Display Grid, and then click View ➤ Grid ➤ Snap to Grid. This second command will make the grid points "sticky" so that when the mouse gets within a certain distance it will automatically snap to the grid element. This makes it a little easier to lay things out symmetrically on the page.

With the grid (Figure 5-5) visible on the page, select the text icon (T) from the drawing toolbar at the base of the window. The cursor will change, and you can click and drag a text box underneath the title using the grid lines to make sure the box is centered. When you let go of the mouse button, a new text box is created and, regardless of the depth defined with the mouse, it will be a single text line in height. Add text by typing, or click outside the text area to dismiss the text box completely. The text box will expand vertically as more text is added, and words will automatically wrap to the next line when you reach the far right of the box.

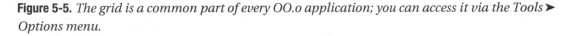

**Figure 5-5.** *The grid is a common part of every OO.o application; you can access it via the Tools ➤ Options menu.*

## EDITING THE GRID

There are a few options available to edit the grid in Impress that can make it more visible or more suited to a particular measurement scheme. To make the grid more obvious, click Tools ➤ Options to launch the main configuration box, and then open the Appearance menu (Figure 5-5) using the disclosure icon (+) on the left of the screen. These are in the main OO.o settings because they affect the whole system. Under the Custom Colors section, scroll down until you see the Impress subheading and the Grid option beside it. Click the drop-down color selector and choose something that will stand out more than the default tepid grey. Finally, click OK to see the change on the screen. This is a universal change, rather than one linked to a particular document.

Remember that the grid is not seen during the final presentation, so it doesn't matter if you choose shocking pink or firebox red.

The next option is to change the measurements. Again, go into Tools ➤ Options, and this time open up the Impress disclosure icon. The Grid has its own section, so choose that. The first two options in here are Snap to grid and Visible grid. The status of these will depend on whether or not you've activated these features as outlined earlier.

The second section covers resolution—or how often the grid dots appear on the slide—and the number of subdivisions between each intersection. The default setting is a 1-cm grid with 1 subdivision, but you may find the slide looks less confusing with a 2-cm/2 subdivisions setup. These settings are available on both the horizontal and vertical planes; by selecting Synchronize Axes, any changes in one plane will be accompanied by changes in the other.

The bottom section defines the extent and strength of the snap that occurs when objects are created or moved.

When typing, note that the context-sensitive toolbar at the top of the page becomes a character-formatting toolbar (Figure 5-6), similar to the one used in Writer. Here you can adjust the font, font size, and style (bold, italic, etc.), and you can also create lists, set the justification, and change the spacing of paragraphs. As these things change, the text box will expand or contract vertically to accommodate everything, but the horizontal spacing remains the same.

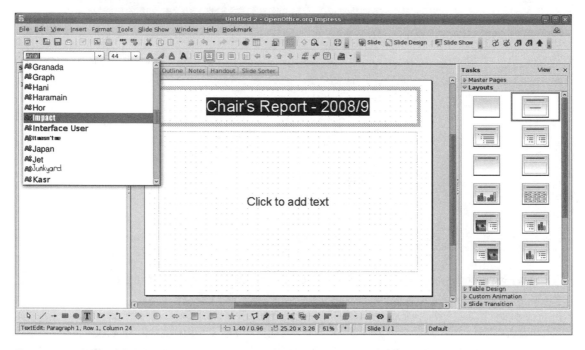

**Figure 5-6.** *Click into one of the regions and begin typing content directly onto a slide.*

Once you have finished editing, click outside the box to deselect it; you can edit the text again by clicking anywhere inside the box, or click one of the edges to reveal a set of drag handles used to reposition or resize the box. Click and drag one of the lines to reposition the box anywhere on the page.

Though you've actually typed in these details, it's possible to use the same variable options explored in Chapter 3; you could, for example, insert the author name by clicking Insert ➤ Fields ➤ Author, or you could add a page number to a slide by doing Insert ➤ Fields ➤ Page Number. The built-in master slides have spaces set aside for these details, and we'll look at these later, in the section "Creating and Editing Master Pages."

# Adding an Image

In addition to text, you can add an image from a file to this slide (Figure 5-7), accomplished in the same way as you added pictures in Writer. Click Insert ➤ Picture ➤ From File, and use the file browser to navigate to an image on your hard disk to insert. You can also drag images from the Gallery (Tools ➤ Gallery) and add them to the page.

At the base of the file browser, click the Preview button to see a thumbnail of the picture before inserting it. If the Link button is enabled, Impress will retain a link between the image on the slide and the original document (as in Writer), meaning that any subsequent changes you make to the picture in an image editor (say, changing it from color to black and white) would show up in Impress next time the document is loaded.

Once an image is loaded, the Picture toolbar will be visible at the top of the window, where you can edit the image border, adjust transparency, or give the picture a shadow. All of the filters discussed in Chapter 2 are available, so it's possible to make a grayscale image from a color image and to sharpen, smooth, or pixellate the image to create the right effect.

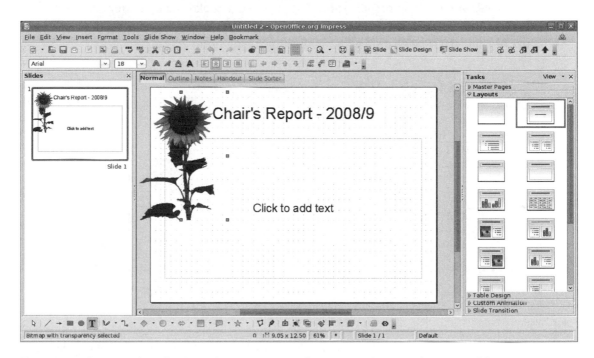

**Figure 5-7.** *The procedure for inserting an image is the same as in any other part of the suite.*

Click Insert ➤ Image ➤ From File and navigate to the image. When using a light image on a light background, it's a good idea to add either a shadow or a line to mark out the edges of the picture. Clicking the shadow button will add an automatic shadow, which can be edited by right-clicking the image, selecting Area, and looking under the Shadow tab. In here it's possible to define the location of the shadow (top-left, bottom-right, etc.), the distance from the main object, the color, and the transparency. The line options are available either by selecting the line icon or by right-clicking the image and selecting from the available options, which include the line width, color, transparency, style (dashed, solid, etc.), arrows (for non-joined-up lines), and corner style. A selection of premade line and arrow styles is available under the appropriate tab; these work in exactly the same way as text styles (see Chapter 3), and so they can be edited and then saved for later recall.

To resize a picture, select it to reveal the grab handles and then push or pull these to the appropriate side. Holding down the Shift key while adjusting these handles will allow you to avoid the dreaded squash and stretch by retaining the images' proportions. You can, of course, squash and stretch images if you like; just keep away from the Shift key.

The other major edit you can perform on an image is to crop it, which is something you may find yourself doing all the time in presentations, because most pictures don't fit the given space without a little tweaking. The advantage of cropping and resizing in Impress rather than with an image editor such as Photoshop or MS Paint is that the rest of the image isn't lost (Figure 5-8). Thus, if you needed to make an adjustment to the slide, freeing up more space for the image, you could reverse the crop to reveal more of the picture or change its aspect ratio without affecting the picture.

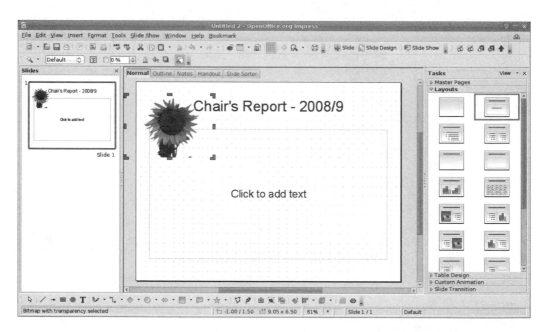

**Figure 5-8.** *Cropping doesn't actually remove any information from the image, so it could be recropped at a later date.*

To crop, select the last icon on the right from the Picture toolbar. This will change the grab handles into crop handles, which look a little thinner, and you can now hide or reveal parts of the image by clicking and dragging. Note that both grab handles and crop handles will snap to the grid if that feature has been turned on. While this is useful for resizing, it can make cropping a little difficult. Turn it off with View ➤ Grid ➤ Snap to Grid to get better control over the cropping process.

If the Picture toolbar is not available, click View ➤ Toolbars ➤ Picture to see it. As with the resize options just mentioned, holding down the Shift key while cropping from a corner will ensure that the crop retains the same aspect ratio as the original image.

Once you have finished cropping, click off the image to deselect the crop tool—clicking the image will reinstate the grab handles, ready for resizing. Crop and resize together are very effective for highlighting a particular part of an image.

You can gain a little more control over the position of the image by right-clicking and selecting Position and Size. The first tab in this dialog box allows you to alter the size of the image, move it around numerically (the x and y values are set out from the left and top edge), or protect the size and/or location, making it impossible later to move the image accidentally with the mouse. If you want to edit later, you'll need to switch this option back off!

The second tab has options for rotating the picture (Figure 5-9). The top half of the box allows you to set the pivot point (the location the rotation will go around), while the bottom section sets the rotation itself. Positive values entered here will rotate the image counterclockwise; negative values will make it spin clockwise. The final tab can be used to change the corner radius of rounded boxes or frames, but it is not usable when editing an image.

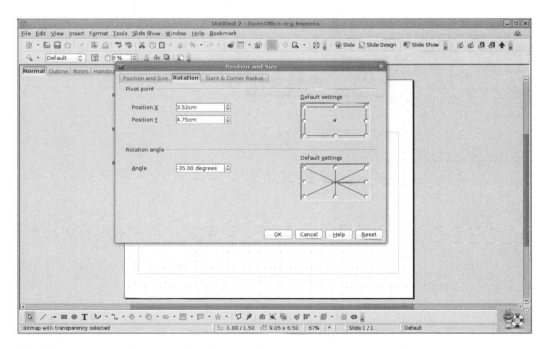

**Figure 5-9.** *Rotation is defined in either positive or negative degrees. Negative numbers turn the object in a clockwise direction.*

# Presentation Structure

Let's slip away from slide design for a while and look at one of the quickest ways of building and editing the structure of a presentation. This is where most successful presentations begin. Good looks and snazzy animations can make a presentation come alive, but if the structure is confused and the content uninspiring, even effects by George Lucas won't help it. For this reason, you're going to design the entire slideshow with absolutely no thought to the visual side of the presentation. At the end of this section you'll have a full-fledged presentation ready to be beautified.

Of course, you could add slides to the presentation using the Slide Pane and add titles and subtitles as you go along, but the following method provides a great overview of the presentation's flow.

Select the Outline tab (Figures 5-10 and 5-11). Note that when you go into Outline mode, a new toolbar (the Outline toolbar) is added to the main toolbar at the top of the window, and the context-sensitive Formatting toolbar (below the main toolbar) will slip into outline mode, which offers just a few text-formatting tools and some item-arrangement buttons. Effective outlines rely on using these two toolbars in tandem; if you're feeling adventurous you could create a new toolbar featuring buttons from both by using the Customize ➤ Toolbars dialog box. In order to concentrate on content, switch off the Task Pane (View ➤ Task Pane) and Slide Pane (View ➤ Slide Pane) to leave an interface that looks like a basic word processor.

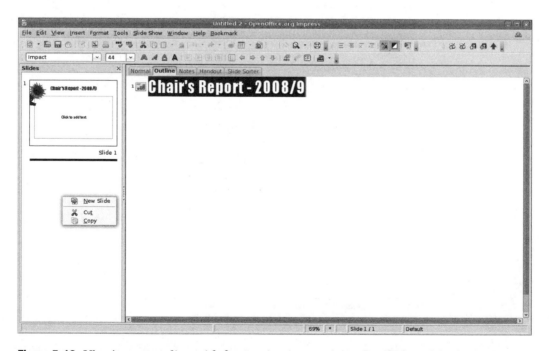

**Figure 5-10.** *Viewing an outline with formatting intact gives a good idea of the look of a piece of text but can seem cumbersome when planning your content.*

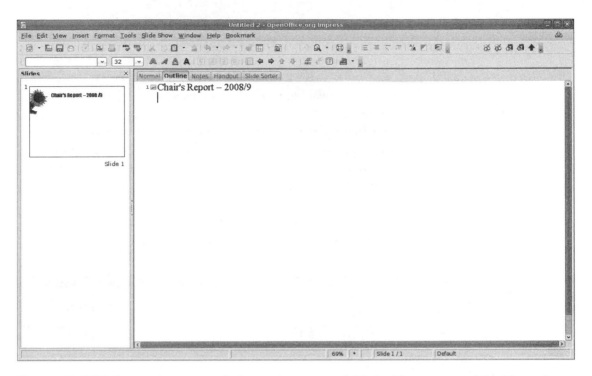

**Figure 5-11.** *With formatting removed, the text is more readable in this context and the hierarchy will be apparent from the position of the text in the window.*

At the top left of the window is a small slide icon labeled 1 that represents the first slide in the presentation To the right of the icon is the text that you previously entered as the title for the first slide.

---

**Tip** If the display looks a little unwieldy with the text formatted as it is likely to appear, click the Format On/Off button from the Outline toolbar (it has the font icon covered by a slider). This will make the text in the outline view plain and will, instead, denote the position of the text using indents. Click at the end of the title from the first slide and press Enter and then press Enter again. Remember, you're entirely unconcerned with the look of the slides at the moment, so don't worry about the font or font size; these will, by default, assume the proportions of the title, list, or content font from the presentation theme.

---

Once you press the Enter key, the cursor will drop down below the first slide icon, add a new one, and label it 2. This is the second slide, and you can add a title for this before pressing Enter again to create Slide 3, and so on until you've added and titled the slides the presentation is likely to need.

Editing any of these involves simply clicking anywhere in the appropriate entry and making changes. This is the basic outline of the presentation set out as a series of titles.

Titles are the fundamental points or ideas around which the presentation is built, so make sure that one flows readily to the next. For example, in your "Anatomy of a newspaper" presentation, it would be illogical to locate a slide titled "Columns and Gutters" before one called "Page size" because the former relies so much on the latter. However, a slide called "Headlines" could appear before or after "Images," depending on the type of newspaper you were discussing.

Because you're thinking in terms of structure here, you can reorder the slides using the Move Up and Move Down arrows on the Formatting toolbar (Figure 5-12). These arrows are also context sensitive, so, for example, if you select Slide 1, the only available arrow will move the slide down the list. However, if you select Slide 2, two more arrows will become available: up and right. To move a slide through the list, click anywhere in the title text and use the down or up arrow to maneuver it into the right place. The numbers will be reordered automatically. Now you can add some content.

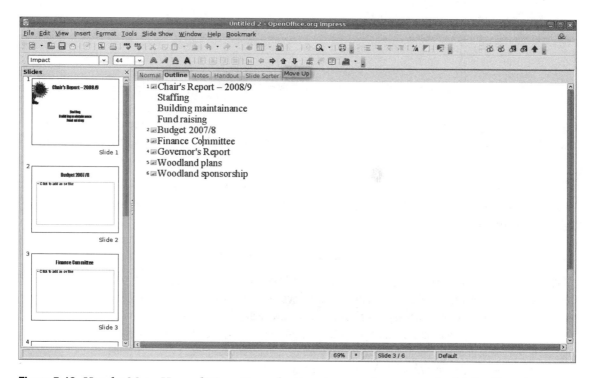

**Figure 5-12.** *Use the Move Up and Move Down buttons to organize content in the Outline view.*

# Content

Go back to the first title, place the cursor at the end of the title, and press the Enter key again, causing a new slide to be added to the presentation and all subsequent numbers to be increased by 1. This is not quite what you want, but it is normal because by default Impress treats each new line of text in an outline as a new slide. We can turn this "new slide" into a child element of the slide immediately above it by "demoting" it one space using the right-facing arrow in the Outline toolbar (Figure 5-13).

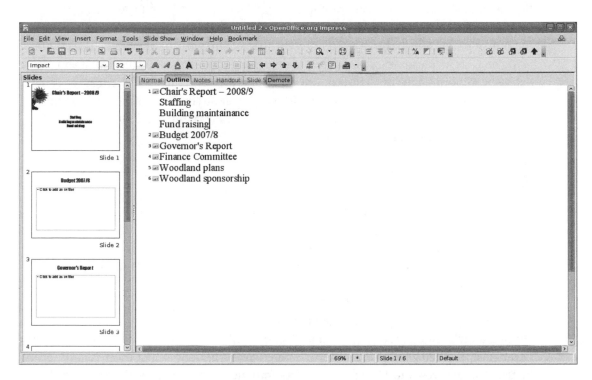

**Figure 5-13.** *Demote and Promote can change the structure of a slide or turn a single bullet point into a slide.*

Impress will automatically treat demoted copy as a list element; that is, it will be introduced with a bullet. But you can switch this off for a particular entry by clicking the Bullets On/Off button (next to the arrows). Subsequent lines of text will inherit this format, so you can add the subtitle, then press Enter, and add the presenter's name. Remember, you're not concerned with formatting at the moment, so everything is going to look like a list.

Note that when you demoted Slide 2, the rest of the slides below it were renumbered with their original designations.

Our second slide begins with a list that also includes a couple of sublists. This structure is created by typing out the list elements and then using the Demote button (or the Tab key) to define where in the hierarchy each element should appear. Clicking Demote on a list item will make it a child of the item immediately above it.

Similarly, you can use the Promote button to turn children into parents. For instance, in Figure 5-13 the second slide looks like it could be a bit cramped, so we can edit the title to remove Margins and then promote Margins to a new slide of its own using the left-facing arrow. If you're working on a more extensive structure, it's worth remembering that the order buttons (Promote, Demote, Up, and Down) work on the selected section. So if you click inside an entry and adjust it, only that entry will be affected, but if you highlight a heading and any lists below it, you can promote or demote all of them at the same time and they will all conform to the structure of the hierarchy. So by selecting Staffing and everything below it on that slide, you can promote everything with one click and then begin constructing that slide properly.

## Hide and Display

As you add more stuff to the outline, things can get a little unwieldy, but the purpose of this exercise is to allow you to work on content without distraction. Having to wade through a long list of lists to get at content is not very efficient. Fortunately, you can hide elements of the outline using the Hide Subpoints button on the Outline toolbar (Figure 5-14).

Let's go back to a slide with lots of information. Selecting one of the parent lists within a slide (i.e., one with child elements beneath it) enables a new button on the Outline toolbar, and clicking it will hide all of the child elements. When this is done, the parent is appended with an underscore before the text to denote that there is content beneath it. To reveal the content again, click into the parent and select the Show Subpoints button.

As with the Promote and Demote buttons, these work on the selected text, so if you selected the first three slides in the outline and clicked the Hide Subpoints button, everything below the titles on those slides would be hidden. The Enter key respects hidden sections too, so if you hid the content of Slide 2, placed the cursor at the end of the Slide 2 title, and pressed the Enter key, it would create a new Slide 3 rather than adding something to Slide 2.

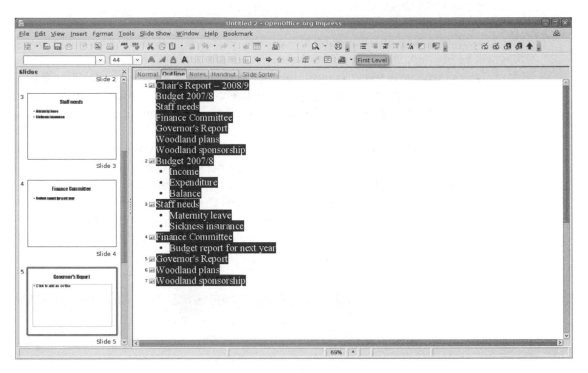

**Figure 5-14.** *Use the First Level button to hide everything except the slide titles. This is good for making structural changes without worrying about the content of each slide.*

## Audition

The final button on the Outline toolbar will launch the slideshow from the currently selected slide and can be used to check whether there's too much going on for a single slide (if something looks crowded in black text on a white background, it will look much worse with added snazzy graphics!). Once that launches—it's full screen—we can either run through the following slides by clicking the mouse or use the Esc key to get back to the outline view.

## Slide Sorter

If pushing onscreen buttons to move slides around seems a bit long-winded or you just want to get a decent overview of the slides themselves, select the Slide Sorter tab at the top of the window (Figure 5-15). This displays each slide as a thumbnail image in the main window, and these can be reordered simply by dragging and dropping slides to new locations.

There are a few ways of selecting multiple slides to move. Firstly, you can click and drag a marquee over every slide to be moved. This selects each slide the mouse touches (they will be highlighted with a thicker border), and these all be moved together. Secondly, it's possible to select a continuous series of slides (e.g., 1–3) by clicking the first and then Shift+clicking the last. Everything in between is selected. Thirdly, you can select noncontinuous slides (e.g., 1, 3, 6, 7) by clicking the first choice and then Ctrl+clicking the rest.

Right-clicking on any slide in here will open a context-sensitive menu that includes a Rename Slide option. This is really useful on longer presentations. Not only is it easier to search for keywords in the slide names than on the slides themselves, but you can also use the names to divide up the presentation into parts that you can then easily select and move around en masse rather than attempting to reorder individual slides. We'll return here in the later section "Multiple Slides." But with the structure defined and satisfactory, it is now time to think about the visuals.

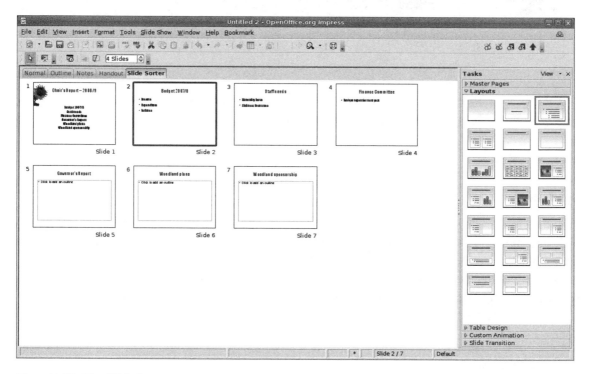

**Figure 5-15.** *The Slide Sorter section is a more visual way of shifting things around. We'll return to this to make multislide edits in the section "Multiple Slides."*

**USING THE NAVIGATOR AS A BASIC OUTLINER**

As with the other parts of the OpenOffice.org suite, you can use the Navigator (Figure 5-16), accessed by clicking Edit ➤ Navigator, to move rapidly around a long presentation. To make effective use of the Navigator, you must label the various elements of the presentation—at the very least you should name each slide by right-clicking anywhere on the slide and selecting Slide ➤ Rename Slide. This text string will then represent the slide in the Navigator. Similarly, clicking on any object on a slide and selecting Rename will allow you to label each part for viewing in the Navigator. Where this works really well is when you have many layered objects and need to edit the one at the very bottom of the pile.

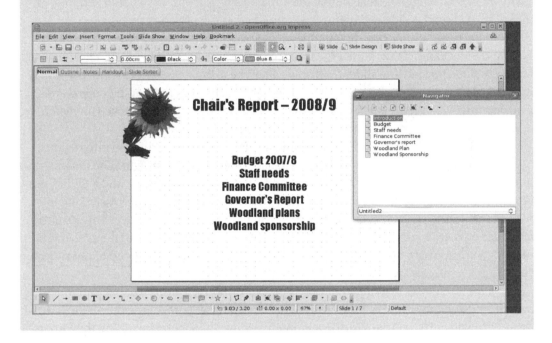

# Creating and Editing Master Pages

One of the things missing from the basic OpenOffice.org install is a wide selection of presentation templates, especially in Impress. However, creating themes is a really simple process, and the results can easily equal anything available in Apple's Keynote or Microsoft's PowerPoint 2008 while still being unique. In this section you'll design a template for the current presentation and then save this as a template so that you can use it at a later date, just as you did with a word-processing document in Chapter 1. For this you will create a number of master pages that will define the visual and positional elements of the slides in the presentation. You can apply these master pages to any slide in the presentation; moreover, you can save and apply them to later presentations as well.

To begin, select the Normal tab above the main area and navigate to the first slide in the presentation. This should be the title slide created earlier and should consist of black text on a white background. Use the disclosure arrow in the Task Pane to open the section labeled Master Pages. This will display the master slides used in the current presentation—just a plain old white one—and any other master slides available in Impress. Creating a theme involves building a new master slide and then applying that to the presentation as a whole.

See how the system works by clicking a few of the available master slides and look through the presentation. The theme is largely visual—we can add backgrounds, graphical devices, branding—and also define the size and style of fonts associated with the different levels of the slide text hierarchy mentioned in the previous section.

As before, we're concentrating on the main area of the interface, so switch off the Task and Slide Panes if they've reappeared. To enter the master slide editor, click View ➤ Master ➤ Slide Master. The slide will display all of the master elements included—which will look like a cascade of different fonts running to the bottom right of the page—and a new toolbar will appear labeled Master View. As always, this can be docked anywhere on the user interface by dragging it toward one edge of the window.

In the Master View it becomes more obvious that each slide is divided into regions, because these are outlined with a border and labeled at the bottom right. The default master slide has a Title Area, an Object Area, a Date Area, a Footer Area, and a Slide Number Area. The Date, Footer, and Slide Number Areas can be switched off by clicking View ➤ Master ➤ Master Elements and then deselecting the element to remove. There's also a Header element in this list, but it is available only in the Notes view—if the presentation needs a header, it's possible to drag and drop the footer element to the top of the slide, or you can add a header space manually later.

The first thing you're going to define is the background, for this will have an inevitable impact on the choice of fonts and colors used in other parts of the production. All of the tools available in normal slide development are available here, including the importing of images, shapes, text, symbols, and clip art. You're going for a combination of calm and casual, so choose something blue and abstract by Scorp84, generously available on Flickr under a Creative Commons license. Creative Commons (`www.creativecommons.org`) is an attempt to fashion copyright law for the Internet age. It allows artists, photographers, and writers to take more control over how their content is used.

---

■**Note**  The image used here can be found at `www.flickr.com/photos/35014792@N00/337187400/` and is available under a Creative Commons license. Ideally, images should be tailored to the format of the final output medium, but they should be at least 1024 × 768. Most data projectors operate at this resolution, but more expensive models may push the resolution up to 1440 × 900 or some other widescreen format.

---

## FINDING TEMPLATES

If premade themes are something you're likely to miss, there are lots of them freely available on the Internet. And, fortunately, Impress does a good job of importing PowerPoint template files too, which vastly increases the number available.

One good source of Impress templates and other OpenOffice.org add-ons is OOExtras (http://www.smalldataproblem.org/ooextras/). This site has a wide selection of templates available for download that are suitable for everything from business or class presentations to more fun projects. Most of the templates are formatted in the older .sti format, but these are still usable in the latest version of Impress. Download one of the files, click File ➤ Open, and navigate to the location of the file. Because the file is a template, it will open up as though it were a new document ready to be used as the basis for your presentation.

The OOExtras site is a community resource, so if you build a useful template (see the later section "Output"), you could upload it for others to use.

You'll also find a good selection of templates at the OpenOffice.org site itself. Just go to http://extensions.services.openoffice.org/ and click the Impress or Presentation tab. We'll discuss additional templates in Chapter 11.

In order to add a PowerPoint theme to Impress, open it with File ➤ Open and select Microsoft PowerPoint 97/2000/XP Template (*.pot) from the file type drop-down. Once the template has loaded, click File ➤ Templates ➤ Save and save the file to MyTemplates. Not only will it then be available in the Master Slides task pane, but it will also be selectable using the wizard that launches when creating a new presentation.

Add the picture using Insert ➤ Picture ➤ From File, and then resize or crop using the handles, as described earlier, remembering to hold down the Shift key to keep the original's aspect ratio. It's standard for Impress to import an image to the top layer of any stack, meaning the content elements of the master slide will initially be obscured by the background picture. To rectify this, select the image with a right-click to see the context-sensitive menu, and then click Arrange ➤ Send to Back. This command, as expected, will reorder the selected image and put it at the very bottom of the layer stack, meaning the various text bits are once again visible (see Figure 5-16).

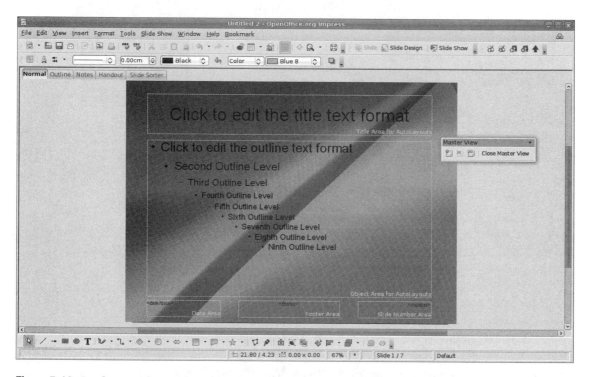

**Figure 5-16.** *Background images will have quite an impact on the color you choose for the rest of the slide elements. For example, this one doesn't suit dark text very well.*

However, the screenshot demonstrates that this reordering has not improved readability because you have dark text on a dark background. There are a few ways to work around this. The first solution would be to "knock back" the color in the background a little. The easiest way to do this is to select the image and then use the transparency control on the Formatting toolbar (which will now have image-editing tools on it) to reduce the strength of the image, as in Figure 5-17, where the transparency is set to 40%. A higher number means more of the background shows through. A second way of achieving a similar result—and a slightly different look—would be to add a rectangle above the image, fill it with white, and then adjust the transparency of that to allow the background image to show through as in Figure 5-18, where the rectangle has 50% transparency.

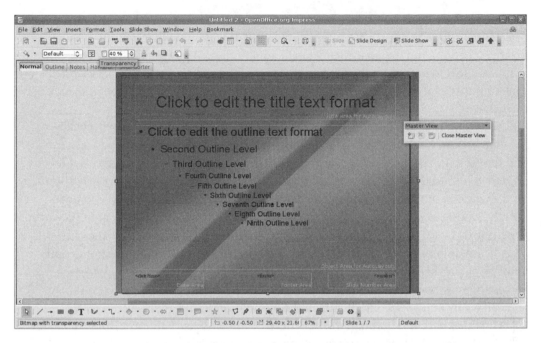

**Figure 5-17.** *Setting transparency on the background image looks OK, but it's not great because it makes the whole slide appear washed out.*

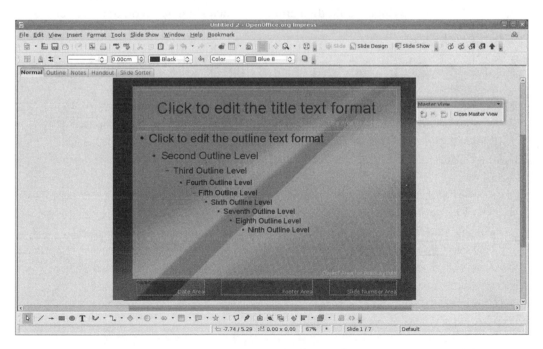

**Figure 5-18.** *This design provides the right contrast, but it also gives the presentation a well-defined border.*

In order to create this effect, which can focus attention onto the content area, you drag guides onto the page (click into the ruler and drag it out with the mouse to the desired location) and then use the rectangle tool from the Drawing toolbar at the bottom of the window to make a shape that covers most of the slide. You fill this with white using the Formatting toolbar, and then right-click ➤ Area and select the Transparency tab. Set the value to 50%.

The result is a transparent shape above everything else. You could right-click ➤ Arrange ➤ Send Backward (which moves the selected shape one layer down) a number of times until the shape was below the text but above the background image, but it is quicker to right-click ➤ Arrange ➤ In Front of Object and then to click the background image (click near one of the edges to avoid selecting one of the text regions) to position the share directly in front of it. Once you have the layering set up, it might be worth revisiting the transparency settings to ensure that the text is visible across the entire slide—remember that it is (usually) the content of the presentation that is important, with the visuals secondary. The real advantage of this method is that, if need arises, you can change the background image to change the feel of the presentation completely, or you can easily build a second theme on the foundations of the first.

The third option is to retain the dark background and use light text. But this can lead to rather intense slides that don't fit with your calm and casual look.

In addition to background images, it's possible to place other pictures, such as logos, onto a page as part of the slide master and then to move other elements around so that they don't cover it. This logo would then appear on each slide based on that master.

### FONTS ON THE SCREEN

Something that presentation planners occasionally forget to do is to put themselves in the audience's place, which can kill a presentation. For example, 12-point serif text may look perfectly acceptable on your bright, glossy laptop display situated a handy 18 inches from your eyes. The same font projected 30 feet away in a lighted room is going to give your audience eye-strain and turn them against you.

Title text will make the most impact at sizes above 40 points, while list entries should be somewhere between 24 and 32 points. All this has an impact on how much information can be packed onto a single slide. Most "experts" suggest that six lines of text on a single slide is a good average.

Font selection is also important when thinking about transporting a presentation from one computer to another. In the next section we suggest using the Microsoft Core Fonts to improve cross-platform compatibility. These are available by default on Windows systems and can be installed on both Mac and Linux machines. A number of these fonts, including Verdana, have been designed to be readable onscreen and thus make for good presentation fonts.

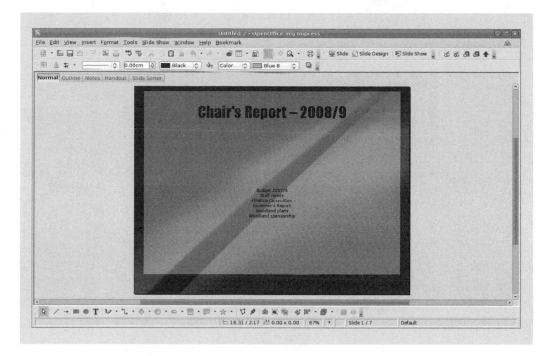

## Font Styles

Now that you have a rough visual impression, you can begin to adjust the look of the fonts and bulleted lists that most people in the audience will be concentrating on. Start with the Title Area, select the whole of the content, and then define the font, spacing, and formatting using the Formatting toolbar. There are options for size, font, alignment, and paragraph spacing, so it's possible to be quite precise in creating the look (Figure 5-19). Remember, though, that while you may have access to thousands of different typefaces, you may be called to present on a strange machine that is not so blessed. Thus, it's best to stick to a few core fonts, such as Arial, Times New Roman, Impact, and Verdana, especially when outputting the final files either to the Web or to PowerPoint, where it's impossible to be sure that some esoteric font will be available. It's also possible to color the text, though it's important to retain a high level of contrast between the text and the background so that everything remains visible.

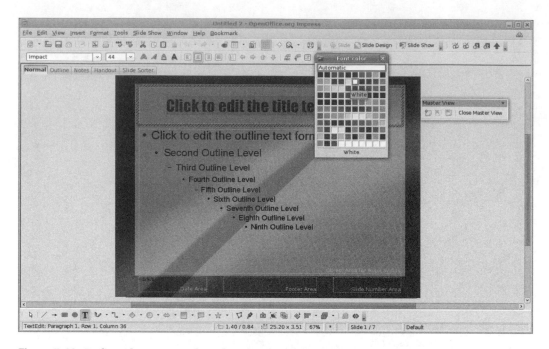

**Figure 5-19.** *Define elements such as fonts, size, and color in the slide master so that you don't have to repeat lots of work later on.*

## Bulleted Lists

The Object Area on this master slide has been defined with outlines in mind (see earlier), so the default text style is a comprehensive bulleted list using a mixture of round bullets and dashes to denote each level. You can redefine this list using either the Styles and Formatting system or by manually editing the master slide. To do the former, open the Styles and Formatting palette (Format ➤ Styles and Formatting), right-click the "level" to be edited, for example, Outline 2, and select Modify. Use the various tabs to edit the style (see the following discussion), and then save the style.

To redefine the whole list, click the cursor anywhere in the text, and then right-click and select Numbering/Bullets to open the dialog box (Figure 5-20).

Each of the first three tabs here—Bullets, Numbering type, and Graphics—has a pre-made selection of bullet options that you can apply with a single click. Bullets are textual objects, such as a circle, a square, and a tick mark, that are often part of a font; Numbering is used for creating ordered lists with consecutive numbers, Roman numerals, or letters; and Graphics has a selection of drawn bullets. Selecting one of these options will apply that bullet type to every level of the outline, so you will need to add any refinements manually using the final two tabs in the dialog box (Figure 5-21).

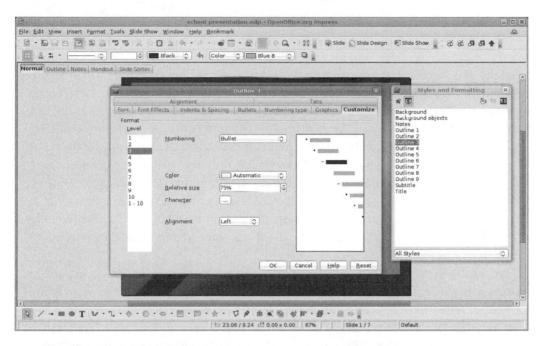

**Figure 5-20.** *The bullets in Impress are based on the same Styles and Formatting system used elsewhere. Everything can be edited.*

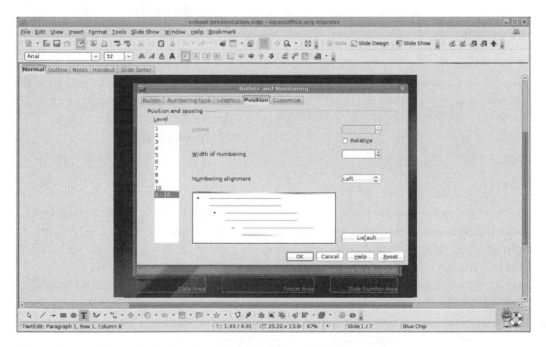

**Figure 5-21.** *Bullets can also be edited manually on the slide master.*

The first of the manual tabs—Position—allows for the relative horizontal positioning of each level of the outline, and this will be represented in the currently used measurement system: cm, mm, feet and inches, points, etc. To edit a position, choose a number from the pane on the left to see the current settings on the right. There are two elements to edit here. The first is Indent, which sets the distance of the element from the left edge of the slide. Click the Relative radio button to see this value relative to the position of its parent. The value can be increased or decreased using the up/down arrow widget. The second editable part sets the distance between the bullet and the beginning of the text. With both of these options it is probably wise to be consistent in spacing, because an inconsistent list can look unprofessional. It's also worth noting that the default settings have been designed to look good. Maybe it would be a good idea to leave them alone!

More extensive editing is available under the Customize tab. Here it's possible to set individual bullets per outline level, import graphics, and add additional characters to numbered or lettered lists.

To configure an individual bullet, select the outline level from the left-hand pane and then, in the Numbering drop-down list, select Bullet. Options available when editing a bullet include Color (selecting Automatic here will make the bullet the same color as the text), relative size, and character. Relative size defines the size of the bullet in relation to the font size of the text; for example, 50% would display a bullet that is half of the font height of the paragraph it is leading off. The Character button will launch the OO.o character selector, where it's possible to choose from a variety of type elements, or glyphs, to use as a bullet. The original list from this master slide used a combination of dots and dashes, but there are many other glyphs included in many typefaces. Just scroll down the list, select a character, and click OK.

It is entirely possible to specify a different character for each part of the outline, but beware—doing this will probably make your slide look horrible. Less is more, and, as with fonts in a word-processing document, any more than two or, in extreme cases, three will overpower the slide and will only make things more confusing. To set the same bullet across the entire list, select the 1-9 option in the Level pane on the right.

## Numbered Lists

Impress (and the rest of the suite) can accommodate many different number/letter types, including Roman numerals (upper- or lowercase), alphanumeric pairs, and letter forms, from any languages included in the installation. To change the unordered list (with bullets) to an ordered list (with numbers), click into the Numbering drop-down and select one of the number options from the list. Again, it's possible to select individual formats for each level—which might be useful, for example, if the first level uses 1, 2, 3, etc.; the second level uses a, b, c; and third uses i, ii, iii—or by selecting 1-9 in the Level pane to configure all levels at the same time.

With any alphanumeric system chosen, a couple of new options will appear in the dialog box. In addition to Color and Relative Size, there is Before and After, which provides an option for adding a prefix or suffix character to each number—for instance, to make numbers look like 1.), 2.), 3.), etc., we'd add .) to the After box—and a "Start at" option, which is useful if you hate the number "1" and would like to start your lists at "2," "3," or "50,000" (Figure 5-22). It goes without saying that consecutive list items of the same level will increase by 1.

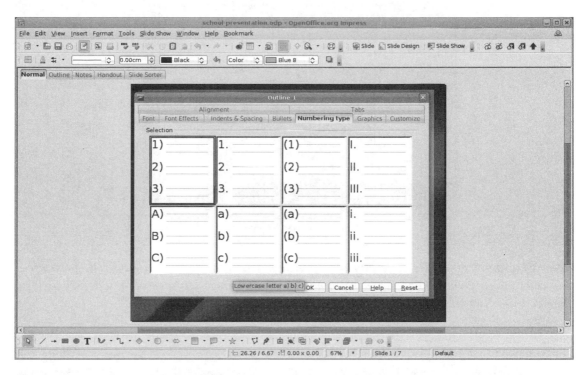

**Figure 5-22.** *Numbers can be formatted using a variety of options, including standard digits, Roman numerals, and alphabetical options.*

## Graphical Bullets

The third type of bullet is simply an image used in place of a number or symbol. In practice, this is likely to be something small and distinct, such as a pinhead, a chalk mark, or a pearl, rather than something complex, such as a photo of a sunset, that will lose all detail when rendered in a 16 × 16 pixel space.

Adding a graphical bullet is similar to adding an image to the page, and it can be done—as earlier—on a single-level basis or for everything, though even simple pinheads and chalk marks will lose legibility well before they get to level 9, so it may be worth using these elaborate bullets only for the top couple of levels.

In the Numbering drop-down, select Graphics (Figure 5-23). Then click Select ➤ From File to launch the normal file browser and pick an image or click Select ➤ Gallery to see a list of all the available graphical bullets on the system.

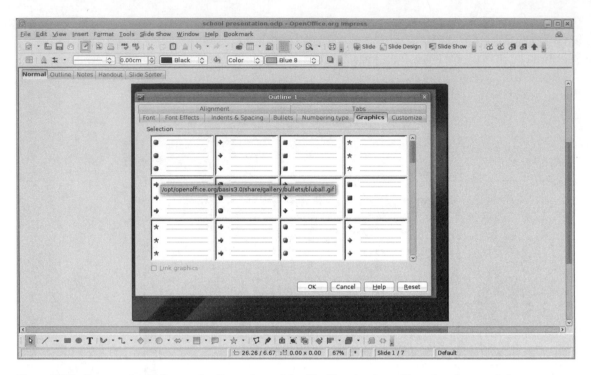

**Figure 5-23.** *Impress includes a selection of graphical bullets in the gallery, but be careful to ensure that your choices complement any backgrounds. Hover the cursor over a selection to see where it is stored on your system.*

## ADDING GRAPHICAL BULLETS TO THE GALLERY

There are two ways to add images to the bullet gallery.

- Manually add an image to the appropriate folder using the file browser. To identify the location of the gallery folder, hover the cursor over a location in the gallery viewer. Click Tools ➤ Gallery to launch the gallery pane.

- The easier option is to drag and drop new elements into the gallery. Images can be dragged from anywhere on the computer system or, with appropriate restrictions and rights, from any web site. The pictures will be stored in the usual gallery location and thus can be edited at a later date if necessary.

Once the graphical bullet is loaded into the system, a few more options will become enabled. These define the height and width of the graphic; use the up/down widgets to increase or decrease the size, and click Keep ratio to prevent the image from becoming distorted.

### Text Areas

The last job is to edit the color and font of the Footer, Date, and Slide Number sections. Once you've completed these edits, this master slide is finished, so click the Close Master Slide button in the master slide toolbox.

## Save As a Template

In order to avoid having to go through this process again later, you're going to save the currently loaded presentation (complete with master slide) as a template (Figure 5-24). Click File ➤ Templates ➤ Save, select MyTemplates as the location for the file, and provide a name. Because you've used the correct method for saving a template, rather than simply saving it in the template format in some random place, the new visual style is available from the Master Slides task pane, meaning it's possible to apply it to any presentation in the future with a single click.

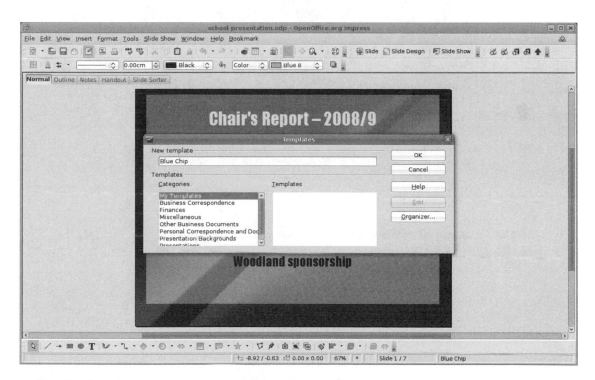

**Figure 5-24.** *Save the document as a template so that it can be reused later.*

More importantly, once the template is loaded, you can go back into the Master Slide section (View ➤ Master ➤ Master Slide) and make a few changes, such as adding a new background, adjusting the fonts a little, and adding a simple image (note that Impress respects any transparency in PNG files) to create a completely different template/theme that can be saved to MyTemplates for later use. Figure 5-25 uses a pair of sunflower images (released by VJ Flicks and Crossing Sparks under a Creative Commons license) to change the total look of the slides. Once you've saved this, it also becomes available for use via the Master Slides section in the Task Pane.

**Figure 5-25.** *The transition from blue chip business to happy hippy took just a few clicks.*

■**Note** The images in Figure 5-25 can be found at www.flickr.com/photos/vj_flicks/382313642/ and www.flickr.com/photos/sparkys/379806096/.

## MULTIPLE MASTERS

Each slide in a presentation can have one and only one master slide associated with it. However, it is entirely possible to have multiple master slides throughout the presentation. If you simply click on one of the entries in the master slide pane, then that will be applied automatically to every slide in the presentation. By right-clicking the appropriate master slide it is possible to select Apply to All Select Slides. In the ordinary slide view (with the Normal tab selected) this will apply the new master slide to the currently viewed slide. But if you went into the Slide Sorter section and selected a range of slides using the Shift+Click or Ctrl+Click method described previously, it's possible to apply a new template to, for example, a section of slides, leaving the rest untouched.

This method can be useful to change the tone of your presentation. For example, you might begin talking about sales figures for the first third of the show, but the second third could be about corporate social responsibility, which might warrant a different style. The last third may move back to a more hard-nosed business look.

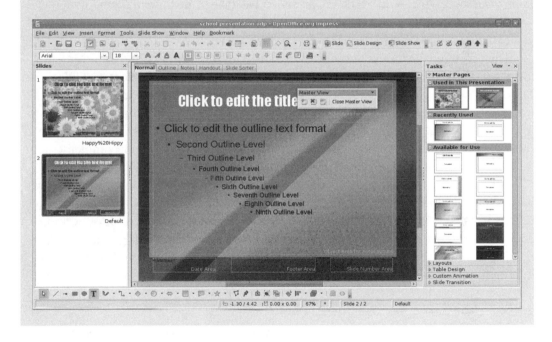

## The Show Must Go On

At this point you have defined the structure of a presentation without any thought to the visuals; and in the master slide, you have designed the visual elements without taking the real content of the presentation into account. It's now time to combine these two elements to create a beautiful, compelling, and, most importantly, informative presentation.

In this section you'll refine the content in relation to the look, add a few dramatic but subtle effects, and prepare everything for the final delivery. It's this last part that tends to be the most nerve-wracking, so you'll use every tool at your disposal to make sure that everything is prepared and that the presentation runs smoothly. But first, let's get everything looking right.

## Transitions

You have the content on the slides, but this may need some editing. The good news is that, though everything so far is based on automated styles and formatting, it's possible to go into individual slides and make edits to the text you added in the outline, add and remove parts, introduce extra images, and basically make sure each slide works individually. It's worth taking your time over this because too much information in a slide can overwhelm an audience whereas too little makes the slide seem pointless unless it contains something vital about which the presenter will take some time to speak.

Let's assume that you've refined each slide so that it does all the work it needs to and you can move on to the dynamic elements of the slideshow.

The first thing to tackle is how one slide transitions into the next, and for this a warning is necessary: Impress features lots of transitions—to see them all, select the Slide Transition heading in the Task Pane—and any one of these can be applied to the entire presentation, to a selection of slides, or individually. As with fonts and bullet types, throwing a mass of transitions into a presentation looks unprofessional and can sometimes lead to tedious pauses in the delivery. Generally it's wise to stick to a couple of complementary transitions to create meaning, remembering to tailor them to your audience.

For example, we could use a fast and smooth fade (called Fade Smoothly in Impress) between most slides—which is quite classy—but add something a bit more obvious, such as Dissolve or a Wipe, to move between sections of the presentation. This lets the audience know you're moving on to a new topic. Wipe and Push transitions give a sense of rising or falling (using Wipe/Push Up or Down, respectively), which could be useful for reinforcing a sales or costs message.

---

■**Note** Transitions have three elements: the slide at the beginning of the transition (A), the one at the end (B), and the transition itself.

---

To add a transition to a single slide, select the B slide from either the Slide Pane or the Slide Sorter window (Figure 5-26). You're defining how this slide should appear. Ensure that the Slide Transition section is displayed in the Task Pane, and choose the appropriate transition from the long list. At the bottom of this pane is a radio button marked Automatic Preview; with this selected, clicking a transition from the list will launch a quick preview of it in the main window.

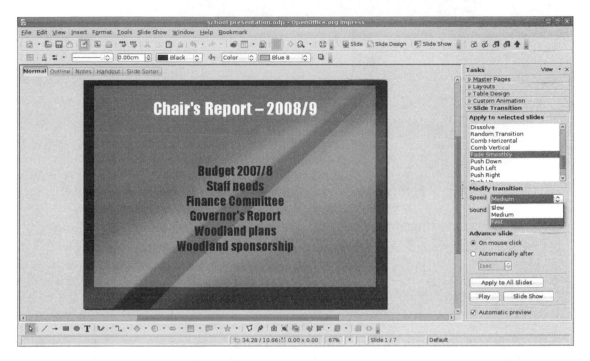

**Figure 5-26.** *Impress has a lot of flashy transitions to move you smoothly from one slide to another. Use them with care, and think about how fast they should be.*

Once you have selected a transition, a few more options will be enabled. Speed changes the amount of time it takes the transition to complete and has three options: Fast, Medium, and Slow. Changes to this element should be made with the final "playback" computer in mind, and the default—in case you end up with a wheezy old Pentium 4—should be "Fast."

The second option allows the addition of a sound to the transition, and Impress comes with a small selection of sounds to cover various uses (Figure 5-27). If none of these suit your needs, select Other Sound from the drop-down list, and use the file browser to add more sounds. It has to be said that sound in presentations often goes horribly wrong unless there is a really good reason to include it, so use sound with caution. Really good reasons might include adding some descriptive narration or background audio for an unattended kiosk presentation and embedding some sound that is to be discussed in the presentation. Once you've chosen a sound, the Loop option becomes available, which will replay the sound from a slide until a new sound is played (e.g., with the next transition) or until <stop previous sound> is added to a transition. You might use this, for example, to create atmosphere; to talk about the company's strong environmental record to the looped sound of birdsong, or to introduce the Employee of the Month with the sound of canned applause.

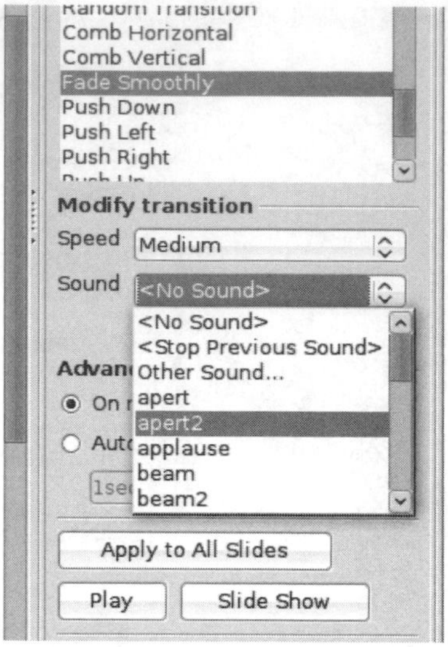

**Figure 5-27.** *You can add sounds to individual slides or animation elements.*

The last definable option in this Task Pane is the Advance Slide section, which has two options: Advance on mouse click (or spacebar press) or Automatically after a certain time. The former is the standard option because it gives the presenter more control over how the presentation is delivered, but the latter could be useful for displaying a selection of images or slides under a well-rehearsed part of the delivery. Even more usefully, this option can help you create slideshows designed to be played automatically without the assistance of a speaker, such as advertising or information slideshows displayed in a company's reception area or foyer—this might even be a good chance to employ a few more of the snazzy transitions.

The final set of options allow you to apply the transition to every slide in the presentation and to audition an individual slide or the whole presentation from this point forward.

To remove a transition from a slide (or slides), select it and then choose No Transition from the drop-down list.

## Multiple Slides

Earlier, when you were moving slides around, you used the Slide Sort tab and a combination of Shift+Click and Ctrl+Click to select a range of slides. With this method it's possible to apply the same transition to a number of slides without having to do everything individually (Figure 5-28). Simply select the slides that need to be configured, and then choose the transition from the list. All edits you make when multiple slides are selected will be applied to all of them, but it's important to remember that these are B slides, which will appear at the end of the transition.

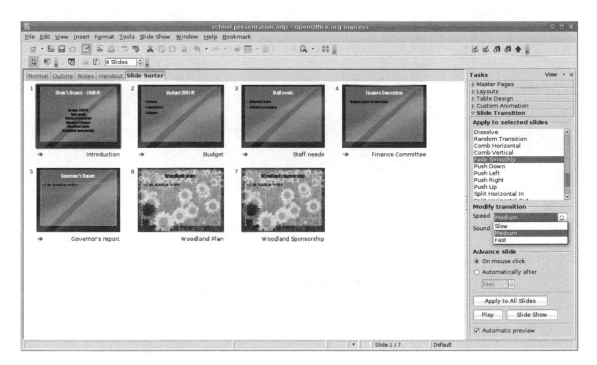

**Figure 5-28.** *Use the Slide Sorter window to apply transitions to lots of slides at once.*

## Custom Animations

While transitions define how each slide appears, a custom animation can specify how each element—a picture, paragraph, or bullet point—appears on a slide. And like transitions it's quite easy to get carried away with the possibilities and turn a rational slideshow into a mad confection of effects that takes twice as long to deliver as the presenter has, waiting for each bullet point to lurch around the screen before falling into place.

You'll take a more sane approach and, again, try to create something classy and targeted that can reinforce a message rather than confuse things (Figure 5-29).

Builds can serve to animate the appearance of any element on a slide, but you'll start with a list. Navigate to a slide with a list on it, and use the mouse to select the list elements. In the Task Pane, select the Custom Animation heading to reveal the build tools. Under the Modify heading, select Add to open the tabbed configuration dialog box.

Impress is able to handle four different types of animation: Entrance, Emphasis, Exit, and Motion Path.

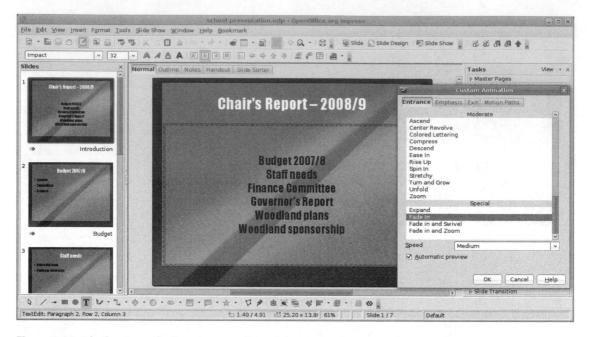

**Figure 5-29.** *The basic goal of a custom animation is to make parts of a slide appear in sequence, though they can serve other purposes.*

### Entrance

This defines how an element appears on the slide and features options similar to transitions, such as fades, swipes, wipes, and spins. This selection is divided into sections covering basic, exciting, moderate, and special transitions (Figure 5-30). Most of the choices here will see the speed option enabled, but further editing is available later.

This is the most used animation, so let's start with it. Choose one of the options from the animation list (the figure shows a fade to follow the rest of the presentation) and click OK. This selection has three list items, and clicking Preview will show that all three points appear at once. Look into the Effect schedule box. It should have three entries, each prefixed with a transition icon (a diamond with some lines coming off the left side). However, the first one will have an additional mouse icon on it denoting that this element will appear on a mouse click. The other two parts have been set to appear at the same time as the first bullet. To change this, right-click the element and choose Start on Click. The other options in here can be used to make the element appear after the previous point (select Start After Previous and see the clock icon appear, and then set the time of the appearance using the Timing menu entry).

Set the third element as well to Start on Click, and then click the Play button to audition the whole slide.

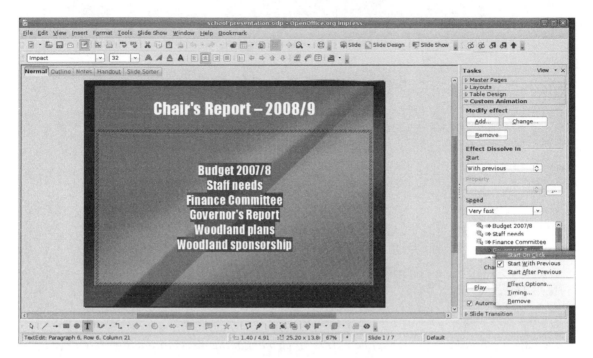

**Figure 5-30.** *Configure the parts to appear one by one. By default all text frames will appear together, so choose Start on Click in the drop-down list for each paragraph.*

Underneath the animation schedule is a pair of buttons you can use to change the order of the effects. These don't change the order of the points on the slide, just the order in which the effects are enacted, so be careful when using them.

## Emphasis

This option serves to highlight one section of a slide and would usually be applied once all of the pieces of text had appeared. In our example, we've set each bullet point to appear on a click, and then the fourth click turns the middle point bright yellow. Under the Emphasis tab (Figure 5-31), select Change Font Color and click OK. It's now possible, using the central part of the Task Pane (now labeled Effect Change Font Color) to select the right color using the drop-down list and to change the speed of the effect. Other options, including adding sound, defining a postanimation effect (such as dimming the text), and setting how the effect should work, are available by clicking the button next to the color list.

Note that the icon next to the element in the effects schedule will change to show that this part has an emphasis effect applied.

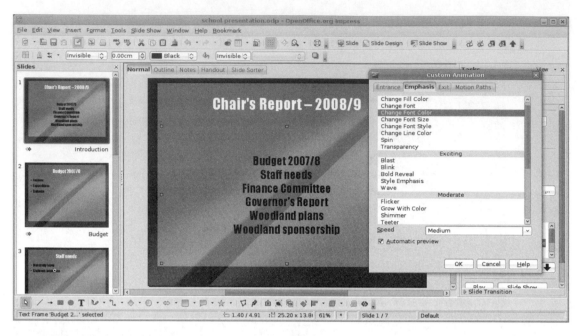

**Figure 5-31.** *Use Emphasis to highlight a particular element in the presentation after it has been added to the slide.*

### Exit

This sets up the method for each part of the slide to disappear. The available options are pretty much the same as for the Entrance tab, but done in reverse. Exit animations are less likely to be employed in professional presentations, but they do have their uses, for example, when fading one piece of text out while fading the next one in. Creating this kind of effect involves simply getting the launch sequence right. To do this with our three-element list would involve the following.

1. Set part one to fade in On Click.

2. Set part two to fade in On Click.

3. Set part one to fade out With Previous.

4. Set part three to fade in On Click.

5. Set part two to fade out With Previous.

6. Set part three to fade out On Click.

Elements with an exit effect will have a different icon in the effect schedule—the line stream to the right rather than the left.

## Motion Path

With this option it's possible to add specific motion to an object; for example, an image of a cloud could float from one side of a slide to the other (Figure 5-32). As with the other effects, it is possible to set motion paths to begin with a mouse click, automatically, or in tandem with another element.

**Figure 5-32.** *The cloud is one of the standard shapes available via the Drawing toolbar. We've added a transparent gradient so that it doesn't obscure the content too much.*

There is a selection of premade paths available via the drop-down list, but you're going to use the freeform path (Figure 5-33). This allows you to draw a path across the slide and then have the object follow that path. For example, you might make the cloud shape appear from the left and drift lazily around one part of the slide before floating off the right edge of the screen. To do this, select the object to be animated (which could be a frame, text element, illustration, or photo), click Add in the Modify Effect section, and choose Motion Paths ➤ Freeform Paths and then click OK. The cursor should now be a crosshair, allowing you to draw the path the object should follow. You can begin this shape outside the boundaries of the slide so that when the slide is shown initially, the cloud won't be visible.

As with other animation elements, there are various options, such as the speed and the launch method for this effect. And it's just as important to use this feature with care because it's very easy to create something tacky if effects are overused or are unsuitable for the audience (Figure 5-34).

**Figure 5-33.** *A selection of paths is included in the application, but it's also possible to create a completely freeform path for an object to follow.*

**Figure 5-34.** *You should use animation with care. The primary reason for any presentation is to impart information clearly and in a form suitable to the audience.*

# Notes and Handouts

So far we've focused on parts of the presentation that are actually designed to be seen by the audience. But Impress makes it easy to assemble the bits that are supposed to be hidden, allowing the presenter to stay in control and deliver a smooth pitch.

Notes are an important part of the production process because they can be associated with a single slide and will move with it if later you reorder the presentation. To add a note, select a slide and click the Notes tab in the main window. The display will show the current slide at the top, with a space for notes at the bottom (Figure 5-35). Click in this space and begin typing the note.

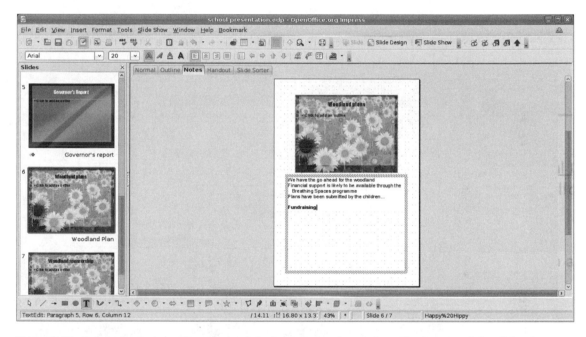

**Figure 5-35.** *Printed notes can be very useful when you're presenting. The image of the slide above the notes means the presenter can engage with the audience rather than looking around at the projection screen.*

When you create notes, the Formatting toolbar works in exactly the same way as the ordinary text formatting toolbar in Writer (because that's what it is), meaning that all the normal word-processing tools are available, including different fonts, type sizes, styles, and paragraph options.

It's possible to change the arrangement of the notes slide by clicking View ➤ Master ➤ Notes Master and editing the layout, just as we did for the slide master earlier. Moreover, it's possible to create new masters for notes pages.

Impress handouts simply display thumbnails of the presentation slides, and these can be handed out—before or after the presentation—to give the audience a copy of the presentation to take away, which might save their making notes. To design the handout sheets, click the Handouts tab and use the Task Pane to define the layout of each page. There are layouts that include 1, 2, 4, 6, or 9 slides, plus an option to include 3 slides and a few notes.

You can print out notes and handouts by clicking File ➤ Print and selecting the appropriate option from the Print Content drop-down (Figure 5-36). When you choose Notes, each slide will be printed out onto a single page, with the notes beneath; choosing Handouts will enable a few options, allowing you to define how many slides should be included on each page.

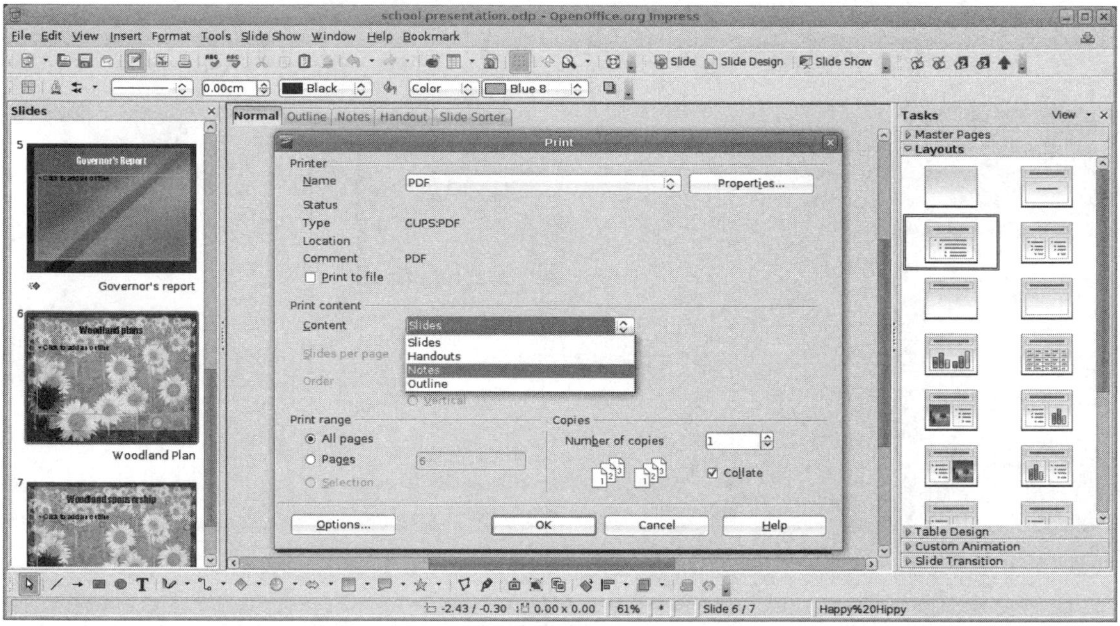

**Figure 5-36.** *Use the Print Content system to output parts of the slideshow selectively.*

**Tip** Presenter notes are really useful and deserve some attention. Firstly, they can contain more information than the slide itself; so a slide might say, "Sales increased 21% in 2008," whereas the notes might break the figures down into regions, quarters, or individual sales teams. In this way, the presenter introduces the subject of the sales increase with the slide and then adds detail for the audience with the notes. Secondly, having notes in her or his hand is likely to give the presenter a little more confidence about the information to impart and could stop her or him from simply reading out the slide contents in full.

# Output

You have designed and programmed the slideshow, assembled the notes, and printed out handouts. The final task is to get everything ready to deliver; how you approach this depends very much on how the presentation is to be given (Figure 5-37).

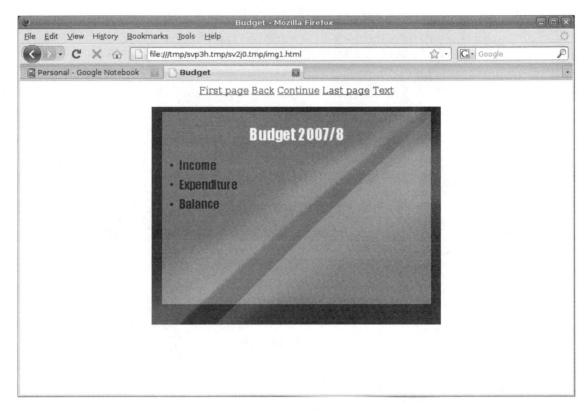

**Figure 5-37.** *The Preview in Browser option (under the File menu) is a great way to see your presentation as a potential web viewer would experience it.*

## Native Format

The best solution is to be able to deliver the Impress slideshow via Impress, which means simply saving the document to a USB drive or a laptop hard disk ready to be opened and played through OpenOffice.org. In this instance, the only things to be aware of—especially if the move from one machine to another also means a move to a different operating system—is that fonts you've used may be unavailable on the other machine. The best way to avoid this is to stick with just a few well-known fonts (Times New Roman, Arial, Verdana, etc.) that are available on all the operating systems supported by OpenOffice.org. Then, if you need to use some fancy font for a heading, make the heading as an image and import it into Impress. The other thing to remember is that if you're likely to edit the presentation later and you have linked images, save those images too in the same directory as the presentation.

## PowerPoint

Fortune favors the prepared, and if your laptop dies (along with the only version of OO.o in the room), a backup of the presentation in PowerPoint format is going to be a lifesaver. Click File ➤ Save as and choose Microsoft PowerPoint 97/2000/XP (*.ppt) from the File type drop-down. Impress has good and comprehensive support, but the transition from one application to another can never be guaranteed problem-free, so it would be useful to check whether the presentation works as expected if you're delivering something on which your life depends (Figure 5-38).

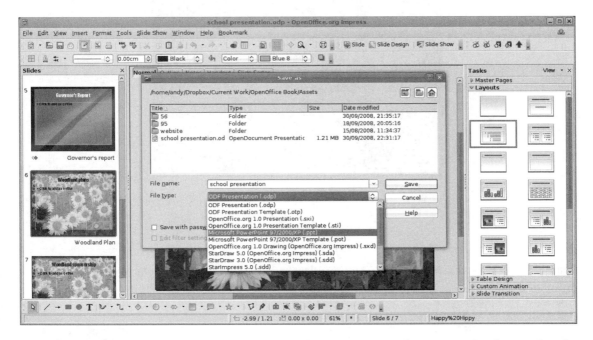

**Figure 5-38.** *Most people experience few problems when exporting to the PowerPoint format. But the more complex the presentation, the more likely it is that problems will be introduced.*

## Self-Contained Package

Outputting the presentation as a self-contained package makes both a useful backup (in case neither Impress nor PowerPoint is available) and a great way of distributing the production either on CD or via the Web. The File ➤ Export dialog box has options to export as a Flash (*.swf) file, as HTML, and various other formats, including as a series of images.

With any of these methods you will lose the transitions and builds included in the presentation, which limits their usefulness a little, but they're a great way of making backups that will run just about anywhere.

## PDF

Impress also features a native Export to PDF filter, which gets its own entry in the list because it's so useful and has so many options (Figure 5-39). To activate it, click File ➤ Export as PDF to see the multitabbed Export dialog box. The first tab allows you to define exactly what is exported (all pages or a range, e.g., 1-6), how images are compressed, and the general PDF options. It's safe to leave most of these as they are. However, if you're e-mailing a large presentation, it might be worthwhile increasing the compression on the images and reducing the image resolution by clicking the appropriate button and setting the value to 72dpi. This is the resolution of most screens. If you've imported any large photos, it shouldn't make too much difference to the view, but it will have a major impact on the file size. Next look under the User Interface tab and ensure that Use transition effects is selected. This will attempt to render the Impress effects with their PDF counterparts.

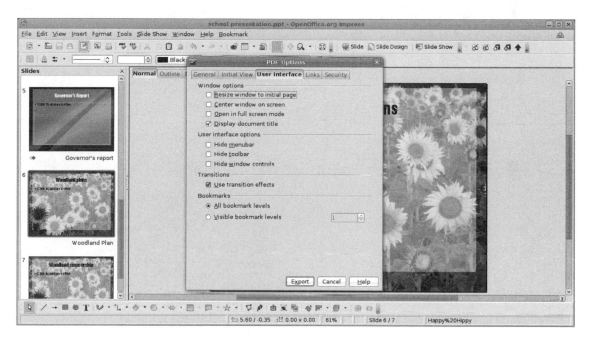

**Figure 5-39.** *PDF is a great option when cross-platform support and document fidelity are important.*

If you're sending something sensitive via e-mail, it's also possible to set a password for a PDF under the Security tab, or change the permissions so it's impossible to print, alter, or even copy any of the content. See Chapter 9 for more on security and sharing.

# Recap

In this chapter you have used OO.o Impress to create a multislide presentation. In the process you looked at the method of building and editing themes, adding themes from other locations and software, and designing the slides themselves. You also added some dynamic effects to the presentation using both slide transitions and animations, and you looked briefly at tools available to make presenting from OO.o a little less nerve-wracking. Finally, you examined the most common output options available for delivering the presentation and distributing it to a wider audience.

There's a little more on Impress, specifically adding tables and spreadsheets to a slideshow, in Chapter 10; we'll also return to the subject of third-party templates briefly in Chapter 10.

# CHAPTER 6

# Creative Draw

OpenOffice.org Draw is commonly seen as one of the peripheral applications in the suite, and yet it's a very capable piece of design software, as well as being a great addition to the package. Draw can handle most design tasks—with the obvious exception of heavy photographic editing—and can be used either as an integral part of the suite or as a stand-alone application (see Figure 6-1).

Draw's core strength is arranging shapes on a page. Just as Writer is used to arrange words into a coherent whole, so Draw can take primitive shapes and other elements and allow you to turn them into a coherent visual product. These shapes may be genuine shapes such as squares, circles, and stars that can be created within the application; more complex items such as curves, spirals, letters, and numbers; and even shapes that are filled with other objects, including photographs, longer passages of text, and spreadsheet tables. Although there are some limited photographic editing tools in the package (they're the same as those you've already encountered in Writer and Impress), Draw is more comparable to something like CorelDraw, Adobe Illustrator, and Visio (for diagrams) than Photoshop or Microsoft Paint.

In this chapter, you'll undertake two projects and a couple of side projects to explore the major tools at your disposal in Draw. The first project is a poster for an event, from which you'll learn the process of building up a complex image using layers, objects, text, and imported images. The methods used will apply to almost any "single-sheet" design job, from a book jacket or advertisement to a business card or flyer; only the dimensions of the page and, perhaps, the amount of content will be significantly different. The second project is a flow chart, which will show you the various object connectors available. This project can be adapted to create everything from network diagrams, organizational charts, and web site maps to process diagrams and family trees.

One of the reasons, perhaps, that Draw is marginalized slightly in OO.o is that, in contrast to a word processor or spreadsheet, it might be seen as a piece of "creative" rather than "productivity" software. In fact, the entire OO.o suite should be approached in a creative manner, and using Draw as an integral part of the productivity workflow can lead to more sophisticated and satisfying work, even with the spreadsheet!

**Figure 6-1.** *Draw is capable of a wide range of design tasks, including posters, floor plans, mind maps, and organizational charts.*

When first launched, the interface of Draw resembles Impress as a Page pane accompanies the main work window. Any new pages added to the document are shown here, which makes navigation easy, but because this project is a single-sheet design, you can dismiss this window by clicking the X in its top-right corner. This maximizes the workspace too. (To get the Page pane back later, look under the View menu.)

The interface follows the typical menus/toolbars approach with the standard toolbar at the top of the window and a context-sensitive Formatting toolbar beneath it. By default, the main window is bordered at the top and left by rulers with divisions set using the default measurement method. At the base of the workspace are two additions: page/layer navigation tools and a series of icons that represent the various "primitives" that Draw is able to use when creating an illustration.

As with the other applications, toolbars can be turned on and off using the View ➤ Toolbars menu—currently enabled toolbars have a check mark—and can also be detached from the interface completely by clicking and dragging the separator (six dots arranged vertically) away from the edge of the interface (see Figure 6-2). They can be refixed by dragging the now detached toolbar to any edge of the interface, where they will dock. Undocked toolbars can be resized and shaped by clicking and dragging any edge just like most other windows on your screen. The icons inside the toolbar will be rearranged to fit the space, and any leftovers will be available via a disclosure arrow at the bottom or far right of the toolbar.

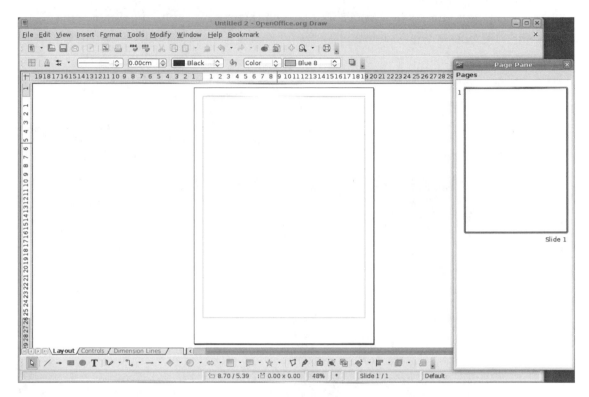

**Figure 6-2.** *Many parts of the interface can be switched on or off to reconfigure the workspace.*

# Setting Up a Page

The page settings in Draw are really important because they determine the size and shape of the final output. This might sound obvious, but illustrations may be used in different settings so it's important to take this into account. For example, an image designed for a CD cover may be destined to be printed on a standard A4 inkjet printer, so it makes sense to think about whether to set up the page with CD cover dimensions, or create an A4 page and then section off a part with the CD dimensions.

The page options are available via Format ➤ Page. In the Page Setup dialog box that appears, the first tab allows you to set up the height, width, and margins of the page, and there is a range of standard sizes such as A4, DL, and Letter available in the Format drop-down list (see Figure 6-3). To create a page that doesn't conform to these sizes, such as a business card, enter the sizes in the Width and Height boxes. The Format drop-down list will display User.

On the bottom right are the options to define the page numbering system, but you can safely ignore that for this project.

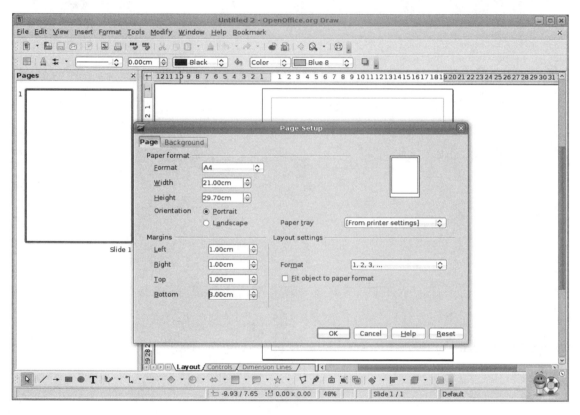

**Figure 6-3.** *The Page Setup box is where you define the dimensions and layout of the basic page. The drop-down list contains a range of standard formats.*

The Background tab provides an opportunity to define the very base layer of the image, and this can be set using a plain color, a gradient, a hatching pattern, or a bitmap. You might set a particular color background, for example, if the final product is destined to be printed on colored card stock or paper, whereas you can use the bitmap option to add a watermark image to the piece or simply to add some background art.

# Layers

One of the things that gives illustration and design software its great power is the ability to situate parts of the production on different layers and then make individual layers visible or printable.

It's sometimes best to think of these layers as individual transparent pages that can be stacked on top of one another and reordered. They make it possible to create an advertisement for both the American and Japanese markets in the same document, for example. The underlying imagery might remain the same, but the textual elements of the ad can be split across layers—English on one layer, Japanese on the other—and these can be switched off or on at the moment of output. Or you can try out different image and headline combinations on various layers without having to worry about scrapping work. More simply, you can build a design over these layers and edit parts without affecting other parts.

Every Draw project starts out with three layers already active, and these are accessible from the tabs at the base of the main window (see Figure 6-4). The layers are persistent and cannot be deleted, although you can edit their appearance somewhat.

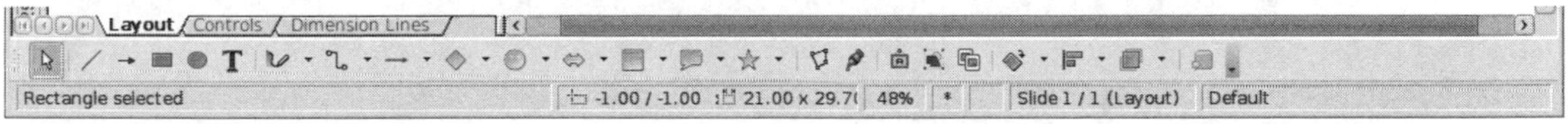

**Figure 6-4.** *The three initial layers in any Draw document are fixed, but you can hide them.*

## Layout

The *Layout layer* is the default content layer for any Draw project. That is, any object created in a project appears on this layer unless new layers are created and selected. On simple projects, you may not go beyond using this single layer, but because the example design is quite complex, you'll be using additional layers later on.

## Controls

The *Controls layer* is where Draw's various form controls are located, and you'll return to these later on.

## Dimension Lines

The *Dimension Lines layer* inevitably contains dimension lines, which are lines that display their length as a label. Dimension lines are a special class of object available in the Lines and Arrows section of the Drawing toolbar. Select this from the available icons, and then click and drag out a line. Hold down the Shift key while dragging to force the line into horizontal, 45-degree, or vertical (depending on which angle you're closest to) position. After the mouse is released, a line is drawn with arrows and shorter lines on the ends, and this will be labeled with the line's length (see Figure 6-5). Right-click the label at the bottom of the window, and select Character to change the font and size.

**Figure 6-5.** *Dimension lines are useful when working on designs that need to translate into the real world.*

Right-clicking on any of the three layer tabs at the bottom of the window launches a context-sensitive menu containing three options. The Insert layer option adds a new layer to the top of the stack, the Modify option launches the Layer Configuration dialog box, and the Paste option pastes the contents of the OO.o clipboard into the layer.

The Modify option is where you can edit the status of the layer. In the default layers, this means giving the layer a title, which isn't displayed, and defining whether each is Visible, Printable, or Locked. Visible and Printable set whether the contents of the layer will be seen onscreen or on paper, while Locked prevents accidental editing of the contents.

Despite the minimal options, this system is very useful. For example, imagine a designer has sent you a rough layout as a .jpg file. This could be inserted into the Layout layer—which would then be set as Visible and Locked but not Printable—then a new layer could be created on which to "trace" the design using Draw's native tools.

User-added layers have a few extra entries in this menu (as described next).

## Add and Edit Layers

In this project, you'll use the Layout layer as a background, use a second layer to contain top-level graphical elements, and use the third for text. You can add a fourth layer for separate text, but that's not needed just yet. You'll start by creating this three-layer structure. Add a new layer to a page, right-click any of the available layer tabs, and select Insert Layer. Give the new layer a name (e.g., Graphics), and click OK (see Figure 6-6). A new tab is added to the interface with the provided name. Do the same again, creating a layer labeled something like Text 1. Note also that when there are too many tabs to fit the space provided, the navigation icons become active. These icons (from left to right) select the First, Previous, Next, and Last layers.

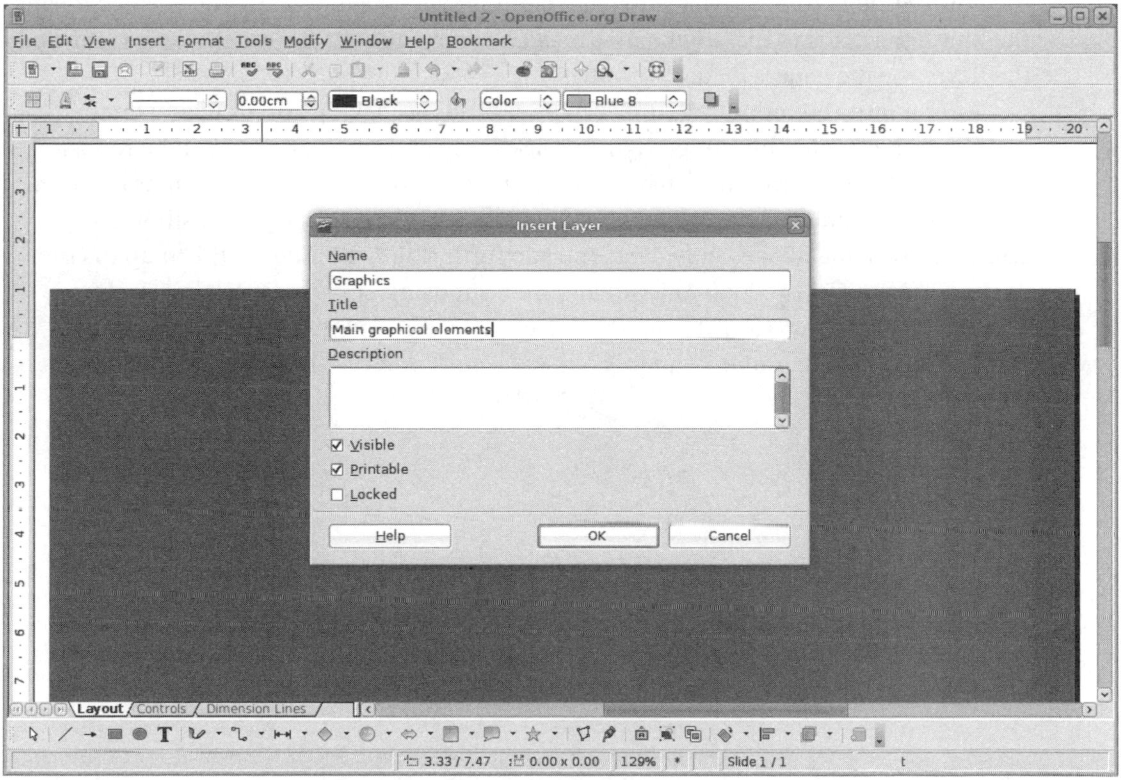

**Figure 6-6.** *Make as many layers as needed but name them sensibly to avoid having to hunt for the object later on. The Name element appears in the tab navigation space, but the other elements are useful for organizational purposes—especially if other people are likely to work on the document.*

If you right-click any of these new layers, the menu will contain the Modify, Insert, and Paste options, in addition to Delete Layer and Rename Layer entries.

The bottom layer contains some visual structure, so ensure the Layout tab is selected, and begin to add some content.

The first element you need is a simple rectangle, which is added by selecting the rectangle tool from the Drawing toolbar, and then clicking and dragging from the top left of the page to the bottom right. For this example project, this foundation object is colored pale yellow by selecting this entry from the area color drop-down list on the Formatting toolbar.

# Bitmap Images

The second element in this project is a series of four photographs ranged across the bottom of the page. Draw handles bitmap images in the same way as Writer; pictures are imported using the Insert ➤ Picture ➤ From file. This launches a standard file browser, allowing you to navigate to the image, select it, and import it with the OK button. Select the Link option before importing to tie the imported image to the original—which means that any edits made to the original image in an editor such as Photoshop will be reflected the next time the page is loaded in Draw.

After images are imported, they can be resized by clicking and dragging on the resize handles (hold Shift to retain the image's aspect ratio), and they can be repositioned by grabbing anywhere inside the images and dropping them on a new location. The various default snap options can make it difficult to get accurate position and size when resizing images, however. You can fix this by switching off the Snap to Grid option (View ➤ Grid ➤ Snap to Grid) and then choosing Tools ➤ Options, selecting OpenOffice.org Draw ➤ Grid from the section selector, and then disabling all of the snap options. These options can, of course, be quite useful, so re-enable them later if you need them.

## NUMBERS VS. PIXELS

Computers typically use two different methods for displaying images, and each of these systems is useful for different jobs. The image types are bitmaps and vectors.

*Bitmaps* are the most common image type you're likely to encounter in daily life because they are the basis for digital photography, scanners, and most images found on the Internet. Bitmap images, which include JPGs, GIFs, and PNGs, are made up of a series of pixels with each pixel being defined in terms of its color. A 1024 × 768 image has more than 784,000 pixels in it, and each of these needs to be described individually, which means large bitmap images can take up a lot of space.

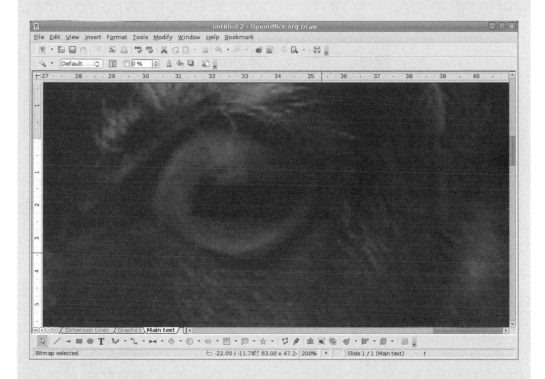

In contrast, a *vector* image is described in mathematical terms. A circle, for example, is described as "circle, 10cm in diameter, red." In addition to being much smaller files than bitmaps, vector images can also be scaled to any size without making the results look "blocky."

On the Picture toolbar—which appears when a bitmap is selected—the Crop image icon is on the far right. Click this to transform the resize handles into crop handles, and then drag these around to obscure parts of the image (see Figure 6-7). If an image is cropped and then resized, the cropping doesn't change, and holding the Shift key will retain the aspect ratio of the cropped image.

**Figure 6-7.** *Image cropping is totally non-destructive in Draw, which is great for experimenting with different layouts. Hold the Shift key to retain the aspect ratio of the original image as you crop.*

After the image collection has been cropped and sized appropriately, you can group them together, which makes moving them around easier, by selecting each one (use Shift-click to select multiple images) and then choosing Modify ➤ Group. The collection can now be moved or resized as though it were a single object (see Figure 6-8).

If you need to ungroup objects later to make large changes to an element, use Modify ➤ Ungroup. However, if you need to make just a few small changes to individual elements without ungrouping, use Modify ➤ Enter Group. Each part will then be selectable, and you can exit the group with Modify ➤ Exit Group or by double-clicking elsewhere on the page.

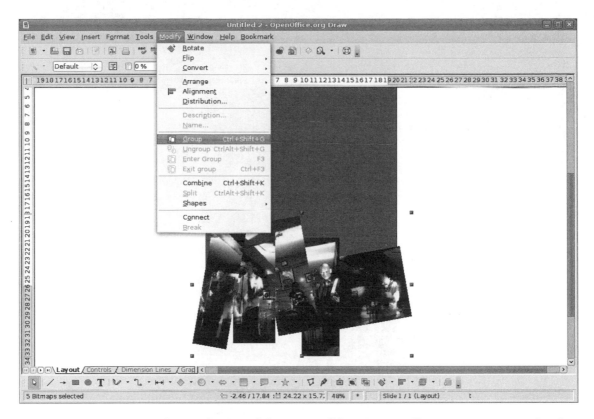

**Figure 6-8.** *Grouping together a selection of objects (Modify ➤ Group) allows you to move and resize them as one.*

The Picture toolbar also contains various options that allow you to transform the image to grayscale, change the image to black and white, apply a selection of filters, and change the alpha channel value of the image via a transparency widget.

# Objects

In Draw, the basic unit of content is an object, and tools are available to edit almost every aspect of an object. In addition to bringing in objects from external sources, such as images, text, and clip art, Draw has a large range of premade "primitive" shapes available with which to create original images, and a Fontwork applet to add graphical text to the production.

At the base of the page, a second thinner rectangle has been drawn about 1 centimeter high and covering the width of the page at the bottom (see Figure 6-9). Not only does this provide space for a piece of text later on, it also covers the slightly uneven positioning of the photographs.

**Figure 6-9.** *Add a second rectangle to the page using one of Draw's shapes. Many other shapes are available, including clouds, smiley faces, and various polygons. Use the small disclosure arrow next to an icon to see the available shapes.*

Just like objects in Writer or Impress and cell backgrounds in Calc, you can recolor any of the shapes that Draw is able to produce. Changing a solid color simply involves selecting the area fill drop-down list from the Formatting toolbar and applying a new color. More extensive options, including gradients and transparencies, are available through the Area button or the right-click ➤ Area menu option (see Figure 6-10).

A second rectangle has also been created to go at the top of the photos (see Figure 6-11), and the color of this rectangle has been changed to match the background color. Next, you'll add a wave to this shape to make it look a bit more interesting.

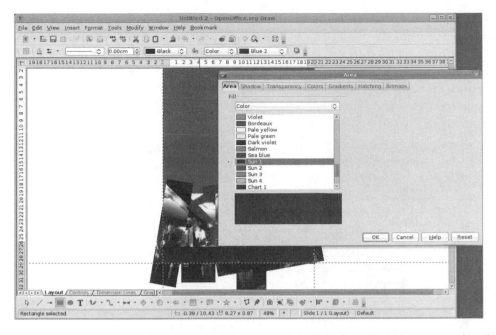

**Figure 6-10.** *Common color management across the suite of applications means familiarity in one part makes for efficiency in all of them. The colors you created in the previous chapter will also show up here if you're looking for a consistent look across documents.*

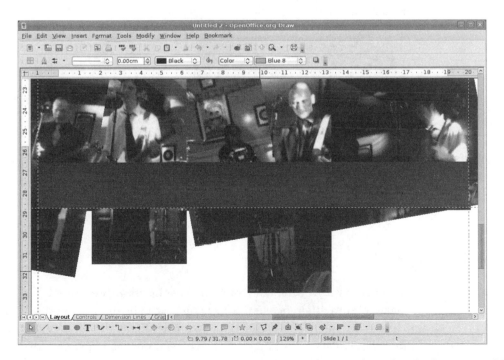

**Figure 6-11.** *Note that objects are always drawn over the top of previously drawn or added objects, so the rectangle covers the uneven edges of our photos.*

Once you've added a significant number of objects to a page, you'll find them much easier to select by using the Navigator. Open it via the compass icon on the toolbar, select the disclosure arrow labeled Slide 1, and see . . . nothing. Only named objects appear by default in the navigator in Draw, so get used to naming significant elements—right-click ➤ Name—to see them show up here (Figure 6-12). To see all unnamed elements, use the display icon (far right), and choose All Shapes.

**Figure 6-12.** *The Navigator is useful in the other applications, but it's absolutely essential in Draw when productions start to get complicated.*

# Curve Editing

In contrast to the bitmap images you've seen far, Draw's native objects are described mathematically. This makes quite a difference in the way objects can be manipulated. For example, a bitmap image of a blue circle is described in terms of the number of pixels in the x and y dimensions, that is, 640 × 640, and then each pixel is described in terms of its color using, usually, the red, green, blue (RGB) method. Bitmaps are also rectangular, so this image also describes the color of the pixels that make up the bounding rectangle. Resizing this object involves adding pixels to increase the size (and working out the colors of the new pixels) and removing pixels to make it smaller. All of these operations degrade the image.

The same blue rectangle created using Draw's method describes the shape (circle), dimensions (640 × 640), and color (blue). Resizing this object simply involves inputting different figures in the dimensions (or color, or shape), and because the image is built from these figures, there is no distortion or degradation in the result. In this way, a poster could be created in Draw using A4 dimensions and then be printed out at A2, A0, or even billboard size without the shapes or text being degraded. The image is always sharp, the edges well defined, and the colors displayed as expected.

With this in mind, select the second rectangle, and choose Modify ➤ Convert ➤ To Curve. The Edit Points toolbar appears onscreen, and the rectangle loses a few of its resize handles. Select the bottom-right resize handle, and note the new additions to the shape—a pair of circular handles on stalks that look like antennae. These are the curve control points. Clicking and dragging the horizontal control point up or down turns the previously straight line into a curve. The horizontal handle has been pulled upwards slightly to add a concave curve to the base of the shape. Next, select the left handle and move the new horizontal control point down slightly to create a wave shape (see Figure 6-13).

**Figure 6-13.** *Use the handles to edit the shape of the curve. This wave was created by pulling the left control point up and the right control point down.*

# The Edit Points Toolbar

The Edit Points toolbar contains the tools necessary to take primitive shapes and turn them into, well, anything you like. If you select any of the various shapes from the Drawing toolbar, draw onto the page, and right-click ➤ Convert ➤ To Curve/Polygon, the new shape displays its control points ready for editing. This toolbar has 11 tools available (see Figure 6-14).

**Figure 6-14.** *The Edit Points toolbar appears whenever you've selected an object that has editable curves.*

## Points

Click the Points button to close the Edit Points toolbar and return to normal editing. The resize handles will reappear as normal allowing you to move and resize the shape. To get back to shape editing and see the toolbar again, right-click, and select Edit Points.

## Move Points

Select the Move Points button to use the mouse to move the control points on the shape. Note that moving, for instance, a corner point of a rectangle will change the shape based on curves rather than straight lines, unless you select the Convert to Curve button (described a bit later). Holding the Shift key constrains movement to the horizontal or vertical planes.

## Add Points

Use the Add Points button to add new control points to an object. These points can then be configured to work on a polygonal (i.e., straight lines) or curved basis using the Convert to Curve button, described later, to create any shape. To actually create the new point, click anywhere on the outline of the object, and then move the new point. If you click and let go without dragging, no point is added. Clicking and dragging an existing control point with this button selected just moves that point.

## Delete Points

The Delete Points button does the opposite of the Add Points button. After a point is deleted, the line it intersected takes the shortest route between the two outer points. For example, to create a square, choose Modify ➤ Convert ➤ To Polygon, and then delete one of the corner points to create a right-angle triangle. To delete, select the control point, and click the Delete Points button, or use the Delete key.

## Split Curve

The Split Curve button breaks apart the curve or polygon at the selected control point. The shape no longer works as a solid object but is a single line with various control points. To rejoin the points, ensure they are positioned on top of one another, and then right-click ➤ Close Object. If the object has a large gap between the two extremities, Close Object adds a new line between the two control points.

## Convert to Curve

If a control point has been defined as a polygon (i.e., a straight line joins it to its nearest control points), selecting the Convert to Curve button turns the control point into an editable curve. If it's a curve, it will be transformed into a polygon. The latter option converts any curvy lines to straight lines.

## Corner Point/Smoother Transition/Symmetric Transition

These three buttons are mutually exclusive. The Corner Point button allows both lines emerging from a control point to be edited independently; Smoother Transition means that edits on one side of the control point will affect the other side, making for a smoother curve; and Symmetric Transition creates symmetric curves on either side of the point. Each point can only be one of these options, but objects can contain points using all three methods.

## Close Bezier

The Close Bezier button closes up a line or curve to create a solid object.

## Eliminate Points

The Eliminate Points button allows the user to automatically reduce the number of control points on a shape based on the shape itself. Imagine you have a line with three points making a V shape with straight lines between them. If you move the bottom of the V in line with the top parts, you get a simple straight line and a redundant control point. If the Eliminate Points button is selected, that control point is automatically removed.

# Back to Editing

The final part of the background section is a small drop shadow on the wave, which gives a nice layering effect. Copy the wave shape using Ctrl+C, paste with Ctrl+V, and then change the color of the new shape to Grey 70% using the color drop-down list on the Formatting toolbar. Right-click ➤ Arrange ➤ Send Backward (see Figure 6-15) to place this new gray shape beneath the other wave and shift it down a bit by pressing the down cursor key a few times. Finally, with the shape still selected, click the Area icon on the Formatting toolbar, select the Transparency tab, and set transparency to 50%.

With that done, you can now lock off the background layer and begin to add more content, so right-click the Layout tab at the bottom of the window, select Modify Layer, and enable the Locked check box (see Figure 6-16). Click OK, and then select the Graphics tab.

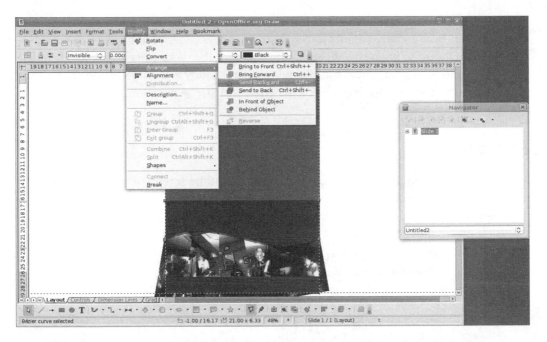

**Figure 6-15.** *Simple shadows can be added to an object by copying it (Ctrl+C), then pasting (Ctrl+V), and then placing it behind the original object (Modify ➤ Arrange ➤ Send Backward) and using a transparent area fill.*

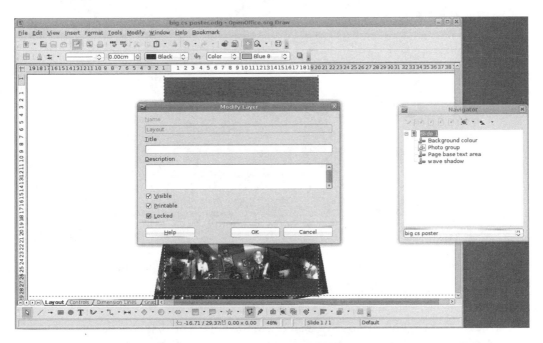

**Figure 6-16.** *Lock off a layer after it's completed so you don't make any accidental edits.*

Onto the graphics layer, add a main image (Insert ➤ Picture ➤ From File), and define a thin border. Now create a slightly larger white rectangle with a thin black border, and send this Backward so it's below the image. Select both the rectangle and the image using Shift-click, and then group them into a single object (Modify ➤ Group), which allows you to rotate it to 5 degrees with right-click ➤ Position and Size ➤ Rotation.

# Fontwork

A closer inspection of the Drawing toolbar at the base of the screen reveals two different text options. The first, on the left side of the toolbar, is the ordinary text tool. Select this to draw a box on the page to house headlines, subheadings, or even paragraph text. The second tool—to the right—launches the Fontwork Gallery, which allows you to apply one of a selection of different shape and color combinations to a piece of text (see Figure 6-17) and then manipulate this as an object.

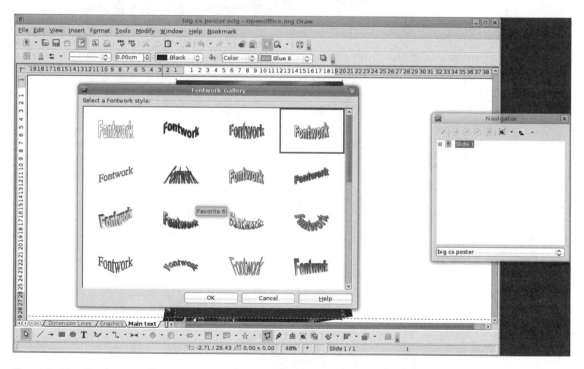

**Figure 6-17.** *The Fontwork Gallery has a selection of premade text designs that can be applied to the page.*

Select one of the options to have it added to the page. The default text says Fontwork; double-click this to make the text editable (see Figure 6-18), and type in the new text. While the text is in this state, you can also change the font, weight, and size using the normal option on the Formatting toolbar. As words are typed, they display normally, but after you click outside the text, the Fontwork effect is applied.

**Figure 6-18.** *After the object is inserted, double-click it to edit the text. The effect will be applied after you click off the text.*

When a Fontwork object is selected, the Fontwork toolbar is displayed that has five icons to define the shape of the object. The following list describes these five buttons from left to right on the toolbar:

- *Fontwork Gallery*: The first button relaunches the Fontwork Gallery allowing new Fontwork objects to be added to the page.

- *Fontwork Shape*: The second button displays a drop-down box for applying a new shape to the object. Select one, and the object assumes that shape. Each shape has a few editable options—usually surrounding the degree of effect applied—and these can be changed dynamically using the yellow dots that appear when a Fontwork object is selected (see Figure 6-19). Click and drag the edit handle around to experiment.

- *Same Letter Heights*: The third button makes all characters in the text stretch to the same height as the tallest letter. The results of this usually look clumsy, but it can sometimes have the right effect. Deselect the option to turn it off.

- *Alignment*: The fourth button defines the alignment of the text, with entries for left, right, center, justified, and so on. It's only really worthwhile if you have text over multiple lines.

**Figure 6-19.** *The yellow dots can be used to edit the strength of any Fontwork effect, such as squash or stretch.*

- *Character Spacing*: The fifth button allows the gaps between letters to be expanded or contracted to create the right effect. In addition to a set of default values, you can also select Custom and define the spacing as a percentage.

---

**Caution** Any Fontwork text is automatically added to the Layout layer, and if this is locked, you can't edit the text. In this case, unlock the Layout layer, then click and hold the Fontwork text until the mouse pointer changes into an arrow with a small box beneath it, and then drag this to a different layer. Relock the Layout layer, and edit the Fontwork text as normal.

---

Although the Fontwork toolbar allows you to work with the look of the letters (see Figure 6-20), you can also use the usual Area, Line, and Shadow tools to make other changes. In the example (see Figure 6-21), edit the gradient to make it smoother by right-clicking, choosing Area, selecting the Area tab, deselecting the Automatic Increments option, and increasing the number to 128. Make the shadow a little more transparent under the Shadow tab, and then make the bend effect a little less pronounced by dragging the yellow shape edit icon toward the top of the page. Then position this so it runs over the main image slightly.

**Figure 6-20.** *The full complement of character controls is available when editing the text in a Fontwork object.*

**Figure 6-21.** *The gradients and text outlines can look a little jagged onscreen, but the printed output is very smooth.*

## FONTWORK: THE MANUAL VERSION

In the example, you used the basic shapes available in the Fontwork system. However, an additional set of options is available through the manual Fontwork system that can be used to add some text to a path; this also works on existing text strings.

To begin, make a new object with the Text tool from the Drawing toolbar. Type some text, right-click the object, and select Fontwork. A new, different toolbar appears on the page, and this is where the path for the text is defined. Use the arch section to create the basic shape, and then use the other options in the toolbox to set how the text sits on the curve, the alignment and orientation, the distance from the curve itself, and the shadow. The text remains editable throughout the use of this system, and Fontwork objects can be re-edited later.

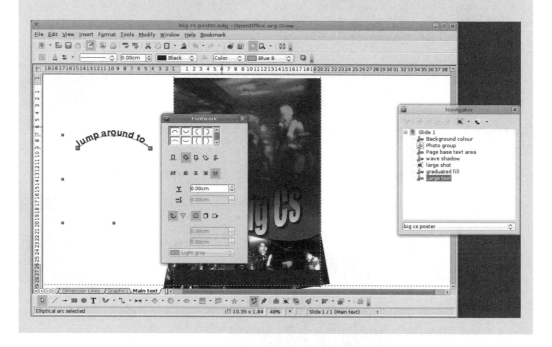

Fontwork objects can be resized normally, but if you need a little more control over individual letters, you can choose Modify ➤ Convert ➤ To Curve and then edit the shapes of letters using the Edit Points toolbar as detailed earlier. When converted, the letters are automatically grouped, so choose Modify ➤ Ungroup to separate them. Remember, however, that after the text has been converted to a curve, it will no longer be editable (as text) so it might be worthwhile to do a copy/paste before converting and moving the editable version off to the side.

Don't worry that the edges of the text look a little "stepped" onscreen; when printed, the edges will be smooth.

# Shape Combinations

The last addition to this layer is a box on the right of the page that will house the main text for the goat-themed poster. You could just add a square, color it Pale Blue, and make it 50% transparent, but it would look better with a few shapes carved out of it. For this, you'll use the Modify menu, which you've previously used to group and ungroup items. However, the Shapes tool (Modify ➤ Shapes ➤ Merge/Subtract/Intersect) can be used to create very complex shapes.

In these examples, you'll work with two primitives—a circle and cross—to look at the ways we can create new shapes (see Figure 6-22).

The first shape is the most obvious. Select both objects either by clicking and dragging around them both or by Shift-clicking on each in turn and choosing Modify ➤ Shapes ➤ Merge. This simply joins together both shapes to create a single new shape. This is ideal for creating arches using a circle and rectangle.

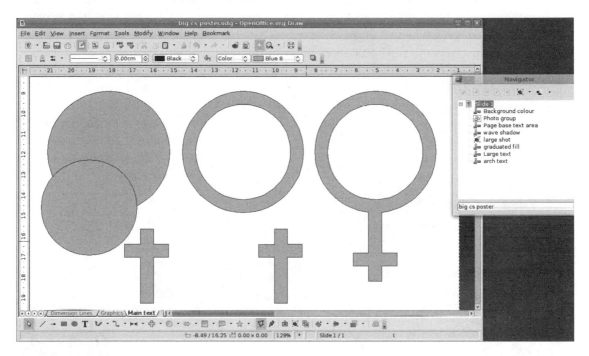

**Figure 6-22.** *By merging, subtracting, and intersecting objects, you can create many complex shapes or simple ones with holes in them.*

The second option (Modify ➤ Shapes ➤ Subtract) subtracts one shape from the other to make a new shape. Overlapping parts are cut out of the primary object. Draw uses the object hierarchy to define the primary and secondary objects, so if, in our example, the circle were underneath the cross, a small section where the cross goes into the circle would be removed. If the cross were at the bottom, however, one of its edges would end up with a concave surface. This is the method used to create "cookie cutter" shapes, which show through everything beneath them.

The final option (Modify ➤ Shapes ➤ Intersect) creates a new shape based on the portions of the two objects that overlap. The original pair of objects will be removed, leaving just the overlap section.

All of these options can be applied to any object, including text that has been converted to a curve (select text, then choose Modify ➤ Convert ➤ To Curve). Do this with the text box on the right of the page, and combine it with a very small Shadow effect to make it look like a physical cutout.

## Text Editing

The final part of this project is adding the text to the page. This is separate from the Fontwork stuff you did earlier and has more in common with the standard text entry and edit tools used in Writer or Impress than Fontwork (see Figure 6-23). Earlier, I created a layer called English Text for this purpose, so select that tab at the base of the window. Lock all of the other layers so you don't accidentally move things around. To lock, right-click the layer name, select Modify Layer, and click the Locked check box.

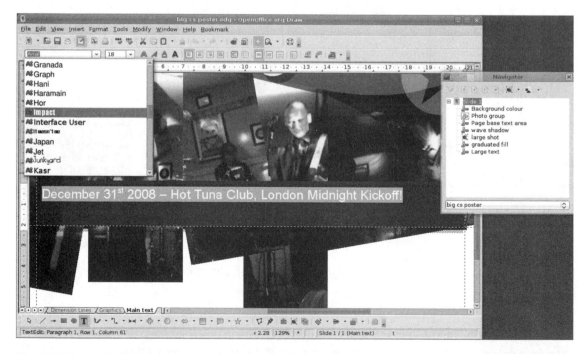

**Figure 6-23.** *Inevitably, there are some very good text-editing options because they come courtesy of Writer.*

Using the normal text icon, draw a box to contain the main text elements (in the example, this appears on the right of the page). This will work in the same way as a text box in Writer; that is, text will autowrap when it reaches the edge of the box, and all of the character and paragraph formatting options are available using the Formatting toolbar or through the Styles and Formatting palette, which is accessed via Format ➤ Styles and Formatting (see Chapter 3 for more on styles and formatting).

# Beyond the Page

It seems quite normal to use the physical paper sizes you're used to such as A4, DL, and Letter when working in OO.o, but there's no reason to be restricted in this manner. After you stop thinking of paper sizes (see Figure 6-24), many new opportunities present them- selves. In this short tutorial, you'll break out from the paper world and use Draw to plan out the renovation of a bedroom. You'll be using real-world measurements and dimen- sion lines to create a full-size plan of the room and then use the Draw Position and Size dialog box to ensure everything needed in the room will fit.

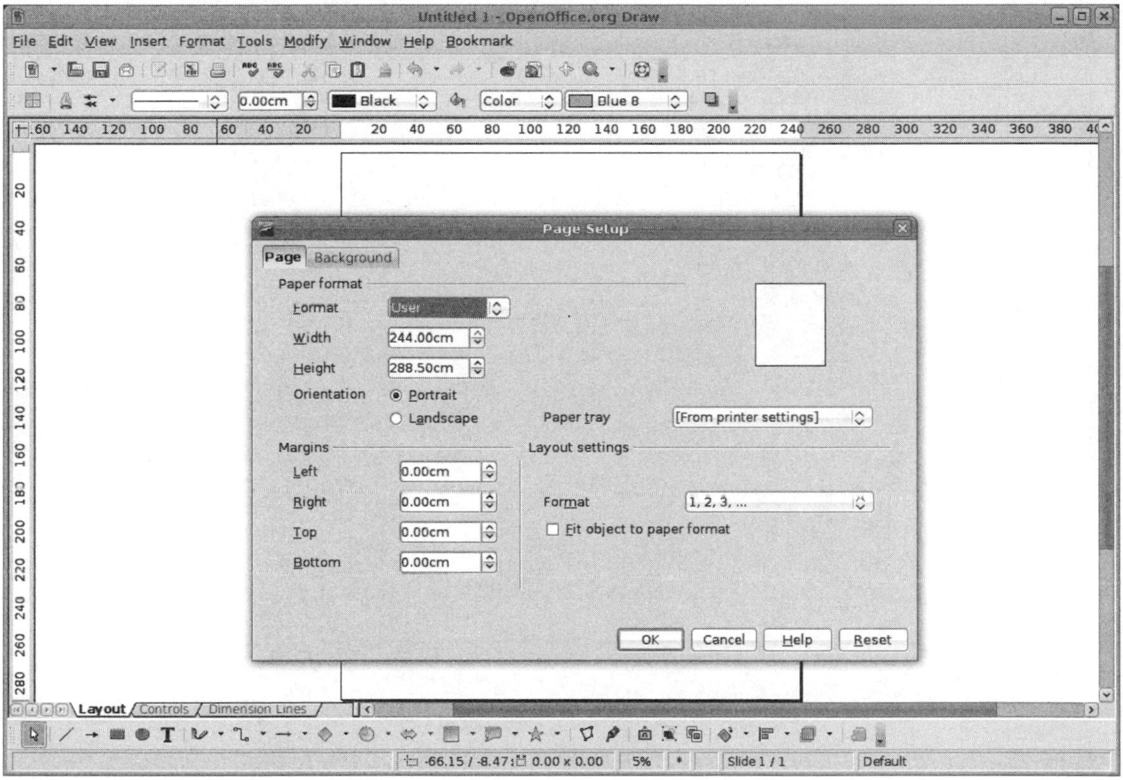

**Figure 6-24.** *Pages don't have to represent paper at all. This, for instance, is a room-size page for planning out some décor.*

After this project is completed, it should give you a better understanding of the potential of Draw *as a visualization tool*. With the precision available in the Position and Size dialog box, you can create accurate floor plans for a house sale or planning approval—or even just to dream—without the cost of specific home design software. Expand things a little further, and curves, gallery objects, and layers make it possible to use Draw to plan out a garden, greenhouse, shop floor, or housing development!

## Setting Accurate Dimensions

Create a new document, and choose Format ➤ Page to open up the page settings. Enter the size of the room in the Width and Height boxes using the default measurement system (see Figure 6-25). If you need to change this to something more familiar, go into Tools ➤ Options, look under the OpenOffice.org Draw ➤ General section, and change the Unit of measurement. Available options include Inch, Foot, Mile, and Kilometer, so you should find something suitable.

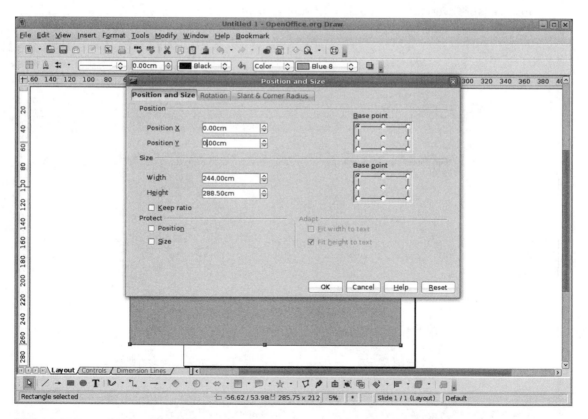

**Figure 6-25.** *Accurate real-world measurements are essential if you want to transfer a design from screen to reality.*

## Setting the Room As the Page

To begin, I've added dimension lines to the x and y planes of the page. Now draw a rectangle roughly the same size as the page/room created in the previous step—don't worry too much about being accurate because you'll get very precise in a moment. This first rectangle will be inserted onto the Layout layer. Right-click the rectangle and select Position and Size, or press F4.

## Performing Precise Editing

Resize the rectangle using the Width and Height options in the Position and Size dialog box using the same values as the page size. In the Position section, ensure the top-left button is selected as the Base point, and set both the Position X and Position Y options to 0. This places the top-left base point on the top-left part of the page, ensuring that the rectangle perfectly covers the page. Because this isn't likely to change, you should also select the Position and Size check boxes under Protect to lock the settings in.

## Adding Objects

The purpose of working with real-world dimensions is that you can now create an object to represent, say, a single floorboard with the real sizes and then duplicate this across the floor, cutting up the objects as necessary to cover the floor. Begin by drawing a rectangle to represent a floorboard, and then choose Position and Size, and input the Width and Height values of a plank—19.12cm × 36.62cm—as in Figure 6-26. Now copy the floorboard and paste it below the first one. Continue copying all across the room, reducing the length of the floorboards on the edges of the floor. Use the View ➤ Zoom menu to get up close to each joint to ensure they're butting up properly.

Now the magic part: right-click the "cut" floorboards, select Position and Size, and see the precise dimensions of any necessary cuts. Double-click a cut object to turn it into a text box, and type in the length of the cut.

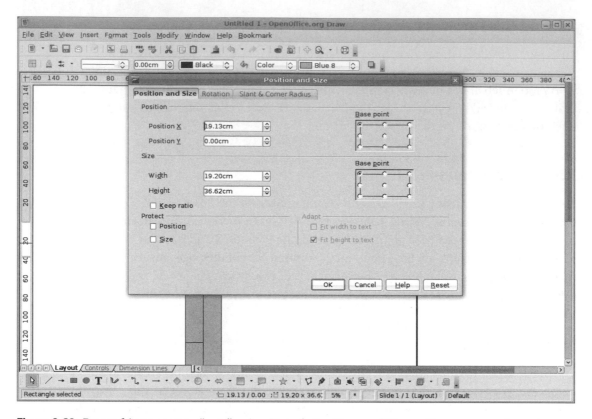

**Figure 6-26.** *By working out your "cuts" using Draw's Position and Size option, you won't waste as much wood when it comes to doing real cuts. Free software can save money in more ways than one!*

## Creating More Objects

After the entire floor is laid, right-click the Layout layer tab, select Modify Layer, and lock the layer. Now is a good time to create a few extra layers—add one for Doors/Windows and a second for Furniture. Remember that dimension lines—when added—are situated on the Dimension Lines layer.

On the Doors/Windows layer, add rectangles using the drawing tools to represent a door and window in the appropriate places with the correct dimensions (right-click ➤ Position and Size to resize) and then lock this off using the layer modification option (right-click layer name ➤ Modify Layer) to prevent further editing because these are fixed elements in the room (see Figure 6-27).

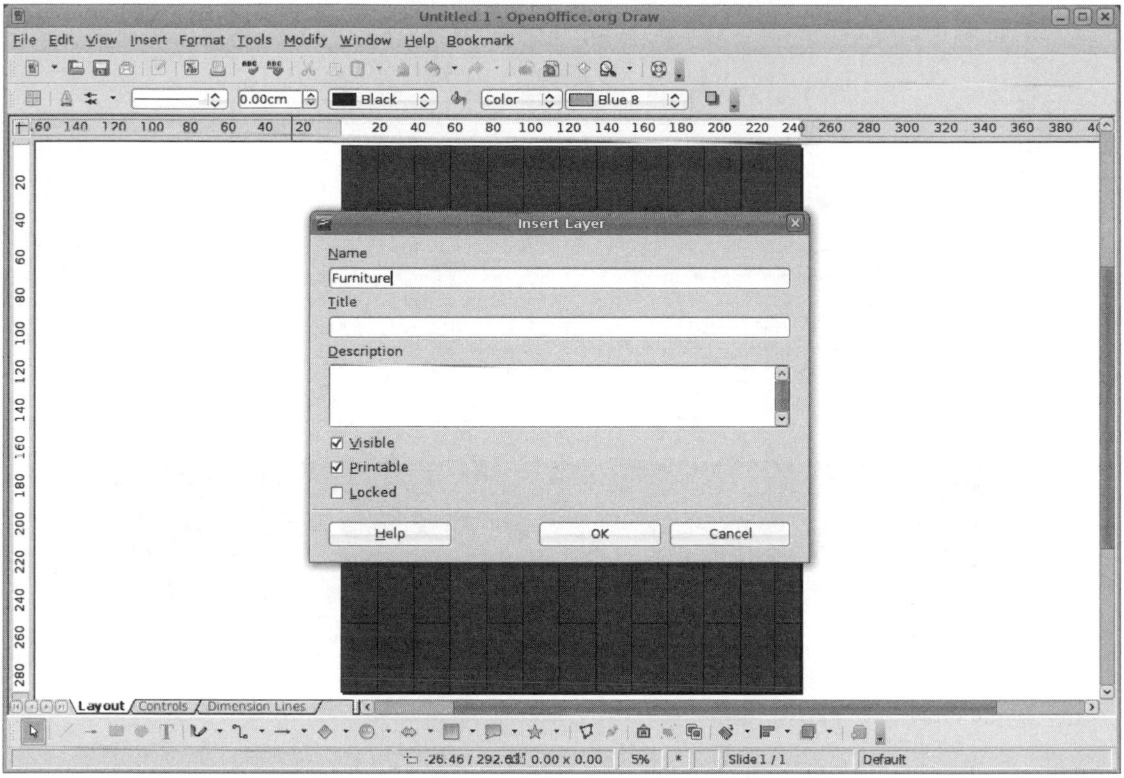

**Figure 6-27.** *By adding objects to new layers and then locking immovable parts, you can edit the space without worrying about messing up.*

## Working with Interior Design

The work you put into the next stage really depends on your time and inclination because it involves creating icons or representations of each element to be added to the room.

In this example, the size is increased substantially because the "room" is so much larger than a sheet of paper. Use dimension lines (see Figure 6-28) to build objects to accurate sizes. Now you'll create a bed shape complete with duvet and pillow rendered with a pretty daisy pattern (see Figure 6-29). You add this pattern by selecting the object, clicking the Area button, and looking under Bitmap in the Area dialog box. Daisy is one of the available patterns but when added using the default size, you won't actually see any daisies unless the zoom level is very high. Fortunately, you can resize the rendition of the bitmap. Select the object again, and click the Area button.

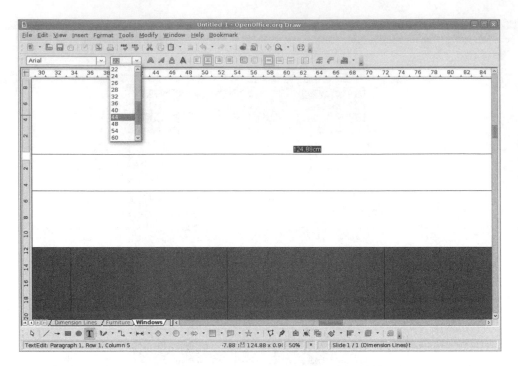

**Figure 6-28.** *Text on dimension lines can be edited by double-clicking it.*

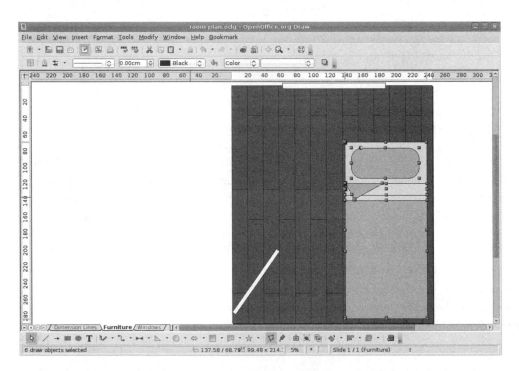

**Figure 6-29.** *You've used a few rectangles and triangles to make an iconic bed to place into the room.*

Again, group objects together so they move as one. The Area tab of the Area dialog box changes depending upon the type of fill applied to an object. Under the Size section, deselect Original, and then add new dimensions in the Width and Height boxes (see Figure 6-30). The settings 20cm by 20cm work well for the duvet. There are also options in this dialog box to offset the bitmap either vertically or horizontally, but this only makes sense if the bitmap in question isn't going to be tiled. So if, for example, you had a single graphic to be applied to the duvet, you could position it using these options.

You could also find real images of furniture to add to the room, and Draw will import .png images complete with transparent backgrounds.

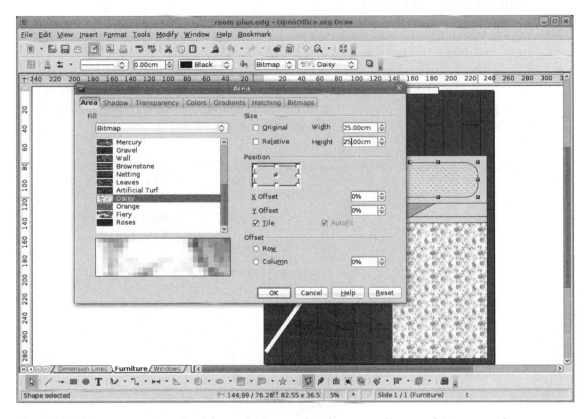

**Figure 6-30.** *Patterns can be edited for scale. Remember, however, these are bitmaps and may not scale up too far.*

Before adding the object to the room, select the whole room, and choose Modify ➤ Group. This makes it possible to move and rotate the object as a single entity.

---

■**Tip** If creating floor plans is something you do often, consider creating your furniture or other object icons using Draw and then adding them to a special gallery to be reused whenever they're needed.

---

## Populating the Room

Right-click the grouped object, select the Position and Size option again, and look under the Rotation tab. Rotate the object by inputting the angle (in degrees) into the appropriate box. The pivot point is the section of the object that will form the center of the spin. With beds, drawers, and so on, the pivot point isn't particularly important, but when doing doors, which have a specific hinge point, it's a good idea to set this correctly, so the door opens the right way.

## Adding New Textures

For the bed shape, you used one of OO.o's included textures to add some variety to the project. If the perfect texture is just not available within the suite, however, you can add new textures, thus making it easier to create unique images (see Figure 6-31). For the example project, you need, for instance, a decent wooden texture to make the floor of this room look right, but textures can also be used to add a brick effect to an architectural drawing or to add a distinctive effect to a piece of display text.

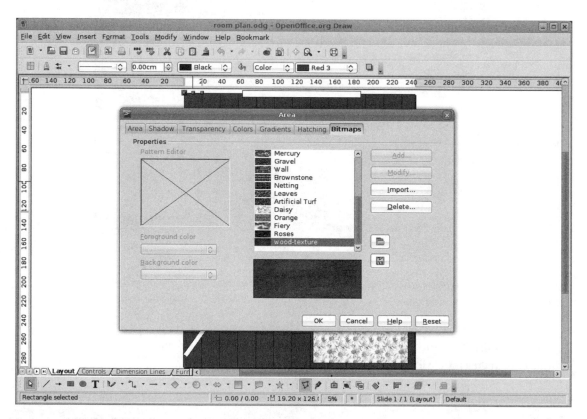

**Figure 6-31.** *This wooden texture (found on the Internet) is perfect for making a floor look more like a floor.*

It's easy to add new textures. In the Area ➤ Bitmaps tab, select Import and navigate to the location of the desired texture. Click OK to have it added to the list. This can be tiled, offset, and resized just like any other bitmap. You can delete textures/bitmaps from the list and even save the entire list as a .sob file using the disk icon, which can then be loaded into other editions of the software—ideal if you work across machines.

## Flow Charts and Diagrams

Another great use for illustration software such as Draw is the creation of flow charts and diagrams. Of course, specialized applications are available for this particular task, but if your needs are not as expansive, Draw's collection of premade flow chart shapes and connector options is an adequate replacement.

These tools can be used to build, visualize, and edit any structure that involves relationships, connections, and hierarchy—projects such as family trees, organizational charts, network diagrams, book outlines, or, as in this example, a visual sitemap for a web site.

As with other projects, you'll start with a simple page setup, and, in this case, you'll use an A3 page with a small margin. One vital component of any kind of organizational map is consistency and an obvious key (see Figure 6-32).

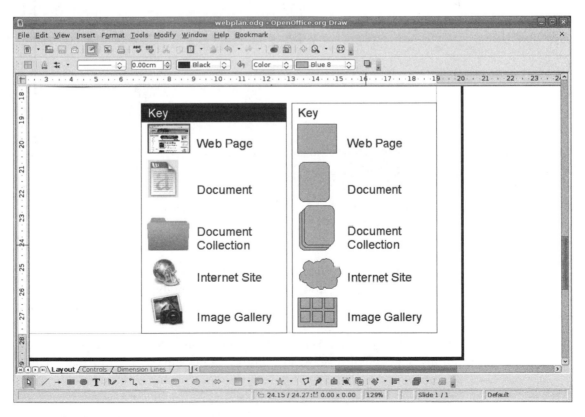

**Figure 6-32.** *Keys can be illustrated or photographic, but they must always be consistent.*

You can represent a web page with the letter W, and as long as the users knew this, and each page was consistently labeled, they would be able to navigate the map. For this reason, you'll begin by constructing a key in the lower right of the page. The other advantage of starting with the key is that after the elements have been designed here—whether full-color images or plain icons—they can be simply cut and pasted to the appropriate section of the map, making construction of the diagram itself really simple (see Figure 6-33).

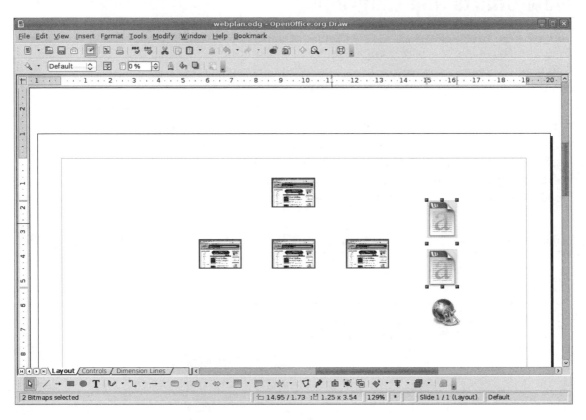

**Figure 6-33.** *Copy and paste ensure consistency in diagram mode, but you could add icons to a special image gallery for reuse later.*

Start by copying the page icon to the clipboard with Ctrl+C and then pasting with Ctrl+V. Grab the newly pasted icon (it will be directly on top of the old one), and drag it to the top of the page. Right-click, and select Alignment ➤ Centered to put the icon directly in the middle of the page.

This will be the home page marker, so give it a title that is distinct from the other icons representing pages. Right-click again, choose Name, and enter **Home Page**. When you click OK, nothing changes, but if you select the icon and look in the status bar (at the bottom of the screen), you can see its name. Or you can open the Navigator (the navigator icon is on the main toolbar), and click the disclosure arrow next to Slide 1. Home Page shows up in the list of assets, and selecting it selects the object on the page.

Use Paste three more times to create three more page icons, and position these roughly in a line a few centimeters beneath the first. Again give these names (Section 1, 2, and 3) using right-click ➤ Name.

## Alignment and Distribution

Depending on your level of pedantry, you may want to tidy the layout up a little, and this is where the Alignment and Distribution tools come in. Select the three second-level page icons by either clicking and dragging around them or using the Shift-click method. Choose Modify ➤ Alignment ➤ Option, where Option is chosen from the six available entries in this menu. The first three deal with horizontal alignment (Left, Centered, Right), and the lower three entries deal with vertical alignment (Top, Centered, Bottom) with the option defining the object edge to be aligned. To line up the three selected elements, choose the Top option. Actually, because your three objects are all the same size, it doesn't really matter which vertical option you choose here, but with objects of different sizes, it can make quite a difference.

While the trio of icons is still selected, choose Modify ➤ Distribution to launch the Distribution dialog box (see Figure 6-34). This dialog box has quite a few different options for distributing objects horizontally and vertically. For this example, you're concerned with the horizontal option, and again because you're working with uniform objects, the actual option chosen isn't that important. The available options distribute—that is, put identical distances between—objects based on either the left or right edges, the object center, or the gap itself, with the outside objects (left, right, top, or bottom) acting as constraining forces. This is especially useful when, for example, you are creating printable forms with spaces for written text entry where lines can be evenly distributed on the form.

Before moving on to the next operation, you need to align the second level of the hierarchy with the first. However, before clicking the Align menu, you must first group together the three icons because the alignment tools work on items individually, so if grouped, each icon is repositioned to the same space on the page. Choose Modify ➤ Group, followed by Modify ➤ Align ➤ Centered (from the first section), and then ungroup so you can go back to individual editing.

Having set the second level of the hierarchy, copy/paste a couple of document icons and an external link icon from the key to the right-hand side of the page (see Figure 6-35 in the next section). You can use the Alignment tool (Modify ➤ Alignment ➤ Centered) to line these up neatly.

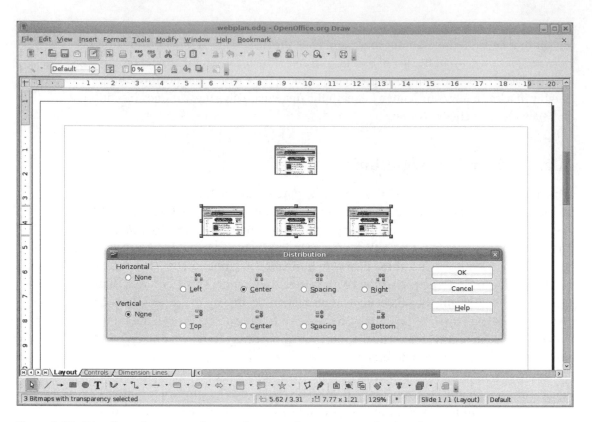

**Figure 6-34.** *Distribute icons evenly to make your chart more professional.*

## Connectors

You now have a series of icons, which, apparently, represent the first layer of navigation in a web site. However, the relationships between each of these elements have yet to be defined; you'll do this with connector lines (see Figure 6-35). Like the dimension lines used earlier, *connector lines* refer to a special class of lines in Draw that have some very useful properties. In this case, you can attach each end of a connector line to an object—thus inferring a relationship—and then have the line expand and move when either of the connected objects are moved.

Select the Connector Lines icon from the Draw toolbar (it's the eighth icon from the left on a default installation) using the small disclosure arrow. This launches a flyout (a second, smaller toolbar with additional options) showing the various line formats; because you'll be using this quite a lot, tear this menu off (click and drag the top of the flyout), and put it inside the window.

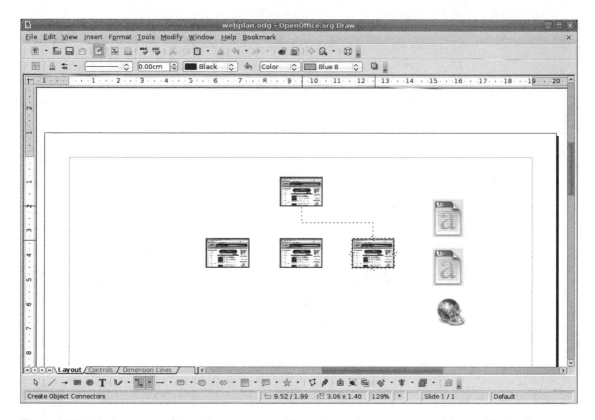

**Figure 6-35.** *Join icons together using connector lines. As you hover over an object with the Connector Lines option selected, a set of handles appear to denote where a connection can be made.*

The Connector tool has four types of line available—Connector, Line Connector, Straight Connector, and Curved Connector—and there are three variations of each to cover the different ways that information might flow along the lines. To define the first set of relationships, you'll use the first option, which creates "square" connections with no arrows (you'll use these to suggest reciprocal links in the web site structure). Click the icon on the top left of the Connector window, and then hover the mouse over the top (Home Page) icon. The icon is highlighted, and a small square box (a connector node) appears in the center of each edge. This is the connection location, so click here and then drag the mouse to one of the second level pages. Again as the mouse hits one of these icons, the icon is highlighted, and the connector nodes are visible. Drop the line end on one of these icons, and the two objects are connected (see Figure 6-36).

To test the connection, click and drag either of the icons to see the line change. The standard connector line is all straight lines and right angles, but other options are available that can be used to suggest different types of relationships. So, in this example, use curved lines to represent secondary navigation elements and use arrow connectors to suggest one-way travel between pages or elements.

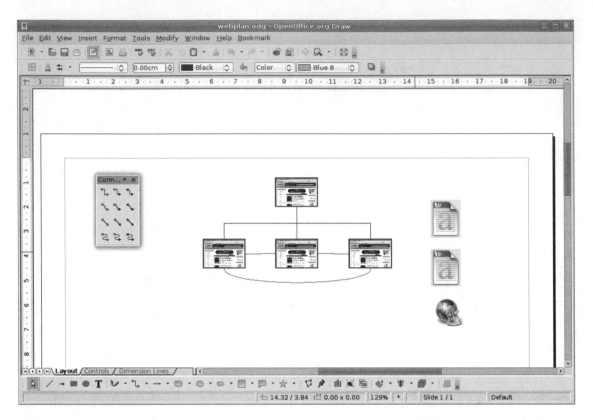

**Figure 6-36.** *Different colors and styles of connector lines can be used to represent different aspects of a relationship or paths through the diagram.*

You can edit connector lines just like any other object, so add a little color using the line color drop-down list because a ton of black lines can be confusing. You can also edit the arrows using the arrow drop-down menu on the Formatting toolbar. There is a large selection of arrowheads available (some not even arrow shaped!), which can be applied to either end of the line (see Figure 6-37). Draw remembers which is the start point and end point of each line created, and these can be redefined using the left (start) or right (end) arrow icons.

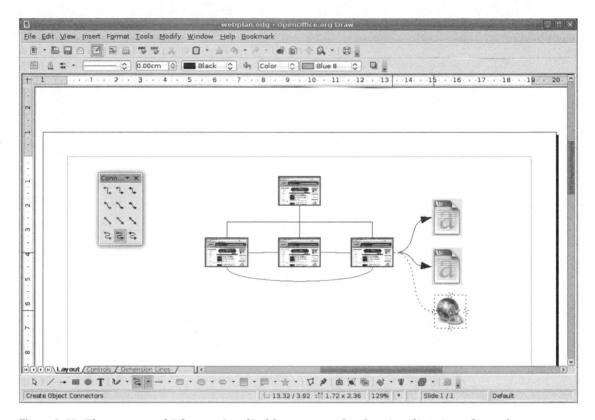

**Figure 6-37.** *The arrows, which remain editable, are great for showing direction of travel on a map or through a web site.*

After the items have been connected, they can be moved around, and the lines that connect them will move in concert, rearranging themselves using the most efficient route between the parent and child objects. You can edit the angle/curve of a line using the center handle that appears when a line is connected, or edit and break the link by shifting around the handles at either end of the line.

Using a combination of shapes, colors, and lines, you can create some extensive sitemaps, mind maps, and anything else that requires organized thinking (see Figure 6-38). It's vital, though, to think in terms of later reorganization and give each significant element a title using the right-click ➤ Name option (see Figure 6-39).

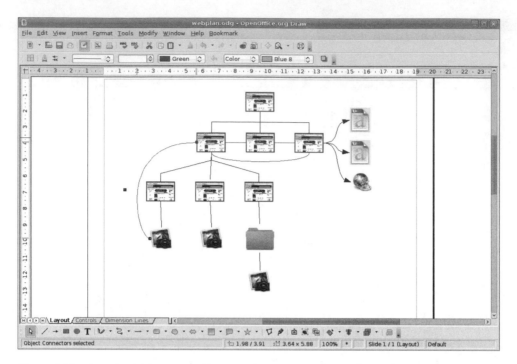

**Figure 6-38.** *Use a combination of line types and colors to denote different elements of a project.*

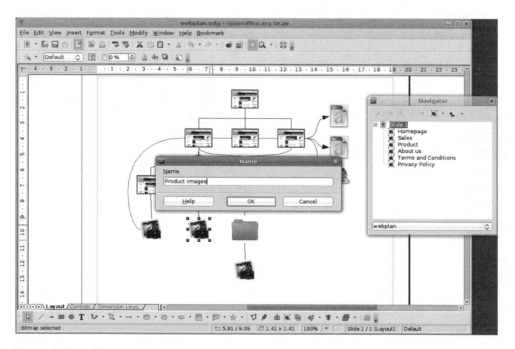

**Figure 6-39.** *Diligently naming objects as you create them will pay dividends when you come to re-edit later.*

# Converting Images

Previously, we talked about the difference between bitmap images, such as the photos you've added to these projects, and vector images, such as Draw's objects and shapes. Both are useful in their own ways, but sometimes it can be useful to convert a bitmap to a vector or vice versa. Draw has tools available for both of these operations, although the process of going from vector to bitmap is the more successful.

---

**Note**  You may need to convert one type of image to another for many reasons. Vector illustrations can be exported as `.jpg` or `.png` files for insertion into web projects or for further editing in an application such as Gimp, Photoshop, or Microsoft Paint. Going the other way—from bitmap to vector—means that simple images can be scaled up to almost any size without loss of clarity, which is ideal for large poster projects.

---

Let's start with the vectorization of a bitmap, which is sometimes called *tracing*. This process works on fairly simple images with a limited color range, but the results can be quite stylish. Begin by inserting an image (Insert ➤ Picture ➤ From File), and resize it as appropriate. Now right-click the image, and select Convert ➤ To Polygon (or look under the Modify menu for this option) to launch the Convert to Polygon dialog box (see Figure 6-40).

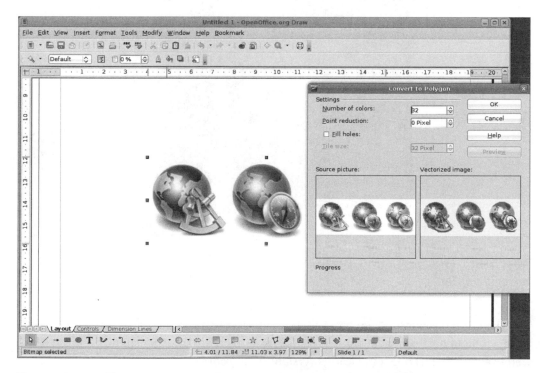

**Figure 6-40.** *You'll get the most satisfactory tracing results when working from simple images. The results will appear more quickly too.*

Select the number of colors to include in the final image. You'll get better results by increasing this to the maximum of 32 colors, although the more colors added, the more complex the final image. The Point reduction option removes any polygon that contains anything less than the value specified here.

The Fill holes option fills up any gaps left by the Point reduction option with the closest (in proximity) color value.

With everything set, click the Preview button to get an idea of what the final image will look like, and, when satisfied, click OK to create the new image. This will completely replace the original bitmap with a fully vectorized, resizable image.

You can edit vectorized images by choosing Modify ➤ Break to break up the individual parts, but beware that this will take some time, and the results are not always what you might expect. That said, simple images such as icons, Mondrian prints, and screen prints with limited colors (see Figure 6-41) can be edited quite well. To see all of the new shapes, open up the Navigator, and set it to display all shapes using the icon on the right.

**Figure 6-41.** *Warhol's Monroe screen print is the ideal vectorization project. By selecting 32 colors in the dialog box, you end up with 32 colored regions that you can easily edit.*

The other direction—from vector to bitmap—is much simpler and quicker, and the results tend to be more satisfying. You'll use Draw to create a button suitable for use on a web site, and then render out various versions of it to cover the different "states" in which the button might appear.

## A Touch of Glass

Spend 10 minutes on the web or with the latest operating systems, and you'll notice that glass is everywhere. This look, designed to provide sheen to a flat surface, not only looks cool but is also very easy to create and adapt to a variety of purposes.

Start with a rounded rectangle shape as shown in Figure 6-42, which is available under the Basic Shapes option in the Draw toolbar. Draw a shape with the dimensions of 7.00cm × 1.5cm (after the shape is drawn, it can be resized with right-click ➤ Position and Size).

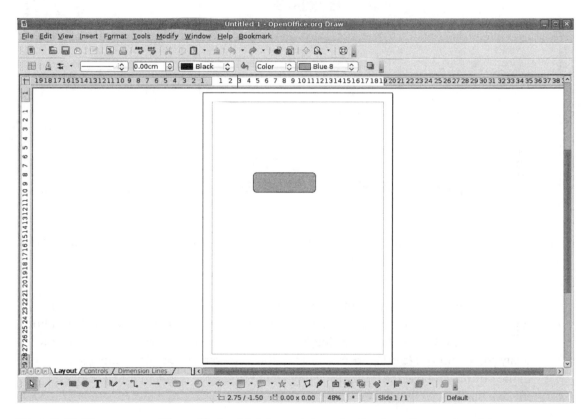

**Figure 6-42.** *The common Glass effect, which is great for web sites, is quite easy to achieve.*

Apply the standard black-to-white gradient to this object using the drop-down options on the Formatting toolbar, and then right-click ➤ Area. In the Area tab, deselect Automatic in the Increments section, and change the value from 64 to 128 steps. Then go into the Gradients tab, set the end color to Grey 60%, and click OK to apply the gradient to the selection. This is the base of the button (see Figure 6-43).

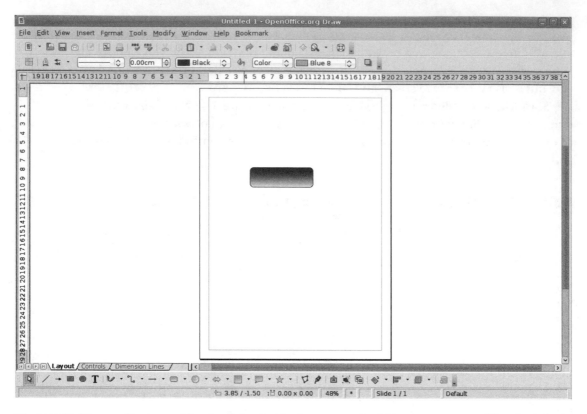

**Figure 6-43.** *The gradient provides the shine for the button, and adding more steps will make it look more glassy.*

Next, copy and paste the button shape (Ctrl+C/Ctrl+V), select the normal rectangle tool, and draw a new rectangle completely covering the top half of the button. Select both objects, and the choose Modify ➤ Shapes ➤ Subtract to remove the top half of the previously copied button (see Figure 6-44). Select the top layer, which is now the bottom half of the button, and use the Formatting toolbar to change the gradient into a color and make it black (see Figure 6-45).

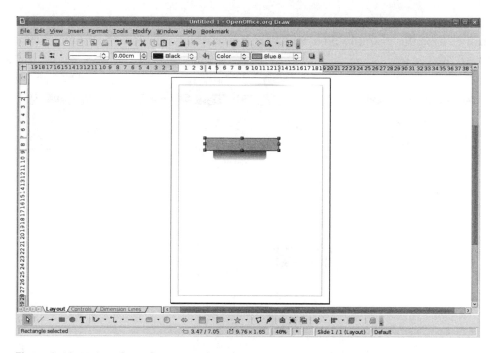

**Figure 6-44.** *Using the subtract tool in this way removes the top half of the front object, leaving the back object intact. It's the best way to create irregular shapes.*

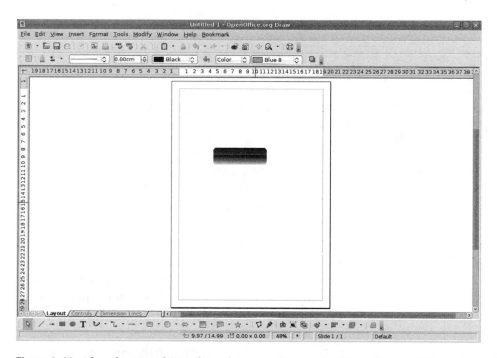

**Figure 6-45.** *After the two objects have been combined, the front object will be reshaded with the same gray-to-white gradient.*

The final job is to add a text box that is the same width as the button, input the text, and then style it (in this example, bold, white Arial) so it stands out from the button itself (see Figure 6-46).

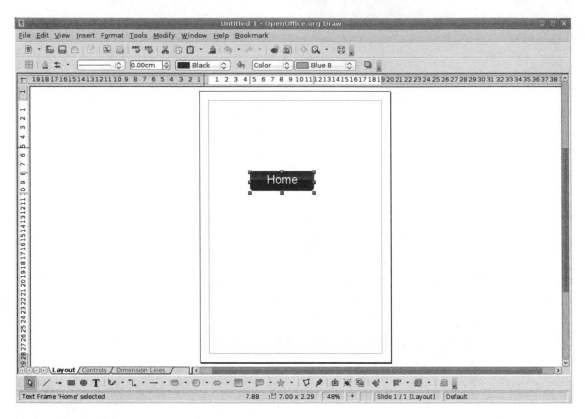

**Figure 6-46.** *You've recolored the front object with a solid black and then added a text box over the top with some white lettering. One button done!*

The button will have three states (normal/over/down), so select and copy/paste the original button twice. Now select the bottom layer of the second button (the original gradient), right-click ➤ Area, and edit the Gray 60% element to a different color in the Gradients tab. Then do the same with the third button.

The result should be three differently "lit" buttons as shown in Figure 6-47.

You could select each one in turn and choose Modify ➤ Convert ➤ To Bitmap, but it might be a better idea to keep the drawings in their vector state and export each one individually as a bitmap. To do this, select the first button, choose File ➤ Export, and select one of the bitmap formats in the File Format drop-down list (.png or .jpg are recommended). Finally, provide a name for the file, make sure the Selection button is enabled, and click OK (see Figure 6-48). The first button will be exported to the computer as a single image. Now do the same for the other two buttons (select each one in turn) to create all three states.

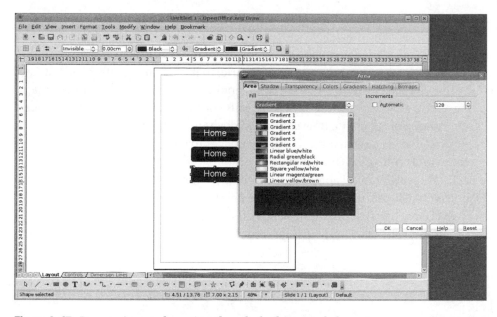

**Figure 6-47.** *By copying and pasting the whole thing and changing one gradient color on the copies, you can create buttons suitable for "normal," "over," and "down," which are the three states typically used in web button design.*

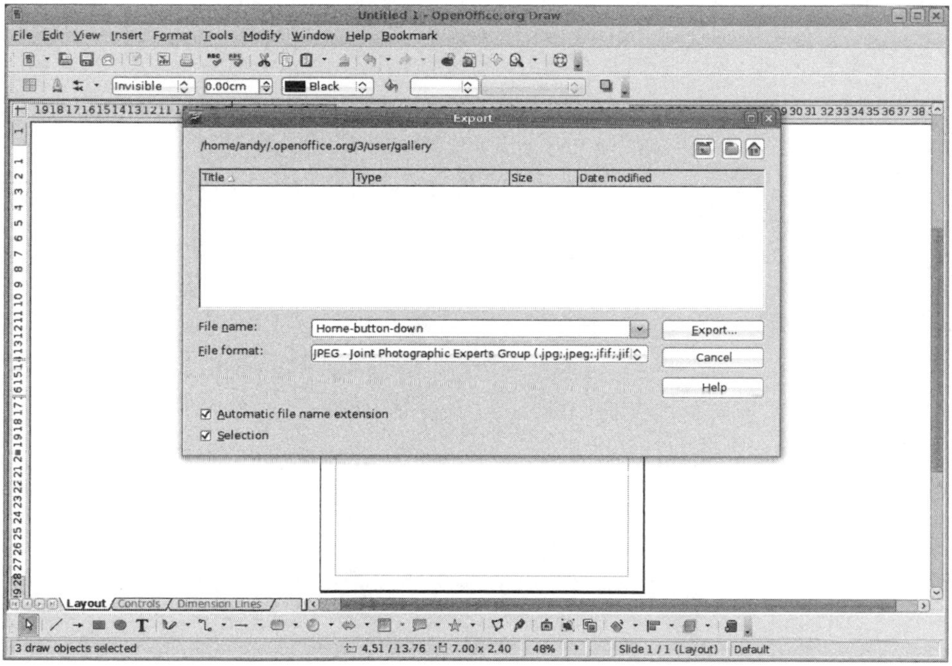

**Figure 6-48.** *The individual buttons should be exported as either .jpg or .png files using the Selection option in the Export dialog box.*

# Recap

In this chapter, we looked at many of the basic drawing tools available in Draw, ranging from simple shapes that can be drawn with the mouse, to more complex designs that require the use of the Shapes tool. You used color, gradients, transparencies, and bitmaps to add variety to the projects; created wacky text with Fontwork; and used a combination of shapes and connectors to create flow charts and diagrams. Finally, we looked at the various tools available in Draw to convert bitmap images to vectors and vice versa.

Using these tools and skills, Draw is capable of some very sophisticated results. However, the package's real potential comes to the forefront when used with other parts of the suite. In Part 2, you'll be putting these tools at the heart of a variety of projects, from adding panache to Calc's charts, depth to Impress slideshows, and interactivity to Writer's web design tools, we still have plenty to uncover!

# CHAPTER 7

# Turn Data into Information with Base

**B**ase, one of the latest additions to the OpenOffice.org family of applications, brings much-needed database capabilities to the suite. Databases are usually thought of as the preserve of either programmers or system administrators working in large organizations, which can lead more casual users either to regard them as too difficult to work with or, more likely, to ignore them altogether. And yet, a simple database can be an asset in so many ways, allowing a user to assemble, sort, and query a dataset to discover relationships that may not be apparent by looking at information in isolation.

The purpose of a database is simple: to turn data into information. This is achieved by giving end users the opportunity to view and manipulate the dataset selectively, filtering out the parts that might get in the way, to see how data elements are related. For example, a large telecom company might have a database of 50 billion records and need to pinpoint all the calls from a particular location, user, or number. At the other end of the scale, a home user might want to see how many e-mails came from a particular friend. Both of these scenarios involve querying and filtering data from a database to create usable information. Databases in OpenOffice.org can be stand-alone entities or can be a data source available to other areas of the suite. To accomplish the latter, a database needs to be registered to the suite so that it can then be accessed using the F4 key.

To add slightly to the confusion, the term *database* can apply to both the software used to manage these processes and the collection of information that is stored by the software.

In this chapter we're aiming for somewhere between the two extremes of database usage. You'll begin with a very simple customer address book—which you will later use to create a mail merge—and then add more information and data types as you go along. In the process of creating this project you will look at the four basic database elements: tables, forms, queries, and reports. You'll also examine dynamic filtering, which on the fly can hide records in which you're not interested, giving you access only to the information necessary to get a particular job done.

In table view (see the later section "The Base Wizards," subsection "Tables"), a Base project looks just like a spreadsheet, with data ranged across columns and rows, which is essentially how the data is stored. It's possible to add data in cells just as you did previously in Calc. More usefully, you can build forms with a variety of widgets (that is, operating system elements such as buttons, lists, and drop-downs), to input data and view records. The table view provides a sortable overview of a large portion of the dataset, while the form view allows you to look at and edit the database as a collection of individual records.

## The Interface

Base is the black sheep of the OpenOffice.org family, in that the interface is markedly different from those of the other applications. The interface still has the menu bar and a toolbar across the top, but the rest of the window is completely different. Partly this is because Base didn't start life as an OO.o project—it grew from the HSQLDB (Hyper-threaded Structured Query Language Database) project. But it also reflects the different way that database software works. Later on, as we progress through the creation of a project, the familiar Writer interface will reappear as Base's form editor.

The main interface is divided in three (see Figure 7-1). At the top is the menu bar and the toolbar. They provide rapid access to a range of tools and options, including the usual configuration stuff, under Tools ➤ Options. The Base-specific options here (under the Base Disclosure icon) show the Connections database (which allows you to connect Base to a selection of industry-standard database types) and the Registered database. The latter is quite important, especially if you change the location of the original database file (i.e., move it to a different folder), because the Edit button will allow you to reassociate the database with a particular file.

The lower section of the application window is split into a database pane, which contains icons for the different kinds of view available—see the later section "The Base Wizards"—and a Task pane with tools for creating new views and accessing existing ones. The contents of the second pane will change, depending on which icon is selected in the first.

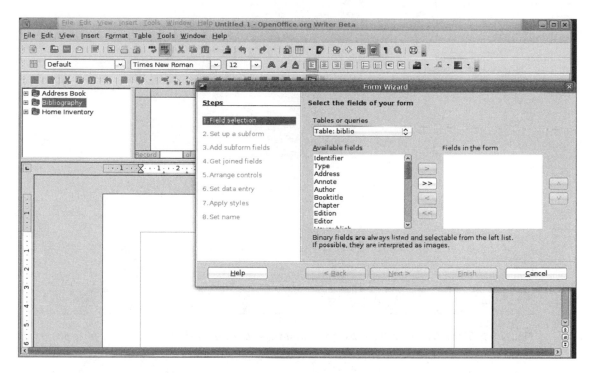

**Figure 7-1.** *The interface in Base is slightly different from the standard application look and feel, but there are a few common points.*

# The Base Wizards

On launching Base for the first time, a wizard offers to guide you through the creation of a database (see Figure 7-2). It is possible to start from scratch, but the wizard makes everything easier, so let's start with that. The first screen allows you to select whether to create a new database, open an existing one, or connect to an external database. Because you're going to define every single element of the database and populate it with information, you'll need the first option, so ensure that is selected. Then click Next to move on.

There are a couple of options in the second and final screen of this wizard. Firstly you need to register the database with OpenOffice.org (see Figure 7-3). This simply means that the application will be aware of the database and its structure and can work with its contents. This way, at a later date, it will be possible to access this information—if necessary—from other applications in the suite.

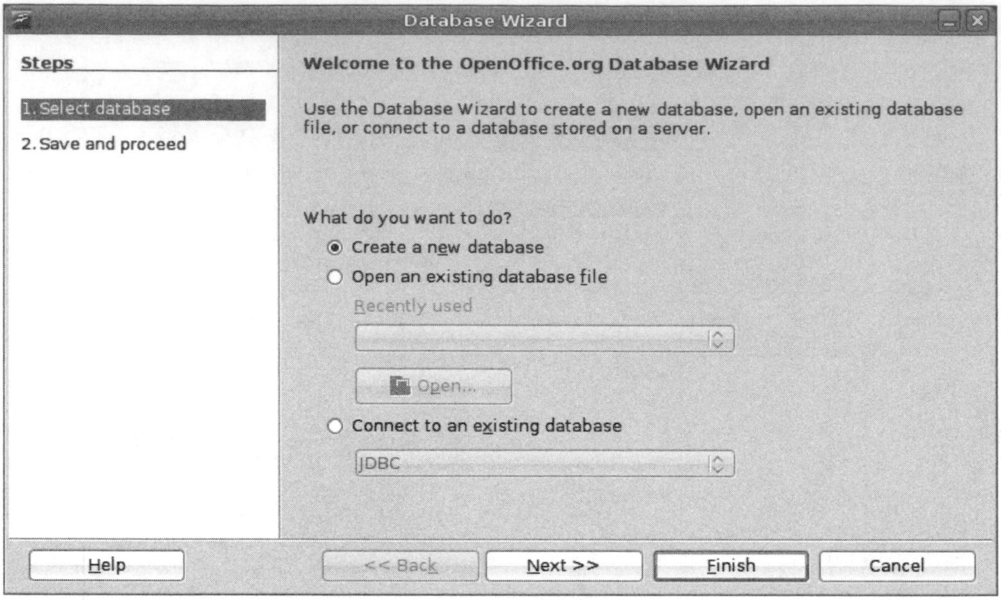

**Figure 7-2.** *The wizards in Base are great at hand-holding, and there is always a summary of what to expect under the Help button.*

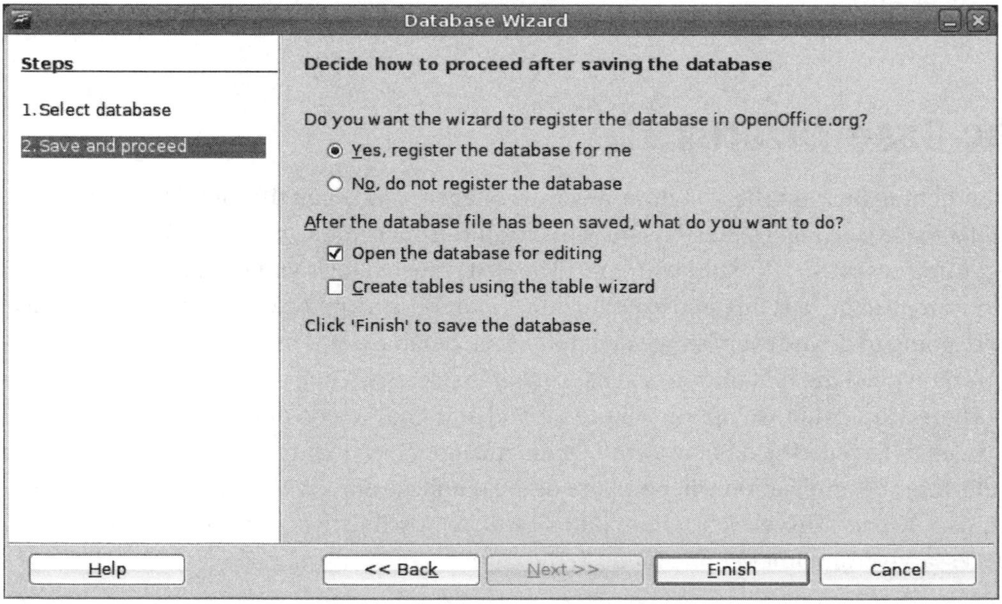

**Figure 7-3.** *By registering the database with OO.o, it becomes possible to use the information in any other part of the application suite.*

In the lower section make sure that Open the database for editing is selected; then click Next again. This will launch the normal file manager, allowing you to save the new database somewhere on the file system. Although saving a project before anything has actually been done to it might seem a little odd, this is the normal way of working with databases. Then, once you begin creating structure and adding data, you won't have to worry about saving, because that is all done automatically.

As mentioned earlier, you're going to look at two distinct ways of working in a database: table view and form view. Base has wizards to cover both methods. You will use these to create basic structure and a form and then employ the available manual options to tweak these to your purposes.

---

■**Tip** An Address data source is already built into Base. It can take address data from the Thunderbird e-mail client (and also Evolution on Linux) and make it usable from within OO.o projects. You're starting a new address book for the purposes of working with a simple data scheme and exploring how it can be expanded at a later date.

---

## Tables

Let's start by creating a new table to hold the data. Tables are the basic organizational structure of the database; typically each row becomes a single record that is divided into sections using the columns. The result looks very like a spreadsheet, but there are a few significant differences between the two forms. For instance, in a spreadsheet each cell is essentially an individual entity within it, while in a database a row usually constitutes a single "record." Moreover, a spreadsheet in OO.o has to be loaded into RAM, whereas you access a database directly from the hard disk. One consequence of this is that once you exit a cell in a database, the information is written to disk; in a spreadsheet the document has to be saved explicitly before it is written to disk.

The general topic of database design can, and has, filled many books, and the intricacies of this job—and it can be a job—are outside the scope of this book.

You're going to begin with a single table. This is where you design the structure of the database, so it's worth thinking through the elements you'll need to include. Note, however, that you can add other fields later on.

In the lower section of the window, choose Tables from the left-hand pane. Then select Use Wizard to Create Table to launch the wizard (see Figure 7-4). The first section of the wizard is built around a selection of different projects, divided into Business and Personal. Select Business, and then use the Sample Tables drop-down list to choose Customers.

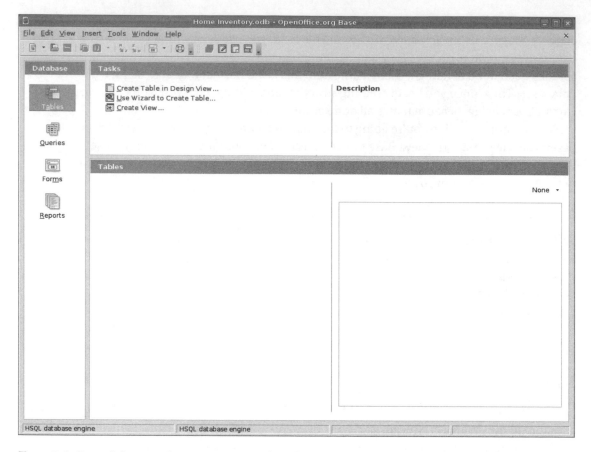

**Figure 7-4.** *One of the most important ways of working with data is through a table, which is accessible via the Tables icon (on the left).*

Below the drop-down is a list of available fields that will show a range of options, depending on the table type selected. In our example, the Available Fields list is populated with options that make sense in a business's customer address book, such as CompanyName, Address, E-mail, Country, and ContactName. You can add these to the table by selecting an entry and using the single arrow between the two columns to move it from left to right. The double arrows will pull every field name from the left column to the right column.

When selecting fields to use, think about how you might have to access data in the future. For example, are you likely to need to visit each client in a potential region or postal code during one trip? If so, you will want to include the CountryorRegion and PostalCode options.

Once you've populated the list on the right, you can use the up and down arrow icons to reorder the information to suit your particular needs. In a traditional scheme this would be something like

CompanyName

Address

PostalCode

PhoneNumber

E-mail

But more can be added or removed, depending on your needs. Once all the fields are set, use the Next button to move on.

In the next section of the wizard, you will define the type of information each field is going to contain. On the left of the window you select the field to edit; options are configured on the right. For your simple address book, all of the entries are defined as Text [ VARCHAR ], which will allow you to enter freeform text into the box. You can also define the length of the entry. This figure is set as number of characters, so, for example, a UK postcode will need to be at least nine characters long and a US ZIP code will need to be five characters long. But the address field will need to be somewhere between 200 and 300 characters.

The Entry Required option will make a field mandatory and prevent a record from being added to the system unless that value is filled out. For example, in your address book, you're going to make the CompanyName and E-mail address required fields, because this is the minimum amount of information you can use to solicit work and send invoices.

It's possible, even at this stage, to adjust the order of fields—perhaps moving a ZIP code field closer to an address field—by selecting a field in the right section and using the up and down arrows to move the entry to a new location.

After clicking the Next button, you can set the database's primary key (see Figure 7-5). This is the unique value the software adds to each record (or row) to identify it internally. The primary key can either be generated automatically by the software or taken from one of the fields defined earlier. You must ensure, though, that any field used is going to contain a unique value. Thus it wouldn't be sensible to base this on a person or a company name because this risks duplication. It's possible to generate the primary key from a combination of fields, which reduces the chance of duplication. But to keep things simple, we've elected to create a primary key and to add a value automatically. The Auto value option will increment the primary key value for each record automatically.

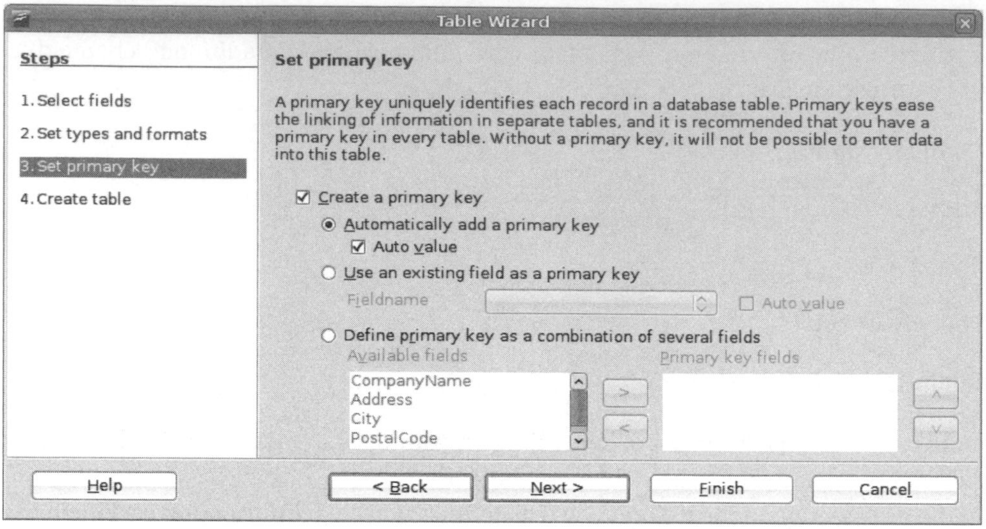

**Figure 7-5.** *Each record must have a unique identifier, which is what the database itself uses to organize information.*

After clicking Next, you have the option to rename the table or to keep it as is and then to select whether to begin entering data into the database, to edit the table manually, or to create a data entry form using the Clear Form Wizard.

You'll be re-editing the table and creating a form later, so go with the first option. You can add some details using the table view. Select Insert data immediately (see Figure 7-6) and then click Finish.

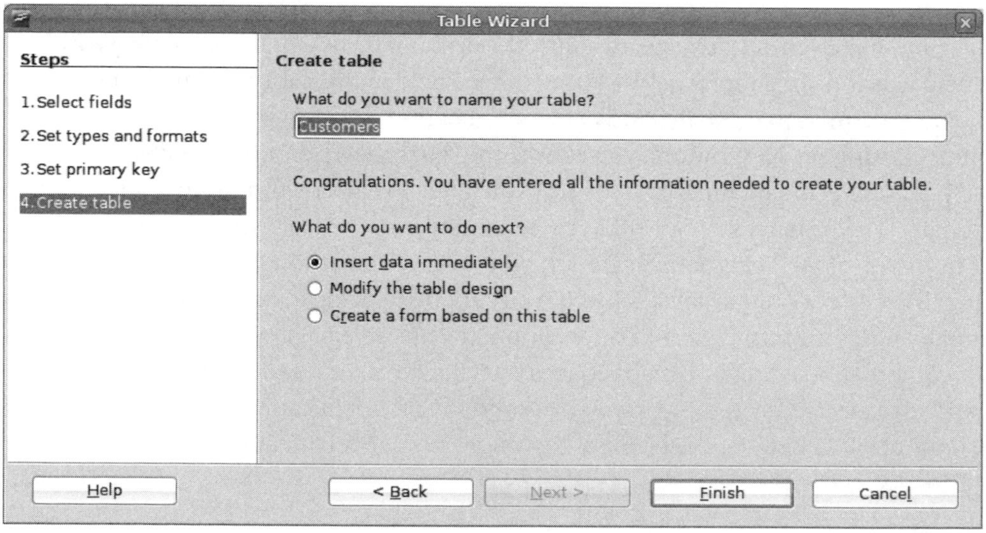

**Figure 7-6.** *The wizard system provides a logical progression through the process of creating the database elements.*

## Types of Information

The way fields are defined in Base affects the kind of information you can add to them. A field type simply configures Base to store and label the data in a particular way, which makes it possible to perform certain functions on them. Many of the field types, such as integer, bigint, smallint, and tinyint, deal exclusively with numerical data, but our database will consist of just a few data types:

Text [ VARCHAR ]—We've used this most because it enables us to add freeform text to a record.

Yes/No [ BOOLEAN ]—Used to define binary options, such as whether a customer has placed an order or whether an invoice has been paid.

Date [ DATE ]—Allows the user to input a properly formatted date into the database, such as the delivery date for a project or the expected payment date for an invoice.

Date/Time [ TIMESTAMP ]—Stamps the record with the time it was created.

# Using Tables

Once the Table Wizard has completed, you'll end up with something that looks very like a spreadsheet, with the field labels defined earlier ranged across the top, below a new toolbar. Resize the columns by dragging and dropping the lines between each label to the desired size (see Figure 7-7). Enter data into the first record by clicking into the first usable column (second from the left and labeled CompanyName in our example) and typing out the information. As you begin to type, note that a second line appears on the spreadsheet, indicating that a record has been added to the database. Once the first column is filled, click into the second one (or use the Tab key to move on) and add the next bit. Do this until each column is filled. Don't worry if part of the record is incomplete because editing a record simply involves selecting the appropriate entry using the mouse and editing the text as normal.

---

■**Tip**  Here's how to preview the table's content: from the main Base Interface, select the Tables icon from the left pane. To the right of the Tables pane is a button labeled None. Click the little arrow to the right of this and select Document.

---

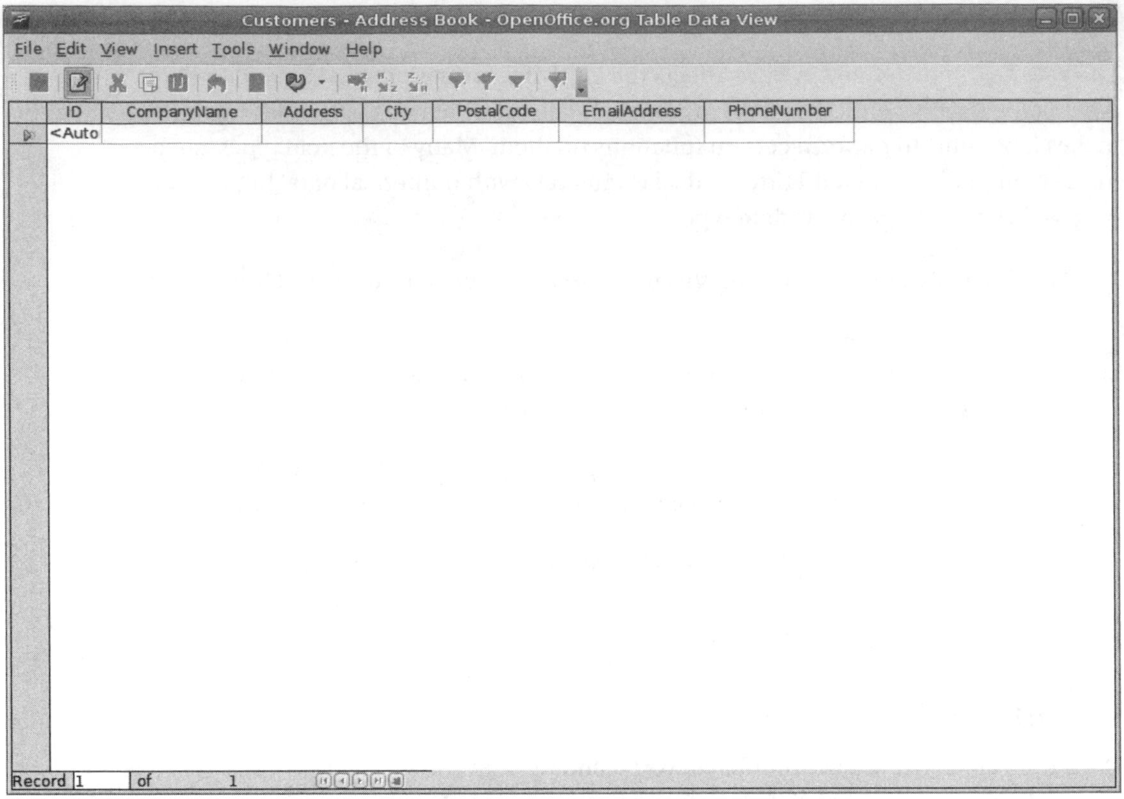

**Figure 7-7.** *Just like a spreadsheet, the database tables are arranged into columns and rows, with the former based on data elements and the latter defining a single record.*

This is the simplest way of adding data to the database. Each record is given its own unique identifier (in our case this is the primary key created earlier, which is an auto-incremented number beginning with 0) and is saved automatically to the system (see Figure 7-8). Once data has been added, click File ➤ Close to close down the current table view and return to the main interface. If Tables is still selected in the left-hand pane, you should notice that the Tables section on the right now has an entry with the name of the table created earlier. Double-click this to reopen the table to add or edit information.

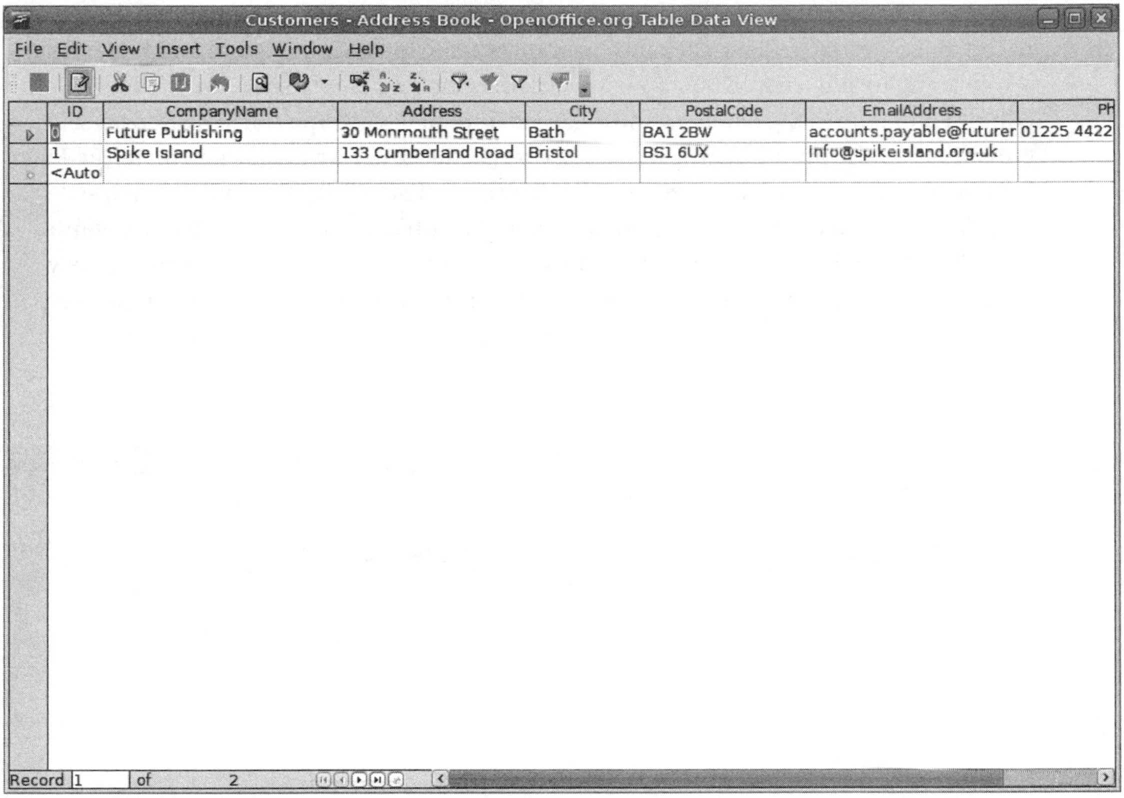

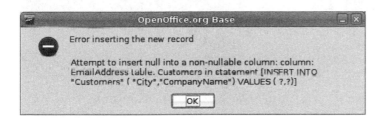

**Figure 7-8.** *Records are saved automatically to the computer once they are created.*

Having begun to enter data into the project, we've identified a shortcoming in the table: there's no space for a "Country" entry. Trying to add information such as Paradise, USA, will lead to an error message (see Figure 7-9) and prevent the currently selected record from being saved.

**Figure 7-9.** *If you attempt to enter data that doesn't conform to the data type provided earlier, an error message will be displayed.*

To remedy this you'll need to edit the table. If the table is open, close it to go back to the main interface. Right-click the Customers table in the Tables pane and select Edit. We're going to add a new field name, so click into the first empty space on the Field Name column and type in the name (Country). Click into the Field Type space next to the new entry and use the drop-down list to select Text [ VARCHAR ] (see Figure 7-10). In the Field Properties section, you can once more configure the field a little more fully, making it mandatory and setting the maximum length of the entry. You can also define a default value for the field, which will be entered automatically into the space every time a new record is created. Because most of our business comes from the UK, it would make sense to put this as the default value. However, since we're thinking of the future, let's leave this blank for now; we'll use a form widget to fill in the information.

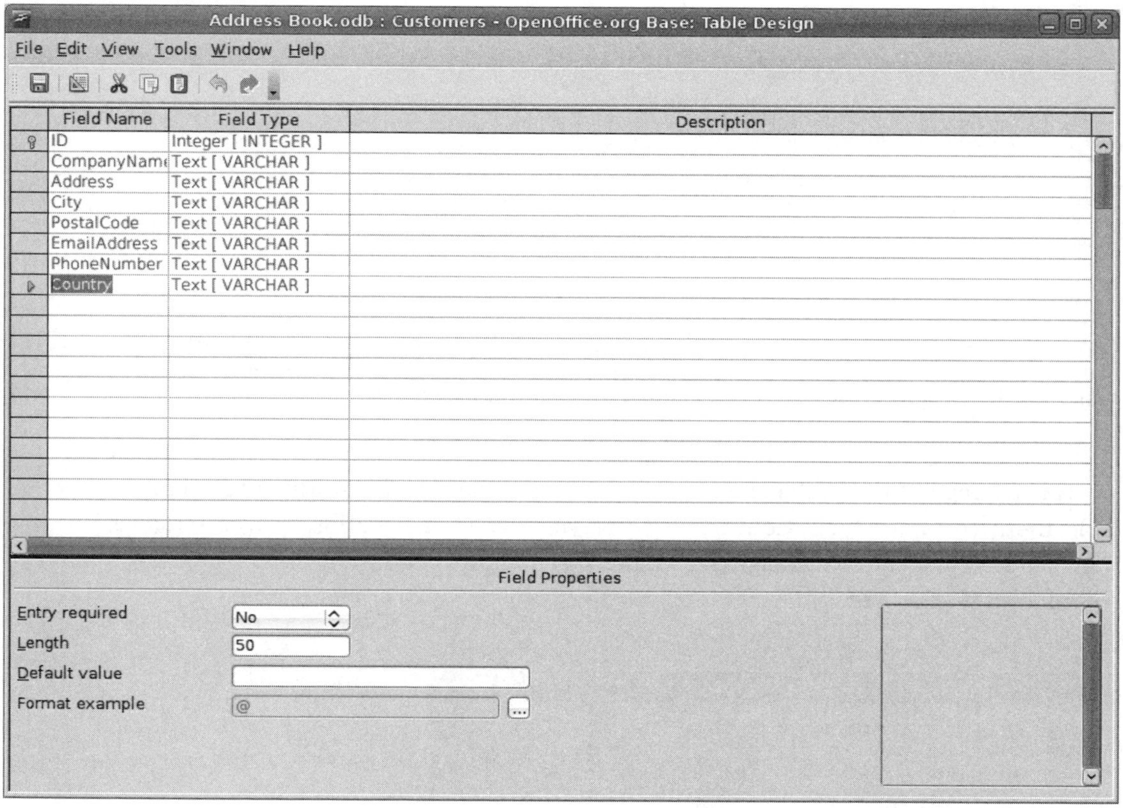

**Figure 7-10.** *Once you have created a table, it's possible to go back and edit it at any time.*

Once the new section has been added, click File ➤ Save to write the changes to the database, and then close down the window to get back to the main interface. Double-click the database to open it and see the new column added to the far right. As with others, click into a space below the column header to enter data.

## The Table Toolbar

The toolbar along the top of a table view has a familiar set of tools for editing and saving records, cutting, copying, pasting, and undoing an edit (see Figure 7-11). A few novel tools are also available.

**Figure 7-11.** *The Table toolbar is divided into sections.*

Immediately to the right of the Undo icon is a Search button. This will launch a comprehensive Search dialog box that can you can use to comb through the entire database (or just a single field name) for a specific word, phrase, or number. Options here allow you to look for the whole word, match the text's case, and look for words at the beginning, middle, or end of an entry. Click Search, and the first record conforming to the search string will be highlighted in red. In addition, the record number that is highlighted will be noted at the base of the dialog box.

Next to the Search icon is the Refresh button. Click this to ensure that you're looking at the most recent view of the database—it's especially useful if more than one person is working on the database at the same time. If you're working alone, though, it's less useful.

Next we come to the sort buttons, which you can use to reorder the records in either ascending (A-Z) or descending (Z-A) alphabetical order. Select a column and then click one of the buttons to use these tools (see the following subsection for more).

---

■**Note**  When you sort using the ascending option, numbers will appear before any records beginning with the letter A. For example, a record for a customer called "123 Graphics" will appear before Aardvark Graphics. With the descending option it's the other way around; that is, records beginning with numbers will appear at the end of the alphabetical listing.

---

Finally, you have the filter buttons, which you can use to display only those records that conform to some criteria. We'll examine this further in the upcoming section "Simple Filtering."

## Simple Sorting

Once you get beyond a few records, the scheme for displaying them in the order in which they were entered begins to make less sense. For example, it might be much more convenient—in terms of finding a record from the table—to sort them alphabetically by company name. To do this, click the CompanyName column heading to select the entire column, and then use the Sort Ascending button on the toolbar. The records will be instantly reordered alphabetically. To get back to the original state—that is, is the order in which the records were entered—select the ID column to the far left and then sort this using the ascending option.

This method is a blunt instrument, but it is the fastest way of reordering data. To have more control over the ordering, use the main Sort button, which is the first of the trio available. This will launch a new dialog box (see Figure 7-12), enabling you to specify which column should be used for the ordering. Crucially, this allows you to sort on more than one criterion. Thus, you could sort first on CompanyName and then on the E-mail address (setting each one to work on an ascending or descending basis), which means that if you had two contacts in the same company, they would also be organized by their e-mail address. Once you have defined a sort criterion, click OK to see the effect on the table.

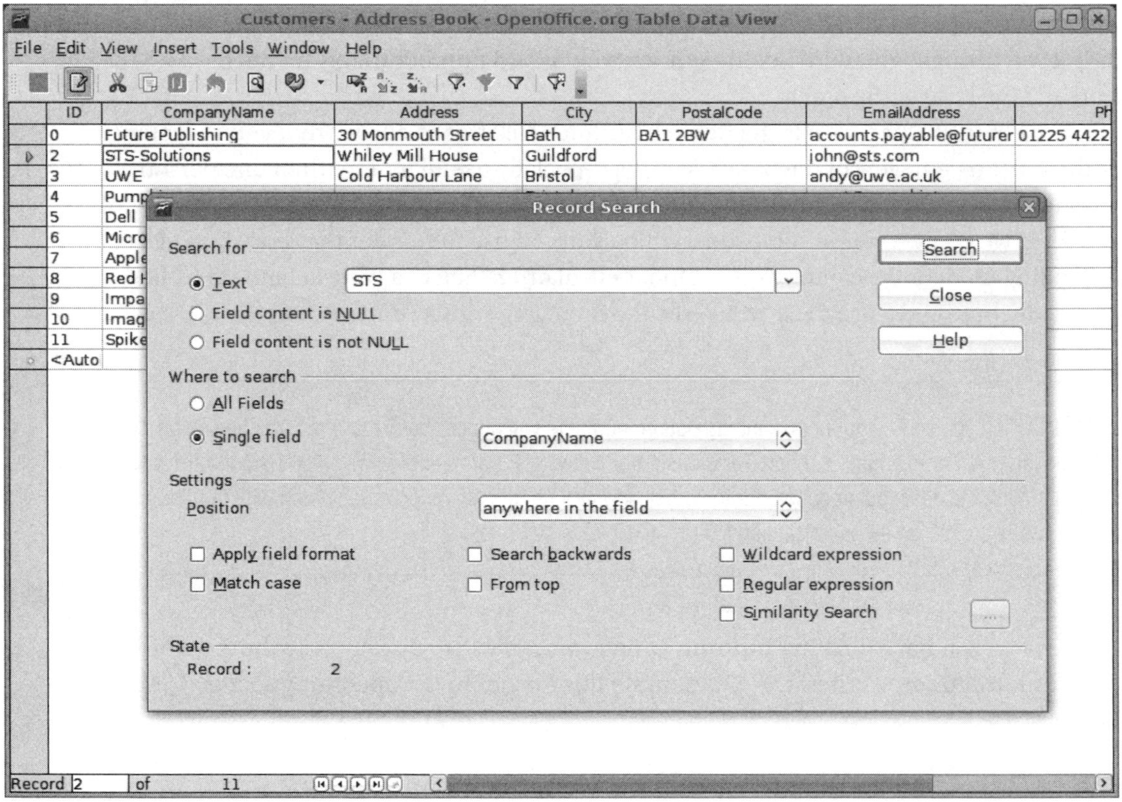

**Figure 7-12.** *The search dialog box allows you to find a specific record in the database.*

## Simple Filtering

For small databases, sorting can be all you need to stay on top of your needs. But once you get beyond, say, a full screen of data, filtering is a much better option, because this will display just the records you're interested in seeing.

At its simplest, you could look through your table of data, select an entry from the City column, and click the AutoFilter button to the right of the toolbar to see only the records featuring that city. As with the search, you can use the main Filter button to create a filter on up to three elements of the database; you can use the final button on the toolbar to remove a filter and show the entire dataset once more (see Figure 7-13).

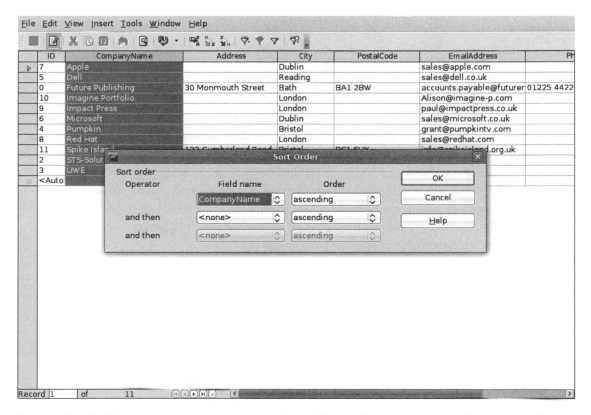

**Figure 7-13.** *The filtering system can take up to three different field arguments, allowing very flexible searching.*

# Using Forms

Tables are not for everyone, and, once you have gone beyond just a few records, having to look along rows and columns to find information can become a hindrance. The solution is to employ Base's forms system to build an interface to the database and use this to input and view records. This is especially beneficial when building a database that other users are likely to be editing, because forms are more user-friendly, allow the user to concentrate on the task at hand (rather than on all the other data), and have coherent labels for each field. You can also add a few widgets to make it easier for the user to input clean, consistent data.

---

■**Note**  OpenOffice.org uses Writer as its table-design tool, so you'll be jumping between the two applications during form building and editing.

---

The form designer itself is really just a specially formatted Writer page, meaning all of the tools available in Writer are right at your fingertips. More importantly, as you'll see later, it's possible to create documents in Writer based on the contents of a database.

In the main interface of Base, select the Forms option from the left-hand pane, and then click Use Wizard to Create Form to launch the wizard. A new Writer window will launch, with the Form Design toolbar attached to the left edge of the window (see Figure 7-14). This will rapidly be overlaid with the Form Wizard dialog box that will walk you through the eight stages of the form-design process.

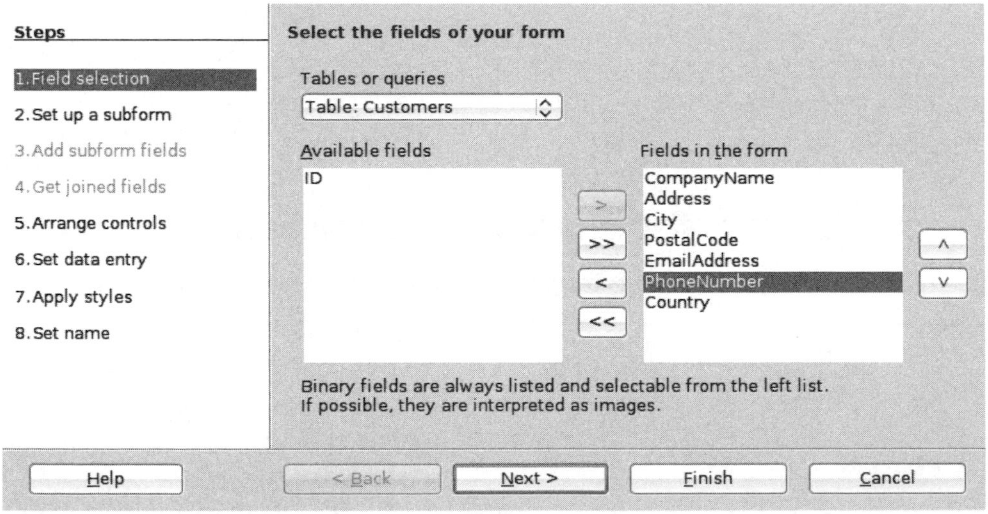

**Figure 7-14.** *Forms can use all or just a few table elements, making it valuable on multiuser systems.*

Begin by defining the field names that are to be included in the form, using the same system as in the Table Wizard (see earlier). Select a field name from the list in the left column, and use the arrows in the center to move it to the right column. These are the fields that will be included. The double arrow will add every field name, while the left-facing arrows will remove a field name. When more than one entry is in the right column, you can select entries and reorder them using the up/down arrows to the right of the list. When this is all correct, click Next to move on.

We're not using subforms at present, so click Next again to get to the Arrange Controls section. Here you can define how the form will be laid out. Four options are available: two columnar, one spreadsheet-like grid, and a multicolumn grid (see Figure 7-15). Choose one of these (the preview in the main window will update as one of the options is selected), and click Next again.

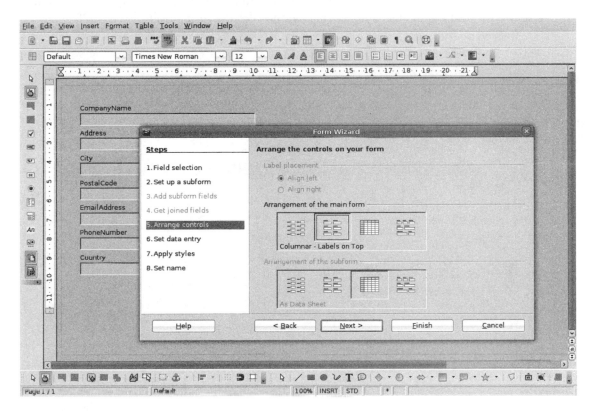

**Figure 7-15.** *The arrangement of the main form can have an impact on usability.*

■**Note** A subform is basically a form within a form that could be connected to a separate database or table. For instance, a student database might contain a subform listing all available courses, allowing you to assign a student to a particular course.

With the Data Entry Mode options, you can set the form to be available only for data entry or for entry and display. The former is useful when there's a separation between those users adding records to a database and those who interrogate the data. Because you're creating a fairly simple project, however, let's stick with the latter option, which will also allow you to view and edit individual records using the form view. Select the option This Form Is to Display All Data, and then add one of the trio of restrictions if necessary. Because you're keeping everything writable, you won't be selecting any of these.

In the next section you can apply one of the premade styles to the form. Again, selecting from the list will dynamically update the preview (see Figure 7-16). Once you have selected a color scheme, choose from No borders, 3D look, or Flat. This will change the appearance of the borders around the form elements and is entirely up to your personal choice. We've opted here for the Flat look because this provides definition and doesn't look too dated. Click Next. The form will remain totally editable later, so if none of the available styles seem suitable, pick the next-best option; you'll get to editing in a moment.

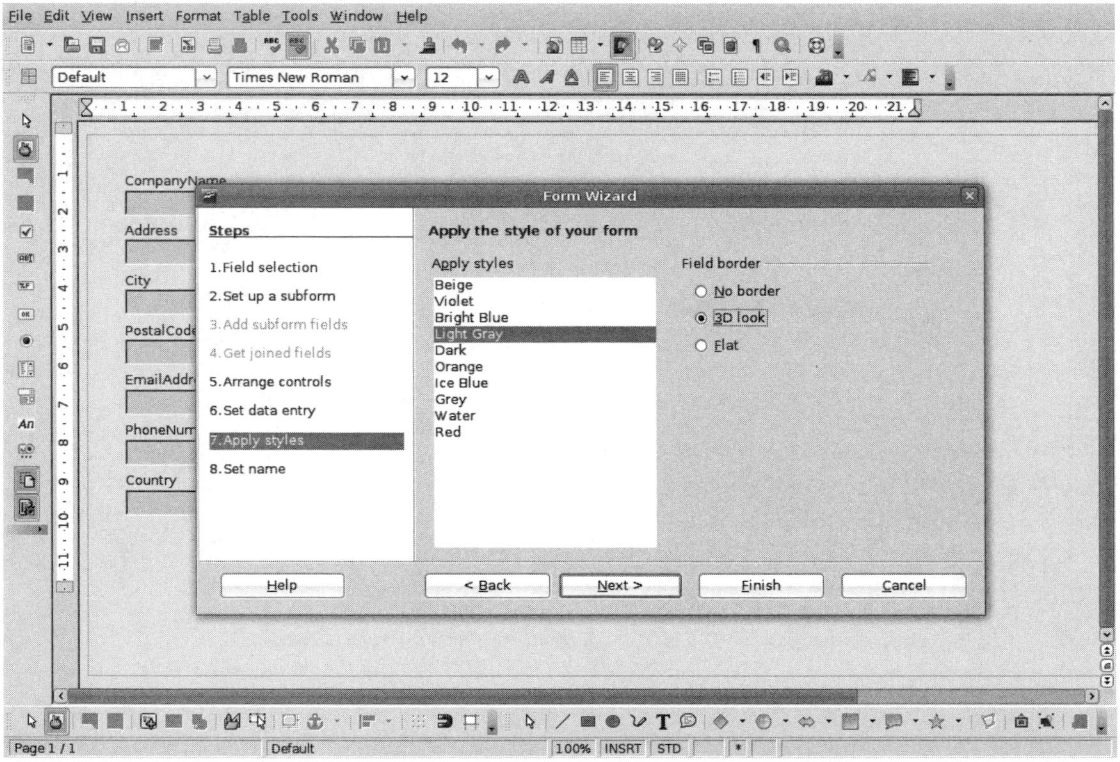

**Figure 7-16.** *There are quite a few premade templates, but it's also possible to redesign the form totally at a later date.*

In the final section of the wizard you can give the form a name. It's important to be distinctive here because it's possible to have more than one form associated with a database, and a nonobvious name might make it more problematic to manage in the future.

The final option in this section is either to work with the form—i.e., begin entering data—or to modify it. Select the latter, and then click Finish to create the form and go into Edit mode.

## Editing the Form

As mentioned earlier, Base's form-editing system opens up an instance of Writer, with the addition of the Form Controls and Form Design toolbars tacked on, which makes it quite easy to perform sweeping edits to the form. For example, right-click any blank space and select Page from the context-sensitive menu. Under the Background tab you can adjust the color using the normal palette, or select Graphic to add a background image using the Browse button. With images, you can set the position of the image—useful for small brand elements—or have it fill the entire page (beware, this can cause image distortion) or tile it. Remember when using a graphic that the intention should be to improve the usability of the form, so anything garish (or pictures of loved ones, say) is likely to annoy users quite quickly. Any image you add in this way will be used as the background on each form page, with the form elements arranged over the top of it.

The form elements themselves are individual parts of the page (well, the default ones are grouped, but we'll deal with that later) and so can be maneuvered around to make the most pleasing arrangement. To make edits to these elements beyond movement, simply double-click to open the Form Control dialog box (see Figure 7-17). This is a persistent box, and so it can be left open as you select different elements ready for editing. All changes will be immediately reflected on the page.

The Form Control dialog box is quite a complex beast, with options available to change the font (click the ellipsis [. . .] to launch the font browser), change the look of text boxes from flat to 3D or borderless, and make the space larger for multiline text. Especially useful if data is being entered by someone else is the Help text box, because anything written in here will be displayed as a tool tip when a user holds the cursor over the form element.

**Figure 7-17.** *The elements of the form are, by default, grouped together with their label.*

One of the things you may want to change is the text box labels because these will initially be displayed using the field name, which, because of the way Base formats "machine-readable" content (as opposed to human-readable), won't have any spaces between the words. Company Name, for example, will be rendered CompanyName. To change this you'll first have to ungroup each element in turn (right-click the element and select Ungroup), and then double-click the label to open the Form Control dialog box. Because you've now selected a single element, the available parts of the Form Control dialog box will be slightly different; you're interested is the Label box near the top. It will contain the label text that was applied by default (see Figure 7-18). Click into here and edit the text as normal. This won't change the actual label in the database, so it's possible to tailor this text to the end user of the form without worrying that big changes are happening in the structure of your database.

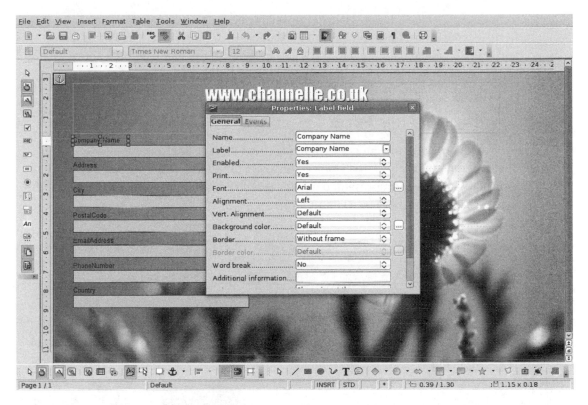

**Figure 7-18.** *Changing the label on a form will have no impact on the database information itself, so you can tailor the label to the audience.*

Making changes to multiple elements is the same as changing a single one. Simply use the Shift+Click option to select multiple form elements, and then edit the common settings, such as border style and label font, in the Form Control dialog box. You may want to change the font to conform with other "branded" documents. But as with any other document, it's probably best not to use lots of different fonts because this will make the final product look messy. Also remember to choose fonts that are readable onscreen at the size they're likely to be seen.

In our example, we have also added a text frame (Insert ➤ Frame), anchored this to the page by double-clicking and selecting the appropriate option, and added a heading for the form. This will become an immovable part of the form.

---

■**Caution** Remember that because you're working in Writer here rather than in the database itself, you must save your document regularly to ensure that you don't lose your work in the event of a crash. Should a crash happen, the OpenOffice Recovery Wizard should kick in and save the work, ready for recovery later. But it's better to be safe than sorry.

---

Once each form element is labeled correctly and the page looks right, you can save and close the window and shift back to the database user interface. The Forms icon should still be selected on the left, and a new entry, with the name defined above, will be visible in the Forms page. Double-click this to open the form in its normal mode.

## Inputting Data in a Form

The normal form view introduces yet another user interface, but this one—with a toolbar along both top and bottom—will look a little more familiar. Because of the way we've set up the database, the form presented initially should be populated with the data from the first record in the database (see Figure 7-19).

**Figure 7-19.** *Use the Tab key to jump between the different parts of the form; use the toolbar at the bottom to create new records.*

There are quite a few redundant toolbars in this view, such as the Form Design and Control toolbars and the Drawing toolbar. You can remove these using the View ➤ Toolbars menu and clean up the interface a little. Ideally, you should leave the Standard toolbar—for copy, paste, etc.—and the Form Navigation toolbar, which, by default, is arrayed along the bottom of the window. As with other toolbars, this is divided into particular regions.

## WRITER'S BIBLIOGRAPHIC DATABASE

One of the most common uses for databases when using OO.o Writer is as a bibliography and citation management system. In fact, Writer ships with a partially built bibliography included, which can be opened and edited to fit in with any research project.

To access the bibliographic database from within Writer, click Tools ➤ Bibliographic Database. It will launch in a hybrid view, with a table at the top of the window and a form at the bottom. Along the top of the window is a toolbar with just a few filter options, which work in the same way as the filters we've covered here. From here, you can delete, create, and edit records just as you have done in this chapter.

The bibliographic database is covered in detail, including how to manage citations and bibliographies in the APA and MLA styles in Chapter 10.

The first section, which takes up almost half of the toolbar, deals with navigating through records and adding or deleting them. On the far left is a numerical box that allows you to enter a number and press the Enter key to jump straight to that record. Next to this is a quartet of arrows that, respectively, moves to the first, previous, next, and last record. In all cases you will be presented with a single record rather than a sea of information as you would in a table.

The fifth arrow icon will create a new, blank record ready to be populated with information. You can also create a new record by clicking the Next Record icon when you're viewing the "Last" record. Once you've created a new record, you can type information into each part. Press the Tab key to shift through the elements without having to use the mouse.

When you create a new record and begin to enter data, the next two icons, which allow you to save a record or undo an entry, will become active. You can use the third icon in this section to delete a record.

The next section offers the same sorting options as are available in the table view. So, for example, clicking the Sort Ascending button will change the order of the records in the form view (it doesn't change the structure of the database itself) to an ascending alphabetical order based on the first element of the form, which in our case is the company name. And, again, the Sort button allows you to sort on up to three criteria.

The next section deals with filters, which, as mentioned before, you can use to remove items from a view that don't conform to particular criteria. For example, if you select the Country element of one of our records (in this case it's defined as UK) and then click the AutoFormat button, any record that doesn't have UK in its Country field is excluded from the view. This information can then be sorted using the sort buttons, navigated through with the navigation buttons, and even refiltered on a different element. Notice that when you apply a filter, the numerical value of "available" records on the far left of the toolbar will change to show the number of records in this particular view. Remove any filters using the last button of this group.

The final button will split the main window to display both the table view and the form view of the database, making it possible to get both an overview of a dataset and a good look at individual records. You can enter data on either part, and it will be mirrored in its counterpart.

## Adding an Interactive Widget

One of the problems of entering data into a database, especially when more than one person is entering this data, is that the results can be inconsistent. For example, one user may type "USA," another may type "America," while another may input "United States of America." Moreover, having to type in the same bit of information over and over again can be tedious. The solution to both of these issues is to provide a drop-down (or combo box) list of all valid entries. Fortunately this process is quite simple. It involves creating a new table for the database and then linking this to the form element.

To begin, go into the Tables section of the main interface and select Create Table in Design View. This will launch the (by-now) familiar spreadsheet-like table view, where you can define new field names and types (see Figure 7-20). We're going for a very simple one-column table, with the Field Name "Country" and a Field Type of Text [ VARCHAR ].

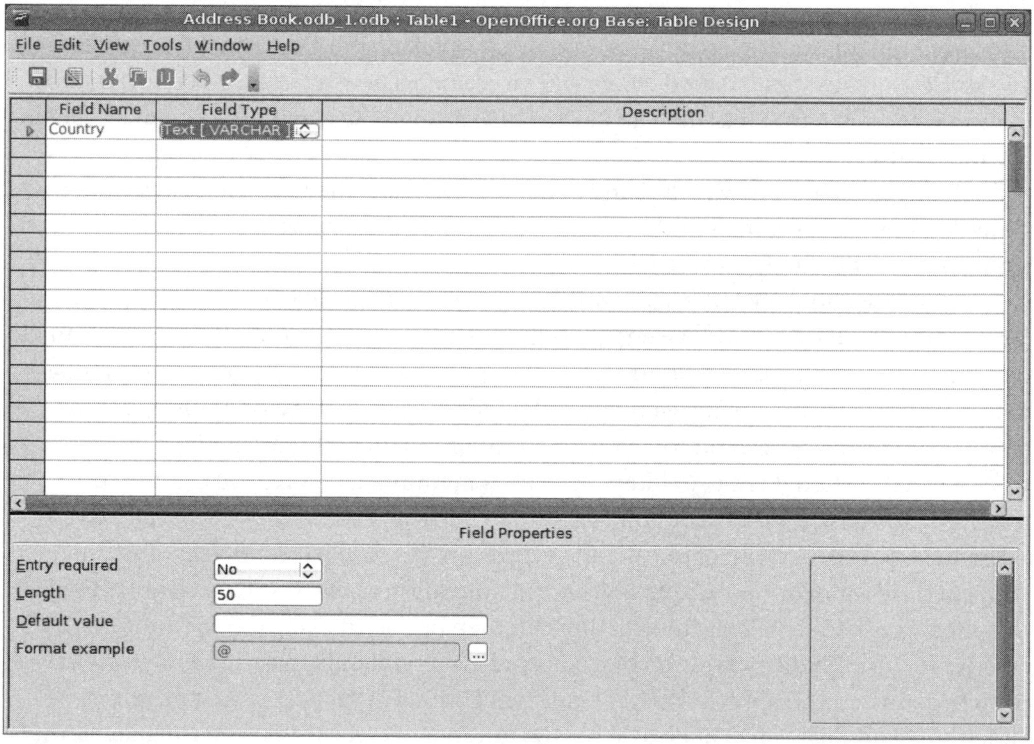

**Figure 7-20.** *Create a new table.*

Click Save, provide a name for the table (see Figure 7-21), and then select Yes when Base offers to add a unique key to the table.

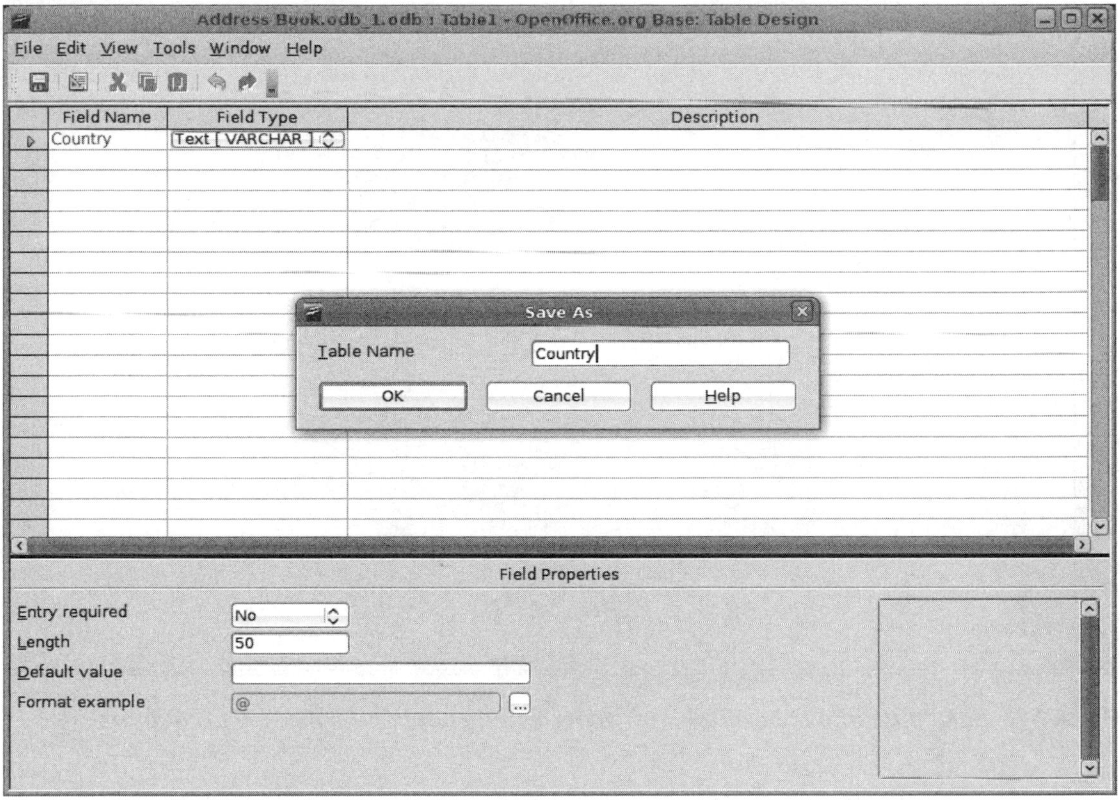

**Figure 7-21.** *Provide a name for the new table.*

Close down the Table window and go back to the main interface. There will now be a second entry in the Tables part of the window. Double-click this to open up the new table, ready for data (see Figure 7-22). As we've defined it, this new table will have a pair of columns to house the identifier and the country name. Add new records and populate the cells with country names. Save the table (File ➤ Save) and then close down the window to go back to the main interface.

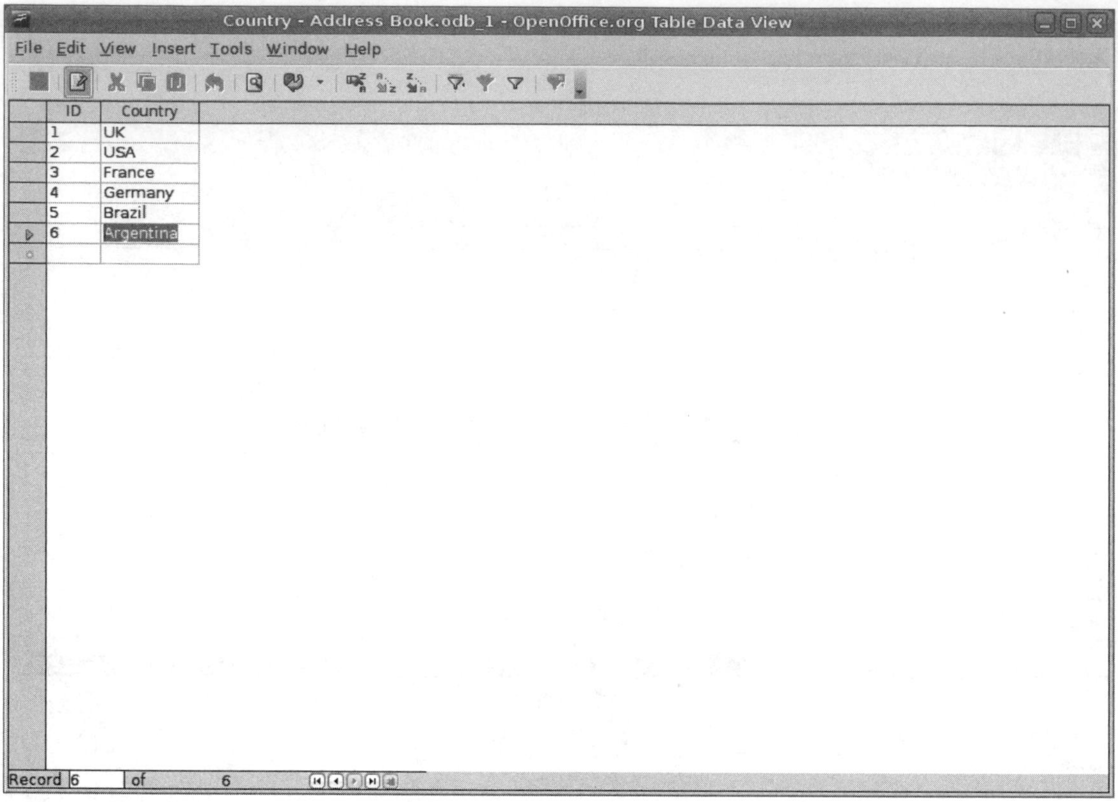

**Figure 7-22.** *Enter data into the new table by typing country names into the second column.*

From the Form Control toolbar, click the Combo Box option (see Figure 7-23) and draw a box in place of the original text box. As you release the mouse button, a wizard will launch to set up the content of the combo box. The first part of this will display a list of available tables from which to draw the data. Select Country (see Figure 7-24) and then click Next. In the second part of the wizard you can select the particular column that will be used to populate the combo box, which in our case is the Country one.

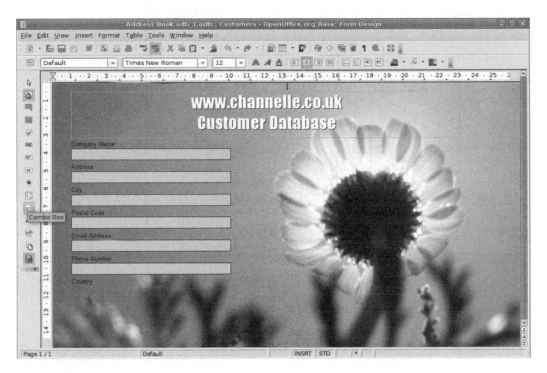

**Figure 7-23.** *You add a combo box to the form to make it easier for users to add consistent data for a particular element.*

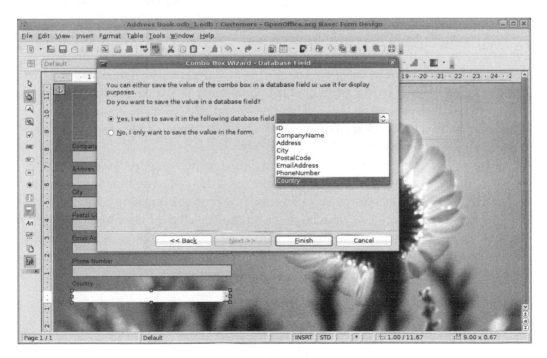

**Figure 7-24.** *Link the two databases.*

Now go into the Forms section, right-click the recently built form, and select Edit. Once in edit mode, select the original "Country" text box, where the user was expected to type out the country title (not the label), and get rid of it by using the Delete key or by right-clicking and selecting Cut. If the Form Control toolbar is not visible in the window, select View ➤ Toolbars ➤ Form Controls to see it.

The final part of the wizard allows you either to keep this data associated only with the form or to send it into a particular column of the table on which the form is based. We're opting for the latter option and we've used the drop-down to ensure the Country field is selected. Click Finish to have the combo box added to the page.

As part of the final formatting, we've double-clicked the form element and added a flat, black border and resized the box to conform with the rest of the page. Click Save to close the window, and then double-click the form name to see the normal form view. The Country form element will now be a drop-down list, complete with arrow. If you click on it, the list from the Country table will be displayed. This is a dynamic list, so if, in the future, you add new entries to the Country table, they will appear in the drop-down.

# Queries

Earlier we looked briefly at the possibilities afforded by filtering out records from the dataset. The problem with filters used in tables and forms is that they are a temporary measure. Fortunately we have a more permanent solution in the form of queries. Basically, a query is defined in the same way as a filter, but it can be saved in its own space on the system and can provide an immediate, targeted view of the data. The beauty of this, of course, is that you could create many different views of the same data that you can then access and modify, depending on the needs of the end user. For example, in the Customer database you have added a couple of columns to deal with "Annual Sales" and "Outstanding Invoices" and set the field type as Numerical data. While it's appropriate for some users to see this information, it might not be for others, so you can create a view that contains everything *except* those sales figures.

Go into the Queries section using the icon in the left pane, and select the Queries Wizard (see Figure 7-25). As with other wizards you've used, this will launch a new window in the center of the screen that will guide you through the process of creating a new view.

The process itself is also very similar to the way you created the table in the first place. In the first section you define the columns to be included in the view. Again, you use the arrows between the two columns to add or remove items and the up/down arrows on the right of the right-hand column to reorder the fields.

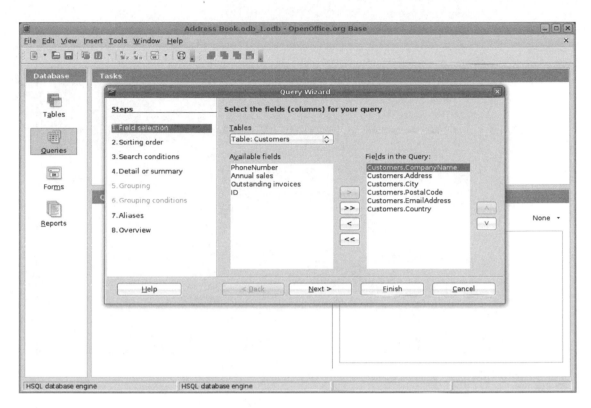

**Figure 7-25.** *Queries work in the same way as filters, but they can be used over and over again.*

The second section of the wizard is similar to the filter options you used earlier. From the drop-down lists you can set the view to sort records based on any field name and then define whether they will be sorted in ascending or descending alphabetical order. It's possible to sort according to four different criteria. For example, if you had lots of contacts within a single company, you could sort first by company name and then by contact name.

You could use the Search section to refine the query further (see Figure 7-26). For example, you could set this view to include only clients from the UK by setting the Fields to "Customers.Country," the Condition to "is equal to," and the value to "UK." It's also possible to skip this and just use the Query tool to show specific fields. You can also skip the Detail and Summary page for now and move straight onto the Aliases section (see Figure 7-27), which allows you to rewrite the column headings (as you did earlier in the form) to make them more useful to the user.

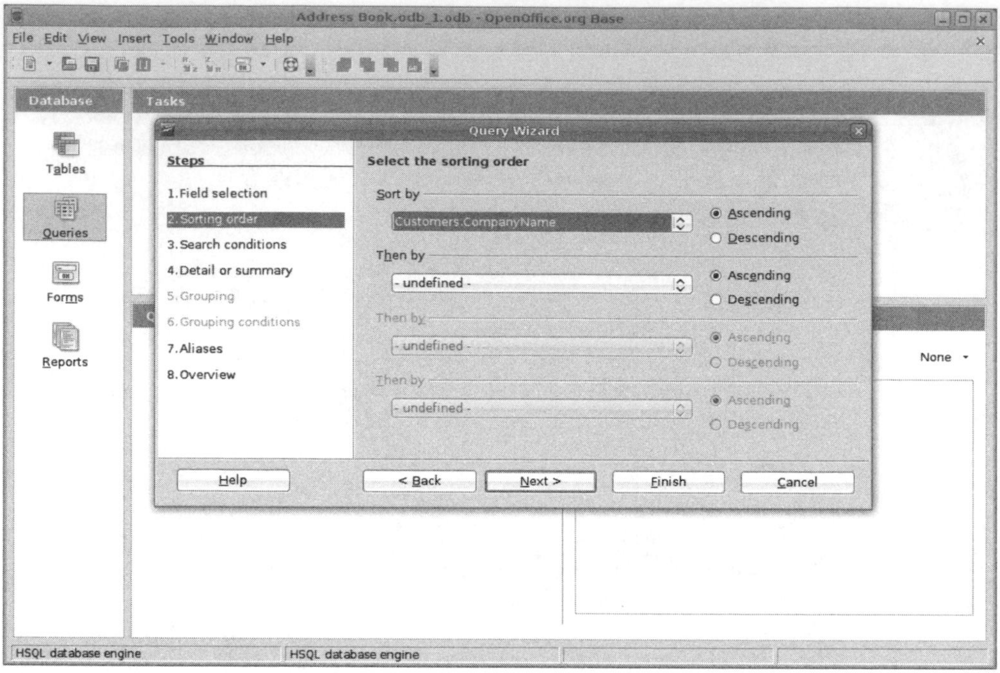

**Figure 7-26.** *You can sort queries according to four different criteria.*

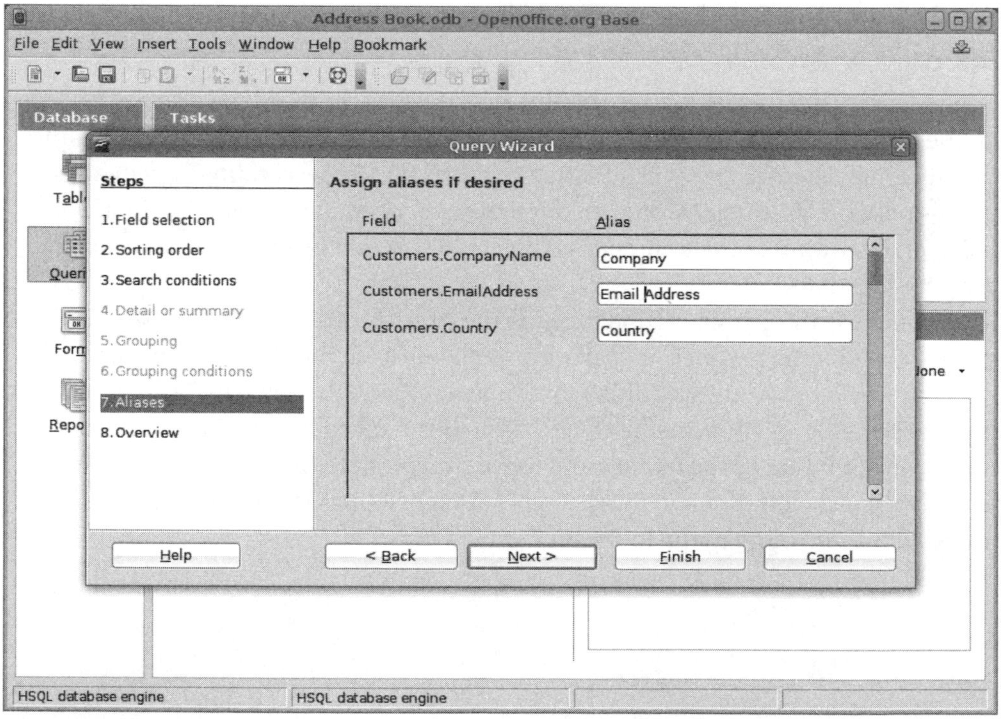

**Figure 7-27.** *Use an Alias to give users a more readable version of the field names.*

Finally, the Overview offers a summary of how the query is defined and also the chance to give it a useful name. Add the name in the appropriate space, and then click Finish to create the view.

To complete this section, you could also create a second query using the wizard that shows just the sales figures for each company.

---

### FORMATTING NUMBERS

Though you've used mostly alphanumeric data so far, that is, entries made up of the letters of the alphabet, punctuation marks, or numbers, there are times when data is purely numerical and needs to be displayed in an appropriate way. For instance, in the example of adding a little sales data to a company address book, you created a Numerical field type. If you've done this and attempted to enter a number and some currency figure or thousands separators, you will have noticed that everything except the numbers were stripped out.

You can solve this problem by selecting the appropriate column, clicking its title in the table view, and right-clicking and choosing Column Format. The formatting dialog box that appears is exactly the same as that used in Calc, so you can select the type of numerical information being used from the left column (in this case Currency) and then select the appropriate format using the right column. Again, more detailed formatting is available in the Format code section at the bottom of the window.

# Linking Tables

The most important thing about databases is that they're not isolated in the same way that, for example, a simple spreadsheet is. This means it's quite easy to join databases or tables together, taking the information from a table in one column and using it elsewhere. Earlier you did this to add a country name selector. But this example is slightly more adventurous and highlights one of the key benefits of using an application such as Writer for the purposes of building forms to use in the database.

Let's begin by creating a new table called Invoices using the Table Wizard. Select Business, and then use the drop-down list to select Invoices. This will provide the most common field types needed for this job. We selected a few of these from the list, but there are some things you need to add, so click Next and use the wizard to add them.

To add a new field, click the + button below the list of fields and then define the Field Name and Field Type using the section on the right of the window. We've added elements for Cost (a numerical field), edited the Status field to say Completed, turned it into a Yes/No option (with No as the default), added a deadline (Date field), and changed the Notes field into a place to note the job specifications. You can edit field names and types at any stage in the wizard process by selecting Set types and formats from the section on the right; you can perform such edits even after the wizard is completed via the normal edit functions.

In the next section we have used the InvoiceID field as primary key for this table (Figure 7-28). In the last section, you input a name and select the option to create a form based on the table and then click Finish.

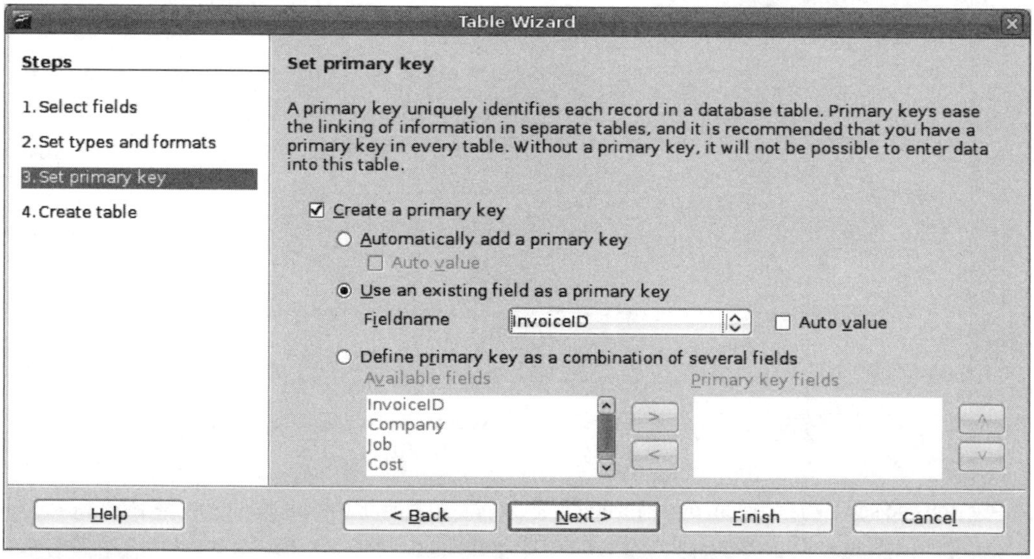

**Figure 7-28.** *On this table, we have defined the primary key based on the invoice number because this will be a useful—and unique—identifier.*

The Form Wizard will now launch, holding your hand through the process of creating a form. Just click all the way through this, pausing only to change the Arrangement to Blocks and to change the Style to Ice Blue/Flat, and then click Finish to create the new form. Finally, select the option to Modify the form, and the normal form-design page will open up.

The default view for these pages is Web Layout, but we want to make this suitable for printing, so click View ➤ Page Layout, and then select Format ➤ Page and change the orientation to Portrait. You can now position the parts of the invoice using a two-column design, with client information on the left, job information on the right, and a standard letterhead-type design across the top. We've also used the method described earlier to link the Company field in this form with the CompanyName field from the first table, providing a drop-down list of all clients in our database. With a printed invoice we might also link together an Address field to input the postal address of the recipient into the appropriate space.

The advantage of using the Customers table to define the customer in an invoice system is that when you add new customers (and their addresses) to the Customers table, this information will automatically appear under the drop-down in the invoice form (see Figure 7-29).

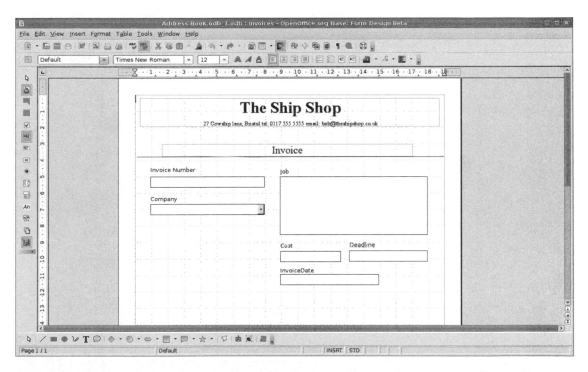

**Figure 7-29.** *The form created here can be used both to enter data and to print it out for mailing to clients or keeping for your own records.*

Remember that each form element will be grouped with its label initially, so you may need to click Format ➤ Group ➤ Ungroup in order to access the individual parts.

Once your form design is complete, click File ➤ Save to ensure that everything is written back to the database. Then close the form down. Now it's possible to enter invoice data into either a table or a form, and, more importantly, you can export the form version as a PDF (File ➤ Export as PDF) for e-mailing to the client or simply print it for mail delivery.

# Reports

The last part of this tutorial covers creating reports based on information taken from the database. These are designed to be printed. In our earlier example, they could be used to create a printout of all work undertaken for a single company, complete with job titles, deadlines, and any payments received, which is ideal when preparing end-of-year accounts or a business loan application.

To begin, go into the Reports section and select the Wizard option from the right side of the window to launch the now-familiar wizard interface (Figure 7-30). As with the form-design system you used earlier, this will also open up an instance of Writer, where the report itself will be constructed.

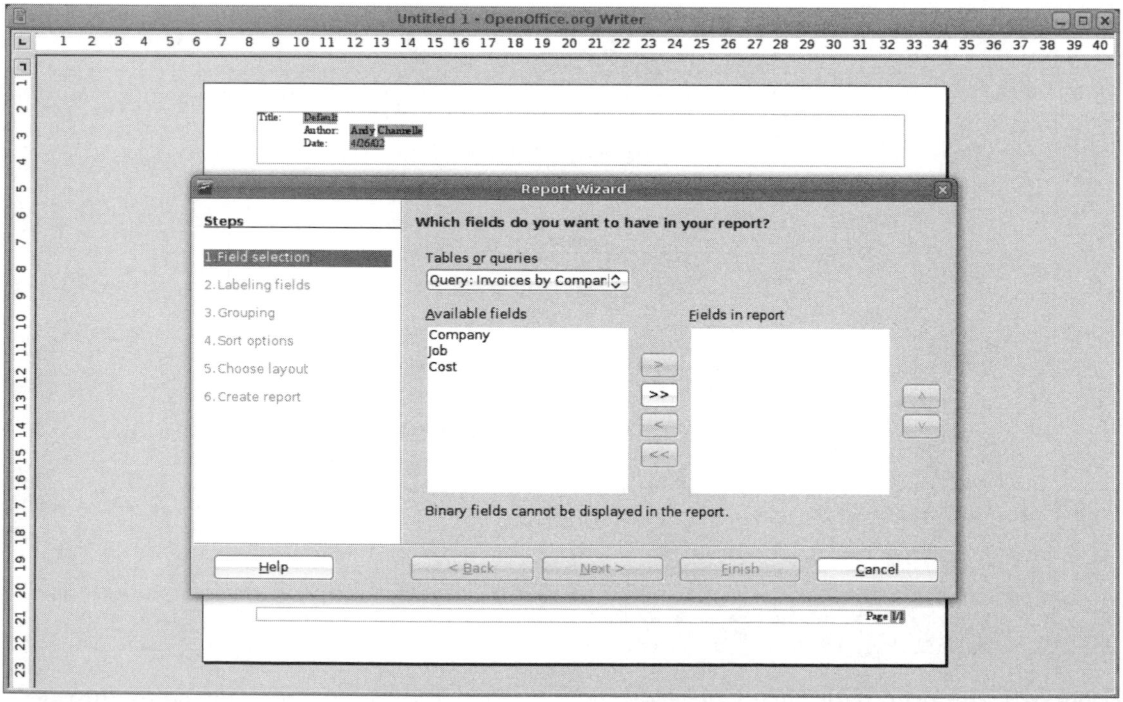

**Figure 7-30.** *As with forms, you can base reports on a subset of the data included in the database.*

In the first section of the wizard, you define the elements to be included in the report using first the Tables or queries drop-down and then by selecting the parts of a particular table using the left/right columns. The second page has options for renaming table headings specifically for this report.

The third page is where you can group different information together under a common heading. In our example, the report will list all of the jobs carried out for a single client under one heading, rather than having all of the details from the invoice repeated over and over, which is what would happen if you ignored the groupings. So select the Company field from the list and click the arrow in the center to push that entry into the right-hand column.

The next page allows you to sort the result. Because we've already set up a group for the report, it will automatically set that as the first—uneditable—sorting priority. You can then sort results using other criteria (Figure 7-31), such as the date or price (note, we went back into our invoice query and added a Date field using the right-click ➤ Edit option).

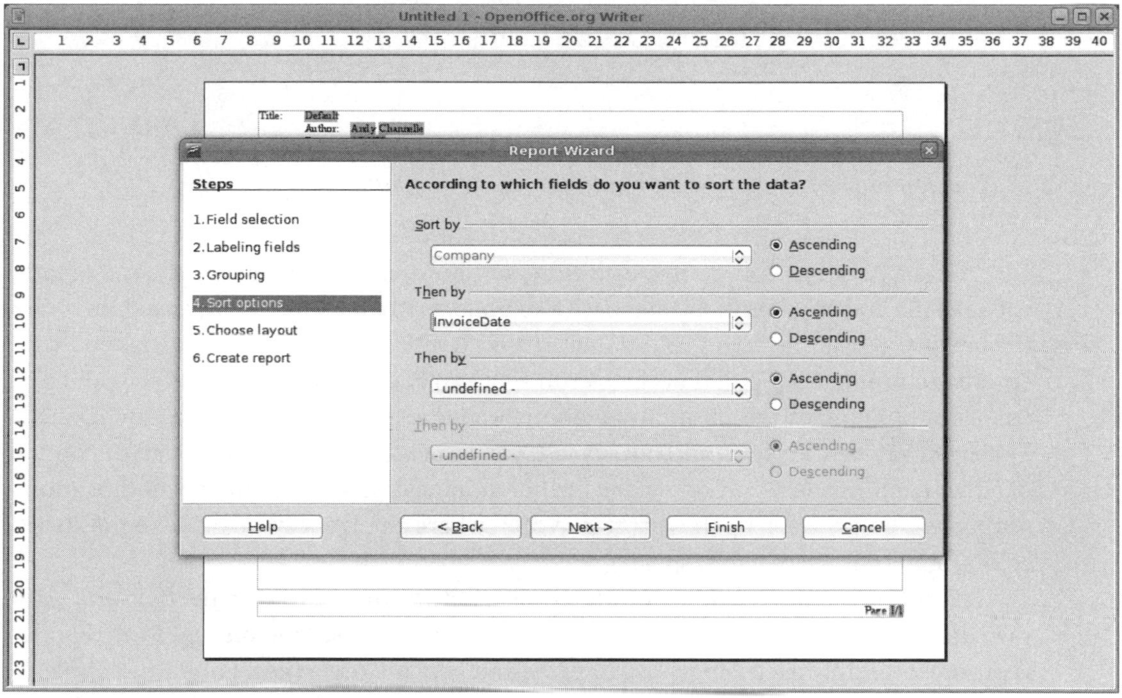

**Figure 7-31.** *You can use sorting to present data in various ways.*

In the penultimate page you can define separate layouts for both the data and the header and footer of the report (Figure 7-32). You can also change the page format from landscape (the default) to portrait. As you make these changes, you can see the effects in the background on the page itself. Though the example is populated with placeholder text, it does give a reasonable idea of what the final report is likely to look like.

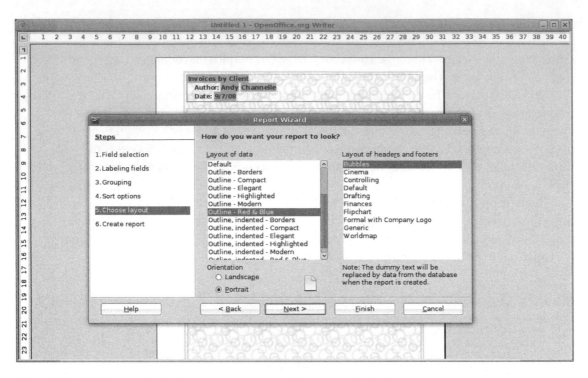

**Figure 7-32.** *The premade designs are a great start for report designing.*

The last page has options to create either a static or a dynamic report. A static report will take the current data in the database and build an unchanging report based on it. In contrast, a dynamic report will simply create a template based on the settings you've entered to produce a report that can be run again and again on the data and so could be useful for building weekly, monthly, or annual reports. If you select the former, clicking Finish will create the report and display it. If you select the latter, you are given the option of either running the report or making further modifications. Choosing the modification option will simply open up the report in Writer, where changes can be made to the styles, colors, and fonts used in the report.

Let's select Create Report Now, which will create a report based on the data and save the configuration you've just done to the database for use later on. Once the report is onscreen, simply click File ➤ Save Copy As and save the report as a standard .odt file. Next time this is opened it will appear in Writer as a standard document. However, in a month's time you could run the report again (double-click its name from the main interface) and see an updated version of it.

# Recap

Databases can be difficult things to use, but Base—through its extensive use of wizards—makes it quite easy to add, filter, and query information and create usable reports. In this chapter you've created a simple contact list and invoice manager using a couple of tables and a couple of forms. You've seen how to build multiple forms for the same table to cater to different users and how you can also use these as dual-purpose data entry/printed invoice pages. In order to get at information, you've used Base's filters and sort tools, which fed into the creation of persistent queries, and you discovered some of the ways that Base can link together tables to take some of the drudgery out of data entry.

Later on (Chapter 10) you'll use the Customer database once more to build a time-saving mail merge document in Writer. But because of the way OpenOffice.org has been built—and because you were careful to "register" your database with the system in the initial stages of design—you can use this as a data source in any part of the suite. You could, for example, grab up-to-the-minute sales figures from the invoice system, feed them into a spreadsheet, and then feed that into a chart in a presentation. Base can also take information from a Calc spreadsheet as the basis for a new database.

One of the guiding principles behind this chapter has been to keep things simple while introducing the fundamental concepts behind working with databases. There is, of course, so much more that could be done with this data, including bringing spreadsheet-like functions into the reporting process, taking dynamic data from the Web (stock prices, for instance), and incorporating it into tables and using forms to grab user input from the Web. There are also a lot of widgets—buttons, lists, check boxes—that you can add to a form to make it easier to capture data from users. However, one of the other fundamental concepts behind working with databases is that things can get very complicated very quickly. If your needs extend beyond the simple projects presented here, we recommend getting hold of a book dedicated to the subject, such as Clare Churcher's *Beginning Database Design* (Apress, 2007), which is part of the same series as this book.

# PART 2

■ ■ ■

# Working Across Applications

So far, you've been working on single applications, but OpenOffice.org is a suite of applications designed to make getting data from one part into another very simple. This means, for example, that you can take a chart from Calc, embed it in an Impress presentation or Writer document, and have the chart update as data is updated in the original spreadsheet; or take an image from Draw, add web-style hotspots, and import the whole thing intact into a Write-based web site.

In Chapter 8, you'll use the suite to create two web page projects, which will rely mostly on Writer to pull together all of the elements, and output them in a format suitable for uploading to a web server or sending out as an e-mail marketing message. In Chapter 9, we'll be looking at the various collaboration options available in the suite, including having multiple concurrent users editing a Calc spreadsheet, sharing documents securely, and setting up the system to work well in an environment where other office suites—in particular Microsoft Office—are in use.

■ ■ ■

# CHAPTER 8

# Building Web Pages

**W**eb pages typically consist of text, images, and other data arranged in a visually pleasing way. The purpose of an office suite such as OO.o is to provide tools to artfully arrange text and visuals, which is perfect for building web pages.

Again you'll tackle two projects in this chapter. You'll begin with a newsletter designed to be distributed via e-mail (see Figure 8-1) and move on to create a small, graphical promotional widget that can be easily incorporated into other sites.

Preparing documents for presentation on the Internet involves ensuring that images are optimized for downloading over slow connections, colors conform to web standards so they look the same—or at least similar—when viewed on almost any display, and the various parts can be pulled together ready to be uploaded via FTP and viewed on the Internet.

Cutting-edge web sites tend to be laid out using technologies such as cascading style sheets, and although Writer is capable of doing this kind of layout, our projects demand a far simpler method. For these projects, you'll define where elements fall on the page by using tables, which is more suited to creating e-mail marketing messages.

If you're attempting to build and manage a large web site, more than five or six interconnected pages, you may find it better to investigate a commercial web editor such as Dreamweaver or an open-source editor such as KompoZer. These editors generate cleaner HTML code, which renders quicker and more accurately, and provide better options for updating content and managing asset collections such as images. They also offer far more sophisticated page-management options than OO.o because they have been designed from the ground up to create web sites.

Writer is a more general-purpose package that nonetheless is capable of handling smaller projects and largely static pages.

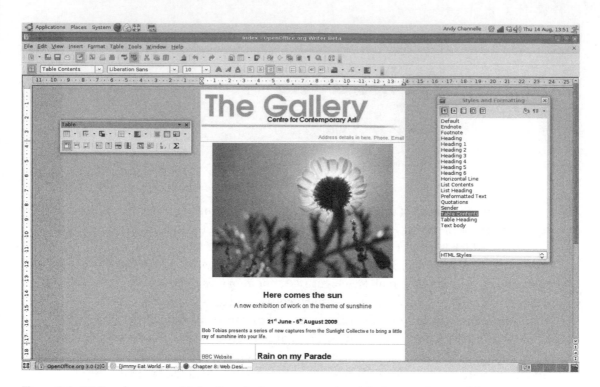

**Figure 8-1.** *Writer does a good job of rendering a page as it might be seen in a web browser.*

# Pages and Tables

As with most of the previous projects, you begin by defining the space that will form the boundaries of the content. To begin, choose File ➤ New ➤ HTML Document to set Writer up in the right mode for web design. This also means you should be working with the Web Layout view (View ➤ Web Layout) rather than the Print Layout view. In drawings, text documents, and spreadsheets, the page dimensions tend to be set within the restrictions of certain printable page sizes.

Most modern web sites are laid out—that is, how the positions of various items on the screen are defined—using cascading style sheets (CSS). CSS is quite a large subject (and beyond the scope of this tutorial), so we'll use tables, which OO.o is rather good at, to create the layout. Tables are very useful on e-newsletter projects because most e-mail clients render them correctly.

On a web project, the project dimensions are defined in terms of the screen space they are likely to take up. This causes a bit of a problem because among the various measurement options available via the Tools ➤ Options ➤ OpenOffice.org Writer/Web ➤ View, the one most useful for creating web pages—pixels—is not available. This means you must define spaces that will be seen in pixels (px) in a format defined for measuring physical spaces (cm). Oddly, after Writer outputs the final page, these values are converted to pixels in the source code.

## CONVERTING CENTIMETERS TO PIXELS

Using trial and error, I've established that the following centimeter (cm) dimensions correspond with the most commonly used pixel (px) measurements. The rough formula for converting centimeters to pixels is px width × 0.023291 = cm.

- 480px = 11.18cm

- 600px = 13.97cm

- 640px = 14.91cm

- 800px = 18.63cm

- 960px = 22.36cm

- 1000px = 23.29cm

- 1024px = 23.85cm

This project is an e-mail marketing newsletter. This will have a header for branding, a large top space for the lead item, followed by a two-column, asymmetric section and a footer. It's a good idea to draw out the layout on paper before starting to organize exactly how the table will be constructed.

Normally, e-mail marketing messages tend to be 600 pixels wide, which should comfortably fit on even the lowest resolution screens, so you need to begin with a table set at 13.97cm. Choose Insert ➤ Table, give the table a name, and set it to 3 columns and 4 rows (header, content 1, content 2, and footer). For the moment, leave the border enabled so you can actually see what you're doing and ensure that the Heading option is not turned on (see Figure 8-2).

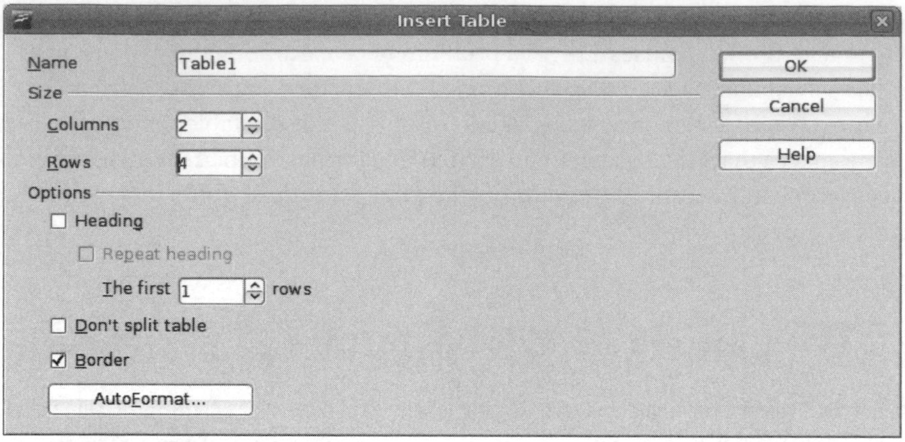

**Figure 8-2.** *When defining tables, rows are the horizontal cells and columns are vertical.*

By default, Writer creates a dynamically resizing table—that is, one that adjusts the table width dependent upon the users' browser window size—that can significantly mess up your layout, so you'll change that shortly.

Click OK to have the table added to the page. Most of the table-editing functions can be accessed by right-clicking anywhere in the table and selecting the appropriate entry. Edits can be made at the level of the cell, row, or column, or on the whole table itself. That's where you'll begin.

Right-click anywhere inside the table, and select Table (or choose Table ➤ Table Properties) to get to the main table configuration dialog box. Under the Table tab, all the options should be grayed out (i.e., not selectable) except for the Alignments option to the right. By default, this is set to Automatic, but if you change this to one of the other Alignment options (for this example, choose Center so the whole table ends up in the middle of the browser window), other options become available.

In the Width setting, enter the number from the earlier list of centimeter/pixel conversions that corresponds to the desired width of the web page (13.97 for 600 pixels). The spacing options will change automatically dependent on the table width, and with Center alignment, the Left and Right settings should be equal (see Figure 8-3).

You'll return to this dialog box shortly to look at the borders, but for the moment, click OK to see the correctly sized table.

You now have a table containing eight equally sized cells, but the header and footer need to be single cells ranged across the middle row, and the right-hand cell of the middle row needs to be smaller. To do the former, click and select the two top cells, then right-click and choose Cell ➤ Merge (or choose the Merge Cell icon, which is the third from the right on the top row, from the Table toolbar). Do the same for the content 1 and footer spaces.

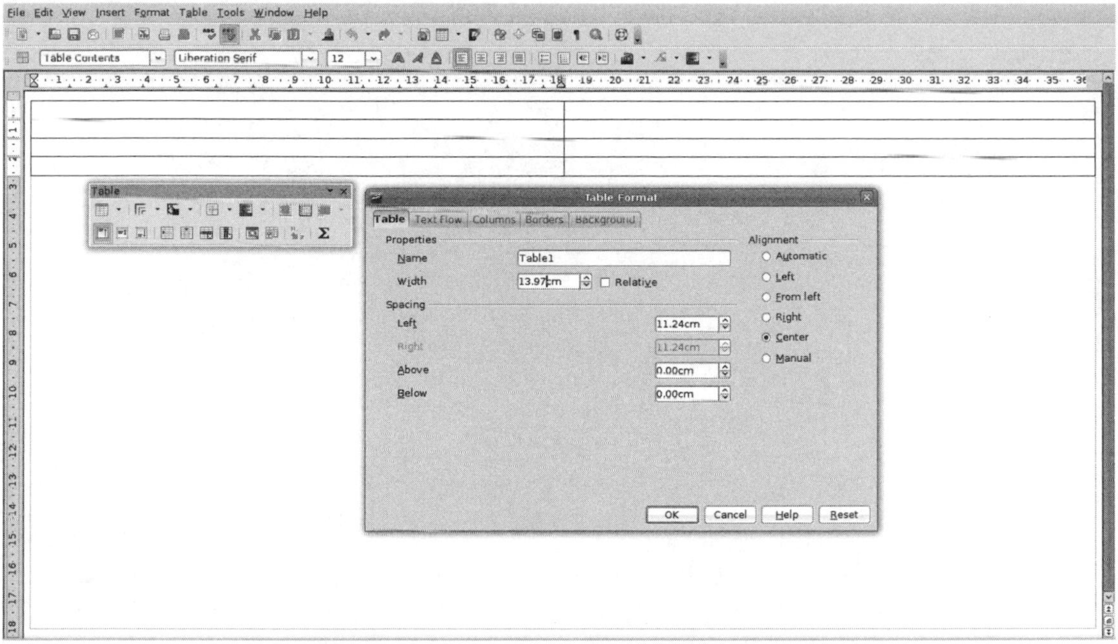

**Figure 8-3.** *Select one of the Alignment options to set the table's overall size.*

To resize the navigation cell (see Figure 8-4), you can either click and drag the line between the cells and drag it to the right, or you can do the same job numerically by right-clicking inside the left cell and choosing Column ➤ Width. As with the table width, the column width is defined in centimeters (with the same formula), and clicking OK changes the display. The column on the right expands to fill the available space. Set the column width to 3.79cm, which equates eventually to 150 pixels.

One of the important things about this kind of message is that it should display consistently across browsers, so you need to define the row height of the header and footer by right-clicking ➤ Row ➤ Height, deselecting Fit to Size, and entering the size as 2.91cm and 1cm, respectively. The two middle rows remain set at Fit to size because they need to expand as content is added.

You now have five areas ready for content (see Figure 8-4), and you can begin creating the e-newsletter. This is also a great time to save this as a template so you won't have to create this structure from scratch if it's called for again later.

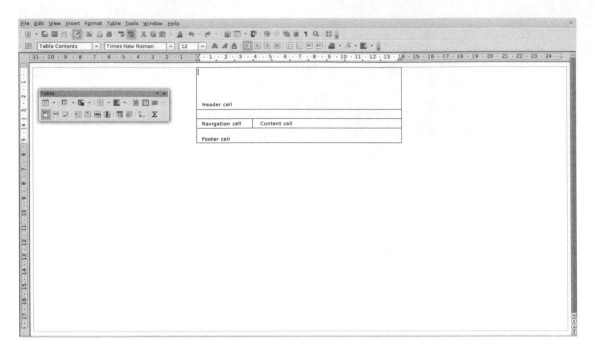

**Figure 8-4.** *Use absolute measurements to ensure your project displays consistently across different platforms and browsers.*

## WEB FILE STRUCTURE

When creating something beyond a single page of HTML, it's a good idea to replicate the file hierarchy that exists on the server that will host the pages on your local machine. So, for example, the main page should be saved (after it's finished) as index.html, and it could be saved into a folder called Home. This is the root folder for the site and should contain a subfolder called Images. Any images destined for the actual page should be saved into this folder and then imported into the project. After it's uploaded, you could access the root folder via http://www.webname.com/home, whereas you could access an image via http://www.webname.com/home/images/imagename.jpg.

To set this up, go into Tools ➤ Options, and look under the Load/Save disclosure arrow for the HTML Compatibility section. Select the Copy local graphics to internet option, and when you export the content to the Internet (later in this chapter), OO.o will attempt to follow the file structure on the web server and save the graphics into the right place.

The four options in the Export section are also important. The HTML 3.2 option outputs HTML content in the most compliant format and should be readable by almost all web browsers. The Microsoft and Netscape options allow a few specific additions that can only be read by post-4.0 versions of the most common browsers, and the OpenOffice.org format retains any OO.o-specific instructions in the code.

# Content

You'll go from top to bottom adding content that will follow this format: the top section will have a masthead created in Draw using a combination of images, shapes, and text and then rendered out as a bitmap; the mid-left section will contain anchors to sections of the main document, external links, and e-mail links; the top content and mid-right section will contain formatted text and images along with other information; and the bottom section will contain only text.

## Adding Graphics

At its simplest, adding graphics to a web page is exactly the same as adding them to a printed page, which in this case involves clicking inside the top cell and choosing Insert ➤ Picture ➤ From File and navigating to the desired image. However, this could mean that after a page has been uploaded to a web site, the images become unavailable (because they're actually on your local machine) and won't display. There are two ways to prevent this from happening.

The first is to build the structure of the web site on the local system, as detailed previously, and then ensure the whole directory is uploaded to the web server via FTP. The second option is to store the images themselves on a remote server and then link to those in the document. Because you've already selected the Copy local graphics to the internet option, the first option becomes the default, and as long as the page is exported correctly (as detailed later in this chapter), everything should work as expected.

---

**Note** The File Transfer Protocol (FTP) is a method for transporting files to and from a remote server. A number of good free software FTP clients are available for Windows, Linux, and OS X, including Filezilla (Windows, Linux, OS X), Cyberduck (OS X), and gFTP (Linux).

---

## Remote Graphics

Remote graphics are particularly good for the production of e-mail newsletters because they tend to use a standard set of graphics for the persistent elements, such as a masthead or company logo, and are not hard-coded into the document. The downside of this method is that the images won't display—either on your machine or on a recipient's—unless an Internet connection is available.

To begin, you need both a local and remote version of the picture. For this project, I've uploaded an image file of the masthead to Google's Picasa web albums service (but any online graphic host will do) and also saved it to the /image folder underneath the root.

You'll begin, as usual, by inserting an image. In web mode, choose Insert ➤ From File, and select the image using the file browser. The important thing is to make sure the Link check box is selected as shown in Figure 8-5. When you dealt with images before, the purpose of this option was to ensure that the image updated on the file system would be updated on the page too, but OpenOffice.org doesn't really care where the linked image comes from, which makes it perfect for our purposes.

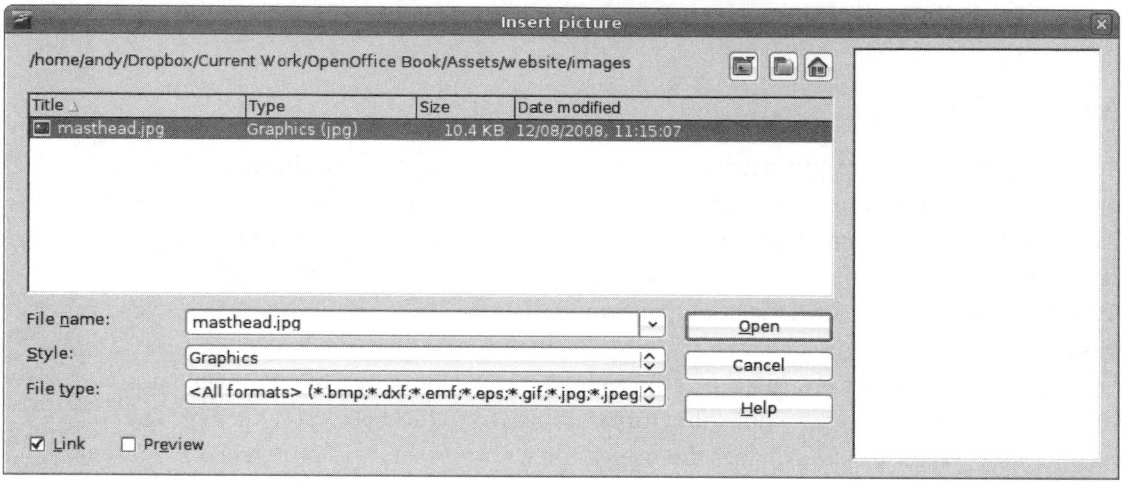

**Figure 8-5.** *Setting the Link option links the onscreen version of the image to its original file.*

---

■**Tip**  Many good image-hosting services are available, including Picasa, Flickr, Photobucket, and even Facebook. These all have private and public options, and to feed an image into a web site, you'll need to set the image to be viewable by the public. In any of these cases, you'll need access to the image's URL to embed it into a site. This can usually be found by right-clicking the image in a browser and selecting the Properties option.

---

Copy and paste the URL of a remote image into the File name text box in the Link section (see Figure 8-6), or use the ... button to launch a file browser and link to a local file. Click OK to see the image inserted into the appropriate cell (see Figure 8-7). This is the local copy of the image, and you now want to substitute this for the remote edition, which means logging in to the graphic-hosting service, locating the full-size image, and copying its URL. In Firefox, this can be accomplished by right-clicking the image and selecting Copy Image Location; in IE7, you right-click the picture, select Properties, and copy the URL from the Properties dialog box or use the embed code options that many image hosts provide.

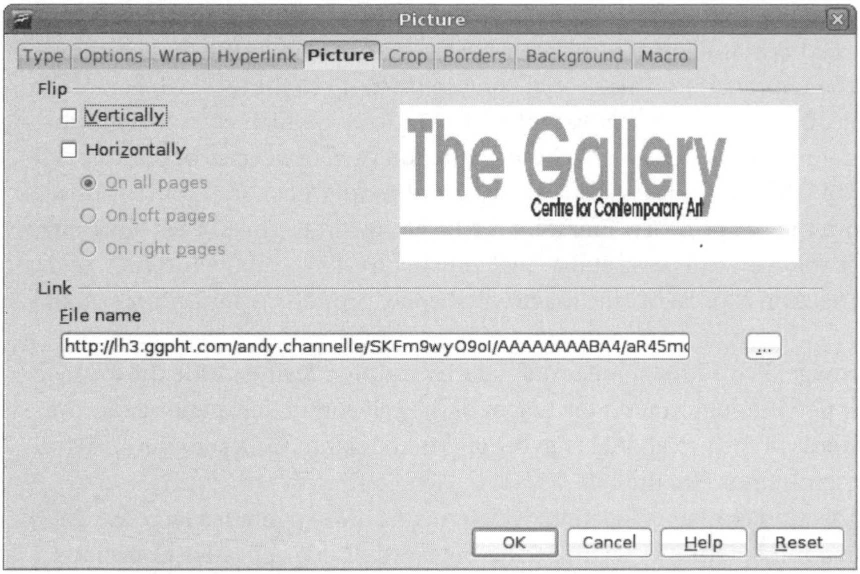

**Figure 8-6.** *You can link images from either a remote (web) source or a local file.*

**Figure 8-7.** *By default, text will not wrap around an image. Select Page Wrap from the Formatting toolbar to apply a wrap.*

With the URL copied, go back to Writer, right-click the image, and select Picture. From the mass of tabs at the top of the screen, select Picture, and locate the File name text box under the Link section. This should contain the path to the local version of the file—for example, `C:/home/images/masthead.jpg` on Windows—which you need to substitute with the remote version. So highlight the path and then use Ctrl+V or right-click ➤ Paste to insert the URL. When you click OK, the image shouldn't change, but it's now being pulled from the image host rather than the local machine. The biggest advantage of this method is that you can now send a single file to anywhere on the Internet, and, as long as a connection is present, the image will display properly—perfect for e-mail newsletters.

Below this image, I've added some text details by simply clicking inside the top cell and starting to type. Although you set the height of the cell earlier, it expands to accommodate the contents of the box should it go beyond that height. It's best to think of the height values as a minimum for the cell.

The second section is a "story" section, which means it will contain a large image (in this case, a beautiful picture by Hamed Saber released under a Creative Commons license) and some formatted text. The image was added, as you did previously, first as a local, linked file, and then the location of the original image (`http://www.flickr.com/photos/hamed/160893800/sizes/o/`) was added to the Link box.

In the top section of the newsletter, the image is simply sitting above the text, which means inserting a hard return (pressing the Enter key) after the image and starting to type. However, the middle section demands a little more refined alignment. Begin by inserting the image with Insert ➤ From File (this project is using a spectacular Creative Commons image of rain by Laffy4K [`http://www.flickr.com/photos/laffy4k/155406168/sizes/l/`]), and then use the mouse to resize it. You also need to align the image to the left by selecting it and clicking the left align button on the Formatting toolbar. Remember if you hold the Shift key while resizing, the image will retain its proportions.

By default, the image comes in with a "top and bottom" text wrap set, which means that the image interrupts the flow of text. To change this, select the image, and then use the Page Wrap option on the Formatting toolbar (see Figure 8-8). Any typed text in this cell will now be lined up with the top of the image and will then range all the way across the cell, just as it would in a printed document.

You may notice that the text is uncomfortably close to the edge of the image. To remedy this, double-click the image to open the configuration dialog box, select the Wrap tab, and increase the Right option in the Spacing section (see Figure 8-8). The size of the gap you add depends upon the design of your page, but for this example, the goal is 5 pixels, which, using the formula shown earlier, comes in at about 0.11cm.

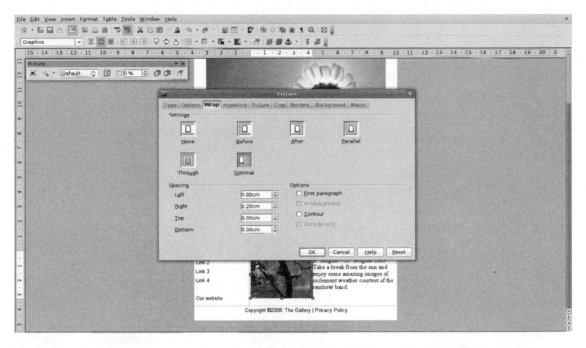

**Figure 8-8.** *The text wrap options are available by double-clicking an image and selecting the Wrap tab.*

Now that the project has images and text, you can see what the final product will look like in a web browser. Writer does a pretty good job of displaying the design, but it's vital to preview in a browser so that any issues that arise are found and solved before the general public gets their eyes on the newsletter. Choose File ➤ Preview in Web browser (see Figure 8-9) to launch the system's default browser and display the page. To be really sure of a design, it's a good idea to test a page in different browsers, for example, Firefox, Internet Explorer, and Opera if you're working on Windows; Safari in OS X; and Konqueror in Linux. This can be done by copying and pasting the URL from the default browser's address bar into another browser.

**Figure 8-9.** *Spot the difference. The big problems that arise when going from OO.o (left) to a web browser (right) involve spacing.*

## Text Formatting

Adding text content in Writer for the Web is largely the same as adding text in Writer for the page with just a few differences. The main difference is that when you're designing a page to be printed or sent out as a PDF, you can be sure of how everything will look because you've defined the fonts and spacing in the document. When designing for the Web, however, you can't be certain that the reader will have the same set up as you do. For this reason, the web development community came up with the idea of *web-safe fonts*. This is a set of typefaces that are available for most computer systems and should render in the same way regardless of the operating system or browser. This was extended slightly by Microsoft into the Core Fonts Initiative, which features Arial, Courier New, Georgia, Times New Roman, Verdana, Trebuchet MS, and Lucida Sans. The number of fonts considered to be web safe in Windows Vista has grown again (see Table 8-1), but if you want to be really accessible it's best to stick to a selection from the seven core fonts or one of those in Table 8-1 that has a check mark in every operating system column.

**Table 8-1.** *The Most Commonly Available Fonts for Each Operating System*

| Font Style | Name | Windows | Vista | OS X | Ubuntu Linux with Microsoft Core Fonts |
|---|---|---|---|---|---|
| Serif | Cambria | | X | | |
| | Constantia | | X | | |
| | Times New Roman | X | X | X | X |
| | Times | | | X | X |
| | Georgia | X | X | X | X |
| Sans serif | Andale Mono | X | | X | X |
| | Arial | X | X | X | X |
| | Arial Black | X | X | X | X |
| | Calibri | | X | | |
| | Candara | | X | | |
| | Century Gothic | X | X | X | X |
| | Corbel | | X | | |
| | Helvetica | | | X | X |
| | Impact | X | X | X | X |
| | Trebuchet MS | X | X | X | X |
| | Verdana | X | X | X | X |
| Cursive | Comic Sans MS | X | | X | X |
| Monospace | Consolas | | X | | |
| | Courier New | X | X | X | X |
| | Courier | | | X | X |

---

■**Caution** Most Linux distributions don't come with the Microsoft Core Fonts included due to licensing issues. They are available, though, and are quite simple to install. In the more common distributions—Ubuntu, Fedora, SUSE, and on—the fonts should be available via the distribution's package manager (just search for msttcorefonts or core fonts), and users of more esoteric fare can visit http://corefonts. sourceforge.net/ for comprehensive instructions on accessing and installing the fonts. After they're installed, you'll need to restart OO.o to make them available. After that, they will appear just like all other fonts in the font drop-down list.

Good design says that documents should be restricted to two fonts, but for this project, you'll just use one, and that's Arial. So you can type text and then add formatting—text size, bold, italic, and justification—as normal (see Figure 8-10).

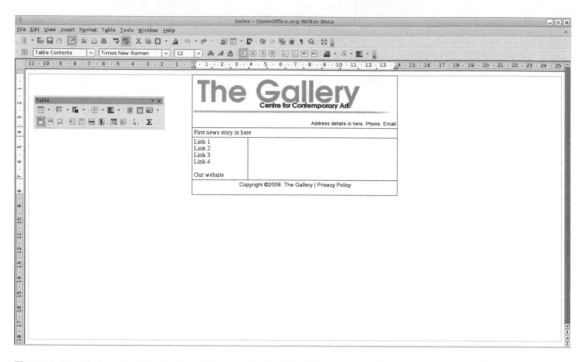

**Figure 8-10.** *It's best to think of a cell as an individual document that can contain anything a normal document can.*

### Predefined Styles

A few predefined styles are available when working in web mode and these correspond to the typical HTML tags such as <h1>, <h2>, <li> (list), and so on. The main styles are accessible from the Formatting toolbar, and the full list can be seen by selecting Format ➤ Styles and Formatting (see Figure 8-11).

Using these in the appropriate places such as headings and lists allows you to define the structure of the page (which is good for search engines) and also makes it easier for the page to adapt to, for example, a sight-impaired user viewing the page with very large text. If elements such as headings and list sizes are defined using the font tools, they may not resize correctly in these circumstances.

To apply a main heading style, select the text to be transformed, and use the style drop-down list, which is next to the font drop-down list on the Formatting toolbar, and choose Heading 1. Although only a few of the available styles are available in here, clicking More launches the Styles and Formatting palette. Use the drop-down list at the bottom of the Styles and Formatting box, and select HTML Styles to see all of the available styles and apply them with a double-click. Color can also be applied to a piece of text in the usual manner, just select the text and use the Font Color icon on the Formatting toolbar to choose the right color.

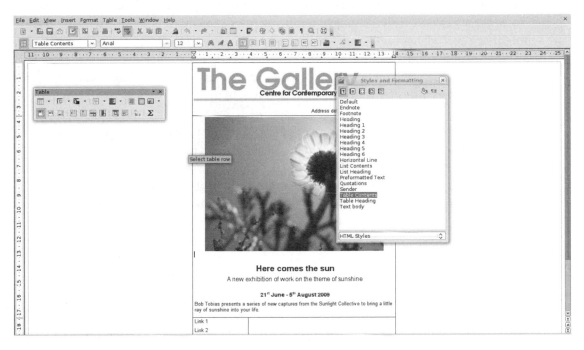

**Figure 8-11.** *A selection of HTML styles should display consistently in any browser.*

## Advanced Table Editing

Whenever a table is selected in Writer (whether you're designing print or web projects), the Table toolbar launches (see Figure 8-12), allowing quick access to the most important editing options. In the past, tables were used extensively to create web pages, but since the advent of CSS, which provides for much better positioning with raw code, tables have been sent back to doing what they do best, which is tabulated data such as spreadsheet. However, in some cases—like the example e-mail newsletter—tables are still a useful tool largely because they're easier to set up and manage but also because they are more likely to display correctly even in older e-mail clients.

**Figure 8-12.** *The Table toolbar contains all the tools needed to manage a table-based design for a web page.*

Options available in this toolbar can be used to add new tables and define visual elements such as background color, border style, and the position of text within the cell. Tools are also available for adding or removing rows and columns, sorting data as you might in a spreadsheet, and even adding Calc-like functions.

The AutoFormat option provides a collection of premade table formats that can be applied to a selected table, and more extensive operations are available via the Table Properties button (the third icon from the right in the bottom row as shown in Figure 8-12).

The table options in Writer offer a good compromise between the easiness of adjusting rows and columns with the mouse and the power and precision of being able to edit numerically. However, tables can be a bit flaky when they're used for web page design, so ensure you preview in the browser often to pick up problems before they get too big. Previewing exports a temporary version of the page to your operating system's /temp directory.

## Links

One of the fundamental innovations of the Web is the possibility to link to pages elsewhere on the Internet. These could be hosted on the same server or located in some far-flung land, but they display as though they were in one place. In fact, this is true of elements from a page, as you saw earlier by taking an image from one web server (Picasa) and displaying it within a different page.

In Writer, almost any item on a page—text or image—can function as a link; they can also work in different ways, including directing the viewer to a different web site, page, or part of a page; launching the viewer's mail client; or downloading a file. We'll cover all of these options and take a brief look at the terminology behind the process of linking.

The most basic link is a text link to a different web site. To insert one of these in the document, highlight a piece of text, and choose Insert ➤ Hyperlink. This launches the Hyperlink dialog box (see Figure 8-13) where you can define the elements of the link. At the top is an address bar to house the URL of the web site you're linking to. This should be entered as a complete web address, including the http:// element at the start. The two buttons next to the address bar will launch a web browser where you can navigate to a web site and then cut and paste the URL, or open a document (i.e., another local web page) where you can set an anchor for a link (we'll look more at this option later).

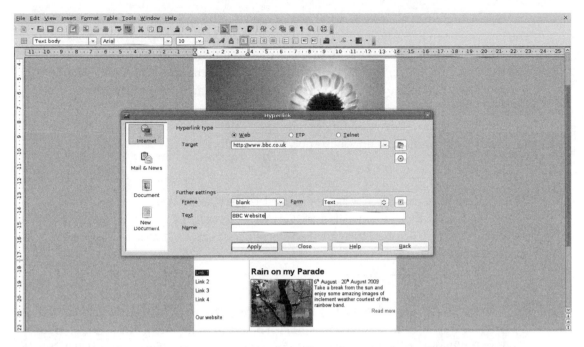

**Figure 8-13.** *Links can open web pages, initiate e-mail messages, and even link to separate documents.*

---

■**Note**  Remember that users may encounter your links with no context, so you should ensure that they are appropriate to your audience; anything that is risqué or even risky should be noted as such. To reinforce the idea of going "somewhere else," it's often a good idea to have external links open in a new window.

---

Now let's move on to the Further settings section of the Hyperlink dialog box. The Frame option defines how the new web site will appear. On a standard page, there are four options:

- *blank*: The linked page appears as a new window or tab.

- *self*: The linked page appears in the same frame as the original link.

- *parent*: The linked page appears in the frameset above the current frame.

- *top*: The linked document takes up the whole window containing the original link.

In practice, the self and parent options are largely redundant because most web sites are no longer built using the frameset model, so it's easiest to think of the blank option as "new window" and the top option as "current window."

The default option—that is, what will happen if nothing is defined in here—is that the link will open in the current window.

The Form option allows you to easily turn a text link into a button by selecting Button from the drop-down list. This will be rendered using the web browser's default button widget, which can look quite nice, and will be labeled using the content of the Text bar just below the Form box in the Hyperlink dialog box.

Finally, you can provide a name for the link, which will be accessible via the Navigator if you need to edit later on. Click Apply to create the link.

---

■**Tip** You can also insert a hyperlink into a Writer document by typing it out (e.g., `http://www.bbc.co.uk`). This is automatically changed into a link using the default options. To have more control, use the method just described. To prevent a link from being applied, press Ctrl+Z right after the link is applied to undo the action.

---

You may have noticed, following the preceding process, that links are formatted in a particular way; they're rendered in a darkish blue and underlined. This is the standard method for identifying links as set out by the World Wide Web Consortium (W3C), but there's no reason you must follow this. After the link has been created, you can highlight the text again and then change the color, font, and underline status as normal. In fact, to be consistent, you should build a new style called Links and then apply this to hyperlinks as you create them.

You can also change the appearance of links using Tools ➤ Options (look under OpenOffice.org ➤ Appearance for the Unvisited and Visited Links options), but this only changes the way that Writer displays links (see Figure 8-14). If you want to change the way a viewer of the final production sees them, it needs to be changed at the paragraph level. To do this, go into the Styles and Formatting dialog box (Format ➤ Styles and Formatting), create a new Character Style called Links (or something similar), style this as you want the links to appear, and then apply this style after the link has been entered.

As it is with text, so it is with an image. Click one of the images added to the page, and choose Insert ➤ Hyperlink. The dialog box launches and the details can be added as you did previously. The Text entry space is automatically filled with the URL of the final link, but this won't be displayed on the page. All the other options, such as Target, work as normal.

An alternative method of adding a hyperlink to a picture is to double-click it to see the Image dialog box, and then select the Hyperlink tab. There are fewer options here, but the most important ones are present. You can also create an image map, which means different parts of an image are linked to different sites or pages (see the "Image Maps" section).

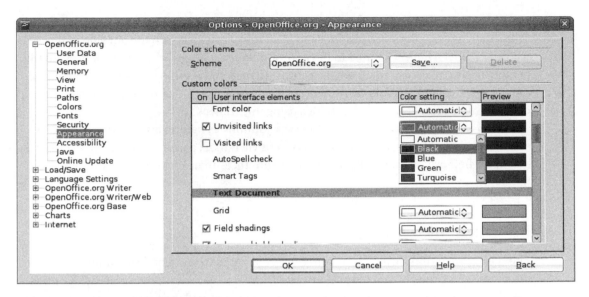

**Figure 8-14.** *Color definitions set in the Tools ➤ Options menu only affect the way OpenOffice.org displays links.*

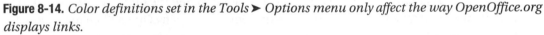

### RELATIVE AND ABSOLUTE LINKS

Imagine you have a web site at http://www.mywebsite.com that has two pages: index.html and, in a subdirectory called pages, pagetwo.html. Using absolute links, the first page is accessible from http://www.mywebsite.com. To add a link in index.html to the second page, you use http://www.mywebsite.com/pages/pagetwo.html. Using relative links, the first page is still at the same URL, but inside index.html, you can link to the second page by using /pages/pagetwo.html. Now this may not seem too much of a difference, but if you were to later move the site to http://www.mynewwebsite.com, the absolute links would all be pointing to the wrong place; however, as long as you retain the structure of the site on the new server, the relative links all still work. This is also true of absolute and relative image links.

## Mailto: Links

One of the more common types of links—especially in e-mail newsletters—is a mailto: link, which can be attached to an e-mail address. When this kind of link is clicked, the viewer's e-mail client is launched with the address of the recipient already added. In fact, you can add some more detail to a mailto: link, which can make filtering e-mails easier later or can just save your audience a little typing.

As you have before, begin by selecting a piece of text and choosing Insert ➤ Hyperlink. This time, however, select Mail and News from the narrow pane on the left side of the window. Add a recipient's name to the appropriate space (this is the e-mail address of the person/account where e-mails will be sent), and then add a subject. In terms of an e-mail newsletter, the subject could be something like "newsletter 17" and then the recipient could set up a filter to capture all queries using this subject.

The Further settings section has the same options as before, but you can leave these alone. Now, when the page is published or sent via e-mail, a user can click the Contact Us link, and their e-mail client will launch with both the e-mail address and subject already filled out.

## Internal Links

The typical hyperlink takes a user from one set of pages to another, but—moving beyond the newsletter project—you may also need to link to pages within the same site. For this, you'll begin by creating two pages, one called `index.html` and the other `writer.html`, and a PDF to be downloaded from the site. Note that you're not using OpenOffice.org's native file formats here, so after typing some text into the first page, choose File ➤ Save As, and change the format to HTML Document (OO.o Writer) (`.html`) before saving the file to a new folder. A warning pops up to confirm that you don't want to use the native `.odf` file (see Figure 8-15). Just click through. Then do the same for the second page.

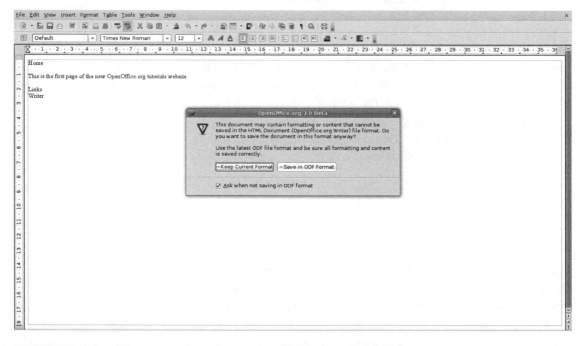

**Figure 8-15.** *OO.o offers a warning when saving files in nonnative formats.*

**■Note**  You can apply styles to existing documents without even opening them. You might do this if halfway through a long, multi-file project, you change a style and don't want to have to replicate this through the other files. Simply open the `.odt` file as an archive (see Chapter 9), and copy the file `Styles.xml` from the document to others in the series. When you open those, the news styles are applied to the existing content.

Create some structure for the site in the root folder (i.e., the site's home) using your operating system's standard options to create the new folders. Add two new folders to the root. Label the first, where all art that will appear on the site should go, as `images`; a second folder, called `downloads`, is used to contain any files (PDFs, Word documents) that can be downloaded by the viewer.

Back in the home page (`index.html`), add and format a short piece of text, and create a section for links. Into this, add a label for the Writer page. Select this, choose Insert ➤ Hyperlink, and select the Document option from the narrow left-hand pane (see Figure 8-16). Click the folder icon next to the Path section to open the file selector, and then navigate to and select the second page in the set.

Again, you can select the target (we've gone for the parent option so the page opens in the current window), and choose either a text or button link (we've selected the latter). Add some text to label the button, click the Apply button to see the new button added to the page, and then click Close.

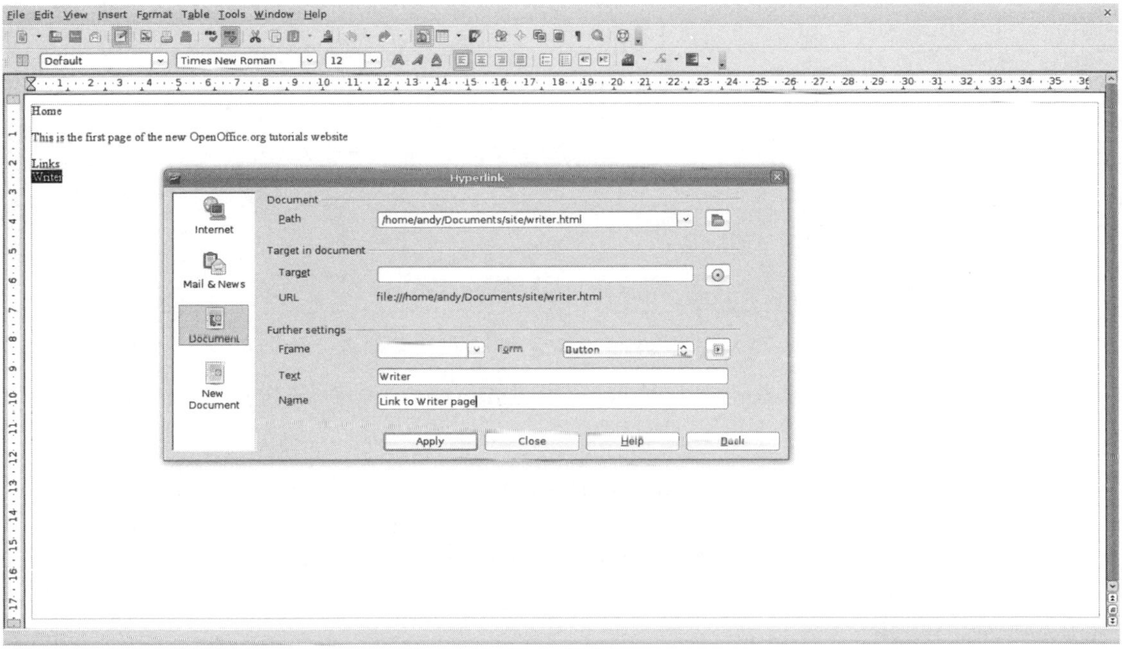

**Figure 8-16.** *Use the Hyperlink dialog box to add links to a preexisting document within your site.*

To test the link, choose File ➤ Preview in Web Browser, and click the newly created button. The Writer page opens.

Using this method, you can link to any page already created on the system. However, you can also link to a nonexistent page, and create this page as you're going along. To do this, add a new piece of text to the page (in this example, use the word "Impress"), and then select it. Open the Hyperlink dialog box once more, but this time, select the New Document option from the left. In the top section, select Edit now if you want to begin editing the page, or Edit later if you're just building up structure and plan on adding content at a later date, and then provide a file name for the document. Under Filetype, choose the HTML Document option because this applies the basic HTML elements (such as ensuring the page opens in Web Layout view) and the correct file extension. The Further settings can be configured as you did previously. Repeat the button building operation to create links to other files within your project (see Figure 8-17).

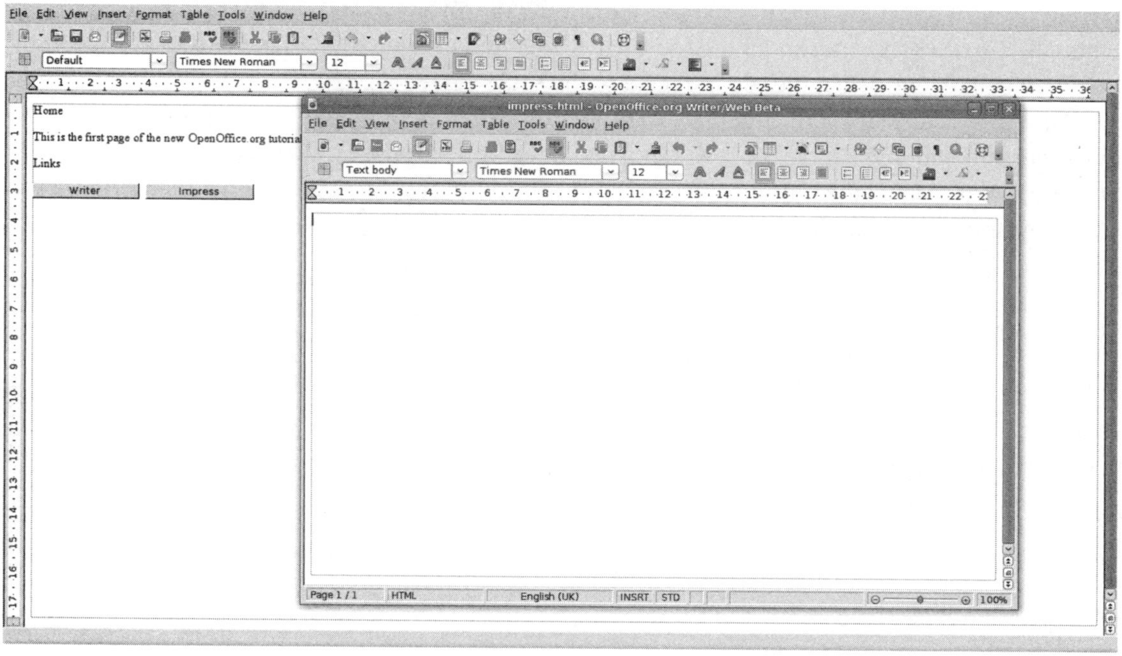

**Figure 8-17.** *The New Document option allows you to define new pages to add to the site on the fly.*

Clicking Apply does two things. First, a new button is added to the page labeled with the defined text, and second, a new page is created using the supplied file name and is launched ready for editing. This can be edited exactly the same as any other HTML page within Writer.

## Links and Bookmarks

In addition to linking to particular documents, you can also link to specific parts of a document. So, for example, in the page about Writer, you might have a section on Writer for Students, a section for Office Workers, and a section for Book Designers, and add links in the first page that go directly to these, so the viewer doesn't have to scroll around looking for the right part.

Setting this up is a two-stage process. First, you must define the locations in the target document and then define the links to these locations. Open up the target page. In this example, create three headings (using the Heading 1 style), and then paste in some random lorem ipsum text.

Highlight the heading for the first section, and then choose Insert ➤ Bookmark. This launches the Insert Bookmark dialog box where you can enter the name for the bookmark (see Figure 8-18). Remember to be logical and consistent about bookmarking because you may end up with lots of them and no way of readily distinguishing where each goes. Now do this for each section of the page. These bookmarks work as anchors for the links on the other page.

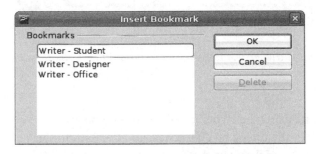

**Figure 8-18.** *Be consistent and descriptive when applying bookmarks to sections.*

You now have two options for adding a bookmark from the Writer document to the index page. The first is to open both pages and position them side-by-side. In the second document, open the Navigator (choose Edit ➤ Navigator or press F5), and then click the disclosure icon next to Bookmarks. You should see the previously created bookmarks. Click and drag one of these to the index document and drop it into the appropriate place (see Figure 8-19). A link is created using the bookmark name in that location. To change the name of the link, select it, choose Insert ➤ Hyperlink, and add a different piece of text to the Text section of the dialog box.

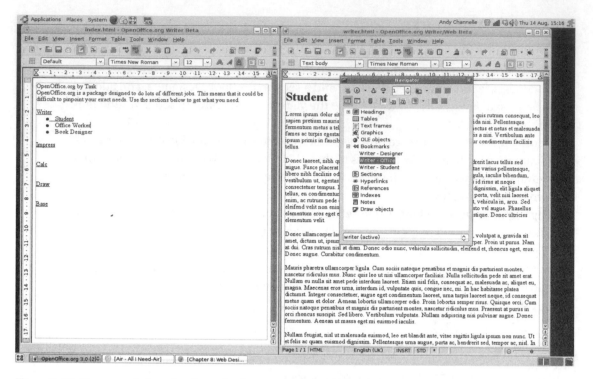

**Figure 8-19.** *Drag-and-drop bookmark placement is the easiest way to link to a bookmark inside a different document.*

You can also add a link to a bookmark using the Hyperlink dialog box (choose Insert ➤ Hyperlink) as shown in Figure 8-20. After the dialog box launches, add the path to the page containing the bookmark as normal and then use the Target in document section to input the name of the bookmark (in this case, it's Writer - Designer). The URL for these sections should have the following format:

```
http://www.sitename.com.page.html#bookmarkname
```

After these links have been defined, save the document and use Preview in Web Browser to ensure that everything is working as expected. Clicking the first bookmark link should take you to the top of the Writer page, and subsequent links should open that page with the linked section at the top of the browser window.

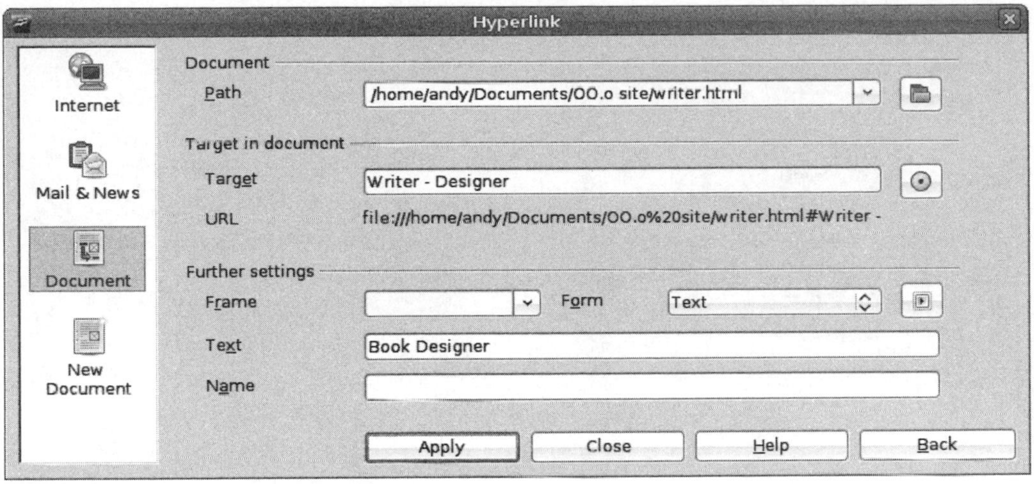

**Figure 8-20.** *You can also specify links to bookmarks manually, but you must make sure the bookmark name is entered accurately.*

## Download Links

The final part of your exploration of links in Writer allows you to define a link on a page that will download a document to the viewer's computer for later viewing. This could be anything from a normal .odt file or PDF to a video, sound file, spreadsheet, or presentation. As with the image links discussed earlier, you can set these links to point to a local file, which will be uploaded to the site after you publish the pages, or to a remote file housed on some other server.

To do the former, select the element—for example an image or text—that will function as the link, and then choose Insert ➤ Hyperlink. The usual dialog box appears from which you need to select Document, just as you did with the web page earlier. Click the Browse button and navigate to the location of the file to be downloaded—the /downloads folder—which will be mirrored on the web server. Use the Further settings section to add more detail as necessary (see Figure 8-21).

When linking to downloadable files, it's good practice to let users know the file size and type they're expected to download before they click the link. The best way to do this in OO.o Writer is to add a short note next to the link, such as Link No1 (2.3MB PDF).

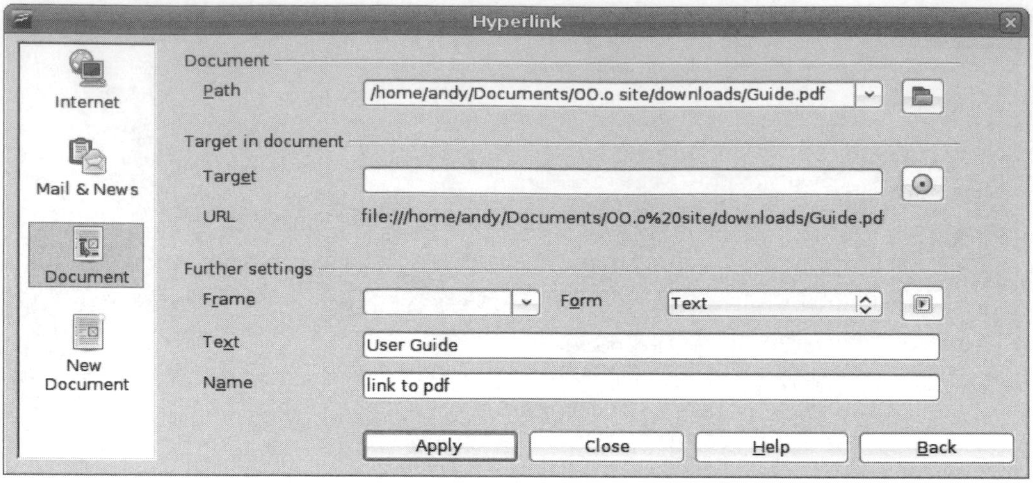

**Figure 8-21.** *Use the Hyperlink dialog box to configure file downloads from your site.*

Using the techniques outlined previously, you can create a pretty sophisticated newsletter or small web site that can be uploaded quite simply to some web space (see the "Outputting Web Pages" section for more on uploading). Beyond the basics of simple editing covered here, it's quite simple to add JavaScript (Insert ➤ Script) to a page, or even embed sound or video files (Insert ➤ Movie and Sound). But now, it's time to move on to a more visual project in Draw.

## Image Maps

You'll create a single image in Draw that will then have links applied to different areas of it. This technique, called an image map, can be used to create banner adverts for web sites, interesting e-mail signatures, or virtual business cards that can be embedded in blogs or social network sites or to create a more visual navigation system. Building an image map is a two-stage process involving creating the image that will be the foundation for the project in Draw and then using OO.o's handy ImageMap editor to create the map itself. This can be invoked from any of the applications in the suite, but we'll go back into Writer because this is where the final image map is destined to be displayed.

You'll begin with an image 480 pixels wide × 300 pixels high, which, using our formula, means a page that is 11.18cm × 6.99cm. You should also reduce the margins on each edge to 0 because you we won't need margins on this project. Using Format ➤ Page, you can also change the background color, and add a gradient, hatching pattern, or bitmap. Choose the gradient and, once again, after it's applied, switch off the Automatic increments option and increase the number of intermediate colors to 128. This makes a smoother gradient.

■**Note** This project uses Andrei Tulai's excellent OpenOffice icon set (http://andrei-t.deviantart. com/). The final image is available at http://picasaweb.google.com/andy.channelle/ OpenOfficeBooks# and is usable under the Creative Commons attribution, share-alike license.

On top of this page, I've used the techniques discussed in Chapter 6—including merging and subtracting shapes, creating new gradients, and bringing in bitmap images—to create a small but attractive image ready to be linked up to other parts of the Internet (see Figure 8-22).

**Figure 8-22.** *This page should end up as a 480 × 300 pixel banner ad complete with loads of links. At the moment, however, it's just a static image.*

After the image has been created, choose File ➤ Export and select .png or .jpg as the file type. Now let's move on to the second part of the process. Back in Writer, create a new web page (File ➤ New ➤ HTML Document) or open one of those created earlier. Click into the document where the banner is going to go, choose Insert ➤ From File, and navigate to the image. After it's placed on the page, choose Edit ➤ ImageMap to open a small applet in the center of the screen with the selected image in it. The interface is basically a pair of toolbars and a work area; the top toolbar is mainly for defining the hotspots that will be clicked in the image. It's divided into five sections covering file operations, hotspot creation, hotspot editing, undo/redo, and link properties. The lower, deeper toolbar is for defining the behavior of those links.

Begin by adding a number of rectangular hotspots:

1. Select the Rectangle button—the second button in the second section of the toolbar—and then draw a rectangle over the element of the image that is to become the link.

2. Hold down the Shift key while dragging to force the shape into a perfect square.

3. Use the other shape buttons to create a circle (hold Shift to keep circular proportions), a polygon (click around an object to add points and create the shape, and then double-click to close the shape), and a freeform polygon, which is just like a freehand shape tool (see Figure 8-23).

4. After a shape has been created, it can be moved around using the Arrow tool from the first section of the toolbar, and the points can be edited using the Edit section. The editing works in a similar fashion to the node-editing tools in Draw (see Chapter 6) and can be used to make complex shapes.

**Figure 8-23.** *The simplest shape to define is a square, but image maps can also handle circles and other more irregular shapes.*

In the example, define link areas to 10 different areas using circles, squares, and irregular shapes; now you can add links.

Select one of the areas to enable the link definition section. In the Address section, you can add a fully qualified URL (e.g., `http://www.mywebsite.com/writer.html`) or the address from a local file (see Figure 8-24). Helpfully, if you click the small arrow to the right of the Address bar, a list of recently opened files is displayed for selection.

The Text bar allows you to define the tool tip that will be displayed as the user hovers the mouse over the link. It's quite important to add some kind of information to this because—depending upon the underlying image—there will be no textual information available normally, and, more importantly, it provides additional information for sight-impaired visitors using screen readers.

Again a Frame option can be set to open the link in a new page or the current page. Links can point to pages within the same site, to pages on a different server, or to downloadable documents.

After a link has been defined, click the Active button (the first button of the last section on the toolbar) to make it a real link. You can also add a little more detail, such as a link name and description, by clicking the Properties icon on the far right.

After links have been added to all of the hotspots, you can save the result ready for insertion into the actual document. Click the Save icon (a disk). This project is using the StarView ImageMap (`.sip`) format, which is a client-side format, so pick that from the Formats drop-down list, and click Save. This saves the file, which can then be edited later.

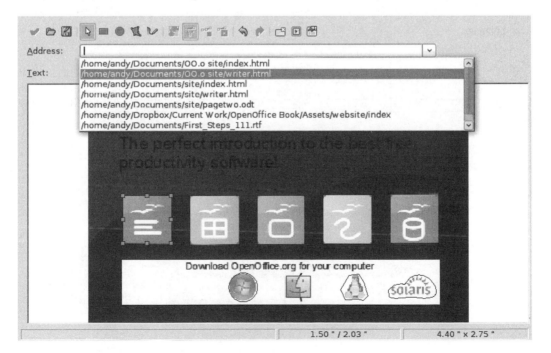

**Figure 8-24.** *The Address drop-down list displays a list of the most recently opened OO.o documents.*

Now, if all of the available hotspots have a link defined, the Apply button will be available. Click this button to apply the map to the selected image, and then close down the window using the Close icon on the title bar.

The image will look the same on the page, but if you check out the code view (View ➤ HTML Source), you should notice that a lot of code is dedicated to defining the hotspots and links. Circular and polygonal hotspots will have very long strings of numbers appended to them because they have to define each point along the lines in terms of numbers.

---

### A WALK ON THE CLIENT SIDE

Image maps come in two different flavors: server side and client side. The difference between the two options is mainly about where the information that underlies the image is stored and accessed, and the names give a clue as to their source. The big problem with server-side image maps is that they rely on additional programs that your web space provider may or may not allow access to. OO.o has facilities for creating two different types of server-side image maps. One of the most significant problems with server-side image maps is that they require use of the mouse, and so your content will be inaccessible to anyone not using a mouse.

Client-side image maps, in contrast, embed the information about where the hotspots are and what action should be taken when they're clicked in the image code itself. This means that after you define the hotspots and links, you don't have to worry about external applications, server availability, or mouse use because links can be navigated using the Tab key. Client-side maps are also easier to create and manage.

| Title △ | Type | Size | Date modified |
|---------|------|------|---------------|
|         |      |      |               |

/home/andy/Documents/OO.o site/images

File name: banner    **Save**

File type: SIP - StarView ImageMap
MAP - CERN
MAP - NCSA
SIP - StarView ImageMap

Cancel

Help

## Outputting Web Pages

The last task on all of these projects is to save the file using the HTML format. When using local files, this is as simple as selecting HTML as the document type. If you've used remote links to graphics as outlined earlier, then the resulting HTML file can be uploaded to a web server as is and will work fine. However, when you're using local graphics, you have to do an extra bit of work to ensure that every element of the site arrives at the server in the correct location.

This section assumes that you have some web space with FTP access and have configured the folders on the server to match the local scheme, that is, there is a root folder called Home and within this are two folders called images and downloads. This discussion also assumes that you have a working Internet connection and all the details necessary to update your web space over FTP.

FTP, as mentioned earlier, is a method for uploading and downloading documents or files to a remote server as though it were a local disk. Most communication with a web server that isn't viewing pages (which has its own HTTP) is handled by FTP.

Fortunately, the developers of OO.o put FTP facilities right into the heart of the application, and to save a web page—including all of the local graphics—to a web server, you just need to provide the right information in the correct format. Choose File ➤ Save As, and, in the space for the File name, use the following:

```
ftp://username:password@hostname/path/to/index.html
```

Breaking this down, the first element (ftp://) defines the protocol that is used to transfer the files. The second part is the username and password that is used to access the site; if these details are not provided, the application will fall back to an anonymous user and a dialog box will appear with a password request. The third section, after the @ symbol, is the URL for the server. This could be either a real name—that is, webspace. com—or an IP address using the dotted quad format, that is, 214.113.11.154. The final part is the path for the file and the file name itself (see Figure 8-25).

The great thing is that after this connection is opened via the Save As operation, it stays open as the document is edited, so every subsequent Save, either through File ➤ Save or Ctrl+S, will be saved to the server. Also, as long as the Save local graphics to the Internet option was chosen earlier, any image embedded into the page will be uploaded to the web space, and the path used to access it will be updated within the document.

Reopening the document later can be accomplished by either entering the full URL using the same format as shown previously in the File ➤ Open dialog box, or by choosing the appropriate entry from the recently opened documents drop-down list.

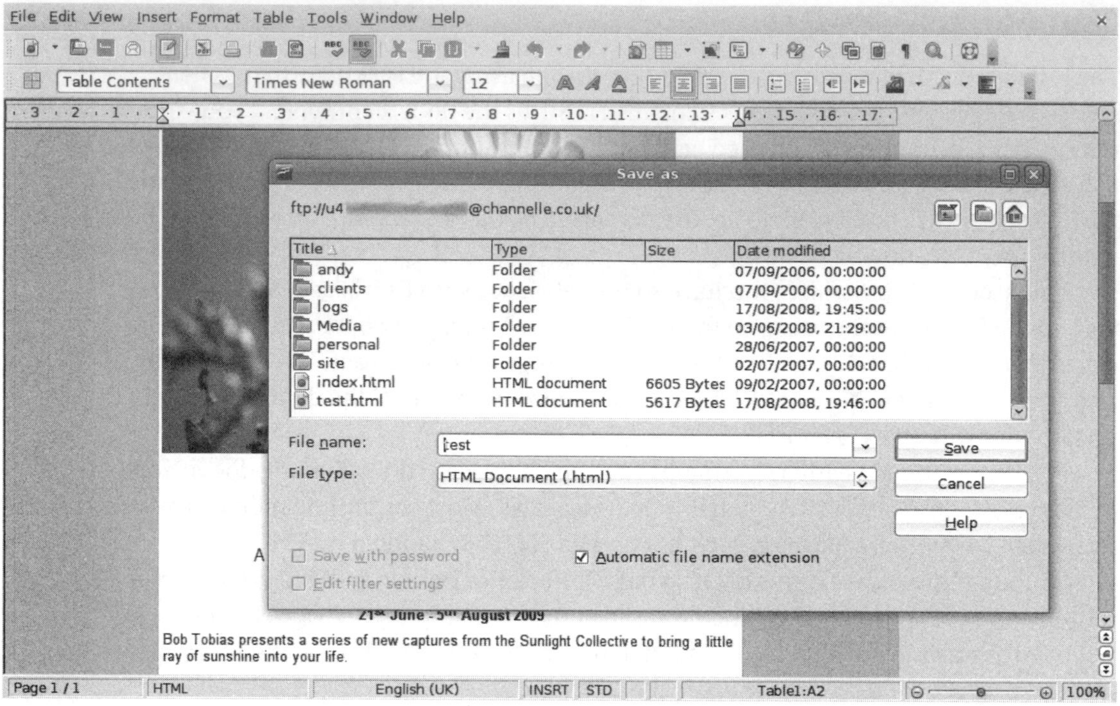

**Figure 8-25.** *The details for your FTP service can be added to the document path (the blurry part in this screenshot) to save remote documents as though they were stored locally.*

---

■**Caution** Usernames and passwords for web spaces should be kept secret. This is not something OO.o is great at because these details are easily accessible while a remote file is open.

---

## The Web Wizard

OO.o also has another trick up its sleeve for users who may need to publish a selection of documents to the Internet but are not concerned with designing pages to house them. The Web Wizard takes a range of files, converts them to a format that can be viewed in any web browser, and then builds a table of contents to make accessing them simple. The Web Wizard won't enable you to create a beautiful site, but it will help you get a selection of documents, spreadsheets, and presentations onto a web server quickly (see Figure 8-26).

The Web Wizard can be launched by choosing File ➤ Wizards ➤ Web Page.

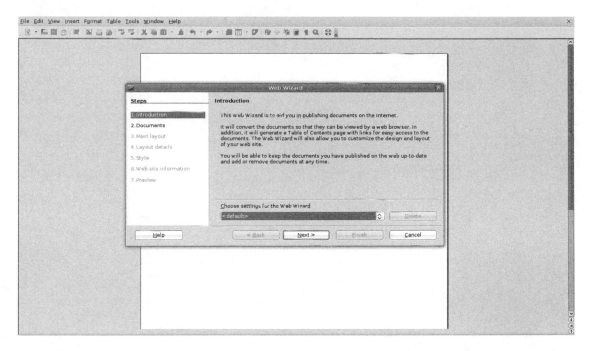

**Figure 8-26.** *Read through the introduction, and then click the Next button to begin working with the Web Wizard.*

Define the documents to be added to the new site. Any document that OO.o can read will be available. The software will suggest the best format to convert the document to, although it's easy to change this. When the documents have been added using the Add button, click Next again.

Choose the layout for the table of contents. Some of the options use Frames so a document can be selected in one frame and viewed in another. Once selected, click Next.

The Layout Details screen allows you to optimize the browsing experience for particular screen sizes and also define the kind of information that will be presented for each file in the site. Details such as the author's name are taken from the file's metadata.

Now you can define the style for the contents page. A range of styles is available from the drop-down list, and these can then be augmented with backgrounds and an icon set chosen using the buttons next to each option.

The Web site information section (see Figure 8-27) is where you should input basic information about your web site or page, such as a description, author details, and copyright information.

In the final screen, you can do two things. First, click the Preview button to reveal what the final site will look like in the system's default browser. And second, you can set the software to create a local copy of the site (i.e., stored on the machine you're using), create a compressed ZIP archive, and upload the entire production to a web server using provided credentials.

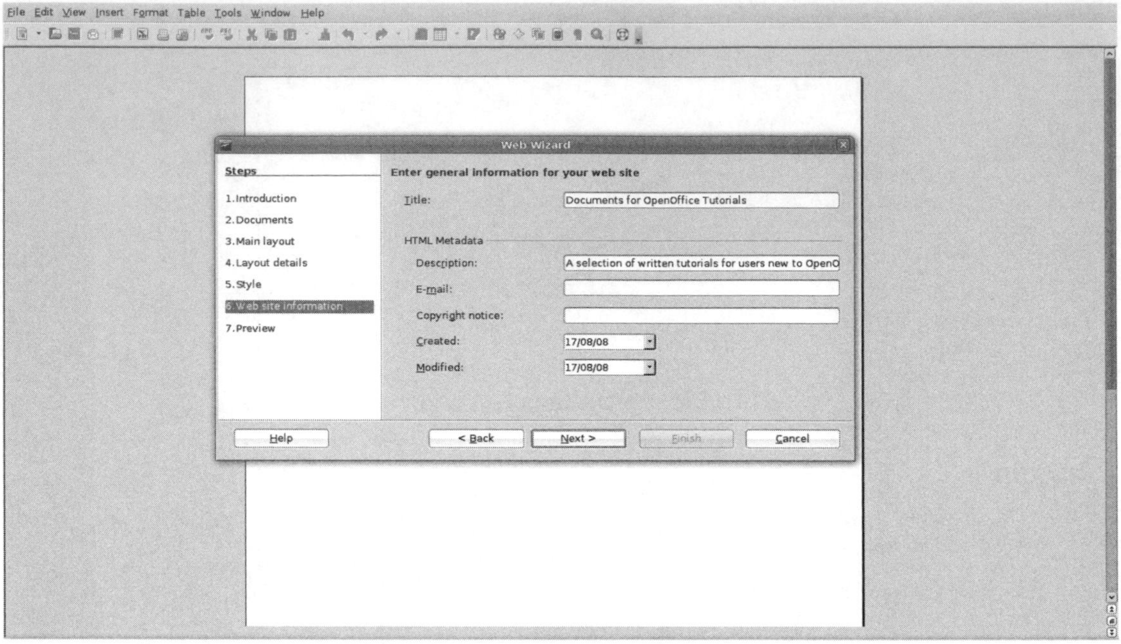

**Figure 8-27.** *All of the information in this section of the Web Wizard goes into the HTML file's head section, meaning browsers will see it, but users usually won't.*

# Recap

In this chapter, you've primarily used two applications to create a small selection of web-based projects. You used tables as a method for laying out an e-newsletter, used Draw to create a banner advertisement and then assigned links to various parts of it, and used Writer's Save As dialog box as a quick and accessible FTP client. Although OpenOffice.org is unlikely to challenge Dreamweaver for the web design crown, it's a capable editor, especially if your needs are not too ambitious. Finally, we ran through one of OO.o's wizards, which can take a series of documents and make a usable collection of web pages with little effort.

Beyond these operations, Writer is capable of working with cascading style sheets, video, and sound to provide even more editing options, and the tools you've investigated in this chapter, especially the table-editing functions, can be put to use elsewhere in the suite to make information more useful in presentations and printed documents.

# CHAPTER 9

■■■

# Working with Others

**C**ollaboration is an important part of document creation for many people, so a piece of software's ability to deal with anything thrown at it can be important. However, file formats are skittish things, and even different versions of the same product—for example, MS Office 2003 and MS Office 2007—will sometimes balk at opening a file from the other. OpenOffice.org has the challenge of transferring data not just across applications, but sometimes even across platforms (see Figure 9-1), which can create additional problems. Despite this, OO.o still manages to open, display, and edit most of these files adequately.

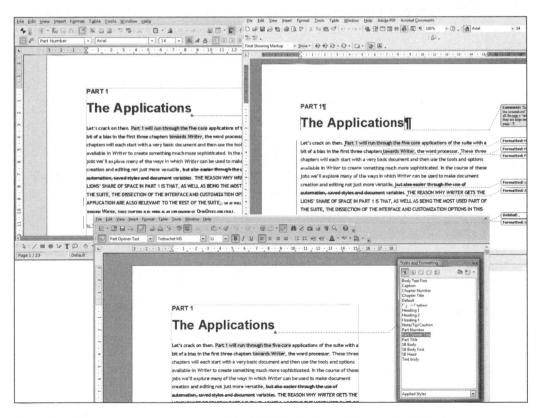

**Figure 9-1.** *The same document opened in MS Word, OpenOffice.org for Windows, and OpenOffice.org for Linux*

In this chapter you'll go through the process of importing and exporting data in the most common formats, learn some of the pitfalls to watch out for in the process, and look at the tools available to make working with others a more fruitful experience. You'll also look at some of the security implications of the world of shared data and learn a few of the ways to use OpenOffice.org to protect the contents of your documents and your work processes.

This last idea—the concept of adding security not just to your work but to the way a document has been created—is seldom discussed. But if you're creating documents intended for public consumption, being able to present a finished document to the rest of the world in a way that doesn't reveal early drafts, deleted sentences, or half-formed ideas (or even the date of creation) can be a very useful skill.

This chapter deviates from the project-based method of previous chapters, but all of the tools we discuss here are designed to be integrated into the document-creation and -distribution process and so will apply to everything we've already covered.

# Document Formats

The native file formats in OpenOffice.org, collectively known as the Open Document Format (ODF), have recently been ratified as an international standard, making them politically suitable for use in public and commercial institutions across the world. Microsoft's competing Office Open XML (OOXML) formats also have this status, and the latest version of OpenOffice.org can use these formats too.

In addition to this software, the ODF formats have been adopted by other productivity packages, including Google Docs, WordPerfect, KOffice, AbiWord, ThinkFree Office, and IBM's Symphony Suite. The ability to import and export all of the most popular global formats (including, in our experience, some "corrupted" MS Office files) makes OO.o the ideal package for those working across platforms.

While OO.o prefers to use ODF formats for saving text, spreadsheet, and presentation documents, it can also use many other formats. The native format extensions are

.odt—Text

.ott—Text template

.ods—Spreadsheet

.ots—Spreadsheet template

.odp—Presentation

.otp—Presentation template

.odg—Graphic

.odf—Formula

.odb—Database file

.orp—Database report

In addition, versions of OpenOffice.org also retain compatibility with the previous versions of these formats, which all begin with .sx for documents and .st for templates.

---

■**Caution** We have occasionally experienced a problem using OpenOffice.org 3 with Windows Vista, where a native .odt file would not be properly saved if an image was embedded in the document. If this happens, you can solve it by going into the OO.o configuration (Tools ➤ Options), selecting the General section (see Figure 9-2) from the left-hand side, and clicking the option to Use OpenOffice.org dialogs.

---

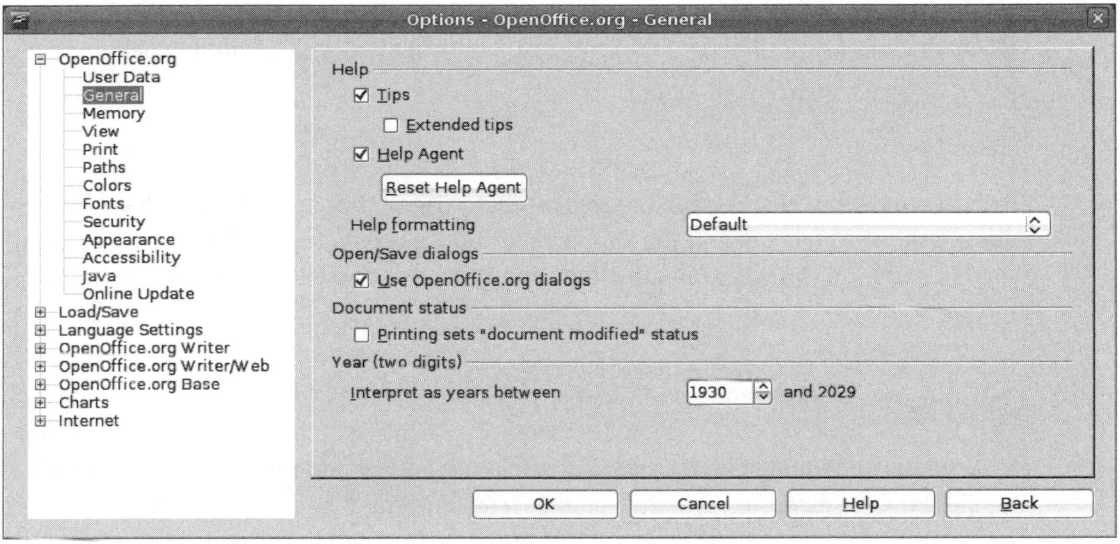

**Figure 9-2.** *If you experience a problem with file management in Windows Vista, go into the Preferences and set OO.o to use its own file dialogs.*

Most of these are available using the typical file management functions, accessible via the File ➤ Open/Save/Export options. By default the software will open and save the native ODF formats (though this can be changed; see the later section "Changing Default Formats"); this is the best choice for storing documents on your hard disk, backing up, or sharing with other OO.o (or ODF-based) users.

One of the interesting things about the default ODF formats is that the file itself is not a single file, but is instead a collection of files and folders pulled together into a standard zip file. To see how this works, navigate to a saved OO.o file, make a copy of it to a different location (usually this can be accomplished by right-clicking on the file and selecting Copy and then Paste into a different folder) and rename the copy so that the file extension is .zip instead of .odt, .ods, etc.

## Windows

Windows typically keeps file extensions hidden from users, so you'll need to make them visible in order to edit them. This can be done on a folder-by-folder basis or can be applied to all folders of a particular type. Open up the folder that contains the copied OO.o file and select Organize ➤ Folder and Search Options. Choose the View tab, and scroll through the content to find the option labeled Hide extensions for known file types. This will be enabled, so deselect it and then click Apply.

Now click the file name to be edited, click it again (this is different from double-clicking), and then edit the file extension. Once you add .zip to the file, the icon will change to a Compressed Folder icon and can be opened with a double-click.

## Linux

Users of most Linux distributions should be able to right-click an icon and select Open with ➤ Other and then choose the appropriate archive utility. Right-clicking and selecting Rename and then changing the file extension to .zip will also allow them to open it as an archive.

## Mac OS X

In OS X you can rename files by selecting with a single click and then clicking the icon. Highlight the file extension and then change it to .zip. You'll be asked whether you really want to keep the .zip extension. Select Yes, and then double-click the icon to extract the contents of the archive to the same directory.

Just as with a modern web site, the ODF formats separate content and presentation (see Figure 9-3), so if you were to look in the file labeled content, you'd see a (just about) readable XML file; if you double-clicked on the styles, settings, or meta files, you'd see an XML rendering of the structure and presentation of the document; and if you checked inside the Pictures folder, you'd see every image embedded in the file.

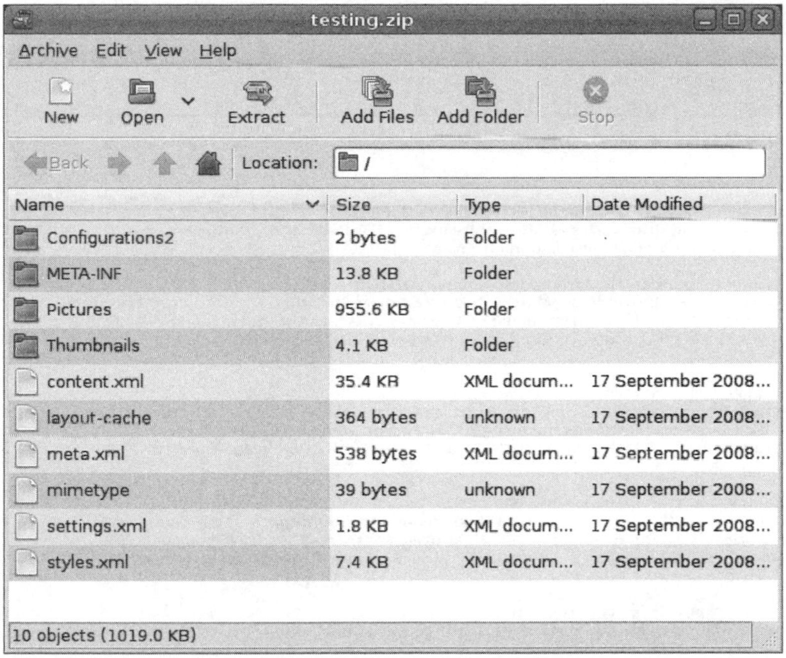

**Figure 9-3.** *If you change the extension of an ODF to .zip, you can access its contents just as with any archive.*

The real beauty of this is that at no point is your data (and it is yours) locked up in some format that you can't access. In 20 years, conservatively guessing that we'll still be using computers and that the zip archive will still be a common format, the information in these documents, including images and metadata (see the later section "Collaborative Work"), will be readily accessible, regardless of the availability of the OpenOffice.org software (see Figure 9-4). Moreover, because no one strictly "owns" the OpenOffice.org software, no company would be able to retire it or remove it from the market, making it likely that the software itself will remain available for the foreseeable future. Data security is about more than just keeping other people's hands off your files. It also means being able to access that data even if your favorite software vendor disappears or their products evolve beyond the current standards.

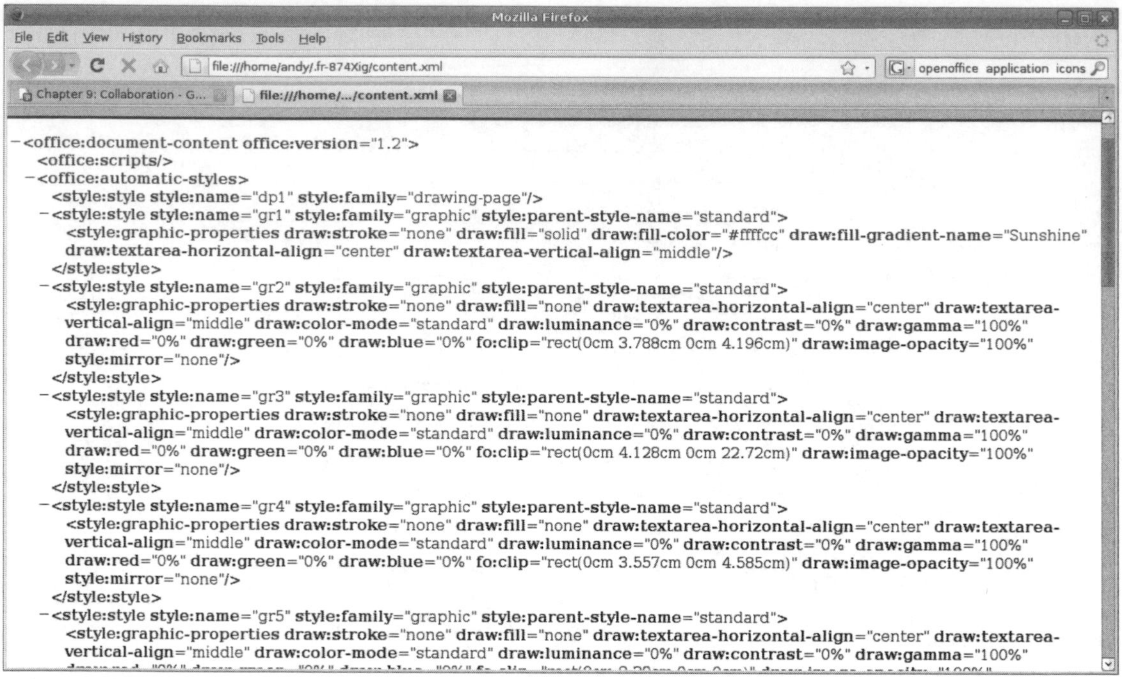

**Figure 9-4.** *Because ODF uses XML, we know that the information contained in the file is safe and will remain accessible even if the formats change.*

## Choosing a Different Format

Whenever you select File ➤ Save as in any of the applications within the suite, OO.o will open your operating system's standard file browser, which can be used to navigate to a location to save a document. Use the Save as File type drop-down list (see Figure 9-5) to select one of the many file formats available, and then click OK to send the file. By default, the Auto Extension option will be selected, which means you don't have to type in the last part of the file name (e.g., the .doc or .odt element).

When opening a new file, the drop-down list next to the file name is quite a powerful sorting tool. For example, click the box and select Text documents, and the file browser will only display files capable of holding plain or formatted text; choose Spreadsheet and it will display all accessible spreadsheet formats. Further down the list are more specific file formats, so it would be possible to restrict the file browser to displaying only .doc files, PowerPoint presentations, or JPEG graphics. Note that this option is universal, so it's possible to open a text file while working in Calc or to open a spreadsheet while working in Impress. The new file will open in a new window.

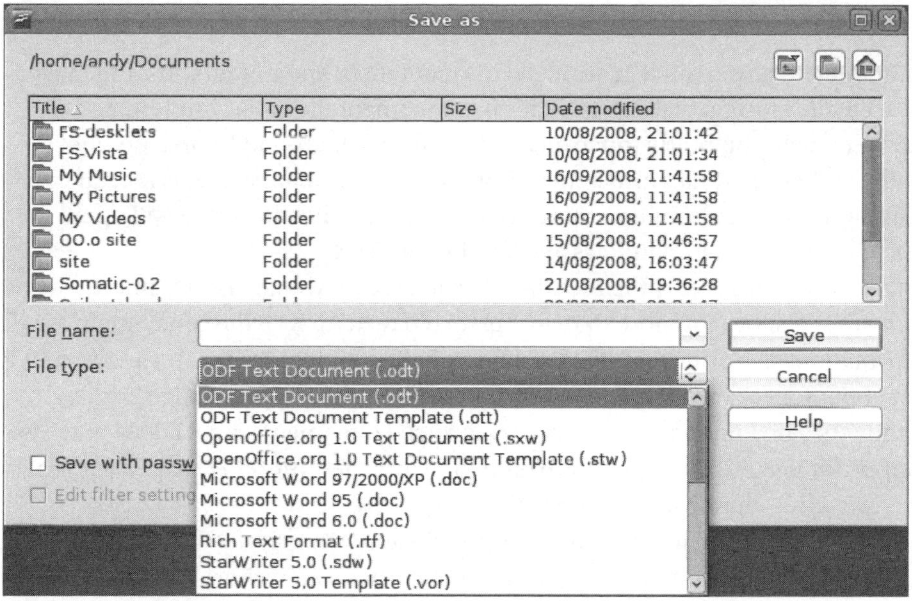

**Figure 9-5.** *Every OO.o application has a range of file output options from the common to the more specialized.*

When working with formats that support multiple versions of the same document (and, obviously, using a file that has versions saved in it), a new drop-down list becomes available that allows you to select which version to open. Note that if you open an old version of a file and then make changes and save, that will become the latest version of the document, though of course other versions remain available.

When sharing documents with users of other software packages (i.e., those that can't handle the ODF formats), you should choose a format based on the content of the document itself. Next we present a series of document scenarios that look at the most appropriate formats for exporting content from OpenOffice.org.

## Document Scenarios

When deciding which format to use in any of these situations, inevitably you must choose between features and accessibility. The most basic formats are also the most universal. This is also true of Microsoft Office formats, where, in general, using an earlier version of the format (e.g., from Word 97 or XP rather than Word 2007) will result in better, more compatible output.

## Text

If your document contains plain text arranged into sentences and paragraphs, the most universally accessible format will be .txt. This is a document file at its simplest, and the content will be readable on pretty much any system, from a high-end PC to a netbook, mobile phone, or iPod. Text files also benefit from being very small, which is ideal if you're e-mailing stuff. All current operating systems have applications that will open a .txt file, such as Notepad in Windows and TextEdit in OS X.

The next step up from .txt is the Rich Text Format (.rtf), which, as its name suggests, provides facilities for more than just plain old text. An RTF file can contain formatting information such as justification, boldface, italics, and underline. It can also hold information about font size and name, headers and footers for the page, page borders, paragraph indents, and line spacing. For more advanced documents, an RTF file may also contain images, though the file formats are limited to just a few bitmap (.jpg, .png, .bmp) and vector (.emf, .pict) options, and even tables.

The third option is useful for the most complex documents that need to be shared among users working across different applications, such as OO.o Writer, Word, and Pages. The common format among these applications is Microsoft's native .doc format (see Figure 9-6). This should render the content of the text, comments, tables, styles, and even metadata, which is the information kept in the document file that is not meant for display, such as tracked changes, deletions, and author data.

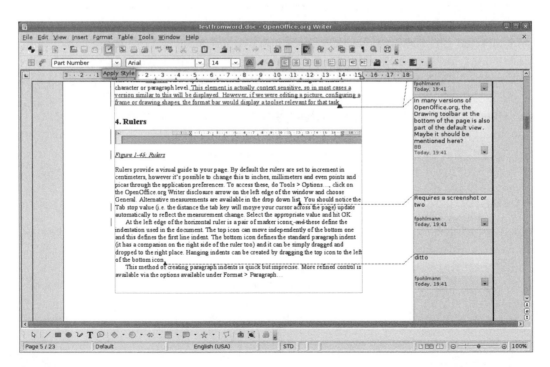

**Figure 9-6.** *In terms of "richness," the .doc format is the best option if you're sharing work among colleagues.*

Table 9-1 compares the features supported in the three document scenarios.

**Table 9-1.** *Supported Features in Text-Based File Formats*

|  | Text (.txt) | Rich Text Format (.rtf) | Word (.doc) |
| --- | --- | --- | --- |
| Text | Yes | Yes | Yes |
| Images | No | Yes | Yes |
| Tables | No | Yes | Yes |
| Formatting | No | Yes | Yes |
| Metadata | No | No | Yes |
| Styles | No | No | Yes |

## Spreadsheet

The most universal format for spreadsheet data is the comma-separated value (CSV) file. This, as the name suggests, contains data in which the cells are delimited by commas. It's slightly more complex in that the columns are separated by commas and the rows are defined with carriages returns. So, for example, the following would be displayed in a three-by-three spreadsheet grid, with the top three cells containing the Package, Version Number, and Web Site headings and the details arranged beneath:

Package, Version Number, Web Site

OpenOffice.org, 3.0, www.openoffice.org

MS Office, 2007, www.microsoft.com

iWork, 2, www.apple.com/iwork

A CSV file will load into almost any spreadsheet application, and the gaps between the commas can take any kind of textual or numerical information.

Most spreadsheets, however, are likely to be exchanged using Microsoft's .xls format, and OpenOffice.org's Calc will open and save these files with little difficulty.

Table 9-2 compares the basic features of the CSV and Excel formats.

**Table 9-2.** *Comparison of Basic Spreadsheet Features*

|  | Comma-Separated Values (.csv) | Excel (.xls) |
| --- | --- | --- |
| Functions | Yes | Yes |
| Cell formatting | No | Yes |
| Borders | No | Yes |
| Macros | No | Yes |
| Images | No | Yes |
| Forms | No | Yes |

## Presentation

When sharing presentations with other OpenOffice.org users, the default .odp format is best. But in all other cases, the best option is to stick with Microsoft's PowerPoint (.ppt) format (see Figure 9-7). In fact, if you intend to give a presentation in front of a group of people on your own computer system, we would still recommend using the PowerPoint format (maybe as a backup to an original .odp file). This way, if a problem occurs with your computer, the presentation could be rescued by running on someone else's. In terms of simple outputting, Impress offers a few even more "universal" options, including saving as a series of PDFs, which could be displayed on almost any device, as an HTML document, or even as a set of images (see Chapter 5). Remember, though, that presentations output as anything but one of the proper presentation formats (.ppt, .odp, etc.) will no longer be editable in Impress. Table 9-3 compares output formats with Impress.

**Figure 9-7.** *If you've invested lots of time and money in PowerPoint templates, your efforts will not have been wasted with Impress. (Template from TemplateWise.com)*

**Table 9-3.** *Comparison of Output Formats for Impress*

|                    | PDF     | HTML | PPT |
| ------------------ | ------- | ---- | --- |
| Transitions        | Limited | No   | Yes |
| Notes              | No      | No   | Yes |
| Animations         | No      | No   | Yes |
| Audio              | No      | No   | Yes |
| Automatic playback | No      | No   | Yes |
| Navigation         | No      | Yes  | Yes |

## OPENOFFICE VERSIONS

OpenOffice is one of the only genuinely cross-platform productivity packages available. With Version 3.0 it takes the tally of natively supported platforms to four: Windows Vista, Linux, Mac OS X, and Solaris. Because it is an open source product, which gives developers the opportunity to study and improve the software, various editions of the software may be available at any one time. And, of course, most of these packages share one important detail (beyond the underlying structure of the software!): the price.

Novell creates a tailored edition of the software for its SUSE Linux system (though it is used by other systems) with different icons and a few extra bells and whistles.

`http://go-oo.org/`

IBM has taken the core of the software, redesigned the user interface to be more familiar to MS Office 2007 users, and released it as Lotus Symphony.

`http://symphony.lotus.com`

NeoOffice was, until the latest release, the only way to get an OS X version of the software with the native Apple interface.

`www.neooffice.org`

OxygenOffice Professional is more akin to the typical OO.o build, but it adds a large collection of photos, clip art, and—perhaps most importantly—templates.

`http://ooop.wiki.sourceforge.net`

The official version—as well as links to many other unofficial ones—is always available from the main OO.o web site.

`www.openoffice.org`

StarOffice is Sun Microsystem's paid-for edition of the software that comes with fonts, extensions, and a range of enterprise support options.

`www.sun.com/software/staroffice`

## Database

As with a spreadsheet, the most universal output option for a database file is either comma-separated values or a Calc/Excel spreadsheet. The downside of this is that none of the forms or structural elements will be included in the export.

### Draw

Draw is capable of outputting a very large number of standard graphical formats, including .jpg, .gif, and .png (all bitmap formats) and .svg, .eps, and .wmf (vector formats).

## Changing Default Formats

When OpenOffice.org is installed on a computer, it will be set with the native ODF files as the default formats; i.e., they will be selected automatically when the user clicks the File ➤ Open or Save option. When working in isolation, it's probably best to keep this setting as is, for ODF documents are going to provide the best fidelity. However, if you're working in a mixed software environment and are likely to be sharing lots of documents with MS Office users, it might be more advantageous to change the default settings to work with the Office formats. This makes it less likely that you'll accidentally send a colleague a document that he or she can't open.

Like most of the big changes you can make in the software, this process begins in the Tools ➤ Options dialog box. Use the left-hand pane to select Load/Save, and then select General (Figure 9-8). You've been here before when defining the URL settings for a web page, but the section you're interested in this time is the Default file format and ODF settings. At the top of this section is a drop-down list for defining which version of the ODF formats to comply with—(there are few reasons to change this)—and then a couple of options for optimizing ODF documents and to warn when not saving in ODF. Because you're changing the default file format, switching off the latter makes sense because it will remove some annoying interruptions. Deselect the Optimization option if you intend to view OO.o's XML files (as mentioned in the earlier section about the zipped file format, "Document Formats") in a plain-text editor. The option, when set, removes programmer-friendly indents and line breaks from the text, thus reducing the size of the file.

Now, what you're most interested in is the two drop-down lists at the bottom of the window (see Figure 9-8). These are linked, so selecting an option in the left-hand list will affect the options in the right-hand one. To set the default format for Text, select that option from the left and then choose the appropriate format—in our case .doc—in the right. Then do the same for Spreadsheet (.xls) and Presentation (.ppt) and, if necessary, the other options.

Next time File ➤ Save as is called up, these formats will be selected automatically in the Save as File type drop-down list, making it more likely that you'll send colleagues the right type of document.

---

■**Tip** One thing you're likely to notice when saving Word documents from Writer is that the file size for similar documents taken from Word itself is likely to be a lot smaller due to the way Writer structures information. Save the same file out in .odt format and it will be smaller still, thanks to the compression included in the file format, though this may not happen if you use lots of .tif images in your documents.

---

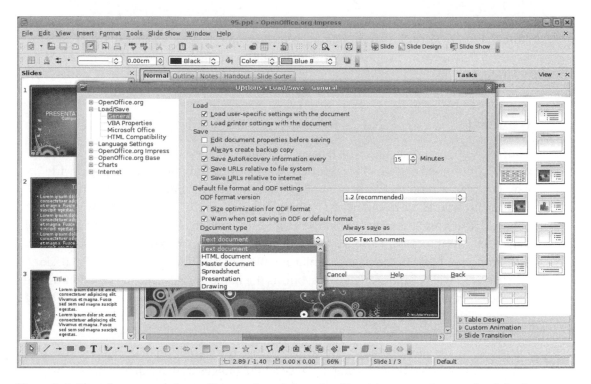

**Figure 9-8.** *If you're constantly sending and receiving .doc files, it's easy to change the default formats across the entire application.*

# Exporting As PDF

One of the most usable export formats, especially when document fidelity is important, is PDF, Adobe's own portable document format that provides genuine "what you see is what you get" output. One of the strengths of PDF is that the specifications for the format have been released, meaning that application and filter developers have been able to add the format to their products fairly easily. It also means that software such as OpenOffice.org has a complete implementation, with all of the compression, security, and resolution options intact. This is great news if you need to share information because almost everybody with a PC will be able to view your output—unless you want to prevent them from viewing it.

It's useful to think of PDF export as "printing to a file" because you can control exactly how the document is output (as you could with a printer) and the final result will (or should) not look significantly different from the onscreen version—especially if you use the Document Preview button. And just as with printing, the PDF export tool is available across the suite and works in the same way whether you're exporting a poster from Draw, a spreadsheet from Calc, or a newsletter from Writer, and so the process of outputting a PDF is exactly the same.

To launch the export dialog box from any application, select File ➤ Export as PDF. Note that there are other export options, which are application-specific, under File ➤ Export. There are a lot of options in here, so we'll go through each tab of the dialog box individually.

## General

The first section here defines which pages are going to be exported. In the Range setting, a set of continuous pages can be exported by separating the start and end pages with a hyphen. For example, 3-7 will print pages three and seven and everything in between. Printing individual pages can be accomplished by separating page numbers with semi-colons (1;5;67), and these two methods can be combined to export ranges and individual pages, for example, 1-5;9;13;30-35. In the Images section you can define how pictures are compressed, which can have a significant affect on the final size of the PDF. Lossless compression will compress image files, but, as the name suggests, no information will be lost. Better compression rates can be accomplished using the JPEG option because this actually removes data from an image file to achieve smaller file sizes. With JPEG chosen, you can define the compression rate (see Figure 9-9)—the smaller the file, the lower the quality of the picture—and you can also reduce the resolution of images as they're imported. This could be important if you've added images from a camera that shoots incredibly high-resolution images and most of each of those images would be lost during the printing process. You can set documents destined for printing on laser printers or even in a professional context to a resolution of 300dpi.

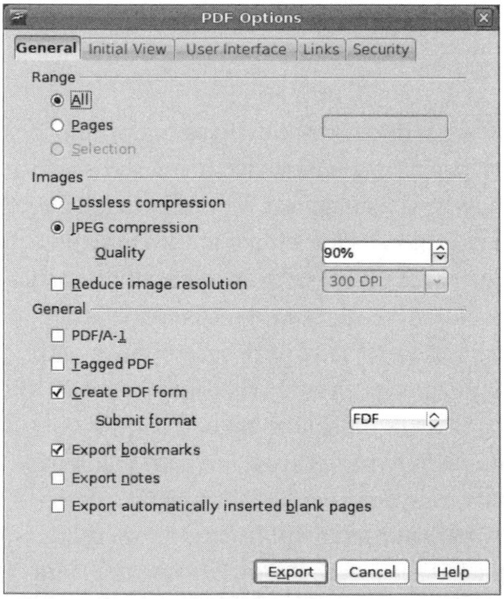

**Figure 9-9.** *Setting up which elements of the document will go into the PDF*

The final section deals with the main PDF type; your choice here will depend on the purpose of the document.

- PDF/A-1: Designed for long-term storage of a document, which means that fonts used inside the document will be embedded into the file, and PDF tags will be included.

- Tagged PDF: Inserts structural information into the file, which can increase the file size considerably, so that it can be viewed on a larger range of devices.

- PDF form: Allows the end user to fill out form elements on their computer before printing or submitting the document. The submission process can be defined using the next section.

- Export bookmarks: Makes any hyperlinks or mailto: links in a document work as they would in a web page.

- Export notes: Includes in the file the notes and comments from the document. This setting can be a security or privacy problem, so if you're selecting it, make sure you know that you're selecting it and not exposing your and your colleagues' thoughts on a project.

- Blank pages: Will retain any blank pages inserted into the document either manually or by styles. For example, if a particular paragraph style has been set to begin on the right-hand page, it won't mess up the layout by removing those blank pages.

## Initial View

The Initial View tab (see Figure 9-10) defines what end users will see when they open the document in their PDF reader. This won't actually change the structure or content of the document, as other tabs can, but will set out the mode of display. The Panes section sets out which elements of the project will be seen. Page only will open the document in a window of its own; adding the Bookmarks or Thumbnails option will make the PDF viewer open up with an additional pane to the left (usually) of the main view with those parts in, which can improve navigation on longer documents. It's also possible to set a different page for a view to open on.

The Magnification option sets the zoom level of the document when it's first open. The options—Fit in window, Fit width, etc.—are similar to the view options in many of the applications. Setting these will not prevent users themselves from changing the zoom level inside the PDF viewer, just set the first look.

The Page layout section defines whether the document is displayed as a collection of individual pages, a continuous column of single pages, or a continuous column of spreads (i.e., where the left- and right-hand pages are shown together). Your choice here will depend on how the document was designed in the first place (see Chapter 3).

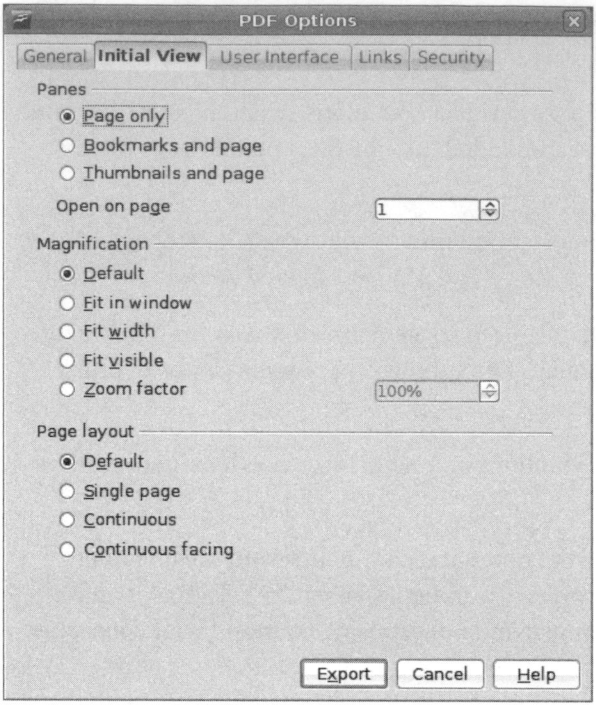

**Figure 9-10.** *These settings define the way the document looks on first loading.*

## User Interface

As with Initial View, the User Interface tab has options for setting how the PDF viewer software works, rather than the document itself. So the Window options can force the document window into the center of the user's screen or open in full-screen mode, and you can set the User interface options (see Figure 9-11) to add or remove elements such as menu bar, toolbar, and other controls from the PDF viewer. These last options are useful if, for example, you want to focus completely on the document (maybe it's a single page) and frills on the margins would detract from your message. Finally, in here it's possible to set up the bookmarks system, with options available for displaying all bookmarks or only those to a certain level. The latter makes it possible to display a long document but to have visible, for instance, only first-level bookmarks (which might equate to chapter headings) and to have bookmarks within a contents page going to subsections of each chapter.

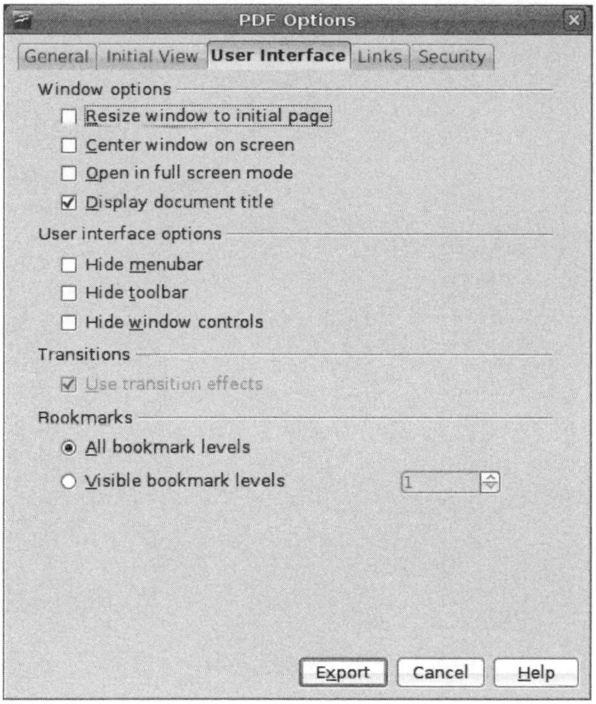

**Figure 9-11.** *Define which parts of the user interface are displayed for the viewer.*

## Links

The Links tab (see Figure 9-12) is where you set out how a document handles HTML and cross-document links. The first option, Export bookmarks as named destinations, turns each bookmark into the equivalent of an HTML anchor, which means that it's possible to link to a specific location in this document from another document.

The option to Convert document references to PDF targets will change the links to other ODF format files (e.g., .odt, .odp) so that they reference a PDF file with the same name. If you created a document called testing1.odt which referenced testing2.odt as a link, selecting this option would render that link as testing2.pdf. Of course, to work successfully with this option, you must export all referenced documents as PDFs before distributing the document set.

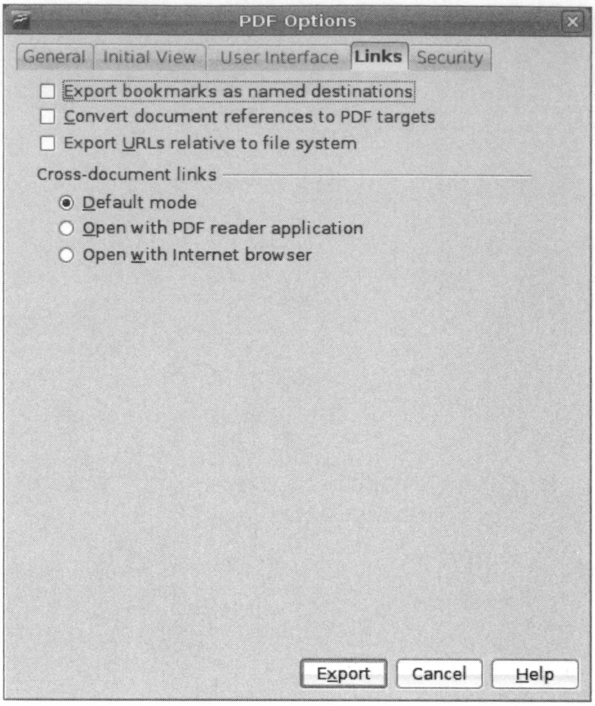

**Figure 9-12.** *Set up how the PDF viewer will handle hyperlinks and document links.*

The option to Export URLs relative to the file system will ensure that documents referenced within a file all point to the same place. Using our example, `testing2.odt` is referenced from `testing1.odt`. With an absolute reference, `testing2.odt` (which you've conveniently put into a folder called `Work`) would be referenced from `testing1.odt` (which is in a user home directory) with something like `C:\Documents\Users\Andy\Work\testing2.odt`. Inevitably, once this document set is moved to another computer (even with the `Work` subdirectory intact), the path will no longer point to the same location. The answer—as with the discussion of links in Chapter 8—is to use relative links. In this case the link to the second document would go to `\Work\testing.odt` so as long as the original document and the `\Work` subdirectory are transferred intact, everything should work as expected.

The Cross-document links section defines how a PDF will handle a link to other documents. The default option will use whatever settings the operating system has configured. The option to Open with PDF reader application will launch the default PDF reader to open new documents—usually a new iteration of the software being used to read the original document—while the Open with Internet browser option will launch the default web browser to display the page. In order for this last option to work, your browser must be set up to handle these kinds of links.

# Security

For some of you, the final tab will also be the most important, because it allows you to set restrictions on how the final document is used (see Figure 9-13). The first, and possibly most commonly used, option is to encrypt the document file. Once this option is selected, a new space becomes active where you can configure a password that will allow access to the file. A reader attempting to read the file will be prompted to enter a password to decrypt it.

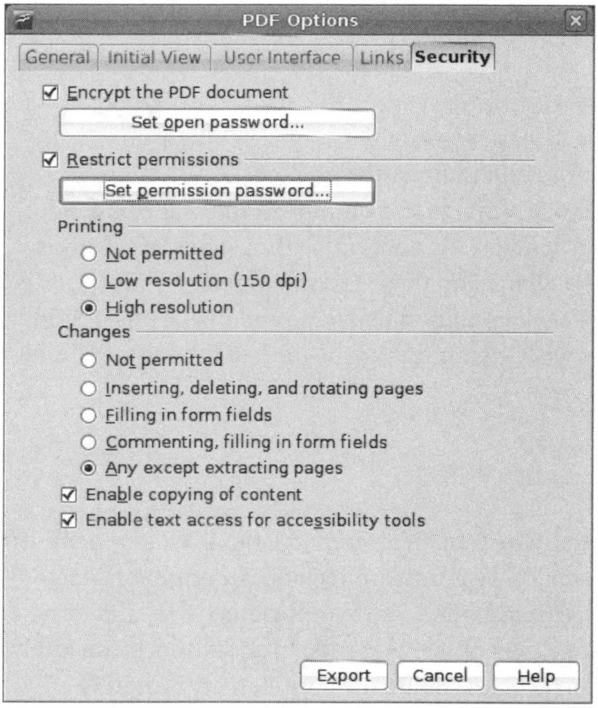

**Figure 9-13.** *Prevent users from copying or printing your documents.*

The second section is far more extensive, and you can use it to restrict how the end user can access the file; once again, this is password-based. For example, you could prevent printing or restrict it to low resolutions only; you could stop the document from being altered totally or allow particular tasks, such as inserting or rotating pages and filling in form elements. The last two options, which are selected by default, enable the user to copy content to the operating system's clipboard for pasting elsewhere and allow screen-reader software to access the text. This is important for accessibility reasons.

---

■**Caution** Adding passwords to different elements of a PDF can give you a false sense of security, because the encryption on this file type is not unbreakable. In fact, a couple of small applications in the wilds of the Internet purport to remove password protection. There are legitimate reasons for these applications to exist. But everyone who uses this format should be aware of its potential flaws and employ something different when transporting nuclear codes, top-secret data, or other information of a sensitive nature.

---

## Tips for Exporting

This section is based on real-world examples of transcoding the most common document types from one format to another. You will learn some of the common pitfalls to watch out for when working on documents across different platforms.

The documents here contain the kind of stuff that is common in the real world. So, for example, you're not going to create a spreadsheet containing thousands of columns and rows, because you're not a Wall Street bank and these text documents, while quite complex, are not going to be overloaded with conditional macros and Visual Basic scripts. The software is capable of handling this work—with varying degrees of fidelity—but that kind of use falls outside your purview.

### Word and Writer

The sample text document is a late draft of the first chapter of this book, which includes not just text formatted using boldface, italics, etc., but applied styles, comments and alterations from multiple authors, images, captions, frames of various types, and content structured by headings, subheadings, and other elements. In short, this is the kind of document likely to test the conversion process. Some missing elements (mainly involving text colors) have been artificially added to test the rendering of those parts. Note that this isn't a review, but a way of highlighting where you may need to focus some attention. Thus, if some element of this file is not mentioned, you may assume that it worked fine.

Taking the file from Word to the Windows edition of Writer kept most of the formatting intact, and, more importantly, the styles employed appeared to work well, including settings for indents, paragraph spacing, and widow/orphan control (see Figures 9-14 and 9-15). There was a slight disparity in the size both applications use for the Small Caps setting, which does have an impact on the way a line falls on the page. We solved this by manually increasing the size of the font for that particular paragraph by one point. When shifting to Linux (with the Microsoft Core Fonts installed), the difference was two points. This problem arises because both Word and Writer "cheat" at creating small caps and, moreover, they cheat in slightly different ways.

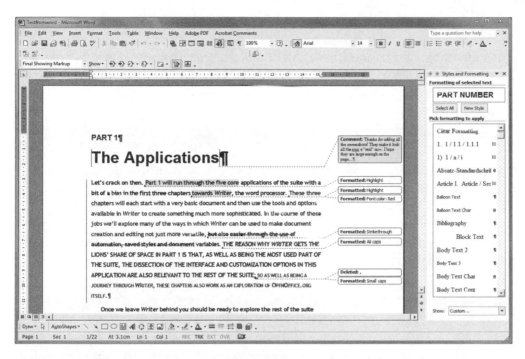

**Figure 9-14.** *A portion of a draft of a complex document featuring styles, comments, and tracked changes*

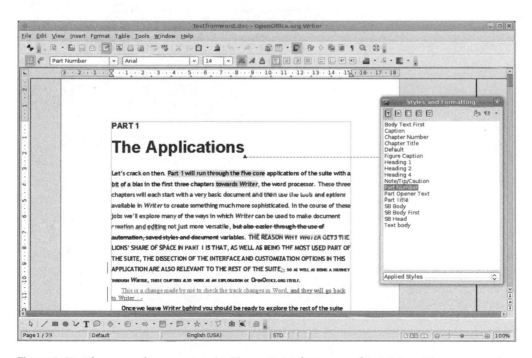

**Figure 9-15.** *The same document as in Figure 9-14, but opened in Writer. Changes made here translated back to Word without significant issues.*

■**Caution**  It's a wise precaution when multiple authors are working on the same document for everyone who will touch the document to have the same fonts installed and for any unusual or esoteric fonts you may use to be legally shared among users.

## FONTS

When you attempt to open a document in Writer that contains fonts not installed on the computer, a Font Substitution dialog box will appear, with a suggestion of the fonts that best match those missing from the document. In most cases, the suggested replacements are fairly good, but substitutions will inevitably lead to some changes in the way text falls in the document. For this reason it's a good idea to look through the document to ensure there are no awkward gaps or problems with anchored images being shunted off to the wrong location.

One way of avoiding significant font-substitution issues if the document is likely to be distributed in its native format is to stick with standard fonts such as Arial and Times New Roman. Of course, if you're outputting the final piece to paper or PDF, you can be a little looser with the fonts.

While the test document did contain a number of fonts, they were pretty standard and so did not differ on the transition from Word to Writer, even when moving to OS X or Linux editions of the software.

Notes and comments were handled well, and a document with Track Changes enabled in Word came through to Writer with the Record option selected. Changes made to the document were denoted in a different color. More importantly, these changes went back to Word correctly marked and annotated with author data from Writer. This is great news because you can be reasonably confident when working collaboratively on documents across the two platforms.

Embedded images also survived the transition and can be edited and cropped as usual. Moreover, pictures that have been cropped in Word will appear in Writer with the crop intact. But because this is not destructive, the image could, if necessary, be "recropped" to expose different parts in Writer.

When it came to taking illustrations from Word to Writer, again fidelity was good. Gradients came through with fewer in-between steps, and transparent gradients with only a single color defined came through with a flat transparency. With little effort, both of these elements can be altered once the document is in Writer.

## Excel and Calc

While it's possible to muddle through any issues with word-processing documents, the same cannot always be said about spreadsheets, where formulas and information may not be readily viewable onscreen. Getting this conversion process right is vital, especially when the household or business budget may depend on it.

For most uses, Calc replicates the tools and options of Excel quite closely, and in our test documents worked without incident. Calc implements the majority of Excel functions (something like 80%), which means all but the most complex documents should import and export correctly. Some of the issues that may arise when taking more complex spreadsheets from Excel to Calc include limitations in the latter's support for pivot tables (named DataPilots in Calc) and functions including INFO and GETPIVOTDATA.

Pivot tables and DataPilots are visualization tools that can be used to summarize the contents (by sorting, grouping, and totaling cells) of one table in a second table, just as "views" can be used in Databases to highlight or take out particular parts of the dataset.

In general Calc will import pivot tables (changing them to DataPilots) fairly well. But, as with other aspects of file formats, the more complex the original file, the more opportunity for problems to be introduced.

However, moving a document from Calc to Excel is less problematic because almost everything available in Calc will transfer well.

With any critical data, you should pay close attention to the document in question and ensure that everything is working as it should.

## PowerPoint and Impress

Due to the more limited formatting options in PowerPoint, our test document transferred quite faithfully both ways between the two applications (see Figures 9-16 and 9-17). One thing we did notice is that presenter notes were marked as wrongly spelled going from Impress to PowerPoint but only on the initial view of the document. Changing slides removed the red wavy lines from the text. One issue that might be significant in terms of custom animations—where sections of text appear in a particular way—is that transferring from PowerPoint removed timings applied to individual parts. We noticed too that the animations such as checkerboard transitions, fades, and wipes were slightly slower on Impress. It's a small thing, but if a presentation relies on tight timing, it might be a good idea to slow things down very slightly before outputting the final PowerPoint .ppt file and, if possible, to test the result on the version of PowerPoint that will host the presentation. However, these differences were small, and in most cases it shouldn't prove problematic.

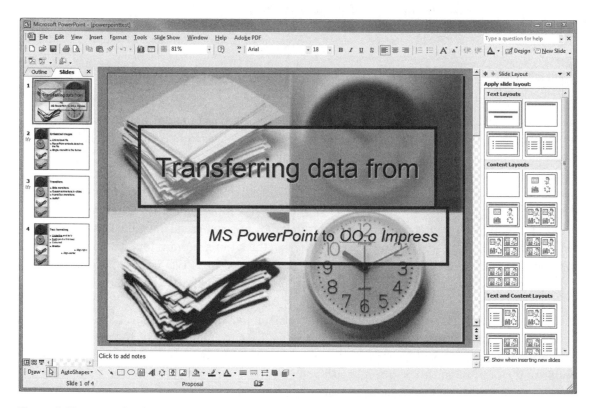

**Figure 9-16.** *A standard PowerPoint file using one of Microsoft's included templates*

**Figure 9-17.** *In the transition we lost some timing information on animations, and slide transitions went a little slower.*

However, the timing issue didn't occur when setting automatic timings for slide transitions. As with Writer, sticking to a core set of fonts available across platforms reduces the potential for conflict, especially if you're saving from Impress with no idea of the machine on which the final presentation may be given.

# Collaborative Work

One advantage of modern software is that it makes working with others a more pleasurable experience. As mentioned earlier, this often involves sharing files with other users. But the real magic happens when authors can share thoughts, ideas, and skills in the same document. OpenOffice.org, and specifically Writer for this section, has a number of cool tools you can use to monitor the stages of creation through which a document passes and that allow one author to comment on another's work. Finally, there are options, as with the PDF security discussed earlier, to share documents securely without fear that they'll fall into the wrong hands.

## Track Changes

When a document passes through many hands, it can sometimes be difficult to work out who was responsible for what changes or, on longer documents, the changes that have actually been made. Track Changes has been designed exactly for this purpose because it will record—as part of the file's metadata—every change made to a document and the name (as defined in the user settings of the software) of the author making those changes. This is great for collaborative writing or editing work, where a solid "paper trail" of changes is an important part of the creative process.

With Comments and Track Changes, each author or editor working on a document will be assigned a color that will be used for both edits and comments, so it's easy to identify the changes made by a particular person (see Figure 9-18).

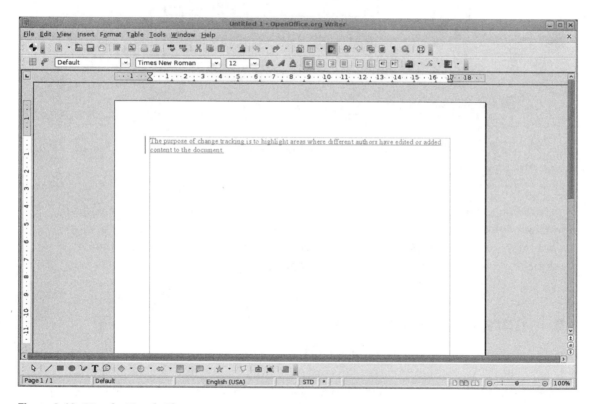

**Figure 9-18.** *Use the Track Changes system to monitor contributions from multiple authors.*

In order to use the Track Changes system in Writer, it needs to be switched on. You can accomplish this by clicking Edit ➤ Changes ➤ Record. The perfect time to do this is when you first create the document, which means that every edit and addition will be logged to the file. The downside of this process is that, once you begin typing, the text will be rendered in your "author color," rather than the traditional black (on our test system it's always a coffee brown for the initial author) and will be underlined, because this is the method by which "changes" are identified. We could solve this via the setting for the Track Changes system. But this is not the best method, because it will also change the way the other authors' changes are denoted.

The best solution when working on an initial draft is either not to track the changes (which is unsatisfactory but can be accomplished with Edit ➤ Changes ➤ Record a second time) or simply not to show the changes. The latter option means clicking Edit ➤ Changes ➤ Show, which will restore the original colors of the document but still record the edits as they happen. Once the initial draft is completed, enabling the Show option once more will recolor the "edits," ready for viewing by collaborators.

The method for displaying edits can be set using the Tools ➤ Options dialog box. Look under the OpenOffice.org Writer section on the left, and then, from the long list of options, choose Changes. Under the Text display setting are three sections for defining the way that insertions, deletions, and attribute changes are shown. There are two kinds of options for denotation. Firstly you can set an attribute such as underlined, double underlined, or italic; secondly you can set a color (see Figure 9-19). The default options are insertion = underline, deletion = strikethrough, and changed attributes = bold; the color is set to be randomly applied, depending on the author. These are sensible defaults and, though it's possible to change insertions, for example, so that they are shown as ALL CAPS and in a particular color, this is probably not going to aid you in the editing process (though we could be wrong).

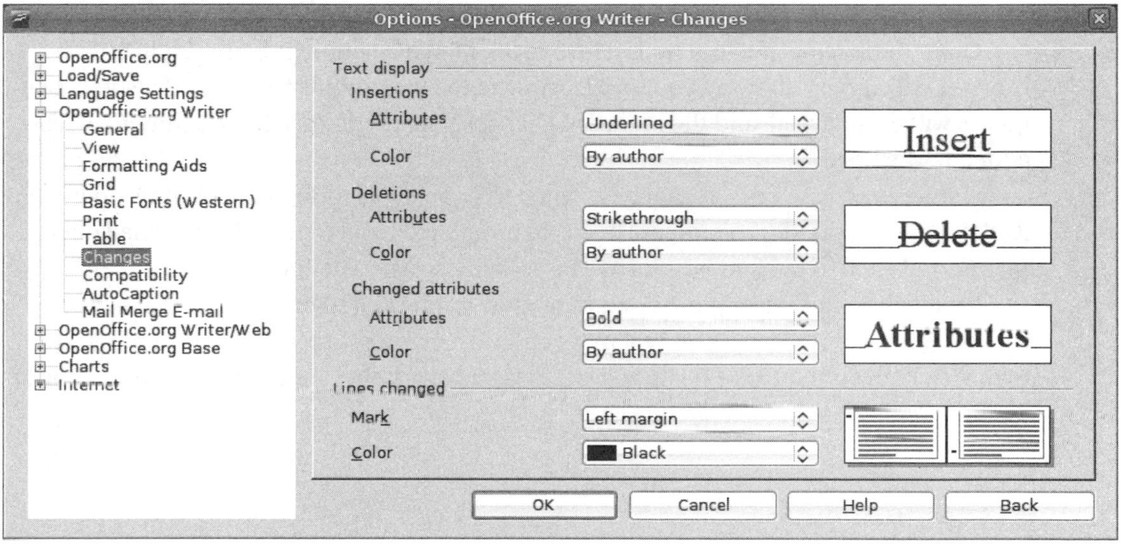

**Figure 9-19.** *Define the way different edits are displayed. By default, each author will have his or her own color.*

Once changes have been made to a document, reveal them once more by clicking Edit ➤ Changes ➤ Show; all the metadata will be displayed using the colors assigned to the authors. Hovering the cursor over a change will pop up a tool tip with the type of edit, the author name, and the date and time of the change using the default date/time formats, e.g., Insertion: Andy Channelle—16/09/08 21:45. A thin horizontal black line will appear in the left margin next to altered lines (though you can change the color and location in the Tools ➤ Options dialog box) to make it easier to find changes as you scroll through the document.

When working on collaborative documents, it would obviously be a mistake to turn off the Track Changes recording; however, you can do this by selecting Edit ➤ Changes ➤ Record.

## Merge Documents

Imagine a scenario where an author has prepared a report and sent that off for review—with the changes having been recorded—by four colleagues. The following day she receives four edited copies of the document. Our author could go through these documents in turn, adding changes to the original as she goes along, but there are two problems with this. Firstly it's time consuming because the writer would have to read through all four new versions to create the definitive one. Secondly, all of these changes would be attributed, in the final version, to the original author, which is no good for later auditing. The best solution is to merge all of the documents into the original using Edit ➤ Changes ➤ Merge Document. Each of the documents will be merged into the original one at a time.

Open the original document and invoke the Merge Document command. A file browser will appear allowing you to select one of the documents to merge. The two documents will be analyzed, and the recorded changes made to the second document will be added to the first.

A color is assigned to the changes, which will appear as though the original document itself had been edited. This process needs to be applied to all four of the returned documents, and each of the four editors will be assigned a different color.

Remember that the original document must not be edited once copies have been sent out for review because this will mess up the merging process. If the author needed to make changes before the review process was finished, she could do so in a fifth copy of the document and then merge this later.

## Accept and Reject

While a document is in the process of editing, it can be useful to have all of that metadata at your fingertips. But as the document progresses, all those changes could become cumbersome. The best solution for this is to comb through the document and Accept or Reject changes (see Figure 9-20). Accepted changes will then be amalgamated into the body of the text—they will become part of the fundamental version—while rejected changes will be lost from the document. It would be sensible, before embarking on this operation, to do a version save (File ➤ Versions) so that "permanent" changes such as these could be reversed later if necessary.

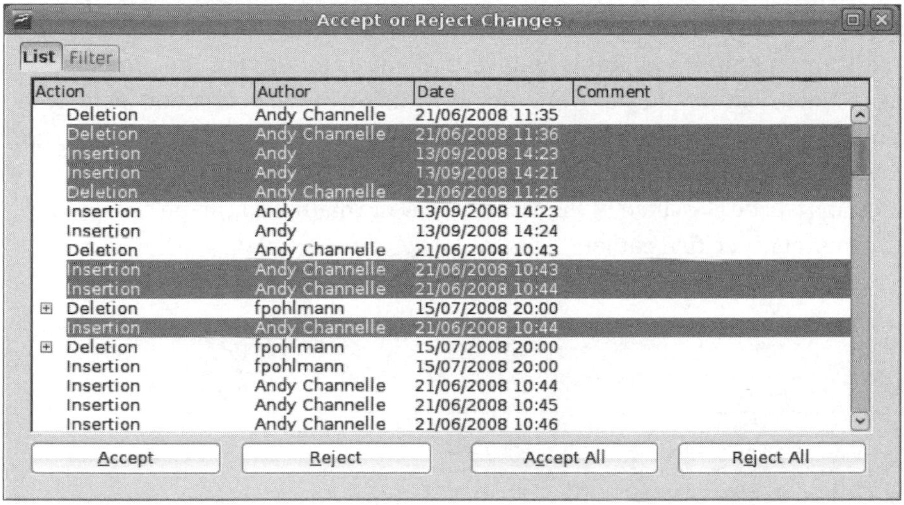

**Figure 9-20.** *Accepted or rejected contributions are rolled into the main document.*

To begin this job, click Edit ➤ Changes ➤ Accept and Reject to launch a new dialog box listing all of the changes made to the document. At the bottom of this dialog box are options to Accept or Reject a selected change.

And the other buttons will do a wholesale Accept or Reject operation for the entire document. You select changes by clicking their list entry with the mouse. As with most standard file browsers, you can make continuous selections by holding down the Shift key, and you can make noncontinuous, multiple selections by clicking with the Ctrl key pressed. Once you've made the selection, click the Accept or Reject button to roll the change(s) into the document. Note that, as you select changes from the list, they will also be highlighted in the document, making this quite a useful way of locating a particular edit.

You can use the Filter tab to seek out specific edits on the basis of the date and time they were made, the author, and the type of action. It works in the same way as filters and sorting systems discussed elsewhere in this book.

---

■**Note** As more metadata is added to a document, the file size will increase. All that information has to go somewhere!

---

# When Collaboration Goes Wrong

When working on projects with lots of authors, things might occasionally go awry. For example, you might send out five copies of a document for review, receive four back with changes noted and colored as expected, ready for merging, and one where the changes have not been recorded. Fortunately, it's possible to compare the new version with the original and note the changes that way.

The process for accomplishing this is almost the same as for merging documents, except in this instance you should start with the new version of the document. So with the new version open, click Edit ➤ Compare Documents and then select the old version using the file browser (see Figure 9-21). The two documents will be merged, and any additions and deletions will be classified in the same way as normally and can be accepted or rejected in the manner specified earlier.

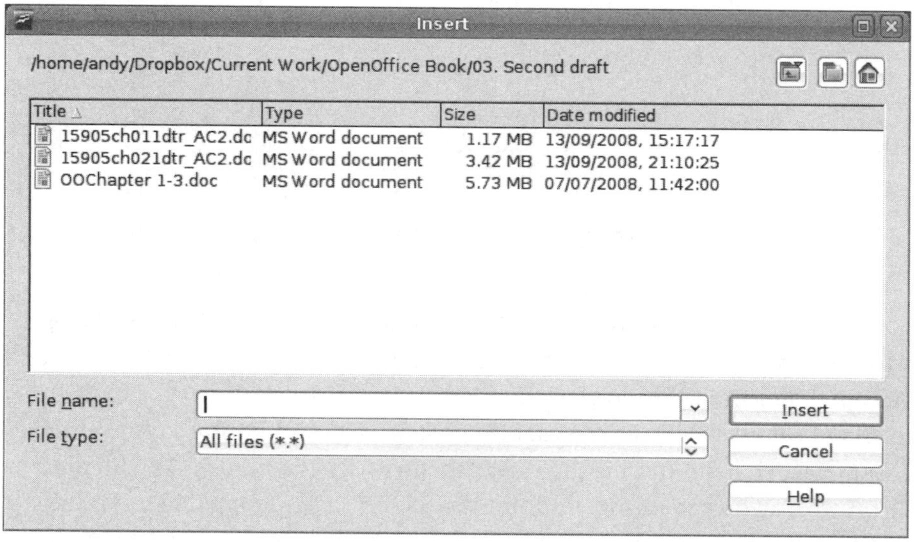

**Figure 9-21.** *Use Compare when one author has forgotten to switch on Track Changes.*

It's important to remember that this procedure must be done using the original document, which means that any comparison operations should be the first part of the merging process. Once you've merged in changes from other authors, the original document will have changed significantly, and comparing to an edited version would inevitably identify the changes made by other authors as part of the original document.

## Adding Notes

While the reason for some changes in a document—for example, changing "colour" to "color"—may seem obvious, others could need a little explaining. For this purpose you can use notes, which work in the same way as the Microsoft Word Comments feature and which look like sticky notes affixed to the margins of the page. In fact, notes are very similar to the marginalia that a teacher might add to the edges of a student's work. You can tie them to a particular section of text and use them to introduce elements of conversation or critique into the document.

You add a note to a document by clicking into a location or selecting an area of text with which to associate it. From the menu bar, select Insert ➤ Note, or press Ctrl+Alt+n (see Figure 9-22). This will add a dashed line into the text at the start of the selection or cursor point (the anchor) and link it to a colored block in the right margin of the page—the color will be the same author color used for the Track Changes system—where you can type out the note in the normal way. And just as with changes made, each note will be identified by the author and the time and date of the addition (see Figure 9-23).

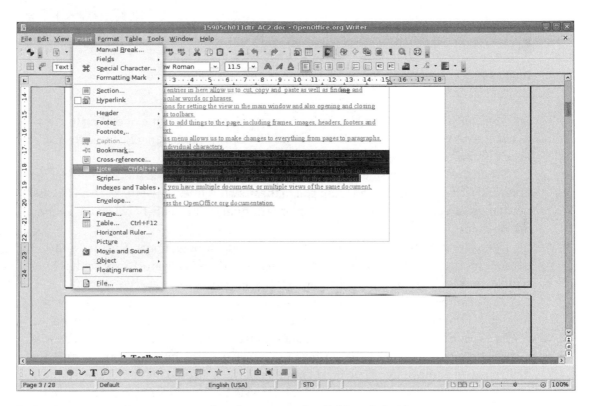

**Figure 9-22.** *You can insert notes using the menu or by clicking Ctrl+Alt+n.*

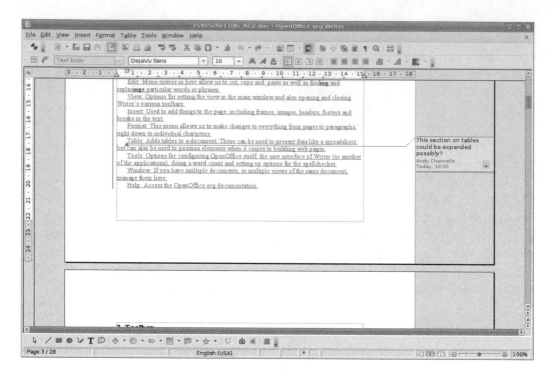

**Figure 9-23.** *Once you have inserted a note, it will move with its anchor text.*

You can edit notes by clicking inside the note blocks and adding or editing the text as necessary. You can edit any author's notes in this way; unfortunately, the software doesn't track these changes as it does normal text.

When the cursor is inside a note, pressing Ctrl+Alt+PageDn will jump you to the next note, and Ctrl+Alt+PageUp will jump you to the previous one. When the cursor is in the normal text area, you can use those keyboard shortcuts to navigate between the anchors for the notes.

There are two other useful methods for navigating through notes. The first, and perhaps more obvious, is to open up the Navigator (Edit ➤ Navigator), expose the Notes section, and click a note in here to jump to it (see Figure 9-24).

The second method is a little more obscure and uses a feature that could easily be overlooked unless you knew it was there. Below the scroll bars to the right of the main window is a trio of small icons: a pair of double arrows (up and down) separated by what looks like a quarter-circle icon (see Figure 9-25). You can use the two arrows to shift the main view up or down by a specific amount. Usually, this would be set to Page, so clicking the down button while on Page 1 would send the view to the top of Page 2. However, it's possible to set this to jump to almost any object type within the OpenOffice.org canon, including Notes. Click the center icon to open the configuration window, and then select the appropriate icon from the collection. Other options here include navigating by Headings, Sections, Pages, Drawings, and Index Entries.

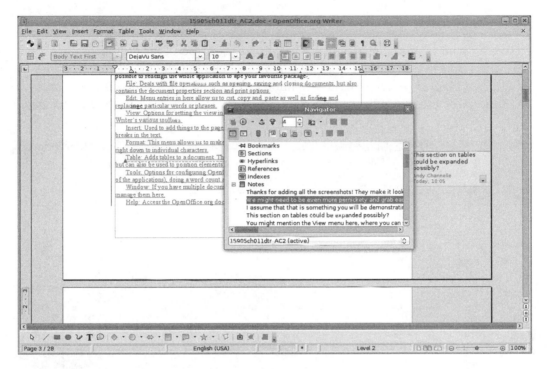

**Figure 9-24.** *You can use the ever-helpful Navigator to pinpoint a note in a long document.*

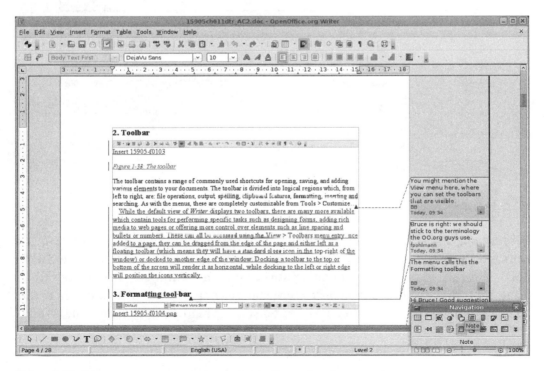

**Figure 9-25.** *There are many ways to navigate through a document.*

## Deleting Notes

To remove a note from a document, use the disclosure arrow at the bottom of the note. This will open a new menu, where notes can be deleted individually, by author, or in totality (see Figure 9-26). It is possible to undo this process (click Edit ➤ Undo or press Alt+Backspace), but remember that the Notes system is not integrated into Track Changes.

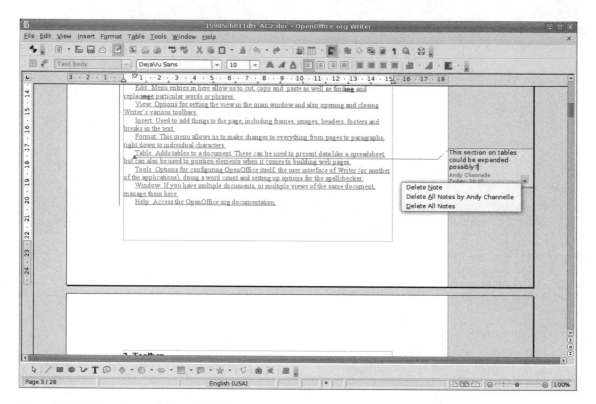

**Figure 9-26.** *Delete one note or all of them.*

## Printing Notes

Because notes are outside of the physical bounds of the printed document, printing with notes is not entirely straightforward. By default, notes that you add to the text will not be included in the printed output; however, you can set things up so that they are printed. From the standard Print dialog box, choose Options and look to the right of the configuration box (see Figure 9-27). The options here are to print the notes only, to add the notes to the end of the document, or to add them at the end of a page. The End of page option may be useful, but it will interfere with the original flow of text in the document and may also mess up slightly the layout of images. Adding the notes at the end will not have this effect on the text. Printed notes will retain their author information and timestamp, which makes this process useful for retaining that kind of information for the long term.

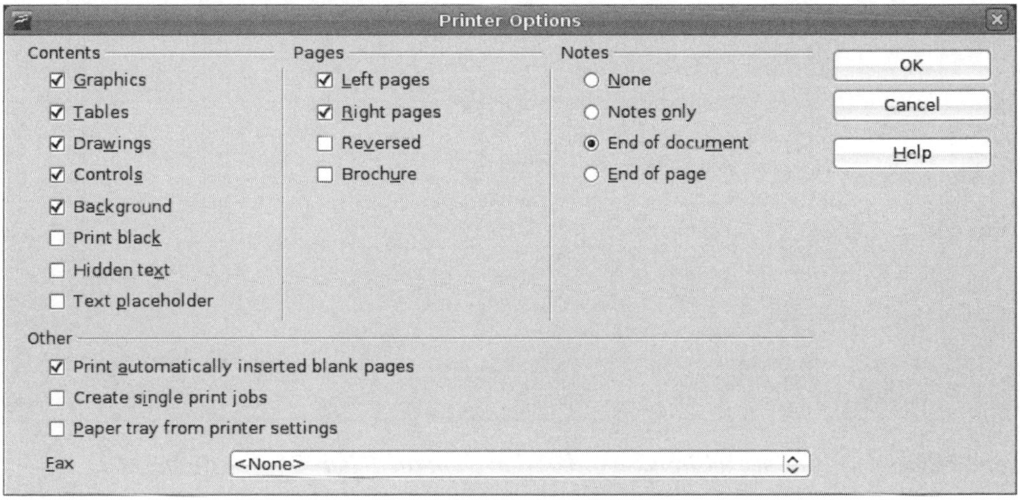

**Figure 9-27.** *By default, notes are not printed, but printing them can be enabled here.*

# Secure Sharing

Some documents are more important than others, and for the most important ones (from any of the applications) OpenOffice.org offers a password-protected security system. This will encrypt your data and will prevent casual users from accessing your private data. Anyone attempting to view a password-protected file will be prompted for the password. Supply an incorrect password, and the document will not open.

To password protect an existing or a new document, click File ➤ Save as, and, in the Save dialog box, check the Save with password option. Click Save—if you're resaving an existing document, you'll be asked if you mean to overwrite the original—and then enter the password for the file twice in the request box (see Figures 9-28 and 9-29). Next time you open this document you'll be prompted for the password (see Figure 9-30).

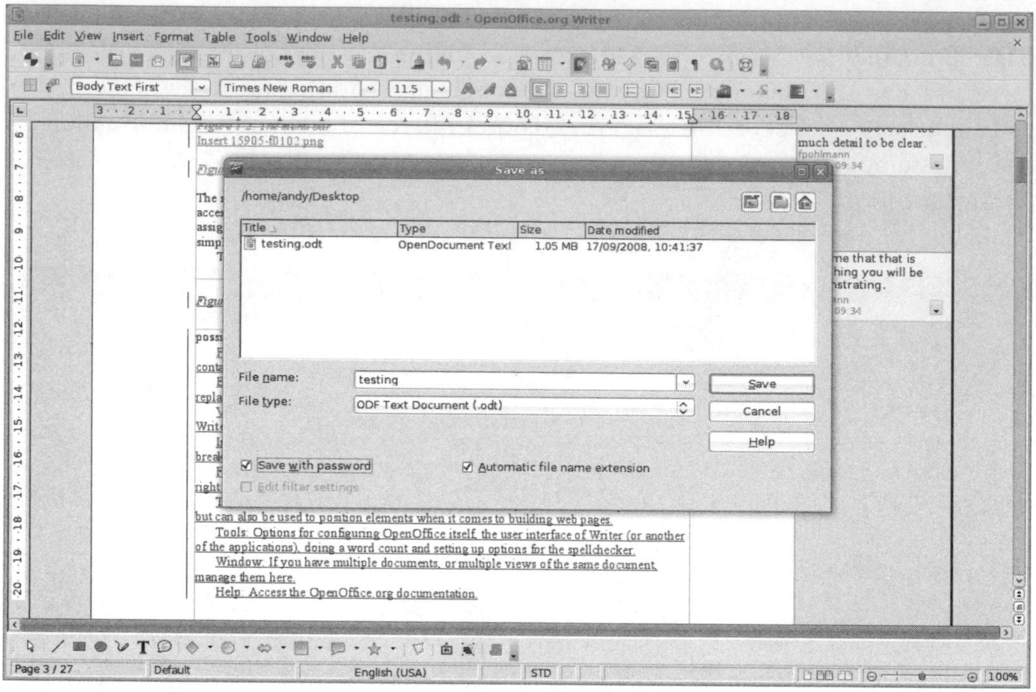

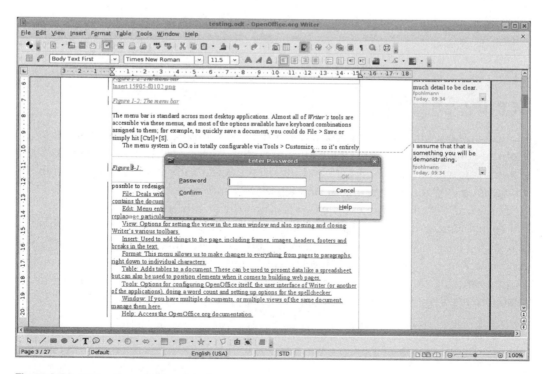

**Figure 9-28.** *Select the Save with password option from the File ➤ Save as dialog box.*

**Figure 9-29.** *Enter the password twice.*

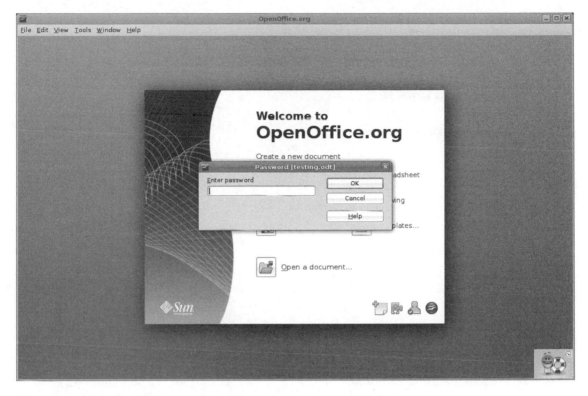

**Figure 9-30.** *Opening the document will launch the Password dialog box.*

To remove a password—once the document is open—perform the same operation (File ➤ Save as), but this time deselect the Save with password option. Confirm the over-write, and the new version will be saved unencrypted.

Because the file is not just password protected but encrypted, attempting to reveal the contents by renaming the file with a .zip extension and attempting to read the content.xml file will not work (see Figure 9-31). As with the PDF format (see the earlier section "Exporting As PDF," subsection "Security"), there are tools on the market that claim to crack the password protection on any OpenOffice.org document. So if you're working on top-secret information, a secondary encryption system may be a worthwhile investment. It's useful, though, for preventing random or casual access to documents such as employment records, private letters, and business accounts.

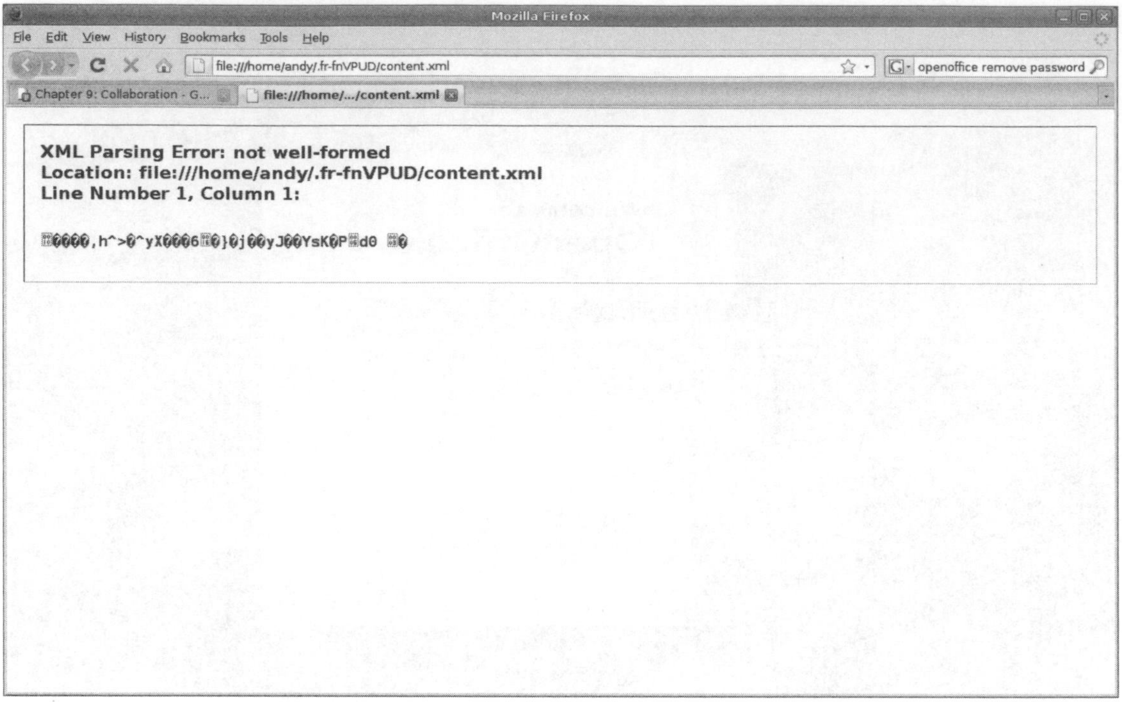

**Figure 9-31.** *The .zip file is also encrypted.*

## Removing Metadata from Documents

While we appreciate the possibilities that access to metadata and editing history provides, there is a downside to keeping all of this information in a single document, especially if that document gets widely distributed. Without taking some precautions, your secrets could be exposed to the world. Metadata is all the information pertaining to the structure and history of the document, and this can include everything from the names of everyone who has edited the document, the length of time it has been worked on, changes made (via the Track Changes system), and all notes associated with the text. In Figure 9-32 you can see a document that has been changed to a .zip file and then had its metadata (from the file meta.xml) exposed with a double-click. In addition to author information, this has data about the number of pages, paragraphs, and images in the document. Deleting this file will remove that metadata from the file. But remember that all that metadata will be regenerated if the document is edited again in OO.o, though the time editing and the creation date will obviously be different.

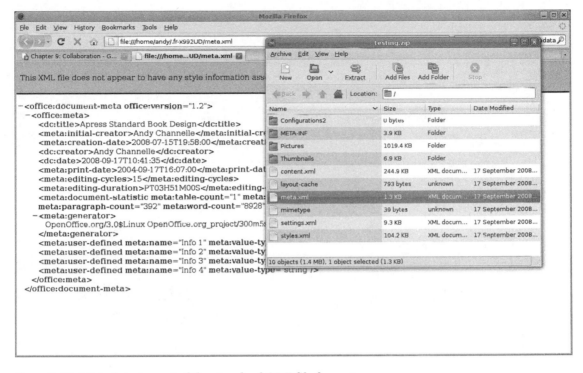

**Figure 9-32.** *Metadata is part of the standard ODF file format.*

Much more (potentially) damaging are the changes and notes kept with a document. In Figure 9-33 you can see how changes appear in the content.xml file, providing a viewer not just with the content of the change (before and after) but also with the author of the edit and the date and time it took place. This kind of information needs to be removed before the document is distributed. Unfortunately, this must be accomplished manually using the Accept and Reject options (as mentioned earlier) and, for notes, using the disclosure arrow. This doesn't take long. But once Accept/Reject All Changes and Remove All Notes have been enacted, click File ➤ Save as and save the document under a new name. This way the "private" version of the document retains all the useful information acquired during the editing phase, and the "public" version is presented as a final document with no discernible history.

**Figure 9-33.** *All the changes that have been made to a document could be exposed this way.*

## Live Sharing in Calc

One of the innovations in the latest edition of Calc is shared documents, a piece of network magic that allows multiple authors to work on the same spreadsheet simultaneously. In order for this to work, the spreadsheet file must be saved to a location accessible by all authors (inevitably) and must be saved in the .ods format.

■**Caution** Sharing spreadsheets across a network invariably raises issues of security and data integrity. If you're undertaking this process with sensitive information, ensure you have procedures in place to protect the network location and the spreadsheet itself. The latter could be handled with the password option mentioned earlier. When a document doesn't have sharing enabled, anyone else trying to access an open file from the network location will see a warning that the file is "locked," with options at the bottom of the pop-up to open either as Read Only, meaning the person won't be able to make any changes, or as a Copy, meaning any changes made will be saved to a different file.

Once these prerequisites have been fulfilled, open the document to be shared and click Tools ➤ Share Document (see Figure 9-34). This will define the document on the server as shared, and other users with access to the server and, if set, any passwords for the file itself will be able to open it up and begin to edit things. When users open the document, they will be informed that they are working on a shared document and that their changes will be rolled into the core version as they save (see Figure 9-35).

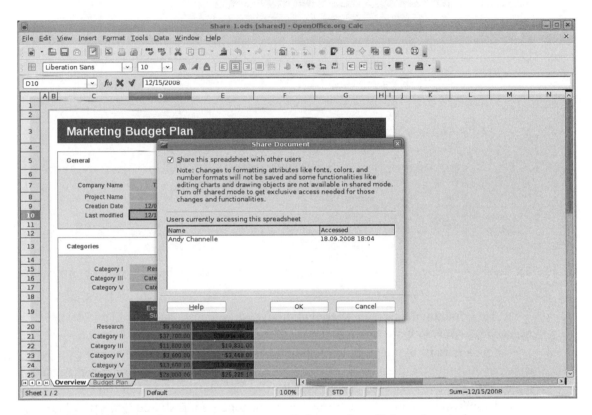

**Figure 9-34.** *Setting up a document—on a network share—for collaborative work*

And as a user saves, the other users accessing the document will be informed that changes have been made by another user and that their version is going to be updated to reflect this. If two users edit and one or the other saves the same cell, the Conflict Resolution dialog box is displayed; this will note the conflicting elements in a list—just as with the Accept/Reject Changes system earlier—and allow the user to select each one (or many of them) and then choose to Keep Mine (as in the current user's) or Keep Theirs (the remote user). It's also possible to Keep All of Mine or Keep All of Theirs.

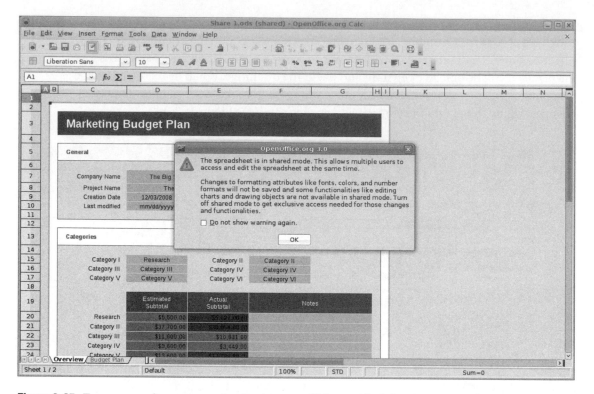

**Figure 9-35.** *Every user who accesses the document will be notified that it may be edited by others.*

Once a document has been shared in this way, it remains shared until one of the users clicks Tools ➤ Share Document once more and deselects the Share option.

There are limits to the number of operations a user can apply when working on a shared document. For example, edits to drawing objects and attribute changes in text (color, size, boldface, etc.) will not be saved in the shared document. For this reason, you should apply any advanced formatting before the document is shared (edits will then assume the formats of the original text) or after.

# Recap

In this chapter, you've looked at the way that documents can be shared and edited in a collaborative fashion. You've learned the ways that authors can keep track of their changes—which is vital to retain accountability and ownership of the creation process—and communicate their intentions through the use of notes within the text.

You've taken a brief look at the process of opening and saving documents in different formats—and the potential issues that can arise—and set up the software to work by default with the most commonly used formats.

You've looked at outputting documents in the popular PDF (Portable Document Format) for distribution either electronically or in print and discovered the ways and means of securing both these files and native OpenOffice.org files. You've also learned how to restrict access to certain features in your PDF, including printing and copying text.

Finally, you took a brief tour through a new feature in OpenOffice.org 3.0 that allows many users to edit the same document simultaneously.

In Chapter 11 you'll go a step further by taking shared documents from the Google Docs service and editing them with OO.o and saving them directly back to the Web.

■ ■ ■

# CHAPTER 10

# Linking and Embedding

It's not uncommon for users of office suites to work primarily in a single application. If this describes you, we'd like to encourage you to experiment, play, and find new ways to create better documents or to improve your efficiency by exploring other parts of the software. Working inside a single office suite makes this easy, for a number of reasons. Firstly, a common core means that it's possible to take some text, a table, or a drawing from one part of the package and insert it in another. This also makes it possible to create a range of documents, such as presentations, invoices, flyers, and letterheads, that use a common theme, color palette, and design, knowing that each application will treat this information in the same way. Secondly, the common toolset means that if you've edited table borders in Writer, you can do the same thing in Impress, giving users a head start on an unfamiliar application before they've even booted up. And finally, using OpenOffice.org means that you could say to your colleagues: "I'm working on a document in Writer and I need to share it with you. You can open it in Word, or, if you don't want to spend a couple of hundred bucks, pounds, or euros, go to http://www.openoffice.org and download your own copy of the software."

In this chapter you're going to undertake a few cross-platform excursions to look at the different methods available for linking and embedding documents and objects in other documents and using data from a separate database to create personalized letters for lots of people. By playing to an application's strengths rather than sticking with a limited subset of features, you get the benefits of both. And the various methods of linking means it's entirely possible to return to a document's original application to make changes and have that updated in the host application. You're also going to take a brief look at OpenOffice.org's macro system, which you can use to automate regular tasks in any of the included applications.

## Mail Merge

The mail merge is one of the most common cross-application tasks you'll come across. Simply put, it involves crafting a letter or other document in Writer and defining areas of that letter where, instead of ordinary typed text, the software will substitute a piece of information from a linked data source, which might include a spreadsheet or any registered database (Figure 10-1). These elements may be names, addresses, interests, or even something like a product name. In a business context, this is great for targeting customers with more personalized mail. But it can also be useful if you're running a club, a scout group, or a church group and occasionally have to send messages to multiple recipients.

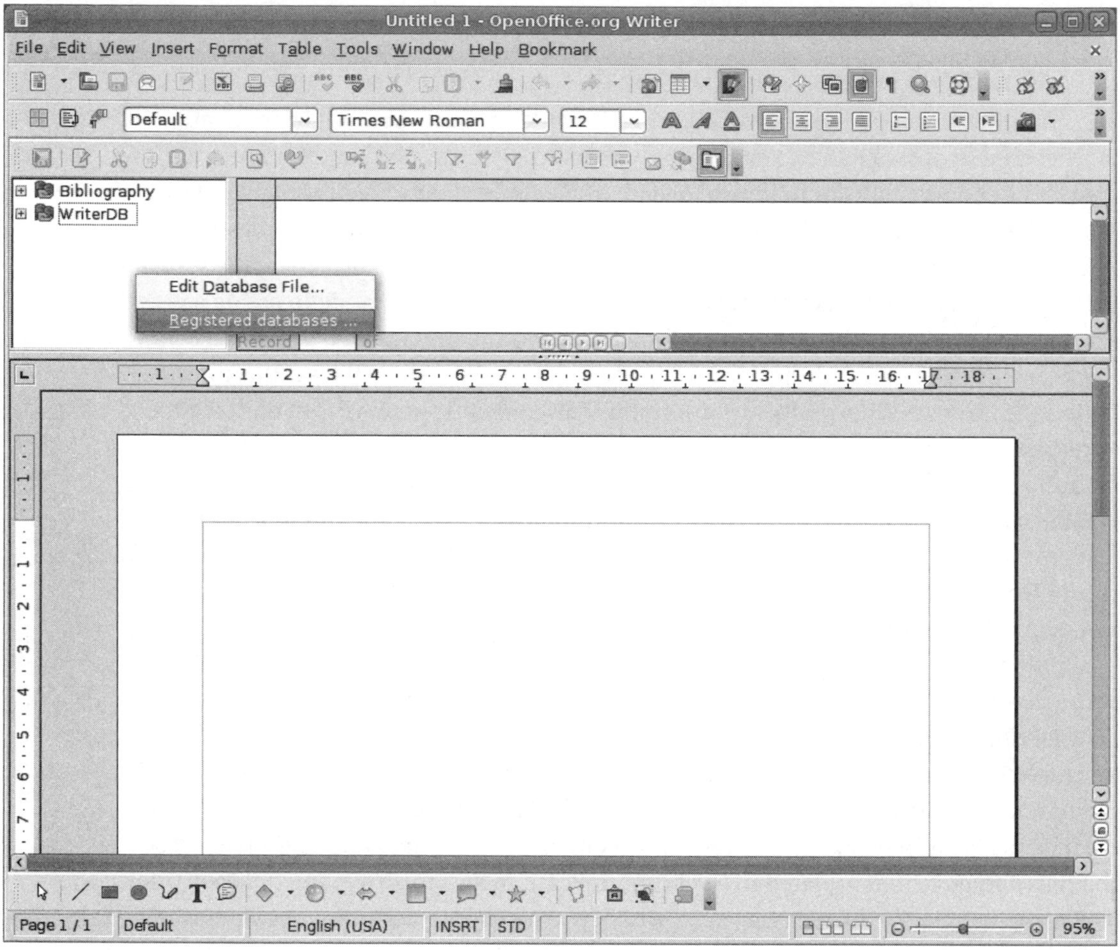

**Figure 10-1.** *Press the F4 key to inspect the databases already registed with Writer and OpenOffice.org.*

The first job before beginning your letter is to assemble the data that will go in the various changeable sections. The process of creating a database was covered in detail in Chapter 7, but briefly, open up Writer and then select File ➤ New ➤ Database. This will launch the standard database wizard. Use the following options as you go through the wizard. Create a new database and click Next, making sure that Register the Database and Open for Editing is selected, then click Finish. Give the database a name and save it in the appropriate location. Create a new table by selecting Use Wizard to Create Table. In the first part of the Table Wizard, select the Personal option and use the drop-down list to select Addresses. This will present a selection of potential fields for the database. Choose those appropriate to your needs, and use the right arrow to add them to the Selected fields column. We've opted for a Title, FirstName, LastName, Address, City, PostalCode, PhoneNumber, and Notes (see Figure 10-2). Not all of these will be used for the mail merge, but it's better to think beyond your current needs when doing this kind of project. Click Next.

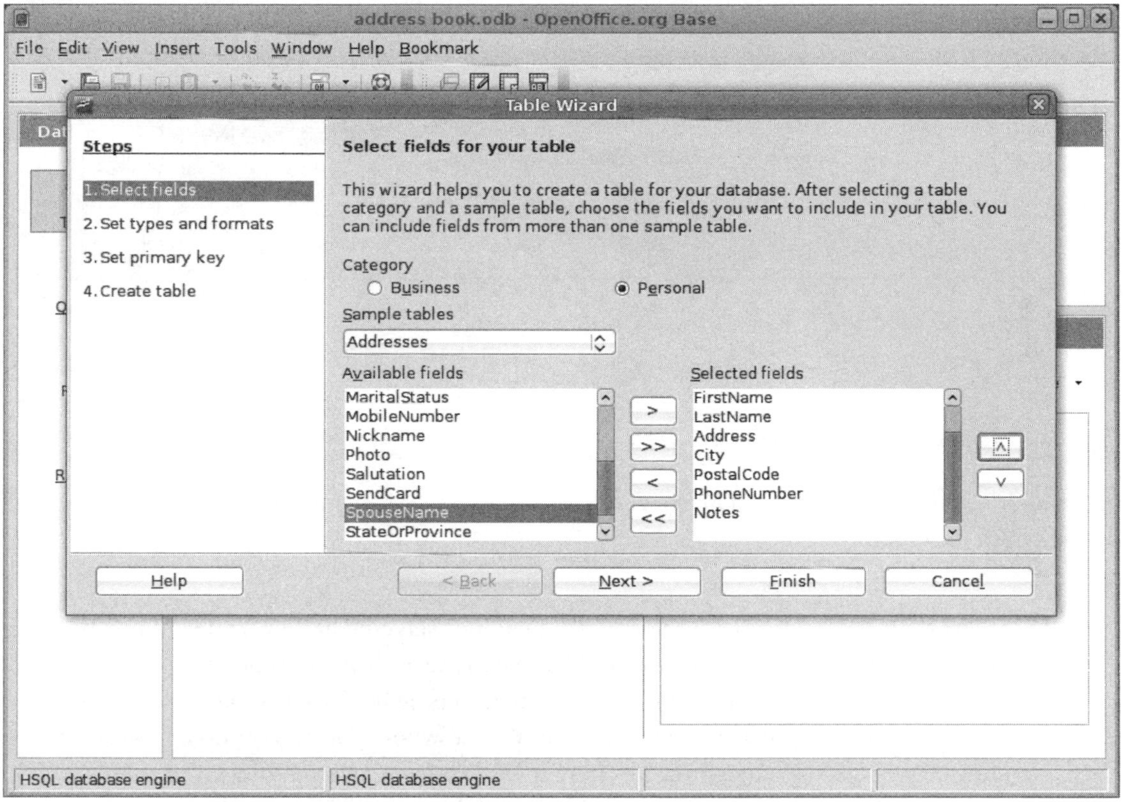

**Figure 10-2.** *Handily, a set of fields appropriate for an address book have already been added to the software. Just choose which ones to include in the table.*

Keep the field types and formats as they are and click Next again. For the primary key we've set Create a primary key. From the options at the bottom of the window we've selected Define primary key as a combination of several fields (in this case, FirstName and LastName). So the key element in the database is the name of each individual (see Figure 10-3). This method is great for address book databases but wouldn't be very efficient on something more extensive, where it might be better just to set the software to Automatically add a primary key. Click Next and then click Finish.

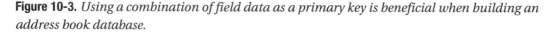

**Figure 10-3.** *Using a combination of field data as a primary key is beneficial when building an address book database.*

The table will appear with the column headings selected earlier. You can now begin adding data (names and addresses) to the table in the appropriate columns.

Obviously, as your address list grows, you can come back to this database and add more entries. But for now let's move back to Writer, where you can set up a new document that will use this data. Back in Chapter 1 you created a letter and saved this as a template, which could be used for this portion of the project. In fact, with a template and a database, most of what you need to complete a rerun of this project in the future is already done. However, start from scratch this time and then save this document as a template for later use.

If you haven't already done so, create a new document in Writer using a standard Letter/A4 format and add your own address details to the top. Of course, if you're working with a preprinted letterhead, you won't need to worry about this.

The first section you're going to create is the recipient's address. Normally, if this were a single letter, you'd type this out on the left edge of the page. But you're working with a data source, so you'll need to add placeholders for each element to be used from the address book database.

---

■**Note** You can check that the data source (the address book) has been registered correctly by selecting View ➤ Data Source or by pressing F4.

---

Place the cursor on the page where the first line of the address will go and then select Insert ➤ Fields ➤ Other. When the Fields dialog box appears, select the Database tab on the top of the window. In the Type section, choose Mail merge fields. When this is selected, the address book database in the right-hand column will gain a Disclosure icon. Click this to reveal the parts of the database you can use in a mail merge (see Figure 10-4).

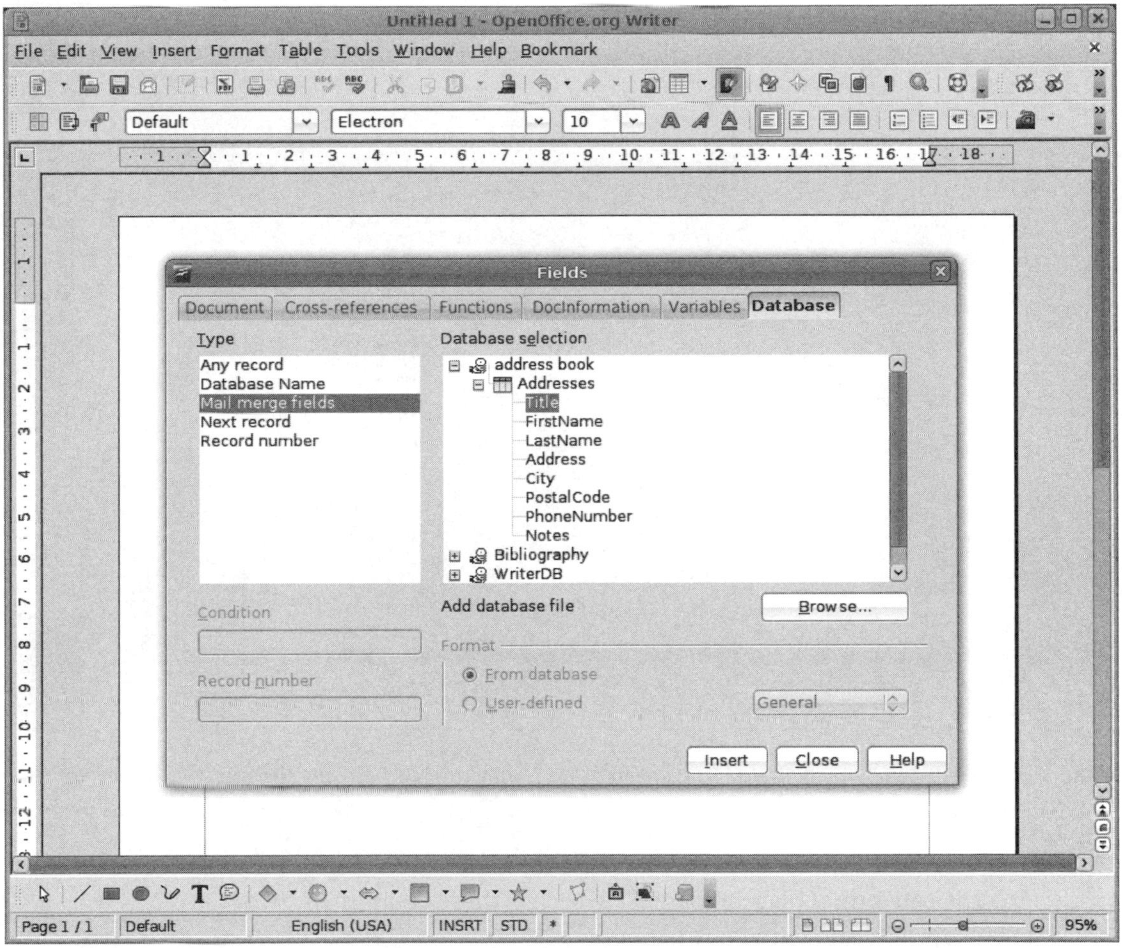

**Figure 10-4.** *Add the appropriate fields to the document in place of real data. The final version will be assembled at print time.*

The first part of the address section is going to be the first name of the recipient, so select FirstName from the list and click Insert. A placeholder will be inserted into the letter page where the cursor was, but the Fields box will not disappear, which means you can now add the rest of the fields for the address and even add non-placeholder text to the document without closing the box (see Figure 10-5). Remember to insert spaces and "Return" where necessary. If you simply click Insert on each element in turn, the final addresses will be displayed in a long line.

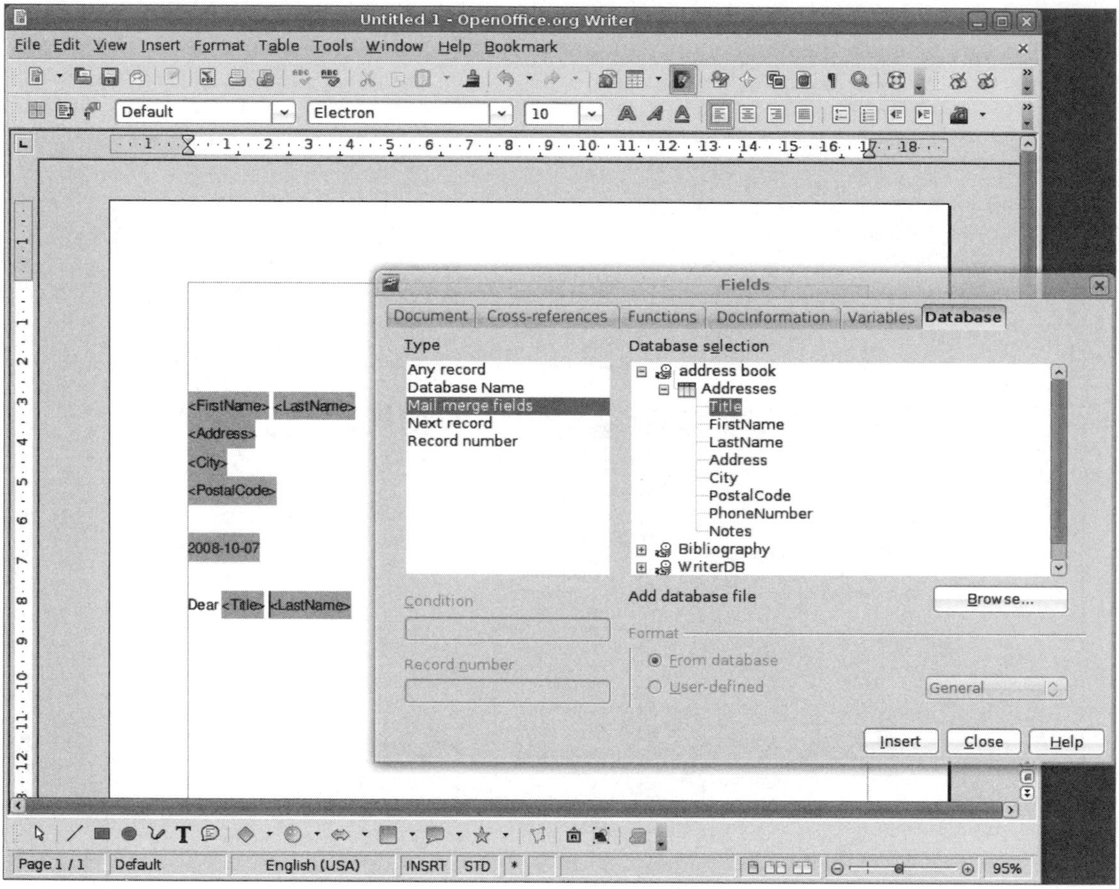

**Figure 10-5.** *When mail merge fields have been added, they will appear on the page with a grey tint. The actual data will not look like this.*

You can format placeholder text in each of these areas in any way; the real text, once inserted, will assume that formatting.

Once you have defined the document using fields, select File ➤ Templates ➤ Save to add the letter to your templates for later use. With the placeholders set and the text prepared, you're ready to begin the mail merge, which happens at the print stage. Select File ➤ Print to begin. A message will appear asking whether you want to print a form letter (see Figure 10-6). Select Yes. In the next section, you'll see the contents of your address database in a table at the top of the window. This has the full complement of filter and sort tools, which means it's possible to select, for instance, just recipients in one city or country from the list. It's also possible to select a range of entries from the database using the Shift+Click or Ctrl+Click method for continuous or noncontinuous selections, respectively (see Figure 10-7).

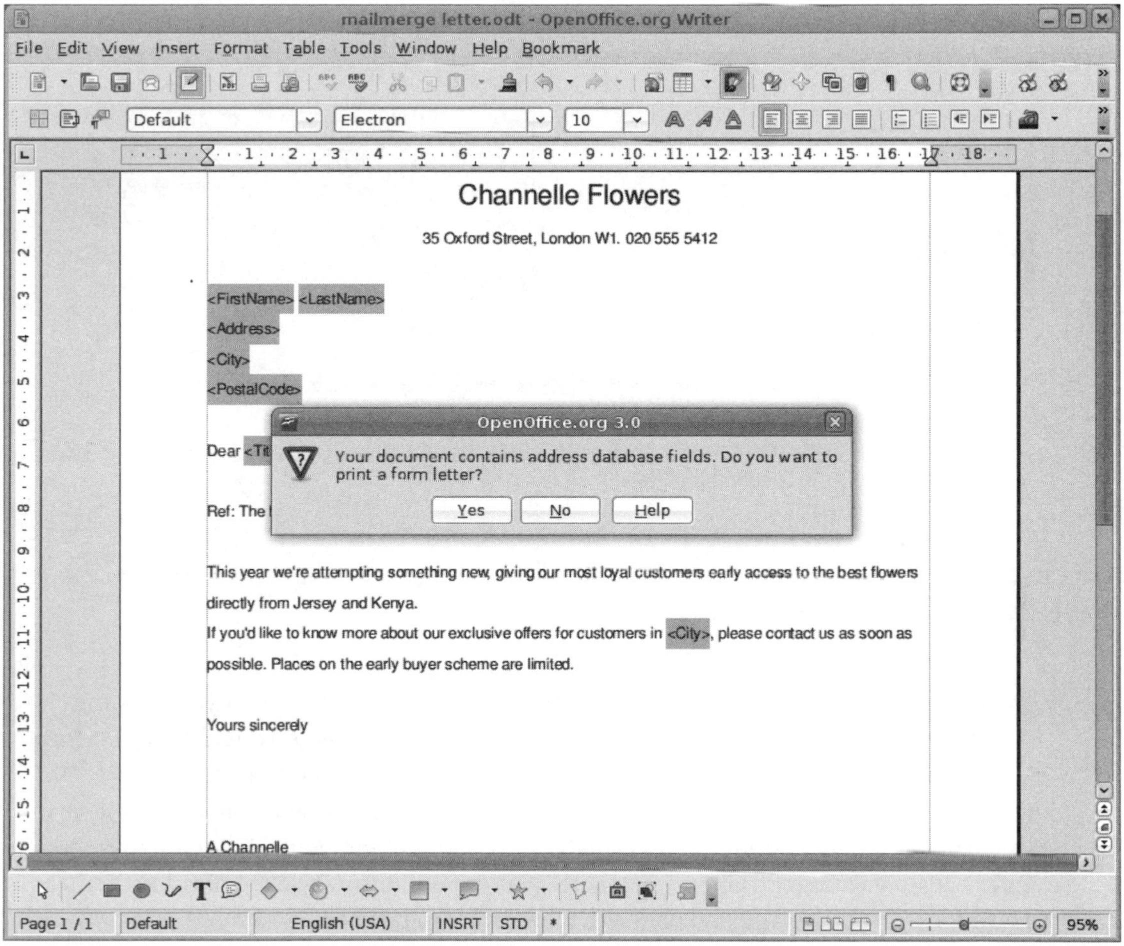

**Figure 10-6.** *Click File ➤ Print; if your document has database fields in it, you'll get a warning before moving on to the merge section.*

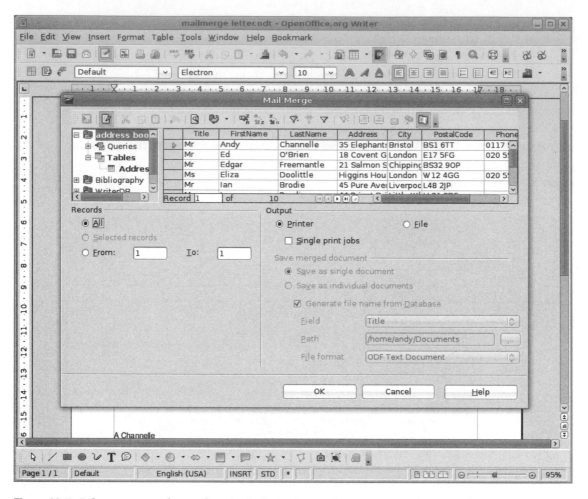

**Figure 10-7.** *Select a range of records to include in the mail merge using the Records section or the mouse. The table at the top is your live database.*

Underneath the database, use the Output section to select whether you're going straight to print or going to create a new file containing the merged documents. Let's go for the latter at the moment, because this will allow additional editing, if necessary. Once File is selected, a few new options will become available, allowing you to create either a single document containing all of the letters or a series of individual files containing one letter each. Selecting the latter will enable yet more options to give the files a prefix (such as "letter 1"), set the path, and define the file format to be used.

When you opt for the direct-to-print option, the file to be printed will be assembled in memory and won't be saved as a file to the computer. If you need to keep a record of sent letters, choose one of the file options and print from that.

Once this is all done, click the OK button to begin the merge, and wait as the file is printed or the letters prepared. If you've opted for the latter, the files will appear on your hard disk quite quickly and can be opened, edited, and printed just like ordinary Writer documents (see Figure 10-8).

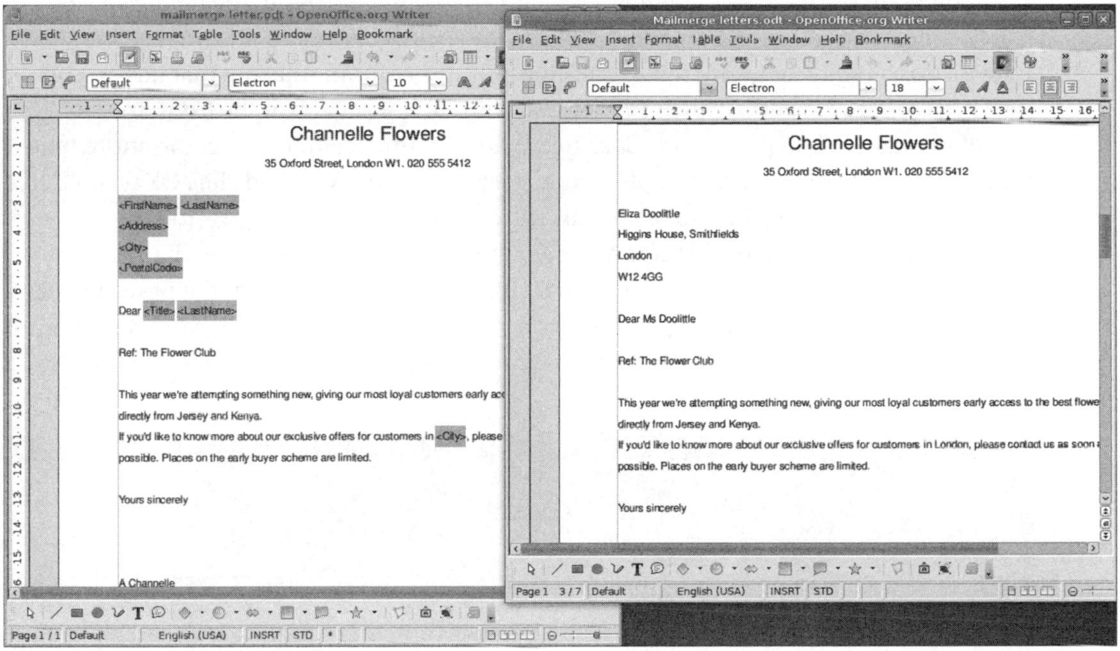

**Figure 10-8.** *Here's the final document next to the merge template. You don't have to restrict yourself to date details; merge fields can go into the body text too.*

We've opted for the manual mail merge system for this tutorial because it's very simple to use and doesn't sacrifice power in a quest for this simplicity. Writer has a Mail Merge Wizard that will enable you to accomplish the same job, available via Tools ➤ Mail Merge Wizard. But a manual approach will almost always lead to a better end product here.

# Bibliographic Entries in Writer

Another great use for the combination of database and word processor is in the management of bibliographic resources for essays, term papers, and dissertations. In fact, this is regarded as so important that Writer ships with a bibliographic database already installed and ready to use.

As you might expect, this operation has two parts. One part involves adding new entries to the bibliographic database as you go through your research. This part should not be neglected because, as with any computer process, you only really get out what you put in. The second part switches to the word processor and happens at the points in your writing where you need to add citations to the text.

To add information to the database, either press F4 or select View ➤ Data Sources to see the bibliographic database listed in the top half of the window. Click the Disclosure icon to open up the bibliographic entry, and then open up the Tables entry. From this, select biblio to see a table containing a selection of default entries in the database. You want to begin by getting rid of these because they're not relevant to this project and, indeed, don't really mean anything. Click the leftmost column (the one that has no content in it) of the first entry, which will select it, and then scroll down the list to the last row of the table. Then press Shift+Click in the first column again to select the entire table. Once selected, the table will turn blue. Now press the Delete key, and click OK when the warning about deleting data appears. This will clear out the table.

You can now begin to add information to the table. You can do this in the Data Sources window within Writer (see Figure 10-9). Or you can go through the Base application itself (right-click the biblio table entry on the top left of the Data Sources window and select Edit Database File). The process is exactly the same as was covered in Chapter 7.

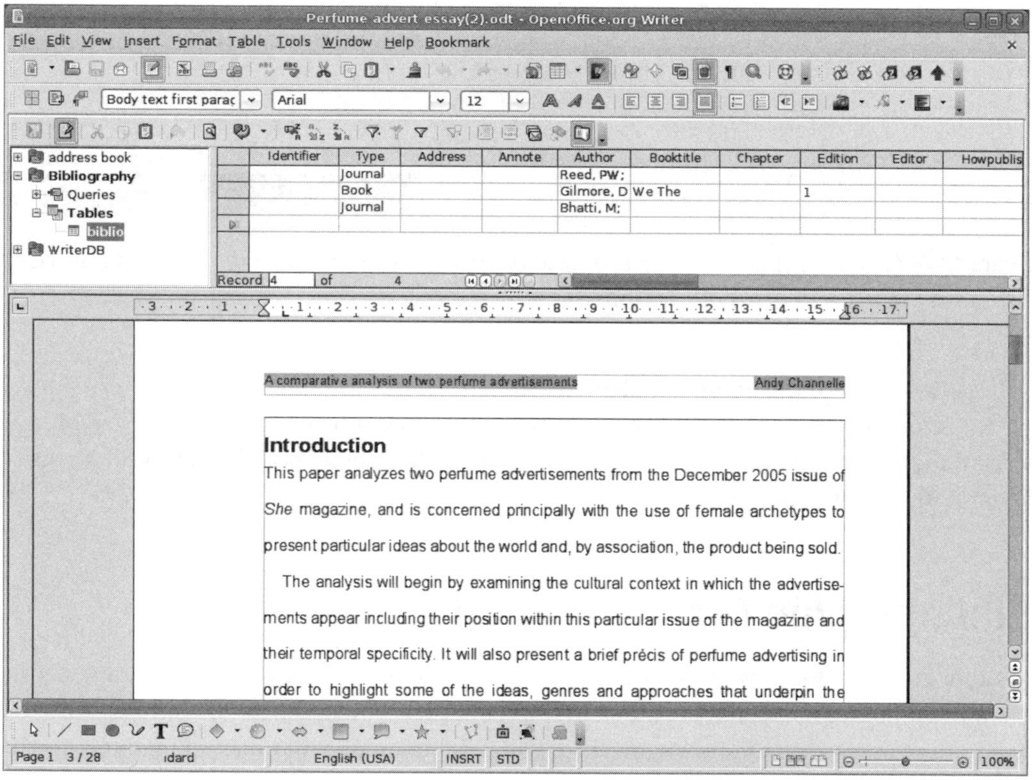

**Figure 10-9.** *Assemble your bibliographic references as you research.*

Note that there are far more column headings available than you'll probably need, because the database has to deal with lots of different types of references, including journals and books. You'll have to decide which sections to use as you add content to the database. Once you've added details such as the author, book or journal name, etc., add an identifier for each entry in the first column. Be careful when adding these, because this identifier is also known as the "short name" for the entry, which will appear as the citation in the text, meaning it should be structured as you'd expect to see a citation in an essay. For this book you might add the identifier Channelle, 2008, which would eventually appear in the text as (Channelle, 2008), with the rest of the details being reserved for the bibliography itself.

Ordinarily, you'll handle database work as you are researching your paper. But it's also possible to add further entries as you write, via either the Data Sources window (F4) or the database itself.

The second element of a bibliographic database is adding citations to the text. This involves simply placing the cursor in the text where the citation is to go and selecting Insert ➤ Indexes and Tables ➤ Bibliography Entry to launch the Insert Bibliography Entry dialog box (see Figure 10-10). Use the drop-down list here to select the entry to insert (the drop-down will list each entry by its identifier or its short name). Click Insert to add a reference to the text.

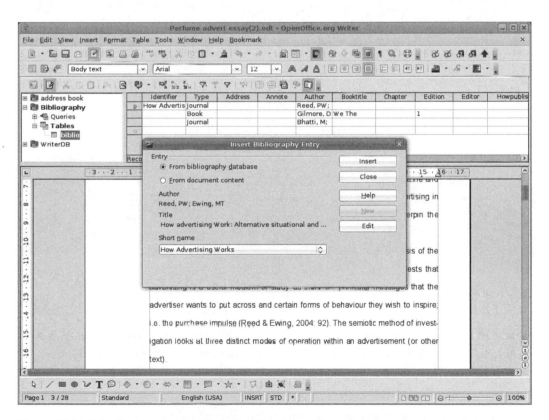

**Figure 10-10.** *The short name (or identifier) is what will appear as a citation in the text, so make sure it contains the information required.*

It's also possible—though a little less efficient—to add bibliographic entries to a document rather than to the database, which you can do, of course, as you write the text. In such a case, select Insert ➤ Indexes and Tables ➤ Bibliography Entry once more. But instead of selecting from the list, click the New button. This will launch a form containing all the details you could possibly want to include in a bibliography. In fact, it's the same information that could be added to the database table earlier. Add the information, click OK, and then click the Insert button. The entry will be added to the text but will not be included in the bibliographic database. You can also click Edit to see a form (Figure 10-11) that you can use to add additional details to either a database or a document bibliographic entry. However, the entries associated with the document will not be saved until the document itself has been saved.

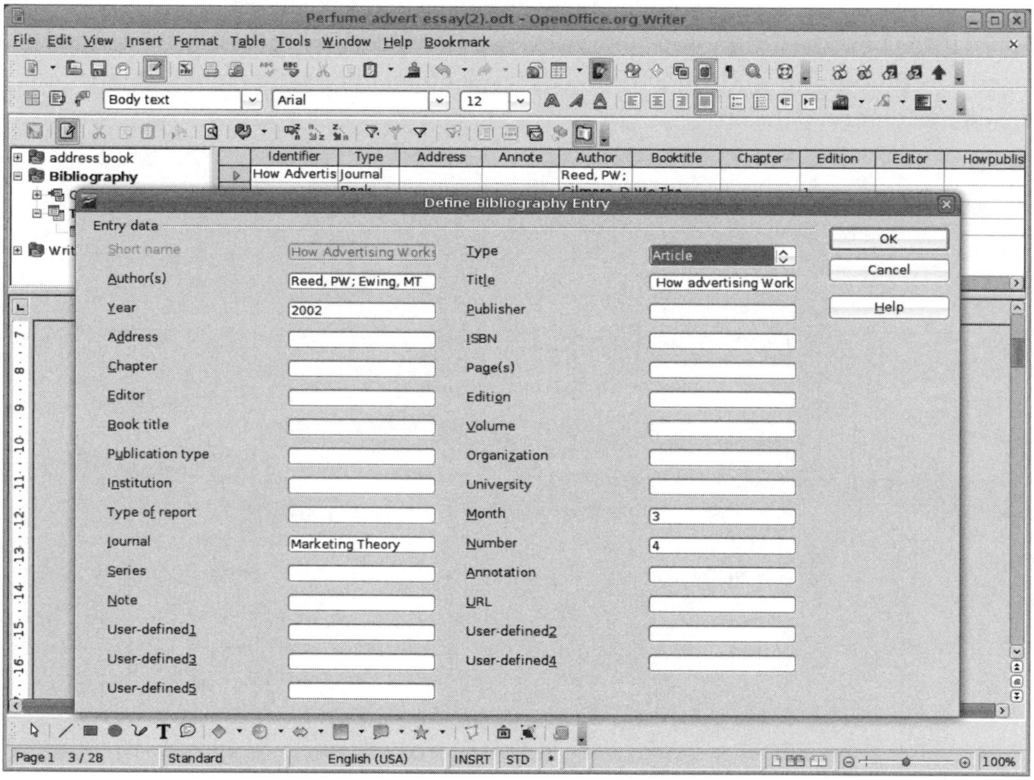

**Figure 10-11.** *Creating bibliographic entries on the fly will keep a record associated with a document but won't add it to the main database. Remember that it's not necessary to fill in everything, just the information you need.*

The entry, once added to the document, will assume the same grey background as any other document variable (see Figure 10-12) and will be updated to include the correct information once the document is printed.

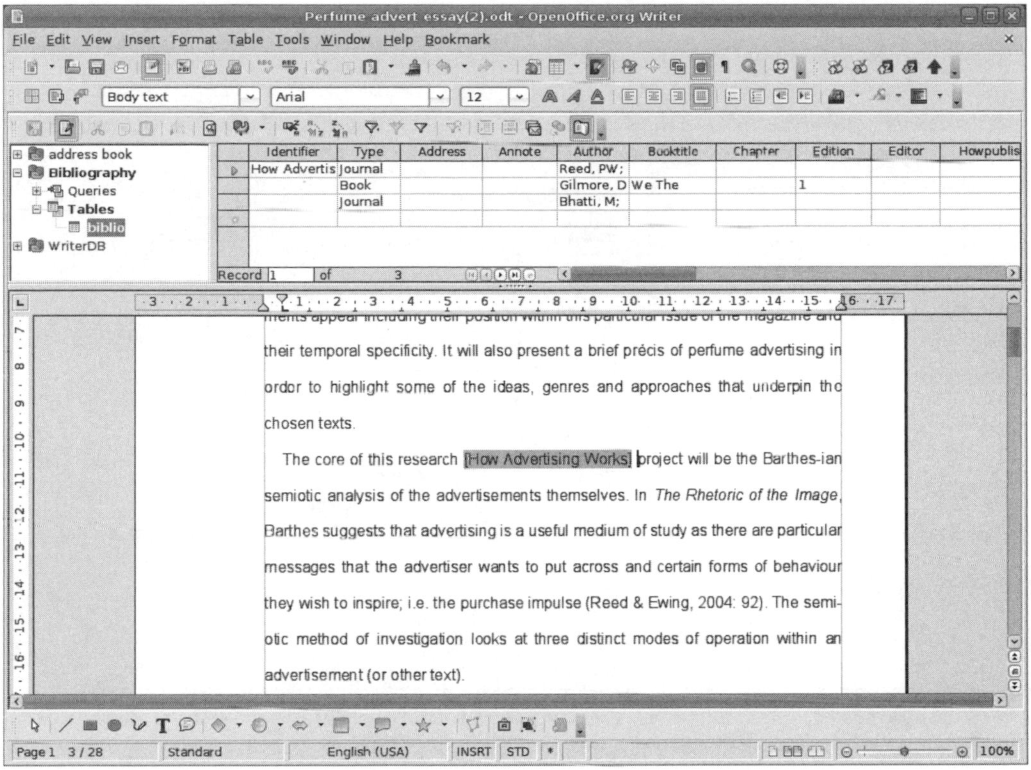

**Figure 10-12.** *Like other "variable" text, citations will appear highlighted in grey. If you edit the identifier text, the citation text will also change.*

The final part of this process is to build the bibliography itself. These entries tend to go at the end of the document, which is the same process you used to create the table of contents in Chapter 3. Click into the document where the bibliography is going to begin, and select Insert ➤ Indexes and Tables ➤ Indexes and Tables. This will launch a new tabbed dialog box into the center of the screen. In the first tab—which is labeled Index/Table—use the drop-down list next to the title Type and select Bibliography. This will set things up for a standard bibliography. However, you may want to change some things. For instance, go into the Entries tab to see the structure each entry will assume. By default this will include the short name, which is not a great idea, so select it from the boxes near the top of the window and click the Remove button (see Figure 10-13). Also remove the colon (:) that will now be in the first space on the line of entries. Depending on how you intend to structure entries, you could add, for example, the journal name by selecting Journal from the drop-down just below Structure and then select Insert. You can also add a character between structural elements by clicking into one of the blank boxes and typing the letter or punctuation mark you want. When doing this part of the project (especially if you're working on a real-world piece of work), remember to structure your bibliography in the form that is acceptable to your institution or organization.

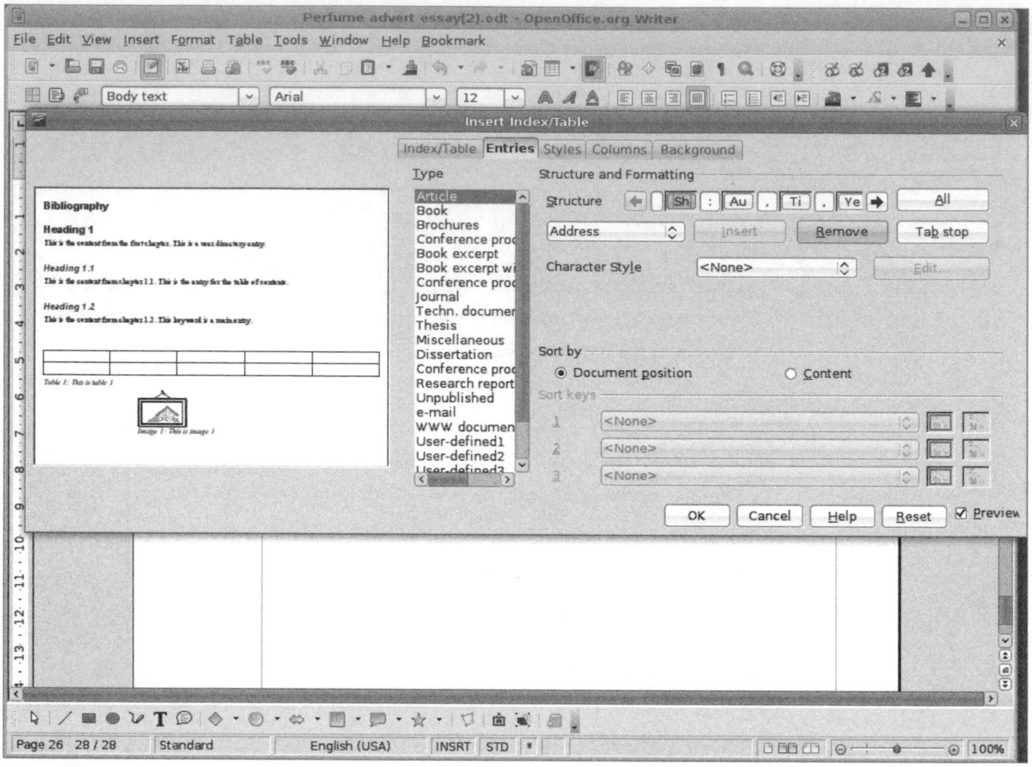

**Figure 10-13.** *Define the look of the bibliography itself following the guidelines set out by your institution or organization.*

---

■**Note**  For more information on using the Index and Tables section of Writer, please see Chapter 3.

---

Following the MLA style, bibliography entries should use the following format:

Rowling, JK. <u>Harry Potter and the Order of the Phoenix</u>. New York: Scholastic, 2003.

In OO.o this translates to

Author[.] Book Title[.] User Defined 1[:] Publisher[,] Year[.]

where User Defined 1 is the city of publication. Each of these parts can then be styled in the appropriate manner (for example, Book Title should be underlined).

The APA style is as follows:

Rowling, JK. (2003). *Harry Potter and the Order of the Phoenix.* New York: Scholastic.

which translates to

Author [. (]Year[).] Book Title[.] User Defined 1[:] Publisher[.]

Note that on either edge of the Year element we've added opening and closing brackets (with appropriate spacing) to enclose the year in parentheses.

As with the table of contents you created earlier, each individual element of the bibliographic entry can be formatted using character styles. These can be applied by selecting the element to format and using the drop-down to select the style. It's traditional, for instance, to make an author's name boldface and a book title italic, so select the element and then use the drop-down to apply those styles.

## CHARACTER STYLES

Character styles are created in the same way as paragraph styles. Format a piece of text in a document and then select it. Open the Styles and Formatting dialog box (Format ➤ Styles and Formatting) and click the second icon along the top to expose the character styles. Find a piece of text in your document that has the formatting you'd like to turn into a style (or create it), select it, and then click the final icon on the right to Create a New Style from Selection. You could also edit an existing style by right-clicking its name and selecting Modify. (See Chapter 3 for more on styles.)

You apply character styles in the same way as you would their paragraph cousins: select some text and double-click the style. Remember, however, that these styles will only change selected text.

# Beginning a Presentation in Writer

In Chapter 6 we mentioned that it was possible to begin a presentation in Writer before actually launching Impress. In this short tutorial you'll look at the benefits of this method, and explore just how much of the presentation effort you can accomplish without even opening up the presentation package. And although this is useful for focusing the mind on the content of a presentation rather than on the visuals, in a practical sense you can use it to turn a paper, an essay, or a report into the basis for a compelling presentation without having to duplicate effort. It's elegant and a time saver!

You'll begin in Writer and create a new document (unless you've just launched the software, in which case a new document will be in the work area) by selecting File ➤ New ➤ Text Document.

Starting at the top, begin to add the proposed title for your presentation, and then press Return to begin adding slide titles. In the first phase of design you're concerned only with the slide titles, so just type out each one and then press Return to drop down to the next line to add the next. You'll end up with a short (or long!) list of titles. Select the whole text (press Ctrl+a) and then use the Styles drop-down, on the left edge of the For-matting toolbar, to select Heading 1. This will turn each of the text lines into a "heading." Now select Edit ➤ Navigator and then choose the Content View button (second button on the left on the Navigator's lower toolbar—see Figure 10-14) to display only the content on the page in the Navigator. Click the small Disclosure icon next to Headings to see a list of the headings on the page.

**Figure 10-14.** *When creating outlines, the Navigator is a vital piece of your kit.*

In Figure 10-15 we have added a few more details beneath each of the titles and given these formats from the styles drop-down to reflect their place within the hierarchy; i.e., the photo names have been designated Heading 2 and the dates have been set to Heading 3. There is also a little unformatted text. On the page, these changes will be signified by a change in the size or formatting of the text, but in the Navigator each level is indented slightly further, which makes it much easier to see the structure.

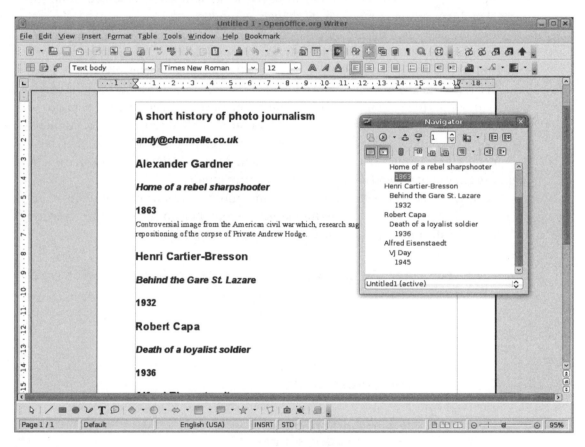

**Figure 10-15.** *The Navigator displays the hierarchy of the outline, with indents denoting parent/ child relationships.*

■**Note**  The method described here is precisely how outlines are created and managed in Writer.

With the Navigator, it's possible to reorder titles by clicking and dragging them to a new location. The other elements will shift around to accommodate the change, and this will also be shown on the page. When doing this type of reordering, you need to be careful to drop the title into the correct place, because moving a Heading 1 section will take all subordinate content along with it (i.e., Heading 2 and Heading 3 content). Thus, if you drop it into the middle of two Heading 2 sections, the lower one will become a child of the dropped-in title. It's not an enormous drawback, but it might be time-consuming to unravel problems if you've made lots of changes without care.

Once you've created the outline, save the document, and then select File ➤ Send ➤ Outline to Presentation. When you actually take this outline into Impress to create a presentation, only content that has been styled using the headings will be migrated. This is great because it means you can create notes for each slide from the body sections of any outline (those portions left unstyled). You could then print out this page as a handout or presentation aid. The other reason why this is useful is for taking an existing document— say, a paper or report—and creating a presentation based on the headings used in the document is that it would be fairly simple, for example, to take the long academic document used in Chapter 3 and create a companion presentation.

The result of taking the Writer document into Impress will look like Figure 10-16 (by default you'll be presented with the Outline view). From then on you can order, reorder, and theme the document just as you did with the presentation in Chapter 5.

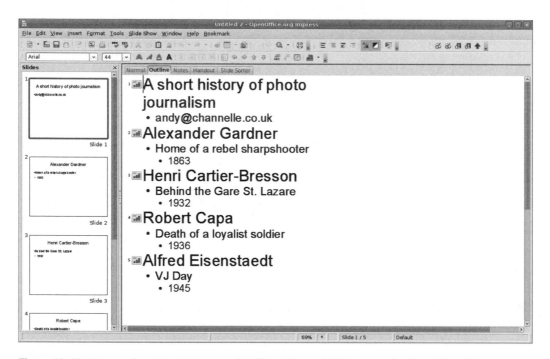

**Figure 10-16.** *Once taken into Impress, the file will work like a standard outline. You can still add new slides (see Chapter 6).*

You can use the other presentation-based entry in the File ➤ Send menu, which is labeled AutoAbstract to Presentation, on those occasions when you want to take not just the headings of a document, but also the body text. The dialog box that will appear when selecting this option includes a widget for defining the number of outline levels to include (the default is 3) and the maximum number of paragraphs per slide that should be taken from the nonheading text. This is set to 1, which is quite sensible because adding long paragraphs of text to a slide is unlikely to make it very audience-friendly.

# Taking a Spreadsheet Out of Calc

Ever since computers were able to launch more than one application, various methods have been available to take information from one piece of software to another. In this section you're going to learn about a few of the ways you could take a spreadsheet or chart from Calc and embed it into a presentation or text document. There are two ways (in technical terms) to accomplish this, and both have their strengths.

Firstly, and most obviously, you could simply copy (Edit ➤ Copy) a selected table from Calc and select Edit ➤ Paste to place it onto a Writer page or an Impress slide. When you paste it into either of these applications, the spreadsheet becomes an object with the same set of properties as an imported image (see Figure 10-17). So, for example, it would be possible to add a border to the sheet, change the anchor from paragraph to page (which makes it easier to reposition the spreadsheet), adjust the size and shape, and define how text should wrap around it. Again, holding down the Shift key when resizing the object will make it retain its proportions. This is quite important in this case because if you squash or stretch an object horizontally or vertically, the fonts inside spreadsheet cells will be squashed and stretched in the same way, making for quite unreadable content. Holding down the Shift key will scale the font correctly.

Spreadsheets inserted into documents will retain all of their original formatting. This is great when you need to add a calendar to a slideshow, for instance. You could create a calendar using an extension (see Chapter 11), format it by means of one of the many autoformats included in Calc (Format ➤ AutoFormat), and then save and embed it into Impress.

This process, called *embedding*, is exactly the same as if you'd clicked Insert ➤ Object ➤ OLE Object and selected a spreadsheet file to insert. The spreadsheet will be "embedded" into the document, meaning that you could take the Writer or Impress document and open it on another computer without any problem as the spreadsheet data is added to the page or slideshow data.

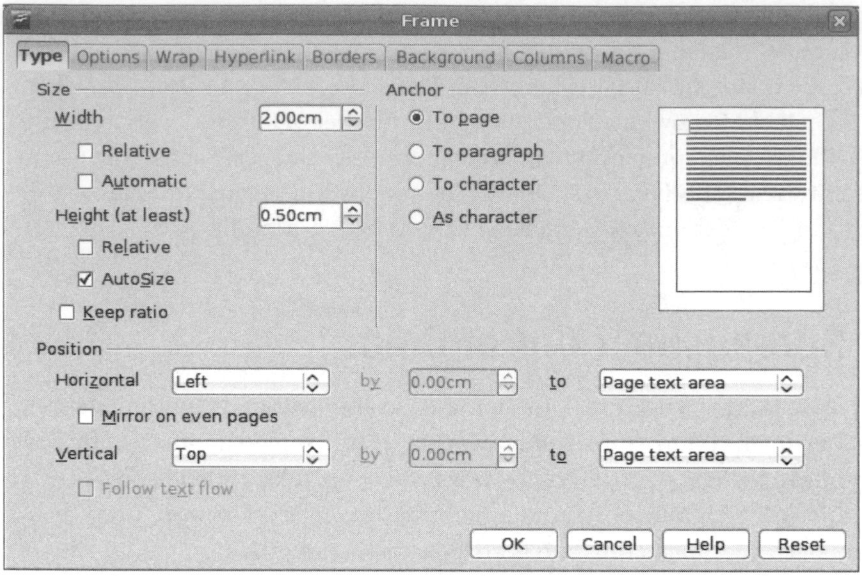

**Figure 10-17.** *You can format embedded and linked objects in the same way you format frames (see Chapter 2).*

You can edit an embedded spreadsheet from within the host application. Simply double-click the object to activate it. When you do this, the object will, to all intents and purposes, become a small, live instance of Calc. The Writer/Impress toolbars will be replaced with Calc toolbars, the table will be furnished with column and row numbers/letters, and the cells will be usable in exactly the same way as in Chapter 4. This means that it's possible to add or edit data, change functions, and even add rows and columns to the sheet.

As this is embedded, changes you make in this side will be included on the page but will not affect the original spreadsheet file. It's great for making quick updates before printing or presenting so that you're always distributing the very latest information.

The second option for integrating a spreadsheet into a page is to link rather than embed. This will include a rendition of the spreadsheet in the page. But it remains tied to the original file, so if you changed the original spreadsheet, the inserted object would be updated with the most current data. To do this, open up Writer or Impress and select Insert ➤ Object ➤ OLE Object. This will initiate a dialog box that allows you either to select an existing file (see Figure 10-18) or to create a new file from scratch (see Figure 10-19). We're doing the former, so select that and then click the button labeled Search to navigate to the appropriate file. Once you've found this, click the Link option—without this the selected document will be embedded as earlier—and then click OK. The document will be loaded onto the page, and you can again resize and move it. And, with a swift double-click, you can edit it (as earlier) as though you were working directly in Calc.

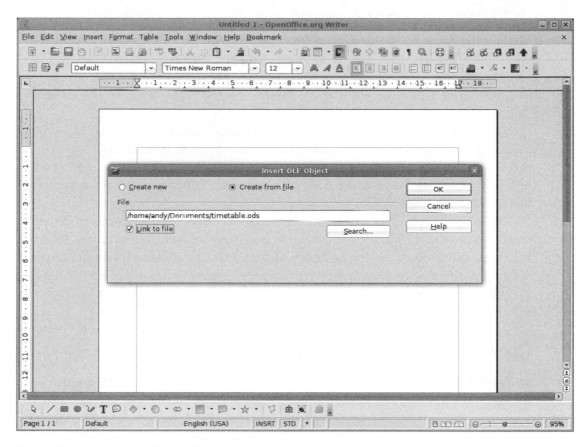

**Figure 10-18.** *Make sure Link to file is selected when importing so that the relationship between embedded document and original document is maintained.*

However, you must keep one very important distinction in mind: there is a two-way link between the document on the Writer/Impress page and the original Calc spreadsheet. This means that editing the spreadsheet in Calc will change the data in the host application, though changes on the page won't be made until the document is reloaded by selecting File ➤ Reload. This method of working is exactly the same as working with linked images (discussed in Chapter 8), but with an extra layer of complexity because changes made to the linked document in the host application will be sent back to the original document and will be visible the next time you open it. The great thing about this is that a document has to be updated only once rather that twice. But beware: this also includes information about font and cell sizes, so if you resize a linked spreadsheet in Writer, the cells and fonts will be changed (on cells included in the linked spreadsheet) in the original file.

---

■**Note** When you insert a linked or an embedded spreadsheet into a document, it will take the range of cells that have been filled with content. So, for instance, if you have added information to cells A1 and Z26, the spreadsheet that is imported will encompass those two cells and everything in between.

---

Employ embedding when you're relatively confident that the spreadsheet date you're including is static (though you can still update in situ) and taking the original spreadsheet file is impractical. It's also the best option for those times when you're sharing with non-OpenOffice.org friends and colleagues, because the information will remain embedded when you output to MS Office formats.

Use linking when up-to-date information from the master spreadsheet is absolutely crucial and you want changes made in situ to pass back to the original document. Linking is also recommended when you're sharing with a fellow OpenOffice.org user and can ship the original spreadsheet with the host document (with appropriate nods to data security, of course).

# Creating a Spreadsheet in Writer

As mentioned earlier, it's entirely possible to create a new spreadsheet in Writer or Impress (see Figure 10-19). To do this, select Insert ➤ Object ➤ OLE Object and choose Spreadsheet from the list of document types. The new object will appear in the center of the window. This time, dragging the resize handles will not enlarge cells but will instead expose more of the spreadsheet in the window. As before when using this window, the toolbar will change to reflect that you're now working in an embedded version of Calc, and the spreadsheet will work as a normal spreadsheet.

If you click out of the object without adding any information, the space will stay blank in the page with a grey border, and double-clicking will open up the spreadsheet tools again.

Note that there is a distinction between editing the object as an object and editing its content. To see this in action, click outside the object and then select it with a single click. Moving any of the resize handles will change the size of the text and cells (with the same potential for squashing mentioned earlier). But if you double-click and then move the resize handles, you will just be changing the size of the view onto the spreadsheet; the cells and text will stay the same size. This "editing the window" is exactly what it sounds like, so it is possible to shift the view of the window and push cells outside the view using the scrollbars and then to click off the object to see only those cells that have been positioned within the window.

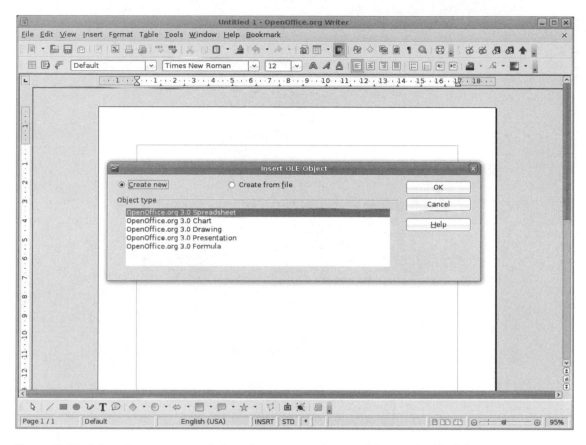

**Figure 10-19.** *Select Create new, and then choose an option to add an embedded document.*

When you create a spreadsheet within another document, it will be saved as an embedded component when the host document is saved. However, it's also possible to save just the embedded part as a completely new document—which is ideal if you're creating a spreadsheet from information contained in a report or a chart and would like later to make it a stand-alone file. To do this, right-click the embedded component and select Save Copy as (see Figure 10-20). This will launch a standard file browser, where you can navigate to the appropriate location and save the embedded file. It will now be available for any other application. Via this method you can use any of the formats supported by OpenOffice.org, including the ever-useful .xls format.

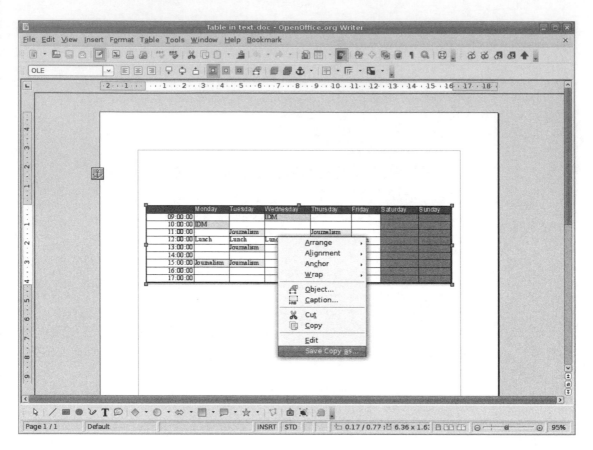

**Figure 10-20.** *To save an embedded spreadsheet as a new file that can then be opened up in Calc or Excel, right-click it and select Save Copy as.*

# Importing Charts

If you just want to take a chart into one of the other documents in the suite from Calc, both the Insert ➤ Object ➤ OLE Object method and the copy-and-paste method work well, but we discovered that the latter was the more useful option. The big benefit of this is that it becomes easy to edit the visual side of the chart without the distraction of the spreadsheet data hanging around. Once you have pasted a chart into Writer, Impress, or Draw, double-clicking it will transform the usual toolbar setup into the standard chart-editing toolbar from Calc. This makes it easy to change the chart type, set the text to scale with the visuals, and switch off the grid lines on the chart (see Figure 10-21).

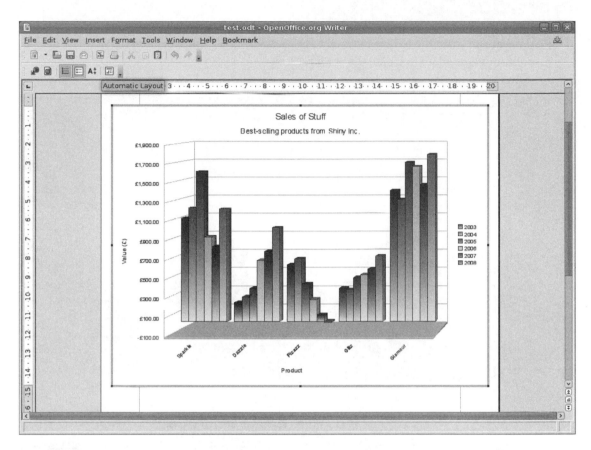

**Figure 10-21.** *Double-click an embedded chart to see the Chart toolbar appear above the main work area.*

Though not many tools are available on the toolbar, right-clicking on an element such as a set of bars in a bar chart or a segment of a pie chart launches a context-sensitive menu that will allow you to define lines, fills, and everything else you can do with these elements within Calc. Just select Object Properties from the list. Double-click any textual element, and that will also become available for editing. You can then simply highlight a section to change the font, size, color, etc., or use the thick edges of the box that appears when you select text to move it to a different location.

Now, when you paste a chart in this way, it is embedded (as earlier) and you can link by means of the Insert ➤ Object ➤ OLE Object menu. But we found it quite troublesome to isolate the chart from its original spreadsheet in an effective way. This could be problematic if you make changes to the coloring or style in an Impress presentation but then need to update the data. Ordinarily this might entail editing the data in the spreadsheet, copying and pasting, and then reinstating the changes made in the host application.

However, a rather nice option becomes available when you click the small Database icon (it's second from the left on the toolbar in Figure 10-22). This will launch a new window containing the data to which the chart relates.

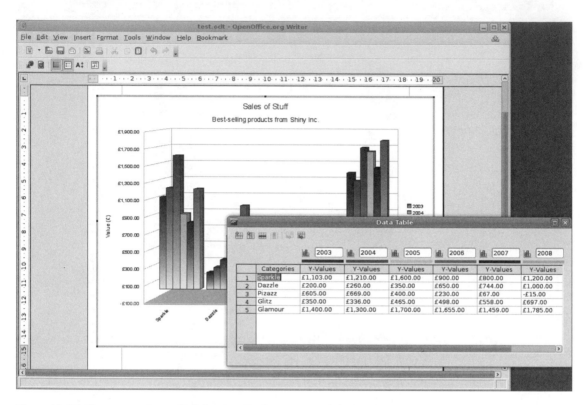

**Figure 10-22.** *You can accomplish basic edits by means of the built-in chart data editor. Beware, however: this only works with numbers and axis labels, not functions or sums.*

This data table window is not a fully fledged spreadsheet instance, so you couldn't, for example, edit any formulas or functions in the spreadsheet. It is simply a tabulated view of the data in the chart and is designed to make it relatively easy to update the contents of a chart without having to leave the safety of the host application. A series of icons along the top allows for the addition and deletion of new elements on the chart, but again any data will need to be input manually rather than via functions. Note that there's no way to get data out of this window either, so don't use it as a replacement for the spreadsheet. You can, however, use it to build a chart from scratch within any of the OO.o applications.

# Creating a Presentation Background in Draw

In Chapter 5 you built a theme for Impress around a couple of images as backgrounds. In this tutorial you're going to create a background in OpenOffice.org Draw and then transfer it to Impress to form the basis of a new theme. During this process you'll explore the options provided in Impress for making changes to this background.

When you first launch Draw, you'll notice that the default page size is designed with printing in mind. You need something to match the standard slide size in Impress, so go into Format ➤ Page and use the Paper Format section to change the Format to Screen and then change the Orientation to Landscape.

For the sake of good design, you should also set the margins on this default page to reflect the content area typically used in the various Impress layouts (see Figure 10-23). So set the left, right, and top margins to 1.50cm and the bottom margin to 2.60cm. This matches the Impress layouts quite well.

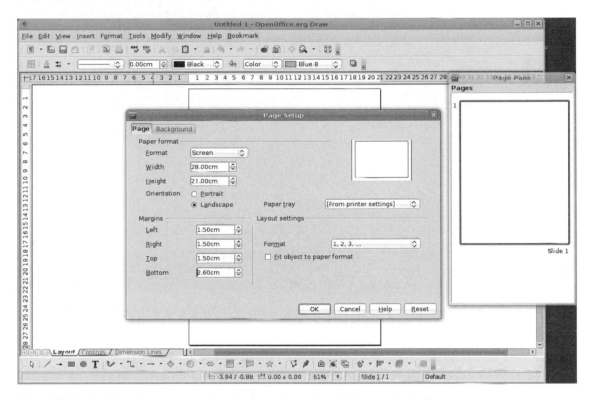

**Figure 10-23.** *Define the screen so that the image matches the page size in Impress.*

The next step is actually to create a background using the standard Draw tools, which are ranged across the bottom of the screen. As you discovered in Chapter 6, a large selection of shapes is available, including stars, clouds, puzzle pieces, and primitives such as circles and squares. You can add these to the page by selecting them from the flyouts on the toolbar and then clicking and dragging onto the page. Holding Shift will keep the shape in its intended aspect ratio. But because these are vector shapes, they can be squashed and stretched without becoming hideous-looking.

You can also twist and curve shapes by selecting Modify ➤ Convert To ➤ (option) (Figure 10-24) or turn them into 3D, and you can insert bitmap images either through the Gallery or via Insert ➤ Image ➤ From File.

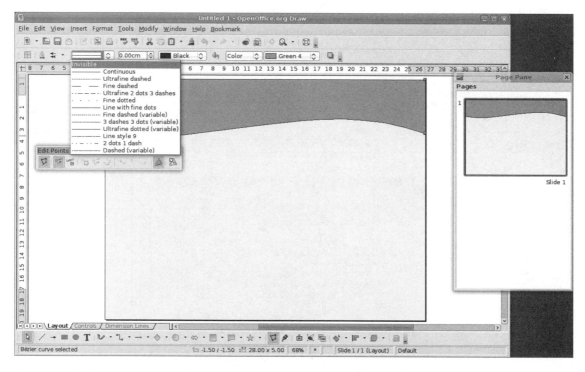

**Figure 10-24.** *When designing slide backgrounds, remember to think about where presentation content is likely to appear.*

Adding pages to the document via the Insert ➤ Slide or Insert ➤ Duplicate Slide menu entries makes it quite easy to create multiple backgrounds for use across different parts or elements of a presentation. For example, if you decide to have a different background for a title page than for a normal bullet point page, and for the sake of file organization, then it's quite a good idea to keep these in the same file.

When you're satisfied with your background, select the contents of a single page (Ctrl+A) and then copy with Ctrl+C before launching Impress.

To begin creating the theme, go into View ➤ Master ➤ Slide Master and then press Ctrl+V to paste the contents of the clipboard onto the master slide. Before clicking anywhere, right-click the center of the drawing and select Arrangement ➤ Send to Back. This will place the image at the very bottom of the stack of page elements.

Using the Master toolbox (which appears as soon as you enter the master slide editor), select the New Master Slide option, and then select the new, blank master from the Slide pane on the left. Copy and paste the second design (if you created one) from Draw, and also send this to the back. Repeat for as many slide designs as you created in Draw. These will all become master designs that can be applied to any slide in the current presentation. Moreover, if you now save the current document as a template (File ➤ Templates ➤ Save), then the designs will be available whenever you launch Impress.

The most important thing about working in this way is that Draw and Impress are so similar and share so much core technology that it's entirely possible to re-edit these images without leaving the comfort of the presentation package. This is because the image has moved from Draw to Impress not as a single image (as our sunflowers were in Chapter 5) but as a discrete series of objects. So you could go back to one of the master slides, select the background of an image, and change its area fill, border, or gradient (see Figure 10-25), or change the text on the header by altering either its color or font or even the content of the text itself. It's even possible to re-edit the control points on a curve.

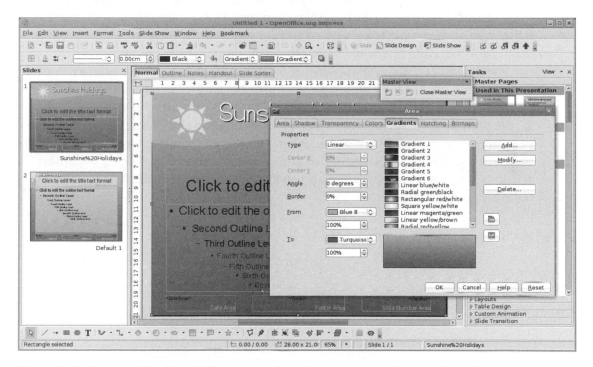

**Figure 10-25.** *Impress is built with the same code as Draw, so every element of the drawing remains editable in the presentation package.*

As with spreadsheets (see the earlier section "Creating a Spreadsheet in Writer"), it's possible to embed or link a Draw image into an Impress presentation, with the same benefits. Linking means that changes made in Draw will be reflected in the background the next time the presentation is loaded and also that changes made in Impress will be pushed back to the original document. Embedding means it's possible to take a totally self-contained presentation on a USB drive without having to worry about accessory files.

# Embedding a Presentation in a Web Site

Presentations, as we saw earlier, are a really good way of getting complex ideas across in a simple manner. In addition to being able to display this information to a "local" audience, you can use Impress to create a presentation that can be embedded into a web page (created with Writer or any other application capable of working with iFrames, which we'll come to shortly) so that "remote" users can also enjoy the experience. This short project begins with an existing presentation, but you're going to craft a few small additions to make the whole thing a little more elegant. Start by opening up a presentation.

When Impress outputs a presentation as HTML (which is what you'll be doing), it automatically adds some navigation options to the top of the screen, and you'll be given the choice of buttons to use during the export phase of this project. These are functional rather than pretty, so you're going to create your own and add them to each slide, allowing the user to navigate back and forth through the presentation.

The hardest part of this job is drawing good-looking buttons. We've used a pair of buttons based on the glassy button project from Chapter 6. But you could also grab bitmap images from the millions that seem to be scattered across the Web or create very simple ones using the arrow shapes (or any other shape for that matter) from the Drawing toolbar. The important thing to remember is that you should eventually define each button as a single object through either turning it into a bitmap (right-click ➤ Convert ➤ To Bitmap) or, more usefully, grouping together the various elements that make up the button (right-click ➤ Group).

## THE HTML EXPORT WIZARD

As with various other parts of the OO.o experience, Impress has a wizard you can use to output well-formed HTML presentations. Invoke this wizard by selecting File ➤ Export and then selecting HTML Document from the File Format drop-down list. Options available in the wizard include automatically advancing presentations, setting the image size (you'll use this shortly), image formats, and sound management, among other options. It's a great system, and the results are good. Just remember either to create a folder or to save into an empty folder in the final stage of output, because the process can create quite a few files.

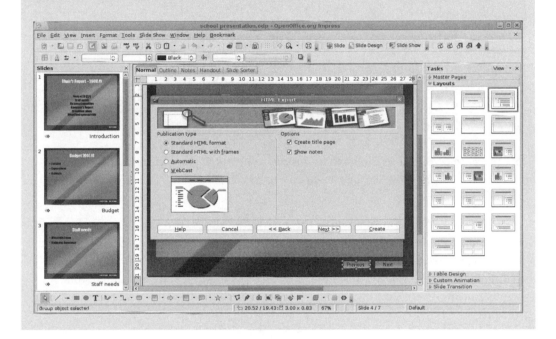

Starting with the first slide, select the button that is supposed to advance the presentation to the next slide. Right-click the button and select the Interaction option from the context-sensitive menu (see Figure 10-26). Next to the section labeled Action at mouse click, select Go to next slide from the drop-down list, and then click OK. Now copy the original button, and then paste a new version of it into the document. Move it somewhere to the left of the Next button, double-click the text to edit, and type *Previous*. Then right-click this button, select Interaction, and change the drop-down list to Go to previous slide. Click OK.

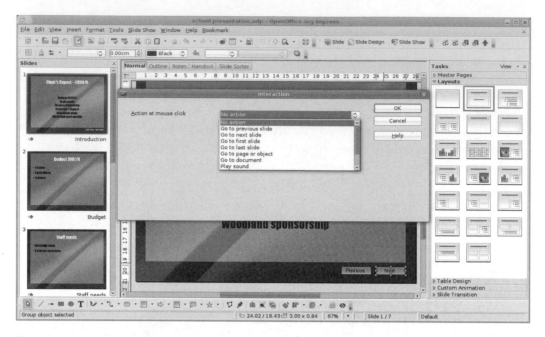

**Figure 10-26.** *Impress makes interactivity simple, which means sophisticated multimedia presentations become possible for even novice users.*

To add the two buttons defined in this way to the slides, you can select both, copy them to the clipboard (Ctrl+C), and then navigate to each slide and paste (Ctrl+V) each button. If you have the whole slide visible in the window, they should both paste into the same location as the originals. Finally, go back to the first slide and delete the Previous button (there's nothing before it!). Then go to the last slide and remove the Next button.

---

**Note** This aspect of Impress is incredibly powerful. You could use it to create interactive projects for students, museums, and kiosk presentations, because it's entirely possible to make these buttons go to any slide, open documents, play sounds, or even run a macro. In short, Impress gives you a fairly powerful multimedia authoring package that can handle custom animations (see Chapter 6), transitions, and sophisticated interactivity.

---

Save the document as a normal presentation, and then select File ➤ Export and choose the HTML Document from the Formats list. This will launch the HTML Export wizard. We've created all of the navigation, so we can race through this quite quickly.

From the first screen, deselect the Title Page and Notes options. In the second screen, select the image format required (we've opted for the default .png format), and then select the resolution at which to export the slideshow. Your choice here will depend on where the presentation is going to end up. Let's choose the middle option, $800 \times 600$ pixels. The third screen has a variety of buttons from which to choose. You're getting rid of these, so select any. Also, deselect the Text Only option, which, if left on, will create a second edition of the presentation that contains only text. The final screen (see Figure 10-27) allows you to define the color scheme of the final production. It obviously makes sense to keep the scheme from the document, so ensure that this is selected, and then click Finish.

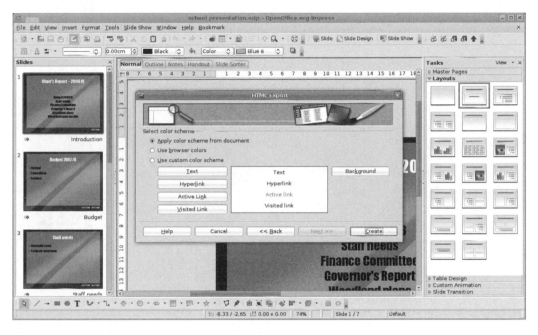

**Figure 10-27.** *When working on your own designs, make sure that Apply color scheme from document is selected.*

Finally, provide a name for the HTML presentation and then select Save.

You will now have a folder full of HTML documents and images (and any other files, such as audio and embedded video). We want to edit each of the HTML files (right-click them in your file manager and select Open With ➤ OpenOffice.org Writer) to remove the navigation buttons at the top. By default, these will be named imgx.html, where x is a number starting with 0 and going up to match the number of slides. In Writer this simply involves selecting the elements and pressing the Delete key.

The only thing left is to embed this document inside another document. For that you'll create a new HTML document (File ➤ New ➤ HTML Document) and then create a floating frame (Insert ➤ Floating Frame). In the resulting dialog box, use the Ellipsis icon to select the first page of the HTML presentation, provide a name for the embedded element, and then switch off the scroll bar (see Figure 10-28). When you click OK, the presentation will be embedded into the document.

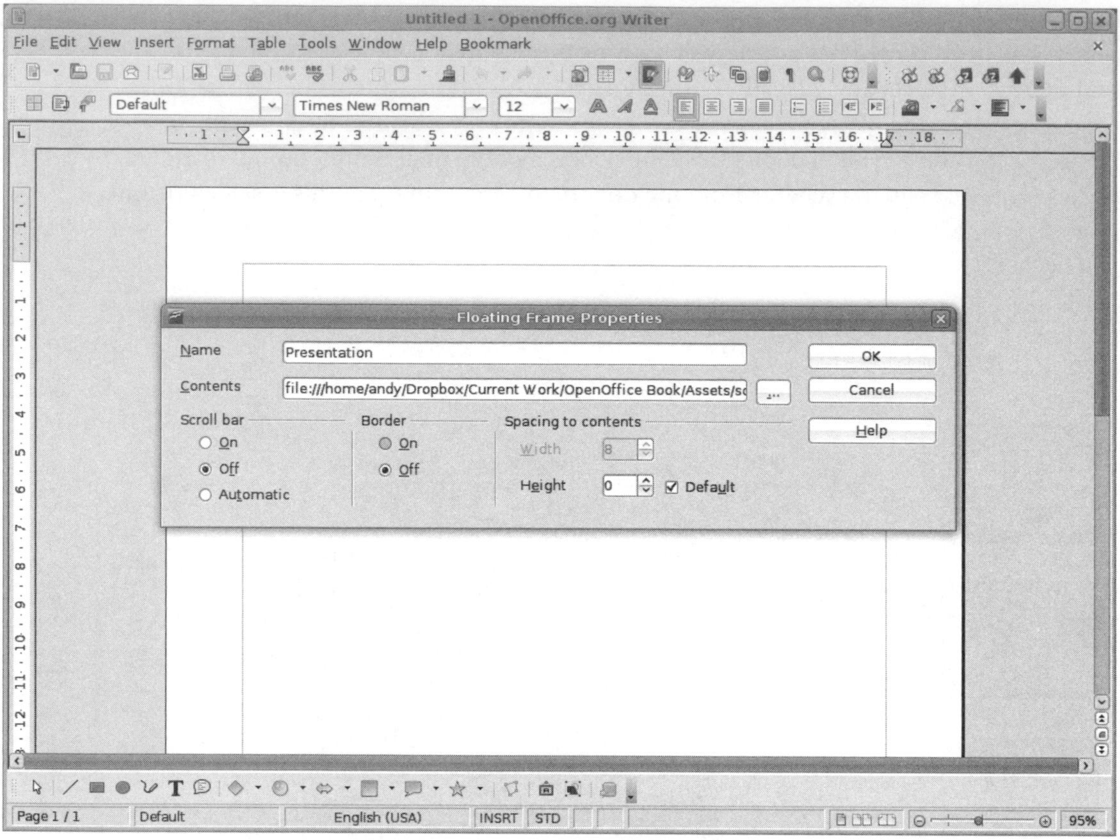

**Figure 10-28.** *Use this section to switch off borders and scroll bars.*

You can embed this HTML presentation into any document capable of displaying an iFrame, so it would be possible to create a presentation that could be embedded into most content management systems, a Google widget, or other display method. It could also be e-mailed to other users in a zip archive, and they'd be able to access the presentation with nothing more than a web browser.

# Recording and Running Macros

Macros, as many users know, can be hideously complicated. It's best to think of a macro as a series of recorded commands. These could be keystrokes, menu commands, or typed content. In fact, back where you defined a piece of AutoText to replace the acronym CZJ with the words Catherine Zeta Jones (Chapter 3), you created a very short and simple macro. But you can also use macros to set things up, such as defining a time sheet in Calc (with appropriate weekly dates), or to batch-process images in Draw (such as converting a lot of vector illustrations to bitmaps).

While they are at the heart of most complex spreadsheet and form-based documents, macros can also be quite simple. It just depends on how much you want to do as a user and how scared of computer code you are. In this short introduction, you'll look at the very basics of macro creation and run through a couple of examples of how they can be used.

Though code has already been mentioned, it's important to remember that using macros doesn't require any programming skills, unless you have very complicated needs or are interested in programming.

It's going to be slightly more complex here, but it's still really easy. Start by selecting Tools ➤ Macros ➤ Record Macro. This will open a small window within OpenOffice.org to signify that every action you take within the window is being recorded. This window has just one button, which you click to stop recording. So, while the macro recorder is running (you'll have to have at least one document open to invoke the command), do a few simple operations. Figure 10-29 shows a name and an e-mail address spelled out (this is the kind of thing that you might regularly add to a document). Once you've added the information, click the Stop Recording button. Recording will finish, and a dialog box will appear where you can give your new macro a name. By default the new macro will be saved under the Basic ➤ Standard ➤ Module 1 section. But it's simple to specify a different location using the options in this dialog box (see Figure 10-30).

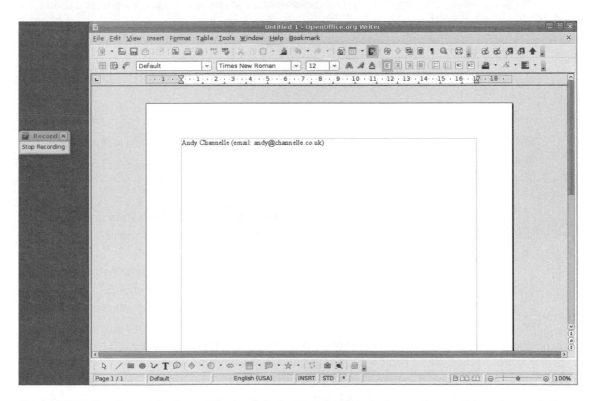

**Figure 10-29.** *The Record button at the top left denotes that keystrokes and everything else are being recorded.*

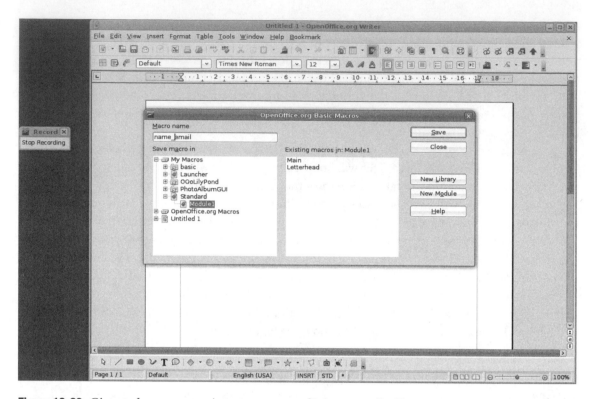

**Figure 10-30.** *Give each macro a unique name to make it easy to find later.*

---

■**Note** Macro names can contain only letters, numbers, and underscores. Attempting to input a space, a dash, or some other punctuation mark will just cause an error.

---

Once you click Save in the dialog box, the macro is saved to the system and can be run at any time by selecting Tools ➤ Macros ➤ Run Macro. Select the macro from the list, click Run, and relax as the text is added to the document automatically.

Now, adding small amounts of text to a document in this way is not terribly efficient because the time it takes you to go through all the commands will probably be more time than it would take simply to type the information with longer pieces of text (for example, boiler plate paragraphs in a legal document). But it's also possible to assign a keyboard combination to a macro, which would make it useful for shorter jobs.

To do this, select Tools ➤ Customize and look under the Keyboard section. Find a vacant combination in the Shortcut Keys section; then scroll through the Category section and use the Disclosure icons to open OpenOffice.org Macros ➤ User ➤ Standard ➤ Module1 (see Figure 10-31) or the location where you saved the recorded macro earlier.

Select the macro itself from the Function window; then click the vacant key combination and press the Modify button. Close the window and go back to the document, where pressing the appropriate key combination (Shift+F10 in our case) will invoke the macro, adding the text to the document.

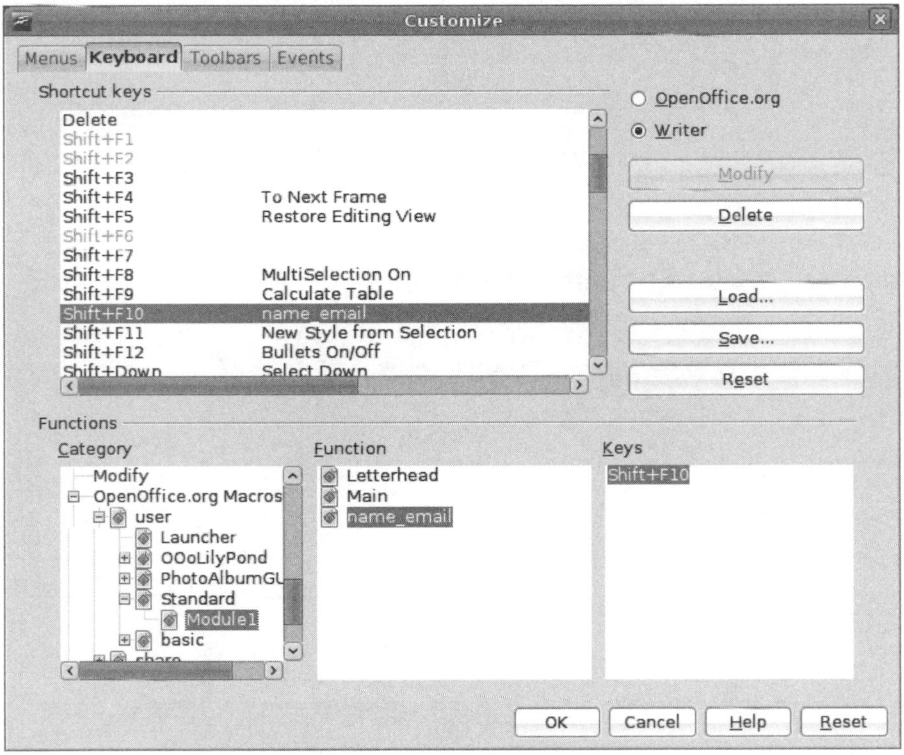

**Figure 10-31.** *You can invoke frequently used macros with a user-defined keystroke.*

Although what you've done is a very simple operation, you can turn almost any task in the various applications into a macro in this way. Combine this with the Interaction buttons you introduced to an Impress presentation earlier and you could create some fairly sophisticated productions.

Heavy editing with the OpenOffice.org scripting language (called StarBasic) is beyond the scope of this book. But one quick example will provide some idea of what lies at the heart of this macro-building process. Select Tools ➤ Macros ➤ Organize Macros ➤ Basic, and then choose from the dialog box the macro you just recorded. The OpenOffice.org Basic editor will open—this is just a simple text editor designed with scripting in mind— with your macro displayed as a series of commands.

In Figure 10-32, the highlighted section of text includes a mistake made during the recording process (a " sign was input instead of @ and we had to backspace to fix it). Though this is not likely to affect the efficiency of the macro significantly, it's a good idea to have things working correctly in case anyone else wants to look at the code in the future. In this case we just need to delete the selected text so that the macro will add the e-mail address directly, without making and then correcting the error.

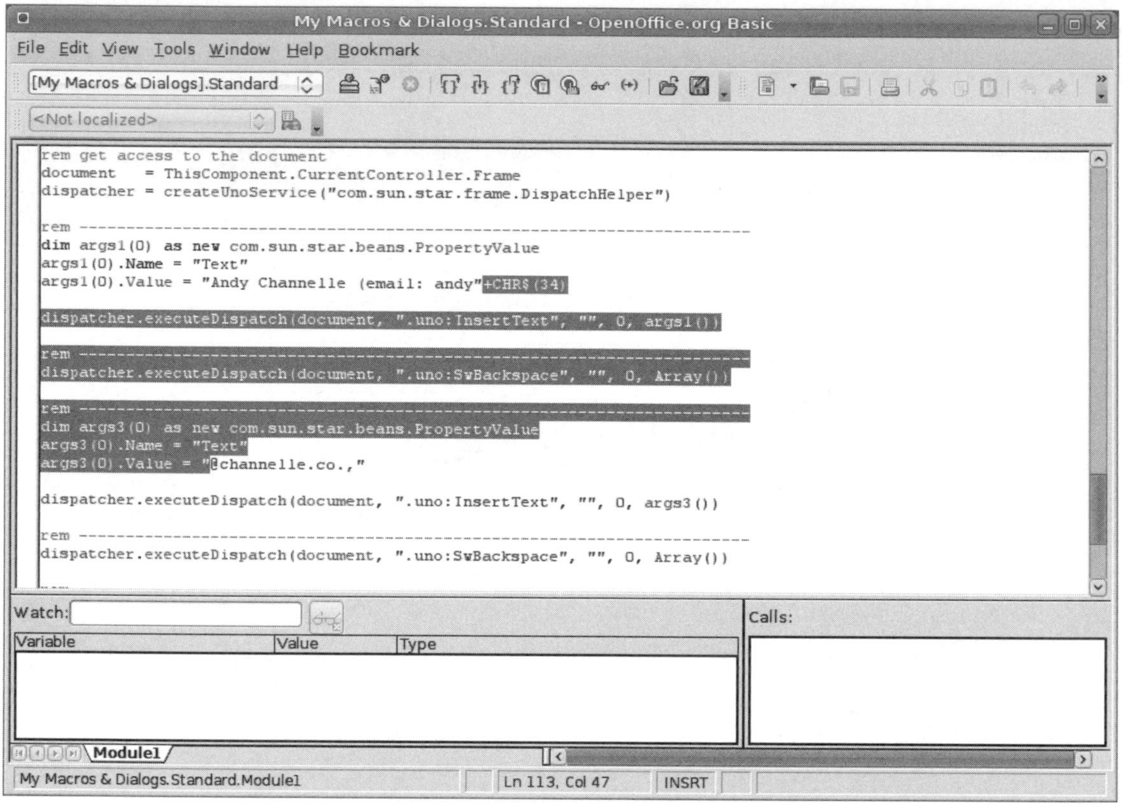

**Figure 10-32.** *Turn away now if you're scared of code! This is the basic environment for macro editing. However, you may never need to look at this.*

# Adding Sections to a Document

In Chapter 2 you created a small newsletter similar in design to thousands of newsletters published in schools, organizations, communities, and churches around the world. In that project you copied all of the text and pasted it into the document or wrote it directly on the screen, which is a common way of doing things when you're working alone. However, Writer is capable of taking this beyond a single user, allowing a designer to create regions for copy (or illustrations from Draw) that another user could edit and then update on the master document before printing or outputting to PDF.

This is such a revolutionary way of working that the major desktop publishing packages have only just integrated such tools into their feature sets—and their makers will charge you quite a lot extra for them too.

So, for an idea of what's possible, let's go back to a newsletter. In Figure 10-33 we've built a frame-based layout in Writer consisting of one frame for the headline, another for a short introduction, and then two main text frames (see Chapter 2 for more on creating and editing frames in Writer). One of these has two columns; the other is a single column but has a tinted background. The traditional way of working would be to cut and paste text into each of the sections (and, indeed, that's what's been done with the top two frames). But you're going to take documents that are still being written and embed them into the two areas set aside for body text.

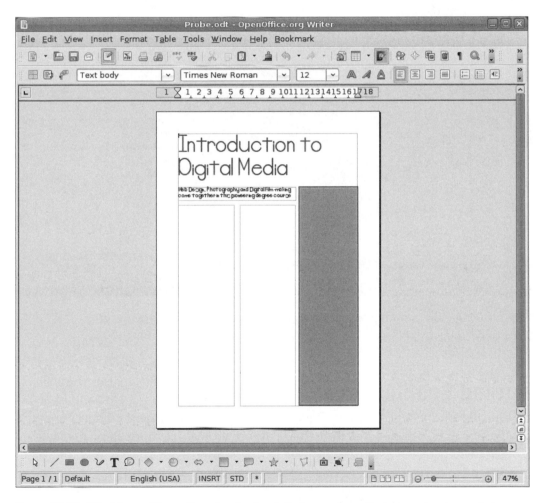

**Figure 10-33.** *Working with sections begins by defining regions that are going to contain content from other files.*

The first task is to choose the location for the embedded text, so select either of the body text frames and then click inside as though you were going to type in there. Now select Insert ➤ Section to open the dialog box (see Figure 10-34). In the New section part of the window, type a name for the section you're creating and then click the Link button under the Link section. This will enable the File name option, where you can click the ellipsis (...) button and navigate to the text file you want to insert.

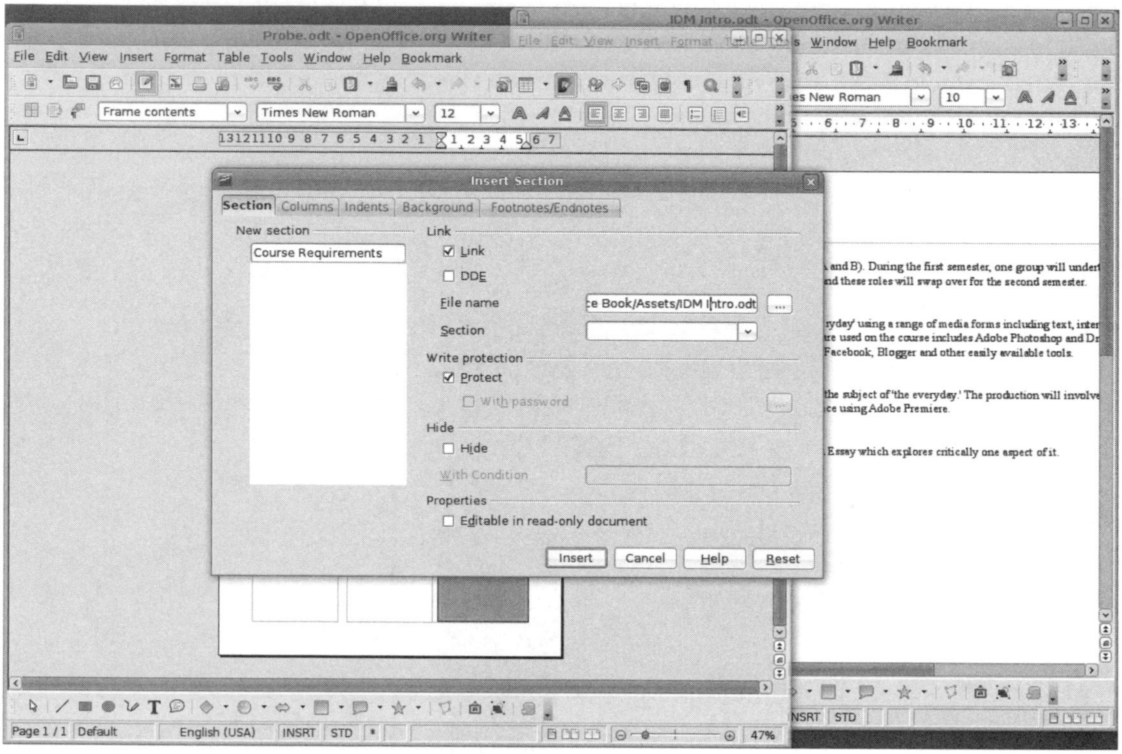

**Figure 10-34.** *Each page can contain many sections that will take content from any other OpenOffice.org document.*

If the document from which you're taking content has sections, you'll also be able to select the section to import from the drop-down list. Finally, if you want to be able to edit the embedded text, deselect the Protection option. Finally, click Insert. The text from the original document will flow into the frame, and you can style it as normal. Do the same for the other frame.

---

■**Tip** Sections are quite valuable if you're creating a document for both printed and electronic output—for example, a print/e-mail newsletter—because the e-version could have sections that match up to the printed version, though styled in different ways, and the text would propagate across both products.

---

And now for the magical part: every time this document is opened, the latest copy from the originating documents will automatically flow into the correct space, with the most up-to-date changes. Moreover, when the author makes significant changes to the text, just select File ➤ Reload to have the latest version embedded. In a production environment, both author and designer would be working on different versions of the same document (so that, for example, spaces and text styles match up), and the sections in the design version (which you might call the master version) would mirror the sections in the writer's version. In this way, a designer could be laying out the newsletter while one or more writers were honing their words.

# Recap

The purpose of this chapter was to introduce you to the potential for sharing the workload among OpenOffice.org's various applications. Using some of the options from the Insert menu, in addition to copy/paste, you've seen how it's possible to take content from any of the applications and embed them into another. Moreover, the Link option creates a two-way relationship between applications and files so that it's possible to make quick edits to an original document without having to interrupt your flow by firing up a different piece of software. The Link option is useful generally. But if you ever work in a group situation, it comes into its own, because it becomes possible, for example, to embed an incomplete spreadsheet into a presentation, safe in the knowledge that the data will always be up to date. Even more impressive, you've looked at the potential for embedding a live document into a space on a book or newsletter page and have it update to include the latest version of the image (which another person could be working on) whenever the document is loaded.

Finally, you took a brief journey into the somewhat scary world of macro recording, editing, and playback, to see how to record multiple keystrokes and menu commands to a file that is ready to play back at a later time.

# CHAPTER 11

■ ■ ■

# Extensions

**H**aving journeyed through the preceding 10 chapters, you'll have a good understanding that OpenOffice.org can accomplish a lot. And when you consider that this software doesn't cost a thing, it's even more remarkable. However, there are some things that OpenOffice.org can't do. But thanks to the way the software is designed and maintained (i.e., it is free, in two ways: it doesn't cost anything, and anyone can access the source code), users and developers have been able to create additions to the package that bring new features or improve existing ones. You've used some of these OpenOffice.org Extensions previously to add cool templates to the software, add random text to a page, and install new dictionaries. The examples cited in this chapter are a mixture of macros, templates, and mini-applets that either extend the user interface or provide new ways of adding content to a document.

In this chapter you'll be downloading and installing some of the most useful extensions available to expand the tools available for particular jobs. Some of these extensions will appeal to just a few of you, whereas others have the potential of really spicing up your documents or changing the way you work, in a good way. After installing the additional software, you'll learn the basics or create a mini-project to understand the ways they work.

Our top-ten list begins with extensions that adjust the application experience (see Figure 11-1). Most of the extensions work with content in various ways throughout the suite. A short final section deals with options that might transform the way you distribute or view documents.

Without exception these extensions are free of charge and will usually ship with the underlying code—or at least a link to the code—meaning that, with the appropriate skills or staff, it's possible to base new extensions on them, maybe "scratching an itch" that no other piece of software can manage.

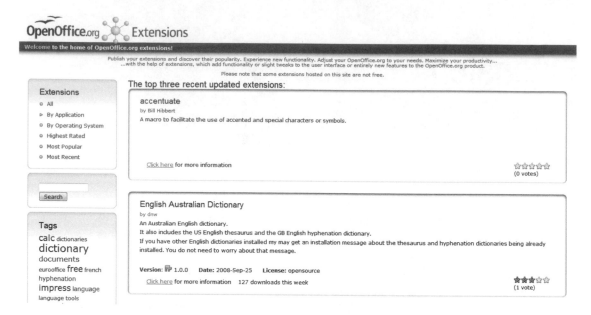

**Figure 11-1.** *You can download all of our top-ten extensions for free from the OpenOffice.org project web site.*

# Installing Extensions

Most OpenOffice.org extensions are installed in the same way and, in the main, are cross-platform; i.e., they can be downloaded and installed on any compatible version of the software on Windows, OS X, Linux, or Solaris. There are some exceptions, notably many of the more complex solutions offered by Sun Microsystems, but in most cases, the extensions are available for all platforms. Some will require your version of OpenOffice.org to have access to a recent version of Java, Python, or some other free scripting languages. The official version of Java can be downloaded from http://java.sun.com or, in Linux, via your normal package manager. Many versions of OpenOffice.org ship with Java already integrated into the software. You can check the state of your software at http://www.java.com/en/download/help/testvm.xml. In a Linux system, open a terminal and type java -version to see which version is installed.

---

■**Note** Since Sun released Java under an open source license in November 2006, a number of alternative installations of the Java runtime environment have been released.

---

With Java installed, it also needs to be enabled within the software. Click Tools ➤ Options and, from the OpenOffice.org section, choose the Java heading. If a Java runtime environment (JRE) is installed correctly, it will be listed in this window (Figure 11-2). Select the most recent version (with the highest version number) by clicking the radio button next to its name. If none is listed and you definitely have it installed, then click the Add button and locate the JRE file manually. Once you've selected a JRE version, a restart will be required to activate it.

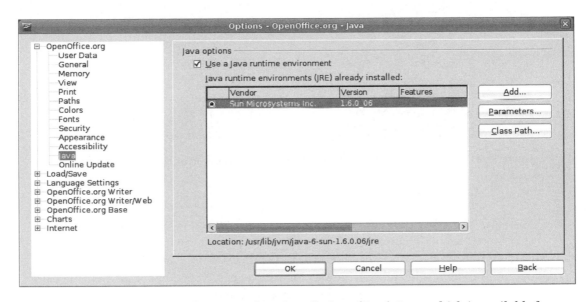

**Figure 11-2.** *Many extensions rely on a working installation of Sun's Java, which is available from the Sun Microsystem web site or via most standard Linux package managers.*

To install an extension, it first needs to be downloaded from the net and saved to some location on your disk. At the end of the discussion of each content extension, we've included a link to that extension. However, these links may change between the date of writing and the date of the book's publication. Nonetheless, most of the extensions are available via http://extensions.services.openoffice.org or http://www.sourceforge.net. Just search using the name.

Go to Tools ➤ Extension Manager and click the Add button. This will launch a standard file browser, allowing you to navigate to wherever the .oxt file has been downloaded and to select it (Figure 11-3). It will be added automatically to the roster of available extensions but, depending on the nature of the software, may need a restart before it becomes usable.

Once installed, the extension will be integrated with the software, and you can safely delete the original downloaded file. You can also disable it using the Extension Manager, which will prevent it from showing up in the interface without your actually removing the extension altogether.

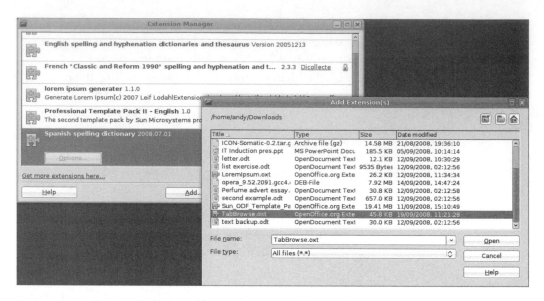

**Figure 11-3.** *Select Tools ➤ Extension Manager to add, disable, or remove extensions to the software.*

You can use the other options in the Extension Manager to check for updates to a selected extension (Figure 11-4)—obviously this requires a live Internet connection— or to disable or remove an extension. The Get more extensions here link will launch the operating system's default web browser on the Extensions section of the OpenOffice.org community site, where new extensions tend to be found.

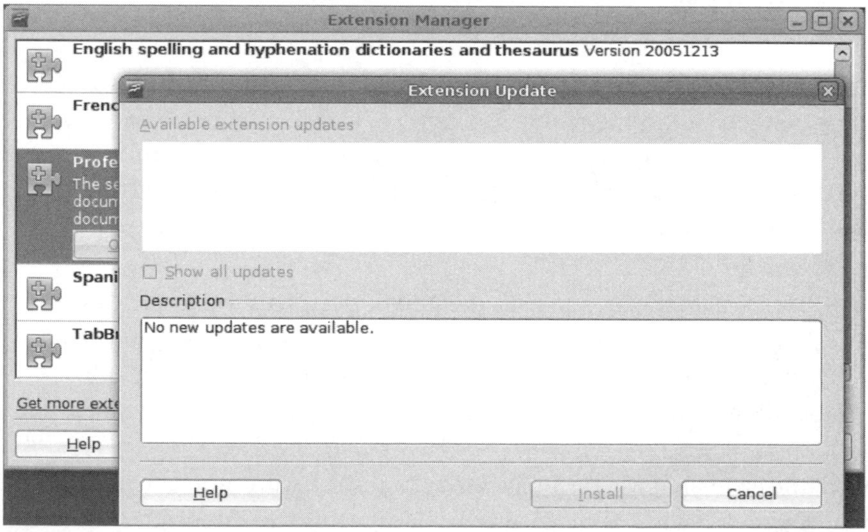

**Figure 11-4.** *Extensions are updated often, and you can upgrade them via the Extension Manager.*

# Interface Extensions

Let's begin our exploration with two extensions that make changes to the OpenOffice.org interface to improve the way you work.

## Tabbed Windows

Tabbed browsing has been an integral part of the Firefox experience for years and for Windows Internet Explorer version 7 and above; this extension attempts to bring the same experience to OO.o. Once you've installed it, you'll need to restart the application to see it working. The extension adds a new toolbar (though it's not yet manageable in the way other toolbars are) to the bottom of the main window, below the status bar. On initial launch it will have a single tab in it, labeled "my window0" (though by the time you read this it may have the name of the document there), which corresponds to the new or existing document you've opened. Click File ➤ New ➤ (document type); instead of appearing in a new window, the document will be added to the tab bar at the base. Click it to see the document.

By default the tabs will be labeled "my window 1," "my window 2," etc. (Figure 11-5). Each name will also be displayed in the title bar of OpenOffice.org itself, instead of the name of the document. This is very helpful when working on related documents such as a selection of pages for a web site or presentations based on the same theme. But beware: this does take up extra space.

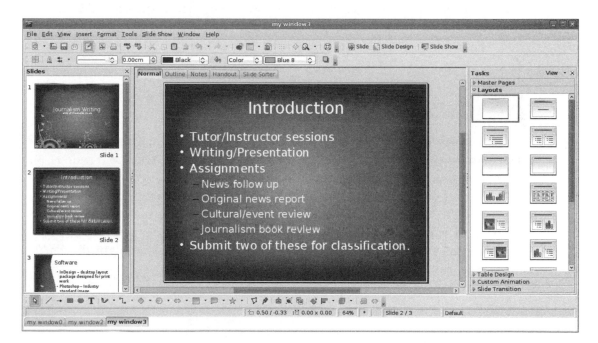

**Figure 11-5.** *Tabbed windows works like browser tabs in Firefox and Internet Explorer 7/8, but they do have an impact on other parts of the user interface.*

In addition to the tabs, the extension makes a couple of significant changes. Before you added the extension, you could close a document without closing the application, by clicking the Close icon (X) at the top right of the main window (below the title bar/window decorations). But this icon is removed once the extension is enabled. This means you will need to close documents by clicking File ➤ Close Menu. This action will close only the currently selected document. Secondly, the Full Screen option (View ➤ Full Screen or Ctrl+Shift+J) will be disabled in the menu, so if you use that feature often, the tabbed browsing extension will be problematic. If you want to keep both tabbed windows and full-screen editing, you'll have to get into the habit of disabling the extension at appropriate times.

Here's the URL where you can find the Tabbed Windows extension:

```
http://wiki.services.OpenOffice.org/wiki/Framework/WorkInProgress/Tabbed_Windows_
Extension
```

## OpenOffice.org2GoogleDocs

This extension acts as a bridge between the online and offline editing suites by providing a system by which you can download documents to OpenOffice.org from a small selection of online suites, edit them, and then save them back to the Internet. This gives you all the advantages of online document sharing—such as the ability to edit your work on any machine with an Internet connection and a browser—but also provides the additional formatting options of which OpenOffice.org is capable.

---

■**Note**  In order to use this extension, you must have Java 6 installed.

---

Install in the usual fashion; then restart OpenOffice.org to launch the extension, which initially will be presented as an extra floating toolbar on the window (Figure 11-6). This works in exactly the same way as a standard toolbar (under View ➤ Toolbars it is called Add-On 1), which can be moved around or docked to any edge of the window. If you use it often, you can place it on the standard toolbar at the top of the window so that the tools are always at hand. In addition to the toolbar, there will be a new menu item, labeled Google Docs & Zoho, on the File menu. This replicates the buttons on the toolbar, but it also has a configuration option—which doesn't do anything yet.

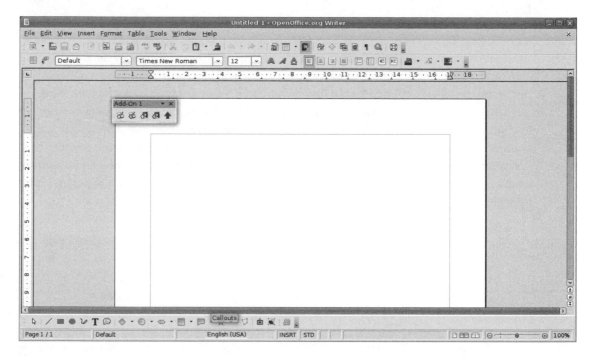

**Figure 11-6.** *The OO2GoogleDocs toolbar is small and can be docked to any part of the OO.o interface.*

The new toolbar consists of five icons. The first two are specific to Google Docs (http:// docs.google.com), icons three and four are for Zoho (http://www.zoho.com), and the fifth you can use to export documents to any WebDAV server. Obviously, to work with either of the online office services you'll need to sign up for an account and have the login details handy.

---

### ONLINE OFFICE SOFTWARE

While not yet capable of replacing a locally installed office package, a number of online office services have emerged that combine basic editing and document creation operations with generous online storage. Google's Docs service is probably the most well known of these products; Zoho's offerings are as good and in some cases even better.

Essentially these are "software suites" that work within the web browser and don't require anything to be installed. Editing takes place within the browser window, and documents are saved to remote servers, meaning you're less likely to lose access to your data—unless you lose your network connection.

Both Zoho and Google offer free services that include access to the applications and storage.

To open a document from Google Docs, select the Import from Google Docs button. A new dialog box will appear with space for your username and password. The Username space needs everything before the @ sign in your Gmail/Google name. By default, the software will request a password every time you import or export a document. Obviously this is the most secure practice, but for convenience it's possible to have the password "remembered" by the extension. Once you have entered your credentials, click the Get list button to see the contents of your Google Docs library (Figure 11-7). On the left is the document name, on the right the date it was last updated. Depending on the number of documents already on the system and the speed of your connection, this could take anywhere from a couple of seconds to a few minutes. Our library of just over 200 documents appeared almost instantly.

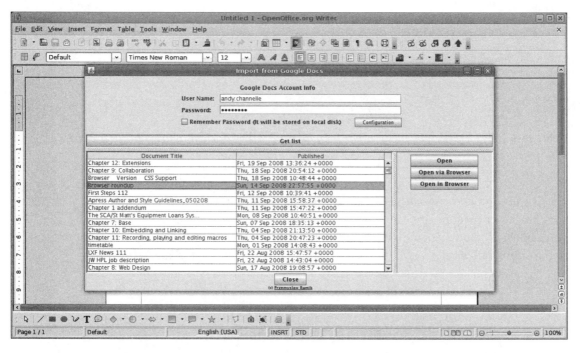

**Figure 11-7.** *Select a file to download from the simple file manager. You can open documents directly in OO.o or via a browser.*

Beside the list of documents are three buttons. The top button will simply download and open the document in the appropriate OpenOffice.org application—spreadsheets will open in Calc, and so on. The center button will launch the default browser and then download the selected file to your computer in the appropriate file format. Google Docs Presentations will download in `.odp` format, word-processing documents will be transferred as `.odt`, etc. The bottom button will launch a browser window with the document in it ready for editing. This is great for checking the contents of a document before downloading it with Open.

Again, documents could take some time to download, especially if they contain a lot of images, but in general it's quite speedy. Once downloaded, the document will be opened in the appropriate application as a native ODF file (Figure 11-8).

**Figure 11-8.** *Google Docs does a good job of rendering the three core document formats from OO.o. The version at the back is running in Firefox.*

Once you have made your edits, you can upload the document again using the Upload to Google Docs button. However, you must have saved a local version of the document before uploading, and the format chosen can have an effect on the performance of the upload process, due to the limits of the Google service. For example, you can save text documents as .doc, .rtf, .odt, or .swx as well as plain .txt or .html, and they will be uploaded in that format. Similarly, you can save spreadsheets as either .xls or .ods. But you must save presentations in the PowerPoint (.ppt) format. If you have saved the document as an .odp, an automatic transcoding operation will launch from within OpenOffice. org before the upload is instigated. Beware, though, this can take some time. It's much easier to resave the document as a .ppt and then upload.

---

■**Note** There are quite a few differences between the feature set of these products and that of OpenOffice. org. As with transcoding from, for instance, Writer to Word, more complex documents are the most likely to cause the biggest problems.

---

Uploading is likely to take longer than downloading, due to the way normal broadband connections work (Figure 11-9). Unfortunately there's no real visual representation of the upload progress (though a dialog box exists for this, so it may be coming); you'll just have to wait for the "finished" message. This is not too much of a problem—because of the Java-based nature of the software, you can get back to editing in OpenOffice.org immediately.

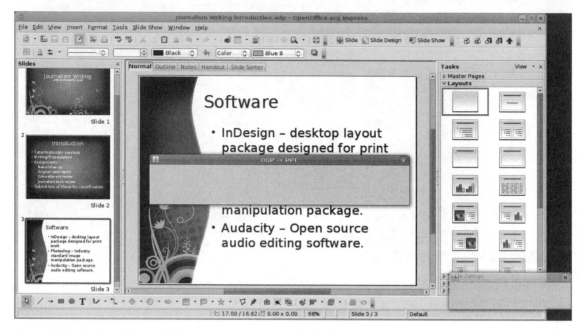

**Figure 11-9.** *Uploading can take some time, especially if the document needs to be transcoded to a different format.*

The process of working with Zoho Docs is the same, except, obviously, you select Upload or Download to Zoho. The Upload to WebDAV server depends on your having the IP address or URL of the server to which you're saving. If you do, click the giant green button, add the server address and file name, and click the OK button. Servers that are already part of your network will be accessible via the ellipsis button. You cannot download documents from the WebDAV server through this extension.

Here's the URL where you can find the Google Docs extension:

```
http://extensions.services.OpenOffice.org/project/ooo2gd
```

# Writer's Tools

Writer's Tools, as the name suggests, is a collection of additions for OpenOffice.org that come as a single extension that features a collection of tools tailored to professional, academic, or just dedicated writers.

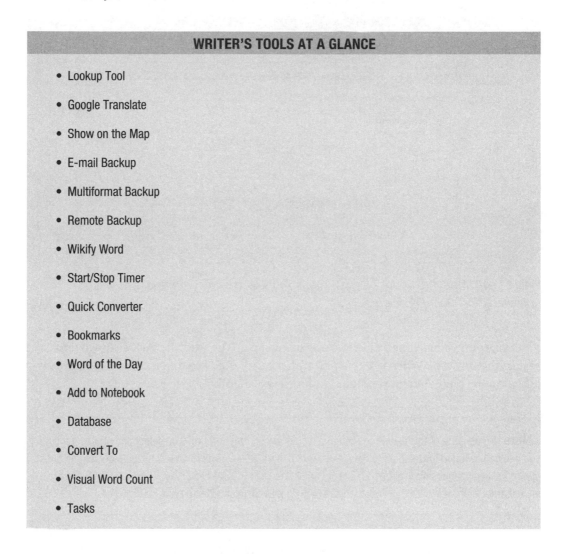

**WRITER'S TOOLS AT A GLANCE**

- Lookup Tool

- Google Translate

- Show on the Map

- E-mail Backup

- Multiformat Backup

- Remote Backup

- Wikify Word

- Start/Stop Timer

- Quick Converter

- Bookmarks

- Word of the Day

- Add to Notebook

- Database

- Convert To

- Visual Word Count

- Tasks

To install, grab the file from the address listed at the end of this subsection, decompress the zip file, and install as normal through the Extension Manager. The zip archive includes a small selection of templates, which can also be installed by the same method. Let's take a brief tour through the options available in this package, because some of them need a little assistance to work effectively. For example, a few of the options rely on the WriterDB database, which is also included in the archive, so this needs to be registered to the system (Figure 11-10). Select Tools ➤ Options and look under the OpenOffice.org Base options on the left. Choose the Databases option and use the file manager to navigate and select the WriterDB database. Remember to save this somewhere sensible because it will now be tied to your installation of OO.o and if the database gets moved, some parts of the Writer's Tools package will stop working.

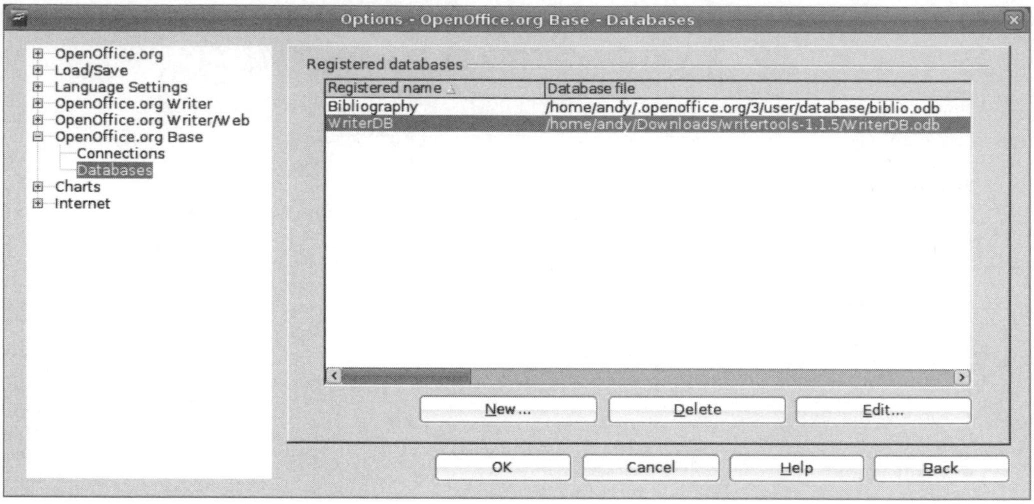

**Figure 11-10.** *Many of the options in Writer's Tools rely on the database, which has to be "registered" in OpenOffice.org.*

Once you've registered the database and installed the extension, close down and restart the software. When it's up and running you should see that a new entry has been added to the menu bar, next to the standard Tools menu.

■**Note** Some parts of this extension require a web browser. The first time you select one of these options, you will be prompted for the path to the file browser (Figure 11-11). The following assume default installations. Windows users should enter C:\Program Files\Mozilla Firefox\firefox.exe. Mac users should enter open -a /Applications/Firefox.app. Linux users should type firefox.

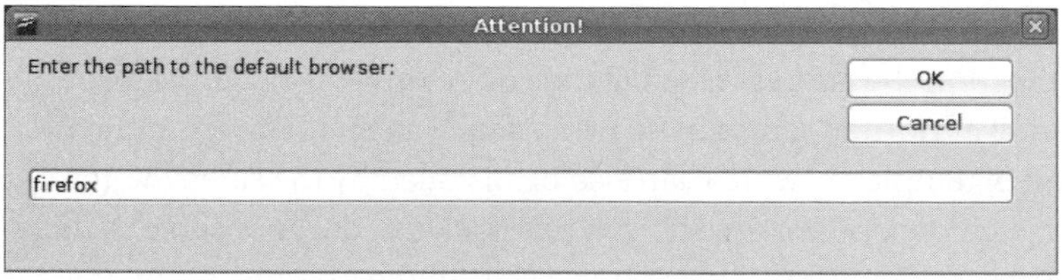

**Figure 11-11.** *The first time you launch one of the applets that need access to the web, you must configure the path to your default browser.*

# Reference

The Writer's Tools menu is divided into logical sections, and the first three entries integrate with different web services. First up is a Lookup tool. Select a word on the page, choose this option, and a dialog box will appear where it's possible to select from a range of reference sources to check that particular word or phrase. Options include Google's "Define" operation, Wikipedia, WorldNet, and a couple of thesauruses. Click one of these to launch the web browser at the appropriate site and page. The second option is Google Translate, which will feed the selected text through an online translation service and spit out a new version. As with the Lookup option, this begins with a dialog box, where the two languages are defined, and then moves onto the Web for the actual translation. The third part of this section of the menu can take a selected postal/ZIP code or place name and display it in Google Maps.

## ADDING NEW LOOKUP OPTIONS

For the technically minded, it's possible to add or edit the Lookup tool to feature favorite reference sites. For example, if you're an academic writer, you might want to search through Google Scholar for certain articles, so it would be worthwhile adding this to the list of options. To begin the editing process, click Tools ➤ Macros ➤ Organize Macros ➤ OpenOffice.org Basic. In the dialog box, reveal the Writer's Tools list in the left pane, choose Tools, and then select Lookup Tool from the right. Press the Edit button. This will open the OO.o Basic editor.

```
Sub LookupTool()

Dim Library As Object
Dim DialogField As Object
Dim exitOK As String, CurrentItemPos As Integer

URLArray=Array("http://en.wikipedia.org/wiki/",_
"http://dictionary.cambridge.org/results.asp?searchword=",_
"http://www.google.com/search?q=define%3A",_
"http://wordnet.princeton.edu/perl/webwn?s=",_
"http://www.askoxford.com/results/?view=searchresults&freesearch=",_
"http://dict.tu-chemnitz.de/dings.cgi?lang=en&query=",_
"http://word.sc/",_
"http://word.sc/thes/",_
"http://www.confusingwords.com/index.php?word=")

ListBoxArray=Array("Wikipedia (En)", "Cambridge Dictionaries Online",_
"Google Define", "WordNet", "Ask Oxford", "BEOLINGUS",_
"Word Source Dictionary", "Word Source Thesaurus", "Confusing Words")

ThisDoc=ThisComponent
LookupWord=ThisDoc.getCurrentController().getSelection().getByIndex(0).getString()
If LookupWord="" then MsgBox (MsgWordLookup, 16, MsgAttn) : End
TranslateTextURL=ConvertToURL(LookupWord)
LookupText=Right(TranslateTextURL, Len(TranslateTextURL)-8)
Split1 = Split(LookupText, "&")
```

The first section you're interested in is the URL array. To this you'll need to add the correct URL for a Google Scholar search. You can acquire this by going to the site (`http://scholar.google.com`) and entering a search term that will yield a piece of code such as

`http://scholar.google.co.uk/scholar?hl=en&lr=&q=new+media&btnG=Search`

The search string comes after the &q= part of the URL. For this particular string, you can forget about the &btnG=Search part. So, following the last line of the URLArray (but before the closing bracket), add the line

`http://scholar.google.co.uk/scholar?hl=en&lr=&q=`

Next you need to add this option to the Selection dialog box, which you do in the ListBoxArray. After the last option, insert a comma and a space and then the menu entry enclosed in quotes, i.e., "Google Scholar."

Click File ➤ Save and then close the editor. Next time you call the Lookup tool, the new option will be available, and selecting it will launch the browser on the appropriate page.

You can also use this method to remove options (we got rid of confusing words), but make sure the order of the URL and list arrays match up, because this is how the dialog box works.

# Backup

You can use the second batch of options to back up documents. The first of these, which you can use to send a backup copy of the document automatically to a Gmail account, takes quite a bit of setting up.

This tool uses Python to do its magic, and so this piece of software needs to be installed. Most Linux systems will have Python by default, but you can check that this is the case by opening a terminal and typing "python." The resulting output will tell you which version is installed. If nothing appears, install Python using your distribution's package manager. In Windows, install the official Python packages from http://www. python.org/, ensuring that you accept the default option, which will install the software to C:/Python25. Python is installed by default on all OS X systems.

In the original Writer's Tools directory is a file called gmail_backup.py. This needs to be copied into the user directory under Linux or into C:/Python under Windows. Once you have moved it, open the file with any text editor (Notepad would be fine, MS Word less so) and look for the section near the top that contains the following:

```
GMAIL_USER = 'address@gmail.com'
GMAIL_PASSWD = "password"
RECIPIENT = "backup@gmail.com"
SUBJECT = "Writer's Tools document backup: " + sys.argv[2]
MESSAGE = "A backup version of an OpenOffice.org document is attached."
```

These are the options that configure the outgoing mail. GMAIL_USER should be your normal Gmail username and GMAIL_PASSWD its associated password. Remember that this document is unencrypted, meaning there is a potential security risk if someone were to steal the machine on which the software is running (Figure 11-12). The RECIPIENT value would typically be the same as the Gmail username. But because of the way Gmail works, you could append the beginning part of the address (e.g., andy.channelle+backup@ gmail.com) and then set up a filter on Gmail to mark each e-mail that arrives with that address with a Backup label. The SUBJECT setting will appear in the subject line of the e-mail, which, again, you could use for filtering purposes, and the MESSAGE line will appear in the body of the e-mail. Once this is configured, selecting Writer's Tools ➤ Email Backup will send the document to the specified address as an attachment.

The Multiformat Backup (Figure 11-13) takes a snapshot of the current document, saves it as a .doc file, an .rtf file, and a .txt file, and then bundles them all up into a compressed zip folder in the same location as the original document. The resulting archive is named with the date and time of the backup. This beautifully simple tool makes backing up in a systematic way easy enough for anyone to use. (There's no excuse for losing work now, though.)

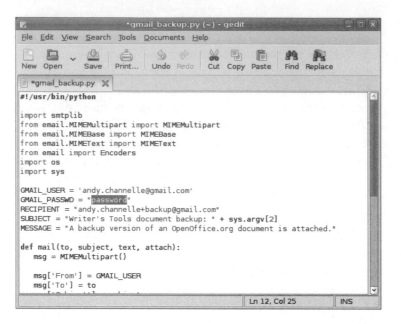

**Figure 11-12.** *Adding your password to this file is a slight security risk on a multiuser system.*

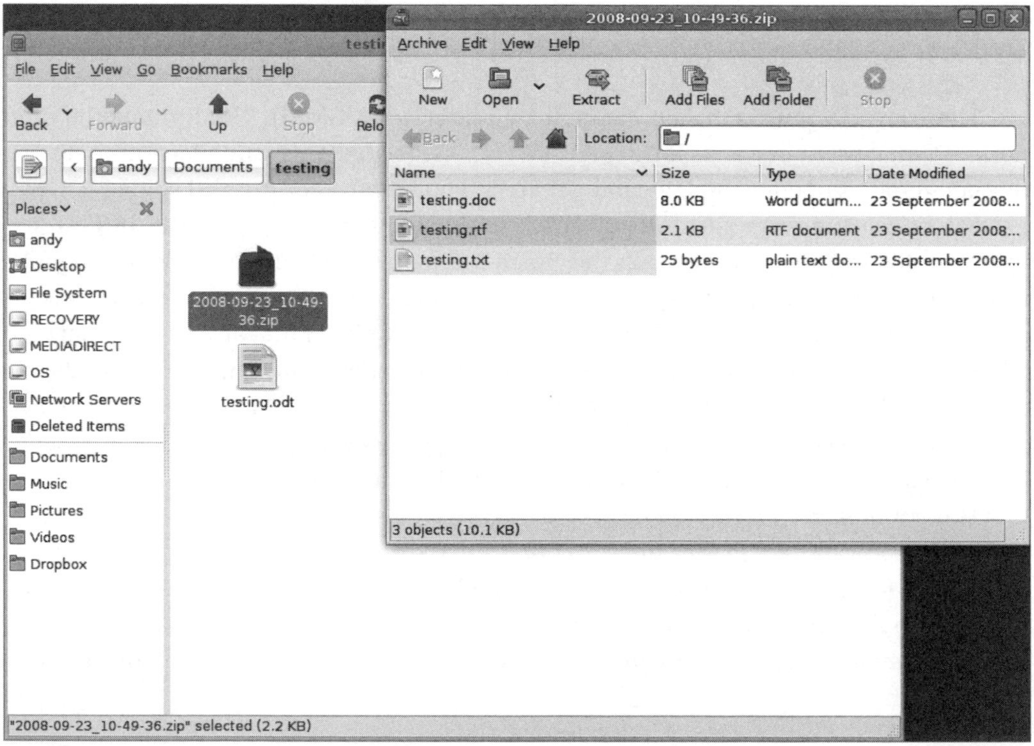

**Figure 11-13.** *Backups in various formats could mean the difference between having access to your files in the future and being stuck!*

Finally for this section, the Remote Backup option will launch a dialog box that allows you to back up a document to an FTP server. For this to work, you'll need the login details for the server and the path to the backup directory. The format for this information is

```
ftp://username:password@serveraddress/path/to/directory
```

For example,

```
ftp://andy:bobtodd@192.168.1.7/docs/backup
```

would send the backup copy of the document using the credentials before the @ sign to a local FTP server and into the directory `/docs/backup`.

## Wikify Words and Documents

The next section contains the single Wikify Word operation, which you can use to build up a collection of documents—they have to be in the same directory—using a Wiki-type structure. For example, let's start with a single document called `Introduction.odt`, which is in a folder called `Project Docs`. Into this, type a small list of other documents to be added to the folder (Figure 11-14). Ordinarily you'd have to create these documents and then add internal links (as in Chapter 8) to the other documents. With Writer's Tools, you can simplify this by highlighting each of the document names and then selecting Writer's Tools ➤ Wikify Word. The selected word or passage will turn into a link. But the option does much more than that. Just as Wikipedia allows users to create links to pages that don't exist and will then create those pages when the link is clicked, so selecting the link in the original document (either by Ctrl+clicking or doing right-click ➤ Open Hyperlink) will create a new document in the same directory as the original, with the link name as its file name. You can then open and edit them as usual.

Here's the clever part: just as with Wikipedia, Wikifying a word that is already a document—in our example you could type the word *Introduction* into one of the secondary documents—would just create a link to the existing document. It's not a complete Wiki system, but it does work well for longer projects that may be built in sections. However, this means multiple authors must be consistent in their labeling because, for instance, `introduction.odt` could be a different file from `Introduction.odt`.

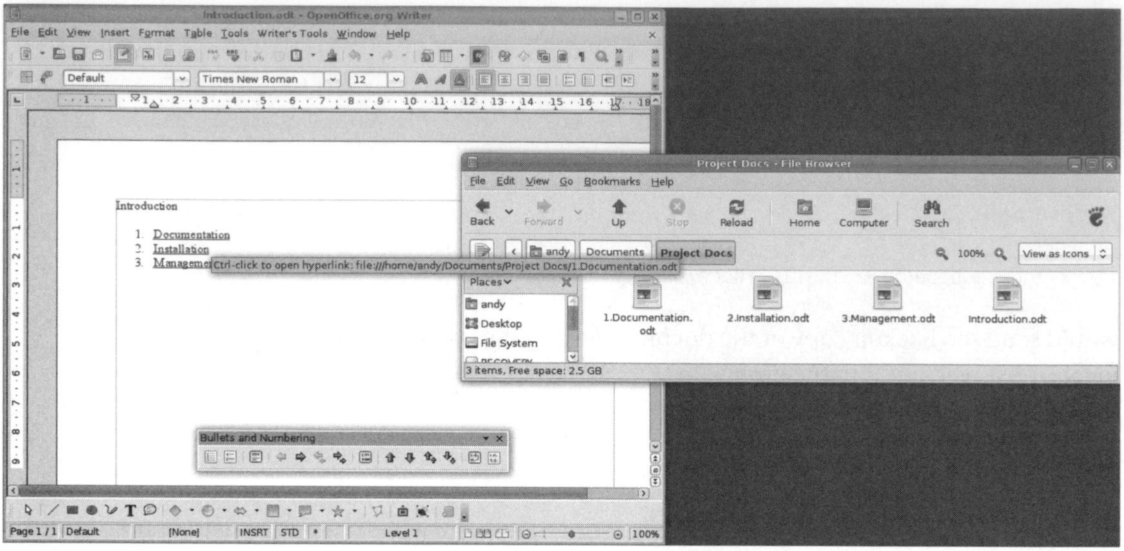

**Figure 11-14.** *The Wikify option is a great time saver if you're working on a linked set of documents.*

## Document Timer

The next section is great for professional authors who may be working on a time = money basis. Simply, the first option will start a timer and the second will stop it and provide a measure of the duration in between. However, there's a little more to it than that because you can save this data, including a word count and date information, as a session assigned to that particular document and you can save it into an OO.o Base database (Figure 11-15).

To see the contents of this database, press F4 or click View ➤ Data Sources, right-click the WriterDB entry, and select Edit Database File. Select the Tables section from the left pane, and double-click the Docstats table. This will open up the table in data entry/edit mode, with each session saved as a single row. The Time Used section is rounded up or down to the nearest minute. You can edit this table in the usual way. For example, we've added publisher data to our particular job, and then the minutes and hours can be summed and used to invoice a client accurately for your time. As discussed in Chapter 7 you can sort and filter this table to provide the best view of your data.

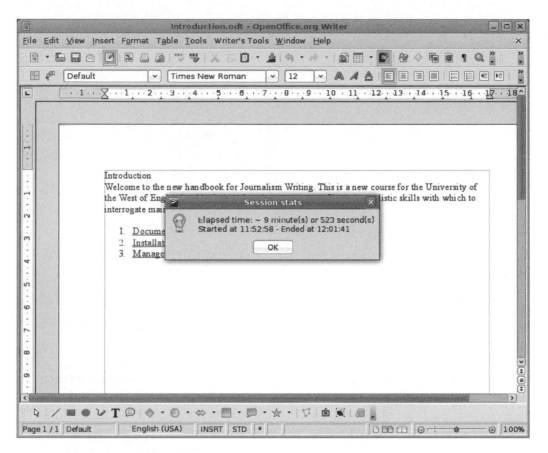

**Figure 11-15.** *Professional writers paid by the hour will appreciate the session timer, which can be tied to a specific document.*

## Bookmarks

There are a couple of different types of bookmarks in OpenOffice.org. Writer's Tools adds another, which is a way of creating links to documents (but not embedded in a document), kind of like a very focused file manager. You can add a document to the list by clicking Writer's Tools ➤ Bookmark Document. This will launch a standard file browser, where you can select an individual document to add to the list. Deleting a bookmark involves selecting the Delete option. Once you've built up a collection of bookmarks, you can access them by clicking Writer's Tools ➤ Open Bookmarks (Figure 11-16). Unfortunately this is not a persistent dialog box, but the bookmarks will stay with the list until they're deleted.

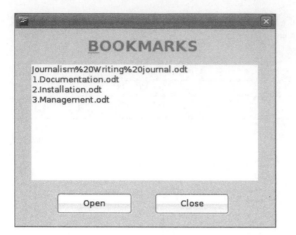

**Figure 11-16.** *You can use document bookmarks to gain rapid access to a selection of documents over the life of a project.*

## Notes and Tasks

After the Word of the Day element (which will display a different intriguing word each day) there are a few database-based tools, the first of which is the Notebook. As the name suggests, this is a place where you can write and store notes and, like the timer settings discussed earlier, access them later via the WriterDB database by double-clicking the Form "Writer's Notebook." You can also add new notes via the database (Figure 11-17). These notes are not the same as the document notes in Chapter 10, because they are not tied to a specific anchor or document.

Below the Database option, which will open the WriterDB file in Base, is a Tasks menu. This opens a dialog box for viewing current tasks from the database. Unfortunately, there's no "Add Task" button here, so you'll need to go into the database (Writer's Tools ➤ Database) and select the Writer's Tasks table or form to add information. We noticed that the tasks list doesn't inherit the date format from the system, so due dates should be entered using the YYYY-MM-DD format.

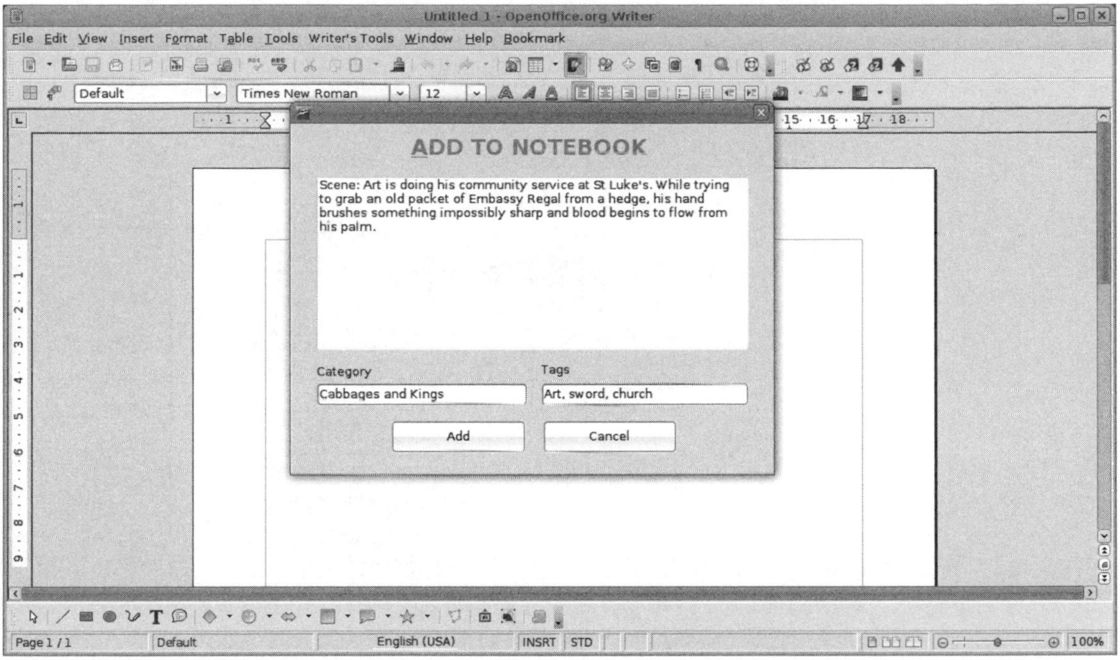

**Figure 11-17.** *You can add notes via the interface, but you must edit and print them through OO.o Base.*

## Miscellaneous Other Useful Options

The Convert to System option allows you to save the current document in Word, RTF, HTML, or PDF format (it's the same as clicking File ➤ Export), but it saves the work of having to define a location and format for the export. It will automatically save the document using the same name and file location as the original.

The Visual Word Count is designed to give a good indication of how far into a project you are. It's great for journalists and students working to a word count limit. Select the option from the menu, input the target word count without any separators (e.g., 18000, not 18,000), and click OK. The resulting dialog box will display the current word count, a percentage value denoting how much has been done, and a standard operating system progress bar, providing a more visual representation of how much work is left to do (Figure 11-18).

Writer's Tools contains a few options that are extremely useful to those who regularly have to create work on tight deadlines or budgets. The Reference and Note/Task options make it easier to work without leaving the confines of the office suite.

Here's the URL where you can find the Writer's Tools extension:

```
http://extensions.services.openoffice.org/project/writertools
```

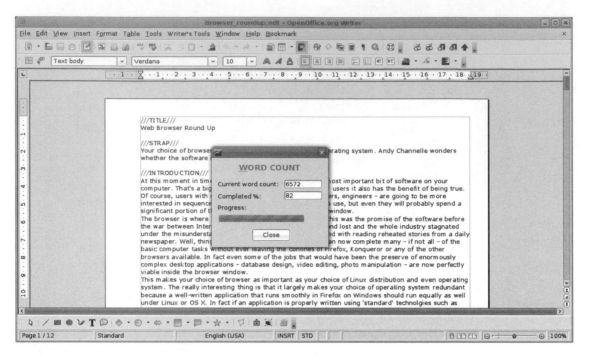

**Figure 11-18.** *Anyone who's tried to work to a particular word count limit will understand how useful this "words to go" tool is.*

# Content Extensions

In addition to working with the user interface, a variety of extensions work on the content of a document.

## OOoHG

OOoHG is an extraordinarily powerful extension designed for creating maps, atlases, and timelines. Unfortunately the project's web site is only available in French (Figure 11-19), so to get the latest version (2.4), select the link on the home page, which is labeled *Téléchargement complet version 2.4*. On the right side of the new page you'll see a section with a selection of links to Windows files (choose the most up-to-date version) and a zip file that contains the extension for Mac and Linux users.

At 27MB, this is quite a large download. With the Windows packages, double-click to install the package and select Start. This will install everything into the default Gallery directory for your OO.o install. If you've installed it in some weird location, this will have to be set in the Extract To bar.

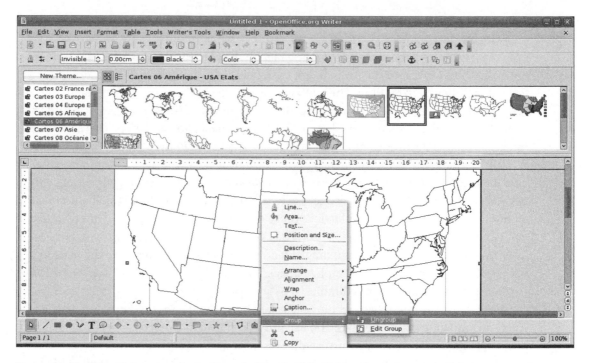

**Figure 11-19.** *Everything may be in French, but the OOoHG package is too useful to pass up. Drag maps out and edit them after ungrouping.*

Linux and Mac users will have to install the galleries manually (Windows users can too if they like). Once the package has downloaded, extract it using your normal archive utility—most modern Linux and Mac systems should be able to access this type of archive file with a double-click—and then copy the files to the Gallery directory for OpenOffice.org. On Linux, the location will be /usr/lib/openoffice/share/gallery (unless you installed it in a different location), while on the Mac it will be /user/library/ Application Support/OpenOffice/org-aqua/3/gallery. If these paths don't work on your system, open up the gallery (Tools ➤ Gallery), open one of the existing gallery libraries, and make a note of the path from the space just above the gallery itself.

---

■**Note**  You'll need root privileges to copy and paste the files from the archive to the Gallery folder in Linux. In Gnome, this can be accomplished by opening a terminal and typing *sudo nautilus*. You'll be prompted for the root password, and Nautilus will launch, allowing you to move the files. In KDE, either use *sudo konqueror* or right-click a Konqueror icon, select Open As, and use root and the root password to open the application in administration mode.

---

You will need to close and reopen the application for the gallery to update. The gallery will now be populated with a large number of French menu entries, which, in turn, open up a gallery on the main part of the gallery interface featuring maps, flags, timelines, and other geographical data. And though the labels are in French, they shouldn't pose too much difficulty in reading. The contents are divided up into a selection of editable "clip art" and noneditable graphics. The former come under the headings *Cartes* (maps), *Carto* (geographical icons), and *Chrono* (timelines). Those labeled *Geo* or *Hist* are bitmap images, which you can edit only in a package such as Paint, Photoshop, or Gimp.

The bitmaps will work well in any of the OO.o packages. But the illustrations provide the most flexible option if you need to create your own version of a map, especially because you can edit them in any package where the Drawing toolbar is available—i.e., all but Base. For the most flexibility let's make a few edits to a map of the United States using the Draw application. Open Draw, click Tools ➤ Gallery, and navigate to the Carte Amerique section. You're going to drag and drop one of the US maps onto the page for editing. This comes down as a complete image, so right-click and select Group ➤ Ungroup to make the constituent parts editable.

From here it is possible to recolor each state individually, for instance, to create an electoral map, or to take one state and expand its size and use that as a basis for another project. In Figure 11-20 we've converted Texas to a curve (Modify ➤ Convert ➤ To Curve) and then extruded it using Modify ➤ Convert ➤ To 3D, which has the effect of highlighting it quite nicely. You could also add labels to states by double-clicking on each one in turn, adding the text, and resizing it to fit.

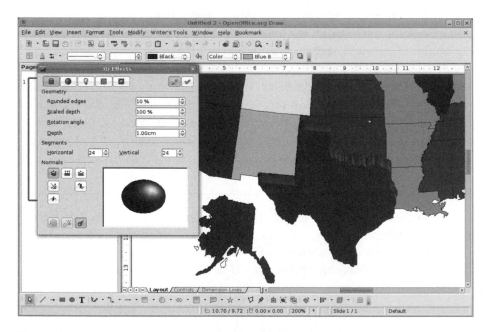

**Figure 11-20.** *Once you have ungrouped maps, you can color them, blow them apart, or treat them with a little 3D to highlight a particular part.*

To find out more about editing images, see Chapter 6; to learn how to build an image map from a map image, see Chapter 8.

Here's the URL where you can find the OOoHG extension:

```
http://ooo.hg.free.fr/
```

## LilyPond

OOoLilyPond is a rather specialized package you can use to create musical notation for integration into OpenOffice.org documents. As the name suggests, it's based on the Lily-Pond software, which is released under an open source license. This means that, in order for the extension—well, it's a macro really—to work, you must first acquire and install the LilyPond software, which you can download from `http://www.lilypond.org/web/install` for Windows and Mac or via your package manager in Linux.

For this extension to work, you must install the stable 2.10.x series, not the development version (2.11.x).

The OOoLilyPond package is installed as a macro, so once you've downloaded and extracted the latest `tar.gz` or zip archive from the project's web site (listed at the end of this subsection), click Tools ➤ Macros ➤ Organize Macros ➤ OpenOffice.org Basic; then select Organizer (Figure 11-21). Select the Libraries tab and click the entry marked My Macros & Dialogs in the Location box. Click Import and, using the file browser, navigate to the location where the archive was extracted and find the file `/OOoLilyPond/basic/script.xlb` in Linux, `C:\Program Files\OOoLilyPond\basic\script.xlb` in Windows, or `/OOoLilyPond/basic/script.xlb` in OS X.

In the Import Libraries dialog box, click OK to move on. You can also create a keyboard shortcut to launch the macro. Click Tools ➤ Customize, select the Keyboard tab, and associate Ctrl+M (or some other combination) with it. Under the Category section, choose OpenOffice.org Macros ➤ User ➤ OOoLilyPond ➤ Main and then, under Function, select Main. Remember to click the Modify button before closing this dialog box. Now use the new shortcut to start the editor, or select Tools ➤ Macros ➤ Run Macro and find the OOoLilyPond macros under the My Macros section.

---

**■Note**  On the first run, OOoLilyPond expects its template files to be in a particular place. If you've installed them somewhere other than the default location, click through this dialog box, click the Config button, and add the path to the template files (they will be part of the original download) in the appropriate place.

---

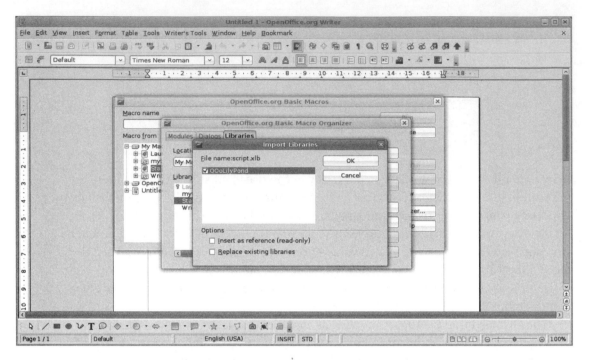

**Figure 11-21.** *Installing the LilyPond extension is a little cumbersome. But if you're interested in printing out music notation, it's second to none.*

A full discussion of the LilyPond language is far beyond this section. But briefly, notation is programmed into the editor a bit like the code for a web page. So we might put

```
\key c \minor \relative c'' { c16 es, d es c es d es c' es, d es c es d es }
```

into the editor and click the LilyPond button. The result is an image of the musical notation, which can be moved around the page like any other image. By means of the Config button it's possible to define precisely how the image is anchored (To Page, As Character, etc.). This can also be changed in the normal way by right-clicking the image and selecting Anchor ➤ (option).

Other things you can do in the Configuration dialog box include defining the image format (.png or .eps), the page template, and the default Wrap option. These are configurable separately for Writer and Impress/Draw (Figure 11-22).

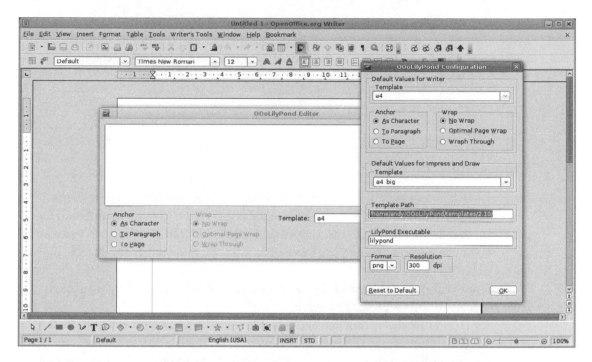

**Figure 11-22.** *OOoLilyPond ships with a few templates built in for Writer, Impress, and Draw.*

To edit a piece of notation once it's been turned into an image, select the image and press Ctrl+M once more. The editor will open, and the LilyPond button will replace the selected image with a new rendering of the edited notation.

For more information on how to get the most from OOoLilyPond, see the parent project's web site at `http://lilypond.org/doc/v2.10`, which includes a complete reference to designing and writing with the software.

Here's the URL where you can find the LilyPond extension:

`http://ooolilypond.sourceforge.net/`

## Oxygen Extras

Oxygen is an edition of OpenOffice.org that includes elements such as templates and clip art. But because it's an open source project, the designers have taken that content and created a series of installable packages that can be added to any version of the software. The installable elements are divided into templates and galleries (see the link following this paragraph) in various languages. One of the clip art packages includes "nonfree" content that has restrictions on how it can be used in a commercial setting. Unlike the

OOoHG gallery discussed earlier, the Oxygen packages are `.oxt` files that you should install through the Extension Manager. These are then accessed through either the usual gallery tool (View ➤ Gallery) or via the New ➤ Templates and Documents menu.

Here's the URL where you can find the Oxygen extension:

```
http://extensions.services.OpenOffice.org/taxonomy/term/34
```

## Calendrier

Calendrier is another macro. But this time, instead of doing word counts or lookups, it actually creates a calendar that can be embedded into a Writer document and then personalized to reflect family or business events. Combined with the PDF output and some good-looking pictures, you could use this to create a great personal gift and a cool marketing publication.

Calendrier should be installed via the Extension Manager. It can then be invoked with Tools ➤ Add-ons ➤ Create Calendar.

In the Calendrier dialog box, select Create big calendar for one month and use the widgets to define the month and year (e.g., January 2009) before hitting Create. After a short time, a new landscape document will appear with the calendar in the center of it. We could now do the same thing for the rest of the year and print out a very plain calendar, but a more stylish solution would be to copy this object (Ctrl+C) into another document, resize it, and add a few personal touches, such as an arresting image at the top and some events in the calendar itself. By pasting into a frame, the calendar portion will be easy to move around and resize, and the table itself will dynamically resize to fit the available space.

Because the calendar is just a standard table, it can be edited in the usual fashion. We could, for instance, change the background color of cells that are part of the previous or next month, change the fonts on the days and numbers, and remove the month/year row from the top of the calendar box and place it at the top of the page.

You can highlight events or dates using either color or text (see Figure 11-23). Once you've finished with January, click the mouse into the last box (January 31 in this case), press the down cursor key to position the cursor beneath the table, and then select Insert ➤ Manual Break ➤ Page Break to create a new page ready for the next month.

With the whole year done, you could print the final production on a laser or an inkjet printer or output to PDF and send it off to a professional printer for longer runs.

Here's the URL where you can find the Calendrier extension:

```
http://sourceforge.net/project/showfiles.php?group_id=87718&package_id=217442
```

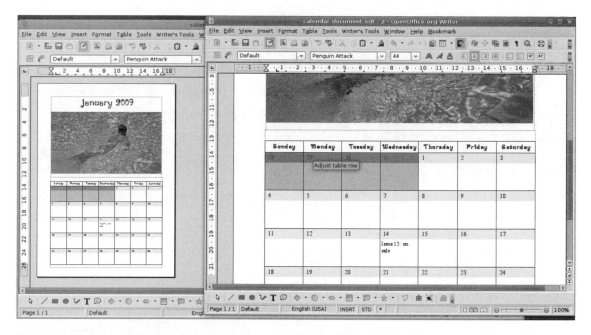

**Figure 11-23.** *Select Window ➤ New Window to get a detailed view of a document while still keeping an overview of the whole design.*

## Calendar for Calc

If you're looking for a more utilitarian calendar, this OO.o Calc template is a great place to start. Download from the link listed at the end of this subsection and then open as a normal document in Calc. The calendar should open up with the current (or next) month defined, because it takes its starting point from your system time and date. The days at the top can be recolored by selecting the appropriate cell and changing the background color using the Formatting toolbar or by right-clicking and selecting Format. You can enter events onto the calendar by clicking inside the appropriate box. We noticed that in the template, the text isn't set to wrap automatically, which can be problematic when adding events. So select the entire sheet, then right-click anywhere, select Format Cells ➤ Alignment, and click Wrap Text Automatically.

When adding events, note that there will be a complex string of data in each cell, which is used for the automatic addition of recurring events. But this can be written over with your text.

Unlike Calendrier, discussed earlier, this template is designed to be used on a monthly basis (Figure 11-24). Thus, if you open it up at the end of January 2009, you will be presented with a calendar for February. This setting can be changed using the yellow-colored parts of the spreadsheet (below the main calendar). But beware: the formulas are moderately complex.

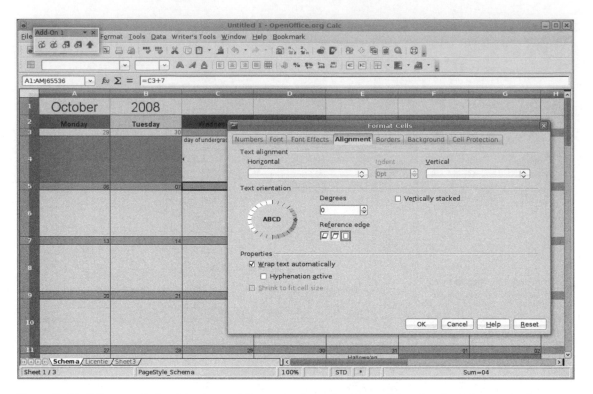

**Figure 11-24.** *Whereas Calendrier is good for annual productions, this calendar is best suited to monthly organizing work.*

Here's the URL where you can find the Calendar for Calc extension:

```
http://extensions.services.OpenOffice.org/project/Calendartemplate
```

## PDF Import

As discussed in Chapter 9, OpenOffice.org has extensive support for outputting PDFs. But this extension, designed by Sun Microsystems, goes the other way, allowing PDFs to be imported into Draw or Impress, preserving the layout, and allowing limited editing of the content. It also offers a cool hybrid export feature that lets files be saved so that OpenOffice.org users can access the ordinary .odt file, while users of other software could open the PDF.

In use, the software is very simple. Once you've installed it, open a document in the usual way, and select Portable Document Format (.pdf) from the File Type drop-down. Navigate to the PDF file you want to edit, select it, and click Open. It may take a few seconds to open, but then the document should appear with an approximately accurate rendition of the layout and all the text in place. Moreover, the text should be editable, making this a useful extension for making small changes to a document.

Note, however, that we had some problems accurately displaying complex multi-column documents from applications such as Quark XPress and InDesign. But for more modest fare (and documents output as PDFs from OO.o) the results were much more useful. In Figure 11-25 we had to make a few adjustments to text spacing, but everything else was pretty much as expected.

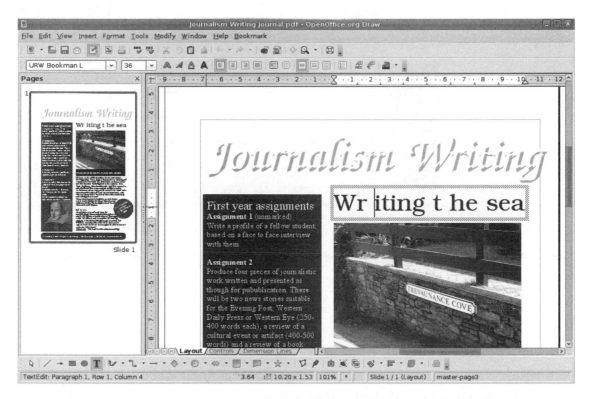

**Figure 11-25.** *There were just a few text-spacing errors in our test document. As with other transcoding operations, complexity will make things more problematic.*

The second option in this package is the hybrid PDF/ODT feature. Exporting a document to this format is the same as a traditional PDF export (see Chapter 9) and will allow all of the typical security options discussed earlier. The big change is the addition of a "Create hybrid file" on the Export dialog box's General tab (Figure 11-26). Select this and save the file as usual. OpenOffice.org users should be able to open this in its native format, and everyone else will be able to see the PDF.

The is an .oxt file, meaning it will install as normal, but you must download the correct version for your operating system. There are packages for Windows, Linux, OS X, and even Solaris.

Here's the URL where you can find the PDF Import extension:

```
http://extensions.services.OpenOffice.org/project/pdfimport
```

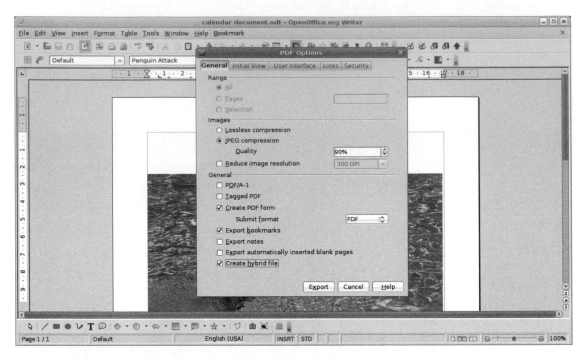

**Figure 11-26.** *The hybrid PDF export is a good choice when you want to retain editability and layout fidelity.*

## Presenter Tools

Presenter Tools is another extension created by Sun. As the name suggests, it adds some extras to Impress to make the job of the presenter easier. This is a platform-specific extension and will only work on a system that can run dual screens. It is also exclusive to OpenOffice.org 3.

In a typical presentation, the presenter will click the Slideshow button on the interface and the first slide will display. If the presenter is well prepared, he or she will have some notes from which to work. Presenter Tools takes advantage of the fact that a person will often present through a computer attached to a data projector, which provides two screens—though typically both displays show the same content. With this extension installed (and the system correctly configured for two screens), the user will click Slideshow and see the actual slideshow appear on the main screen—which is assumed to be the data projector—and the Presenter Tools on the secondary screen (Figure 11-27). The extension also adds an additional item to the Slideshow ➤ Slideshow Settings dialog box, which allows the user to configure which monitor displays the presentation.

**Figure 11-27.** *Two screens are better than one, especially when you're giving a presentation. On the left is the view the audience will see, on the right the Presenter Tools.*

The Presenter Tools screen is very dark—great for contrast—and displays a large version of the current slide, a smaller version of the next slide in the sequence, and a Control Dock at the base of the screen (see Figure 11-27). This can be used to advance or reverse slides, switch on the notes, or view a contact sheet of slides and also displays the current time and elapsed time for the presentation. When notes are active, the layout changes, and the notes are displayed in the largest section, then you can use a pair of Zoom icons to increase or reduce the text sizes. The previews shown in the Presenter Tools screen follow the main screen exactly so the presenter will see animations, movies, and transitions that have been applied to the slide.

---

■**Tip**  If you're carrying presentations around on USB drive or e-mailing them to colleagues, you can use the Sun Presentation Minimizer (`http://extensions.services.openoffice.org/project/PresentationMinimizer`) to reduce the file size of your productions. This will also ensure that embedded images are available when the remote user attempts to deliver the presentation.

---

If you regularly give presentations with external screens, this is about as close to an essential extension as you will find.

Here's the URL where you can find the Presenter Tools extension:

`http://extensions.services.OpenOffice.org/project/presenter-screen`

## PhotoAlbum

The final extension in our top ten is great for both personal and professional projects. The former could be simple image slideshows of your holiday trip to the Rockies, the latter might be a rotating slideshow of ads or product images in the lobby of your company's building. The purpose of this extension is to take a folder full of images and create a presentation that can then be shown as normal. And despite being a tiny extension (the download is just over 9kb), this comes complete with a graphical user interface and some surprisingly sophisticated options (Figure 11-28).

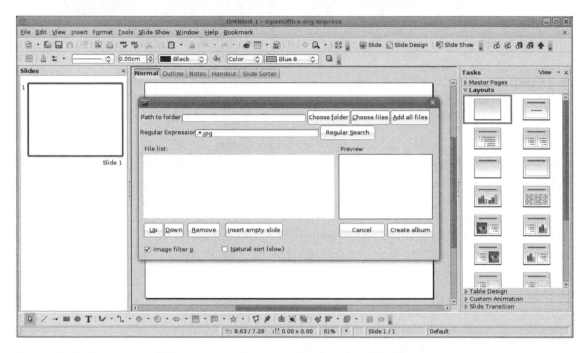

**Figure 11-28.** *You can use this tiny extension to make photographic slideshows.*

Begin by installing through the Extension Manager, and then close down and restart OO.o Impress. The interface to build a new slideshow is accessed through the Tools ➤ Add-ons Create Photo Album. To begin, click the Choose folder or Choose files button. The former allows you to take the contents of an entire folder, while the latter can be used to select a range of individual files using the mouse and the Shift key for a continuous range and the Ctrl key for multiple, noncontiguous files. Once you've accomplished the selection, click Add all files; the selection will be added to the slideshow File list. Select one image to see a preview on the right.

By default, images will be added to the list in alphabetical order, but this can be adjusted using the Up and Down buttons beneath the list. The Remove button will take the currently selected image out of the running order; you can use the Insert empty slide option to add a break in the slideshow for titles or other Impress content.

The Natural sort option, which may take some time, attempts to sort through a batch of images the same way a human might, even though it's within the bounds of alphabetical sorting. For example, if you have a list of images named `fishing1.jpg`, `fishing 2.jpg`, `[] fishing 10.jpg`, and `fishing 11.jpg`, a typical sort procedure will put fishing 10 and fishing 11 after fishing 1 but before fishing 2. Natural sort attempts to work around this.

The Image filter option ensures that only supported image files are pulled in from a folder of content.

Once the files have been added to your list, click Create album to build the album from within Impress. The result is a new file—remember to save—that contains each selected image on an individual slide. The images will be resized to fill the page while retaining their aspect ratio. This means that portrait image will have white bars on each vertical edge and that very wide landscapes will have bars on the top and bottom.

Slide 1 is left blank to be used as a title page.

To complete the production, we changed the background color on all pages to black—which looks better when projected (Figure 11-29)—and then added transitions between slides (open the Slide Transition section on the right, select Smooth fade, and click Apply to All Slides), and set each image to display for six seconds before moving to the next slide (under the Advance Slide section, choose Automatically and set the time).

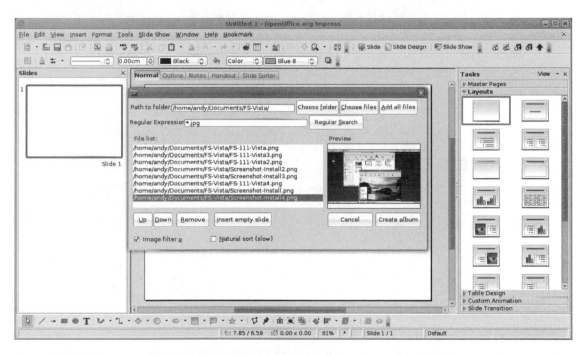

**Figure 11-29.** *Images are dynamically resized to fit the appropriate space. The bars on the top and bottom look better with a black background.*

**Tip** You can add new slides to a presentation by clicking Tools ➤ Add-ons ➤ Add Images to Existing Presentation.

One of the important points to remember is that images added to a slideshow in this way are linked rather than embedded, so if you intend on transferring the slideshow to another computer or want to distribute it more widely, you'll need to embed them. The easiest way to do this is to resave the presentation in the .ppt format.

If you have a soundtrack or an audio narration to add to your slideshow, ensure that the track is edited to the length of the presentation (or that the timings in the presentation coincide with the track length). Then add it as a sound using the Sound ➤ Other Sound drop-down in the Modify Transition section of the Slide Transition palette. This will then start (and restart) when Slide 1 is displayed. To make it really smooth, put a fade at the end of the sound.

## LOOPING A PHOTOALBUM SLIDESHOW

In this brief exploration of the PhotoAlbum extension you've built a very simple slideshow that advances through each image automatically. This is a great tool for creating advertising presentations that are to be seen in a store or a company's reception area. However, although you've dealt with movement through the slides, the presentation will come to an end at some point, so you need to configure it to loop right back to the beginning once the last slide has displayed.

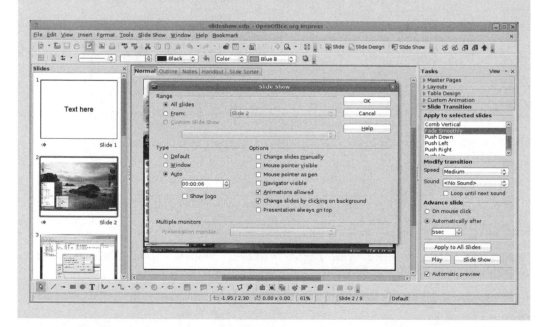

Go into the Slideshow menu and select Slideshow Settings under the Type section. Select the Auto option and then define the time between displaying the final slide and looping back to Slide 1. This period of time is in addition to the display time for the slide set earlier, and a countdown will display on the screen between the last and first slides. By setting the pause to 0.00, it's possible to transition from last to first. Then if you've set a transition for the first slide, it will be displayed in the loop, making for a seamless presentation.

Here's the URL where you can find the PhotoAlbum extension:

`http://extensions.services.OpenOffice.org/project/PhotoAlbumGUI`

# Recap

This chapter has introduced a small selection of the available extensions for OpenOffice. org. You have examined the various applications and worked on the application itself and on content. But it's important to note that we've only scratched the surface here. Because of the way that OpenOffice.org is developed and maintained, there is a constant supply of new extensions, macros, and templates being released by companies and community developers alike. And the really great thing is that most of these are released under an open source–type license (see the appendix). This means that people are free to use, explore, and redesign the packages for their own particular needs or for the community as a whole. Because the community is dynamic and diverse, things are changing all the time, so it's a good idea to keep an eye on the `http://extensions.services.OpenOffice.org` web site for reports of exciting new offerings.

The flip side of this is that if you create something special using OO.o, sharing it with like-minded users might be a good idea. Not only will you be giving back to a community that does so much for users, but you might even expand your own skills as new challenges arise. It might even be fun!

To help keep you up to date with changes to installed extensions, OpenOffice.org 3 has a new notification system that will, if you're online, check automatically for updates to the software itself and the extensions. If something is available, an icon and a speech bubble will appear on the top right of the main window, with a list of possible updates. If the notification concerns extension updates, clicking the icon will launch the Extension Manager, ready for updating. It's also possible to force a check by selecting Tools ➤ Extension Manager and clicking the Check for Updates button.

■■■

# The Beauty of Free Software

**O**penOffice.org has been written and released under a free-software/open source license. For end users, the chief advantage of installing open source software is that usually it doesn't cost any money, which, in political terms, makes it free, as in "free beer." However, there's an important addition to this, because open source software is also free as in "free speech."

This concept was outlined by Richard M. Stallman in 1983 when he set out to create a free variant of UNIX called GNU. Stallman's operating system dream has not been fully realized, even though the GNU ethos was adopted by Linus Torvalds when he began the Linux project. But the important concept of "copyleft" and its attendant GNU General Public License (GPL) did come out of Stallman's project.

The GPL, the most popular free-software license, defines four essential freedoms in relation to computer software:

- To use the software for any purpose

- To study the source code of the program and alter it to suit your particular needs

- To redistribute the program to other users

- To release altered editions of the software so that the entire community can use and build on it

A prerequisite for the last of these conditions is free access to the source code of the software, so you'll typically find a copy of this wherever you can download a free-software project. There are many other free-software or open source licenses that have been crafted for particular software projects or methods of working.

Despite the hacker ethic that appears to pervade the free-software community, many projects are backed by large multinational corporations, including Google, Sun, IBM, Intel, Hewlett-Packard, and even Microsoft.

OpenOffice.org uses a version of this license called the Lesser GPL (LGPL). This allows developers to include elements not covered by open source licenses, as long as they don't prevent the software from working. This means, for instance, that Sun can build its "official" version of OpenOffice.org, called StarOffice, and include elements such as fonts, photos, and clip art, without having to release those parts using a permissive license.

Although OpenOffice.org is a large and significant free-software project, it is by no means the only one. The software that "runs" the Internet is built on free-software principles: the core of Apple's OS X is a UNIX variant called BSD, Google's entire infrastructure is built on many open source projects, and, if you have a set-top box to record TV, a hardware firewall or wireless router, a portable media player, or a digital music player, the chances are that it's running free software somewhere. Even many cell phones rely on a stripped-down version of the Linux operating system to make everything work.

## Do Something

Because many of these projects rely on community to advance, improve, and increase their profiles, there is always a need for developers and, crucially, users who can get involved. And, fortunately, you don't have to be an elite hacker who thinks in C++ to make your mark. Applications often need translation and documentation services, graphic designers (those pretty icons have to come from somewhere), template builders, and coders. But even bug reports and advocacy (making sure friends and family know about a great free product) can make a difference.

## More Information

- http://www.gnu.org

- http://www.gnu.org/copyleft/gpl.html

- http://www.gnu.org/copyleft/lgpl.html

- http://www.opensource.org

- http://www.openoffice.org

- http://www.linuxfoundation.org

# Index

# You Need the Companion eBook

**Your purchase of this book entitles you to buy the companion PDF-version eBook for only $10. Take the weightless companion with you anywhere.**

We believe this Apress title will prove so indispensable that you'll want to carry it with you everywhere, which is why we are offering the companion eBook (in PDF format) for $10 to customers who purchase this book now. Convenient and fully searchable, the PDF version of any content-rich, page-heavy Apress book makes a valuable addition to your programming library. You can easily find and copy code—or perform examples by quickly toggling between instructions and the application. Even simultaneously tackling a donut, diet soda, and complex code becomes simplified with hands-free eBooks!

Once you purchase your book, getting the $10 companion eBook is simple:

❶ Visit **www.apress.com/promo/tendollars/**.

❷ Complete a basic registration form to receive a randomly generated question about this title.

❸ Answer the question correctly in 60 seconds, and you will receive a promotional code to redeem for the $10.00 eBook.

THE EXPERT'S VOICE™

2855 TELEGRAPH AVENUE | SUITE 600 | BERKELEY, CA 94705

**Offer valid through 06/09.**